MANCHESTER'S FINEST

How the Munich air disaster broke the heart of a great city

David Hall

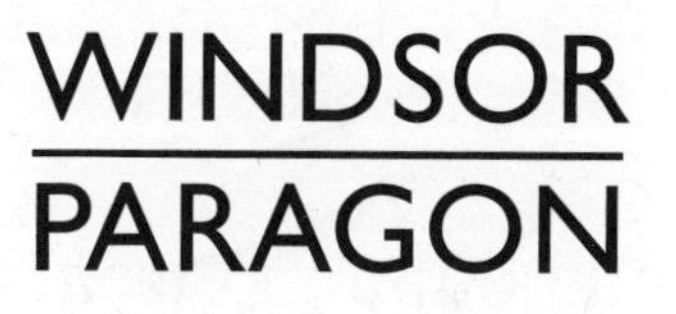

First published 2008
by Transworld Publishers
This Large Print edition published 2008
by BBC Audiobooks Ltd
by arrangement with
Transworld Publishers

Hardcover ISBN: 978 1 405 64923 0
Softcover ISBN: 978 1 405 64924 7

British Library Cataloguing in Publication Data available

Printed and bound in Great Britain by
Antony Rowe Ltd., Chippenham, Wiltshire

MANCHESTER'S FINEST

On 6 February 1958, British European Airways flight 609 crashed in a blizzard on its third attempt to take off from an icy runway in Munich. On board were the Manchester United football team, returning from their 3-3 draw against Red Star Belgrade, as well as a number of journalists and other passengers. Twenty-three of the forty-four passengers and crew aboard died in the crash. News of the disaster sent shockwaves around the world.

Manchester's Finest tells of this terrible air crash, but it is also the story of the immediate aftermath of the disaster and its effect on the city of Manchester. David Hall's poignant and very personal memoir remembers a season long gone, when a patched-up team, carried along on a great wave of emotion, came to embody the heart and soul of a great city.

To my children,
Kathryn and Thomas

In memory of my Dad,
Eddie

Three generations of Reds

CONTENTS

FEB 6th 1958
MUNICH

ACKNOWLEDGEMENTS

I would like to express my thanks to those who have helped me to tell this story. Alan Robertson, Beryl and Olga Townsend, Mary Walker (née Morris), Sandra Webb, Norman and Madge Williams and Tony Willis, for giving their time to recount their memories and allowing me to tell some of their stories. Neil Berry for sending me his book *Johnny: The Forgotten Babe* (Brampton Manor Books). My daughter, Kathryn, for her invaluable research efforts, particularly the many hours she spent poring through newspaper archives. The *Manchester Evening News* for allowing me to quote so extensively from what was at the time my main source of information, and their librarian Susan Hayes for the help she gave with the research. David McGowan, written archives researcher at the BBC. Staff at the Manchester Libraries archives and the National Newspaper Library, Colindale. The *Barnsley Chronicle and South Yorkshire News*, *Charles Buchan's Football Monthly*, *Daily Express*, *Daily Herald*, *Daily Mail*, *Daily Mirror*, *Doncaster Chronicle*, *Manchester Guardian*, *News Chronicle and Daily Dispatch*. The team at Transworld: especially Doug Young for commissioning the book; my editor Giles Elliott who became a Manchester United sympathizer in spite of being an AFC Wimbledon fan, and who encouraged me to ensure that my story came through without getting lost in everybody else's accounts; Daniel Balado for editing the copy, checking all the facts and cutting my many repetitions; and Sheila Lee for finding so many pictures that give a feel for what it was like at the time. Finally, I would like to thank my wife Fran for putting up with all the years of living with a family of Reds even though she says she's a City fan.

PROLOGUE

THE FLOWERS OF MANCHESTER

One cold and bitter Thursday in Munich, Germany,
Eight great football stalwarts conceded victory.
Eight men will never play again who met destruction there,
The flowers of English football, the flowers of Manchester.

Matt Busby's boys were flying, returning from Belgrade,
This great United family, all masters of their trade;
The pilot of the aircraft, the skipper Captain Thain,
Three times he tried to take off and twice turned back again.

The third time down the runway disaster followed close:
There was a slush upon the runway and the aircraft never rose.
It ploughed into the marshy ground, it broke, it overturned,
And eight of the team were killed as the blazing wreckage burned.

Roger Byrne and Tommy Taylor, who played for England's side,

And Ireland's Billy Whelan and England's Geoff Bent died.
Mark Jones and Eddie Colman, and David Pegg also,
They all lost their lives as it ploughed on through the snow.

Big Duncan he went too, with an injury to his frame,
And Ireland's Jackie Blanchflower will never play again.
The great Matt Busby lay there, the father of his team;
Three long months passed by before he saw his team again.

The trainer, coach and secretary, and a member of the crew,
Also eight sporting journalists who with United flew.
And one of them was Big Swifty, who we will ne'er forget,
The finest English keeper that ever graced their net.

Oh, England's finest football team its record truly great,
Its proud successes mocked by a cruel twist of fate.
Eight men will never play again who met destruction there,
The flowers of English football, the flowers of Manchester.

Anon.

On 6 February 1958 a BEA Elizabethan class Airspeed Ambassador charter aircraft carrying the Manchester United football team back to England from a European Cup tie in Belgrade needed to stop at Munich to refuel. When Flight 609 touched down at Munich's Riem Airport the United party were met by blizzard conditions. Snow and slush covered the runway. Conditions for flying were difficult and hazardous, and once the aircraft was refuelled there were two attempts to take off, both of which were aborted due to engine problems. When a third attempt was made, at 3.04 p.m., the aircraft failed to get airborne. It overshot the runway, went through a fence and crossed a road before one of the wings struck a house. Seven of the players—Geoff Bent, Roger Byrne, Eddie Colman, Mark Jones, David Pegg, Tommy Taylor and Billy Whelan—were killed instantly, along with the club secretary, the first team trainer, the first team coach, eight sportswriters, one of the aircrew and two other passengers. Two weeks later the aircraft's co-pilot and Duncan Edwards, one of the most promising young players ever to come out of England, lost their battle for life, bringing the final death toll to twenty-three. Two other United players, Johnny Berry and Jackie Blanchflower, were so severely injured that they were never able to play again.

For people who lived in Manchester at that time, and for football fans throughout Britain, it was one of those moments like Kennedy's assassination or 9/11 when everybody remembers exactly where they were and how they heard that terrible news. I was an eleven-year-old schoolboy and I'd been going to Old Trafford to watch United with my dad for two years. I'm over sixty now, but tears still come to my eyes whenever I think of the moment I first heard the news, or when I think of the words of 'The Flowers of Manchester', the ballad that was written anonymously within weeks of the disaster.

According to a report in the *Manchester Guardian* on 3 March 1958, the song was first heard in an upper room of the Princess Louise pub on High Holborn in London, where a group of people who called themselves the Ballads and Blues movement met every Sunday night to listen to a collection of new and traditional songs. 'The Flowers of Manchester', the report said, was one of three songs that had appeared in the Ballads and Blues programme, all of them dealing with the tragic events of 6 February. Each was different in mood and character, but the late fifties was the beginning of the folk revival, and they all fell within what was defined as the folk tradition. All three ballads were being sung at the Ballads and Blues club before the end of February, and each of them evoked a deep emotional response from the audiences.

In the case of two of them, this, the *Manchester Guardian* writer said, had less to do with the quality of the songs themselves than the tragic nature of the accident. The first, 'Manchester Mourns', by Dominic Behan, the brother of Irish playwright Brendan Behan, was in the heroic Irish tradition; Behan sang of 'gallant and brave boys; footballers great and true'. The second song, 'The Munich Tragedy' by Joe Moss, was written to an American tune with words predominantly in the American idiom. It had an air of the hillbilly about it which was about as remote from the world of Manchester football as it was possible to get. The third song, however, was right in the mainstream of the ballad tradition. It was emotional too, but it was free from bogus sentiment; it was the eloquence of the words that brought the tragedy vividly to life.

The words of 'The Flowers of Manchester' appeared in a folk magazine, *Sing*, in October 1958, but no music accompanied it. According to the magazine the lyrics had been sent in anonymously with a note saying it should be sung to the tune of 'High Germany'. The song was first sung for wider public consumption by Mick Groves of the Liverpool-based folk group The Spinners. Mick was a United fan from Salford and he sang it unaccompanied on The Spinners' first album *Quayside Songs Old and New*, released in 1962. I first heard it being sung by Terry Whelan at the Pack Horse on Bridge Street, Manchester, in 1964. Terry was one of the resident singers at the Wayfarers Club, a folk club at the pub a crowd of us used to go to on a Saturday night. I got the words of the song from The Spinners album, and when I set up a folk club myself when I was at university in Dundee I used to sing it regularly. I particularly remember doing it at a concert when I shared the bill with The Spinners and the American folk singer Tom Paxton. During the holidays a whole crowd of us used to hitch-hike around Ireland, often singing for our bed and breakfast on the way; a rendition of 'Flowers' would always bring tears to the eyes of those present, not to mention fond memories of the Irishman Billy Whelan, who lost his life in the crash.

Nobody knows for certain who wrote the song, or who first sang it at Ballads and Blues. It is often attributed to Ewan MacColl, but that is not correct. At the time it first appeared MacColl was a regular at Ballad and Blues and he probably knew as much about it as anyone in Britain. He said he had seen several texts on the Munich disaster but 'The Flowers Of Manchester' was certainly the best. McColl also collaborated with The Spinners on their version, which may go some way to explaining why for so many years he was rumoured to be its writer.

Since 2001, before the home match that is closest to the anniversary of the disaster, fans have gathered under the Munich Memorial at Old Trafford to sing 'The Flowers of Manchester'. This is now a regular event.The number of people attending increases every year and it is recognized by the club, which fixes temporary boards on the wall under the memorial for fans to leave floral tributes. With its re-emergence, the mystery of the authorship of the song was, for many, cleared up. Tony Davis of The Spinners told a contributor to the United fanzine *Red News* that it had been written by Eric Winter, the Mancunian editor of *Sing* magazine. He'd published it anonymously in the magazine because it was the custom of folk singers to write anonymously at that time; they believed it gave the material more credence. This claim was backed up in Winter's obituary in the *Guardian*: 'his song, The Flowers of Manchester, prompted by the Munich Air Disaster, was recorded by The Spinners'. The only doubt in my mind about this is the fact that the writer of the *Manchester Guardian* article that was published just over three weeks after the disaster was none other than Eric Winter. Would he have praised his own song so highly while dismissing the other two that had been written in the wake of the disaster?

Some of the words that are sung now, in what has come to be accepted as the official version, are different to the words of the original that I used to sing, notably the line 'There was ice upon the wings and the aircraft never rose', which has been changed to 'There was a slush upon the runway and the aircraft never rose'. At the inquiry just after the disaster the German authorities contended that ice on the wings had caused the crash and that the pilot, Captain James Thain, who survived the crash, was at fault because he had not had them de-iced before take-off. When the song was written, therefore, ice on the wings was accepted as the cause of the crash. But Thain's position was that what little ice there was on the wings was thawing, and de-icing was not necessary. For years he lived under the cloud of blame and he fought to clear his name, maintaining that it was a build-up of slush on the runway causing deceleration of the aircraft and preventing safe flying speed from being attained that was the cause of the disaster. The German authorities, who were legally responsible for the state of the runways, would not accept this, and the British Government did not want to embarrass the West German Government so soon after the war. In the end it took eleven years and four inquiries, two British and two German, to clear the name of Captain Thain by establishing that slush on the runway was the sole cause of the crash.

There is, I believe, one other small but important change that should be made to correct a major omission in the song. In the foreword to his book *Johnny the Forgotten Babe*, Neil Berry, the son of Johnny Berry, points out that the lyricist of 'The Flowers Of Manchester' is not the only anonymous person in this story: 'My father was a member of the Manchester United team and was on the plane that day. The injuries he sustained prevented him from playing football again.' Of the eight players who died and the two who were never able to play again, right-winger Johnny Berry is the only one who is not mentioned in the song. As we mark the fiftieth anniversary of the disaster, it would be appropriate to make sure that along with the others Johnny is not forgotten by changing the line 'And Ireland's Jackie Blanchflower will never play again' to 'And Johnny Berry 'n' Jackie Blanchflower will never play again'.

* * *

Flying is a lot safer now, probably the safest form of travel. I fly thousands of miles every year on business and for pleasure and I have no fear of it. But to this day I cannot board an aeroplane without at least a thought of Munich flashing through my mind. In that mad scramble for seats on one of the budget airlines, I'm always reminded that Bobby Charlton, Bill Foulkes and Harry Gregg, the survivors of the crash, were sitting near the front of the aircraft; those who died were all sitting at the back. At that moment before take-off, just before the wheels leave the ground, I think of the aircraft that 'never rose'. Until we're safely up in the air and beyond the perimeter fence of the airport the image remains of the broken aircraft lying in the snow at the end of the Munich runway. 'It ploughed into the marshy ground, it broke, it overturned…'

In the course of writing this book I've spoken to many older United fans who were supporting the team at the time of the disaster, and for them, like me, the word 'Munich' means only one thing: that cold and bitter Thursday when the football team we followed was destroyed. Munich is a great city; I've visited it many times, landed at its airport, made a television travel programme there. But whenever I hear its name the first thing that comes into my head are the words of 'The Flowers Of Manchester'. The song takes me straight back to that time in the middle of the 1950s when Manchester was still a great manufacturing city and one of its teams won the affection of the entire British nation with their displays of footballing skill. In 1958, when disaster struck, Manchester United were going for the same fabulous Treble of league championship, FA Cup and European Cup that saw Alex Ferguson knighted forty-one years later.

Football then was a very different game to the one we know today, and the lives of the players were more in touch with the mainly working-class support that football enjoyed. Pay during the season was only £20 per week, with a £4 bonus for a win, and £17 a week in the summer months. It wasn't a great deal more than a lot of the supporters earned. The players lived in modest semi-detached club houses or in lodgings close to Old Trafford. A lot of them didn't have cars, and many travelled in for matches and for training on public transport, shoulder to shoulder with the fans. The club was very much part of the community, and when tragedy struck, the whole city—Red, Blue and uncommitted—went into mourning. The film and television script writer Colin Shindler is a lifelong Manchester City supporter, and in his book *Manchester United Ruined My Life* he expresses the feelings of everybody who was in Manchester at that time: 'I was devastated by the news of the crash. Everybody in Manchester was. I am informed that the nation wept—possibly wherever football was played tears were shed—but not like they were in Manchester. It was a death in the immediate family... There was no City/United divide on this.

The great City and England goalkeeper Frank Swift died at Munich, but our tears were shed for us—the city of Manchester.'

Manchester's Finest is about the people of Manchester and their lives, and about the place of a football team in the heart of a city. It's about a time when that city was paralysed as the news of the deaths of its football heroes came through; a time when, in the weeks immediately after the disaster, a patched-up team came to embody the heart and soul of the city as, carried along on a great wave of emotion, it reached the FA Cup Final. It was a time when memories of the Second World War were still fresh in many people's minds and Germany was still regarded as the enemy; when the care given to the crash victims by the German doctors changed these views and helped the reconciliation process. *Manchester's Finest* is about family and community and the links that bind them together through shared allegiance to a football team, and about the creation of a legend that was built into an international brand which gradually, in the eyes of many people, became distanced from the very community it was part of.

CHAPTER 1

ONE COLD AND BITTER THURSDAY

It was getting dark as I walked down our road on my way back from school and the street lights were already on. Heavy black clouds filled the sky. 'Good,' I thought, 'snow's on its way.' It was certainly cold enough. I was looking forward to snowball fights, to making snowmen and big long icy slides down the middle of the road. But then I thought, 'Oh no! What'll happen to United's game against Wolves at Old Trafford on Saturday?' My dad had promised me that we'd go to the match against the league leaders but it would surely be called off if there was too much snow.

At the top of the road, just after the telephone box on the corner of Greenbrow Road, there was a row of four neat little redbrick houses followed by a pair of semis. The trouble was there was a big Alsatian dog at one of the semis. I didn't like Alsatians; I'd heard too many stories about them turning on people and biting them, and there were quite a lot of them on our part of the estate. I walked slowly to see if it was around, because I wasn't going to walk past it if it was. Better to take a detour than risk being attacked by it. But no, the coast was clear. Maybe it was too cold for the dog to be out. I quickened my pace, almost breaking into a run to get past the dreaded house.

After the houses there was a stretch of grass that had a long row of three-storey flats backing on to it. I used to go to some of them on a Saturday morning to collect the football pools bags for church. On the other side of the road open fields stretched all the way to the Newall Green pub and to Shenton's Farm about half a mile away. Beyond that, country lanes weaved their way into the Cheshire countryside. After years of living in inner-city Manchester, Wythenshawe was like living out in the country. It was the garden suburb that everybody in the slums of Hulme, Ancoats and Ardwick wanted to move to.

By February 1958 we'd been living in Wythenshawe for a couple of years. We'd moved from a terraced house on Grey Mare Lane not far from Bradford Pit, three doors away from my Gran Kearney's. Apart from the green fields and the open spaces all around us in place of the chimneys and the gasometers and the pithead winding gear I'd grown up with, the biggest change for me was the smell. We'd still get the thick pea-souper fogs out here—Wythenshawe might have been on the edge of the countryside but it wasn't far enough away from the old industrial areas with their chimneys belching out black smoke to be clear of the smog—but the air was much fresher and there were none of the foul odours of industry. Where we'd lived in Bradford was bad some days when the wind was in the wrong direction and the stink of Clayton Aniline came drifting across our back yard. On Wastdale Road, where we now lived, the smells came from Shenton's cows when he let them out on our field and they wandered on to our road, or from the fertilizer they used on the market garden at the end of the road.

In the summer holidays we'd play all day in the fields, making dens, slinging a rope over one of the top branches of a tree to make a swing, or playing football on the pitch that had been trampled down near the scout hut. The fields were carpeted with flowers, a blaze of shining yellow buttercups and bright white daisies, and kids would go home with great armfuls of flowers for their mams. But in the winter all that open space made it feel a lot colder than it had been when we'd lived among the tightly packed terraces and factories of Bradford and Beswick.

Wearing short trousers didn't help. A year earlier I'd passed my eleven plus and got a place at St Bede's, one of Manchester's Catholic grammar schools. It was the junior seminary for the Salford Diocese, run by priests with a monsignor as the head, and the rules were strict. In the Upper Third you were not allowed to wear long trousers. Whatever the weather you had to wear shorts, which meant chapped legs for most of the winter. How was it that the cold and the rain always seemed to get up inside your trouser legs to make your legs red raw?

On the field just opposite the flats was the pond where we used to go to catch frog spawn and fish for newts in the early summer, but that day it was frozen over. There was a jagged crack and a hole near the middle where some kid must have gone through when he'd tried sliding across it. Probably got a battering from his mother for his pains when he got home, wet and muddy and shivering.

That afternoon of Thursday, 6 February 1958 it was bitterly cold, but apart from that, it was just like any other afternoon. School had been boring as usual and we'd got some of that dreaded algebra to do for homework. We'd started doing it just after Christmas and I couldn't make head or tail of it. Neither could my mam and dad. They'd stay up for hours with me at night trying to help me with it and make sense of it, but how could you add up and multiply letters? It didn't make sense. We were in for another long night of scratching our heads. But who cared about algebra? These were exciting times. One of Manchester's football teams was winning the affection of the entire British nation with their skilful displays on the pitch; Manchester United was the team. In the second half of the 1950s they were the top team in Britain, and they were my team and my dad's team, and his dad's team before that.

The 1950s was a time when United captured the imagination of the footballing world with the fruits of their youth policy. Every other club in the country decided they wanted to get in on the act. No longer was it necessary to live by the chequebook and the transfer system when there was so much talent to be tapped in Britain's schools. United's manager Matt Busby was the man behind it all. In the 1930s he'd played for Liverpool and Manchester City. After the war, their ground having been wrecked in a wartime bombing raid, United needed a young manager to try to rebuild the club, and the man they appointed was Matt Busby. Within two seasons he'd won the FA Cup, beating Blackpool 4–2 in a match that is regarded as one of the greatest ever Cup Finals. Four years later, in 1952, Busby's first United team won the league title after finishing runners-up in all but one of the previous five seasons.

But by this time the team was getting old and new faces and younger legs were needed. Busby dismantled his championship-winning side to give youth its head, and he was handsomely rewarded with back-to-back titles in 1956 and 1957. The average age of the side that won the championship in 1955/56 was just twenty-two—a feat that had never been achieved before. The following season United entered an exciting new competition pitching the champions of the national leagues from all over Europe against one another for the prize of the European Cup, and at their very first attempt United reached the semi-final. The young team Matt Busby had built seemed destined to dominate football for many years.

On Wednesday, 5 February 1958 the team had drawn 3–3 with Red Star in Belgrade, a result that took the Reds through to the European Cup semi-final for the second season on the run. Despite the efforts of that night and the long journey home from Belgrade, it looked on form as if on Saturday against Wolves the Reds would close the four-point gap at the top of the table, putting them just one victory behind Billy Wright's side, and ready to increase their efforts for a third successive league title. For me there was no problem. Matt Busby's Babes were invincible. I hadn't seen them lose a match at Old Trafford since I'd started watching them two years earlier, in the 1955/56 season. I couldn't wait for Saturday to come, and I couldn't wait to read Tom Jackson's report on the Red Star match in that night's *Manchester Evening News* when I got home.

Along with Alf Clarke, his opposite number on the *Manchester Evening Chronicle*, Tom Jackson was particularly close to Matt Busby and the whole of the United team. Both of them had a column in the United programme and both were Red through and through. There was never any pretence at objective reporting, so for me their reports were great. We were an *Evening News* house so my main source of information about United was Tom Jackson. It was good and it was reliable, because it was very much in

United's interest to keep the reporters on the two local papers happy and make sure they had all the latest news as well as regular access to the players.

Wastdale Road was a dead end, and our house was near the end of it. Just beyond it there was a wooden fence across the end of the road, fencing off the big market garden. Beyond that on the other side of Clay Lane was the very fine-looking redbrick chimney and boiler house of Baguley Sanatorium. My dad said it was where they burned all the bits they took out of people in operations there and at Wythenshawe Hospital, which adjoined it. Over the road from our house were the white-painted old people's bungalows and community centre of Johannesburg Gardens. In the middle was a beautifully kept lawn with a rose garden at the top of it. Our front windows were slap bang in the middle of the gardens on the other side of the road, and my dad always said there was nowhere you could live that would have a better view than we had. We'd been lucky to get a house in Wythenshawe, and even luckier to get this particular one. My mam and dad had fancied this part of Wythenshawe, and when they were on the council waiting list they'd come out to look around here and seen this one when it was being built. As soon as they saw it they decided it was the one they wanted, and they went down to the town hall to put their name down for it.

The house itself was quite funny-looking really. For a start it was in the middle of a terrace—quite unusual for a newly built house in Wythenshawe at that time—but it also had two front doors right next to each other. The proper front door had glass in it, but then there was one next to it that we called the side door. It was in a little porch which housed the dustbin and the coal hole. It was the door we always used; the front door was for visitors. I went in through the side room, where we kept the Hoover and bikes and things like my dad's tools.

The side room led into the kitchen, at this time of the year the warmest room in the house, because as well as my mam doing the cooking we had an electric fire in there as well. One bar of the electric fire was on; two would have been a bit extravagant, a bit too expensive, and it wasn't cold enough for that. My younger sister, Joan, was sitting at the kitchen table, crayoning. My mam was cutting potatoes up into small pieces and putting them in a big pan. Good, tater ash for tea. My favourite. As she worked she sang:

I'll take you home again, Kathleen,
Across the ocean far and wide
To where the fields are fresh and green.
I will take you home again, Kathleen.

She stopped singing and looked at me. 'You look perished, David,' she said. 'The kettle's on. You stand in front of the fire while I make you a cup of tea.' But all I wanted to know was had the paper boy been round to deliver the *News* yet. As Mam poured the tea, she asked me about school and about what homework I'd got. Had I found out how to do that algebra yet? 'But before you start on your homework,' she said, 'can you light the fire in the front room in time for your dad getting back from work? It's already set. All you need to do is put a match to it and then make sure it doesn't go out.'

I took the matches into the front room. It was freezing in there; no central heating in those days. It was so cold that there were bits of ice on the inside of the windows, and when you breathed you could see your breath freezing in front of you. I was glad my mam had already done most of the work, laying the fire. I lit the firelighters and small flames soon started to lick around them and the coal. But it was going to need a bit of a boost. I wasn't supposed to, but I got a sheet of newspaper from under one of the cushions and held it in front of the fire to make it draw. My dad used to light the fire like this. Sometimes it would catch fire, then there would be panic to get the paper into the fire before it fell on to the rug in front of it, so I was very careful, pulling it away at the first sign of scorching.

I sat there watching the flames licking around the coal, yellow and red with purple and blue in the middle, until I heard the paper boy. As soon as the *Manchester Evening News* was delivered I made a bee-line for it and turned to the sports pages at the back to read Tom Jackson's report on the match in Belgrade the day before. Under the headline 'It May Be The Spaniards Next, But United Will Never Have A Tougher Fight Than This!' he began with: 'Now I'm ready to wage my last Yugoslav dinar that even though it may be the strutting Spaniards of Real Madrid who Manchester United will be set to face in the semi-final of the European Cup, they will never have a tougher fight on their hands than the one they survived here against the challenge of Red Star. Believe me.' The report went on, 'this match that ended with the rivals gaining three goals each and United through to the last-four stage by the barest possible goal margin on aggregate had everything to send the blood running fast through the veins'.

What a great match it must have been, and what an

adventure to fly what seemed to me like halfway across the world to play a football match. Some of the players themselves, it had been reported before they left for Belgrade, felt they were taking a step into the unknown by venturing beyond the Iron Curtain. I'd read one report that said right-half Eddie Colman's mum had been so concerned that she'd made up a food parcel for him containing fruit, biscuits and a packet of tea. I tried to imagine what it would be like to travel all that way to play football, or even just to watch it. For a lad who'd never been any further from Manchester than North Wales it all sounded very distant and exotic. But that was the thing about supporting United. It wasn't like any other football team. In those early days of the European Cup it was all a huge romantic adventure, and I followed every episode avidly. Tom Jackson's words really conveyed the spirit of that adventure.

> How else but by sheer, at times almost desperate, determination and drive, the deafening roars of 50,000 people ringing in their ears—and some remarkably strange decisions by the Austrian referee—could Red Star have pulled back three goals and got within sight of forcing a replay? It wasn't that the United defence cracked. It wasn't that the forwards, brilliant in the first half, faded out of the game. To my mind the pendulum swung in Red Star's favour directly they took full toll from a penalty kick which I'm sure nine out of ten referees wouldn't have given.

'Here we go again,' I thought. 'That's the trouble with this European Cup. To win it you've not just got to beat these clever foreigners with all their tricks, you've got the foreign referees to contend with as well.' From what I'd read about them they sometimes seemed to have a different rule book from the one we had. Tom Jackson confirmed this view. 'How ironic,' he continued, 'that big Bill Foulkes, who had an outstanding game at right-back, should have conceded the penalty when he made what seemed to me a perfectly legitimate tackle on Red Star centre-forward Tasic. From that moment onwards the Yugoslavs were able to come back into the game with a chance of saving the match because the United players seemed dubious about going hard into the tackle in case they might be penalised further.'

I never missed reading Tom Jackson's reports in the *Evening News*. It was a bit like having your mate or your mate's dad telling you about the matches you hadn't been to. A real Red telling you what he'd seen, and what he thought of the match. What a job it must have been, getting paid to travel all over the place to watch United and to be so well in with the club that you were almost part of it. Even better than being a train driver, and that was saying something, because that was what I really wanted to do when I grew up.

Further down the page in that night's *Evening News* there was a selection of comments from the match reports that had appeared in that morning's national newspapers. Praise for the spirit of the United players and for their performance along with criticism of the referee were the main points made by most of the football writers who'd gone with the team to report on the match. The *Daily Mail* said that 'Manchester United were nearly scared into a replay by Austrian referee Karl Kainer—pronounced mud in Manchester touring circles … He would have been howled off an English ground for his niggling anti-tackling phobia.'

The *Manchester Guardian* described it as 'a battle of wits and guts and rugged tackling… the Austrian referee's performance on the whistle assumed the proportions of a flute obbligato due to the frequency with which fouls were committed by both sides'. Other papers, the *Evening News* said, had reported on the unbearable tension of the second half when every ounce of spirit had been wrung from United's brave hearts and the match was described as a rough, tough tale of tempers and crazy decisions.

The Yugoslavian press had seen things very differently. 'United were unsportsmanlike and often unscrupulous,' *Politika* reported. 'In the second half the British felled opponents in an impermissible manner. Many times we asked ourselves where was the renowned British fair play? That is only a legend. There was not a single professional trick they did not use to bring themselves out of difficult positions and were often unscrupulous when they tackled and pushed and tripped.' I couldn't believe those words. To me United were everything that was good about football. Attack-minded, flowing football, hard but fair—all that was best about the British game. Clearly they played football differently in other parts of the world.

We'd got used to seeing United going forward, but in this game they'd obviously been up against it in the second half. Like all true fans, though, Tom Jackson concentrated on all that had been positive about the display. 'The real story of this full-blooded cup tie,' he wrote, 'is not so much how United had their backs to the wall in the second half, but how they virtually made sure of victory by an inspired forward display in the opening half. Here was the United attack in their greatest and most polished mood of the season, with Tommy Taylor the architect in chief, and the young Bobby Charlton—the best forward on the field—and Dennis Viollet the goal-snatching spearheads.'

And the defence? It was good to read in the report that they'd played brilliantly as well. 'Those three goals against might suggest they panicked under the weight of Red Star's heavy pressure. Not a bit of it. Gregg, Foulkes, Mark Jones and Roger Byrne never lost their heads in matching the Yugoslav forwards, who put much more bite into their play than they did in the first leg at Old Trafford. Foulkes takes top marks because he was the coolest and surest United defender all through the game.' It was good to see Bill Foulkes getting star billing. It was usually Duncan Edwards, Roger Byrne, little Eddie Colman or one of the forwards who took the plaudits. Foulkes was as hard and solid and dependable as you'd expect of a former coal-miner, but he'd faced competition for the right-back spot and had only recently re-established himself in the team after a spell of being kept out by Ian Greaves.

Clearly it had been a good all-round team performance, another job well done in Europe. Tom Jackson summarized his report with the words, 'That's the story at Belgrade—a battle which will be long remembered in this European Cup which has produced so many tense and dramatic struggles for United.'

The journalists who covered United's matches were close to the team. They flew with them to their European away matches and stayed with the team party. None were closer than Tom Jackson and Alf Clarke, and alongside his piece in the *Evening News* was Jackson's interview with the captain Roger

Byrne in which he gave his impressions of the match. 'Fouls galore, but not dirty' was his summary.

> But I am confident that the way we played in Belgrade, especially in the first half, we are capable of giving the best teams left in the Cup a very good run for their money. All the United players set themselves out to win the match with Red Star. I'm sure we would have done so had not our luck been out as far as the referee was concerned, especially when he gave that penalty against us. I'm told there were 37 free kicks for fouls in the match—26 against us and 11 conceded by Red Star. From that you might think it was a dirty game, but I wouldn't say that, even though there were one or two instances of individuals playing the man instead of the ball. When a team is able to pull back a goal or two after trailing well behind it gives them every incentive to fight all the harder. Red Star certainly gave us a fight after our forwards had produced such grand form in getting three goals ahead. They were a much better side than in Manchester and I've never been more pleased to hear the final whistle than I was in this game.

What a captain, and what a team to support. United were the centre of my life, and going to Old Trafford the most important thing in it. I wouldn't dare say it at the time, because it was probably a mortal sin, but it was even more important than going to church. 'Roll on Saturday and Wolves,' I thought. 'We'll cut that lead to two points.' Elvis was top of the charts that week with 'Jailhouse Rock', but I didn't care about that. My favourite song was the 'Manchester

United Calypso' and I was singing it to myself as I went into the kitchen to help set the table for tea.

Manchester, Manchester United,
A bunch of bouncing Busby babes,
They deserve to be knighted.
When they're playing in your town
Take a trip to that football ground;
Take a lesson and you will see
Football taught by Matt Busby.
Oh Manchester, Manchester United,
A bunch of bouncing Busby babes,
They deserve to be knighted.

Our little back kitchen was warm, and it got warmer as my mam opened the oven to get the tater ash out. Condensation clouded the window that looked out on to our frozen back garden. The gate-legged table was set, ready for tea as soon as my dad got in from work. He always got in just before six o'clock, regular as clockwork. He worked in the office of a cotton warehouse on Dale Street in town and always finished at five o'clock. Most lads' dads that I knew worked in engineering works, mainly in Trafford Park, but my dad had always been a clerk in the offices of the cotton traders that still dominated the centre of Manchester. He was, however, already looking for other work. By the late 1950s Manchester's once great cotton industry was dying, and he knew the work wasn't going to last for long. Many of the great, solid-looking Victorian warehouses that lined Portland Street, Whitworth Street and Moseley Street were already half empty.

Wages were low because there was no longer any money in the industry that had once been the foundation of Manchester's wealth. My dad used to get £6 a week—quite a lot less than he'd have been getting if he'd done an engineering apprenticeship after he'd left school—but my mam worked wonders on it, always managing to get a good bit of meat to make a meat and potato pie or a hot pot. And there was nearly always a pudding to follow: lovely apple pie with the lightest pastry I've ever tasted, or a creamy rice pudding with a thick skin on the top. Tonight was no exception, but my dad was a few minutes later than usual.

The clock on the kitchen wall above the electric fire was pointing to five to six when the side door burst open and my dad came rushing into the kitchen. It was a moment when time stood still, one that is still clearly etched on my brain fifty years later. Even now I can hear the words he blurted out.

'United have been wiped out.'

For a few seconds I didn't understand what he was saying. Then he went on: 'Their plane's crashed. It's in the stop press of the *Evening News*. Get into the front room and get the news on the wireless.'

The tater ash was forgotten. All of us—me, my mam, my dad and my sister—rushed into the living room where the fire I'd lit an hour earlier was blazing, taking the chill off the room. My dad went to the big radiogram in the corner and switched on the six o'clock news on the BBC Home Service, just in time to hear the chimes of Big Ben and the newsreader say, 'Here is the news. An airliner carrying the Manchester United football team crashed in Germany this afternoon.' We didn't really hear the rest of the headlines: Lord Hailsham challenging Mr Thorneycroft's suggestion that Britain was on the road to ruin; anybody allowing dark smoke to come from chimneys would be liable for a fine of up to a hundred pounds. They were all irrelevant. They just passed over our heads until the newsreader got back to the main story.

> A British European Airways charter plane carrying the Manchester United football team crashed after taking off from Munich Airport, at about three o'clock this afternoon. The weather was said to be poor at the time. BEA stated about half an hour ago that the plane was carrying a crew of six, and thirty-eight passengers—including a baby. They say they believe there are about sixteen survivors, including some of the crew. A Reuters report from Munich says that survivors include the Manchester United players Gregg, Foulkes and Charlton. Reuters says that two other survivors are Mr Peter Howard, a *Daily Mail* photographer, and his assistant Mr Ellyard, both from Manchester.

As the unemotional BBC voice listed all the members of the United party who had gone to Belgrade, the sports writers who were believed to be on board and others who had been booked to travel on the plane, the fact that my dad's words were right drove home like a hammer blow. If the report was saying that Gregg, Foulkes and Charlton had survived, surely the rest of the team had been wiped out; but there was very little information at this stage, as the newsreader confirmed: 'Those are the names of nearly all the thirty-eight passengers believed to be on board. It is not possible to say yet what has happened to most of them.' Other than that he was able to say that the plane was an Elizabethan, that it had landed at Munich to refuel and should have arrived in Manchester about an hour ago. The Lord Mayor of Manchester, it was reported, had spoken of his deep grief at this terrible tragedy. He concluded by saying that yesterday United had drawn 3–3 with Red Star Belgrade, putting them into the European Cup semi-finals for the second season running, and that they had been without question the most successful post-war English side, before moving on quickly to the next item about the Commons debating an Opposition motion attacking the Government's industrial and social policies.

We didn't want to know about the rest of the news. Not interested. My dad went over to the radiogram and switched it off. We were in a state of shock. It was as if we'd just been told that members of our own family had been killed in a terrible accident. You felt you knew all of those players. They brought us joy and pleasure and excitement on the football field every week; the sense of loss was indescribable. But more than that, there was a sense of disbelief. It was hard to comprehend what we'd just heard; it couldn't have happened; but if it was on the BBC it had to be true.

We trooped back into the kitchen in silence. I was in tears as my mam served the tater ash. Good as it was, no one had any appetite for it, nor for the apple pie she'd made to follow it.

We wanted to know more. We were desperate for more details. But what we'd heard on the six o'clock news was all we were going to get that evening; no more information, and nowhere to get any. By this time the paper shop over the fields at Greenbrow Road shops was shut, and even if it hadn't been it wouldn't have had the late city editions of the *News* or the *Chron*. We didn't have a television, but for those who did, there was no more on the six o'clock television news than there had been on the radio. Coverage then was a far cry from the rolling channels and live satellite feeds of today.

Everybody who was in Manchester at that time remembers the moment when they first heard the news. My wife's cousin, Mary Morris, was living in Chorlton on Medlock, not far from the city centre. 'I remember it was snowing, very cold that afternoon,' she told me.

> I'd just come in from school, and at the time my mam used to have the couch in the middle of the room in front of an open fire we used to have in them days. It was always there lit when we got in from school. My brother James was already in and he was sitting there in front of the fire. My mam had made a cup of tea because it was cold, and she was upstairs changing the bed, ready to do the washing the next day. It was about ten past or quarter past four and we both sat down with the television on and all of a sudden the programme was interrupted with a news flash saying news had just come in that the plane carrying Manchester United had crashed. I remember getting up straight away and running to the bottom of the stairs, shouting to tell my mam. So she left what she was doing upstairs and came down. Then we sat there, the three of us, just listening to different things that were coming through about what actually happened. When my dad came in he said, 'I know, it's all over town, everyone's talking about it.' So all four of us just sat there and we couldn't say

anything. I don't even think we had our tea because it was just so much of a shock.

Norman Williams was one of the real diehards who had been watching United since the 1935-36 season. He was at home in Droylsden when he first heard the news. He was a postman but he was off work because he'd broken his leg while on his way to Highbury to watch United the previous Saturday. 'I was reclining in my chair at home,' he recalled. 'It was cold and the fire was on, and as I sat there a knock came on the door, about half past four or quarter to five. It was the paper lad. He knew I was a big United supporter so he wanted to let me know that United's plane had crashed. When I got the paper from him the stop press said no more than the lad had been able to tell me. There was hardly any detail about what had happened so I just sat there wondering how bad it was.'

Norman's wife Madge was at work when she first heard the dreadful news.

I was working in an office at the time at Laurence Scott's in Openshaw and the boss came up to me and said, 'Madge, I've got some bad news for you.' So I said, 'What is it?' I thought something must have happened to Norman, but he said, 'It's about the team.' I could see it was difficult for him to tell me so I said, 'What about the team?' He still couldn't bring himself to tell me so he said to my friend working next to me at the next desk, 'Take Madge outside.' He followed us outside, and it was then he told me that United's plane had crashed.

'I don't believe it,' I said.

'I'm sorry,' he said, 'it's true. You'll see it later on. But I want you to go home now. You're upset.'

So I went home, and when I got there Norman was very upset. He was sitting there with his leg propped up and I said, 'Oh God! I don't know what to say to you!' and we both had a cry. Then we started hearing on the radio what had happened. We heard that Matt Busby was very poorly and Duncan Edwards was very, very poorly and we started to hear about the players who had been killed. I remember they mentioned Tommy Taylor's name among those feared dead and that upset me because I idolized Tommy Taylor. I thought of his mother because she used to sit next to us at the match.

After our tea, that had remained largely untouched, I'd still got my homework to do for the next day—all that dreaded algebra for maths. There was no way I could concentrate on quadratic equations though. As we waited for the next radio news bulletin I kept seeing in my mind's eye all the players, especially David Pegg, who for some reason had become a favourite of mine. I don't really know why that was. Perhaps it was because as a boy you always got passed down to the fence at the front of the terrace, and David Pegg out on the left wing was always one of the closest players to me. And when he played he always seemed to be chewing gum. David hadn't played in the match in Belgrade. He'd been kept out of the team since just before Christmas by his great rival for the number eleven shirt Albert Scanlon. But he'd be back; he was too good to be out of the team for long. That night it was impossible to accept that I would never see him or the rest of the team again.

CHAPTER 2

WIPED OUT

It was nearly six o'clock before I'd got the news that, in my dad's words, United had been wiped out, but others, like my wife's cousin Mary Morris, had heard a lot earlier that Thursday afternoon. Many of my friends also got their first news of the crash when they switched on the television for *Children's Hour* at five o'clock, only to see newsreader Richard Baker saying, 'And the reason you've come over to the news studio is that we have to report a serious air crash at Munich Airport. We haven't full details yet, but the aircraft that has crashed is an Elizabethan. It was on charter from British European Airways and travelling from Belgrade to Manchester. The crash was at Munich Airport. On board was the Manchester United football team returning from the World Cup [*sic*] match in Yugoslavia. With them were sports writers of Fleet Street newspapers and, as far as we know, team officials. Twenty-five of the passengers and crew are believed to have died.'

Earlier on that February afternoon one of those sport writers, Alf Clarke, who'd reported on all of United's games for years for the *Manchester Evening Chronicle*, had telephoned the paper's sports desk to say that he thought the flight would be held up by bad weather. By three in the afternoon the *Chron* had 'gone to bed'. The final city editions were leaving the newspaper's offices on Withy Grove when news of the terrible disaster came chattering through on the teleprinter in the newsroom: 'Manchester United aircraft crashed on take-off... heavy loss of life feared.' That was all. The report was unconfirmed, but it went into the stop press of the late city editions of the *Chronicle* and the *News*. By four o'clock the first news of the disaster was out on the streets of Manchester.

As the news was breaking that afternoon, Jimmy Murphy, Matt Busby's wartime friend and now his assistant, was on his way back to Old Trafford from Cardiff. Murphy was manager of the Welsh national side, and a World Cup qualifying game against Israel had coincided with the Red Star fixture. Murphy had told Busby that he would rather go to Yugoslavia than Ninian Park, but his manager told him that his place was with the Welsh side. When he got to Old Trafford, Alma George, Matt Busby's secretary, broke the news to him that the charter flight the team was on had crashed. Murphy was stunned, and at first he couldn't take it in. Alma told him again, but still it didn't sink in. Then she started to cry. She told him that many people had been killed, though she didn't know how many, but some of the players had died. Murphy just could not believe what he was hearing. He said later, 'The words seemed to ring in my head. Alma left me and I went into my office. My head was in a state of confusion and I started to cry.'

As soon as he regained some of his composure he took over arrangements for informing wives and relatives of the party. He was joined in the terrible task by assistant secretary Les Olive, but they often had to wait several minutes to be able to make an outgoing call as the club's telephone system was jammed with incoming calls. Chief scout Joe Armstrong was sent out in a taxi to call on relatives. As he left the ground there was a steady trickle of people coming to the ticket office on the forecourt of the ground to buy tickets for the fifth-round FA Cup tie against Sheffield Wednesday, which was due to be played at Old Trafford the following Saturday.

Armstrong found that many of the relatives he went to call on were not at home. A lot had already left for the airport to meet their loved ones on their triumphant return. They were joined at the airport by fans. One of them was seventy-eight-year-old Joe Hartley, one of United's oldest supporters, who never missed welcoming the team back from their European adventures. Joe sat in the lounge with a red and white scarf around his neck. When Matt Busby's wife Jean arrived he laughed and joked with her, talking excitedly about the team's success the day before. Around them, also waiting for the flight to come in, were some of the players' wives and girlfriends.

BEA Flight 609 was scheduled to arrive at Manchester's Ringway Airport at five o'clock. But at 4.30 p.m. the airport's public address system crackled into life and BEA hostess Jean Swainton spoke softly into the microphone. 'People waiting for BEA Flight 609 from Belgrade should call at the reception desk in the main hall,' she said.

Silently, those who were waiting were led to a lounge. There, BEA airport station manager Gerard Payne told them there had been a serious accident but that full details were not yet known. Mrs Busby collapsed in tears. Two other wives clutched each other screaming, and a woman's voice cried out hysterically, 'All wiped out!' Hostesses tried to comfort them, saying that there were some survivors. Joe Hartley slumped forward in his chair, head in his hands.

Tea and brandy were served, and taxis were

ordered to take the players' wives and girlfriends home. Inside the main hall a woman wearing a white coat whispered, 'There are only ten left. I've just heard it on the radio.' Then Joe Hartley phoned news of the tragedy through to United chairman Harold Hardman at Old Trafford.

Down in the dressing room at the ground a small group of apprentices and youth team players were cleaning the boots of the first-teamers. Their activities were halted when one of their trainers came in and told them that the plane carrying the first team back from Belgrade had crashed. At first the seriousness of the situation didn't register. In fact, the first reaction, some of those who were there recalled later, was to laugh about it; maybe somebody had broken a leg or something, giving one of them their big chance in the first team.

One of the apprentices was fifteen-year-old Nobby Stiles, who went on to distinguish himself as a tough-tackling wing-half not just for United but for England's 1966 World Cup-winning team. Nobby lived at home at the time in Colyhurst, a predominantly Irish Catholic inner-city area of tightly packed terraced houses dominated by the huge St Patrick's Church on Livesey Street. The area was a breeding ground for boxers and for good footballers. As well as Nobby, United's Wilf McGuinness, Brian Kidd and Carlo Sartori, Stan Bowles of QPR and John McGrath of Newcastle came from this area. My Uncle Tommy was in the MacSweeny Pipers, an Irish pipe band that was based at the church, and he told me how some of the band members who knew Nobby and his family said that it was only when he was on his way home from Old Trafford that the horrible truth hit him. By the time he was changing buses in town there were late city editions of newspapers out on the street. Nobby, they said, grabbed a copy off a newspaper seller, and his first thought was how strange it was to see the faces of Roger Byrne, Geoff Bent, Eddie Colman, Mark Jones, David Pegg, Tommy Taylor and Billy Whelan staring out of the front page. They should have been on the back page. And here on the front page it was saying they were dead. 'Eddie Colman can't be dead,' Nobby thought. He cleaned Eddie's boots. None of them could be dead, but especially not Coly. But that's what the *Evening Chronicle* was saying in big black headlines. Nobby remembered feeling sick as he got on the Colyhurst bus. When he got off he knew no one would be at home so he went into St Pat's, where he prayed that the *Chronicle* had got it wrong.

The news was very quickly all over Manchester, and the city went into a state of shock. On the streets, victory placards on the news-stands saying 'United in the semis again' were replaced by 'United disaster'. As the winter sky darkened, anxious, news-hungry crowds began to gather on street corners in a city centre that still bore the scars of German bombing raids carried out during the Second World War. Much of the city had been obliterated during the Blitz, and many of its finest buildings had been destroyed. Some estimates say that up to 70 per cent of Manchester's Victorian and Edwardian buildings were destroyed by German bombs. For three nights prior to Christmas 1940, Luftwaffe bombers dropped incendiary bombs, and for a time the whole city was ablaze; many of the fine historic cotton warehouses of Portland Street were set alight or razed to the ground. Within a mile of Albert Square, and the Town Hall, 165 warehouses,

150 offices, five banks and over two hundred business premises were destroyed or so severely damaged that they had to be demolished. By 1958 most of the demolition work was complete, but some gaunt shells still stood, the ghosts of past Manchester glories, to remind Mancunians of those wartime atrocities, and there were bomb sites all over the city centre, levelled out and covered in black cinders. Most of them were used as car parks. This was the city that was trying to digest news of a terrible tragedy in Germany, a country that was still thought of by many as the enemy.

Beryl Townsend had been following United home and away since 1955. She went to all of the matches with her sister Olga. They were part of a group of friends that included Norman and Madge Williams who had set up an unofficial supporters club that met at a pub on Dale Street in the centre of Manchester every week. Beryl was working in an office on Canon Street, and she too remembers the moment she first heard the news.

> The caretaker there knew I was a big United supporter, and at half past three [*sic*] he came up to me and said, 'I don't know if you've heard, but United's plane has crashed.' At first I didn't think it could have been true because I was convinced they'd been coming home early that morning and if there had been any problem we would have heard by that time. I knew they had to be home as early as possible because they'd got the game on the Saturday against Wolves, and also we'd been told that one of the Old Trafford directors [George Whittaker] had died and they had to get back to attend his funeral. So

> I said to the caretaker, 'I think you must have got it wrong. Maybe it was the journalists who were coming home this afternoon. I'm sure the team were due home this morning.'

But what the caretaker had said had got Beryl worried. 'I was sitting there at my desk getting more and more upset,' she continued. 'I couldn't concentrate on what I was doing, so not much more work got done that afternoon. The time dragged on. Outside it was getting dark. Then, at about ten to five, my boss's wife came into the office and she spoke to him and said, "I'm sorry but it's true about United."' Beryl still found it hard to believe. She said to her boss, 'I'm sorry, but I can't work any more. I've got to get out and find out what's happened.'

Beryl recalled the scene in the centre of Manchester when she left the office:

> I walked up Market Street and everybody was standing around in small groups and talking. On the news-stands the headlines on the latest edition of the evening newspaper said 'United Plane Crash'. So we were all buying the paper trying to find out what was going on. I just didn't know what to do with myself, whether to wait in town in case I got more up-to-date news or whether to go home. In the end I got on the bus and went home to see what news I could get on the radio and television. My sister Olga came in just after I'd got back. Her boss was a United fan and he'd told her what had happened so when she got back home we both sat there crying because nobody knew who was alive and who was dead at that time.

As the twilight gathered and Manchester's uncomprehending workers began to make their way home, news of the disaster spread quickly round the city. Tony Willis lived in Clayton, just round the corner from where I used to live in Bradford before we moved out to Wythenshawe. He'd only just moved to Clayton himself from nearby Ancoats, which was only about half a mile from the centre of town. Ancoats was the world's first industrial suburb. It's now on Britain's list of sites for proposed World Heritage status, but then it was like a vast graveyard, the totally unloved, uncared for, forgotten heritage of the once mighty powerhouse of King Cotton's capital—Cottonopolis. It was while he was living there surrounded by derelict canals, former steam-powered cotton spinning mills, terraced housing and the filth, muck, soot and grime of two centuries of industrial output that Tony started watching United with his dad. By early 1958 his family had moved out to Clayton, not far from the Aniline, but Tony loved Ancoats. For a child it had been an exciting playground, and he loved it so much that he'd insisted on staying on at St Alban's School where all his mates were. He travelled to and from school on the trolley bus along Ashton New Road.

> I can remember getting off the bus at Clayton Aniline that afternoon at about four o'clock. As I got off there were people coming out of work and waiting for buses because there were very few cars then. As I walked past I became aware of a lot of people talking about United. I didn't quite catch it all, but I knew something had happened, so I got home as quickly as I could and then I was told what had occurred. We'd

just got a television, and my abiding memory is of the picture that came on. There was just the one picture of the wrecked plane in the snow, and it kept coming on all that night. That's all we were shown, and I can still see it now in my mind's eye—this grainy black and white image of the wreckage; just the remains of the plane with the snow filtering down on to it. There was talk over the picture—people just talking in general about what had happened—but there wasn't a lot of information. We didn't know very much about it at first, other than that something terrible had happened.

In factories throughout Manchester work stopped earlier than usual as the news began to filter through. Mather and Platts was a huge engineering works in Newton Heath that made generators, transformers and components for power stations. They employed nearly seven thousand people, and Alan Crookall was one of them. He remembers vividly how that afternoon the whole factory just ground to a halt. 'You could hear all the machines all over the factory going off until the whole place was silent,' he told me. 'Nobody in that factory could believe what had happened; that the casualties were so bad.' And one of those casualties, Alan soon discovered, was somebody from Mather and Platts he knew well. *Manchester Guardian* football writer Donny Davies was the headteacher of Mather and Platts apprentice school, and as the chairman of the apprentices committee, Alan dealt with Donny on a daily basis. They learned that afternoon that he was one of the journalists who had perished in the crash. As the list of the dead became known that day, many Mancunians like Alan were touched personally by the tragedy.

In the United heartland of Trafford Park the first sketchy radio flashes that had been heard in the offices and works canteens that afternoon had stunned the work force. Many were United fans, and as the factory hooters sounded and work finished at the nearby factories dozens of men, women and boys came running to the locked offices of the ground. There at Old Trafford, and in the dark, smoky industrial suburbs that surrounded it, were the diehards who'd spent their lives living through the team's ups and downs, standing on the open terraces through rain and snow, peering through the fog at shadowy figures on the far side of the pitch before the days of floodlights. To many of them the players seemed so close they were like family. They all stood together, in incredulous groups, around the newspaper sellers and their display bills.

* * *

Old Trafford stood on the edge of Trafford Park, the world's first and biggest industrial estate, and of the Port of Manchester. Although Manchester was thirty-five miles from the sea, its port was still ranked as the fourth most important in the UK, thanks to the Manchester Ship Canal and the direct access it afforded to the sea. The canal ran through Trafford Park, making it well suited to the import of raw materials and the export of manufactured goods to the world. The Park was a major employer, the industrial home of the Co-operative Wholesale Society, which had a major food packing factory and a flour mill there, and over forty other major companies, many of them connected with food processing and with engineering. It was a major economic success story for Manchester and its working people, and among the big employers was Metropolitan Vickers, known to everyone as Metros, or MetroVicks. It was here that John Alcock and Arthur Brown first met each other and talked the company into building and supplying the Vickers Vimy Aeroplane which they flew non-stop across the Atlantic in 1919.

During the Second World War, Trafford Park was Britain's biggest arsenal. The Metropolitan Vickers Company adapted its machinery when war broke out in 1939 to produce the 'Manchester' and the 'Lancaster' bombers. A thousand Lancasters had been produced in Trafford Park by the end of the war in 1945. MetroVicks also produced other armaments and war supplies including radar equipment, control systems for anti-aircraft guns, automatic pilot systems for aircraft, aerial compasses and bomb defusing equipment. The Ford Motor Company also re-jigged the machines at their Old Trafford factory for the production of Rolls Royce Merlin engines for fighter planes. All this meant that Trafford Park was a prime target for German bombers, and one of the places that was hit was Old Trafford. In March 1941, the main stand was destroyed along with the dressing rooms and the club's offices.

When football resumed after the war the ground was derelict, there were no training facilities, and United had a £15,000 overdraft. That's when Matt Busby stepped in. Matches had to be played at Maine Road, the ground of Manchester City, but Busby, newly returned from the war himself, started to put into practice ideas he'd formed about the game during his playing days with Manchester City and

Liverpool in the thirties. Until this time football managers had been largely office-bound, but Busby put on a tracksuit and got out on to the training ground with the players to show them what he wanted and how he wanted the game to be played. His first Manchester United team was already in place when the club returned to Old Trafford. With a few shrewd buys and his revolutionary new style of management, he'd soon created a team that became one of the most attractive footballing sides in the country.

In the years immediately after the war football attendances were high. Demobbed soldiers, starved for years not just of top-class football but of all forms of leisure activity and entertainment, crowded into football grounds and into dance halls, theatres and cinemas with their wives and girlfriends. There were lost years to be made up. My dad was no exception. When he got back from his wartime service in India he started watching United again, and it was all very different from the United he'd watched before the war when the side was struggling in the Second Division and Arsenal and Huddersfield were the top teams. Like my dad, Norman Williams supported the team back in the bad old days in the 1930s. 'I never thought then, when I was six years old,' he told me, 'that United would one day become such a great team. I used to look at Arsenal as a kid and I was jealous, and I'd say to my dad, "Why can't we play like Arsenal, Dad?" ' I asked Norman what it was like when he first started watching United, and he said he remembered some of the players they had at that time were absolute garbage.

Billy Bryant and a fellow called Smith were two

I remember in particular. But as soon as Matt Busby came after the war he got rid of both of them right away. They lasted for three months at the most. Bryant went to Bradford, I think, and Smith went to Blackburn. But by the time Busby came there were some good players on the books as well, like Johnny Carey, Johnny Morris, Henry Cockburn, Allenby Chilton, Jack Rowley and Johnny Aston. In fact, I think the war cost us titles. I think with some of those players who were around at that time we'd have won the league earlier if it hadn't been for the war.

In the 1946/47 season, when football returned to a national league instead of being divided into northern and southern leagues as it had been during the war, United finished second, one point behind Liverpool, in the First Division championship. They finished the next season and the season after that as runners-up again. My dad and the friends he went to the match with had never seen a United team riding so high in the league. By this time he was going to all of United's matches, home and away. For the away matches he went with the same group every week on a coach from the newsagent's near North Road in Clayton. One of the group was the wife of United full-back Johnny Aston, who lived in Clayton. My dad knew Johnny well and used to go into work with him on the bus when Johnny was on his way to training at Old Trafford.

The highlight of that late 1940s period was the 1948 FA Cup Final against Blackpool. United had dominated the competition that season, reaching Wembley by scoring eighteen goals in five ties. My dad had been to all of them, and he wasn't going to miss the final. He didn't have a ticket, but he went down on the day with my Uncle Tommy, who'd also been to all of the matches, hoping to buy one from a tout. But he didn't have much money and by five to three he still hadn't got a ticket. Then, seeing his red and white rosette, somebody came up to him and offered him a seat at face value. When he got into the ground, just as the teams were lining up, he found that his seat was just next to the royal box and he had a perfect view of what has been described as the greatest FA Cup Final ever. Blackpool led 2–1 until the 69th minute when, after constant pressure, United turned the game around and finished as 4–2 winners.

The reality was, though, that in spite of the fact they had won the Cup in such fine style, the league title continued to elude them. Norman Williams felt the problem was that by this time the war years had taken its toll on the group of players Matt Busby had inherited. Having said that, he added that from the end of the war until 1952 they were an absolutely brilliant team to watch. 'One touch, two touch, great dribbling skills. We had Jimmy Delany with his pace and the subtle touches of Charlie Mitten on the other side. But my favourite was Jack Rowley.' It was a team that finished runners-up in the league three years on the run, then fourth, then second again before finally cracking it. When United won the league in 1952 it was their first championship for forty-one years. And this was only the beginning. Matt Busby had put a scouting system in place to comb the land for the country's finest young players and bring them to Old Trafford, where he brought them up according to his footballing philosophy. Over the six years since he'd arrived at Old Trafford, so successful were Busby and the back-room team he'd put together to groom the youngsters that United won the FA Youth Cup for five successive seasons, starting from its inception in the 1952/53 season.

The team that won the league in 1952 was basically the team that had won the great Cup Final against Blackpool in 1948. In Manchester they were legends, but they were ageing legends: Johnny Carey, the captain, was thirty-three, top scorer Jack Rowley was thirty-two, and most of the others were around thirty. By 1952 the first wave of Babes—Roger Byrne, Mark Jones, David Pegg, Jackie Blanchflower, Dennis Viollet—were knocking on the first team door. Busby had already begun to introduce the first of them into the team: Roger Byrne played on the left wing or at left-back, new signing Johnny Berry was on the right wing, and Mark Jones got the odd game at centre-half. Towards the end of the 1952/53 season players like Duncan Edwards, David Pegg, Jackie Blanchflower, Dennis Viollet and Bill Foulkes all began to get a game or two. It was the beginning of the Busby Babes—a name Matt Busby himself never liked. He always preferred the Red Devils nickname that they soon acquired.

One of the key figures in the United set-up was chief scout Joe Armstrong. The way Joe used to operate was that he would always talk to a lad's mother, not to the father. One of the key players he brought to United was Bobby Charlton. With all his connections with Newcastle through his uncle, Jackie Milburn, a lot of people thought he'd go to St James's Park, but representatives of other clubs were calling round at the Charlton house almost every day. By this time, though, United had captured the imagination of the country with their youth policy, and Bobby Charlton said to Joe, 'I don't know what you're worrying about, Mr Armstrong. I'm signing for United.'

By 1955/56, the season when I first started watching the Reds, Matt Busby had replaced all of the old guard with a team built around youngsters he had taken from school; all but three of them were developed through the juniors and the youth team. That season they took the First Division by storm, winning the league with an eleven-point margin over second-placed Blackpool, which equalled a record shared by Preston, Sunderland and Aston Villa that had stood since the previous century. The achievement was remarkable in that it had come so soon after winning the title in 1952, with an almost completely new team. Roger Byrne and Johnny Berry were the only players from the 1952 championship side in the 1956 side, and they went on to win the league again the following season.

This was the team that, if the reports and the rumours that were flying around were to be believed, had been wiped out that Thursday afternoon.

* * *

By six o'clock a special late edition of the *Manchester Evening Chronicle* was on sale in the city centre. 'About 28 people, including members of the Manchester United football team, club officials, and journalists, are feared to have been killed when a BEA Elizabethan airliner crashed soon after take-off in a snowstorm at Munich airport this afternoon,' it stated. 'It is understood there may be about 16 survivors. Four of them are crew members.' A late final edition of the *Manchester Evening News*, out on the streets about the same time, carried the stark headline

'United Cup XI Crash: 28 Die. Plunged Into Houses At Munich, Exploded. Survivors Saved In Blazing Wreckage.' These first reports were inevitably confused, but what was very clear was that there had been a major catastrophe involving United. 'One of the greatest disasters to befall British football struck Manchester United this afternoon,' the *Evening News* said, 'when the plane carrying the £350,000 wonder team crashed at Munich. At least 28 of the 40 aboard were killed; some reports said higher casualties were feared.' According to these first reports the BEA Elizabethan had just taken off and climbed to sixty feet when it crashed on the outskirts of the city.

By this time a crowd of around a hundred, mainly workers on their way home from the factories of Trafford Park, had gathered outside the ground. Men in bowler hats and white collars stood side by side with men in cloth caps and overalls, waiting for news. There, in little groups, the muted conversations were steered by the same emotions. Disbelief was the main feeling. It wasn't true; it can't have happened; the reports were exaggerated. The Reds had too much of an emotional hold on the people who were gathered here for them to be able to accept what they'd heard. Many had spent a lifetime living through the team's ups and downs as though the players were their own children from their own families. There was also sympathetic concern for the bereaved families, as well as reminiscences of great games they'd been to and great performances by the young players whom the reports were saying were dead. 'To think,' one man said, 'it was only yesterday afternoon that everybody was all over the place in our factory trying to find out what the score in Belgrade was.' Then, as the news sank in, talk turned to how well the team would have done in the forthcoming fixtures. 'The way we've been playing, we'd have murdered Wolves and Sheffield Wednesday. It's a cruel blow, especially as we were just hitting top form.'

Mr Robinson, who lived next door but one to us on Wastdale Road, worked in Trafford Park. He came round to our house that evening to see if we'd got any more news. He said he'd stopped at a pub near Old Trafford on his way home from work and nobody there had been able to bring themselves to accept the full extent of the tragedy. An old man in the corner said he'd first seen United at the Bank Street ground in Clayton when he was a kid fifty years earlier, and he'd watched them through thick and thin, including the time in the 1930s when they nearly went down to the Third Division. A young man in overalls had come in, pulled a bundle of programmes out of his pocket and thrown them down on the bar. 'Best team in the world,' he said, 'and they're all gone. I've been collecting these tokens all season to get a Cup Final ticket, and there's no chance of that now.'

As the night wore on more bits of information came through on news bulletins that interrupted the scheduled programmes on the wireless, and from neighbours calling in with details they had picked up from the television. The story that was emerging was that the plane carrying the team back to Manchester from Belgrade had stopped at Munich to refuel. When they touched down in Germany they were met by blizzard conditions; snow and ice covered the runway and beyond. Conditions were obviously hazardous, and once the aircraft was refuelled there were two attempts to take off, both of which were aborted due to engine problems. On the third attempt, the aeroplane overshot the runway, crashed through a fence and crossed a road; then one of the wings struck a house. Seven of the players, Roger Byrne, Geoff Bent, Mark Jones, David Pegg, Billy Whelan, Eddie Colman and Tommy Taylor were killed instantly—as well as the club secretary, the first team trainer, the first team coach, eight sports writers, one of the aircrew and two other passengers. Matt Busby was seriously ill. He'd suffered fractured ribs and a punctured lung, the reports said, as well as injuries to his legs. A hospital statement said, 'We do not have much hope of saving him.' His condition was grave and he'd been given the last rites. Duncan Edwards, Johnny Berry and Jackie Blanchflower were all in a critical condition; most of the others were lying in hospital with varying degrees of injuries.

Television reports continued throughout the night, but because we didn't have a television in our house we didn't see any pictures of the crash. Nor did we see United chairman Harold Hardman breaking down as a television reporter said to him, 'I know this is a terrible shock to you.' But, recovering quickly, he gave this message to supporters: 'Keep your hearts up. We shall carry on whatever our losses and we shall still have a good team.'

We had to wait until nine o'clock for the next news on the radio. The great big mahogany radiogram in the living room was turned on again, and we heard a list of the names of the members of the Manchester United party who were known to have survived: 'Matt Busby and the following players: Gregg, Wood, Foulkes, J. Blanchflower, Edwards, Morgans, Berry, Charlton, Viollet and Scanlon'. After listing other known survivors, the newsreader went on to confirm our worst fears: 'The people believed to have been on the plane who are so far unaccounted for are, of the Manchester United party, Walter Crickmer (secretary), Bert Whalley (coach), T. Curry (trainer) and the following players: Byrne, Bent, Colman, Jones, Whelan, Taylor and Pegg.' Unaccounted for. The newsreader had not actually said the word, but we knew they were dead; the heart of the team. Roger Byrne and Tommy Taylor who played for England's side and Ireland's Billy Whelan and England's Geoff Bent had died; Mark Jones and Eddie Colman and David Pegg also, they had all given their lives on this far-off, snowy airfield.

'Wiped out.' I couldn't get those first words of my dad's out of my head as the newsreader went on with the terrible news. To me and to many that evening, United had indeed been wiped out.

Others 'unaccounted for' included all of the sports writers of the Manchester and national newspapers who'd flown with the team to report on the match and a number of individuals who had booked on to the flight. One of the sports writers was Frank Swift of the *News of the World*. Big Swifty died in hospital that evening. He'd played for Manchester City for seventeen seasons and had been the greatest goalkeeper of his day. The Queen, it was reported, had sent a message to the Minister of Transport and Civil Aviation and to the Lord Mayor of Manchester in which she spoke of her deep shock at the news of the accident and sent her sympathy and that of the Duke of Edinburgh to the relatives of those who had been killed and to the injured. President Tito of Yugoslavia had also sent his deepest condolences to the Prime Minister, Harold Macmillan.

By the time of that bulletin, an account that *Daily Mail* photographer Peter Howard—one of the survivors of the crash—had telephoned to his office in Manchester that evening, after climbing back into the wreckage to help with rescue work, had also come through. He said it was snowing when they landed at Munich to refuel before taking off again for Manchester. When the pilot tried to take off, there seemed to be a slight engine fault. The pilot stopped, then tried a second take-off. That didn't seem satisfactory either, so he taxied back to the apron to get things checked. On the third take-off, when they crashed, Mr Howard said he thought they were 'about at the end of the runway, only a bit above the ground'. The plane suddenly appeared to be breaking up, accompanied by a rolling sensation. There wasn't time to think, and for some seconds there was 'just a deadly silence'. Another report the BBC carried was from a German correspondent who said the plane had crashed into a wooden barracks at the end of the runway and burst into flames, but it wasn't totally burnt out.

In that nine o'clock news bulletin we also got the first reaction to the crash from the Football League. That night the management committee had an emergency meeting to discuss the immediate consequences of the disaster. United's match against Wolves on the Saturday, billed as the outstanding league match of the season, they decided would not be played. The other ninety clubs in the league, it was agreed, would play their matches and observe two minutes' silence before kick-off. Flags at all grounds would be flown at half mast and all 990 players would wear black armbands as a tribute to their colleagues. In the tradition of the entertainment business, it was felt that the show had to go on as soon as possible.

Again, we didn't listen to the rest of the news. Nothing else counted. We'd lost our football team. I think it was the news of the postponement of the Wolves match that really brought it home. I'd been looking forward to the match for so many weeks, and now it wasn't going to be played. Would we see any more matches at Old Trafford? In the midst of the despair of that evening it didn't look possible. No more roar of the crowd as the red shirts appeared from the tunnel on the halfway line; no more Roger Byrne trotting out at the head of the team; no more towering Tommy Taylor headers; no more jinking, hip-swivelling Eddie Colman sending opponents the wrong way. All unimaginable.

The radio was switched off and I tried to get back to my unfinished algebra homework, spread out on the gate-legged table in the living room, but it was no good. My dad sat down and tried to help me, but it didn't mean any more to him than it did to me. It was as much a foreign language as the five French sentences I had to translate. And anyway, how could you think about maths and French when there were so many questions to be answered about the plane crash? What had happened in Germany that afternoon? Why had the plane made a third attempt to take off after trying and failing twice? Surely they must have known there was something wrong? Why hadn't they just stayed there until the weather got better or the problem was sorted out properly? Such questions would be asked throughout Manchester for many months to come.

I usually had to be in bed by ten o'clock, but there was another bulletin on the Light Programme at half past ten and I was allowed to stay up to see if there was any further news. Sure enough, we got a fuller account of what had happened than anything we'd heard all night when they put out a report from Donald MacKay of Radio Free Europe. Our old radiogram crackled a bit as we listened to his words.

> This is Donald MacKay reporting from Munich, Germany. Late this evening, rescue and clearing operations were continuing around the wreckage of the British European Airlines [sic] plane which crashed near Munich this afternoon. Snow was falling when the plane crashed into a house one hundred yards from Munich's main commercial Riem Airport at four minutes after four, Munich time, and snow continued to fall most of this evening. Rescue workers led by the Lord Mayor of Munich himself, Thomas Weimar, worked painfully in mud and wet snow around the shattered plane. Normal airport traffic was not disrupted by the tragedy. Many of the casualties were thrown free of the wreckage and lay in the snow. At the time the plane crashed, visibility was estimated by the control tower at a mile and a half, but as darkness grew late this afternoon the only light was from the burning plane itself and from the work lights of the firemen and rescue squads reflected by the snow. The first words of the survivors, the witnesses of the crash and the wheel marks made by the twin-engined chartered aircraft itself seem to confirm early reports that the plane barely, if at all, became airborne, before crashing on the fringe of the airport.

I sat on a cushion on the floor leaning against the radiogram, my ear pressed against the speakers. This was more detail than we'd had in any of the previous reports, and acceptance of that afternoon's tragic events was slowly sinking in. My mam brought me a cup of cocoa as the report went on. 'A German customs man I talked to who saw the crash said his impression was that the plane burst into flames and crashed even before leaving the ground to any real extent.' One of the survivors of the thirty-eight passengers and six crew members, sports reporter Peter Howard of Manchester, said this was also his impression. Speaking from his hospital bed to reporters tonight, Mr Howard said his impression was that the plane apparently lacked power to take off.

Information on who exactly was dead and who was alive, who might be able to play football again and whose careers were over, was very confusing, and that is one of my overriding memories of that night and of the next few days—bewilderment and confusion. What was clear already, however, was the extent of the tragedy, the loss of so much young talent, and the fact that United would never be the same again. I wasn't the only one in Manchester that night who went to bed with tears in his eyes.

CHAPTER 3

FOOTBALL TAUGHT BY MATT BUSBY

It was late when I went to bed that Thursday night, much later than usual, and I hadn't got the algebra done, or any other homework for that matter. My room was freezing. None of the bedrooms had any heating, and getting into bed in the middle of winter was a bit of a test of character because the starched cotton sheets we had were even colder than the room itself. When you got into bed it was like sliding in between two sheets of ice. The shock it gave you was like jumping into an icy pool of water, so the routine always had to be the same: get your clothes off and pyjamas on as quickly as possible, dive into bed and roll up into a ball, and gradually edge your feet further and further down the bed as you began to warm it up a bit.

That night was as cold as any I can remember; everything I touched in the bedroom felt icy. A shaft of light cut into the room from the electric light on the landing, and as I lay in bed I could see the framed picture of United I had on the wall at the end of the bed. I've not got it now, but I can still see it: a glossy black and white team photograph with the shirts coloured in red and the Popular Side in the background. My dad had put it into an old wooden frame he'd got from work. It was the team that had won the league in 1956, and, although Matt Busby had made some changes, the players on that team photo are still for me the Busby Babes. I looked at it and tears came to my eyes as I thought about the players and some of the games I'd seen them play. This was my team, and it had been annihilated that afternoon. Of the eleven players in the picture, six were confirmed dead and four were in hospital, and we didn't know if or when they would ever play again.

The goalkeeper who looked down from my bedroom wall was Ray Wood. Ray had been at Old Trafford for years and was one of the players who provided a link with Matt Busby's first great United team, the one that won the Cup in 1948 and the league championship in 1952. He'd been signed from Darlington in 1949 and made his United debut that same year, but it wasn't until the 1953/54 season that he established himself as first-choice keeper. He was a very good shot stopper, though his handling of crosses sometimes let him down. 'You didn't get miracles from Ray,' Matt Busby once said, 'he was just there when it mattered.' A few weeks earlier he'd lost his place in the team when Harry Gregg arrived at Old Trafford bearing the tag 'The World's Most Expensive Goalkeeper'. Gregg was a more commanding figure who made the penalty area his own personal territory. In contrast to Wood, Gregg was totally dominant in the air. He had a massive determination to make any cross that came his way his own, and once he committed himself to getting a ball he usually got it, and then immediately looked for a way to start United back on the attack. Both keepers, we knew from the news reports, had survived the crash. Gregg was one of the few who walked out of the wreckage; Wood was in hospital with bruises and flesh wounds.

The right-back in the picture was Bill Foulkes. Bill was an ex-coal-miner from St Helens, and a reliable, no-nonsense, hard-tackling right-back who for the first few years of his United career kept his job down the pit. ‘A big, rough, tough and reliable lad from St Helens’ was the way Matt Busby described him. Foulkes was another of the survivors who had walked away from the crash. But then, everybody else on that picture, from left-back all the way through to left-wing, was either dead or seriously injured.

Roger Byrne was the captain, the man I’d seen lifting the championship trophy, and because he was a bit older than most of the other players he was seen as something of a father figure. Byrne was captain before I started watching United. He was a local lad from Gorton who made his debut in 1951 and became club captain in 1954. When United won the league in 1952 he played on the left wing, but when Busby wanted him to play there permanently he wasn’t happy and asked for a transfer. Busby backed down and quickly made Byrne a left-back, a position he soon made his own, not just for United but for England also. According to what you read about the team he commanded a lot of respect in the dressing room and he was a key figure in making the Babes the team they were. I remembered him particularly for his pace, and because on the pitch he always appeared to be such a cool, confident character. Matt Busby had a high regard for him, describing him as ‘an aristocratic footballer, majestic in his movement’.

> Roger was so fast—one of the fastest full-backs of all time—but at the same time he controlled his movement beautifully, like Nureyev. He would go up the wing to attack, but always had the speed to get back before the opposition could make anything of it. Often he would give

the other fellow a bit of a start before running to catch him, just to keep things interesting. Roger was brilliant at intercepting passes. He could read a situation very quickly and make a move to counteract it. And he had the knack of jockeying wingers into positions where he could tackle them before they could make a move. Great as they were, Stanley Matthews and Tom Finney never played well against Roger. In fact, I don't think Stan liked playing against him at all.

Little Eddie Colman was one of my favourites, a real local lad, born and brought up in a two-up-two-down terraced house in Archie Street in Ordsall, just by the docks about a mile from Old Trafford. He was one of the youngest players in the team. He'd only made his debut in the 1955/56 season but he'd made the right-half position his own. He was one of those players who was a joy to watch, and he'd established himself as a great favourite with the supporters at Old Trafford. Eddie used to entertain the crowd with an impudent array of skills, in particular a body-swerve that left defenders for dead. He also had the ability to see and deliver a pass that could instantly tear the opposition apart, and he was able to control the ball instantly with either foot. One of his favourite tricks, I remember, was to receive the ball on the touchline and beat an opponent just by body-swerving and rolling the ball back and forth with the sole of his boot. Matt Busby described him as 'the little stylist with the wonderful shake of the hips and great control of the ball'. But we'd never see that body swerve again because Eddie was dead.

Centre-half Mark Jones came from a mining

village near Barnsley, and had captained England schoolboys before making his United debut as a seventeen-year-old in 1950. Off the field he was a gentle budgerigar collector, but on it he was a hard rock of a man, the classic centre-half, big, strong, hard-tackling and commanding in the air, the linchpin of United's defence. I always found it amusing that, young as he was, whenever you saw a picture of the team—like the one that had been taken a few days earlier on the steps of the aircraft, before they flew to Belgrade—Mark was always wearing a trilby like one of my uncles. As well as that he smoked a pipe, even though he was only twenty-four, and he was reputed to be something of a father figure, always on hand to make sure none of the younger players overdid it when they were out. Mark, too, was one of the dead.

Then there was Duncan Edwards. I knew he was good, but I didn't realize at the time that I was watching one of football's all-time greats—perhaps the greatest footballer this country has ever produced. He was a power-house, end-to-end type of player—tall, strong, fast, and blessed with limitless stamina. He played at left-half, but he could have played anywhere as he was two-footed, a great tackler, strong in the air, a fine passer of the ball, and the possessor of a fierce and accurate shot. One minute he'd be back, clearing off his line, the next he'd be surging forward at the other end. There were just no weaknesses to his game. He made his United debut when he was only sixteen, and two years later he won his first England cap—the youngest England player so far that century. His legs were like tree trunks; he always wore his shorts hitched up, folded over a couple of times at the waistband, to leave his massive thighs uncovered. In 1957 he'd played in nearly all of the first team matches, but he was still in the Army on National Service so he played for them too, as well as turning out regularly for England. Within a twelve-month period he played just short of a hundred games for United, England and the Army. Matt Busby described Edwards as 'the player who had everything'.

> He was so big, so strong, and so confident. And so young. We used to look at players in training to see if we might have to get them to concentrate more on their kicking, perhaps, or their heading, or ball control, whatever. We looked at Duncan, right at the start, and gave up trying to spot flaws in his game. Apart from anything else, he could move upfield, brushing players aside as he went, and lash in goals when we needed them. Nothing could stop him and nothing unnerved him. The bigger the occasion, the better he liked it. He had no nerves before a game. While other players would have to be pacing up and down a dressing room, rubbing their legs, doing exercises and looking for ways to pass the time, Duncan was always calm. He was a good type of lad too. Duncan didn't want to know about the high life. He just wanted to play and go to his digs or go home. He lived for his football.

Duncan Edwards was in a critical condition, fighting for his life in the hospital in Munich.

At thirty, Johnny Berry was the old man of the team, and he was one of the few players in it who had not come up through the ranks at Old Trafford. After

Matt Busby had spent eighteen months trying to sign him from Birmingham City, he joined the club in the 1951/52 season, and had been a regular star of the side in the number seven shirt ever since—only losing his place to Kenny Morgans a few weeks before the crash. As well as the classic winger's abilities, in particular his tremendous knack for getting to the goal-line and sending in dangerous crosses, Johnny was a determined little player who had the heart of a real competitor. He had an eye for goal and he was cool under pressure, as he showed when he stepped up to take the vital penalty against Blackpool that secured the title for United in 1956. Now Johnny's condition was described as very serious indeed. He was suffering from shock and concussion, he had an eye injury, and he had lost consciousness. Morgans was also among the injured in hospital, with concussion and suspected fractures. Kenny was only eighteen, an outstanding prospect who seemed to have the footballing world at his feet. After making his debut earlier that season, he had put in some excellent performances and unexpectedly ousted Berry from the right-wing position. His nippy style of play and confident ball control looked set to make him a firm United favourite for years to come, but how bad were his injuries? Would he ever be able to play again?

Liam Whelan, or Billy as he was known to all the fans, was a traditional inside-forward with a great eye for goal, a body-swerve nearly as good as Eddie Colman's and the ability to put his foot on the ball and slow the game down. He was a brilliantly gifted player, tall, graceful and tremendously skilful, a real genius with the ball at his feet. Billy, we all knew, was a devout, teetotal Catholic lad from Dublin who had chosen soccer ahead of Gaelic football after winning medals for both. He'd been spotted by United and brought to Manchester when he was seventeen. Although he too had lost his place just before the crash, to Bobby Charlton, he was still young and I'd had no doubt he was going to be back. If he had a problem about his game, it was probably because of his shyness and the fact that he wasn't very assertive. Matt Busby said, 'I don't think he knew just how good he was.'

Tommy Taylor was another member of that 1956 team who had come from a mining background, and another who was an England regular. For me he was the most exciting player in the team. I'll never forget how high he used to be able to leap to head the ball. He signed for his hometown team, Barnsley, in 1948 when he was fifteen and scored a hat-trick in his second game for them. He joined United five years later, in March 1953, for a then record fee of £29,999, and scored on his debut against Preston with a stunning header. Tommy was a powerful centre-forward who was great in the air, so good that he ranks with the all-time great centre-forwards. He was also a clinical finisher with both feet, and an unselfish player who would always put somebody else in on goal if he had a clearer chance. In fact, he always seemed to be just as happy making goals as scoring them.

Dennis Viollet was another Manchester lad, a natural goal-scorer with lightning reactions in the box. With his electric pace and wonderful dribbling skills he was the ideal striking partner for Tommy Taylor, who was so accomplished in the air. He would spot Tommy making a move for the ball, either in the air or on the ground, and could work out where to position himself to take advantage. He could read a situation before a defence could. And not only could he take chances, he could also create them with wonderful touches of skill. It was always a bit of a mystery to me why he didn't get into the England team, especially because he had such a good partnership at United with Tommy Taylor, an England regular.

Left-winger David Pegg was another lad who came from a coal-mining background, this time from Doncaster. It was hard to believe that he was only twenty-two years old when he died; he'd made his United debut over five years earlier at the age of seventeen, and by the time I'd started watching them he was an established face in the Old Trafford set-up. He was quick, and he had a decent shot, but his greatest strength was his ball-playing skills. A natural left-sided player, rather than go outside the full-backs, his favourite trick was to cut inside and go for goal himself. That said, he was also a very good crosser of the ball. Many a goal came when he put the ball on to the head of Tommy Taylor.

David Pegg was one of my favourite players, but he had a rival for the left-wing berth and for a few weeks before Munich he'd lost his place to Albert Scanlon. Albert was a tricky two-footed winger whose speed was his most effective weapon. He kept Pegg out on merit and put in some brilliant performances, especially in the 5–4 win at Arsenal the previous Saturday when he had been the star man. But Pegg had real class and I always thought he would be back. It was interesting to hear what Matt Busby had to say years later about the two of them and their rivalry. 'David Pegg,' he said, 'was a great asset then and would always have been a great asset to any team because he was a natural left-flank player. David was very, very clever. He was our best left-winger by a mile. Albert Scanlon was a good direct type of winger, but David was the kind you do not find very often.'

And then, of course, there was Matt Busby himself, the father of this great young team, who was lying in hospital, his injuries extensive, his condition critical. 'Please God,' I prayed, 'don't let him die as well.'

When I looked up at that photograph that night it was still almost impossible to believe that many of these flowers of English football had been destroyed. So many great footballers who would never play again. This United team had been on the verge of greatness. Most of the players had not yet reached their peak and fresh young talent was emerging all the time to complement the skills of the 1956 and 1957 championship-winning side. There was healthy competition for some of the positions from players like Kenny Morgans, Albert Scanlon, Alex Dawson and Wilf McGuinness, and good reserve cover for just about every position provided by the likes of Geoff Bent, Ian Greaves, Jackie Blanchflower and Freddie Goodwin. But for me, the most exciting of the young players coming through at that time was Bobby Charlton. He'd played in the Red Star match, and, thankfully, he was one of the survivors of the crash.

One of my most treasured football memories is going with my dad to see the match against Charlton Athletic at Old Trafford at the beginning of October 1956 when eighteen-year-old Bobby Charlton made his league debut. He had joined United as an amateur in January 1953. Two years later, on his seventeenth birthday, he turned professional, and the same season he helped United to lift the FA Youth Cup. Right from the start he looked like a special sort of footballer—an elegant attacking player with a good eye for the telling pass and a powerful shot. For the game against Charlton Athletic, Roger Byrne, Duncan Edwards and Tommy Taylor were all away on international duty, so Bobby Charlton got his chance coming in at centre-forward for Taylor with Geoff Bent coming in for Byrne and young Wilf McGuinness deputizing for Edwards. Wilf was a Manchester lad who'd come up through the youth team. He was a very promising, tough-tackling wing-half who'd already made a few first team appearances. Geoff Bent was another local lad, from Salford. Another good ball winner, he could play on the right side of defence as well as the left, and was noted for his speed, distribution and calmness under pressure. If he'd been on the books of any other English team, Bent would certainly have been a regular first team player, but unfortunately he found himself behind captain Roger Byrne in the United squad. I've always thought Geoff Bent's death at Munich one of the most tragic, because he didn't really need to be there.

Back on that October afternoon in 1956, the Charlton Athletic match was the only time I saw Geoff Bent play, and he, along with Charlton and McGuinness, gave the team a very youthful look. In the absence of Roger Byrne, Johnny Berry, United's most experienced player, captained the side from outside-right. We got into the ground early and I got a place on the fence on the Popular Side, almost on the centre line. The cartoons in the match programme made a bit of a play on the fact that it was Charlton versus Charlton, and it was Bobby not Athletic who took the eye that afternoon, scoring two cracking goals in a fairly comfortable 4–2 win for United. Johnny Berry and Billy Whelan got the others.

Bobby Charlton also played in the first ever match I went to see at Old Trafford. Before we moved to Wythenshawe I'd been asking my dad if I could go with him to see United for a long time, and eventually he agreed to take me to an FA Youth Cup match against Newcastle United in the 1955/56 season. The FA Youth Cup was of massive importance to United at that time. It was an Under-18 knockout tournament, and in Matt Busby's opinion it was essential for United to win it in order to show that their policy of finding and nurturing the best young players really was the best way to guarantee the club's future. Youth team matches attracted big crowds to Old Trafford, and the United youth team was simply unbeatable. They won the Cup for the first five years of its existence, going forty-three games without defeat.

As we approached the ground that afternoon the first thing I became aware of was the smell. The distinctive smell around Old Trafford was like nothing else I've ever come across. I can still recall it to this day, but to try to describe it is difficult. To me it was the smell of heavy industry, slightly acrid, certainly not very healthy. My dad said it was something to do with Procter and Gamble's soap works, which was nearby. In the 1930s it was the biggest soap and candle factory in the world and by the late 1950s it was employing over eight hundred people, producing brands like Fairy Soap and Camay.

There were around twenty thousand in the ground for the game, and no wonder that these Youth Cup games attracted such big crowds, because what a game it was! The lads in the youth team had only one thought in mind and that was to attack, and that afternoon they ran out 7–3 winners against a good Newcastle team. It was exciting to watch, and above all it was entertaining. United conceded three goals, but they were always going to score more with the talent they had in that team and their absolute commitment to driving forward. It's over fifty years ago now, but I still think about that first game I went to because the young players who came through from the youth team in the 1950s were the embodiments of Matt Busby's approach to football, and they laid the foundations for everything Manchester United now stands for—winning the game, and winning it in style. Football as taught by Matt Busby. Over the years this philosophy has provided much drama, excitement and entertainment and its still there to this day in Alex Ferguson's United. In April 2007 I attended a match at Old Trafford that ranks with any from that time, a match that carried on the traditions established in the 1950s, one that Matt Busby himself would have been proud of. For those who weren't around at the time, United's 7–1 annihilation of AS Roma in the second leg of the 2006/07 Champions League quarter-final was a bit like what watching the Busby Babes was like.

That FA Youth Cup tie against Newcastle was, like the Roma game, a great team effort, but what I remember it for more than anything else was the performance of one man who went on to embody the Manchester United spirit more than anybody else. Seventeen-year-old Bobby Charlton scored a hat-trick and was the outstanding player on the pitch. Grace, elegance, power, and a thunderous shot—all the attributes of a great attacking player. Bobby Charlton had them all, and they were all there on show that afternoon in a performance I've never forgotten.

*   *   *

Watching United in the 1950s at any level—first team, reserves, youth team—was watching the beautiful game. But it was all set in some distinctly unlovely surroundings. With its mills and factories and its mile upon mile of inner-city terraced houses, the Manchester of the 1950s still looked like the city from which mass industrialization had spread across the world. Its rivers and canals were dirty and polluted, the city constantly blotted out by thick yellow pea-souper smog. Standing on the edge of one of the biggest industrial estates in the world, Old Trafford was particularly badly affected, and the atmosphere around the ground was unhealthy. Apart from the smells there was the constant fog. Even when the sun was shining there always seemed to be a constant haze and on bad days, when there was a match, players at the other end of the pitch would be quite indistinct as you peered through the gloom to watch.

In the early fifties I was too young to go with my dad—or at least that's what he and my mam said. Instead I had to be content with his reports when he got back. We were living on Grey Mare Lane then between Bradford Pit and Grey Mare Lane Market, and my dad was still going to the matches on the coach from Clayton. Our house was in the middle of a row of terraces and we were surrounded by railway lines, canals, a chemical works, a coal pit, a gasworks, a coke works, and dozens of mills, foundries and engineering works. The smell from the factories and the chemical works made the atmosphere rancid and acrid and created a semi-permanent greeny yellow smog. When you put clean clothes on they were dirty in no time. I think we were still a bit of an unhygienic nation then: a bath maybe once a week on a Saturday—if you had one—and your clothes washed once a week—if your mam went to the wash-house or had a boiler.

In the winter we rarely saw the sun from one week to the next. When the fog was really bad it invaded our school, St Brigid's RC Primary just round the corner next to the church on Mill Street. The fog would make the classrooms cold and damp until the boiler warmed up and heated the frozen pipes, which clanged with the steam, and then the fog disappeared. The fog could be so bad that I remember one night going to the New Royal pictures on Ashton New Road, and when we came out it was so thick that it was difficult to find our way home because we couldn't see the names on the streets.

According to a survey conducted in the 1930s, the area we lived in was the unhealthiest place in Britain. We were an island in the middle of Manchester, surrounded by all the remnants of the industrial revolution. All around I could hear the hooters from the engineering works signalling the beginning and end of shifts. On a Saturday or a Sunday morning I'd go for a walk with my dad through this industrial landscape. It had its own sort of magic. We'd go past the Lancashire Hygienic Dairies grocer's shop on our corner, where sugar and butter and other essentials like dried peas were all sold loose, and bacon was cut on a great big slicing machine with a dangerous-looking blade. At the traffic lights we'd turn right along Ashton New Road and walk past a pub on every corner towards Clayton Aniline. The Clayton Aniline Company manufactured textile dyes which were exported all over the world. It had been there for nearly eighty years, by the side of the Ashton Canal, which provided a plentiful supply of water—the key raw material in dye manufacture. All I knew about this place, though, was that it was some sort of chemical works, and the horrible smell from it used to hang over the whole area. It was so bad that it made rotten eggs smell quite fragrant.

Opposite the Aniline we'd turn down Bank Street towards Phillips Park. My dad always used to tell me that this was United's first ground. It was before his time, but his father had seen them play there. Just beyond the place where United used to play was the back entrance to Phillips Park, with the broad sweep of the Red River flowing through it. The Red River was the River Medlock and it wasn't really red, or at least the river itself wasn't red (it was more of a dirty brown), but its banks were covered in red brick and it all looked rather splendid.

After a short walk along the river and through the cemetery, the excitement really began when we came out on to Forge Lane—a dark corridor of mining and engineering. On one side, just down a short side street, was the great pithead gear of Bradford Pit with the wheels at the top whirling round as the coal was hauled up from the depths of the earth. On the other side was a place that I thought must be what hell was like. Johnson's Wire Works stretched all along one side of the road with big double doors opening up on to the road to reveal a gloomy, machine-filled interior illuminated by the flickering lights of fires set at intervals across the vast shop floor. There was something that was fascinating about the sight, but it was also a bit scary, and I was always reluctant to walk close to it. I always felt happier walking along the other side of the road at what I regarded as a safe distance from the flames.

On the next street at the back of our house there were gaps in the row of terraced houses where they'd been bombed in the Blitz and the houses had been pulled down to leave what we called crofts. On one of them, immediately behind our house, there was an old wrecked lorry that provided hours of amusement as we played at loading it up and driving it. Other crofts were utilized as cricket and football pitches, or for building dens and playhouses, and on bonfire nights we had our 'bommies' on them. Summers always seemed warmer then, and on Saturday nights we would sit on the back step and listen to the roar of the speedway from Belle Vue.

Ancoats was only a short walk from where I lived, and I talked to Tony Willis about living in that part of east Manchester, and about the part that football played in our lives from an early age. Tony's dad used to take him to watch United at Old Trafford one week and City at Maine Road the following week. 'You might have a favourite team, and in my case it was United,' he told me, 'but it didn't matter. It was football, and we wanted to watch it whoever was playing.' That's the way it was then. Manchester didn't just have one good team, it had two. Most people supported one or the other, but just because you supported one it didn't mean you hated the other. We both remembered plenty of United supporters who went to watch City with their mates who were City fans, and vice versa. 'And you didn't support United then just because United were winning all the time,' Tony added.

I can remember in the 1954/55 season we got beat three times by City. We got beat in the Cup and in the two league games that season. I can remember the Cup game at Maine Road because Allenby Chilton was still playing that season and he got sent off for swearing at the ref. Roy Paul and Don Revie were playing for City and they both went to the ref and said, 'Let him stay on,' but he was off and we got beat 2–0. One of the reasons that game sticks in my head is because the crowd was so big and we were so crushed that they let all the little kids over the white wall and on to the track around the pitch. And then we got beat 5–0 by them at Old Trafford in the same season, and Roger Byrne, Duncan Edwards, Mark Jones, Bill Foulkes and Jackie Blanchflower were all playing that day.

But I was always United. I think that was only because as a boy I identified more with that team because they were so young. City were a great team and I enjoyed watching them because we all loved football so much then, but to us they were old men. They weren't really, but they were to us. With United you could see something in them that was closer to yourself because the Babes weren't much older than you were and they were such great footballers. There was a newness and a freshness about them, and a freedom in the way they played—something that you'd not seen before. United really were a breath of fresh air.

Tony also recalled the hours of playing football on the croft with everyone trying to copy the skills of the Babes.

Near us, everyone practised Eddie Colman's body-swerve, or at least tried to, when they were playing on the croft. We didn't have much in the way of greenery around there, but a croft would do. As kids we were very territorial. You'd only have to move two or three streets away and you were in someone else's territory. Our territory was Woodward Street, which was lined with two-up-two-downs. You walked straight in off the street into the parlour, which always had to be nice. Then you walked through to the room where you lived and there was a big brown enamel sink in the corner with a block of carbolic soap and a lead pipe sticking out of the wall with a tap on the end of it—cold, of course, no hot water. But because you were a kid that didn't seem to matter. Life was good as a kid. For me at least. We didn't have a lot, but hey.

It was a time when everybody used to stick together because we couldn't survive on our own. There was a collectiveness, a cohesion between everybody in that community; there was an understanding that if you didn't stand with one another you wouldn't survive. When we were kids we had an invisible support network. You had the woman next door to come in and help if your mum got ill—but God forbid that ever happening because your mum couldn't afford to be ill. It was the women who got us through, not the guys. Your auntie took you to school and picked you up and done the old fella's cut up because he could never have done it on his own. Then there was Mrs Simpkins who was almost like a soothsayer, giving good advice and delivering kids and laying out and washing the bodies when somebody died. All of these things were part of the network and the tapestry of life that kept us going.

Tony still lives in Clayton, very close to where I used to live on Grey Mare Lane, and we talked for a long time about the way it used to be there when we were young and Matt Busby was getting a team together that looked as though it would conquer the world. The football was always big with us, as it was with most kids at the time. We lived for football in many respects. We'd spend all our days playing out, cricket as well in the summer. We'd put our coats down at one end or a couple of bits of wood for the goals or the wickets and we'd got a game. We even used the gable ends of the terraced houses. Not that the people who resided in them thanked you for it, but there were goalposts and wickets chalked on to a lot of them. We always found a little bit of space to play. We remembered how on glorious summer nights in places like Ancoats, Bradford and Colyhurst all the kids would be out playing, inventing their own forms of amusement. The girls would throw their skipping ropes around the gas lamps to make swings and the lads would kick a tennis ball against the gable end of a house. These were the kind of nights when any child felt comfortable and secure, and all those you loved so dearly sat outside. Chairs usually confined to the kitchen were brought out. Some of the women sat on the doorsteps with cups of tea, chatting with neighbours, catching up on gossip as the sound of Radio Luxembourg came from one of the houses: 'We are the Ovaltinies, little girls and boys!' Life was poor in money but rich in love and affection; few material possessions, but a wealth of concern and warmth. These were working-class nights in a working-class street in a working-class city, nights when nothing could spoil the bliss, apart from the wail of 'Time for bed, come on in!' This was the Manchester that was the background to the rise of the Busby Babes, the sort of atmosphere and environment that had nurtured most of them.

By the time I started to go to watch United, we'd moved from Bradford, with its pit and wire works and terraced houses, to Wythenshawe. When I left St Brigid's Primary School, my mam got a card from my teacher, Miss Gahan. She said she would be sorry to see me go because it had been a pleasure for her to have me in her class, but we were moving to a better place. It made it sound as though we were going to heaven. In a way, it was. We'd got a brand-new house with a garden at the front and the back and miles and miles of Cheshire countryside starting at the end of the road. Wythenshawe was Manchester's largest district, a massive new housing estate that was created as a so-called 'Garden City' where an overspill population could be rehoused away from what was regarded as the squalor of inner-city areas like Ancoats, Ardwick, Bradford and Beswick. But in its early days the estate had its problems. The houses were better and the air was fresher, but the upheaval and resettlement of such large numbers of people took little account of community spirit, as the estate was built initially without many amenities or services. Another problem was that there was very little employment directly to hand and people had to travel six or seven miles into town, as my dad did, or get special buses to Trafford Park. Still, Wythenshawe felt like a brave new world—just as it did for me at Old Trafford.

* * *

The first league match I went to was against Aston Villa in February 1956. It was a top of the table versus bottom of the table game on a bleak mid-winter's day. We got into the ground early and made for the middle of the Popular Side. There, almost opposite the players' tunnel in the middle of the main stand on the other side of the ground, my dad took me down to the railings and took his place a few steps up the terrace just behind me. Villa, without an away victory all season, were facing a United team still holding an unbeaten home record after fifteen matches, but it didn't matter to me. It could have been the Cup Final as far as I was concerned, so excited was I to be at my first proper United game. As we waited for the kick-off, the Beswick Prize Band played a selection of music and United's mascot, Jack Irons, walked round the pitch. What a sight he was—long red tail-coat with white trousers, a red and white bowler hat and a red and white umbrella.

When United ran out on to the pitch, there was one player who stood out above all the others. He was one of the biggest, he had his shorts hitched up around his waist so that they were shorter than anybody else's, and as he ran out he kept leaping up into the air with great enthusiasm. It was Duncan Edwards, and it looked as though he couldn't wait to get started.

Roger Byrne won the toss and United began by attacking the goal to our right, at the Stretford End. Playing conditions were difficult. The pitch was covered in about an inch of snow and it must have been rock hard underneath. Players were sliding about all over the place, and it looked cold and wet out there. I don't know whether it was the conditions or the spirit of the Villa team, who were clearly still clinging to the hope that they could avoid relegation, but it was hard going for United. Billy Whelan, playing at inside-right, eventually managed to get a goal and United came out with a narrow 1–0 win. Inside-right, my dad said, was the one position that was causing a bit of a problem. First Jackie Blanchflower had been tried there, then John Doherty. They'd both been in and out of the team, but now Matt Busby had found this exciting young prospect from Dublin.

From that first game onwards I was hooked. For a nine-year-old Old Trafford was a magical place. Not only was it the football ground where you could see the most exciting players in Britain, but there were the views from the terraces and the fascination of the industrial hinterland that surrounded the ground. It was a landscape of dozens of chimneys that belched smoke skywards from the coal-fired furnaces of Trafford Park. Behind the Popular Side terraces and stand with its structural steelwork by Edward Wood was one of the biggest and tallest factory buildings I'd ever seen. There were great piles of coal and railway lines behind the high wall that surrounded it, and on top of the building were two or three huge black things that looked like great big coal tenders or hoppers. On top of them, looking like tiny insects, there were always two or three men looking down on the ground on match days.

Then there were the docks. Thirty-five miles inland it might be, but Manchester had some of the biggest docks in the country. If you approached the ground over the Trafford Road swing bridge you could look right into the heart of the docks along the Ship Canal on either side. Like United and Old Trafford, the docks were in Salford and Stretford, but they were very much a Manchester enterprise and the port was a thriving centre for Britain's exports at a time when the country was still a leading manufacturing nation. Throughout the fifties it was one of the biggest docks in the country, handling around sixteen million tons of cargo every year. Everything about the docks was big, especially the enormous gantries that stood there. I was fascinated by it all, and one Saturday we even got on to the docks before going to the match. A Royal Navy submarine was visiting Manchester and it was open to the public for viewing. That was unbelievably exciting, and a bit scary—going on board a submarine and having a look round. I even got to look up the periscope.

By the beginning of April 1956 United's only challengers for the league title were Blackpool. Unbeaten at Old Trafford in all nineteen league matches that had been played there that season, United went into the game knowing that victory would seal the championship. It was the biggest match I'd been to so far, and it was a chance to see Stanley Matthews in action. That was the great thing about going to football matches then: you wanted your team to win, but you also wanted to see the famous players from other teams, and you'd enjoy seeing them play well. My dad knew the gates would be locked well before kick-off so we set off early. It was just as well, because he was right about the size of the crowd. The gates were closed a quarter of an hour before the match started when there were over sixty thousand packed into the ground and thousands more queuing up at the turnstiles outside. We were safely inside the ground by then, at the Stretford End, between the goals and the corner flag. We'd worked our way down to the front and I'd got a place on the railings, but the ground got so full and there was such a crush before kick-off that the police let some of us lads at the front over the railings on to the grass that surrounded the pitch.

Conditions were ideal as the teams came out on to the pitch, and just before kick-off, as the captains tossed up, the Blackpool mascot, dressed in a long tangerine cloak and a tangerine turban, came to the centre spot and put a live duck down there. Roger Byrne lost the toss and United began by attacking the Stretford End, where we were, but soon the ball was at the other end, and within ninety seconds of the whistle blowing Blackpool had taken the lead with a header from Perry after a throw-in by Stanley Matthews.

At half-time United were still a goal down and it was beginning to look a distinct possibility that they would suffer their first home defeat of the season. But the crowd was behind them: the main stand had risen to the players as they trooped off the pitch at half-time even though they were a goal down. I was right up near the goal-line on what would be Blackpool's right wing in the second half, so there would be a really close-up view of Stanley Matthews' dribbling skills. But there weren't as many Blackpool attacks as there had been in the first half. In the second half there was a confidence in the United team and around the ground that the Reds would pull it off, which they did with a goal from Tommy Taylor and a penalty converted by Johnny

Berry. Even then there were a few scares; it took two magnificent interceptions by centre-half Mark Jones to ensure that United got both points. When the final whistle blew, the crowd went mad. United were champions with two games to spare. My first season watching them, and they'd won the league. And what a great game it had been to clinch the title: two top teams with everything to play for and an exciting ninety minutes played in front of a packed crowd.

Plans were made for the league championship trophy to be officially presented after the last game of the season against Portsmouth. In the meantime, in the *Manchester Evening News* on the Monday night following the match, the first thoughts of Roger Byrne, ever the sportsman, were for another team and another player, for Manchester City had reached the FA Cup Final for the second year in a row. 'Well, it's all over now,' he said, 'and what a thrilling climax to the season. Players and spectators alike could have wished for nothing better than to have taken part in such a game. We only hope at Old Trafford that the Cup Final at Wembley will be half as exciting, then everybody will be happy. We have done our share towards the double. It's up to Roy Paul [the City captain] and his boys to complete the show!' And that's the way it was. City were rivals, but they were a Manchester team and players and fans alike wished them well. Byrne also showed real feeling for his adversary that day, the great Stanley Matthews. 'The only two unhappy things concerning last Saturday,' he continued, 'were the fact that the "boss" was absent and that Stanley Matthews was on the losing side. The least we could do was to put on an exhibition that would have done Mr Busby proud had he been there to witness it. Secondly was the fact the “maestro” has still to win his League Championship medal. He was so near, and now he is as far away as ever. “That is football,” as Stan admitted to me after the game.’

You’d go to Old Trafford to see United win, but you’d also go to see the likes of Stanley Matthews play well. I loved watching Tom Finney too, and Nat Lofthouse, and Jimmy McIlroy. These were players you just wanted to see. The fact that they played for the opposition didn’t stop you from liking them or wanting to see what they could do. It wasn’t like it is now, when kids are so partisan that they boo good players if they play for the opposition. You certainly didn’t boo any of them then. In fact you were waiting for something special to happen because you knew they were good, and your love for football transcended the fact that you were a United supporter or City supporter. If you saw something happen in the game that was good you applauded it regardless of who created it. You wanted it to be your team, of course, but if someone else did something well, you clapped. First and foremost we were fans of football. All that’s lost in the game now.

United’s last game of the 1955/56 season was at home to Portsmouth and the League Championship trophy was to be presented at the end of the game. Although the title had been won, the new champions were out to hold on to their impressive unbeaten home record. The early editions of the *Manchester Evening News* commented on the fact that it was fitting that United were again at full strength. This meant that Johnny Doherty was playing at inside-right rather than Billy Whelan, who had still not fully established himself in the first team, and Ian Greaves was still keeping Bill Foulkes out of the right-back berth. The ground was packed again, the gates locked well before kick-off. With the league title in the bag the crowd was in carnival mood on a beautiful spring afternoon. But the Reds did a thoroughly professional job on the pitch and retained their unbeaten record at Old Trafford, a goal from Dennis Viollet giving them a 1–0 win.

Five minutes before the end of the game the magnificent old First Division championship trophy was brought out and put on a stand just above the players' tunnel on the halfway line. This was the signal for all the kids who were lining the fence around the ground—and a few of the dads as well—to climb over the fence and crouch like sprinters waiting for the starting gun to race to the tunnel when the final whistle went to get a good view of the presentation. The whistle blew and the race was on. Most people headed for the nearest red shirt on the pitch. I finished up next to a laughing Ian Greaves who tried to explain to the adoring fans surrounding him that the game wasn't over. The ref, he said, had blown for a free kick, not for the end of the game. Everybody thought he was kidding, but eventually we realized that there were another few minutes to play and we made our way back to the goal-line. Play resumed, and then a couple of minutes later the ref blew his whistle again. This time it was the end. The players raced for the tunnel, chased by the crowd who were converging on the pitch from all four sides. There was much back-slapping, but eventually all the players made it safely to the tunnel where Roger Byrne led them up the steps by the side of it. When he turned towards the pitch with the trophy in his hands there was a great roar from the crowd, who by this time were covering every blade of grass on the pitch. Champions!

As champions, United were invited to enter a new competition which was open to the title winners of each country on the Continent. It was called the European Cup. The previous season, Chelsea, who had won the league in 1955, had been invited to enter the first ever European Cup. They turned the invitation down, following pressure from the football authorities who at that time were resolutely anti-European. Football League secretary Alan Hardaker was notoriously quoted referring to continental opposition as 'wogs and dagoes'. But Matt Busby and the United directors didn't go along with that. They thought taking on the best sides in Europe would be good not just for United but for English football, and they knew they had a side that was good enough to take on Europe's best and re-establish supremacy in the sport Britain had given to the world. So United entered the brave new world of European football in defiance of the English football hierarchy.

That Thursday night in February 1958 as I lay in bed with the covers pulled tightly around me to keep out the freezing air, all these memories and more—of football and Manchester and where we lived—flooded into my head. Football was one of the things that defined your life; it was part of your identity, where you came from. I kept thinking of matches I'd been to and players I'd watched. Over the two years that I'd been going to see United, I'd read all I could about those players. I felt I knew them almost as well as my own family.

CHAPTER 4

THIS GREAT UNITED FAMILY

In the pubs of Manchester that night there was no music or laughter, and there was only one topic of conversation. How were United going to be able to carry on? Grown men were in tears. Manchester was stunned, as was the whole sporting world. Fans couldn't or wouldn't believe it. *Daily Express* sports editor Robert Findlay recalled how scores of anxious fans rang him on the sports desk that night almost pleading with him—'Say it isn't true.' Unfortunately it was true, but the picture remained confused, not just for the fans but for those who were much closer to the events and to the people involved. When Spurs right-half Danny Blanchflower, who went on to captain their great 1961 Double-winning team, rang the desk to ask if there was any news of his brother Jackie, Findlay couldn't tell him. When, later in the evening, he got some news about Jackie, it was no pleasurable task for Findlay to ring Danny back to tell him that although his brother was alive he was so badly injured that he might never play again.

The annual Manchester Press Ball was due to be held on 6 February at the Plaza Ballroom on Oxford Street. Jimmy Savile was the manager at the time, but as soon as he heard the news of the crash he put a sign up outside saying 'Press Ball cancelled'. Then he locked the doors and sat around with his staff listening to the reports as they came through on the radio. Slowly and agonizingly that night the news from Munich filtered through and the death toll mounted. Of the twenty-one confirmed dead, they learned, seven were United players and three were club officials. Secretary Walter Crickmer was the longest-serving official with the club. He'd been at Old Trafford for twenty-eight years altogether, twenty-one as club secretary, and had just been awarded the Football League's gold medal for long service. Tom Curry, a Geordie from South Shields, was regarded by Busby as the best trainer in soccer. He'd been at Old Trafford since the mid-1930s after a playing career at Newcastle United and Stockport County. Bert Whalley had been with the club for twenty years. His playing career had been cut short by an eye injury in 1948, which is when he joined the coaching staff at Old Trafford. Bert had looked after the young players, especially the Youth Cup team.

As well as being England's soccer capital, Manchester was also England's second city in the newspaper world, and it was here that all the nationals had their northern offices and printed their northern editions. In their offices around Withy Grove hard-bitten newspapermen sobbed as it became apparent that sports journalism had also suffered a savage blow. Newspapermen are used to reporting tragedies, but these eight men who had died were friends and colleagues doing the job they lived for. Every newspaper was affected. Alf Clarke of the *Manchester Evening Chronicle*, Donny Davies of the *Manchester Guardian*, George Follows of the *Daily Herald*, Tom Jackson of the *Manchester Evening News*, Archie Ledbrooke of the *Daily Mirror*, Henry Rose of the *Daily Express*, Frank Swift of the *News of the World* and Eric Thompson of the *Daily Mail* had lost their lives. The only survivor from the press corps was Frank Taylor of the *News Chronicle*, and he was so seriously injured it was feared he wouldn't survive. Mr H. J. Bradley, general secretary of the National Union of Journalists, said that night, 'The disaster has just about swept the north of England, and Manchester in particular, of its leading sports writers. I cannot recall a greater disaster to journalism than this one.'

Three others had lost their lives in the crash: Tom Cable, who was a cabin steward on the flight; Mr T. B. Miklos, a Manchester travel agent who had organized the charter flight for United; and Willie Satinoff, a wealthy Manchester businessman and racehorse owner. Satinoff's interest in charitable work had brought him into close contact with Matt Busby and he'd travelled to Belgrade as a guest of United. It was rumoured that he had been in line for a vacant seat on the board.

So it wasn't just a football team that had been affected by the tragedy, but inevitably that evening it was the players the fans were thinking about. Down in Ordsall near the docks, and less than a mile from Old Trafford, Salford Lads Club became a focal point for supporters from that area. Eddie Colman had always been a member of the club and he used to spend a lot of his time there, often taking his team-mates there with him. It was just round the corner from the two-up-two-down on Archie Street where Eddie had still been living with his mum and dad, where many a Saturday night got started for Eddie and his colleagues, sitting in the parlour sharing a jug of beer with his mum, dad and granddad. Then he'd take them round to the club. All of his family had close connections with the club, and that night its doors opened and mourning supporters who'd got used to seeing Eddie and his team-mates in there began to gather, trying to find some comfort in community feeling.

Whenever you talk to people about that night, one thing that comes across is this sense of people needing to get together in the same way that a family draws together when they hear of the death of a loved one. Beryl and Olga Townsend's house became another focal point, for the group of Stretford Enders they used to go to all the matches with. The two sisters were desperately trying to get whatever news they could when, as Beryl recalled, there was a knock on their door.

> About seven o'clock all the people we used to go to the matches with turned up at our house. They all lived in Colyhurst and Ancoats and places like that, but our house near Ardwick Green was always the place they used to congregate. That night they all piled in and we were switching between the two television channels we had then and all the radio stations. At first we just couldn't find out who had died at all. There was so little real information coming through. Then later on we heard the news that Bobby Charlton had survived. Some good news at last, but as soon as they said Bobby's survived I said, 'Billy's dead.' Billy Whelan was my favourite player, and when everybody asked me why I'd said that I said, 'I've just got this feeling. Bobby's taken his place in the team and I've just got a feeling about Billy.'
>
> I loved them all, but Billy was my favourite. I always remember going to Goodison Park when we were playing Everton and we were standing behind the goals. Billy was having a really great

game and this Everton fan said, 'That boy could turn a ball on a sixpence.' And I was really pleased. I think it was just his sheer class that I liked. Another game I remember well was when we played Burnley at Turf Moor on the Good Friday in 1957 and Billy got a hat-trick. The thing was that before the game I had been wondering if he would play because Billy was such a good Catholic and in those days if you were Catholic you could refuse to play on Good Friday on religious grounds. I wasn't even sure if I should go to the match myself. I thought, 'Should I be going to a football match or should I go to church?' But I went and I was delighted I did because we won the match and Billy got his hat-trick. I wouldn't have wanted to miss that.

Beryl was a big Johnny Berry fan as well.

His pace and his balance were wonderful. He was a beautiful footballer to watch. And he's not always got the credit he should have. But I thought Johnny Berry was a great player. Then there was Tommy Taylor. The way Tommy used to head the ball was just fantastic. There was just something about all of them. If you didn't actually see them play, it's difficult to explain to people just how good they were because you can't see them on television. And off the pitch they were such gentlemen. Mark Jones was a lovely man; so gentle, and really nice. He was like a father figure to them even though he was young himself. Only a couple of years older than some of them. In pictures of them he'd always be sitting there smoking his pipe, and when they were outside he always had his trilby on. I remember seeing one picture of him in the paper with a budgie sitting on his shoulder. There he was, this big, gentle giant of a man with this little bird. They were all really nice people, though. And they were close to the fans. Not like the footballers of today. There was never a question of kids being pushed to one side if they wanted an autograph or something like that. But all I was concerned about was whether I could watch them play or not. That's how all of us lot were, and we'd all help each other out, like the way we did with one lad who worked down the pit. He had an accident so he couldn't work. We were only earning around two pound a week then, but we all chipped in sixpence each so he could see the game. That's how fans were.

While the Stretford Enders were waiting for news at Beryl and Olga's house, their mum was still out at work. She worked for Smallman's, the caterers, and that Thursday she was at an exhibition at City Hall.

My father went to pick her up, and when he met Mum as she finished work he said, 'You want to see our house. It's a bit like the Stretford End at the moment.'

'Why?' she said. 'There's no match or anything tonight is there?'

'No,' my dad said, 'but United's plane has crashed and all the crowd that Beryl and Olga go to the matches with have come round to our house.'

'Ah,' my mother said, 'I was wondering what was going on. Everyone has been standing around in groups talking, but I didn't know what was going on because I've been so busy.'

Then my dad said to her, 'Frank Swift could be one of them,' and that really upset her because Frank was a director of Smallman's and she knew him very well.

Frank Swift had been taken out of the wreckage alive, but he died later that night in hospital. Beryl said her mum was absolutely devastated when she got the news. He was a much-loved figure, not just in Manchester football circles but in the football world in general. Big Swifty, the finest English keeper that ever graced their net, had been Manchester City's goalkeeper from 1933 until his retirement in 1950 when he'd taken up football journalism, as well as a directorship at Smallman's. He'd played with Matt Busby in the City team in the 1930s and Busby was a great admirer of his, so much so that he'd tried to sign him for United after the war, but City wouldn't let him go.

Frank Swift's sad departure from the soccer scene along with his newspaper colleagues added to the grief of the disaster. With his death football lost one of its all-time greats who would be remembered not just for his daring dives at the feet of advancing forwards, his masterly tips over the bar and his long throw-outs to the wings in place of the old-fashioned drop-kicks, but as a big, genial jester whose ready wit and pleasant personality were loved by millions. Although he'd hung up his boots years earlier he was still escorted to his car after every match he reported on by dozens of young autograph hunters, and he'd always sign the lot of them. *Manchester Evening News* football writer Eric Thornton recalled one occasion when he was walking along Euston Station platform with Swift after an international match when a little boy shouted through the barrier, 'Give us your autograph, Mr Swift, I've been waiting a long time.' Without hesitation Frank turned back, dropped his bag and wrote in the lad's book, 'Best wishes to my pal, from Frank Swift.'

'He was a smashing bloke,' Beryl said. 'He had a party one time and my mum introduced us to him. We had a photograph taken with him and we almost disappeared because he put his hands round us and his hands were so big. Absolutely enormous hands, but what a lovely man. My mum was a supervisor at Smallman's and whenever Frank had a private party at his home my mum used to be the one he'd leave in charge because he knew he could trust her. She was due to do a party for him that Saturday night, but of course he died on the Thursday. She ended up doing the catering for his funeral.'

The Townsends' house was a sombre place that night. Beryl remembers their friends staying there until late that night, switching from radio to television and from one station to another, trying to piece together what had happened. 'It was really weird,' she said. 'None of us seemed to know what to do with ourselves. People had come to congregate at our house as though there was something we could do about it, but there was absolutely nothing we could do other than hang around and wait for whatever bits of news we could get.' All they'd got were their memories of the players and the matches they'd been to, of this great United family that they had come to associate with so closely.

The first match we went to was on 12 February 1955. City beat us 5–0 at Old Trafford, but that didn't put us off and we really started going regularly at the beginning of the 1955/56 season. From then on it just virtually took our lives over. They were so good, that team, that once we'd started going to watch them literally nothing and nobody got in the way of us watching the Babes. We were fortunate because we had Burnley, Blackpool and Preston in the First Division so they were all very local and it was easy to get to see them, especially on a Saturday afternoon. All through the summer you'd save up to go to the away games. I even used to walk home from work to save the money to make sure I could get to the Babes. I only got about a week's holiday and I used to save my days for all the mid-week games.

The thing was, no matter where we went across the country, everybody loved the Babes. We went down to Luton for one game but because so many of our boys were missing on Army service we had to play what was basically our reserves. We were winning 2–0 and a Luton supporter standing behind me said, 'If this is your reserve team I wouldn't like to be playing the first team.' But everywhere we went there was just so much respect for that team because they had so much style and they were so attractive to watch. It was just incredible, the buzz everywhere you went to watch the Babes. You could sense the excitement. That was the impact that they had. It was a fantastic feeling; you could feel the warmth and affection for them everywhere you went. And you never saw a boring game. In the 1950s and on into the early sixties if you saw less than four goals in a match you felt as though you'd been deprived.

It's no wonder football was so popular then—plenty of goals, plenty of excitement and a lot of entertainment. And it was cheap: no more than two shillings (10p) to stand on the terraces and watch a First Division football match—the real working-class game that everybody could afford. People couldn't get enough of it. You had your own team that you supported, but it didn't stop you going to see other teams, especially if some of the big stars of the day were playing. Football just wasn't as tribal as it is now. 'Yeah,' Olga said, 'we'd even go to Liverpool if United weren't playing. There was none of this nastiness that there is today.'

Beryl remembers going to watch Everton quite regularly too. 'I used to go to Goodison Park to watch Everton because Johnny Carey was manager there. I went because he was a United player, and I went to support Everton because they were his team.' She also recalls going to watch United play Preston at Deepdale in a mid-week match. At the ground she met some soldiers who were stationed at the nearby Fulwood Barracks where they were doing their National Service. The soldiers came from different parts of the country and all had their own teams, but above all they were football fans. They'd come out that night because they wanted to see United; they were particularly keen to see Tommy Taylor who they regarded as the greatest centre-forward of the day. It didn't matter that he didn't play for their team. It was a time when great players were great players whoever they played for, and you went to a match to be entertained by them and to applaud their skills. And the Busby Babes were emerging as one of the all-time great teams.

* * *

After winning the league in 1956 the young champions were in peak form the next season. By October they were undefeated in the league and they'd sailed through their first two-legged European Cup tie with a 12–0 aggregate win over the Belgian champions Anderlecht. And Anderlecht were no mugs. In fact the first game in Belgium, United's first ever in Europe, was fairly close, the Reds coming out 2–0 winners. The return leg was played under the floodlights at Maine Road because United had no lights of their own at this time, and on a pitch that was covered in great pools of water. But they put on an attacking display that would have annihilated any team in the world. What a performance! Just imagine a win like that today, 10–0 against a bona fide domestic champion club. There could not have been any better vindication of United's defiance of the football authorities to play in Europe. Even Matt Busby was incredulous at his young team's performance. 'It was the greatest thrill in a lifetime of soccer,' he said after the game. 'It was the finest exhibition of teamwork I have ever seen from any team. It was as near perfect football as anyone could wish to see.'

By this time Billy Whelan had established himself in the team as inside-right and Bill Foulkes had won back his place from Ian Greaves at right-back. The team had a settled look about it, with Ray Wood in goal; Bill Foulkes and Roger Byrne the full-backs; an

Above Walking down the Warwick Road.

Left The Author with sister Joan, 1957.

Below (Left to Right) Olga Townsend, Frank, Swift, Beryl Townsend.

Left Bradford Pit.

Below Market Street and the Kardomah Café, where the players used to go after training.

Above Back of the main stand, Old Trafford, in the 1950s.

Right Piccadilly and the Guinness clock on a rainy night.

United v Atlético Bilbao, Maine Road, 6 February 1957.

Roger Byrne leads the team ou
for the last match at Highbury, 1 February 1958.

UNITED TOPICS

by TOM JACKSON

of the "MANCHESTER EVENING NEWS"

Champion going, United! Six points from the last three games, including such formidable away tests as Luton and Wolves, have really boosted the club's title aspirations. You won't get Ma
is
be
chi
alr
inc

the importance of having effic
reserves on call. At Luton,
Foulkes, Eddie Colman and Dur
Edwards were all missing beca

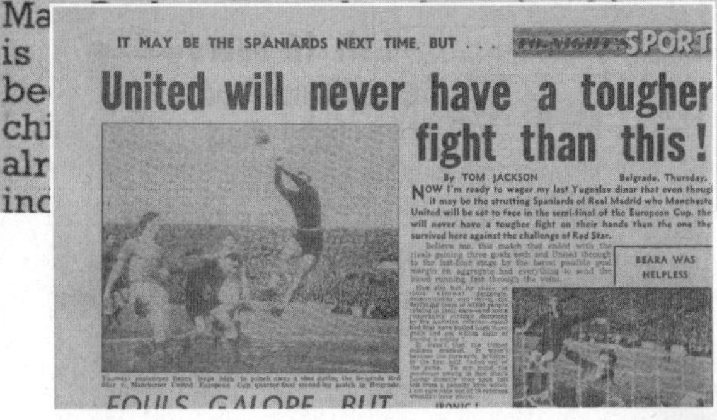

IT MAY BE THE SPANIARDS NEXT TIME, BUT . . . SPORT

United will never have a tougher fight than this!

By TOM JACKSON Belgrade, Thursday.

NOW I'm ready to wager my last Yugoslav dinar that even thoug it may be the strutting Spaniards of Real Madrid who Manchester United will be set to face in the semi-final of the European Cup, the will never have a tougher fight on their hands than the one the survived here against the challenge of Red Star.

BEARA WAS HELPLESS

FOULS GALORE BUT

Tom Jackson's programme notes and his last report on the Red Star match.

Right Players, officials and journalists board the chartered BEA Elizabethan which was to crash at Munich.

Above The final team talk. Matt Busby gives his briefing to the team before their pre-match meal in Belgrade.

Below Bobby Charlton scores his second goal in Belgrade to give United a 3–0 lead on the day; 5–1 on aggregate.

Manchester Evening News

LATE FINAL

UNITED CUP XI CRASH: "28 DIE"

Plunged into houses at Munich, exploded

SURVIVORS SAVED in BLAZING WRECKAGE

ONE of the greatest disasters to befall British football struck Manchester United this afternoon when the plane carrying the £350,000 wonder team crashed at Munich. At least 28 of the 40 aboard were killed; some reports said higher casualties were feared.

Pulled from blazing wreck

Ministry inspector flies out

Sport's biggest tragedy

The Busby genius

WAS V.I.P. BABY ON THE PLANE?

BRIGHTON CONSPIRACY TRIAL

Bennett shouts: I didn't swindle tax

Fuchs—Serious trouble

Jockey Joe Childs dies

Dentists: 'Pay is down one third'

12 buses join ice-skid toll

Man drops 20ft.—glass saves him

FLYING BAN LIFTED LAST YEAR

ROUND ABOUT

United star may never play again—Tragic families

ABOVE: Those who died. RIGHT: Some of those who escaped.

MATT 50-50: EDWAR 'GRAVE': BERRY CON

50 doctors battle to save their lives

FIVE German surgeons fought desperately to-day to save the life of MATT BUSBY, Manchester United's famous manager critically injured in the disastrous Elizabethan air crash at Munich. First dramatic message from the Rechts Der Isar Hospital said: "He is lying between life and death." Then came brighter news—"He is somewhat improved," but to-night it was still "touch and go."

One surgeon commented: "We are pleased with the progress he is making, but he is still very ill.

And a doctor who spoke to Mr. Busby this afternoon said afterwards: "He is still very critical, but a bit better than yesterday."

Another doctor said: "His chances are now 50-50.

"One lung apparently has collapsed completely. His fractured ribs apparently punctured the lung."

Back in Manchester, the city was flooded with false rumours that Mr. Busby was dead.

Inquiries and telegrams from all parts of the country poured into the "Manchester Evening News" asking the dreaded question, "Is it true?"

The Munich hospital commented: "The reports are entirely false. They did not come from us."

MORALE AT ITS HIGHEST

TO-NIGHT the four most critical cases apart from Mr. Busby were United players JOHN BERRY and DUNCAN EDWARDS, sports writer FRANK TAYLOR, and pilot Kenneth Rayment.

"All five are still not out of danger," said a hospital official.

Morgans and Wood were "very cheery" and Charlton should leave hospital within the next day or two.

Mrs. VERA LUKIC was transferred to nearby Terlach Hospital with internal injuries. Her baby daughter with facial burns was sent to Munich Eye Hospital.

An army of 50 doctors are working without sleep to save their lives.

"I don't think Edwards will be able to play football any more," said one doctor.

Four doctors are at Mr. Busby's bedside all the time.

Professor Georg Maurer, chief of the surgical section, said:

"It will be necessary for Mr. Busby to remain here for three or four weeks.

"He is conscious part of the time and responds somewhat to questions with a nod.

Mr. Busby has a tube running through his throat to help his breathing.

He has extremely serious chest injuries in addition to several fractures.

Twenty-one of the 44 aboard the plane perished.

Mr. D. Ballantine, British Consul in Munich accompanied by his wife, visited British patients in the hospital to-day.

He looked into the oxygen tent covering Mr. Busby and tried to talk with him. Mr. Busby had difficulty in talking because of the pipe in his throat.

HOSPITAL STAFF WONDERFUL

BEA

We will remember them . . .

ROGER BYRNE

BENT

COLMAN

DESPITE the many thousands of words that have been written about the terrible air disaster on February 6 that cut down so many Manchester United players and officials, I find it difficult to realise they will no longer delight us with their skill and courage.

United had become world-famous, even to a greater extent than Arsenal in their palmy years. They owed a great deal to the sportsmanship, the ability and the team spirit of great men like Roger Byrne, Geoffrey Bent, Eddie Colman, Mark Jones, Bill Whelan, Tommy Taylor, David Pegg, and Duncan Edwards.

To the relatives of these lovable young men who lost their lives I extend, on behalf of many "Football Monthly" readers who have asked me to do so, and my staff, our deepest sympathy. May time heal the deep wounds inflicted.

And to those United members severely injured, like Matt Busby and Johnny Berry, I sincerely hope they will soon be restored to complete health; and that before long they will be able to take up life's threads where they were broken.

To me personally, it has been a great shock. I had seen them, at Highbury the previous Saturday, give a wonderful exhibition of Soccer, one of the best for many years. I thought then, United, blossoming further with more experience, would become the finest Soccer machine of the century.

Adding to the shock was the loss of so many journalistic friends with whom I had travelled to many corners of the earth and spent so many happy hours.

They were able men who wrote about the game and players without fear or favour.

Since the war, Manchester United have been without rival in League, F.A. Cup and European Cup.

It was a team of experts playing for the good of the side as a whole. And now some of those experts have passed away, their parts in the victory plan will not be overlooked or forgotten.

England, too, will sorely miss the artistry and wholehearted work of Byrne, Edwards and Taylor.

I have been in the company of these outstanding players many times. Their modest, unassuming behaviour was a credit to their club and to their country.

Every day that passes, I receive messages of sympathy from all over the world. I pass them on to United officials with a sad heart. With the memorial words of former heroes: *"At the going down of the sun and in the morning, we will remember them."*

CHARLES BUCHAN.

JONES

WHELAN

TAYLOR

PEGG

DUNCAN EDWARDS

4

Tribute from *Charles Buchan's Football Monthly*, April 1958.

incredible half-back line of Eddie Colman, Mark Jones and Duncan Edwards; and the most exciting forward line in Britain with Johnny Berry on the right wing, Billy Whelan at inside-right, Tommy Taylor at centre-forward, Dennis Viollet at inside-left and David Pegg on the left wing. For me, they were the Busby Babes. That was the team in the *Manchester Evening News* photo that I had on my bedroom wall.

In Europe, United were English football's pioneers; no other club before them had competed against the best teams from the Continent in a knockout competition. It was all a new experience, not just for the manager and players but for the spectators as well. For those first European matches Maine Road was packed and the atmosphere was electric, the novelty of seeing a football match being played under floodlights adding to the mystique of it all. During the course of that season the European seed was sown. Manchester witnessed the all-conquering skills of Di Stefano, Kopa and Gento of the great Real Madrid side in the semi-final, but on the way there they'd seen United score ten times against Anderlecht, then hang on against Borussia Dortmund before a remarkable quarter-final against Atlético Bilbao. The first leg was played in Spain in January 1957, and it was a tough task for the Reds. Bilbao had lost only one match at home in the previous three years and on a snow-covered pitch United went down 5–3. The tie was poised for a great second leg at Maine Road. United's European games were still being played there because the floodlights, which they'd started building by now at Old Trafford, were still not ready.

We got to Maine Road early for the Bilbao match and bagged a place on the whitewashed wall that ran along the side of the pitch. There was a light covering of snow all over the pitch and the mist that swirled over it made the main stand on the far side of the pitch indistinct. As the ground filled up and the tension built the mist seemed to get thicker so that by the time the teams came out and lined up for the national anthems of Spain and Great Britain, the players and officials were shadowy figures. The roar from the crowd as they kicked off must have been heard in the city centre more than a mile away, and right from the start Bilbao made their tactics clear: they were there to defend their lead. United piled on the pressure but the crowd groaned as chance after chance was missed. Then, four minutes before half-time, came the breakthrough. Duncan Edwards came surging upfield and let fly with a piledriver that was heading for the net when Bilbao centre-half Jesus Garay lunged out and blocked it. The ball spun up into the air off Garay's leg and dropped right into the path of an unmarked Dennis Viollet, who calmly put it into the net.

The half-time break seemed to drag on for ever and you could feel the tension in the air as the teams came out for the second half. Only forty-five minutes to go and two goals to get against a resolute defence. Could United do it? Of course they could. Within minutes of the restart the crowd roared as Viollet put the ball in the net again, but the celebrations didn't last for long as the linesman's flag was up for offside. A minute later Billy Whelan had the ball in the net, but the German referee gave another offside decision. United were being robbed. From where we were he didn't look offside. But, like many a United team that came after them, this team never gave up. Tension mounted as they piled on more and more pressure, and in the 71st minute they got their reward. Tommy Taylor, who'd led the line magnificently all night, swerved around Garay and shot fiercely to beat Carmelo in the Bilbao goal.

The scores were level. The crowd went wild. Every man, woman and child packed into Maine Road was urging the Reds on. But Bilbao continued to defend resolutely. Then, with five minutes to go, man of the match Tommy Taylor moved out to the right wing. His marker Garay followed him, but Taylor beat him and headed for the goal-line. As he did, little Johnny Berry moved into Taylor's position in the centre. Taylor rolled the ball across to him and Berry gave Carmelo no chance with a right-foot shot into the corner. The crowd erupted with the biggest cheer I've ever heard at a football match, and they continued cheering until well after the last of their heroes had left the field. They say you could hear the roars that night all over Manchester.

'El Magnifico, Manchester United!' wrote Tom Jackson in his report in the *Manchester Evening News* the next night. 'You can say it, like the men of Bilbao, in Spanish. You can say it in a dozen different languages if you wish, yet even now, in the cold light of today, that nerve-tingling and inspired fighting football of the Busby Boys which has swept them into the semi-final of the European Cup has brought the world to their feet.' The Babes had defied the odds by turning a 5–3 deficit from the first leg into a 6–5 victory, to win the right to challenge the European champions, Real Madrid, in the semi-final.

Over forty years later on that great night in Barcelona when Alex Ferguson's United won the Treble in such dramatic fashion, I was on the Ramblas as United fans partied all through the night.

I sat having a beer with a Red of my age. The last three minutes in the Nou Camp had been as exciting as anything any football fan is ever likely to experience. The 1999 FA Cup semi-final replay against Arsenal with Schmeichel's penalty save and Giggs's wonder goal had been a titanic struggle—one of the all-time great games to have been at. But United's greatest game ever? From a fan's point of view we had no doubt that it was Bilbao. Everybody I have spoken to who was at that match is in agreement on that point.

United lost the semi-final 5–3 on aggregate, but it had been a remarkable achievement for the young team and there was no shame in going out to what has always been regarded as the greatest club side in the history of world football. On the home front United won the league again and were set for a remarkable league and Cup Double, only to have it snatched from their grasp by an injury to goalkeeper Ray Wood very early in the final against Aston Villa. In the days before substitutes, playing with ten men for more than eighty minutes on the Wembley turf was too much for any team. But we knew they'd be back again, because the team Matt Busby had built seemed destined to dominate football for many years. Such was the power of the Babes that they seemed almost invincible. Nothing, it seemed, would prevent the young braves of Manchester United from reigning for the next decade.

The glory of supporting this team was not so much the trophies they won but the way they went about winning them. What I remember most about them was that, although they had good defenders, the attitude of the whole team was directed at scoring goals. Matt Busby had brought together at Old

Trafford the most talented group of young footballers that had ever been seen at one club. They were the elite, the Sandhurst cadets of the football world, not only in their efficiency on the field but in their bearing after they had been in action. After training the players were encouraged to use the facilities at Old Trafford—a game of snooker or table tennis in the games room. It was here that the players met socially and the spirit of friendship, which helped to make the club great, grew. Every professional at Old Trafford was made a member of the YMCA and many spent their afternoons there, while others spent their afternoons on the golf course.

They were a generation of players who in their outlook still had the attitudes and values associated with the hard days of war and ration books. Today they'd be regarded as young men who were old before their time. Mark Jones was married to June, his childhood sweetheart from Barnsley; he had a young son, and in his spare time he bred canaries and budgies. It was the sort of lifestyle Matt Busby encouraged for his young players. 'It's a good thing for a player to settle down and start a home,' he used to tell them. 'It will make you more mature as a person and help with your football.' Duncan Edwards was every bit the model professional. He never went 'gallivanting at night', as Busby used to say. 'He was never in any trouble. Going to the pictures was about his only night life. He lived for the game and his only concern was making himself and keeping himself fit for it.' For Busby, 'club spirit' and a commitment to the club as 'family' were the qualities he prized most in his young players, and he and his assistant Jimmy Murphy worked tirelessly to instil them.

It helped to create a strong bond with the fans. It's

one of the things that always comes up when you talk to supporters from that time. Madge Williams told me as I sat having a cup of tea with her and her husband Norman in their front room in Droylsden, 'No one could take their place, could they, Norman? They was great, those lads. I used to see them a lot in Manchester. When they'd finished training they used to all come down Market Street and go in Kardomah Café. Do you remember that? I used to see them coming down and they used to all go in there and have a coffee. Nothing like the players of today. I mean, Duncan Edwards used to go around on a bike and he used to go on the bus to the match. Would you get players doing that now? No way would you.'

The main ingredient of this spirit that Matt Busby and his backroom staff so carefully fostered was a sense of togetherness, a sense of being part of a great United family. Most of the out-of-town lads were put into lodgings at Mrs Watson's boarding house at 5 Birch Avenue, where youth team players straight from school shared digs with men who had already established themselves in the first team. One of them was Duncan Edwards. A lot of the fans used to call him 'Tank', but he was known as 'Brush' to the players he shared his digs with because of his obsession with tidying up and keeping the place smart. He was known to tell some of the younger players that the main thing to remember was to make sure that shirts and shorts were always clean and that socks were well darned because a smart team starts off with high morale and will play football as neat as their appearance. At Birch Avenue all the players shared the same table, and conversation was usually about football. It was here and at other carefully selected lodgings as much as on the pitch and on the training ground that they developed their club spirit and became United players. The house was on a small estate that was just a short walk from Old Trafford, and generally the players would walk to the ground, mixing freely with the fans. 'We walked up Warwick Road with Tommy Taylor on our way to the match one day,' Madge recalled. 'We asked him if he was playing, and he said, "Yes. If I don't get killed by a bus first!" Chester Road, which we had to cross, was busy even in those days. He was a lovely lad, and his mother was a sweet lady as well. But they were all nice lads.'

Every Saturday night, all of United's reserve and first team players used to meet up in a pub for a drink before going to a dance hall—usually the Locarno in Sale. Beryl Townsend remembers those Saturday nights.

> All the players used to go there, and Duncan and his girlfriend used to come to collect Tommy and David and the others. He'd put them in a taxi to get them home because they were always kalied. Tommy was a right drinker, but then if you think about where he was from it was no surprise. Like so many of them he came from a mining community, and after working down the pit all day a lot of miners liked a pint. So Tommy was used to a drinking culture. But Duncan got into trouble himself because he used to have a bike and he went out on it one night with no lights on and he got told off by Matt Busby. Busby fined him for showing the club up. On the pitch they were magical, though, weren't they? But off it they were just ordinary lads.

With me working in town I used to see Tommy and the rest of them coming out of Kardomah Café at lunchtime. They were always out in town among ordinary people, and I think that's why the crash hit the city so much because they were used to them being around. They were part of the city life. They weren't distant. I remember we were on the bus going to Levenshulme one day and Albert Scanlon got on with his first wife Josie, who we knew because she used to be in Olga's class at school. There were no flash cars then. They didn't seem as materialistic in those days. They played for the love of the game. They'd got talent but they just seemed to love playing football and it didn't seem to matter to them that they were on a small wage. They did what they loved [to do] and you were never disappointed when you went to see them.

Footballers certainly didn't have 'celebrity lifestyles' in the 1950s and there was very little about them in the newspapers other than team news and match reports. One of the only sources of information about players and their lives was *Charles Buchan's Football Monthly*, and I was an avid reader. In the May 1957 edition one of their columnists, John Thompson, wrote, 'I suppose the next danger for Manchester United is that they will become as disliked as Arsenal were at the height of their glory [in the 1930s]. There are peculiar specimens among our fellow countrymen who are irritated by success and snipe spitefully at those who gain it. Manchester United are unlikely to be put out by these mean and jealous little men. They are big enough to shrug them aside … and to carry on enjoying every game as they so obviously do. Long may they flourish! They have brought a glint to our tarnished reputation.'

* * *

For the time being, at least, United's supporters and admirers far outweighed the 'mean and jealous little men', and they were looking forward to 1957/58. It was going to be United's big season. By this time Matt Busby's biggest problem was not who to put in the team, but who to leave out. When United qualified to enter the European competition again in 1957/58 it was clear where the club's priorities lay. Busby wanted a side that was good enough to win everything. The 1957 FA Cup had been snatched out of his grasp because of the injury to Ray Wood, but his Babes were capable of reaching Wembley once again. Having secured the league championship in 1956 and 1957 they could certainly match the great sides of the pre-war years, Huddersfield Town and Arsenal, and win it, like them, for a third successive time.

The campaign started well with victories over Leicester at Filbert Street, then Everton and Manchester City at Old Trafford. It was the perfect launch pad for a new title challenge. Their scoring record was remarkable, twenty-two goals coming in the opening six games. Yet when they lost for the first time it was not by just an odd goal, but 4–0, to Bolton at Burnden Park. It was a team that didn't do anything by half measures, which was one of the things that made them so entertaining to watch. In Europe, United strode past Irish champions Shamrock Rovers before beating Dukla Prague 3–1 on aggregate to reach the quarter-final against Red Star Belgrade.

In January 1958, as the tie with Red Star approached, United made good progress in the FA Cup with a 3–1 win at Workington and a 2–0 victory over Ipswich at Old Trafford to see them through to the fifth round, where they would meet Sheffield Wednesday. In the league they were in second place behind Wolves. The Yugoslavs came to Manchester on 14 January, and by this time the United team had a different look about it: Harry Gregg had taken over from Ray Wood in goal after a December transfer from Doncaster Rovers; eighteen-year-old Kenny Morgans had come in on the right wing in place of the ageing Johnny Berry; Bobby Charlton had got the inside-right berth in preference to Billy Whelan; and Albert Scanlon had the upper hand in his duel with David Pegg for the position of outside-left. Charlton and Eddie Colman scored the goals that gave United the edge in a 2–1 first-leg victory.

The form in the run-up to the second leg was encouraging. A 7–2 win over Bolton, with a hat-trick from Bobby Charlton, two goals from Dennis Viollet and one apiece for Duncan Edwards and Albert Scanlon, was just the result United needed before visiting Highbury for their next league match, then leaving on the tiring journey behind the Iron Curtain. And what a match the Highbury one was. United and Arsenal thrilled all those who were packed into the stadium on that Saturday afternoon with a magnificent display of attacking football. Nine goals were scored: four by Arsenal, five by United. That game on 1 February 1958 typified the Busby Babes. They played with such flair and enthusiasm that they thought nothing of conceding a few goals in their efforts to score at least one more. The *Manchester Guardian* report is enough to confirm that team's legendary powers. United kept 'one or both wing-halves always poised on the frontal limit of defence, ready to move forward and make a sixth or seventh forward'. This left large gaps in defence, but 'always Manchester's forwards promised to score more goals than their defence yielded'.

It was the last match the Busby Babes ever played in England.

For the match the following Wednesday in Belgrade, United announced that the club would be hiring an aeroplane to transport the squad there and back. In December 1957 United had made a mid-week journey to Czechoslovakia for the second-leg tie with Dukla Prague, but the return flight was delayed by fog and the team was forced to divert to Amsterdam; they eventually completed the journey by sea and land with only hours to spare before a league match away to Birmingham City. A tired United, lucky even to have made it to the ground on time, could only draw. In an attempt to do all that was possible to get back in good time for the weekend's match at home to top-of-the-table Wolves, United's management hired a private plane for the two-thousand-mile round trip to Eastern Europe. Although the flights would still be at the mercy of the weather, at least the team would be able to make their own time and would not have to conform to an airline's schedules and routes.

They'd made it there all right, but they hadn't got back, and most of them were never going to get back, to play Wolves or anybody else. As I looked up at those faces staring down from the picture on my bedroom wall it was still hard to believe. But that was only because I didn't want to believe it. Nobody wanted to believe it.

I asked Beryl Townsend and Norman Williams, if it hadn't been for Munich, how long did they think it would have been before United lifted the European Cup? Beryl believed they would have done it that season. 'We would have done it the year before if it hadn't been for Real Madrid. They were the greatest club team of all time and it was just our bad luck that we had to meet them in the semi-final. I think we'd have made the final if we hadn't had to play them. But by 1958 that Real Madrid side were starting to get older and the Babes were going from strength to strength. I think we would have done it in 1958, that's how great that team had become.' Norman thought it would have taken longer. 'I would say at least two years. But we would have done it because those lads were maturing so quickly.'

The crucial factor was that by February 1958 Matt Busby had got together a team that had strength in depth. It was almost the beginning of the modern squad system—he'd got good cover for every position. There was this sense that we were watching a team that was on the threshold of greatness, on the way to becoming the greatest club side Britain would ever see. Years later Bob Paisley said Manchester United would have dominated soccer for the next ten years with that team. On that dreadful Thursday night in houses throughout Manchester, disbelief soon gave way to a terrible sense of loss and of being cheated by a cruel twist of fate.

Sleep was impossible. As I lay awake replaying in my head some of the matches I'd seen them play, there was one game above all others I kept thinking about, the greatest game I saw the Busby Babes play, the game at Maine Road the year before when they'd overcome all the odds to beat Atlético Bilbao. It epitomized everything that was great about that side: the outstanding individual skills, the team spirit, the sheer grit and determination, and the commitment to attack, attack, attack. And the date was 6 February 1957—exactly one year earlier, to the day.

CHAPTER 5

A CITY IN SHOCK

I woke up early on the Friday morning. It was the cold that did it. It was still dark, but my bedroom door was ajar, and by the light that spilled in from the landing I could see the thick ice glistening on the inside of my bedroom window. My mam and dad were already up. I could hear them moving around in the kitchen downstairs, but I wasn't ready to brave the cold. I pulled the blankets up over my head and wriggled further down into bed.

You always tried to put off the moment when you had to get out of your warm bed into the icy air of your bedroom, but this morning I needed to get up in time for the seven o'clock news on the wireless. Had Matt Busby survived the night? And what about Duncan Edwards and Johnny Berry? As I lay in bed I felt a deep sense of personal loss. I still couldn't quite believe that the players I'd been expecting to cheer on against Wolves the next day would never play again.

My mam came to my room with a mug of tea to warm me up and a kettle of boiling water to take into the bathroom for a wash. There was no hot water, she said. Then she gathered my school uniform up, saying she'd take it downstairs to put in front of the electric fire in the kitchen to warm up. I could go downstairs to get dressed in front of the fire after I'd had a wash. I tried to keep as many of the bed covers over me as possible while I drank the tea, but as soon as you raised yourself up off the pillow the bedclothes came up with you and an icy blast came cutting in under the blankets. Still, I'd have to brave the cold air sooner or later. If you moved quickly enough it wasn't too bad. So, covers off, dressing gown on, and a quick dash to the bathroom with the kettle of hot water. Into the sink with the water, a quick splash on my face, and a dash down to the nice warm kitchen where my clothes were as hot as toast.

It was five to seven—just enough time to get my clothes on before the seven o'clock news on the Home Service. But did I want to hear it? Did I want to leave the warmth of the kitchen to go into the cold front room to hear things I wished I didn't have to hear?

I followed my dad into the living room. There was ice on the windows and it was nearly as cold as my bedroom. My dad switched the radiogram on, and there was nothing on the news to take the chill out of our bones. 'Here is the seven o'clock news for today, Friday the seventh of February,' the newsreader said. What had happened overnight? I wondered. Had there been any more deaths, or could there have been a miracle? Could some of those reported missing have been found alive, thrown clear of the plane and lying in the snow? But no. Nothing had changed. Sixteen of the survivors were in hospital, some of them seriously injured; seven others had been released from hospital after treatment. They included Bill Foulkes and Harry Gregg. Apart from reporting on the messages of sympathy that had been coming in from football clubs all over the world, there was nothing new. But the newsreader did say, 'Our reporter is coming through to us from Munich shortly and it is hoped to give a recording of his latest dispatch in the eight o'clock news bulletin.' I'd just be able to catch that before setting off for school.

Breakfast was silent. It was as if there'd been a death in the family. My dad had been following United since the 1920s. He'd supported them throughout the 1930s when they were in the Second Division and in danger of going down to the Third. When he got back from war service in India he became part of that great post-war boom in English football, following United home and away all the way to the great 1948 Cup Final against Blackpool. Now his team had been wiped out. Even now, the morning after, the mind couldn't take it in. The flowers of English football were dead, crushed in one awful moment at Munich Airport.

At eight o'clock the BBC did indeed have a piece from their own reporter, Ray Colley, who'd flown to Munich the night before in a special Viscount airliner taking senior BEA officials and engineers to the scene to investigate the disaster. 'He telephoned us just over an hour ago,' the newsreader said, 'after interviewing some of the survivors.'

> One of them was Harry Gregg, the twenty-three-year-old Irish goalkeeper who was recently transferred to Manchester United for a record fee. He told Colley that he'd sensed that an accident was about to happen. He wasn't hurt, and as soon as he could he obeyed the shouts to run in case the plane caught fire. Then he saw that there wasn't any fire and Colley says he immediately ran back and took a leading part in rescuing survivors trapped in the wreckage. At the moment, says our reporter, inches of snow, which fell steadily through the night, hide and soften the remains of the wrecked aircraft as it

lies where it came to rest two hundred and seventy yards beyond the end of the runway.

In Chorlton on Medlock, Mary Morris was up early as well—albeit for a different reason.

It was about half past six, and we were up because the house across the street was on fire. Everybody in the street was up because it wasn't a very big street. Straight away we put the radio on. News kept coming through about the crash and of course we were getting more and more upset because all the names were coming through with details of what had happened to them. When the firemen had put the fire out I remember my mam opening the door and asking the firemen if they wanted a drink of tea because it was still cold and snowy. All the firemen came in, and different people in the street came in as well, because my mam was making tea for everyone.

While the firemen were in our house I was crying and one of them said to me, 'There's no need to cry. The lady in the house over the road is all right; she hasn't been hurt.' So my mam said, 'She's not crying about the fire, she's crying about the crash.' I can still see the fireman standing in our front room with his big white hat and can still hear him saying to me, 'You know how strong firemen are and you know how they are supposed to be very tough people? Well, we all cried last night.' After the firemen had left, me and our James couldn't go to school that day because we were both too upset.

Snow must have blanketed most of Europe that morning. It was long before anybody had ever heard anything about global warming, and the winter was a bitterly cold one. Like Munich, Manchester was in its icy grip the morning after the disaster. The electric fire was still on full in our kitchen as I put my Marmite sandwiches into my schoolbag alongside my attempts at my maths and French homework. Cap on and navy gabardine over navy school blazer and it was off into the cold morning air.

Outside, everything was white; there had been a thick frost during the night and a sprinkling of snow. It was a short walk up our road past the flats to the bus shelter on Greenbrow Road. I'd got my football boots laced together and slung over my shoulder because it was football on Friday afternoons for the Upper Thirds, but it didn't seem right to be playing football this particular Friday afternoon. Maybe our matches would be abandoned out of respect for the dead.

At the bus stop there was the usual long queue stretching out of the shelter, shop workers and office workers going into town and schoolkids from the estate who'd passed their scholarships going to the grammar schools and technical schools that were closer to town. A lot of the people in those queues every morning knew one another and there was usually plenty of good-humoured banter, but this morning most were silent and the mood was sombre. Many looked as though they'd been up all night.

The bright red bus drew up at the stop and everybody piled on. I always went upstairs because you didn't have to stand up there; if you stayed downstairs, the bus always got full before it got off the estate and you had to stand up and give adults your seat. Upstairs was for the smokers, so as I walked up the steps I entered a thick fug of cigarette smoke. Condensation dripped down from the nicotine-stained roof. Heads were buried in the morning papers whose pages contained the first reports of the tragedy.

There were a few empty seats and I moved up the top deck of the bus to sit next to Mr Penter, a friend of my dad. His son Paul had been in my class at primary school and the whole family were Blues—big City fans who went to most of their games. He was reading the *Daily Express* and had it open at the photo news section, which he showed me. Under the headline 'Shattered In One Dramatic Second—The Finest Soccer Team Since the War' were cigarette-card images of the players who were my heroes. Against one line of pictures the terrible words 'Dead or still missing early this morning', against another the words 'These are the ones who survived the crash'. There were tears in my eyes as I read the few short paragraphs above those familiar faces and the tribute that followed. The paper said that when the airliner crashed it was carrying the greatest team in British soccer since the war. 'You may support another team,' it said, 'a great one or a small one, but you are likely to concede that United were the greatest club. Not only because they had been League champions and winners of the Cup. But also because they brought a higher art to post-war football and provided the thousands who go to see them with the kind of pleasure other teams seldom give.'

It was true. They *were* the greatest team in Britain; they were going to be the greatest team in the world. And they were my team. But the *Express* tribute had it right: whoever you supported at that time you were prepared to concede that United were the best. City fans of that era like Mr Penter and his family were no exception. City had a very good team in the 1950s. They were losing cup finalists in 1955 and went back to win it in 1956. Manchester was the soccer capital of Britain: there was nowhere else to touch it. But even dyed-in-the-wool City fans knew that the Busby Babes were a bit special. What's more, as a Manchester team and England's first representatives in this exciting new European competition, the majority of City fans wanted United to do well, and the sense of loss and grief they felt was shared that morning by football supporters throughout the land.

The piece in that morning's *Express* went on, 'Above all they were young. That was the creed of Matt Busby, the great player who became their manager and whose flair for finding brilliant youngsters built them into an all-conquering team. It was not just in Britain that their name had a magical sound. They were ambassadors. In many small towns in Europe where English is not understood, faces will light up at two names—Winston Churchill and Manchester United.'

Ten years later I remembered those words as I stood by a roadside shack at the top of a mountain pass in the former Yugoslavia. I was a student hitch-hiking to Athens. My route had taken me all the way down the Yugoslavian coast almost as far as the Albanian border; then there'd been a turn eastwards into the mountains through Titograd towards the town of Skopje before the main drag down from Belgrade into northern Greece. On a dirt road high in the mountains I stopped for a drink with my hitch-hiking partner and the two American girls who'd given us a lift. We were in the middle of nowhere drinking the local lemonade when a ragged little boy of about ten wandered up to us. I don't know what his language was—Serbo-Croat I suppose—and he didn't speak a word of English, but 'Manchester United' brought instant communication. He told me the name of the place we were in and I pointed to myself and said, 'Manchester.' 'Manchester United!' he replied instantly, and his face lit up at the magical sound, just as the piece in the *Daily Express* had predicted on that dark February morning just after Munich. 'Yes, me,' I replied, 'Manchester United.' Then, 'Bobby Charlton, Bobby Charlton' we both said, and we started to run around on this mountain top, laughing and kicking an imaginary football. We weren't to know it at the time, and we wouldn't have thanked anybody for telling us, but out of the death and destruction in the slush of that runway a legend was born.

As the morning wore on we started to hear more about how the City of Manchester was beginning to react to the tragedy that had engulfed it. After receiving news of the disaster the previous evening the Lord Mayor of Manchester, Alderman Leslie Lever, had opened a Manchester United Disaster Fund. It was proposed, he said, to establish a suitable permanent memorial, the form of which had not yet been decided, though it would be in accordance with the feelings of public opinion. It would also be a reflection of the role the team played in the world of sport. Alderman Lever had been up all night taking messages of sympathy. 'I have never known in the whole of my life public opinion so stirred,' he said, 'and I am sure that all sections of the city, the country and the world will be anxious to join in the establishment of such a worthy memorial. Manchester

United were ambassadors of this country in every sense of the word. They brought honour and glory by their skill and genius. The city also mourns these pressmen who by their close liaison throughout the years with the team gave them impetus and encouragement to do the great things they did do. We mourn these talented journalists who served their country no less than their team.' Early on the Friday morning the first donation to the fund was received. It was 1,000 guineas, from Great Universal Stores.

By 9.30 a.m. groups of relatives of the injured players began to gather at Ringway Airport. Duncan Edwards's fiancée Molly Leach was one of the first there and was surrounded by friends. She pleaded with waiting reporters, 'Don't ask me questions.' Half an hour later assistant manager Jimmy Murphy arrived. Chain-smoking as he paced up and down the departure lounge, he said, 'I am too grief-stricken for words. I cannot get to Munich quick enough to check on the boss and the boys.' At 10.50 Jimmy, along with the first of two groups of relatives, left Ringway on a BEA plane to Paris to connect with a flight to Munich. The next group out—Mrs Berry, Mrs Wood, Mrs Viollet, Mrs Blanchflower and Mrs Scanlon—left before noon for Amsterdam to connect with a KLM flight to Munich. Superintendent Fred Waddington of Lancashire Police also flew out to Munich, from London Airport. His division, Stretford, included the United ground, and during his years there he had got to know all of the players and officials closely. His grim task was to make a positive identification of some of the dead.

Outside Old Trafford, a simple notice read 'Training cancelled'.

For me, half past nine was the time that school

started. Nothing that had happened the day before changed the fact that we'd got Maths, French, Religion and English that morning. What had changed was that as we waited to line up there was nobody playing football and nobody playing 'wally', the game that involved kicking a tennis ball against the high gable-end wall of the covered playground without letting it bounce more than once. Instead, lads stood around in small groups, and there was only one topic of conversation: how they'd found out about the crash the previous afternoon. Bernard Murray said he was on his way home from school when he met his granddad. 'He was coming home from work,' he said, 'and he was crying. I hadn't heard anything about the crash in Munich up to then and when he told me I was shattered.' Kevin Sheehan said that when he got home from school his mother told him that there had been an air crash at Munich and it was feared that some of the United players had been killed in it. They had a television at their house and they watched it continuously for the rest of the evening until it closed down for the night. He said his older brother was in the middle of his draughtsman's exams at Salford Tech and should have been studying; he didn't know how he was going to get through the exam he'd got that day. For Danny Murphy, the day before had been a good day as he celebrated his twelfth birthday. When he got home from school he opened his birthday cards. Then he and his mate went outside to play football. But no sooner had they gone out than his mam came out to say there had been a news flash on the radio, and that put an end to his birthday celebrations. That morning he said his dad had put up a black-edged copy of the *Manchester Evening News* in their front window showing the team that had flown out to Belgrade for that game with Red Star.

When Jimmy Murphy arrived at the Rechts der Isar Hospital in Munich he was stunned by what he saw. Matt Busby was in an oxygen tent, and he told Jimmy to 'keep the flag flying'. Duncan Edwards recognized him and spoke. Murphy was given the job of rebuilding the team. Suddenly the responsibility for the survival of Manchester United was laid on his shoulders. Life would go on despite the tragedy, and Manchester United would play again, but in those first days after the crash the idea of seeing a Manchester United team play again was inconceivable.

A few lads had brought transistor radios into school; another who lived right next to the school slipped out at playtime to listen to the latest news; so we too managed to learn a bit more about what was happening in Munich. Reports were coming through about Harry Gregg and Bill Foulkes, both of whom had survived the crash and walked out of the wreckage. Foulkes, it seemed, was the last man to come out alive from the burning plane. The two of them had been sitting together near the front of the plane. It appeared to be Matt Busby who was giving most cause for concern on the Friday morning. Doctors had operated on him for five hours throughout the night, and a statement had been issued saying 'Seven others are in grave condition. But in Mr Busby's case, every minute that we manage to keep life in him is precious.' Seven dead. Matt Busby close to death. Seven others in a grave condition. The feeling that morning was that United really had been wiped out. There was a growing feeling that our team was gone; that we'd never see them again. A terrible question was crossing everyone's mind: would the club survive? And what would happen if we got relegated or thrown out of the league because we didn't have any players?

We were all young, and it was difficult to come to terms with the scale of what had happened, to get beyond thinking about the loss of the football team that so many of us supported, and a feeling of being cheated. But it wasn't just about a football team being destroyed. That morning it was about twenty-one men losing their lives with at least half a dozen more in mortal danger; not just footballers but club officials, journalists, businessmen and a member of the cabin crew: and it was about their wives and families waking to the desolation of the loss of their loved ones. Looking back, it was obscene to elevate the death of a footballer above that of an airline steward or a travel agent. But the loss of something so fresh and creative that played such an important part in our lives felt like a different level of calamity. For young supporters in particular it was difficult to think beyond the team and the players we felt we knew so well who had lost their lives.

Tony Willis remembers the same sort of reactions at his school, and has the same sort of feelings about them now.

> I remember the kids talking about it the next day, you know the way that kids do. We viewed it in football terms, as seven footballers [dead]. We didn't see beyond that, as family men with wives and children and mothers and fathers. We didn't think very much about all the other people who had been killed and injured either. All I can remember is talking in football terms about how terrible it was that football had

suffered such a great loss. It felt in some ways that we'd been robbed; that the people that we'd seen playing and the expectations that we'd had of them had all been taken away from us. We'd been told this was only the start of this great team and we hadn't seen, as Matt Busby told us all the time, anything like the fulfilment of what they would go on to achieve. We were young ourselves at the time and because they were only just a little bit older than us we related very closely to them.

At my school, St Bede's, one of the lads who lived nearby went home for his lunch and came back with that morning's *News Chronicle* and *Daily Dispatch*. The brutality of the tragedy was brought home in one piece that began 'English football suffered the worst disaster in its history at Munich airport yesterday. Manchester United, whose name shone like a beacon across Europe's soccer scene, must inevitably cease to exist as an effective unit for some considerable time.' That was it. That summed up the feelings throughout Manchester that morning. How could United carry on when just about all the team were dead or lying injured in hospital? At school that dinner time, as we tried to find black armbands to wear for football that afternoon I knew I'd never see Roger Byrne or Tommy Taylor play again; no more David Pegg, chewing gum as he ran down the wing, or Eddie Colman twisting this way and that; no Mark Jones or Billy Whelan or Geoff Bent. And would I ever see United play again?

The *News Chronicle* summed up the mood in Manchester that day. Under the headline 'Manchester—A City Stricken With Grief', reporter

Eric Dowd wrote, 'It was as if every family had lost a personal friend. A city staggered under the blow. Manchester became a city of mourning. At first it was unbelievable . . . Only 24 hours before there had been the jubilation of more success for the team which had brought so much honour. And now . . . A deep, dark tragedy that goes into almost every home. Manchester United had become more than a football team. To the man-in-the-street this was the symbol of how British sportsmanship, good honest Lancashire endeavour, the boy-next-door, could reach the top.'

At school that afternoon it was going to be football as usual for the Upper Thirds. Out of respect for the dead we decided we shouldn't play so soon after the crash, but the school authorities insisted that life and the timetable had to go on. Those of us who didn't have school dinners sat on the wooden benches in Our Lady's Corridor eating our sandwiches—Marmite for me, cheese or fish paste for most of the others (no meat because it was Friday). Running the length of the corridor with its marbled floor were school photographs dating back to its early days in the last century. In happier days we'd study them carefully to find the lads who were on the same photo twice—the ones who'd been on one end of the line when the photographer had started to take the photo and then run round the back to the other end while the photographer was making his slow pan along the line. Today, though, there were more important things to do and we spent all of our lunch break searching around for something we could wear as black armbands when we were playing football that afternoon. We felt we had to do something. It was the sort of scene that was being repeated in schools and workplaces throughout the city. Everybody felt they should be making some sort of gesture, but nobody really knew what to do. At the Manchester clothing manufacturer E. Raffles and Company workers observed a minute's silence. Mr Ralph Raffles said, 'Everyone is deeply affected. One man here told me they were his life.'

Football at school that afternoon was a joyless affair. Nobody had their heart in it. For me it was particularly dismal. When I'd looked on the teamsheets that were pinned up outside the changing rooms I was in the seconds. If you didn't make it into your house First XI you were left to play with all the lads who weren't interested in football and couldn't play. They'd stand around talking to their mates in the middle of the pitch as the game went on around them and if the ball came anywhere near them they'd give it away or kick it in the wrong direction. It was always a useless game, but if you played well there was always the chance you'd get picked for the firsts the following week. Down at the playing fields I put my blue and white St Chad's shirt on and, along with a lot of the other lads, carefully tied a black lace round my arm before lacing up my great clod-hopping leather football boots with their rock-hard toe caps. At least they had good studs, which wasn't a bad thing because it had thawed a bit during the day and the pitch we were on was a bit of a mud bath. I don't remember anything about the game except that in the second half I was running for the ball when Ed Corrigan, a friend from my old primary school in Wythenshawe, St Peter's, who was on the other side, booted it straight at me. The heavy leather ball, covered in mud, hit me full in the face. It didn't half hurt, but you didn't let anyone see, so for the rest of the game I ran around spitting mud and blood.

The game had to go on, just as life had to go on for Manchester that grey day. However deeply they had been affected by the dreadful events of the previous day, United fans had to go to their offices and factories as usual. Beryl and Olga Townsend both went to work that day. 'Yeah, I had to,' Beryl said.

> But I said to my boss as soon as I went in, 'I'm not going to be able to do anything today,' and he said, 'It's all right, I understand.' You couldn't believe it that day: it still hadn't sunk in properly. It was like being in a fog. I just couldn't believe that a few days before I'd been talking to Tommy Taylor at Highbury, after the Arsenal game. He was sitting in the front of the United coach eating an apple and he smiled and said hello. We said to him, 'Tommy, you put us through it today,' and he laughed and said, 'We put ourselves through it!' And that was the last any of us ever saw of him. We were never going to see him or any of them again. That was what made it so strange. We just didn't know what to do with ourselves at all.

* * *

Olga's memory of that Friday was just that 'Everyone was walking around in a dream. I was thinking we'd wake up and it would all go away. But it didn't.'

Far from going away, the news just seemed to get worse during the course of that Friday. The city was flooded with rumours that Matt Busby was dead. Small crowds began to gather around the offices of the two Manchester evening papers, the *News* and the

Chronicle, waiting for any details as they came through. Enquiries and telegrams from all parts of the country poured into both papers, all of them asking the dreaded question 'Is it true?' The Rechts der Isar Hospital in Munich put out a statement: 'The reports are entirely false. They did not come from us.' But the message didn't get through to the majority of the people of Manchester and the rumours continued.

The city was in a state of shock—even the newspaper sellers were silent; they sombrely sold copies of the *News* and the *Chronicle* with their poignant pictures and dreadful stories on the front page. The whole of the city was in mourning. Everybody, Red, Blue and uncommitted, was stricken with grief. Chorlton on Medlock, where Mary Morris lived, wasn't very far from Maine Road, and nearly everyone round there apart from her family were City supporters. David Shawcross, who played for City, lived next door to her gran and granddad, just round the corner. 'So of course all the kids round there used to be City because David used to come out and play and kick the ball around with them,' Mary said. 'I think there was only me and our James who were United really. But then when the crash came they were all just as upset. Everybody took it very badly. Not quite as much as me. They didn't have to take the day off school like me, but everybody did get very upset.'

That Friday afternoon when she was off school, Mary remembers an old lady from round the corner coming to her house. She had a framed picture of United on the wall of her living room and she told Mary that twice on the Thursday afternoon the picture had fallen off the wall for no apparent reason. 'What's to do with you today?' she'd said to it each time she picked it up and hung it back up on the wall.

As the long, sad day wore on, spontaneous moves were made to honour the victims and take care of the relatives. United supporter Raymond Gray from Stretford suggested that fans should go to the ground the next day to pay silent tribute and that they should pay their admission price as usual to go to a special fund. Boxing promoter Jack Solomons offered to stage an open-air tournament in Manchester in aid of dependants of the victims, and the Hallé Concerts Society discussed a tribute in music. Others were more concerned about how the team was going to carry on: the Salford Businessmen's League discussed the idea of approaching Manchester businessmen to start a fund to help dependants and to rebuild the team. Behind the Iron Curtain, where United had played their last match just two days earlier, the Yugoslav FA suggested that the European Cup should be renamed the 'Manchester United Cup' in memory of the team. A spokesman for Red Star, the team United had knocked out, said that season's European Cup should be awarded to United. Their proposal was immediately backed by Real Madrid, the holders of the trophy, who had beaten United in the previous season's semi-final. If you were a United fan, it was nice to hear these things, but it was no consolation for the fact that your team had been wiped out. On that Friday afternoon it was hard to see how they would ever be able to play again.

The thousands who had been on the terraces to share the great victories of the Busby Babes were staggering under the blow. They saw United not just as a football team but as one of the greatest international ambassadors their city had ever had.

United had put Manchester on the map. In that night's *Manchester Evening News* Piccadilly car park attendant Leonard Bright of Gorton summed up these feelings. 'Manchester United have not just been a football team,' he said, 'but a great prestige booster for Manchester.' To many there was a great sense of personal loss. Looking back over his thirty-six years as a United supporter, corporation plumber John Quinn of Longsight said, 'When you have followed a team all that time and shared in their successes and defeats, when disaster strikes them it becomes a personal loss.'

* * *

When I got home from school the *Evening News* hadn't yet arrived and there was no news on the radio or television until six o'clock. It was all a far cry from today with our twenty-four-hour news channels. I'd got more homework to do, but how could I concentrate on algebra and French verbs? Anyway, there was all weekend to do it.

There was still an air of unreality about it all. I still couldn't quite grasp that I wouldn't be going to Old Trafford the next day to see United play Wolves and close the gap at the top of the table. But when the paper finally arrived the grim reality was all over the front page. 'Matt 50–50: Edwards "Grave": Berry Coma' the headline said; '50 doctors battle to save their lives'. Under the headline was a special *Manchester Evening News* radio picture showing Matt Busby in an oxygen tent in the Munich hospital with a German nurse standing by his side. 'Five German surgeons fought desperately to save the life of Matt Busby,' the paper said. The first dramatic message from the Rechts der Isar Hospital said: 'He is lying between life and death.' But it was all very confused because the report went on to say 'Then came brighter news—"He is somewhat improved." One surgeon commented: "We are pleased with the progress he is making but he is still very ill." Another doctor said: "His chances are now 50–50."'

As I read further, it didn't get any better. 'Others lying critically injured in hospital are United players Johnny Berry and Duncan Edwards and sports writer Frank Taylor. A nurse said Berry was "very, very ill—dangerous". He has lost consciousness.' Duncan Edwards was just as bad. 'I don't think Edwards will be able to play any more,' said one doctor. Later, the hospital reported that Mrs Vera Lukic, wife of the Yugoslav attaché in London who was on the flight with her baby daughter, and co-pilot Kenneth Rayment were critical. 'But we do not believe that any one of these cases is hopeless,' declared Dr Georg Maurer. 'An army of fifty doctors are working without sleep to save their lives.'

German doctors, I thought, working night and day to save United. I thought the Germans were supposed to be the baddies. It was only thirteen years since the end of the war in Europe and anti-German feeling was still running high. They were still seen as the enemy. The war comics I used to read depicted German soldiers as Fritz, the evil Hun. But German nurses and doctors were now the heroes of the hour, working tirelessly to save British lives. And all of this was happening in Munich, a city I'd always associated with Hitler and the Nazis. It all felt very strange.

But would the efforts of all these doctors be enough? In the stop press the latest statement from the hospital said that Berry's condition had worsened slightly. A *News* reporter at the hospital, it said, had seen Mr Busby, Rayment the co-pilot and Taylor, a journalist. In the next room were Berry and Edwards. 'I heard Edwards say, "I am dying. I am dying."'

The news just got worse and worse. 'Matt Busby's not going to make it,' said my dad grimly when he got back from work and came into the kitchen where my mam was steaming fish for tea.

The six o'clock headlines confirmed how bad things were for some of the survivors. 'Here is the news. In Munich, five of the fifteen still in hospital after yesterday's air crash are seriously ill. Matt Busby had been given the last rites by a priest that afternoon. He was lying inside a transparent oxygen tent breathing heavily under the influence of sleeping drugs. Relatives on their way to Munich are being delayed by snowstorms on the Continent.' The snow was everywhere. 'It's been snowing over much of England and Wales,' the headlines went on. 'More snow is officially forecast for most parts of Britain, and it may be heavy in the Midlands and the South tomorrow.'

The main report started with the latest news about the survivors from Reuters correspondents in Munich. Matt Busby was said to be a little better. 'During the night,' the newsreader said, 'he had been the most critically ill of the survivors, but he had shown some improvement this afternoon. The man now most seriously ill is Johnny Berry, Manchester United's outside-right; the co-pilot of the aircraft, Captain Rayment, is also said to be "in very bad shape". Duncan Edwards, Manchester United left-half, is said to be a little better than he was this morning; Frank Taylor of the *News Chronicle* is in "pretty bad shape still". The condition of the others still in hospital is said to be more or less unchanged.'

I was in tears. We knew that seven of the team had been killed in the crash; how many more deaths were there going to be? Would there be any of the team left?

The bulletin went on to report on the difficulties the relatives of the survivors had had to face to get to Munich that day. 'Five of them who went by way of Amsterdam were diverted to Frankfurt because of continuing snow at Munich. They were going on by train, but a railway spokesman in Munich said this afternoon, "We are snowed in, and all that is running now is emergency traffic."' Then questions surrounding the three attempts at take-off were raised as it was reported that 'Four of the five surviving members of the crew of the BEA Elizabethan appeared before the press at their hotel in Munich this afternoon. The pilot, Captain Thain, was asked about the fact that there had been two false starts before the final attempt to take off yesterday afternoon. He replied that there was "nothing peculiar about it"; he had just not been satisfied. The engines were giving full power, but their note was "varying".'

We switched off the news and went into the kitchen for our tea. My dad said he'd never seen town like it was that day. There was a terrible sadness hanging over the city and the only topic of conversation was the air crash and rumours of more deaths. The bleak mood that day was summarized in a letter in that night's paper:

> Standing on the outside, seeing and feeling the horror as one who is not a football fan, I now realize how much affection and admiration this city felt for United. Last night in the Tatler

> News Theatre there were very few laughs no matter how funny the show was. There was a heaviness, an anxiety over everyone. This morning the passengers on the buses had their heads bowed, studying the latest reports. There was a newspaper in every hand. If anyone spoke it was about the plane crash. Even in the blackest fog there has never been such a heaviness over the city. Even the noise of the traffic seems to be subdued. Although I have never met them personally nor seen them play, I, a 22-year-old office worker, feel the full tragedy of this loss.

That's exactly the way my dad said it was. From the young office girl at his place of work who didn't have the slightest interest in football to the old fellow who worked in the warehouse who was a rugby league fanatic, everybody felt a deep sense of loss.

We didn't get a morning paper in our house, but that day my dad had got hold of most of them and brought them home with him. After tea I spread them out on the floor of the living room in front of the fire and read some of the condolences that had come in from around the world. All the headlines were saying the soccer world was in mourning that day. Soccer, it was reported, poured out its condolences to Manchester United. Many of the papers carried reports from Italy where sports fans had their own disaster of 1949 cruelly recalled. Turin, the team that wore Manchester United's red and white colours, then lost 18 players in an air disaster. Turin were Italian champions in 1946 –7 –8 –9 and contributed nine of the Italian national side. Their secretary Gino Giusti said: 'The hearts of all Italians go out to

Manchester United. We know what it means. We went through the torture and hell of a similar catastrophe.' Real Madrid, the team that beat the Busby boys in the European Cup the previous season, sent this message from manager Antonio Calderón: 'This is one of the best teams in the world and the world will mourn their losses.' The club United had eliminated from the European Cup the day before the tragedy, Red Star Belgrade, issued this statement: 'The boys from Manchester United played so well and they were such a good team that the management of Red Star has decided to propose to the management of the European Cup that Manchester United should be proclaimed the honorary champions this year. It is impossible to believe that such a team of excellent sportsmen have been struck by such a terrible accident. The news will cause deep sorrow to all Red Star players and all sportsmen of our country.' Yugoslavian newspapers followed Red Star's example and said that United should be made honorary champions. The cup should 'go to the football masters who were only prevented by bad luck from winning it'.

By now, some twenty-four hours after first hearing the news, the sense of disbelief, of not being able to comprehend the terrible news was giving way to the reality; the realization that we would never see that great team again—that even if Manchester United were to go on, things would never be the same again. The sense of loss throughout British football was acute, and a deep sadness settled over the game and all those involved in it. Willie Waters, chairman of the Scottish League said, 'I feel a great personal loss in this tragedy. Matt Busby is a close friend of mine.' Ted Drake, the manager of Chelsea, spoke for London and the South when he said, 'We have always held Manchester United in the highest regard both on and off the field. A great side, great sportsmen. It's a terrible shock.' Walter Winterbottom, the manager of the England team, remarked, 'How stunning this blow is to everyone! Only last Saturday Matt Busby said they ought to win the European Cup this year. This is bound to affect the England team. Some great players will be missing after this tragedy. One cannot begin to think at the moment how we will replace them.' Until I read this last comment I hadn't given the England team a thought, and I don't think many United fans had on that day. But 1958 was a World Cup year. Roger Byrne and Tommy Taylor were both regulars in the England team, and they were both dead; Duncan Edwards had already won eighteen full England caps, even though he was only twenty-one and he was fighting for his life in a Munich hospital.

That night the pubs and clubs of Manchester were largely empty and silent. Wherever people gathered they talked in hushed tones of the tragedy. The cinemas and theatres didn't do good business either. Most people stayed at home, ears to the radio or eyes glued to the television for the latest news about the life-or-death battles going on in Germany. For those, particularly those in their teens and twenties, who wanted to get away from it, Elvis was on at the Theatre Royal in *Jailhouse Rock* and Decca's Dynamic Deneage Sensation, Terry Dene and his Dene-Aces, were on at the Hulme Hippodrome. For those with young children, the pantomime season was still going strong. Many a distraught dad had had to sit through Ken Dodd, Norman Evans and Eve Boswell in *Aladdin* at the Palace Theatre or David Nixon as Buttons in Emile Littler's Laughter Pantomime, *Cinderella*.

All over the city that Friday night, in hotels, pubs, clubs and restaurants, the dark shadow of the disaster which had turned Manchester into a city of grief darkened the glitter of its social life. Most events went on as planned—dinners, dances and parties—but they were subdued affairs. Porters at the city's hotels, where many of the players were regular visitors, were mourning 'old friends', and in the restaurants and dance halls the players used to frequent staff were still stunned at the loss of the young stars they had got to know so well. At the Midland Hotel a two-minute silence was observed before the start of the annual dinner dance of Bramall Park Golf Club, and waitresses went about their tasks with tears in their eyes. At the Plaza Ballroom coins and notes came tumbling in as ballroom manager Jimmy Savile stopped the annual staff dance of Walker's Showcards to raise money for the Lord Mayor's Disaster Fund. For as long as Jimmy could hold his breath, the dancers showered copper, silver, pound notes and ten-bob notes on to the ballroom floor. The company's managing director, Mr Ralph Walker, said, 'We are deeply sympathetic with the relatives and friends of the dead. This is our small way of saying thank you for the entertainment they have given us in the past.'

Like many other families, we didn't have a television. They were expensive, and those people who did have them generally rented them. But even renting a television cost about ten bob (50p) a week, and with my dad's low wages it was too much. But Friday was always the night when me and my sister Joan went round to some friends to watch their television. It was always a good night, with Michael Miles's *Take Your Pick* and *The Army Game*, but whatever was on the television was always turned off when the whole family got down on their knees to say the rosary. Our friends, the Buckleys, were an Irish family with seven children ranging from five or six to early twenties, and each would take a turn to lead one of the mysteries of the rosary. Tonight was no exception, but this time our prayers were all more focused. *Take Your Pick* was turned off, and as we all knelt down Mr Buckley said, 'Tonight we pray especially for all the United lads who lost their lives in the crash yesterday and we pray for Matt Busby and the rest of the boys in hospital that their lives may be spared and that they have a full recovery.'

By the time we'd finished the rosary and had some supper it was nearly time for the BBC *Nine O'Clock News*. When it came on I saw television pictures of the crash for the first time. The first shot showed what remained of the aircraft, but even looking at it there on the television screen, with the snow fluttering down on to it, it was difficult to comprehend that the football team I'd been looking forward to cheering on the next day had perished in that wreckage. Over the pictures the reporter's voice said that snow had been falling at the scene of the crash, hiding much of the remains of the aircraft, but this film had been taken when there was still only a little snow and telerecorded as it came over the Eurovision. Then, over a shot of the house which the plane's wing caught, the reporter explained that the wreckage was lying about three hundred yards away from it. The pictures showed bits of debris and luggage scattered over a wide area, and then there were pictures of men in tin hats examining the scene. The commentary informed us that before it grew dark, all the injured had been taken out of the plane and taken to hospital.

'The most pressing work done,' it continued, 'the focus of attention shifted to discovering the cause of the accident. BEA experts flew out from London, but their investigations are now being held up by heavy snow. This is a case in which the twisted remains of the aircraft spell tragedy not only for the relatives of those involved, but for lovers of football throughout the country and throughout the world.'

Mr Buckley got up and said 'God rest their souls' as he switched the television off. Me and Joan got our coats and thanked Mrs Buckley for letting us come round to watch their television. It was cold outside and we walked back quickly along Greenbrow Road to the top of our road. We didn't say very much. It was coming home to me that it wasn't just a football team that had died, it was twenty-one individuals, all of whose lives were precious; all of whom left grieving families and friends. Almost certainly the team, in some shape or form, would go on, but those seven players' lives would never come back, nor would the lives of all the others who had perished—the club officials, the journalists, the steward who had died and the ordinary members of the public who were unfortunate enough to have been on United's aircraft. These thoughts were going to be difficult ones for me and for many supporters to contend with over the coming weeks. There was a terrible tendency only to have concern for Matt Busby and the players. But no life lost on that plane was less valuable than any other, even though for a United supporter it was difficult to think of anything but the team and the losses it had suffered.

When we got home my dad had that night's *Evening News* on his lap. He'd been listening to the reports as they came in on the radio. Underneath the picture of Duncan Edwards at the top of the page he'd written 'Better' in red biro; under Johnny Berry's picture he'd written 'Unchanged'. We looked again at the picture showing Matt Busby in an oxygen tent with the German nurse by his side. My dad had read Busby's biography—it was one of my Christmas presents the previous year—and he remarked how strange it was that when Matt was six years old a German sniper's bullet had killed his father on the Somme. Now here he was in this German hospital and the wheel had come full circle: the Germans were fighting night and day to *save* his life.

CHAPTER 6

UNITED WILL GO ON

There was no group of people in Manchester more affected by the tragic events in Munich than the staff who were left at Old Trafford. Those who had lost their lives in the crash were friends and colleagues; the players were as close to some of them as their own sons and brothers. But already that Friday, as the boss fought for his life, those who were left were having to turn their thoughts to the business of keeping a football club going. The front page of Friday night's paper may have been completely dominated by news of the crash and the progress of the survivors, but the back page was devoted to football matters. The headline 'Club To Play Out All Fixtures' was the first indication for me that, although the team had been wiped out, the club would go on. 'Manchester United are going to carry on with all their fixtures—English and European Cup-ties and English League games—because they believe it is their duty to the public and to football. Mr Harold Hardman, the United chairman, will discuss the position with his fellow directors at their next meeting, but it is not yet possible to say when they will be able to field a team again.'

The 'United will go on' message came over strongly in another piece on the back page. Under the headline 'The Future Is In Their Hands', a reporter named in the by-line as 'the Captain' wrote:

From the stricken shell of Manchester United

will rise another great team. For the spirit of the world-beating side of yesterday will live through this grievous Munich tragedy and will be inherited by the boys who are the team of tomorrow. Sportsmen the world over have paid their tributes to this wonder club. But none of the thousands of admirers who have been numbed by this catastrophe can pay the everlasting tribute that is in the hands of every single player on United's books. It is in their power to ensure that the great traditions of a great club survive. And such is the spirit of every man, woman and boy who play a part in the intricate running of this Old Trafford machine that we believe the future of the Red Devils could not be in better hands. Here are the boys who can be the Busby Babes of the future.

The article went on to list the young members of the United squad, excluding those who were lying in hospital.

The same message came through from Jimmy Murphy after he had been to see Matt and the boys in their Munich hospital beds. 'I have seen the boys,' he said. 'Limbs and hearts may be broken, but the spirit remains. Their message is that the club is not dead—Manchester United lives on. My boss and my greatest friend, Matt Busby, would want me to tell you that the Red Devils will survive this. We have a motto at Old Trafford which means "Work and Wisdom". The work of the country's finest players and the wisdom of the country's finest manager have made us what we are. It is going to be a long, long struggle, but together, we hope to be back there again.'

So the die was cast. These emotions, coming so

soon after the crash, were to gather pace and momentum over the coming weeks and months leading to a remarkable progression to that season's Cup Final, carried along on a huge wave of public sentiment and to the European Cup on a May evening at Wembley ten seasons later. The team that had been wiped out would, we were all convinced in our grief at that time, have gone on to become one of the greatest football teams in the history of the game. But with the death of that team came the birth of a new Manchester United, and of a legend: the club that rose from the ashes and went on to become one of the most famous and successful clubs in the world. And nobody epitomized that dogged spirit of rebirth and renewal more than the twenty-year-old who had been the best forward on the pitch in Belgrade and who was now in hospital in Munich. Bobby Charlton said he had been thrown a hundred yards from the plane when it crashed, but he wasn't feeling too bad.

In the depths of the despair of the Friday afternoon, just over twenty-four hours after the disaster, a message of hope was already beginning to glimmer. The future lay with a new generation of Babes. The average age of the remaining squad was just nineteen. The majority had never played a first team game, but over the next few emotional months they were thrust into the limelight. For some it would prove to be too soon and they would never realize their full potential; others would go on to become household names, not just for United but for England, including a young wing-half who was listed among a group of amateurs who had represented Manchester United's youth team in their last game against Newcastle—one Norbert Stiles.

Chiming in with that declaration of United's

resolve, the Football League Management Committee decided that, with the obvious exception of the United v. Wolves match, the full league programme would go ahead on Saturday afternoon. A statement issued by the secretary said, 'They have come to their decision after careful consideration in accordance with the tradition of the League and feel that the Manchester United club and those affected by the accident would wish it to be so.' Still, it was a controversial decision, and not everybody in the football world agreed with it. Mr Bert Tann, manager of Bristol Rovers, for one:

> The matches should be postponed out of respect for Manchester United and the wives and relatives of those killed or injured. If this had happened in any other organized sport in this country there would have been no thought of continuing with the programme. It smacks of complete disregard for the feelings of those who mourn. It is all very well to say the show must go on, but there is far more to it than that. Those who criticize professional soccer will be further fortified in their stand when they know the Football League have come to this deplorable decision. Critics will say the need to make money transcends all other feelings. Bristol Rovers will travel to Nottingham feeling numbed inside and we have very little stomach for the job of playing football.

Leeds United manager Raich Carter also came out strongly in favour of postponement. 'No games should be played until they have all been laid to rest,' he said. 'We have got a competition here. We expect our players to fight to win, and people go to watch them—to enjoy themselves. But this is so depressing that nobody will enjoy themselves. It's all right saying the show must go on. But this is the first time anything like this has happened here and it goes deep. I shall be seeing Manchester United players running around the park all afternoon. They were at Leeds recently. We could do with points in view of our league position, but even if we get licked, who will care? The result doesn't count any more.'

But not everybody in the game was in agreement. Eric Taylor, manager of Sheffield Wednesday, spoke for those who thought the fixtures should go ahead. 'If we tried to interpret the wishes of those who have gone and those still suffering I think we should play,' he said. 'They played the game to the end, and our best course is to follow their example.' Most important, though, as the debate raged in the football world, were the views of some of those who were most closely affected. Danny Blanchflower, the cultured Spurs and Northern Ireland right-half who went on to captain the Spurs Double-winning team of 1961, had just seen his parents off at London Airport; they were flying to Munich to be at the bedside of their son Jackie, who lay severely injured. After they'd left he said, 'I will play against Manchester City tomorrow unless there is an overnight change in Jackie's condition.' And United chairman Harold Hardman made it clear that he 'wholeheartedly agreed' with the Football League's decision to carry on with the next day's programme. 'I sincerely urge all players to turn out and play the game in the normal way,' he said. 'This would be the best way of paying tribute to everyone concerned in this tragedy. I am confident our manager Mr Matt Busby and the other players who lie injured in Germany would wish it so.'

Those wartime echoes again—and they were never to be far away over the coming months. Many football supporters of the day—my dad's generation—had fought in the Second World War; memories of those days and of lost friends were still fresh, as were the sentiments of fighting on in honour of those fallen comrades. In that sense at least, the committee's decision was very much in tune with national feeling. Certainly the *Express* reported that telephone calls to the paper were supportive. 'We want to make our tribute to Manchester United, and the only place we can do it is at a football ground' was a typical comment. Also in tune with the spirit of the day came a further pledge from Harold Hardman: 'We will undertake our full League, FA Cup and European Cup commitments as soon as it is humanly possible to do so. We have a duty to the public and a duty to football. We shall carry on even if it means we are heavily defeated.'

That Saturday morning Manchester, along with most of the country, woke up to snow. Blizzards had swept across Britain during the night, bringing chaos to transport and threatening the day's sporting programme. Eight inches of snow had fallen on the Yorkshire coast at Whitby, seven inches in the West Country and South Wales, and there was deep drifting in many parts of the country. Roads were blocked in the Peak District, and it was reported that at Edale, where the Peak Park Planning Board was developing a 'Switzerland of the Midlands', skiing conditions were ideal that weekend. Ideal for skiing but not for football, so after all the debate it looked likely that at least some of that day's league programme would have to be cancelled anyway.

Manchester itself escaped the worst of the weather and that Saturday, with no match to go to, I went with my mam and dad and our Joan to see our two grandmothers, my Gran Hall in Beswick and my Gran Kearney who lived ten minutes' walk away on Grey Mare Lane in Bradford. We put our best clothes on and got well wrapped up to face the arctic conditions on our walk up to Greenbrow Road to get the 101 bus into town. On the bus my dad got all-day tickets for us all. Our bus got into town at Piccadilly Bus Station. For me, this was the centre of Manchester. Running all along one side was Piccadilly Gardens, where they always had the city's Christmas illuminations. Beyond that was Piccadilly itself, with Woolworth's and Littlewoods and the grand-looking building of the BBC. At one end was London Road, leading to the city's main railway station, and at the other was Market Street with Lewis's and all the big stores. We had to go through Piccadilly Gardens and down Oldham Street to get to Stevenson Square, where we would catch a trolley bus down Ashton Old Road to get to my Gran Hall's, or one down Ashton New Road to get to my Gran Kearney's.

I found the city centre a fascinating place, especially around Piccadilly. On this bitterly cold Saturday morning we made a little detour to get some tomatoes to take to our grans. As we crossed the top of Market Street to go down Tib Street it was surprising how normal everything appeared to be. Apart from the Union Jack flying at half mast on the BBC building and on some of the big stores, it seemed just like any other Saturday morning. Crowds spilled off the pavements along Market Street as, collars up to keep out the cold, people rushed from shop to shop. Those with children had to stop outside Wile's, the big toy shop on Lewis's corner, and the kids, seemingly oblivious to the cold, stood with noses pressed longingly against the windows, gazing at all the toys, train sets and model planes. The prices were beyond the reach of my mam and dad, and those of most of the kids looking through those windows, but you could always hope. The window I liked best was the one that had all the jokes in, things like black face soap and itching powder. At least some of them were affordable.

We hurried past Wile's and down Tib Street with all its pet stores. Through these windows you could see glass cages full of kittens and rabbits and little mongrel puppy dogs looking longingly out at anybody who stopped to peer at them. There were tanks full of goldfish and cages full of blue, green and yellow budgies, and in the corner, tortoises crawled all over one another. Further down the street, by the side of Smithfield Market, were the barrow boys. On a Saturday a number of streets in this area were occupied by people selling vegetables and other items from a barrow, a flat cart about six feet long on two wheels and two legs to stop the cart from tipping over. They would all shout out the produce they had for sale as you passed by. 'Get yer finest Blackpool tomatoes 'ere!' Most people agreed that it was from the barrow boys around Tib Street that you always got the best tomatoes. Their carts had a canvas canopy to keep the rain off the produce, and electric lights that shone brightly on their colourful displays. According to my dad, some of these barrows had been coming here for many years, the business handed down from father to son.

When we'd got our tomatoes we cut across to Oldham Street on our way to Stevenson Square and went past the Lyons corner café where we would go as a treat on a Whit Friday after the Whit walks. Inside, steam rose from two giant hot water urns on the counter. But there were no treats for us this morning.

A side street halfway down Oldham Street led to Stevenson Square. The only shop there was Manchester's main record shop which we had to walk past on the way to our bus stop on the other side of the square. 'Look at all them Teddy Boys in there,' my mam said as we hurried past. Lads in long jackets and drainpipe trousers crowded into little booths to listen to Elvis Presley's 'Jailhouse Rock', which had been at number one in the charts for the last three weeks. Apart from the record shop there were no stores in the square, just lots of large buildings surrounding it that had been converted to warehouses which sold clothes direct to the public. Stevenson Square was the trolley bus terminus that served places like Ashton, Stalybridge and Hyde out to the east of Manchester.

I liked the trolley buses. They were powered by overhead electric lines, they were smooth and quiet, and they accelerated quickly. The journey to the stop on Ashton Old Road where we got off for my Gran Hall's took less than ten minutes. On our way we went up the steep Pin Mill Brow and through the Blitz-ravaged Ardwick. We passed the ends of mean little cobbled streets packed with tiny two-up-two-down slum dwellings scattered among small textile factories, engineering workshops, pubs, off-licences and corner shops. It was a scene that was already beginning to disappear from the Manchester landscape. Corner shops in particular were becoming something of a museum piece. Some were being converted into houses, others were being pulled down altogether and they weren't being replaced. The only new retail premises being erected were the latest American import, supermarkets, and shopping parades on the new housing estates, like our shops at Greenbrow Road in Wythenshawe.

We got off the trolley bus at Viaduct Street, which was dominated by the massive bulk of the London Midland and Scottish Railway's high viaduct, built of Staffordshire blue bricks. In the shadow of the viaduct were some tiny run-down back-to-back houses. It was here that a few rag and bone men and their families lived; their horses and carts were kept out on bombed sites between the houses, or in sheds under the arches. Once we'd got through rag and bone land we walked by the side of the high wooden fence that ran along the railway line. On the other side of the road was Nansen Street School, the secondary school my dad and his brothers had gone to in the 1920s. It was a three-storey Victorian building with a flat roof that was surrounded by an iron railing. This was the school playground and my dad told me they used to play football up there on the roof with nothing but that four-foot-high railing between them and the forty-foot drop to the cobbled streets below.

Between the school and my gran's house on Baslow Street was the football pitch on Donkey Common, or the rec as it was known. The side of the rec nearest the railway line had a little park now with some kids' swings, but the other side still had the red shale football pitch my dad and his brothers used to play on. He said my Uncle Jack was the best player—

a big stopper centre-half—and he remembered his team winning the cup and taking it back to my gran's to have it filled with dandelion and burdock.

After crossing the rec we went down the back entry to my gran's and in through the yard with its outside lavatory and flag-floored scullery built on to the back of the terraced house. My gran's living room was dark and gloomy. There was just one window looking out on to the back yard, which was overshadowed by the houses on either side and next door's lean-to scullery. My gran was sitting in her wooden rocking chair in front of the big black leaded kitchen range. In the middle of it was an open grate with a welcoming coal fire blazing in it. To one side there was an oven, and on the hob in front the kettle was boiling. On the back wall there was a scrubbed wooden table with a horsehair settee behind it. Dark lino covered the floor, with a rag rug in front of the range.

My dad took the black kettle off the range to brew some tea while my gran took a stone jar off a shelf and poured two glasses of dandelion and burdock, one for me and one for Joan. As she did she talked about the crash. 'It's all that anybody round here is talking about,' she said, 'even the City fans.' My dad commented on the fact that everybody you spoke to seemed to have been affected by it. 'There's a real sense of personal loss in every family,' he said. 'It's been like losing one of your own. I don't think there's ever been a tragedy like this that has touched the hearts of so many millions.'

'Didn't you know some of them?' my gran said.

No, my dad replied. It was Johnny Aston he used to know, and he'd played in the 1948 team. This was a new young team which had replaced the team he used to watch every week after the war. Now that we'd moved to Wythenshawe he'd lost touch with Johnny, but he'd heard that he'd got TB and had been in the sanatorium at Abergele.

My mam's sister, my Auntie Cissie, lived a few doors away from my gran, so when we'd finished our tea and dandelion and burdock, my mam went to see her sister and took our Joan with her. She always seemed to be all right with my Gran Hall, but I'm not sure they got on all that well. My dad was a Protestant and my mam was a Catholic. We were brought up as Catholics, and I don't think that went down very well with my dad's family. Manchester didn't have any of the extreme religious bigotry of Belfast or Glasgow, but there was a fair bit of rivalry between Catholics and Protestants. We used to call the kids from Newall Green, the state primary school near us, the 'Proddy Dogs', and to them we were the 'Catty Cats'. The rivalry extended into the family and one of my mam's proudest moments was the day when my Gran Hall was talking about one of the hymns they used to sing at the Congo—the Congregational church she used to go to—and I piped up to say it wasn't one of their hymns because it had been written before the Reformation so it must have been a Catholic hymn.

Once my mam and Joan had gone, my gran asked my dad to look at some insurance policies. One-penny policies they were, with the Wesleyan and General and the Co-op. This was boring, so I went out to look at the trains. At the front of my gran's house there was a railway line, but you couldn't see anything because there was a high brick wall running along the side of it. All you could see from the house were the voluminous clouds of smoke and steam that drifted across Baslow Street and into the front of the house, if there was a door or window open, bringing with it soot and the pungent, sulphurous smell of burning coal. To see the trains you had to walk down the road. About a hundred yards from my gran's, just at the start of the rec, there was an old iron footbridge crossing the railway to Viaduct Street on the other side, and from there you could see the trains as they went past. I don't know what line it was, but near the bottom of the bridge there was an old plaque that said 'Lancashire and Yorkshire Railway'. My dad said it was a circular line that went round the centre of Manchester; it joined the line to Leeds out of Victoria Station with the line out of London Road Station. Whatever it was, I only ever saw goods trains going past. They came clanking along slowly, pulled by dirty black locomotives that belched out evil-looking smoke. They'd take ages to get past, wagon after wagon. The last one was always the guard's van, with its open platform at the back where the guard would stand and wave to you as he went past. But that Saturday afternoon there weren't even any goods trains, so after about half an hour I went to play on the roundabout in the little park.

When I got back, my mam and our Joan had returned from my Auntie Cissie's and it was time to walk round to my Gran Kearney's. Before we left, Gran Hall got a tin box down from the mantelpiece and gave me and our Joan our customary threepenny bit (just over 1p).

The ten-minute walk to Grey Mare Lane took us past the wash-house at the baths. It was a place that had always fascinated me, with its tiled walls and rows of boilers and women in turbans standing talking or folding their washing in the steam-filled room. My Gran Kearney, my mam's mother, had lived on Grey Mare Lane since coming over from Ireland after the First World War. Before moving to our new house in Wythenshawe we'd lived three doors away, and I'd started school at St Brigid's. Manchester City's Eastlands Stadium stands within a hundred yards of the spot now, but historically it was United territory, close to the Bank Street ground in Clayton where the club started life as Newton Heath. Although my dad wasn't a Catholic, both sides of the family were Reds. He'd started watching them in the 1920s when City were Manchester's big team and United were languishing in the Second Division. When he got back from India after the war he followed Matt Busby's first great team home and away with his brother-in-law, my Uncle Tommy. Together they went to the 1948 Cup Final, when United beat Blackpool 4–2. He kept his ticket till the day he died.

Gran Kearney was old and frail, and she was confined to her bed, which was downstairs in the front parlour. My Uncle Tommy, the youngest of her four children, still lived there. We all looked into the front parlour to see my gran, and my mam stayed in there, fussing around her, making sure she was comfortable. I went into the back room where my Uncle Tommy was polishing the side drum he played in the MacSweeny Pipers, the Irish pipe band based at the neighbouring parish of St Pat's in Colyhurst. He'd always wanted to play the bagpipes in the band, but in an accident at Dunlop's where he worked he'd lost two of his fingers and couldn't play the pipes.

When my dad walked in the conversation turned again to the crash, and the old days when they used to follow United all over the country. Then they chatted about that afternoon's fixtures and the question of whether any matches should be played that day. My dad didn't think they should be playing, but Uncle Tommy thought the games had to be played and that the silence would pay tribute to United's lost players. He said the game that followed the silence would be its own tribute as well: a good, hard, clean game was the best recognition footballers could give to their fellow players. Anyway, carrying on is in the spirit of United, and it is what they wanted. 'Well, if they are playing,' my dad concluded, 'the Football League should ask all clubs to contribute to the Lord Mayor's Disaster Fund.'

*   *   *

When they were not affected by the weather, the matches were going on all over the country and on that afternoon of Saturday, 8 February soccer stood in silent tribute to United on the blackest day in the history of British football. All over the country, Football League and amateur club alike, and all over Europe too, the flowers of English football were remembered and honoured. After the huge crowds of the immediate post-war years, fans had begun to drift away, but on this freezing, snow-bound February afternoon the game's missing millions returned to show their respect for the greatest club side Britain had ever produced. In just the way Manchester United would have wanted to be mourned.

'Abide With Me' was sung at many British grounds, then at three p.m. precisely, wherever the weather allowed football to be played, a hush settled over the packed terraces. For two minutes tens of thousands of heads were bared and bowed. The only things that moved were the club flags flying at half mast and the odd piece of paper blowing across the pitch. All was still and silent. Then the referees' whistles blew and the games commenced—everywhere except at Old Trafford, where the biggest game of the day, the one that was going to have a big say in whether the league championship trophy was going to stay in Manchester or move to the Midlands, should have been in progress. Instead, the wind blew across the empty Stretford End and through the deserted main stand as the proud championship flag flew at half mast over the ground. All around the ground factories and warehouses flew the Union Jack at half mast, while outside stood small groups of supporters, not sure exactly where it was appropriate to be but drawn to the ground to make some sort of tangible expression of their grief. Young and old stood with tears streaming down their faces, gazing at the flag as it fluttered forlornly.

Beryl and Olga Townsend were both there in the grieving crowd, paying their respects. There didn't seem to be anywhere else to go. 'We just didn't know what to do with ourselves at all,' Beryl said, 'so we all went down to Old Trafford. We all met on the Saturday morning and thought, "What can we do?" Because we knew the game had been cancelled. We decided that if we could get in touch with the club we would find out if there was anything the fans could do to help the families.'

It was exactly one week to the hour since they'd been watching the Reds in that last great game at Highbury. For all those, like Beryl and Olga and their friends from the Stretford End, who had packed into Highbury the previous Saturday afternoon, whether they were wearing the red and white of Arsenal or the red and white of Manchester United, it was one of those games it was a privilege to have been at. All agreed that it was a fitting final appearance in the English First Division for the Babes.

Just one Saturday on and outside Old Trafford grown men were in tears as they mourned a loss they felt would never be replaced. Many were workers on their way home from their Saturday-morning shifts in the factories of Trafford Park. United was part of their lives, and match-day routine never varied: work on Saturday morning; a couple of pints with your mates at the pub; then straight to the match. They didn't want that routine to change; they didn't want to believe everything had changed. Some of them came simply to maintain that routine, others because they thought there might be some sort of memorial service outside the ground at three o'clock. But as kick-off time came and went the small crowd began to disperse, trudging past the ticket office with its pathetic notice saying 'All reserved tickets for the Wolves match are sold'.

Not far away, fifty birds fluttered around an aviary in Kings Road, Stretford—the great love of Mark Jones's life. Now his wife, twenty-five-year-old June, had decided to give them away to anyone who would like one of them in his memory. Mrs Jones, who was expecting another baby in July, had gone with her two-year-old-son Garry to her parents in Wombwell, a mining community near Barnsley where she and Mark grew up together. At Wombwell Parish Church that afternoon a prayer was said for the men killed in the crash during the wedding of twenty-one-year-old Irene Jones. Irene was Mark's sister. With the same adversity-defying spirit so characteristic of her brother when he was the pivot of the United defence,

Irene had decided to go through with her wedding plans despite the tragedy that had befallen the family, telling friends that she thought that was what Mark would have wanted. Their mother had died just three months earlier. At the time of her death Irene had been planning her marriage for some time, and just before she passed away Irene had let her see her wearing her wedding dress of white lace. Subsequently, Irene had wanted to adopt a more sombre outfit, but Mark had insisted that she should be married in the dress her mother had seen her wearing. It was this, more than anything, that had persuaded Irene that her brother would have wanted the wedding to go ahead as planned.

At Manchester University the students were due to hold their annual Rag Day on Shrove Tuesday, which this year fell on 18 February, and in the run-up to Rag Day, students would often dress up and come into town to perform a few stunts and sell their *Rag Rag* magazines. But that day they'd decided to call off all events, including the Shrove Tuesday Rag Procession and the Rag Ball. Fun and merriment were not the order of the day and would not have been welcomed by the majority of the citizens of Manchester. At my gran's, it was nearly time to go home. I went into the front room to see her. Outside it was already starting to get dark, and as the number fifty-three buses went past the reflection from their lights flickered across the ceiling of the room. Before leaving, my mam had to do some shopping for her mother. She made a cup of tea, or 'tay' as my gran used to call it, and I stayed with her while my mam and Joan went out to the Lancashire Hygienic Dairies grocer's shop on the corner, and to the greengrocer's and the sweet shop on Ashton New Road.

My gran sat up in bed and reached for a bottle of Lucozade and a small glass on a bedside table. She poured me a glass—always one of my treats when I went to see her. Then she had her 'tay'. She poured it carefully into the saucer, as she always did, and blew on it to cool it down before drinking it. I talked to her about United and the crash. 'Don't worry,' she said. 'They were all good boys. They should all be up in heaven now. Anyway, let's have a song. Sing "Danny Boy" for me.' It was something she always asked me to do, and I was always happy to oblige because she would give me sixpence (2½p) for my efforts. I started singing to her:

Oh Danny Boy, the pipes the pipes are calling,
From glen to glen and down the mountain side …

But singing it this afternoon wasn't easy. It sounded so sad and mournful to me. My voice started to crack and tears welled up in my eyes. But I struggled on with it as best I could.

The summer's gone and all the flowers are
dying …

It was too much. I burst into tears and couldn't carry on.

Gran took my hand and looked kindly at me. 'What's the matter, my little goson?' she said.

'They're all gone,' I sobbed. 'I won't ever see them again. I should have been at the match this afternoon. I'll never see them play again.'

'Oh, but you will,' she said. 'You will see them one day. They'll make a fine football team up in heaven and they'll be able to carry on for ever doing what they love doing so much. And, I'll tell you what. That Dublin lad, Liam Whelan, will be the captain. He was a good lad. They say he'd have made a very good priest if he'd not been such a good footballer.' She smiled. 'I'll be seeing them soon you know. It's not long before I'll be joining them up there.' I knew she was old and she was ill, but she'd never talked about dying before. The thing was, she didn't seem to be worried about it. Her faith made her convinced that death wasn't the end. 'Those boys will be playing for ever, and I'll be there to see them.'

I hadn't managed to finish 'Danny Boy', but she gave me my sixpence. Then she got a sweet bag from the bedside table and gave me three Kendal mints. By this time my mam and Joan were back with the shopping and it was time to go home, but not before we'd listened to the football results on *Sports Report*. I went into the back room where my dad and my Uncle Tommy had the radio on. Many matches had been called off because of the weather, but of those that were played, City had lost 5–1 to Spurs at White Hart Lane, Preston had beaten Chelsea 2–0 at Stamford Bridge, and Luton had put seven past Sunderland. But the main headline that afternoon was the way in which the two minutes' silence had been observed so impeccably.

By the time we left my gran's it was dark. We walked up to the bus stop on the New Road. It was just in front of the sweet shop that my mam used to take us to with our ration book when we still lived round there. The day shift had just finished at Bradford Pit and groups of miners were crossing the road from Forge Lane. A few came and joined our queue. My dad knew one of them, a small, wiry fellow with a sallow complexion. He was somebody from the regiment he'd gone out to India with; he told me later he'd been captured by the Japs and had been in a prisoner-of-war camp for nearly eighteen months. My dad started talking to him at the bus stop. For the first time since we'd got the news about the crash on Thursday night, the conversation wasn't about United and the disaster. They talked about old Army friends and about what had happened to them, and they talked about India and the places where they'd been stationed.

'I see Nehru is at it again, passing round the begging bowl,' my dad's friend said. 'It's in this morning's paper that he's getting a loan of £80 million from America and he's asking us for another £16 million. I know India's the poorhouse of Asia, but I don't see why we should be giving them hand-outs. We never get any gratitude for it and they've destroyed our cotton industry now that they've started making it themselves and under-cutting us.' My dad reminded him about all the poverty they'd seen in India, but this fellow would have none of it. 'I'll tell you what,' he said, 'India's always acting against our interests and America's interests. They're more interested in Russia than us. I think all the money we're pouring in there is money down the drain.'

The bus came, and they carried on talking when they got on. It wasn't far into town, so we all stayed downstairs, sitting opposite one another on the long bench seats at the back near the platform. As we went down the New Road towards town, past Baylem's furniture store where my dad first met my mam when they were both working there after leaving school, the conductor came downstairs to collect the fares. He was a black man—quite unusual in those days because it was before the first waves of Commonwealth immigration reached Manchester.

'Hello,' he said to my dad and his friend. 'I've not seen either of you for a bit.'

'Hello, Sambo, how are you?' my dad's friend replied.

The conductor didn't seem to be put out by the way he had been addressed. He was, it seems, the only black conductor working on the trolley buses, and this is what everybody called him. 'I'm all right,' he said, 'but how have my team got on today? Anybody heard the results?' My dad gave him the bad news that City had been thrashed. 'Well, at least we've still got a team,' the conductor said. 'It's terrible what's happened to your lot.'

When he'd collected our fares he went to his little cupboard under the stairs, where the conductors kept their brew cans and the paperwork they had to fill in. He got a bag of sweets out and gave me and Joan a spearmint chew each.

When we got to town we hurried across Piccadilly to get our bus to Newall Green. I liked Piccadilly in the dark. It was an exciting place with all the neon lights on the side of Lewis's that overlooked the gardens and on the other big buildings at the Market Street end. A huge neon Mother's Pride loaf took up most of the front of the building next to Lewis's department store, and a big red neon Guinness clock hung above the shoe shop on the other side of Piccadilly. The clock said quarter to six as we made our way to the hot chestnut cart on the corner of Portland Street and Parker Street, where the buses went from. There was a warm red glow coming from the coals in the bottom of the cart and we warmed ourselves up as we stood there getting four penn'orth of chestnuts to eat on the bus going home.

By the time we got home the *Evening News* had been delivered. 'Busby Better' the main headline said, 'But Three Stars Won't Play Again'. Above it were three smaller headlines: 'Johnny Berry—Still A Chance', 'Edwards Won't Walk For Years' and 'Germans May Accuse Pilot'. Underneath the main headline were the words 'Matt's order: Carry on, Jimmy', then came the words that all of Manchester had been waiting for. 'From a city 6ft deep in snowdrifts,' *News* reporter Douglas Slight wrote, 'I am phoning the news Manchester and all Britain is waiting anxiously to hear—the greatest soccer manager in the world is winning the fight for his life.' Matt Busby, the report went on, had opened his eyes that day and said, 'I am feeling a little better.' By the side of it there was a picture of Busby fighting for his life in that oxygen tent, his daughter Sheena keeping vigil at his bedside.

On the six o'clock news on the Home Service the appalling weather conditions throughout Britain that day had taken over from the crash as the lead story. Snowdrifts up to ten feet deep had affected Scotland and the north of England, with more snow and frost forecast. Road and rail traffic had been severely disrupted; villages had been cut off; telegraph wires had been blown down; road and railway lines had been blocked; and many of the day's sports fixtures had been called off. Scotland had seen its worst blizzard for more than ten years, and the RAC described conditions in the west of the country as the worst for forty years. Trains from London to Edinburgh were up to seven hours late. After this the bulletin moved on to the crash. Mr A.H. Millward, chief executive of British European Airways, had said he couldn't say what had caused the crash, but one thing that had to be looked at was the weather and the effect of snow on the aircraft.

At least the icy conditions in Wythenshawe gave me a bit of a break from thinking about the crash. After we'd had our tea I went out to play on a big long slide some kids had made in the middle of the road outside our house. Making a slide when the weather was icy was a favourite pastime. We would spend hours perfecting one, only to come out the next morning to find someone's mam had put salt on it. Our road was particularly good for slides because it was a dead end and, as nobody near us had a car, there was never any traffic on it. The slide that night was a good one, a long, thin sheet of ice glistening in the light cast by the street lamp outside our house. For a time, all thoughts of the disaster were put out of my mind as I concentrated on going as fast and as far as I could down the icy path. I went back up the road past Mr O'Malley's house to take a great long run at it before launching myself sideways on to it to slide more than thirty yards down the road, the cold night air biting my cheeks as I went. The great thing about a good slide was that the faster you ran at it, the further you slid, though after a bit it did tend to get a bit worn in the middle, and that would slow you down. All quite thrilling really, but all over quite quickly. My mam called me in at eight o'clock.

When I got inside I spread the paper out on the floor in front of the fire. An orchestral concert was playing on the radio. My dad had always liked classical music; he used to take me to the Hallé Proms in the summer. Under the words 'The terraces were empty at Old Trafford this afternoon after the United airliner disaster at Munich' there was a 360-degree view of the empty ground. There were also some readers' letters. As I went through them with the rather solemn, sombre music playing on the radio, they seemed to sum up the emotions of those days just after the crash, none more so than this from Leslie Holt of Cheetham: 'There are no words … no pious sermons … nothing that can convey all our feelings at the bitter tragedy. I have never met Mr Busby or his proud warriors. I remember them … for the pleasure they gave me.' Another letter suggested the club should be renamed Manchester Phoenix.

The 'United will go on' message came over strongly in several of them, like the one from a group of women supporters from MetroVicks, the engineering company that was such a big Wythenshawe and Trafford Park employer. 'We are just a few female supporters of Manchester United and we would like to express our deepest sympathy to all the relatives. We would also like to send a message to the team that will take this great club forward. It is now up to all you young players to show the country and the world what you are made of, so come on lads, and bring more glory to your club and the memory of your lost team-mates.' H. Lamb of Ancoats Lane made a similar point: 'The young lads of the Youth Team were meant to be the giants of tomorrow. Tomorrow is here now. There is nobody else. These lads have a tremendous burden to carry, a great name to live up to, they can't do it alone. So let's see the supporters who were there every week while United were at the top there every week from now on to give them the support they so dearly want.'

Looking at those letters fifty years later, I was struck by a sense of a very different world. It was, for instance, the age of Sputnik and man's first attempts to explore space, as a letter signed simply 'A Mourner' reminds us: 'United's plane crash has brought the most horrifying disaster for several years. Surely, then, why isn't more time and research spent on perfecting our present-day methods of transport rather than on sending up Sputniks and space missiles? This long-neglected demand can be ignored no longer. Why don't the scientists realize we must crawl before we can walk?' It was also a world in which religion played a much more important role in people's lives and a lot more people went to church; a world in which people were not afraid of coming out in public to profess their faith. 'A Pilgrim' from Sale wrote, 'I will be flying to Lourdes next Monday. May I say to the relatives and friends of the players, officials and journalists that their intentions will be foremost in my prayers; that Our Lord may comfort them in the knowledge that the work of their loved ones has brought such pleasure to countless millions; that their memory will live on in our hearts wherever and whenever footballers, and particularly Manchester United, play. Thank God for them all, and may they rest in peace.'

Above all, this was a world in which football and footballers were very different. I can't think of anything that tells us more about the contrasting lifestyles of a modern footballer and a footballer of the 1950s than this letter about Roger Byrne from the principal of the Salford Hospital Management Committee School of Physiotherapy:

> To the world at large and to followers of football, Roger Byrne will always be remembered for his prowess as a footballer, but to us in the School of Physiotherapy he will be remembered for his fine character and loving personality. He was a part-time student in training and had been with

> us for over four years. He had a special concession from the Chartered Society of Physiotherapists to undertake this training part-time over six years instead of the usual three years full-time. He was well liked and popular with the staff and the students and was determined to make a success of his training. At no time did he presume on the fact that he was something of a national hero, and he was completely without conceit and self-satisfaction. He took his place with the other students and worked industriously and steadily. As a result he was successful in passing the preliminary examination of the Chartered Society and was preparing to take the intermediate examination later this year. We feel that we, personally, have lost a great friend, and the physiotherapy profession one who would have had much to bring to it.

I found out a bit more about the last hours before the crash in a report from Vinko Sale, one of Yugoslavia's leading sports journalists, writing from Belgrade. He'd been at the farewell banquet after the match where Matt Busby had said, 'There were many surprises for me in the second half of the match and the most pleasant surprise of all is the close friendship of all of us here. I do hope we meet more often.' Sale said the evening had been spent in a gay mood and he'd never forget those young faces, 'so happy that night when they sang so gaily'. After the banquet Busby had allowed the players to go to a night club. With them were some of the Red Star players along with journalists from both countries. Tommy Taylor made friends with the young Red Star player Dragoslav Sekularac. He invited the Yugoslav to visit him in England, and Sekularac invited Taylor to spend his holidays that summer with him on the Adriatic coast. When they parted at about two a.m., Taylor said, 'So long until May, when we'll meet up in the World Cup in Stockholm, and after that on our holidays in Dalmatia.' Sale was with the party that saw United off from Zemun Airport. Before the door of the plane was closed, Matt Busby said, 'I do not remember more pleasant days and evenings than those I have spent with you in Belgrade.'

On the nine o'clock news on the Home Service the suggestion that the weather was the cause of the disaster was given greater substance as the bulletin gave the first details of the preliminary report on the crash issued by the Federal German Ministry of Transport. It said that investigation of the causes of the accident had established that there was nothing wrong with the engines and that the probable reason for the plane not becoming airborne was ice on the wings. It was also reported that the first survivors of the crash to return to Britain had arrived at London Airport that afternoon. They were the *Daily Mail* photographer Peter Howard and his assistant Edward Ellyard, and they confirmed the stories we'd started to hear about the bravery of Harry Gregg.

Mr Ellyard said that Harry Gregg was one of the heroes of the disaster. He rallied the fit survivors to help those who were trapped or badly injured, then dashed back into the plane to get a baby out. I couldn't help thinking back to the derby at Maine Road that had been played just a few weeks earlier, and Gregg's dash out of his area to slide feet first through the mud to get to the ball before an on-rushing City forward. My dad thought he was mad; if he'd mistimed his run and his lunge for the ball the forward would have had an open goal. As it was, he timed it perfectly and cleared the danger. Perhaps it was that sort of decisiveness that he'd shown on the football pitch that had him rushing back into the plane to save the lives of others without a thought for his own safety.

CHAPTER 7

MANCHESTER MOURNS

On the Sunday morning I served at eleven o'clock Mass at St Peter's in Newall Green, which was our church. I was an altar boy there and, if you were not serving at one of the earlier masses, you were expected to be there on the altar at eleven o'clock. There were about seventy altar boys altogether so there was usually a big turn-out, and this Sunday was no exception. The altar boys' bit of the sacristy was packed. It was a long changing room with hooks down one side where we hung our black cassocks and white lace-trimmed cottas, and underneath there was a bench with wire compartments beneath for our black patent leather buckle shoes. As usual there was a bit of a commotion as lads scrambled to find their own altar clothes and shoes. 'Me shoes have been swiped! Who's got me shoes!' was a common cry. Then everybody crowded around Norbert Hannett, the head altar boy, or whoever else was Master of Ceremonies that day, to get picked as one of the six 'torches'—the torch bearers who knelt three on each side of the altar. It was good being a torch because there was always something to do when things got boring—playing with the wax that dripped down the candles and making little wax balls that you could flick across the altar at the three torches on the other side. All the rest who weren't torches would be 'top step' or 'bottom step', kneeling on the steps that led up to the altar and lounging on them 'Roman orgy' style during the sermon when everyone else was sitting down.

At eleven o'clock precisely the long procession filed out of the sacristy doors led by the thurifer, who swung the thurible with the lighted charcoal in its base sending white clouds of perfumed incense into the air. Next came the two acolytes carrying up high the big candles in their silver candlesticks, then the torches, followed by all the rest of us, with the MC and the three priests at the back. By the time the priests got out of the sacristy doors, those at the head of the procession would already be on the altar. It was solemn High Mass, sung in Latin, and the church was always packed. The choir sang 'Kyrie Eleison' and 'Gloria in Excelsis Deo' and we joined in, and at the end there were prayers for all those who had lost their lives in the terrible disaster at Munich and more prayers for the speedy recovery of those who were still in hospital.

Outside church, after Mass, there was always a small group who'd stand for ten minutes or so talking about football. One of the men who was always there was Mr Caesar, a tall Irishman who seemed to be as devoted to United as he was to the Catholic Church. He was a real fan who went to all the matches; you never heard him say anything bad about the team or any of the players. By the time I got out of the sacristy that morning the group was already immersed in an animated discussion about how United were going to carry on.

'United have got to carry on,' one said, 'but where are the players to replace the Roger Byrnes, the Tommy Taylors and the Billy Whelans?' The biggest problem, many felt, was the fact that they'd taken so many reserves to Belgrade. Why, when they could only play eleven men, had they taken seventeen? They knew what the team was going to be before they flew out there. Billy Whelan, David Pegg and Johnny Berry had lost their places earlier that season to Bobby Charlton, Albert Scanlon and Ken Morgans, and they didn't play in Belgrade but all three were still great players. It was the same for Geoff Bent and Jackie Blanchflower, who were pretty useful but were never going to line up against Red Star. What a difference it would have made if they'd all stayed at home. We'd still have the nucleus of a very good, experienced team, rather than having to throw so many untried reserves in at the deep end.

'I think they should ban air travel,' Mr Caesar said.

His son Pat, who was in the sixth form at St Bede's, wouldn't have that. 'Look,' he said, 'we're in the space age now. How can anybody talk about banning air travel in this age of space? You can't put the clock back and put a brake on progress. Football teams have got to fly to get to matches abroad. How are Brazil supposed to get to the World Cup in Sweden this summer if they can't fly? Anyway, even if they travel by train, what guarantee is there that they won't have a crash? It's not any safer. Look at that crash at Lewisham last year. Ninety people got killed in that.'

'AC Milan must think train travel is safer,' his dad countered. 'They've just cancelled their flight to Germany and they're going to travel by train to meet Borussia Dortmund in the second leg of their quarter-final this week.'

When I got home from Mass we listened to *Two Way Family Favourites* on the radio, as we always did on a Sunday lunchtime. The reports that came through from Munich that afternoon were starting to get a bit better, particularly those on Matt Busby. The latest bulletins from the hospital said that Busby,

Frank Taylor the *News Chronicle* reporter and Jackie Blanchflower were improving. On the six o'clock news a British European Airways doctor was quoted saying that both Busby and Taylor were off the danger list, although they were still very ill. 'Operations were performed this morning,' the report continued, 'on John Berry and Captain Rayment, the co-pilot, who are still both unconscious. The hospital bulletin said that Duncan Edwards's condition was unchanged and was still serious. All the other players are doing well and some may be discharged from hospital tomorrow.' But details were still confusing and contradictory. Only that morning in the *News of the World* it had been reported that Dr Georg Maurer had said it was most unlikely that Berry, Edwards and Scanlon would be able to play football again. The BBC newsreader concluded the section on Munich with these words:

> Manchester United's assistant team manager, Mr Murphy, who is now in Munich, has expressed the club's thanks to the doctors and nurses and the people of Munich and to airline officials for all they've done for the victims of the crash and their relatives. After the preliminary report last night by German experts, which said that the disaster was probably caused by icing on the wings of the aircraft, a full inquiry is now to be made by the Federal German Civil Aeronautics Board. The commander of the wrecked airliner, Captain Thain, who flew home yesterday after giving evidence to the preliminary inquiry, will be available if the German authorities want to question him again. Our Bonn correspondent,

reporting from Munich, says it might be quite a long time before the findings are known. In the meantime it has been emphasized that last night's report should be regarded as an interim statement.

After that we listened to the rest of the six o'clock news—me in my usual place, sitting on a cushion on the floor in front of the big mahogany radiogram, and my dad in one of the armchairs by the fire. My sister was in the kitchen with my mam helping to clear up after our tea. The next item on the news was of particular interest to my dad. A memorial to the twenty-seven thousand men of the Commonwealth armies who died during the campaigns in Burma and Assam had been unveiled that morning near Rangoon. My dad had spent nearly all the war in India and Burma; many of his mates were among the twenty-seven thousand who gave their lives. He was still in touch with some of the survivors. I had uncles we used to go to see who weren't really my proper uncles who'd survived the horrors of the Japanese prisoner-of-war camps in Burma. We used to go and visit them and my aunties sometimes on a Sunday afternoon in Droylsden and Rochdale and places that were two long bus rides away from Wythenshawe. The war was never mentioned, and as we sat down to a Sunday tea of luncheon meat and salad served on the best china plates followed by tinned fruit and jelly, it was impossible to conceive of the horrors these men had been through just before I was born.

I got up from my cushion on the floor, lifted the lid of the radiogram and looked at the illuminated dial inside it. The outer circle was red and the inner one green; both had the names of far-off places on them—Luxembourg, Hilversum, Helsinki. Where were all these places, and what was their news like? Was it all about death and disaster, as ours was? The fire was low in the hearth so my dad went out to fetch a shovel of coal to get it going again. I sat down on the settee in front of the fire. Something was troubling me.

'Why did they try to take off three times when the plane had ice on its wings?' I asked when my dad came back. 'The pilots and the ground staff must have known it was there, and they must have known it was dangerous.'

It was a question that was being asked in pubs all over Manchester that night—the start of a debate about the causes of the crash and who, if anyone, was to blame that was to go on for many years. That night it all seemed a terrible waste. If only they'd cleared that ice from the wings, perhaps it would never have happened. If it hadn't happened, United would have beaten Wolves and would have been on their way back to the top of the league.

'If, if, if,' said my dad. 'What's happened has happened and nothing will change things. If things had turned out differently for me when I was in India, I would have been one of the twenty-seven thousand commemorated on that memorial.'

I knew what he meant. He didn't talk about it, but my mam had told me. When his regiment was sent into Burma to meet the advancing Japanese army, it was wiped out. My dad was saved because shortly before the push he contracted malaria, and instead of going into the jungle with his mates he was in hospital in Quetta.

For an eleven-year-old it was a lot to take in—forced into confronting the great tragedies and mysteries of life. Being on an aeroplane that couldn't get off the ground because it had too much ice on its wings; sitting in one seat on that aeroplane and walking out of the wreckage with hardly a scratch; sitting in another further down the plane and—instant death. Why is one life taken while another is spared? Why was my dad one of the few in his regiment who was spared from the carnage of the war in the jungle and where would I be if he hadn't?

* * *

It was still cold and grey on Monday morning, but there had been a thaw. The snow had started to turn to a cold, wet porridge that was being washed away by the icy rain that now fell from the leaden sky. Mild weather was forecast for England and Wales. I got up early to listen to the seven o'clock news on the Home Service and it was back to the normal round of politics for the headlines. It was the height of the Cold War, and the main story was about Prime Minister Harold Macmillan telling Russian premier Nikolai Bulganin that before a summit conference could be arranged there must be a reasonable prospect of achieving concrete results. Munich was down to the third item. It was reported that two of the survivors, the co-pilot Captain Rayment and Johnny Berry, had got worse. That was about all it said.

I wanted to know more, but we didn't get a morning paper, so on my way to the bus to school I went to the newsagent's to use some of my precious one shilling (5p) spends to buy one. I spent 2½d (1p) on a *Daily Herald* because the headline shone out optimistically: 'It's Better News This Morning Of The Red Devils. Busby Out Of Danger.' On the smoke-filled top deck of the bus I read the previous night's bulletins on Matt Busby and his two seriously injured players. 'Busby: Off the danger list,' it said. 'Slow but gradual improvement throughout the day. Edwards: Off the danger list, and has improved considerably. Berry: Unchanged, still critically ill.'

The news gave me a little bit of a lift on that cold, wet morning as the bus made its way slowly along the narrow roads of the estate. Matt Busby was going to get better and Duncan Edwards would be back—maybe not that season but certainly by the next. The only bad news that morning seemed to be about Johnny Berry, still unconscious on a bed of crushed ice. Nurses changed the bags of ice around Johnny every hour, and he was also being given special drugs to cool the blood. Both Berry and Captain Rayment, the report said, had serious brain injuries and they were both receiving the same treatment. A lower blood temperature helped brain tissue to heal more quickly and also reduced shock and helped a patient to weather the crisis. It was a treatment similar to one that had saved a woman described in the press as the 'deep freeze mother'; she'd been unconscious for 169 days after a street accident. Professor Georg Maurer, the brilliant forty-nine-year-old brain surgeon, was personally supervising their treatment. 'Berry and Rayment are our most serious cases now,' he confirmed. 'Then come Mr Busby and Duncan Edwards.'

The *Daily Herald*'s chief sports reporter, Peter Lorenzo, said that he had talked to Matt Busby the day before. He was, he said, the first newspaperman to speak to him since the tragic crash on Thursday, and he still didn't know that his wonder team had been wrecked. 'As I entered his ward in the Isar Hospital,' Lorenzo wrote, 'his eyes flickered in recognition through the plastic oxygen tent. He raised his left arm in greeting. I clasped his hand through a flap in the tent and said, "Hello, Matt." He whispered, "Hello, Peter. It's good to see you!" He was obviously in pain. But in his tired eyes I caught a glimpse of the magnificent fighting spirit which has helped to keep him alive.'

One of the things I remember very clearly from that time was the quality of the newspaper reporting. By the Monday after the crash it was being given less and less prominence in the BBC radio and television reports; the national newspapers and the Manchester evening papers were the only real source of information for a Manchester public anxiously waiting for any scrap of information on the progress of the survivors. Writers like Peter Lorenzo brought us close to the events in that Munich hospital hundreds of miles away. It helped that the newspapermen of the time were close to the team and to the players; there was very little of the animosity that characterizes the relationship between some of the big clubs and the popular press today. And, despite the fact that they were rivals, the newspapermen themselves were close to one another. The writers who were reporting from Munich were mourning the loss of their own colleagues too.

'Alongside Matt,' Lorenzo's report went on, 'lay another friend of mine, Frank Taylor, a sports writer of the *News Chronicle*. His right leg and left arm were broken in the plane crash. He said, "Hello, Peter. It's great to see you again. I'm feeling fine." Doctors have ordered that none of the more seriously injured survivors be told that 21 passengers died in the crash. When Frank asked about my colleague George Follows, who was one of the victims, I had to tell a white lie. I said he was doing fine. Frank replied, "That's good. George is a tough nut."' George Follows was another of the journalists who was United through and through, and he used to admit this quite unashamedly: 'I reckon I take the prize as the world's most biased football reporter.' Like many of the journalists who lost their lives, Follows was a good friend of the players; among his best pals was skipper Roger Byrne. The two men had just made a TV documentary together. It was never shown.

Lorenzo also informed his readers that Duncan Edwards had come out of a coma and had recognized and spoken to people. He had also taken some soup. And Jackie Blanchflower was said to be much better. He thought they'd both be playing by next season. In Ward 256 the less seriously injured players—Ray Wood, Albert Scanlon, Dennis Viollet, Bobby Charlton and Ken Morgans—were reported to be laughing and talking together. Viollet, his head swathed in bandages, said, 'It's going to take a long time to get over the shock that we will never again play alongside Roger Byrne, Tommy Taylor, Eddie Colman and the rest of our pals and team-mates who died. But once we get over it we'll be all right. We all want to play football again. We hope to do so very soon.'

Towards the bottom of the page a short paragraph confirmed that an official German report on the air disaster issued on the Sunday had said it was probably caused by ice forming on the wings. A BEA spokesman in Munich warned that the inquiry was not yet complete, but he agreed that icing during take-off was one of the possible causes of the accident.

I turned to the sports pages and there was a picture of footballers from two teams standing around a football pitch, players from the German teams Eintracht Frankfurt and Reutlingen. All of Germany's First Division matches on Saturday afternoon had been stopped in the thirtieth minute, at the approximate time of the disaster two days earlier, to pay tribute to the dead of Manchester United. All Italian games were stopped in the fifteenth minute, and an estimated hundred thousand Spanish professional and amateur footballers wore black armbands. Under the headline 'It's Up To You, Jimmy', Peter Lorenzo wrote, 'Jimmy Murphy leaves here tomorrow morning to tackle the biggest job of his life. Matt Busby, the Manchester United manager, still fighting for his life in hospital, whispered to him this morning, "It's in your hands now, Jimmy. Go to it, keep winning … and keep the lads happy." Murphy lifted the flap in the plastic oxygen tent, gripped his lifelong friend's arm, and left to begin his great task.'

That Monday morning, people who had taken the Friday off school or work had to go in to face their teachers and bosses. One of them was Mary Morris. 'I was always in trouble at school,' she said, 'because me and my friend Barbara were always talking. We used to tell everyone in the class about going to see United and about what we'd done at the football, and our teacher used to give us lines about the way United had played. If they'd played badly on the Saturday he used to make us write these terrible things about them. But when we got into school that Monday morning we didn't get into trouble because he was just as upset as we were. He was a United supporter and he used to go to Old Trafford himself.'

On the Monday, Manchester mourned as the bodies of its famous footballing heroes were flown home and I mourned with them. It was strange. They were footballers. I didn't know any of them personally, but they felt like people you knew. For many people at the time it was like death in their own family and everybody wanted to pay their last respects when the bodies of all twenty-one victims of the crash were to be flown from Munich to London on the Monday afternoon. At Munich Airport, grey-uniformed police formed a guard of honour to salute the coffins as they were put onboard a special BEA Viscount plane. Before the plane took off there was a simple ceremony attended by the British consul general in Munich, the Mayor of Munich and representatives of the Bavarian Football Association. There were wreaths from the Bavarian State Government and from the City of Munich, and silent groups of airport workers watched as more wreaths were taken on to the plane, which had had its fuselage windows screened. Then the little group of mourners filed silently through the plane where the coffins were stacked. The plane flew to London first, where the coffins of David Pegg—who was being taken straight back to his parents' home in Doncaster—and Billy Whelan—who was being flown to Dublin—were taken off. After that it would make its way to Manchester with the bodies of the remaining five players, the three club officials, the eight journalists, all of whom were Manchester-based, and the other three victims. It was to be met at Manchester Airport by the directors of the club, and the bodies were to be taken to Old Trafford, where they would lie that night.

That evening was cold and wet—a miserable

Manchester winter night. When I got home from school I stood in front of the fire to dry out and waited for the paper to arrive. When it did, it had dramatic pictures on the front page showing for the first time the full horror of the crash. Taken only seconds after the impact, they showed the ferocity of the blaze. Huge flames and smoke billowed from the twisted wreckage. It was hard to see how anybody had got out of it, yet just below these pictures was one of Bill Foulkes revisiting the disaster scene and retrieving from the debris a bottle of gin he had bought in Belgrade, and another of Bill with Harry Gregg and Jimmy Murphy onboard a train just before leaving Munich. There was a report on the departure of the special flight carrying the coffins from Munich, and the route from Ringway to Old Trafford that would be taken by the coffins later that evening. A club statement said it was the express wish of the club that supporters and those who wished to pay their respects should do so at various points along the route, and not make the ground the focal point. The bodies were due to arrive at Ringway at 8.25 p.m. and to head off for Old Trafford in a procession of hearses at about 9.20 p.m.

Me and my dad left home at about eight to get the bus to the bottom of Princess Parkway where it met Altrincham Road, just by the Royal Thorn pub. There we waited in the rain. The crowd lining the route grew to three deep, and all stood in silence. The flight from Munich was delayed and we stood for a long time at the bottom of Princess Parkway on that freezing February night. I think it was about ten o'clock when a murmur went through the crowd as the low drone of an aircraft was heard in the distance.

'That's them. That's their plane coming in.'

At the airport, the Lord Mayor of Manchester, other civic leaders and directors of the club waited to meet the aircraft and pay their respects to the dead. When the plane landed it taxied towards the waiting mourners. When the doors were opened and the steps rolled up to the aircraft, more than fifty wreaths and sprays, many of them in United's red and white, were unloaded first from the plane. Then came the coffins. One by one they were carried out of the plane, and each was taken to a waiting hearse. By this time more than two hundred thousand mourners were lining the streets all the way from Ringway Airport to Old Trafford.

At the bottom of Princess Parkway, about an hour after we'd heard the heavy drone of the plane's engines, another murmur went through the crowd as another sound was picked up. It was the distant roar of motorcycle engines cutting through the silent night air. We peered over the roundabout and down Altrincham Road, and then the headlights came into view, approaching slowly through the rain. Past the Royal Thorn pub they came and round the roundabout to where we were waiting. The procession of hearses was headed by a police motorcycle escort. As they drove slowly past, everything looked strangely anonymous. Where was Roger Byrne and Tommy Taylor? Which of the coffins was Eddie Colman's, Mark Jones's, or Geoff Bent's? Many of the people around us were in tears; some were kneeling down in the mud, heads bowed in silent prayer. We watched as the cortège disappeared into the distance, towards the Wythenshawe Road roundabout. That was all that was left of United, our football heroes who'd been set to conquer the world.

The crowd around us started to melt away into the

night. Some stayed where they were for a few minutes, staring straight ahead before turning and walking away. Some were walking away from the team they loved, because they knew they'd never be able to bear going to a match again. Further up the road, the sad procession continued to move through the throng. All along Princess Parkway cars were parked nose to tail, and mourners crowded on to the roundabouts, turning them into mud baths in the pouring rain. Many girls were wearing club colours, and they wept when the dead passed by. Along the entire route, the crowd, up to four and five deep in places, stood silent and bareheaded in the driving rain. They were the men, women and children of the Old Trafford terraces; many more of them had never been to a match, they just felt they should be there. The next day's *Evening News* told us about some of those people:

> People like 71-year-old Harry Hope of Silver Street, Moss Side, who had rooted for the Reds for more than forty years. In cloth cap and raincoat he stood white-faced for hours. People like the widow who said, 'My husband used to follow United. That's why I'm here.' People like the Teddy Boy with tight blue jeans who said, 'I'm a City fan really, but...' He nodded to his blonde girlfriend. 'She's a United fan. She cried her eyes out when she heard.' People like the girl who walked to Northenden from Didsbury. 'I have never seen United play,' she said, 'but I felt I wanted to come.' There were many people like Mrs Ivy Cornthwaite of Bath Street, Moss Side, who simply said, 'It is like losing one of the family.'

Beryl and Olga Townsend went down to Old Trafford and stood on Chester Road, as near to the ground as they could. Despite no one being allowed down to the ground itself, there were more people lining the roads near Old Trafford than anywhere else on the route. 'Even people who weren't interested in football were so upset about it that they came out to pay their respects,' Olga said. The rain continued unabated, and as the coffins came slowly past them Beryl remembers saying to herself, 'Oh, Billy isn't with them.' Because Billy Whelan's body had been flown directly to Ireland she couldn't pay her tribute to him, and she says now that she found that absolutely heartbreaking.

The coffins were taken to lie overnight in the gymnasium under the main grandstand at Old Trafford before being passed on to relatives for the funerals. Today, that gymnasium is the place where the players' lounge has been built, where those who succeeded the Babes gather after a game for a chat and a drink with their family and friends.

It was gone eleven o'clock when I got home with my dad that night. We were both cold and wet, but we felt we had done what had to be done, paying our last respects not just to the players, but to the club officials, the journalists and all who had perished just a few days earlier. Seeing that long procession of hearses moving slowly through the rain had really brought it home: all these people were dead and we would never see those footballers again. I took off my soaking wet gabardine mac and my mam put it on the back of a chair in front of what was left of the fire. It had to get dry before half past six the following morning because I was serving at seven o'clock Mass and it was all I'd got to go to church in, and then on to school.

* * *

I was up at quarter past six. The earlier you got up the colder it seemed to be, and there was no staying in the warmth of my bed for an extra five minutes this morning because I had to be in the sacristy ten minutes before the start of Mass to get my cassock and cotta on and get the wine and water poured and out on to the table at the side of the altar.

On my way to church I looked up Greenbrow Road to the bus shelter at Tuffley Road, and there was the usual long queue of men in overalls, with butty bags over their shoulders, stretching out of the shelter as they waited for the early buses to Trafford Park. It was a time of full employment, the days of Harold Macmillan's 'never had it so good' Conservative Government. Although the cotton industry was in decline, Britain was still very much the workshop of the world, and the engineering works of Trafford Park provided employment for thousands of Manchester men and women.

Throughout the night and into the early hours of the morning thousands of supporters had kept vigil at the stadium as the football world mourned the passing of the Babes. From before dawn, workers heading for the lathes and grinding machines of Trafford Park stopped off at the ground, standing with caps off and heads bowed to pay their last respects. A groundsman said, 'It has been a remarkable sight, seeing men on bike and on foot paying homage.' All through the day the supporters continued to come. Beneath grey skies, housewives, workers and schoolchildren all stood with their heads down to pay their silent tributes. One of the first to arrive at the ground was Mrs Betty Clarke, who lived close by in Old Trafford. 'I stood in the rain for three hours to see them last night,' she said. 'I never knew them personally, but they were to me every mother's ideal of a son.'

Everyone went to the main entrance—the nearest point to the gymnasium where the coffins, draped in black, were placed on tables. There were more than twenty wreaths there, and in front of them a policeman stood guard. No one was allowed into the gymnasium. One of the people outside it was fifteen-year-old schoolboy Alan Bower who had taken a day off from Eccles Grammar School to pay his last respects. Alan, a centre-forward in his school football team, idolized Tommy Taylor. 'I never met him,' he said, 'but I am more determined than ever to try to emulate his play and sportsmanship.'

That day I had to go to the dental hospital just near town. I'd had toothache since the previous Friday when the ball had hit me in the face. Our local dentist had looked at it and said I'd got an infection in my gums from all the mud that had smacked me in the teeth and I'd need special treatment. At the hospital they said I'd need a root filling but first of all they'd have to get all the poison drained off. It was going to be a big job, and the treatment would take a few weeks. So for me, the weeks after Munich are remembered for almost daily visits to the dental hospital where I'd spend hours in the chair surrounded by a huge group of students as their professor drilled and probed deep into my gums and told them how to go about this highly advanced bit of dental surgery.

When I got out of the hospital at the end of that first visit everything in the centre of Manchester had been brought to a halt as the first funeral, that of Willie Satinoff, was held. He was the friend of Matt Busby who had been to Belgrade as a guest of the club because, it was rumoured, he was a candidate for the seat on the board that had been left vacant by the death of George Whittaker just before the crash. The story is still told in Manchester that Satinoff was one of two candidates for that seat; the other was Louis Edwards. There was one seat left on the flight to Belgrade so Satinoff and Edwards tossed up for it. Edwards lost the toss, and he went on to be offered the directorship that led to the creation of the dynasty that ruled at Old Trafford for more than forty years. Satinoff, of course, won the toss, and that Tuesday his funeral was being watched by thousands of mourning people in Manchester.

Sleet fell as hundreds gathered outside the Manchester Jewish Hospital before Satinoff's funeral procession of over sixty cars moved away. As it crossed the city centre on its way to Southern Cemetery, it was watched by all sections of the city—businessmen, doctors, lawyers, errand boys and women with shopping bags—all standing silently under a sea of umbrellas. Later that day came one of the biggest funerals of all, that of *Daily Express* football writer Henry Rose. A thousand taxi drivers offered their services free to anyone who was going to the funeral and there was a six-mile queue to Southern Cemetery. The cortège halted for a moment outside the *Daily Express* offices in Great Ancoats Street where Rose's colleague Desmond Hackett wrote in the style of Henry, 'Even the skies wept for Henry Rose today . . .'

Throughout the day the news bulletins on the condition of Johnny Berry and Duncan Edwards kept changing, but it was the condition of Edwards that was causing most alarm. That night's paper reported that he was unconscious and that he had taken a sudden turn for the worse. Doctors were alarmed at the unusually high percentage of nitrogen in his blood. Johnny Berry was also still in acute danger. He'd been unconscious for five days—'not a good sign', the hospital's deputy administrator said. But the news about Matt Busby was good again. He had recovered so much from his injuries he could now be treated as a normal patient: he had been allowed to have a drink of beer and was eating well. Jackie Blanchflower was also reported to be improving.

That night my dad said we'd have to get a television. Although we'd listened to all the reports on the radio and read the papers avidly, there was film coming out of Munich we'd not been able to see any of in our house. We could have gone to the pictures to watch the newsreel footage but that would have meant going to town where the Tatler News Theatre was showing the Manchester United Air Tragedy. 'Graphic Newsreel Scenes', the advert in the paper said. 'Also we pay tribute to this great team by showing glimpses of their past glory. Plus normal supporting programme of Bugs Bunny and other cartoons.' Just above it the advertisement for the Manchester News Theatre said, 'Comedies. Cartoons.' And then, 'With sorrow and pride we present on the screen Tribute to Manchester United.' Somehow it didn't seem appropriate. We'd give the pictures a miss.

But it wasn't just the news from Munich that had swung my dad about getting a television. The next day, history was going to be made. There was an important by-election at Rochdale and it was going to be the first televised by-election. My dad wanted to see it. The result was going to come in on television as it was declared, and he wanted to see Rochdale pronounce judgement on what he regarded as the current dead-end Tory Government and vote the Labour man in to capture the Tory seat. Rochdale, my dad said, was important. Hugh Gaitskell, the Labour leader, had said: 'Its outcome is of supreme importance to the nation and indeed to the world. We say that there should be summit talks, that we should agree to suspend H-bomb tests and that we should work towards a neutral zone in Central and Eastern Europe.'

My mam and dad had held out against getting a television for a long time. It would distract me from my homework, they used to say. But the real reason was the cost. Not many people could even think about buying a television; most people used to rent. And with my dad earning £6 a week and television rental about ten bob a week it would mean a huge chunk out of the family income. But I think the combination of Munich and the big political stories of the day like the Rochdale by-election, nuclear tests and the attempts that were being made to set up summit talks with the Russians made my dad feel that, in spite of the cost, we would have to have a television. We would go to Northenden on Saturday morning to have a look in all the rental shops there.

* * *

Wednesday morning dawned, and news about United and the crash had disappeared from the headlines for the first time to be replaced by concern for the health of Winston Churchill. The eighty-three-year-old former Prime Minister, it was reported was indisposed and had been ordered by his doctors to stay in bed. Apart from the fact that Bobby Charlton had left hospital, what news there was from Munich wasn't good. A doctor said there had been no change in the condition of the injured survivors still in hospital. Johnny Berry, Duncan Edwards and Captain Kenneth Rayment were still in acute danger; the condition of three others, Matt Busby, Jackie Blanchflower and the journalist Frank Taylor, had improved but was still serious.

An apparatus known at the time as an artificial kidney was taken to Munich to be used in an emergency operation on Duncan Edwards. After his condition had deteriorated the night before, telephone calls were made to London and Vienna for this rare piece of medical equipment, but none was found available. Eventually the Munich doctors had discovered that there was one at Freiburg in south-west Germany—more than two hundred miles away. It was sent by road with a police patrol car, racing through the night at over 60 mph. When it arrived at 10.40 on the Wednesday morning, doctors were waiting to load it into a lift and take it up to the fourth floor. One of two specialists who also drove to Munich from Freiburg during the night explained that the artificial kidney would be connected with Edwards's bloodstream.

In Manchester flags were again flying at half mast in the city centre as more funerals of players, officials and journalists took place. On the Wednesday were those of Roger Byrne at Flixton Parish Church and Manchester Crematorium; Billy Whelan in Dublin; David Pegg near his family home in Doncaster, where his dad had been a miner; Frank Swift; Eric

Thompson of the *Daily Mail*; and Archie Ledbrooke of the *Daily Mirror*. Manchester florists reported a tremendous demand for wreaths and sprays. One said, 'We have received hundreds of orders, mainly from ordinary people. Many have no connection with the dead.' A wholesaler reported that they'd had to send for extra supplies from Holland. As cortèges left the ground, workers from Trafford Park came to pay their last respects. Where families requested that funerals should be private, the United followers stayed away from gravesides but lined the procession's route to look on in tearful silence.

As the funerals continued and we grieved for the dead, we dreaded hearing the news that was coming through from Munich. The condition of some of the survivors was so serious we feared the death toll would rise. The usually lively and exuberant city was still hushed and sombre. In pubs and workplaces there was still only one topic of conversation: 'How will United recover from this?' Every day at school we listened to the reports on Duncan Edwards and Matt Busby. Those on Edwards's deteriorating condition especially stick in my mind. In spite of their seriousness, we were convinced he would pull through. He was a big, strong, lion-hearted player. On the pitch he'd always appeared indestructible. It was inconceivable that he would die. With so many lost, he became a symbol of survival. But Matt Busby was older and according to the reports we were getting his condition was more critical than Big Duncan's.

In our house we remained glued to the radio for every scrap of news, and in every report things seemed to change. In one there'd be a glimmer of hope, a slight improvement; then within hours that hope would be dashed. On Wednesday evening we switched on the six o'clock news as usual when my dad got home from work, and it was bad. 'A statement about the Manchester United player Duncan Edwards, issued from the hospital in Munich within the past hour,' we heard the newsreader announce, 'says according to Reuters that his life is in "acute danger". An emergency operation had been performed on him that morning and the artificial kidney had been attached to two points on one of his veins, to try to purify his bloodstream.' But then, just before bedtime, there was better news on the 10.30 p.m. bulletin: 'Within the last hour, Professor Maurer, the head of the Munich hospital where most of the survivors of the air crash are being treated, has said that the condition of the Manchester United player Duncan Edwards has improved. Professor Maurer said that Edwards was still unconscious and critically ill, but the artificial kidney was doing its work. On Thursday evening a British European Airways doctor in Munich said there had been a dramatic improvement in his condition. Earlier, Professor Maurer had said that Edwards had regained consciousness soon after five o'clock that morning for the first time since Sunday. He had drunk a little milk and spoken a few words. To me, that was it. He was going to recover and he'd be playing again. It never entered my head at that time that even if some of the critically injured players did survive, they might never be able to play again.

One piece of news that cheered my dad up a bit was the result of the Rochdale by-election. The Conservatives had been thrashed. Labour had romped home in the 'TV by-election' to win a marginal seat that had been held by the Tories at the last two

General Elections. Television presenter Ludovic Kennedy had come second for the Liberals, the Tory very much bottom of the poll. The message from the Labour papers like the *Daily Herald* and the *Daily Mirror* was loud and clear: for the Government it was another 'Give Up! Get Out!' notice in unmistakable terms. My dad said Labour would get back in at the next General Election. I wasn't bothered about the political news; what I wanted was details from Munich. By Thursday, though, just one week after the crash, it was no longer the main headline even in the *Evening News*. The lead story was a Defence White Paper published that day that contained dramatic and far-reaching changes in the pattern of Britain's nuclear age defence system. Britain, we learned, was building a ballistic super rocket bigger and better than America's, and the latest V-bombers of the RAF were going to carry a new super bomb.

As the week wore on and news of the survivors continued to trickle through from Munich, more funerals of those who had lost their lives in the crash took place, on the Thursday Geoff Bent at St John's Church, Pendlebury; Bert Whalley at Trafalgar Square Methodist Church in Ashton and Dukinfield Crematorium; Tom Curry at Gorse Hill Methodist Church in Stretford and Manchester Crematorium; Alf Clarke of the *Manchester Evening Chronicle* at Manchester Crematorium; and Donny Davies of the *Manchester Guardian* at St Ann's Church and Manchester Crematorium. Jimmy Murphy took time off from his efforts to bring football back to Old Trafford to attend as many of the funerals as he could get to. He headed a party from United at the funeral of Bert Whalley. Many members of the youth team and former players Johnny Aston and Henry

Cockburn also attended. Nearly all of the playing staff and the surviving club officials were representing the club at these funerals, and again thousands took a few hours off work to pay their respects. In the city centre, newspaper workers, many dressed in black, left Kemsley House and stood silently in the street as a last tribute to Alf Clarke. Traffic lights were ignored and traffic halted as the fourteen-car cortège made its way through the city centre. Mourners crowded the chapel of Manchester Crematorium, among them Manchester City manager Les McDowall and goalkeeper Bert Trautmann.

Along with pieces on the funerals, the *Evening News* also reported each day on contributions that were being made to the Disaster Fund, like that of thirteen-year-old Roberta Ormerod from Handforth in Cheshire. Although she'd only been to see them twice, United were the great love of her life. Every weekend for the past three seasons she had read every newspaper report on the matches, then cut them out and pasted them on her bedroom wall. Roberta had been near to tears for a week and had made a sacrifice for the team she idolized. At Christmas she had been given £2 for a long-playing record she had set her heart on. But her first thought was to help the club, and she sent the money to the Disaster Fund.

But not everybody in Manchester had been affected in the same way. On the same page, the paper also told its readers that police were hunting a fair-haired man whom they had tagged the meanest thief of the year. He'd walked into the Clubhouse Tavern in West Gorton, ordered a beer, then vanished with £6 collected for the Lord Mayor's Disaster Fund. Licensee Mrs Veronica Edwards said, 'He can have no conscience, because the pot containing the money was clearly marked.' The man had gone into the pub shortly after opening time. Mrs Edwards served him, then went to put her baby to bed. When she returned to the bar he had gone, and the first thing she noticed was the gap on the bar where the glass containing the money had been. Her husband George said, 'It's only a small pub and we were proud of the amount. We hoped to make it £10 by the weekend. But we will carry on—just like Manchester United.'

In that week of funerals that followed the air crash, it wasn't only Manchester in mourning. Three of the seven players who had lost their lives were from Yorkshire mining communities. On the Wednesday, workers from Trafford Park who were gathered at Old Trafford had watched as half of the second team left the ground in three cars to attend the funeral of David Pegg in Doncaster. Wilf McGuinness, Colin Webster, Shay Brennan, Bobby English and Alex Dawson travelled across the Pennines to the sort of industrial landscape so many of their team-mates had come from. When they arrived at the church at Highfields, aproned women, miners in their pit muck and groups of small boys stood bareheaded and sad in the cold wind. Above it all, the mournful siren song of the Brodsworth pit buzzer sounded a requiem for their dead friend. The *Doncaster Chronicle* described how 'through the sad streets of Coppice Road, where David had once kicked the toes from his shoes playing with a small ball, came the cortège. A solemn, slow procession of twenty cars . . . And it was perhaps then, the Yorkshire paper added, that these silent people who lined the route realized that David Pegg had actually died. Before, it had seemed too awful to be true. All the shops were closed and every house had its curtains drawn as the procession made its way to St George's Church. Alongside the family mourners and the United players in the church were Albert Quixall, Alan Finney and manager Eric Taylor from Sheffield Wednesday and many of the Doncaster Rovers team including wonder boy Alick Jeffrey. During the funeral sermon the vicar of Woodland said, 'It was inevitable that David, a young man of such fine character, should win for himself a place in the hearts of the people of this village and indeed in the hearts of all who came to know him. Despite the honours that came to him through his wonderful skill as a footballer David remained unchanged. He remained humble; he remained the same with loyalty and affection for his friends. Indeed his loyalty to this village remained unchanged.'

Tommy Taylor and Mark Jones were both Barnsley lads, and the people of Barnsley were immensely proud of them—feelings summed up by one local miner who wrote to the *Barnsley Chronicle* and *South Yorkshire News*.

> As a miner I would like to pay tribute on behalf of the many miners in this district to Tommy Taylor and Mark Jones whose deaths have brought great sorrow and many a heavy heart to young and old in this community of ours. Familiar as we are to disaster and misfortune in a mining area, the suddenness of this terrible air crash has shaken us to the very core. It is hard to realize that no more can we follow with interest the career of these great players, who rose from the very shadow of the pit heaps to achieve fame. On the field of play they set a shining example of whole-hearted effort and gentlemanly play. They

> will be missed, and football will be the poorer for their passing, but for many, many years, wherever miners meet, their names will be recalled and their triumphs re-lived.

In the same paper, Barnsley manager Tim Ward had this to say:

> What fine lads they were, and how pleased we always felt to hear of their fine achievements with Manchester United; they were a great credit to the game on and off the field and they always remained unaffected by the greatness they had earned for themselves. Football was their life, and whether playing in a world famous stadium or on the side of a pit stack in their native South Yorkshire, they would always give of their best and enjoy every moment of every game. How they loved to talk football, and what a pleasure it was to talk to them. Football is all the poorer for their passing. We were very proud to know them both. Well played Tommy. Well played Mark.

Ward also revealed the contents of a remarkable letter he had received from an inmate of HM Prison at Dartmoor.

> Dear Mr Ward, on hearing of that terrible disaster which overtook that grand team, Manchester United, the Governor kindly gave permission to the inmates to open a voluntary subscription out of their earnings which (believe me) are round about the entrance fee to the Spion Kop at Oakwell. The money has been sent

off and it is hoped it will be put to whatever purpose is best suited. This gesture is to show appreciation, sympathy and respect to those who are bereaved, the club and football in general. Football can ill afford to lose such fine examples of the game, and regarding Barnsley's own loss in Mark Jones and Tommy Taylor, may I request that if the opportunity arises, you will convey to their relatives my deepest sympathy. I saw them play and admired their sportsmanship. I shall always remember them.

The Barnsley paper was full of tributes to Mark Jones and Tommy Taylor for several days, and thousands of men, women and children from the mining communities they came from turned out for their funerals. Taylor was buried in his village of Monk Bretton. Former team-mates, representatives of the Football Association and Football League and other sporting organizations together with civic representatives and hundreds of Barnsley men and women attended the service at Monk Bretton Parish Church. In the town centre flags were at half mast on the Town Hall and other public buildings, and at Barnsley's Oakwell ground, where Tommy had played before his record transfer to United. As the funeral procession made its way from the home of Tommy's parents through streets lined four deep, it was exactly a week to the hour that the ill-fated plane had taken off from Munich. Many in the crowd wore red and white rosettes—the colours of Tommy's two teams, Barnsley and Manchester United—trimmed with black ribbon. Eleven boys in football kit of red shirts and white shorts stood outside their school as the cortège passed on its way to the parish church, where a short and simple service was held. Players from Barnsley FC formed a guard of honour as Tommy's coffin was carried out, and at his graveside a bugler sounded the 'Last Post'.

Among the many tributes to Tommy Taylor that poured into the *Barnsley Chronicle* was one from local Justice of the Peace Mrs W. Gillespie, which is redolent of a different age, when footballers, however famous they became, were always part of the community they came from.

> Sometimes in the summer, looking down from my window on to the bowling green at Smithies, I would see a figure striding across the green, tall, clean-limbed, a symbol of English manhood. It was Tommy Taylor, 'Tucker' Taylor as we affectionately called him, who had come for a game with the lads. The lads were his friends from childhood. He made friends and he kept them. His shy smile and his quiet 'Hello' were so very much his nature and his sincerity. It seems incredible that fame and success could change a lad so little, but his reflected glory shone on Smithies like a torch. We had watched him grow up and our thoughts went with him on all of his travels. I know I speak for all of Smithies when I say he was loved by us all. He was a fine young man, an example to all youth, for it wasn't for the sake of an England cap or the selfish hope of a season's fame that he always played the game.

The next morning, at the home of Mark Jones in Kings Road, Stretford, friends and neighbours including Manchester City captain Dave Ewing attended a short service conducted by the Dean of

Manchester before the cortège left for the church in Wombwell. Two bunches of snowdrops from an old age pensioner and a wreath from sixteen Todmorden schoolboys were among the floral tributes that carpeted the lawn. A wreath of red and white carnations in the shape of a football from Jones's widow, June, and his two-year-old son Garry was placed on the coffin. June said, 'Mark was everything that is good, and I'm not just saying that because he's gone. They called him the gentle giant, and though he could dislike people he could never hate anyone. He would never have a bad word for any team that beat United, or even players who kicked him.'

When the funeral party arrived at Wombwell it was met by United players and officials, who were joined by representatives of Barnsley FC, Sheffield Wednesday and Wolves, along with Bill Shankly, who was then manager of Huddersfield Town. The Rector of Wombwell conducted the service and told the congregation, 'It has been truly said again and again during the past few days that it has been the saddest week in the annals of British sport. The details of the recent happenings on that tragic February day are so well known to us that they remain indelible in our minds.' But there had also been, he said, a demonstration of the best qualities of human sympathy and understanding. He referred to the delight Mark had given to so many thousands of football fans and commented on the way in which sport could override the barriers of distrust between nations. He described Mark as having remained unspoiled by the fame he won.

The last of the funerals was held that Friday. As Eddie Colman's coffin was carried into St Clement's, Ordsall, a woman handed in a wreath inscribed

'From the immigrants of Yugoslavia'. She said they used to support Red Star, but since coming to Manchester ten years earlier had followed United. After the service thousands lined the cortège's route along Regent Road and Eccles New Road as it made its way from St Clement's to Weaste Cemetery. Among them were parents with their children, many wearing red and white scarves and football socks. Waiting for the cars to arrive at Weaste Cemetery were more big crowds, many people carrying sheaths of flowers for which they'd queued at local florists.

Eddie was a local lad, and many people knew him. They took time off work to attend his funeral and most local bosses either closed down for a couple of hours or turned a blind eye to the absenteeism. But not so at one local factory. When twenty-seven workers returned to the works of Boxmakers (Manchester) Ltd they were locked out. Twenty-two women and five men were sacked because they wanted to see Eddie off. Eddie lived near the Salford factory, and some of the girls who left their workplace knew him. They were only away for half an hour but it was enough to get them their cards. The workers claimed that the firm's production director made them wait in the rain to collect their pay and refused to let them into the factory to collect their belongings. Instead he sent a foreman out with their property. The works manager, a United supporter for fifty-three years, said, 'We had a collection for wreaths for Bent and Colman and the works flag has been flying at half mast ever since the disaster. We have the greatest sympathy for them, but if industry allowed everyone to walk out just to watch a funeral, the wheels would just stop.'

That day nearly all the United players and

members of staff were attending funerals. On Chester Road in Stretford traffic was diverted as more than five hundred people gathered outside St Anne's RC Church to pay their last respects to United secretary Walter Crickmer. The altar boys who assisted the parish priest, Father J. Edmondson, were Jimmy Murphy's son Philip and United Youth players Nobby Lawton and Nobby Stiles. After the Requiem Mass fourteen policemen led the funeral procession from the church to Stretford Cemetery. A further 250, many carrying wreaths and sprays, were there, among them former players Johnny Aston, Stan Pearson and Jack Rowley. Many wept. One corporation bus driver was so overcome with grief that he fainted.

For other people, too, it was all too much. Fifty-four-year-old John Bunn, a United fan from Northwich, was in such a state of depression that he stabbed himself to death. At his inquest his doctor said he had been called to see him on the Monday following the crash but he refused to be examined. Later, the doctor was called to the hospital where Bunn was found to have about twenty wounds in his neck and chest. His sister said that just after the doctor had left her brother's home on the Monday she saw him at the top of the stairs stabbing himself with a scout knife. The Mid-Cheshire coroner returned a verdict of suicide while his mind was disturbed.

For most people, though, by Friday some semblance of normality was returning to their lives. Things had to go on. United, it was clear now, would go on as a football team, and for everybody else there was school and work to get on with. That day, for the first time since the disaster just over a week earlier, there was no reference to it on the main national news. Wars and strikes and politics had taken over again. Mr Macmillan, back from a Commonwealth tour, stated that the countries with populations of British descent now had a stronger loyalty and affection for the Crown and the Old Country than ever before; and in answer to a question about the Rochdale by-election he said he had no intention of abandoning his task. King Faisal of Iraq, it was announced, was to be head of a new Arab Federal State formed by his country and Jordan. The French Defence Minister said that all necessary measures had been taken to feed French troops blockaded in Tunisia, and that France was ready to pay compensation for civilian casualties of a French air attack on a Tunisian village. And there was no work for forty-five thousand British Motor Corporation workers because of a strike at a Birmingham rear axle factory. For the second day since the disaster the headline in that night's *Evening News* was not about the disaster. Instead, the Manchester University students, who had decided to go ahead with their Rag Week, had taken over. 'Rag Students Raid Second Atom Plant' the headline said over a story about a raiding party who had made a 600-mile dash across the Scottish Highlands to hang a ten-foot Rag banner at the heart of one of Britain's top secret atomic power stations.

Throughout this week of funerals, offers of help flowed in to United from all over the football world. It was reported that the great Hungarian footballers Zoltan Czibor, Ferenc Puskas and Sandor Kocsis, who had remained abroad after the Hungarian uprising of 1956, had announced that they were prepared to play for United. All three were awaiting permission from FIFA to resume playing and would welcome the chance to come to Old Trafford. In the midst of tragedy, here was something that was exciting. Other than Bert Trautmann at City, there were no foreign players in Britain at that time, and now there was talk of three of the best playing for United—the Three Musketeers of the Mighty Magyars forward line that had thrashed England 6–3 at Wembley in 1953 to end the legend of England as masters of world football. It was a small beacon of hope in a dark week during which the whole of Manchester seemed to be grieving. But none of these messages and offers of help could alter the fact that the Busby Babes were no more. The heart had been ripped out of the team.

CHAPTER 8

KEEP THE RED FLAG FLYING

Throughout the week after the crash, as all the funerals took place, Manchester still seemed to be dumbstruck by what had happened. When I talked to people about that week, what Madge Williams said she remembered particularly was the silence all over the city.

> It was so quiet. Everywhere you went, everyone was feeling the trauma of everything. It was a solemn place to live, Manchester. That week after the crash when all the funerals were taking place was a horrible week. Everywhere you went everybody was quiet, and when they saw you they'd turn their heads away because they didn't know what to say to you. It was very sad. And when you went into a shop there was no chit chat with the shopkeeper or anything like that. It was all hushed, everything was very hushed, and you were frightened of buying a paper because you didn't know what the latest bad news was going to be. It was very sombre; a very depressing time.

But somehow life had to go on, and for Manchester United that meant getting back to playing football. When, the day after the crash, Matt Busby had managed to whisper to his friend Jimmy Murphy 'Keep the flag flying', the responsibility for the survival of Manchester United was placed on his shoulders. But how do you get a team together and continue playing football in the midst of so much suffering and grief? Murphy was faced with the most remorseless task ever faced by anybody in sport. He had been an integral part of the creation of the Busby Babes, working with the reserves and juniors, honing them, ready for the final push into the first team. Few at the club had been closer to these boys, yet now, even as they were being buried, he was faced with the task of replacing them. Before he left the Rechts der Isar Hospital, a pale and drawn Jimmy Murphy told reporters, 'Manchester United will field a side against Sheffield Wednesday in the Cup on Saturday [15 February]. It may not be our strongest side, but the Busby spirit will be there. Goalkeeper Harry Gregg and Bill Foulkes are coming with me by train tomorrow and if the doctor agrees to let them out of hospital, so will Bobby Charlton and Ken Morgans. Charlton and Morgans definitely won't play on Saturday and I can't see Gregg or Foulkes playing either, but I will leave it to them. They are tough lads, although I fear the reaction will certainly hit them soon.'

It seemed incredible that there was going to be a match that Saturday, but that was the plan. In the papers on the Monday morning after Murphy's announcement there was a reminder that the eleven players who turned out for United in that first match would not be the only ones who would be affected: 'There will not be the usual heart about the Sheffield Wednesday players when they start their preparations today for their Cup-tie at Old Trafford,' the papers said. Eric Taylor, the Wednesday manager, said, 'It is an unfortunate position to be in, to have to play United in their first game after this disaster, when we are just as much upset as anyone. But if United feel they would rather not play for another week, we are agreeable to fall in with anything that may be decided.'

But United were determined to play. On the very day their team-mates' bodies were being flown back from Munich, United played their first practice match since the disaster when two full teams took part in a game lasting about half an hour each way at White City. Assistant trainer Bill Inglis was in charge. After the session he said the players were all determined to pull out something extra to make up for the club's great loss. Later, wing-half Freddie Goodwin spoke for all the players when he said that everyone at Old Trafford realized that the players the club had lost had set a fine example which those who were there now had to do all they could to follow. Full-back Ian Greaves confirmed that everyone would give all they'd got for the club, and he hoped they would be able to cheer up those players in hospital by recording a win. The message that came across from all the players was that they were all determined to make a special effort.

Watching them in training was one of the old boys, my dad's old friend Johnny Aston, who was the right-back in Matt Busby's first great team after the war until ill health made him quit football. After watching them he said, 'The playing spirit of these boys is as high as it was at the end of the war. Our ground was blitzed, but you know what a recovery we made then. The family spirit of Manchester United lives on. It will pull them through.' But from the medical room of a silent, shocked Old Trafford came more bad news: Wilf McGuinness, the highly promising young wing-half, was almost certainly out for the rest of the season. The mystery injury that had kept McGuinness out of action for the previous three weeks, and consequently off the ill-fated Belgrade flight, had been diagnosed as cartilage trouble and he would have to go into hospital for an operation. That was the news that greeted Jimmy Murphy when he got back from Munich. It was a big blow. McGuinness was one of the few left who had a reasonable amount of first team experience with around twenty outings going back to the 1955/56 championship-winning season.

The situation at Old Trafford was critical, and full of uncertainty. One thing that did become clear very quickly to Jimmy Murphy and club officials was that, however much they might desire it, United would not be ready to get a team out to face Sheffield Wednesday in the Cup as early as Saturday. Straight away, therefore, the club got in touch with the Football Association to ask them for a postponement of the fifth-round tie. An official of the association said a decision would be made the next day. United proposed that the match should be played the following Wednesday night, 19 February, and the Sheffield Wednesday manager Eric Taylor honoured his earlier commitment that the club would be happy to fall in with any rearrangement. United also asked the FA whether newly signed players would be eligible to appear for them in the Cup even if they had already played for another club that season. Chairman Harold Hardman said, 'We simply have to keep the flag flying. It's most difficult for everyone, yet the game must go on, and we shall have to do our best with limited resources. I do know that all our youngsters at Old Trafford will give of their very best, and we can't ask them to do more than that.

Some of them have not yet fully developed and it's a bit difficult imagining them coming up against experienced, well-built players, but it seems that will have to happen.'

On the day when the first of the funerals was being held in Manchester, a special meeting in London attended by Sir Stanley Rous, the FA secretary, and members of the Challenge Cup committee discussed all aspects of United's immediate problems. They gave answers to three important questions that Harold Hardman had submitted to Lancaster Gate. First, United's fifth-round tie with Sheffield Wednesday could be postponed and played at Old Trafford on Wednesday, 19 February. Step two in the FA's efforts to lend every possible assistance to United was the waiving of the fourteen-day qualification rule affecting newly signed players, who could now be drafted into the team at a moment's notice. The third step was to agree that Cup-tied players who had already appeared for another team in that season's competition would be allowed to turn out for United, even if signed only twenty-four hours before a match. There was, however, one small proviso to this: if the club was thinking about signing a player who had already appeared in a previous round they would need to contact the FA, and each case would be considered on its individual merits.

In London that afternoon Harry Gregg and Bill Foulkes stepped from a train at Liverpool Street Station into a barrage of arc lights and flash bulbs. They were the first players to reach England after the disaster. With them was Jimmy Murphy. Earlier the three had landed at Harwich after travelling by night ferry from the Hook of Holland. Neither of the players would say anything about their experiences or future plans. Murphy said that he was 'pleased we left our injured players and Matt Busby much better, which cheered us up for our long journey'. The two players, he added, were 'not feeling too good as yet' and he didn't know whether they would be fit to play football in the FA Cup fifth round. 'There is a lot to be done and only time will tell about our future programme.' At the station, crowds thronged around them as, escorted by policemen, the three were ushered away. Cries of 'Good luck, lads!' followed them as their taxi sped away under grey skies to the hotel where the players' wives were waiting to go home with them.

In that night's *Evening News*, commenting on the decisions the FA had made that day to help United, Eric Thornton wrote, 'Questions of a likely team for next week's Cup tie remain in the air.' The issue would not be fully examined until Jimmy Murphy was back from Munich. Then he would be able to give some sort of indication to the board and assistant secretary Les Olive as to when and which of the club's experienced players would be available for first team duty again. Only then would it be known how many gaps would have to be filled. 'It may mean that United will enter the transfer market in a big way,' Thornton continued. 'On only a few occasions since the war have they opened their chequebook and bought ready-made stars ... Fortunately they have the money. During the last eight years alone their profits have aggregated over £140,000. But even a good bank balance does not entirely simplify the rebuilding of a team capable of holding its own in senior soccer.' Thornton was actually the paper's City correspondent, but in those days immediately after the crash Eric stood in for his dead colleague Tom Jackson.

Until we got the new television in our house, we were still dependent on the *Manchester Evening News* and BBC Radio for all our news from Munich, and the news that was coming through wasn't good. With Matt Busby still so close to death—he received the last rites a second time—and Duncan Edwards and Johnny Berry seemingly fighting losing battles, football was the last thing on our minds, or on any Mancunian minds. But, as always, life had to go on. Jimmy Murphy's obvious problem was to get a side out for the next match. 'I had no players, but I had a job to do,' Jimmy Murphy said. But in the days immediately after the crash he also had to attend to the needs of the survivors returning to the club in a state of shock, to console the bereaved families, and to attend as many of the funerals as he could get to. Rival clubs offered helping hands. Liverpool and Nottingham Forest were the first to respond by asking if they could do anything to assist. Soon every club in Lancashire and many from other parts of the country had offered to loan players. United's acting secretary, Les Olive, revealed that 'Manchester City, Bolton, Preston, Blackpool, Chelsea, Liverpool, Grimsby and Northampton are among the clubs which have offered help with players, but no specific men have been mentioned'.

I remember the week after the crash as a very strange time because despite all the funerals and the pall of tragedy that was still hanging over Manchester, talk in the city was slowly beginning to come round to football matters, and to the sort of team Jimmy Murphy would be able to put out in the first games. And while the front pages of

Manchester's evening papers were still dominated by the news that was coming from Munich, the back pages of the evening papers were full of news from Old Trafford about Murphy's attempts to get a team together for the Sheffield Wednesday match. It had already been reported that goalkeeper Harry Gregg and right-back Bill Foulkes did indeed wish to play in the FA Cup tie; accompanying that news there was intense speculation about who might be joining United. One name that came up was John Charles's brother Mel, the play-anywhere wonder boy from Swansea; another was Blackpool's England international inside-forward Ernie Taylor. It was also suggested that Murphy might make an offer for the Welsh winger Cliff Jones, who was also at Swansea. United's need for players was desperate, and the change of rules that had been made by the FA to help them in their time of need allowed Murphy to begin his rebuilding by signing Taylor for £8,000.

Taylor was signed on the Friday, as the last of the funerals were taking place. That same day it was also announced that Luton Town had generously agreed to release Jack Crompton, United's goalkeeper in the 1948 Cup-winning side, so that he could return to the club as trainer/coach. On Saturday morning all of United's available professionals and amateurs reported to Old Trafford and went across Chester Road to White City for a two-hour training session as part of a plan to bring everybody back to peak fitness as quickly as possible. Murphy had an idea of the likely shape of the team to meet Sheffield Wednesday, but the session gave him the chance to try a few things out. At The Cliff, United's training ground in Lower Broughton, a trial game was held in which some of United's amateurs and boys from teams in the Federation of Boys' Clubs took part. Nine of these boys, mainly from Gorton and Wythenshawe, had been offered trials. The search for the next generation of Babes was already on.

What I remember more than anything about that Saturday, though, is how a bit of excitement was brought to our house, something to lighten the gloom of those horrible days. Me and my sister Joan caught the bus to Northenden with my dad to go and look at televisions. At last we were going to get our own set. We went round the three rental shops—Fred Dawes, Park Wireless and Radio Rentals. Most of the televisions were between seven shillings (35p) and ten shillings (50p) a week. My dad was uncertain. He wanted us to have a television but at those prices it was going to be a sizeable chunk out of his wages. But at Radio Rentals the manager said they'd got some reconditioned sets with a fourteen-inch screen for six shillings (30p) a week. That was more like it. My dad felt we could just about afford that, so the rental agreement papers were filled in, the deposit was paid and arrangements were made for them to come round the following Friday to fix up an aerial and deliver the television. My dad asked if we could get it any earlier than that because there was a rumour that highlights of United's Cup match against Sheffield Wednesday might be shown. The manager said he'd see what he could do, but it was unlikely. The installation people were very busy because there had been a big demand for televisions over the past week.

At three o'clock that afternoon all the fifth-round FA Cup ties, with the exception of United's match against Wednesday, were played, and there were no real shocks. The two Third Division sides still in the competition, Scunthorpe United and Darlington, were knocked out; Bristol Rovers visited their neighbours Bristol City and beat them 4–3 and in the all-London tie Fulham beat West Ham by the odd goal in five. Bolton Wanderers beat Stoke City 3–1 and the other two games ended in draws. Of all the ties played that day, the biggest surprise was the defeat of Bishop Auckland, winners of the FA Amateur Cup for the previous three seasons, by near neighbours Stockton.

Football was getting back to normal, but United still hadn't been able to get a team together to play their first match after the crash. On the front page of that night's *Evening News*, though, there was a picture of Bobby Charlton giving a cheery wave as he left Munich by train, and underneath it was a picture of Harry Gregg in action again as he leapt for the ball during the training match at White City. Foulkes was also in action again; neither he nor Gregg, it was reported, showed any ill effects from the crash. Gregg, in particular, made some fine saves. They both looked as though they would be able to play against Sheffield Wednesday, but the team wouldn't be announced until the morning of the match, along with the selection of a new captain.

The bad news was again about Duncan Edwards. 'Today' the *Evening News* report from Munich said 'is a day of crisis for Duncan Edwards. He is critically ill, but conscious. Emergency calls went out to blood donors early today when he had a haemorrhage. Police cars rushed people of the same blood group to the hospital shortly after 2 a.m. After transfusions the bleeding was stopped.' I thought about Germany and the Germans again. In the days just after the crash kids had been going round saying,

'It's the Germans! It's the Germans who've done it! They've got United!' They were the baddies; they were supposed to be our arch enemies. But now ordinary German people were standing alongside the doctors and nurses at the hospital doing all they could to save our footballers. Just over a decade earlier we were bombing their homes and workplaces, and they were bombing ours. Now these people were getting up in the middle of the night to give their blood in an effort to save Duncan Edwards's life. These people couldn't be bad.

In spite of all their efforts, Professor Maurer said that the haemorrhage had left Big Duncan in a worse condition than he had been in the day before, and Dr Graham Taylor, the BEA medical officer, said it was too early to say whether the artificial kidney, which had been used twice in three days to cleanse Edwards's blood of excess nitrogen, would have to be applied again. Doctors in Munich were amazed by his tremendous strength and his will to live. Dr Taylor said, 'They really admire his fighting spirit. He has plenty of pluck apart from his splendid former physical condition, and the doctors feel these are helping to pull him through.' He added that Edwards was conscious all the time, but very restless. 'I told him this morning to keep quiet and not talk any more than was necessary. He said he understood.' Maybe Duncan Edwards would pull through. Could he even be playing again next season? Throughout that weekend thousands of people went to the grave of his wing-half partner, Eddie Colman at Weaste Cemetery.

In London on Monday, 17 February more than a thousand people attended a memorial service at St Martin-in-the-Fields for the victims of the crash, and there was another big congregation in Manchester

Cathedral at a service commemorating the eight sports writers who were killed. Why had the tragedy of the Munich air disaster struck home all over the world, and why had this particular accident caused such a widespread expression of sympathy? These were the questions posed by the Bishop of Chester at the London service.

> It is due not solely to the drama of the setting or the fact that skilful players and writers, well known and admired, have been killed. It is rather due, so I believe, to the character of the team to which these players belonged and to the fine spirit they have created and upheld. Those well qualified to express an opinion have spoken of the quite outstanding quality which Manchester United have built up during these last ten years. Under the genius of Matt Busby, young men have not only been trained to a high standard of technical efficiency, but they have also been inspired with a loyalty to their club and to the game which has been a pattern to all who have aspired to the best man can achieve. When we remember that during the season a million people each week in this country watch professional football, we can appreciate the responsibility laid upon these young players. They are admired, glamorized, imitated. They have a responsibility not merely to play efficiently, but to play well. It is because Manchester United have acquitted themselves so splendidly in the wider, as well as the more limited discharge of their duty, that the team has become a by-word for good play and good spirit wherever football is played.

For me, nobody embodied values like these more than Bobby Charlton. As the bishop was addressing a congregation that included players, managers and directors from clubs ranging from Arsenal to Woolwich Polytechnic, and representatives of football clubs and associations from all over Europe, Bobby was back at his home in Beatrice Street, Ashington, Northumberland, getting ready to begin his comeback. At first, though, he wasn't sure whether he would ever want to play football again. Bobby had escaped from the aircraft with relatively minor injuries and there was no doubt that he was going to be physically fit enough to resume playing football within a relatively short space of time. But the mental scars were deep, so deep that they were never to go away. He was still only twenty years old and he'd seen close friends and team-mates die in horrific circumstances. 'They were all people who were quite personal to me,' he said later. 'Tommy Taylor, David Pegg, Eddie Colman—they were close, really close. I spent so much time with them. Tommy and David and me were in digs in the same area and we all had mining backgrounds.' But Charlton's best mate was Duncan Edwards. They were such good friends that they used to stay with each other's families when they were both apprentices at Old Trafford. Edwards was only a year older than Charlton, and when Bobby arrived at Mrs Watson's lodgings when he first came to Manchester, Duncan had already been there for twelve months and was only a few weeks away from becoming a regular first-teamer. But Duncan took him under his wing and, almost from day one, they became mates, both of them United through and through. Now Duncan was close to death in the hospital in Munich.

Newspaper reports began to emerge saying that it

was the Charltons' family doctor who found the word that persuaded Bobby to play football again—and the word he used was 'comrades'. The doctor, it was said, told Bobby that he had been in the RAF and had seen many of his friends shot down but there was no alternative other than to go on and go up again the next day. 'I expect to see you at Wembley,' he said. In the days and weeks immediately following the crash references to the war were never far away. The players who had perished were closely associated with the wartime generation, and it was appropriate that so many of the tributes echoed these experiences. 'At the going down of the sun and in the morning, we will remember them' were words that were often used in tributes to the players who had lost their lives while on duty for their club and country.

It was less than two weeks after the crash but thoughts were now turning more and more to getting back to playing football. I remember being particularly anxious to find out when Bobby Charlton would be back. To me, and to many at that time, he became a symbol of hope—one of the youngest and brightest stars who had survived the disaster to carry the club forward playing football in the manner of his fallen comrades; a symbol of the phoenix rising from the ashes. I read every report I could get my hands on and listened to all the rumours that were going round. Some were still saying that he couldn't face playing again, but then came a piece in one of the national newspapers that said that he'd been to Ashington Hospital to have the stitches taken out of his head and on his way home he'd bought a football and met up with some of the lads from Beatrice Street where he'd been brought up. His mother, Mrs Cissie Charlton, was reported to have said, 'As soon as I knew he was going to buy the football I knew everything was fine. It's just a matter of time before he'll be his old self again. He's still badly shaken, but determined to get back in trim as soon as possible.' Later, Bobby Charlton said of that time, 'Obviously life had changed and it would never be the same again for anyone at the club. It wasn't for yourself any more; you weren't trying to build a career or anything like that. You were giving everything you had for Manchester United and the lads who didn't make it at Munich. In the hospital, along with the other survivors, I had asked the question: what can we do? It was simple enough, really. We could just play in a way that showed we would never forget the lads who died at Munich.' That is what Bobby Charlton went on to do, serving Manchester United with honour and great distinction, first as a player and then, as he still does, as a director and ambassador for the club.

Football was due to return to Old Trafford just thirteen nights after news of Munich had reached the city. Bobby Charlton hadn't recovered sufficiently to play in that match, but Bill Foulkes and Harry Gregg had—the first of the survivors back to play for the lads who'd died. Manchester's days in limbo were due to come to an end, and excitement grew at the thought of getting back to playing football again. Bobby Charlton was, however, planning to be at the match. When the *Manchester Evening News* phoned him in Ashington after he'd got back from the hospital, he said, 'I'm going to do my best to come down to see the Cup match on Wednesday.' As for serious training, he said, 'I hope to return to Manchester after a week up here and start training again. But it will probably be three weeks before I can play.' That was great news.

On Monday, two days before the Sheffield

Wednesday match, it was reported that Jimmy Murphy was the busiest soccer boss in Britain as he fought against time to put together a new team. He had taken his squad to Blackpool for a two-day tonic before what was shaping up to be the most important game in the history of Manchester United. It also got the young players away from the gloom that was still hanging over the city. At 9.30 a.m. they started their training session on a field just off the promenade, next to the Norbreck Hydro Hotel where they were staying. Throughout the day Murphy repeatedly had to leave the lads with newly appointed trainer-coach Jack Crompton to return to the hotel to make desperate efforts over the phone to clinch transfer deals. But in spite of all the offers of help that had come flooding in to Old Trafford, he didn't meet with very much success in his frantic quest to draft some experience into the side. So far the only actual deal that had been done was the signing of Ernie Taylor.

One of the players Murphy tried to sign was Burnley's international left-winger Brian Pilkington, but Burnley's controversial chairman, local butcher Bob Lord, made it clear that sentiment certainly wouldn't be swaying him. The club turned down United's offer, and Bob Lord didn't make himself very popular in Manchester when he launched into an outspoken attack on people who think they should give away their star players to United:

> Some people have got hold of the wrong idea. Of course clubs will help United. But not to the extent of parting with their star players. Surely we are not expected to help United win the League, the European Cup, the FA Cup and the Central League. I don't want to be unfair or

unkind in any way, but clubs still have a duty to themselves. I am sure that every club offering help has in mind the idea of assisting United to complete their fixtures and carry on. I am sure every club is ready and willing to help out with reserve players for that purpose, but football is big business. With all our sympathy and sorrow we just mustn't let this thing get out of focus. Help? Certainly. But star players? It cannot be done.

While Jimmy Murphy continued to work round the clock to get a team together, Matt Busby was lying in his Munich hospital bed still unaware that his team had been wiped out and doctors decided that it was still too early to tell him that seven of his players had been killed in the crash. The manager, we were learning from reports from the hospital, was showing signs of improvement every day, so much so that he had asked his doctors if they could get a new pair of glasses for him to replace the ones he had lost in the crash. Without them he had been unable to read any of the papers reporting the deaths of the Busby Babes. But, fearing that learning the bad news might affect his own recovery, doctors managed to divert his questions and requests.

On Tuesday, some of the gloom that had hung over Manchester was lifted for a short time in the city centre where large crowds of businessmen, office girls and shoppers were out in the winter sunshine for the Manchester University students' much-debated Shrove Rag. In spite of suggestions that it was being held too soon after the disaster, it seemed, if anything, to be welcomed a bit more warmly than in the past, because it brought some light relief to a city that had been stunned by twelve days of mourning. But after the several hundred students had made their uproarious way through the city centre, most of the excitement subsided. A bit of a party atmosphere continued throughout the afternoon as groups of musicians went round rattling their collection cans and selling the *Rag Rag* magazine; on an old bomb site on Deansgate you could pay 1s 6d (7½p) for a pancake cooked over a brazier, or have your name attached to a balloon in the hope of winning a prize for the one that travelled furthest. But even the students didn't think some of the planned stunts were right: two female pharmacy students who had planned to do a strip-tease on the Deansgate bomb site to raise some cash decided to call their performance off.

When my dad got home from work he said all the talk in town that day had been about the way spivs were cashing in on the match that everybody wanted to be at. Tickets that had been bought at Old Trafford the day before were being offered on the black market at double and treble their face value. Spivs were asking 10s (50p) for a 3s 6d (17½p) ticket and 5s (25p) for a 2s (10p) ticket. Boys and youths, it was said, had started it. When the tickets had gone on sale they'd made several trips to the ticket-office windows and got as many as they could. Black market tickets were then, as they are today, a fact of life, but the general feeling around Manchester seemed to be that it was disgusting that people were cashing in at a time like this.

In stark contrast to this, in that night's paper British European Airways announced that they would give an artificial kidney machine to the Munich hospital in appreciation of all that was being done for the survivors of the crash by the hospital staff. BEA's director of medical services said it would be similar to the one the hospital had on loan for treating Duncan Edwards. But in spite of having the very latest in medical technology to treat him, the news coming from the hospital had taken yet another turn for the worse. Edwards was 'rather weak and showing some signs of distress'. Johnny Berry's condition, however, was showing slight improvement, even though he was still only semi-conscious; Jackie Blanchflower was improving; and there was good news about Ray Wood: X-rays had shown no head fractures.

As Duncan Edwards fought for his life in the hospital in Munich, United prepared to play their first match. Despite all his efforts, and all the goodwill that had been shown to United, Jimmy Murphy hadn't been able to get any other experienced players to strengthen his team for the meeting with Sheffield Wednesday. It looked as though United's future was going to be in the hands of the reserves and youth team players. Before Munich, reserve and youth team matches had always attracted big crowds so we were familiar with a lot of the players. At school that day the talk was all of inside-forward Mark Pearson, centre-forward Alex Dawson, centre-half Ronnie Cope, and of Freddie Goodwin, who had been described as the 'best reserve team half-back in Britain'. Harry Gregg spoke about the match and the contribution that some of these young players would be making in an interview that was carried in several of that morning's papers. He said he thought United could win the match but that there were far more important things on the minds of everyone at Old Trafford.

The main job we will be out to do tonight is to

show the world that Manchester United will rise again, that we are determined with all our hearts to see that new ambition come true. We not only have to play our hearts out, as we shall do. We older and more experienced players have to set an example. That we are determined to do. And I regard tonight's Cup-tie against Sheffield Wednesday as a memorial to those boys we so well remember … I'm sure that too goes for the youngsters who will be stepping out tonight in the red shirts that carry the battle honours of many a far-flung soccer field. Since my return I have had the chance to know better these boys who now carry the banner of Manchester United. I can tell you that in such players as Alex Dawson, Mark Pearson and in all of them I find the great enthusiasm, pride and spirit of determination that took United to the heights. Whatever the result tonight they will send a message to manager Matt Busby that will help him on his way to recovery.

That's the way it was being regarded by everybody in Manchester that day. They were going to be doing it for the boys that night. The stage was set for a remarkable, emotion-packed night, the like of which football had never seen before and has never seen since. Throughout the day, at schools and in offices and factories throughout Manchester, there was only one topic of conversation—the match and who was going to be playing in it. The morning's papers had described it as the match the whole world wanted to see. Under the Old Trafford floodlights eleven men of Manchester United were going to run out to play the most emotion-charged game of football that had ever been played; a football match the whole sporting world wanted to see; one that had captured interest, concern and feelings throughout the non-sporting world. It seemed that day that, apart from Sheffield Wednesday and their supporters, the whole nation was behind United. Whatever team they supported, football fans from all corners of Britain felt as though they had been affected by the disaster, and they were all right behind the Reds as they prepared to take their first step on the road to recovery. Such feelings were summed up in a letter to the *Daily Herald* from a football fan in faraway Plymouth. 'Manchester United,' he wrote, 'were a work of art, created by wonderful Matt Busby. Wherever Englishmen went, irrespective of what club he supported, he could speak with pride of them. We have all suffered a great blow, but Manchester United will rise again. Other youngsters, imbued with the same spirit, will follow in the footsteps of the beloved players who graced the Old Trafford turf with such distinction.'

The drama, the excitement and the tension built up as the day wore on, and just before kick-off there was another dramatic turn of events. During the course of the day a transfer drama unfolded as Jimmy Murphy tried to beat the clock to sign Aston Villa left-half Stan Crowther, and possibly another First Division player, in time for the kick-off. Murphy knew he didn't have enough experience in the team. After four long hours of strained attempts at team selection the night before he and the United directors had been forced to give up; they knew they needed some older heads. Crowther was one of the players on their list, and his move from Aston Villa was completed just seventy-five minutes before the teams took to the field. The England Under-23 left-half made a dramatic dash from Birmingham to Manchester that afternoon before making his mind up whether or not to sign for United. Murphy had already included him as a possible for that night's line-up after receiving FA permission to play him even though he was Cup-tied. The surprise choice was a twenty-year-old Wythenshawe lad, Shay Brennan, who was selected for his first game at outside-left. Brennan was an A team player and an inside-forward who didn't even have much reserve team experience. He'd played only three times for the reserves so no one was more surprised than he was when he was told he was playing.

But as well as the team news in that evening's paper there was a grim article on the front page about the worsening condition of Duncan Edwards. A bulletin from the hospital said he'd grown weaker following further treatment with the artificial kidney. Use of it had developed into a vicious circle which was gradually sapping his strength and reducing the ability of his blood to clot.

Meanwhile, United's youngsters got ready for the biggest game of their lives. The future of the Red Devils was in their hands. All the young players selected for the game, the *Evening News* reported, were thrilled and determined to do their best for the club. That afternoon they'd received a telegram from Munich: 'Good luck and best wishes from the Boss and all the boys.' 'Murphy's Chicks', the paper called them, and it predicted that they could upset Wednesday. 'Tonight,' the headline said, 'boys will step into men's boots.'

The match drew a crowd of over sixty thousand, who ventured out on a cold February evening to see United start out on the long road back. Fans came in black ties and red, white and black rosettes. Chairman Harold Hardman made it clear that the club would continue in his message on the front cover of the programme: 'United will go on … the club has a duty to the public and a duty to football. We shall carry on even if it means that we are heavily defeated. Here is a tragedy which will sadden us for years to come, but in this we are not alone. An unprecedented blow to British football has touched the hearts of millions. Wherever football is played, United is mourned.' Inside there was a message to those in the Munich hospital from Old Trafford: 'Our thoughts are constantly with those who still lie in Munich … Among them is our dear manager, Matt Busby, and we know that his first concern is always for his players … we recall his words to Jimmy Murphy: "Glad to see you, Jimmy, how are the lads? Look after them for me." ' Then in the middle of the programme, under the heading 'Manchester United', there was a blank teamsheet. Spectators were told to write in the names of the players. Few did. Instead, each name, as it was announced, was cheered resoundingly. Harry Gregg in goal and Bill Foulkes at right-back had returned after the traumas of Munich, other names were not so familiar. A great complex of emotions swept around the ground. Spectators wept openly, many wore red-and-white scarves draped in black.

Before the kick-off, the crowd stood in silence for a minute in memory of those who had died and the ghost of greatness past hovered over the stadium. Then came an avalanche of pent-up emotion. There was nobody in that crowd who didn't have a lump in their throat as the red shirts came out of the tunnel into the lights, led by new captain Billy Foulkes. Like the players, many in the crowd were wearing black armbands; others had black centres stitched into their red and white rosettes. There was a football match to play, but as the teams lined up for kick-off it was the tragedy of Munich that was uppermost in the mind of everyone there. Beryl Townsend went to the match straight from work with some of the boys she worked with. 'When the team walked out,' she recalled, 'it was them [the Babes] that walked out. There was a presence that night. For me it wasn't a makeshift team, it was them. I'll never forget it as long as I live. It was awful, and the atmosphere was hysterical, not like a football match. Poor Sheffield Wednesday didn't stand a chance that night. I had to feel sorry for them because if they'd beaten us everybody would have hated them.'

Right from the start, Sheffield Wednesday were swept out of the way on that great wave of emotion. United hurtled into attack, playing with all the unity and cohesion of a team that had been playing together for years, not as a motley collection of players pressed together in a desperate emergency. Once they'd kicked off, the football began to take over and Foulkes and Gregg the two survivors of the crash, were cheered loudly every time they touched the ball. Some fans inadvertently shouted the names of dead players as the excitement of the game began to take over. That night, Wednesday had the toughest job in soccer, and they didn't have a chance. Murphy's Manchester United were playing for the memory of their friends who had died less than a fortnight earlier, and a running commentary was being relayed by telephone to the less seriously injured players in hospital in Munich. On a night charged with emotion the passion of the crowd urged the makeshift team on, with Wednesday perhaps more affected by the occasion than United's young players.

Nobody in the crowd had really known what to expect, but within a quarter of an hour it had become clear that this scratch side was more than holding its own. The defence was never in trouble, and the forwards quickly settled down to the familiar United pattern of play—attack, attack, attack. Ernie Taylor was at the heart of everything, encouraging the youngsters around him, directing play, spraying out passes. Then, what a roar there was when a corner kick from the left by new boy Shay Brennan beat the Wednesday goalkeeper Ryalls and curled into the top of the net for United's first goal! It was, Brennan said later, as if an invisible Tommy Taylor had risen high above everybody in the area to turn it in. From that moment it was clear that nothing could stop United. In the second half the Reds continued to surge forward. They were rewarded with another goal from Brennan and a third from Pearson five minutes from time. At the final whistle the thousands of supporters packed into the ground exploded in a great frenzy of cheers and upstretched arms and as the players walked off the field, the ecstatic crowd cheered to salute the new Babes.

United were playing again! But it was much more than that. This team, hastily put together and comprising two survivors of the disaster, two experienced players bought at the last moment, and young lads scarcely out of United's nursery, had beaten First Division Sheffield Wednesday to reach the quarter-finals of the FA Cup. The crowd turned for home, their heads full of memories of a remarkable game, though their hearts remained heavy with thoughts of Munich. The new team had carried on where the Babes had left off, and the fans had played a massive part in it. Sheffield Wednesday had been swept out of the way on a wave of emotion, the like of which had never been seen in a football ground. Right from the start there had quite rightly been no sympathy from Sheffield Wednesday. They paid United's patched-up team the courtesy of going at them as hard as they could, but they were beaten because this new United were too good for them. They were beaten for skill, for strength, for commitment and for teamwork. Playing in the Wednesday side that night was Albert Quixall, who was to join United in a record transfer deal the next season. 'I don't think anyone who played in the game or who watched it will ever forget that night,' he said. 'United ran their hearts out, and no matter how well we had played they would have beaten us. They were playing like men inspired. We were playing more than just eleven players, we were playing sixty thousand fans as well.'

Outside the ground the thousands who hadn't been able to get in had stayed where they were all through the game. At first they'd hoped to get a ticket from one of the touts, even though by this time prices had gone up to ten times' face value. When they realized they were not going to get into the ground, they had stayed out there, feeling it was the place they ought to be, listening to the sound of soccer history being made. That night on the floodlit turf of Old Trafford Manchester United took the first step to recovering its heart, and so did every supporter who was inside and outside that packed ground. United were back. The heavy burden of mourning that everybody had been carrying for the last two weeks was eased, and the crowd felt they were on their way back to a more rational and understandable world of football.

If all the people who have since claimed to have been at that match had been there, the crowd would have been nearer to a quarter of a million. I was one of the ones who didn't go, and I've regretted it ever since. I wanted to be there, but my dad didn't manage to get any tickets for us. But really I think it was just that he couldn't face going. He was still too upset and didn't want to see a patched-up team filling the boots of the men who should have been there. He did take me to a few of the games that season, including the first league match that was played, against Nottingham Forest, and the sixth-round replay against West Brom. But for him the team had died, and nothing would ever be the same again. From the end of that season he never went to see the Reds again. He continued to support them for the rest of his life, but at a distance, second-hand, through the radio, television and newspapers.

One person who was there was Bobby Charlton. He'd been driven down to see the match by his uncle, and it was possibly that night, with seven of his friends dead and Mr Busby and his mate Duncan Edwards still hanging on to life in hospital, that he decided once and for all that it was his duty to go on. Winning from then on was to become a duty; an act of remembrance in honour of his dead comrades, not something to be indulged in or even celebrated. Charlton said he hoped to return to Manchester to start full training after another week recuperating at home in Ashington.

That morning's papers were unanimous in their praise for the new United. Manchester United were born again last night, they all said. 'The bright new Red Devils made their entrance at Old Trafford last night like the Red Devils we used to know,' enthused the *Daily Herald*. 'Their victory was more than just another win,' said the *Daily Mirror*. 'It was a memorial to the men they mourn and the men in Munich.' All agreed that Shay Brennan was man of the match. 'Seamus Brennan became the first hero of the new Babes,' said the *Daily Mail*, 'and Alex Dawson is set to be a power in the new, so impressive Manchester United set-up.' The victory had been one that Manchester had been hungry for and it was the start of the path back to better times when supporters could live for the football again.

That night we learned that there was a new man reporting on United for the *Evening News*. David Meek, who went on to do the job for nearly fifty years, had taken the place of Tom Jackson. In his first report he said, 'Forget the idea that the crippling blow of Munich has put paid to Manchester United ... I saw enough last night to convince me that Old Trafford is far from down and out.' Man of the match for him too was Shay Brennan, but, he added, 'the real hero last night was the boss, manager Matt Busby. Heroes too were his dead right-hand men who had helped to give United such a wealth of reserve talent so that in their time of need there were players capable of stepping nobly into the limelight.'

United had taken their first step back from the ashes of Munich. In the next round they would meet West Brom.

CHAPTER 9

BIG DUNCAN HE WENT TOO

With their victory against Sheffield Wednesday, United won their first big battle since the crash, but just over twenty-four hours later Duncan Edwards lost his. The 'Big Boy' of English soccer, the giant of Manchester United, succumbed to his injuries in the early hours of the morning of Friday, 21 February. For many it was the biggest and cruellest blow of all: he, more than any of the others, symbolized the spirit of the Busby Babes, and in the days immediately after the crash it had looked as though he might survive. With his death the light finally seemed to go out, and the full impact of Munich was brought home. For the second time in a fortnight thousands of United fans in offices, factories, schools, shops and homes were silenced as they heard the tragic news—the death of the most talented Babe of all.

'Team-mates Weep As Edwards Dies' ran the headline. The lion-hearted Edwards, it was reported in the *Evening News*, 'died peacefully in his sleep at 2.15 a.m. today after a desperate last-minute battle to save him. Nurses at his bedside—well used to suffering and sudden death—broke down and wept as the flame of life for which they fought so hard flickered out.' First to be told were Edwards's parents and his fiancée Molly Leach; then his colleagues had to be told. Ray Wood, Dennis Viollet, Ken Morgans and Albert Scanlon, four of the less seriously injured who were still in the hospital, wept as Professor Georg Maurer, who was with Edwards when he died, gently broke the news to them. The more seriously injured, Matt Busby, Johnny Berry and Jackie Blanchflower were not told.

The news was devastating. It brought back all the pain of those hours just after hearing about the disaster. Like many, I'd convinced myself that Big Duncan would survive. I'd even imagined him playing again. But it wasn't to be, and with the massive injuries he had sustained it was never likely to be. 'If there is any consolation to be had from this black day for Manchester,' the report went on, 'it is this. Had Edwards lived he would never again have been the dashing hero of the Busby Babes. No more would he have been capable of the dazzling breakaways and the flashing footwork that brought the Old Trafford crowds to their feet. It is more likely that the 21-year-old Edwards would have been a permanent invalid.'

I got the news on the eight o'clock Home Service bulletin, just before leaving for school.

> In Munich early today, the Manchester United and England player Duncan Edwards died of injuries he received in the air disaster fifteen days ago. His injuries included severely damaged kidneys, and in the fight to save his life doctors used an artificial kidney which had been specially sent to Munich. A week ago one of the doctors said that only Edwards's tremendous physical strength had kept him going. No ordinary person would have survived so long. Edwards, who was twenty-one, was the Manchester United left-half and had played for England eighteen times in full internationals. His selection had been almost automatic since his first game against Scotland in

1955 when, at the age of eighteen and a half, he became the youngest player ever to appear for England.

In Ashington that morning, it is said that there was no paper on the table when Bobby Charlton sat down to eat his breakfast.

'Duncan's dead, isn't he?' he said to his mother.

Just as I was hearing about the death of Duncan Edwards on the radio, the March edition of *Charles Buchan's Football Monthly* was delivered. Smiling out from the front cover as he laced his boots up in a corner of the dressing room was Duncan Edwards. The magazine, which was the football bible for lads of my age at that time, had obviously gone off to the printers before the crash and had been out on the news-stands just before Duncan died. Seeing him there on the front cover of my favourite football magazine as he got ready to take to the field only added to the sense of loss.

The tributes flowed in. Professor Maurer said, 'I do not think anyone other than this young man could have survived so long. His resistance made us admire him.' When England team manager Walter Winterbottom heard the news, he said, 'It was in the character and spirit of Duncan Edwards that I saw the true revival of British football.' It was generally agreed that here was a footballer who would, had his life been spared, have gone on to be the greatest footballer of all time. Matt Busby had no doubt about it. Years later, in his autobiography, he had this to say about Edwards: 'He was a colossus. Whatever was needed, he had it. He was immensely powerful. He was prodigiously gifted in the arts and crafts of the game … His confidence was supreme and infectious. No opponent was too big or too famous for Duncan … If there was ever a player who could be called a one-man team, that man was Duncan Edwards. His death, as far as football is concerned, was the single biggest tragedy that has happened to England and to Manchester United. He was then and has always remained to me incomparable.'

It was a view shared by his friend Bobby Charlton. A few years ago, while I was filming at the Black Country Living Museum in Dudley, I was talking to one of the re-enactors in the nail-making shop about Duncan Edwards. He said he'd been at the unveiling of Duncan's statue outside Woolworth's in Dudley Market Place in 1999, and Bobby Charlton had said a few words. He'd said that he still found himself thinking about Duncan a lot. He'd seen all the players who in their time had been called the best in the world—Puskas, Di Stefano, Pelé, John Charles—but not one of them had been as good as Big Duncan. There was no other player in the world like him then, and there had been nobody equal to him since. Charlton said it wasn't in his nature to dramatize things or to dispense fulsome praise. A man is a good player or he is not. A few are great, and they deserve respect. But Duncan Edwards was simply the greatest footballer of them all.

Duncan Edwards's greatness had been clear for all to see since he first turned out for United's all-conquering youth team. Even then he looked like an international, and in 1954 he became the youngest player up to that time to win a full England cap, at the age of eighteen. 'I think even the sight of him in those youth matches used to put the fear of God in some sides,' Bobby Charlton said of him. That was confirmed by opposition players. United fan Alan

Robertson lived at Colyhurst. 'I used to play football myself,' he told me. 'I played with a lad who played for City and he used to play with us at the parks on the weekend. Then City got drawn against United and this lad we used to play with said that all the lads in the team said, "I'm not marking him." He said nobody wanted to have to play against him. When the match did come round it was foggy and all of a sudden, this City lad said, "Someone comes running out of the fog and it was him. So we all scattered. Gospel truth. It was unbelievable." But what a player he was. He was a giant of a lad with a heart just as big, and he could do anything on a football field. He would have played for England until he was forty.'

* * *

The day after Duncan Edwards's death, and three days after United had beaten Sheffield Wednesday in the Cup, they were back in league action for the first time against Nottingham Forest at Old Trafford. The club was absolutely committed to completing that season's league programme as well as playing their Cup matches, but there were plenty of people around who felt they were only doing it because they felt they had an obligation to do so. This view was summarized in a letter to the *Daily Herald* that said, 'Manchester United are being morally coerced into continuing League football when to do so is completely unrealistic. It seems forgotten that they are human. The strain they suffer is unknown except to those who bear the burden. Far better if their record was expunged from the League table and their remaining fixtures fulfilled as friendlies. Then with their place in Division One assured, they would have a fair chance to experiment and regain their poise after their shattering blow.'

Reading a letter like that now reminds me that in the weeks immediately after the disaster there was still a huge amount of uncertainty about how United would carry on, in the immediate future at least. There were all sorts of rumours and suggestions flying around, including one that had come from the organizing committee of the European Cup: if United weren't able to play all their matches their place in the competition could be taken by City, who would represent United and the city of Manchester. But the United directors continued to make it clear that the club was going to fulfil all its fixtures, and now that the first game had been played my dad felt he was able to start going again, particularly as there was to be a memorial service on the pitch before the kick-off of the first league match against Nottingham Forest.

Before setting off for the match that Saturday afternoon we listened to the one o'clock news bulletin on the radio. It said that Matt Busby continued to make good progress, as did Jackie Blanchflower and the sports writer Frank Taylor. The condition of Johnny Berry and of Captain Rayment, though, was unchanged; both were still on the danger list. But two of the players, Dennis Viollet and Ken Morgans had been discharged from hospital that morning, although they wouldn't yet be able to make the train journey back to Manchester.

It took us nearly an hour to get from our house to the ground, changing buses at Barlow Moor Road, and we only just got there in time. The gates had to be closed before the service with a record crowd of over sixty-six thousand crammed into the ground. The queues for the main terracing along the Popular

Side and behind both goals, where we usually went, were long. When the dreaded 'ground full' bells started to ring on the gates, my dad said we should try the paddock. We didn't usually go there because it was more expensive. There was no boys' entrance to the paddock at the scoreboard end so we dashed along the side of the main stand between the players' entrance and the railway line to the Stretford End paddock. We just about made it. The bells on the gates started to ring just after we'd got in, signalling to the gate men that their gates had to be closed.

I've still got the programme from that match. No picture on the front, just the simple words 'United Will Go On' with a message from club chairman Harold Hardman:

> On 6th February 1958 an aircraft returning from Belgrade crashed at Munich Airport. Of the twenty-one passengers who died twelve were players and officials of the Manchester United Football Club. Many others still lie injured. It is the sad duty of we who serve United to offer the bereaved our heartfelt sympathy and condolences. Here is a tragedy which will sadden us for years to come, but in this we are not alone. An unprecedented blow to British football has touched the hearts of millions and we express our deep gratitude to the many who have sent messages of sympathy and floral tributes. Wherever football is played United is mourned, but we rejoice that many of our party have been spared and wish them a speedy and a complete recovery. Words are inadequate to describe our thanks and appreciation of the truly magnificent work of the surgeons and nurses of the Rechts der

Isar Hospital at Munich. But for their superb skill and deep compassion our casualties must have been greater. To Professor Georg Maurer, Chief Surgeon, we offer our eternal gratitude. Although we mourn our dead and grieve for our wounded we believe that great days are not done for us. The sympathy and encouragement of the football world and particularly of our supporters will fortify and inspire us. The road back may be long and hard but with the memory of those who died at Munich, of their stirring achievements and wonderful sportsmanship ever with us, Manchester United will rise again.

The first thing I always used to turn to in the programme were the cartoons on page three by George Butterworth and Frank Smart, but there were no cartoons in this programme. In their place were details of the various memorial services to be held that day and the next in memory of those who had died: an Inter-Denominational service to be held before kick-off that day; a Protestant service at Manchester Cathedral the next day; a Jewish service at South Manchester Synagogue on Wilbraham Road; another Inter-Denominational service at the Albert Hall on Peter Street; and a Roman Catholic service with Mass in the presence of the Bishop of Salford at Belle Vue Speedway Stadium.

The paddock was packed and I couldn't get down to the front, but we got near a crush barrier and I was able to climb up on to the concrete block that supported it and see over the heads of the crowd. Snow was falling softly on the pitch right up to the time, 2.45, when the Dean of Manchester led the official party out from the players' tunnel. Among them for the brief service in memory of the victims of the disaster were the Yugoslav ambassador and representatives of the Yugoslav Football Association and Red Star. It felt strange seeing these people on the pitch. It was the height of the Cold War, yet here we were joining in a service with representatives of a country from behind the Iron Curtain. At the time high-level exchanges were going on about nuclear disarmament and summit talks in London, Washington and Moscow. The US State Department had criticized Russia's refusal to link summit talks with disarmament negotiations through the United Nations. The Soviet Union had just carried out its third nuclear test in forty-eight hours, and President Tito of Yugoslavia had accused Western powers of trying to sabotage a summit meeting with counter proposals and evasions. It was a time of fear. People thought there was a real danger of nuclear war, which could wipe out a city like Manchester. The Soviet Union was the enemy and Yugoslavia was one of their Communist Eastern Bloc allies. They were sinister and frightening, and if you were a Catholic these Communist anti-Christs were the very devil himself. Yet United had been to their land and played a football match against them, and here they were on the pitch at Old Trafford joining in a religious service. All very strange.

The entire crowd stood bareheaded as prayers were said, including one for the club, hoping that it may 'continue to contribute to our delight and to hold its place in the high traditions of sport and sportsmanship'. A girl of about fifteen or sixteen was standing nearby, sobbing inconsolably. She was wearing a red and white scarf with the names of all the team embroidered on to it, and against the name of each player who had died she had stitched a black diamond. After a reading from

Pilgrim's Progress and a minute's silence, it was time to think about the football.

As Billy Foulkes led the team out for his first league match as skipper, the snow that had been falling stopped. Forest kicked off. They were soon at the United end and had a shot that went just over the bar. But then Ernie Taylor's class began to show as he set up a couple of attacks. Taylor, until recently, the brilliant inside-right partner to the great Stanley Matthews at Blackpool, was proving to be an inspired buy. Now he was commanding United's midfield, although I don't think we called it that then. He was the archetypal scheming inside-forward, and he was in a class of his own. Everything was flowing through him, and if any of the young team seemed unsure what to do with the ball the safest thing seemed to be to slip it to Ernie. Things looked promising. 'They're playing well, you know,' an old fellow standing near me said. But no sooner had he said that than Forest took the lead, and they went in at half-time 1–0 up.

The snow had started again, and the muddy pitch was beginning to cut up. The Beswick Prize Band came on for their customary half-time music programme, but this time, instead of the usual marches and music from the shows, it was made up of hymns and solemn music including 'Abide With Me', 'Lost Chord' and Handel's *Largo*. The music reminded us of the sadness of the occasion. The crowd fell silent, but when the teams came out at the end of half-time we knew we were at a football match again.

In the second half, urged on by wave after wave of cheers from the record post-war crowd, United slipped into gear and mounted attack after attack in the softly falling snow. With twenty minutes to go, that man Taylor had a shot turned round for a corner, and from the goalmouth scramble that followed, Dawson scored. United had got a point from their first league match.

Watching that game was a strange experience. You expected to see all the familiar faces, but this was a new team we were watching. No Tommy Taylor in the number nine shirt; no Roger Byrne at number three. All the old heroes were gone; but at least we were back playing football.

The Forest game was typical of the league matches United played to the end of that 1957/58 season. The patched-up team won only one of the fourteen remaining fixtures after Munich and managed five draws. For me and for many of the younger fans it was a new experience. I'd started watching the Reds in 1956 and I'd never seen them do anything other than win. We had been spoiled by success, and by the quality of the football we had got used to watching. Now all that had changed.

On Sunday morning, all the talk outside the church after eleven o'clock Mass was about the two matches United had played that week. The Forest game had been decisive, Mr Caesar thought, and United should have won. We were well on top in the second half, and what it showed more than anything was that the win against Sheffield Wednesday in the Cup was no flash in the pan. They'd certainly deserved their point. Others weren't as sure. They'd not played as well as on Wednesday night; there just wasn't the same inspiration. 'What do you expect?' said Mr Geoghan when he emerged after counting the collection. It would have been too much to expect of such a young, inexperienced team after all the emotional and physical strain they'd been under. Mr Caesar agreed. 'They did well enough,' he said. 'When the combination play improves a bit—and it will do with a bit of time and when the passing gets a bit sharper—they'll be back to their old winning ways. All they need is a bit more match practice.'

The conversation then turned to the World Cup, which was to be played in Sweden that summer, and to the damage that had been done to England's prospects by the crash. The draw had been made in Stockholm the previous week and it had put England into the toughest group with Russia, Brazil and Austria. But England's chances had already slumped badly. The crash had not just pegged United back; it had, according to many commentators, put the whole of English football back by at least ten years. Many continental countries had been impressed by the revival of the England team over the last couple of seasons, and some had made them favourites to win the competition. But Roger Byrne, Tommy Taylor and Duncan Edwards were key members of the national team; David Pegg, Mark Jones, Eddie Colman, Dennis Viollet and Bobby Charlton were also potential members of the squad. They were all good enough to be playing for England. Until a few weeks earlier it was beginning to look as if England had what it took to win the World Cup that year. In austere, postwar Britain, Busby's Babes represented hope and optimism. But when that Airspeed Ambassador crashed into the snow at the end of the runway in Munich, that dream was shattered. The blow to United had been a terrible one, but it was nearly as big a blow to England.

In town that morning Manchester Cathedral was packed for the memorial service to the victims of the disaster. About two thousand people attended, and admission was by ticket only; a crowd of non-ticket holders, many wearing red and white scarves, filled the doorways, waiting to take any seats if they were left vacant. Everyone fell back respectfully to make way for the small groups of family mourners in black. In his address, the Dean of Manchester, the Very Reverend H. A. Jones, said that there was a family feeling about United unlike anything he had ever known. 'We are all conscious of having lost a friend,' he said.

That night we went to Belle Vue to join more than six thousand people filling the Kings Hall for the Catholic memorial service. It was strange to be going there for such a sombre occasion. The Kings Hall was the venue for the Belle Vue Circus, which we used to go to every Boxing Day for the altar boys' Christmas treat. I also knew it as a boxing arena because my Uncle Jack, who was a sergeant in the Manchester police, had begun to take me there for the Northern Counties ABA Finals, which the police used to promote. But tonight it was very different. Instead of the clowns and the lions and the cheers for the boxers, solemn High Mass was being sung in the presence of the Bishop of Salford, Bishop Beck. Canon Sewell, parish priest of Matt Busby's parish of St John's, Chorlton-cum-Hardy, said in his address that from a survivor of the crash who was sitting next to Billy Whelan on the plane there had come a lesson for all of us. In those frantic final seconds when everyone realized that a dreadful crash was imminent, Billy said to his companion, 'This may be death—and I'm ready.' 'All of us,' said Canon Sewell, 'should always be ready.'

Beryl Townsend was there, and she told me she

was fine until the priest came to Billy's last words. Then it was just too much for her.

> Later, I wrote to Billy's mother in Dublin and sent her some money for masses to be said for him. She wrote back to me and said, 'God and his Holy Mother obviously loved him and needed him more than we did.' And I thought, 'What a marvel.' At that time I was ready to murder [pilot] Thain for even attempting to take off the third time and I wasn't happy that Matt Busby had let him, but here was Billy's mother who'd just lost her son and she was so forgiving and was so prepared to accept the will of God. One of the things she did tell me, though, was that before the trip to Belgrade Billy hadn't been feeling very well and he'd asked to go home to see his mum. But Matt Busby had said he couldn't because it would look bad if he didn't go. It was just at the time that he'd lost his place to Bobby Charlton, and if he didn't go with them it would have looked as though he wasn't happy about Bobby being in the team. But Billy just wasn't like that. She also told me later how he used to get upset because he thought some of the fans at Old Trafford didn't like him. He was a very sensitive lad.

After that first exchange of letters just after the crash, Beryl and Olga became friends with the Whelan family, and they have stayed in regular contact with them ever since.

> When I asked Billy's sister, Rita, once about how they got to know about the crash, she said

they didn't know that Billy had died until about ten o'clock that [Thursday] night. When I said to her I knew at half past three she just couldn't believe it. Of course they didn't have television, and the first they had heard about the crash itself had been about half past five. Rita said, 'I'll never forget it because this man turned up in his brewer's uniform to say there'd been a plane crash. But Mammy just couldn't take it in. Then it wasn't until about ten o'clock that the whole thing was confirmed. Mammy didn't even have a phone with not having much money, so we had to go to a neighbour's down the street who had a phone to try and find something out. But we couldn't find out anything and nobody could contact us because we didn't have a phone. In the end we had to rely on the police to tell us Billy was dead.'

* * *

Just a few days later, despite the fact that Britain remained in the icy grip of a deep freeze, thousands lined the streets of Duncan Edwards's home town, Dudley, in the heart of the Black Country, for his funeral. The Black Country was a region of heavy industrial activity based on coal mining and iron working; it had got its name in the middle of the nineteenth century when thousands of furnaces and chimneys filled the air with smoke, and the mining of the coal, ironstone, fire clay and limestone turned the ground inside out, creating vast expanses of industrial dereliction. By the middle of the twentieth century, when Duncan was growing up, little had changed. His father, Gladstone Edwards, worked nearly all his life in a local ironworks, and Duncan had first kicked a ball surrounded by the smoke and fire of the nail-makers and chain-makers that filled the town when it was still at the heart of industrial Britain's 'metal bashing' region. This was the place he knew, and this was the place where he was brought back to be buried.

From the early hours wreaths from countless admirers arrived at his parents' home on the town's Priory Estate and were laid out on the frozen front garden. One was shaped as a football, another in the form of a six—Edwards's number in the United and England teams. Among the twenty-six family mourners were Mr and Mrs Dorman, whom Duncan had lodged with in Manchester. They were there at the special request of his mother and father. Edwards had represented town and country as a schoolboy while attending Wolverhampton Street School in Dudley, and as the cortège passed the school, pupils lined up on either side of the road to pay their last respects to their most famous old boy. Reserve goalkeeper Gordon Clayton—Duncan's best friend—and Bobby English, both from United, were among the pall bearers; the others were his England team-mates Billy Wright of Wolves, Ronnie Clayton of Blackburn Rovers, and Ray Barlow and Derek Kevan from West Brom. From United, Jimmy Murphy was there with a party of club directors and players. In his funeral address, the vicar said, 'We are proud that the great Duncan Edwards was one of our sons. His football record needs no praise for it is known throughout the world. Talent and genius we shall see again, but there will be only one Duncan Edwards.' Five thousand mourners saw the cortège leave the church where Duncan had worshipped as a boy, and traffic came to a standstill as drivers stood by their vehicles with heads bowed as it was driven along the two-mile route from the church to the town cemetery.

That night I prayed that Duncan's would be the last of the funerals, but it was by no means certain. It was reported from the hospital that the plane's co-pilot, Captain Kenneth Rayment, who had been at the controls at the time of the crash, was sinking fast. Doctors refused to admit defeat, but they held little hope. Matt Busby, though, was clearly on the road to recovery. He was, we were told, in cheerful spirits and making good progress, but he had still not been told the full extent of the disaster. Johnny Berry was still giving a lot of cause for concern. According to the latest reports he had shown slight improvement over the past eight days, but it had been too gradual to be noticeable day by day, and he was still on the danger list. It didn't sound good, particularly when I recalled that in the days just after the crash, reports stated that Duncan Edwards was showing some signs of improvement.

They didn't come any braver than Duncan Edwards, but after he died it was revealed that he had a secret fear of flying. The day after his funeral we were reminded starkly once again of the dangers of flying, this time right on our doorsteps. Winter Hill is the moor that stands above Bolton to the north of the town, and on Thursday, 27 February, three weeks to the day of Munich, a chartered Bristol 170 airliner crashed in the snow there with the loss of thirty-five lives. The aircraft had been chartered to take a party of motor trade agents from the Isle of Man to the Exide battery works at Clifton, near Manchester. It crashed, without any apparent explanation, on snow-covered moors less than a quarter of a mile from the

ITV transmitter, 1,500 feet up on Winter Hill. Aeroplanes and snow again. It seemed that it was a fatal combination.

Flying seemed like a dangerous business; something to be avoided. There just seemed to be so much that could go wrong and, as with the crash at Munich, there were lots of questions to be asked about the Winter Hill crash. Why was the aircraft anywhere near Winter Hill when its route from the Isle of Man to Ringway Airport ran south of Wigan, about eight miles away? Why was it flying so low? Was there a fault in the plane's radio and navigational systems? Air travel was still in its early days. There were no budget airlines and it was all a far cry from today when millions think no more of stepping on to an aeroplane to fly off for a short break than they would of getting on a bus. Statistically it is now the safest form of transport, but that wasn't always the case. Around Manchester alone there had now been two major plane crashes in the space of less than a year. The first came on 14 March 1957 when a BEA Viscount flying into Manchester from Amsterdam came in too low, smashed into a row of houses on Shadow Moss Road close to the end of the runway and burst into flames. All twenty occupants of the plane, fifteen passengers and five crew, were killed, as well as a woman and her son who were in one of the houses. Two houses in the neat row were completely demolished, another was badly damaged. At the time of the Munich crash, there was still a gap in that row of houses and a lot of concern remained among residents living close to the airport about the dangers they lived with.

Shadow Moss Road and Munich both involved buildings in or close to the flight path at the end of the runway. As the debate about Munich raged it had been suggested by a number of experts that if there had been no building at the end of the runway at Riem Airport the aircraft's failure to take off would not have been as serious. It was only because one of the wings had hit the building that the aircraft broke up and burst into flames. If it hadn't hit anything it would have been brought naturally to a halt as it ploughed through the fields on the perimeter of the airport and there would have been no serious injuries or loss of life.

Now the same questions were being raised about Munich as those that had been raised about the Manchester crash. Why did the authorities allow houses to be built right in line with the end of the main runway? Papers in Munich were now suggesting, just as the Manchester papers had done a year before, that many lives could easily have been saved. Unlike the row of houses on Shadow Moss Road, the house on the edge of Riem Airport was the only one in the area, surrounded by acres of open fields. The Munich papers were claiming that if the house had not been there the plane would have had plenty of room to skid to a stop on its belly. The usual results of a belly landing were, at worst, a few broken bones and concussion. The crash, following the Viscount disaster the year before, it was being suggested, might have global repercussions affecting the international regulations about the siting of airports. The debate was reported in the Manchester papers, the *Manchester Evening News* making the comment, 'Sooner or later the authorities must realize that houses in line with airport runways—it has been repeatedly stressed in the *Manchester Evening News*—are a terrible, unnecessary risk.'

Duncan Edwards was not alone in his fear of flying: many people, not least those in football circles, were uneasy about it, and Munich reignited a debate that had been going on in English football for some time about whether teams should be allowed to fly. It seems inconceivable now when all of our big clubs jet all over the world to play pre-season tours, when eight of the twenty Premiership teams take regular flights all through the season to play in Champions League and UEFA Cup matches, and when most teams use domestic flights for league games, but until June 1957 clubs were banned from flying to and from league matches. Should that ban be re-imposed?

The ban was introduced in 1949 after a plane carrying almost the entire Torino football squad crashed into the hill of Superga near Turin killing all thirty-one aboard: eighteen players, club officials, journalists accompanying the team, and the plane's crew. The team was returning from a match against Benfica in Lisbon in early May. The Italian airline's Fiat G212CP flew into a thunderstorm on the approach to Turin and encountered conditions of low cloud and poor visibility. After descending so that the pilot could fly visually the plane clipped a wall and crashed into the hill. Italian authorities cited the low cloud, poor radio aids and an error in navigation as factors contributing to the accident. It was the biggest tragedy ever in Italian sports history as it claimed the lives of the players of a legendary team: Torino won the last Serie A title before football in Italy was interrupted in 1944 by the Second World War; after the conflict the club landed four consecutive titles (1946 to 1949). At the time of the crash Torino was leading Serie A with four games left to play in the season. The disaster seriously weakened the country's national side, too, which had included up to ten Torino players. The club would not claim another title until 1976.

United were back and were playing and, in the Cup at least, they were winning, but the Torino disaster also gave an indication of what the long-term consequences might be, not just for United but for English football in general. Torino were the United of Italy at the time. Many of the top football names in the land were killed, and nine years later, after the 1958 crash, many Italian observers said that even then a full recovery had not yet been made. Immediately after their crash, for instance, Torino played the last four games of the season with their youngsters, just as United did. But, unlike United, all the teams that played against them insisted on playing their own young players too so that Torino would finish as champions for the fourth year in a row. At the time of the Munich disaster they were fourth from the bottom of the Italian league. On hearing news of the crash, Torino club secretary Gino Giusti made clear what the consequences had been for his club and, by implication, what lay in store for United. 'We have been struggling to keep in the First Division ever since,' he said. 'Sixteen of the eighteen players we lost were internationals. Then the eighteen were worth 600,000,000 lire; today they would have been an asset of at least 1,000,000,000 lire. And to think that we are now so hopelessly in debt we had to give up our glorious old ground, where we won our post-war league championships. Now we share the municipal ground with Juventus.'

United themselves were still considering whether they should fly again. The decision had been made that United wouldn't pull out of the European Cup, but how they would get to the next match was still open to question. Chairman Harold Hardman had said, 'Regarding the European Cup, we shall carry on to the end, even if it unfortunately means that we are heavily defeated. But meanwhile, I don't think we shall do any more flying for a while.' Blackpool, however, who were due to go on a close-season tour of Australia, said they were not worried by the prospect of a 12,000-mile flight. Still, a club official couldn't confirm an Australian report that the eighteen players would fly in groups of six on three separate aircraft.

But would United fly again? Would they even play in Europe again if it meant flying to their matches? The semi-finals were looming, and it was confirmed that United would not need to fly when they were paired off with the winners of the quarter-final tie between Borussia Dortmund of Germany and AC Milan of Italy without a draw, because the overland route to both these places could be covered within a day. Under a gentlemen's agreement the organizing committee agreed unanimously to the pairing to give United as few travel problems as possible, when it was pointed out to them that United were reluctant to travel by air. On hearing the news, captain Bill Foulkes said, 'It's a load off my mind and an extremely helpful arrangement. I think United should definitely go on with the European Cup, but at the moment I don't want to fly.'

The question of footballers flying to matches didn't only affect United. With the World Cup coming up in Sweden that summer the FA made an announcement that all players selected for the party would be asked 'How would you like to travel? Air or sea—the choice is yours.' It would have been easy for the FA to be dogmatic about it and insist that, because of the difficulties involved in transporting a big party of players and officials across a continent, everybody would have to fly. The fact that they gave the players a choice showed that they recognized the tremendous impact of Munich and the worries so many players had about having to fly.

The FA were right. There was a real fear of flying at the time, and it was now affecting Manchester City, who had an end-of-season tour of the USA and Canada arranged for May. Three of their first team players refused to fly. Manager Les McDowell said that none of the players would be forced to go on the tour. He said that many of the players didn't like the idea of flying after what had happened to United so the City party would go to America by sea in May and return by sea in mid-June; but because they had such a heavy match programme while they were there they would have to take some internal flights in America and Canada, and therefore none of the players would be forced to go on the tour. The disaster was also having repercussions in American sporting circles. It was reported that the crash had alarmed many baseball clubs. It was only through frequent air travel that widely separated teams could keep to their fixtures, so the American baseball league formed a pool of players from which any club that had suffered seven or more injured in an accident could rebuild their side.

For my family and most other people we knew, flying wasn't an issue. Along with thousands of others from Manchester, we went to North Wales for our holidays, staying in a converted bus in somebody's big, rambling garden on a hillside near

Penmaenmawr. For the well-to-do it was the beginning of the package holiday era and fear of flying wasn't going to deter those who could afford to go to exotic places like the Italian Riviera. Less than a week after the Munich crash the *Manchester Evening News* carried a holiday guide that featured two islands in the sun, Sardinia and Sicily. Sardinia, it said, was now coming within tourists' reach for the first time. That year several well-known travel agents had arranged accommodation there, and by chartering special aircraft they had brought down the cost of an inclusive holiday with air travel below that of an ordinary return ticket by scheduled airline. Once you were there you could hire a boat complete with crew for 5,000 lire, or about £2 17s (£2.85) per day. On the same page, Wings advertised holidays by air from Manchester 'at prices you can afford'. Once a fortnight, the advert said, on Saturdays from 24 May to the end of September, a Viking aircraft of the Eagle fleet would take off direct from Ringway Airport for Saragossa in Spain where an experienced courier would be waiting to escort the party on a fifteen-day coach tour of southern Spain. All this for only fifty-four guineas (£56.70). And for those who just wanted to soak up the sun, Lunns King Flight Holidays were offering a fortnight on the Costa Brava with air travel from thirty-eight guineas (£39.90). Lunns would be using luxury Viscounts on many of their King Flight Holidays. But with all the air crashes at the time, how many takers would they have for these exotic new holidays? I for one didn't fancy the idea of flying, even if my family had been able to afford it.

Today we don't think twice about flying and statistically it is clear that it is the safest form of travel. But there's no doubt that at the time, flying was more unpredictable and dangerous, and many people found even the idea of it frightening. In spite of this, less than three weeks after the crash, the question of flying was again being raised at Old Trafford. The players, it was reported, were going to have to decide whether or not they would go by plane to their European Cup semi-final. Chairman Harold Hardman said, 'The sooner we can get the players' feelings on this question the better. I shall arrange a get-together with them and Jimmy Murphy to test their reaction. We can't compel anyone to go by air, but although they may not be very keen just now, their confidence may return.' My only thought at the time was that lightning couldn't strike twice. But I knew that if I'd been in a plane crash and seen all of my friends die around me, like Bill Foulkes, there was no way I would want to fly again so soon after the event.

CHAPTER 10

MURPHY'S MARVELS

That last week in February the arctic conditions returned with a vengeance as Britain was swept by the worst blizzards since 1947. The north-west was particularly badly affected, and the *Manchester Evening News* headline on Tuesday, 25 February read 'Snow High As Houses. 11 Trains Lost: Scores Of Cars Trapped.' But when you were a kid, snow just meant good fun. On winter evenings everybody would be out slinging snowballs at one another, some with half-bricks hidden inside them, or sliding down the middle of our road on a long, glistening sheet of ice. Other teeth-chattering evenings were spent pushing each other through the slush-filled streets on home-made sledges until the shrill cry of Mam's voice whistled through the cold night air to beckon us in for bed.

But every night, before going out to play in the snow, I continued to look at the paper to find out what the latest news was from Munich. By now the papers were beginning to be dominated by news about the H-bomb. The House of Commons was facing a vital issue—in what circumstances Britain would use the bomb. Mr Duncan Sandys, the Conservative Defence Minister, declared that if faced with an all-out, overwhelming attack by Russian conventional forces, the Government would use the H-bomb rather than submit to defeat and occupation. Most Labour MPs were totally opposed, and in the Commons they shouted 'Suicide!' when Mr Sandys said, 'To me it is inconceivable that the free peoples would meekly surrender their liberties without a fight.'

It was now three weeks after the crash and the first thing I did when the paper arrived every night was to look for news of Matt Busby and the others who were still in hospital. Thankfully, Matt was getting better. He was conscious now and was able to talk to his visitors, but he still hadn't been told what had happened. I and the whole world had known about it for three weeks; everybody knew except the boss. It didn't seem right, but all the reports said it was being done for the best. If he'd heard the terrible news it would have set back his recovery. After the crash he had fought on in the Rechts der Isar Hospital in Munich drifting in and out of consciousness and for weeks nobody dared tell him what had happened. 'How are the boys?' he'd ask his son, Sandy. 'They are all right,' came the reply—a white lie born of the best intentions. For his wife, Jean, each visit had become agony—thinking up new things to talk about, trying to evade the only subject that was on both of their minds.

Then, just before the rebuilt team was due to play the sixth-round Cup game at West Brom, we read the first reports of how the news was broken to him. Although he was still very ill, Matt clearly had an idea of what had happened, so we read about a German priest calling in to see him. 'How is Duncan Edwards?' Matt asked. He spoke no German, and the priest spoke no English, but he understood what the manager was saying. The priest, it was reported, thought quietly for a moment and then, deciding he could not tell a lie, shook his head slowly. Matt understood. Then the priest left and Mrs Busby came into the room and stood over him. 'So, young Duncan is dead,' he said. Tears filled her eyes. 'How is Roger?' Matt asked after a short pause. Jean shook her head. 'And Tommy … and Eddie … and Bill?' Jean didn't speak; if they were dead, she just shook her head. Pausing between each name, Matt mentioned first the eight dead players and the three members of his staff who had been killed. Only the dead. And each time Mrs Busby shook her head, knowing why it was her husband had named only those who had perished: they were the names no caller to his bedside had ever included in their conversation. Then, with the worst over, Jean Busby told him all there was to tell about the disaster, including naming the dead sports writers, who were all his friends. She hid nothing. The long succession of white lies had ended. She also told him how the survivors were doing and how the team was getting on. Here there was some good news: Bobby Charlton was back in training and there was a possibility that he would join Bill Foulkes and Harry Gregg in the team to play West Brom in the Cup.

That night, the *Evening News* reported that Matt Busby was given sedatives to help him to sleep and by the next morning he seemed to be getting over the acute depression that had set in when he first heard the grim details. Doctors kept an anxious eye on his progress in case delayed shock set in now that he had been told the full story of the disaster. Feelings at the hospital about the wisdom of Busby being told the full story were mixed. Most of the doctors there wanted to keep the news from him until he was back at full strength; others, however, were relieved that at last this bridge had been crossed. One doctor said, 'Although Busby definitely did not know about the deaths—as some people suspected—there can be no doubt that at the back of his mind he had more than a suspicion. He had been noting the boys who had come to visit him, such as Gregg, Foulkes, Morgans and Viollet, and doubtless he had put two and two together.'

Bill Foulkes, the new club captain, was unveiled by the *Evening News* as their new columnist. In the first of a series of articles headed 'United Will Regain Greatness' he spoke for the first time about the crash and some of his dead team-mates.

> When I was a lad I used to dream that one day I might captain a great team like Manchester United. Now my dream has come true, but I wish it hadn't. This great honour is one I could have well done without, for I realize only too well that I am captain because my very good friend Roger Byrne perished in that terrible crash at Munich. The fearful moments of the actual disaster and the sickening feeling as we hurtled along at the end of the runway when most of us, I think, realized we were not going to get off the ground, are beginning to fade. But the people themselves I shall never forget. For they were not just my colleagues, they were my friends.

He went on to write about Roger Byrne, his qualities as a captain both on and off the field and the way they had partnered each other as full-backs for several seasons. 'It is for his sake and for the memory of all our other friends who lost their lives at Munich that Manchester United must carry on,' he wrote. People had asked him if he thought United would ever be great again, and his reply was always an emphatic yes. 'There is something about this club that according to those players who have been around a bit, you don't find anywhere else.' There was no doubt in anybody's minds now that United would carry on, and going on the results they'd achieved so far they were going to carry on successfully. There was now, Foulkes said, a very different mood in the dressing room.

> Before this tragedy the spirit of United was a carefree one. We were always laughing and clowning. The lads often played practical jokes on each other. Even at Belgrade, before leaving on the fatal journey home, we had great larks messing up Bill Whelan's hotel room and arranging a birthday party for Eddie Colman. Now the spirit is a different one, but it is just as vital and will be the bond that will make United the team with a difference. There is no joking like there was. The atmosphere is tense—but there is plenty of spirit, as I think our Cup win and league draw have proved. We are determined to make United great. It may take a long time, but I think we shall do it.

Nobody embodied that change in the spirit of the dressing room more than twenty-year-old Bobby Charlton, who had by this time been back in training for a week. It must be difficult for today's supporters to imagine Bobby Charlton as one of that carefree band of young players Bill Foulkes referred to. He's now regarded by many United fans who never saw him play as the pillar of the United establishment, synonymous with the suits who run the club; the quiet, sober figure acting as ambassador for his club, for football, for his country and for his adopted city. To them he's a grave, remote figure associated more with the big business that Manchester United has become than the footballer of immense promise who flew out to Belgrade as a carefree youth and returned to Manchester as a man determined to remember his dead friends by making United great again.

Bobby Charlton was, from the time he first joined United, shy, as he has always been. But as a young player, sporting a quiff of blond hair in the style of Elvis, his shyness didn't stop him taking part in a few of the practical jokes and youthful pranks Bill Foulkes referred to. I wonder how many supporters today would associate Charlton with one story I remember from the *Evening News* in the 1950s: he was, it was reported, in a car driving along Piccadilly with Wilf McGuinness and Shay Brennan firing water pistols at passers-by. That Bobby Charlton was a different person, a gifted young footballer who inhabited a different life prior to Munich. It was the Bobby Charlton who was always singing 'Peggy Lee and Frank Sinatra', as one of his Ashington neighbours once told a reporter. 'He always used to be singing. After Munich I never heard him sing aloud again.' But Bobby Charlton's return to training raised my spirits no end, as I think it did for the whole of Manchester. He was the youngest of the Babes and, after his friend Duncan Edwards, the brightest prospect in a team full of bright prospects. With his return there was a real feeling of 'United Will Go On'. He brought with him hope, a sense of optimism. There was going to be a future after all.

* * *

As we neared the end of that dread month February, both Manchester and football were beginning to regain some semblance of normality. Everybody had grieved; now the message was 'let's get on with the game'. It was the message coming from Old Trafford and it was the message opposing managers were having to get across to their own players. Nowhere was this expressed more eloquently than in an article in the *Daily Herald* by West Brom manager Vic Buckingham as he prepared his team to face United in the sixth-round tie at the Hawthorns on Saturday, 1 March.

> If I were Jimmy Murphy I would go into the West Bromwich Albion dressing room just before next Saturday's game and say, 'Look, lads, I know you are very sympathetic towards us. I know you want Manchester United to rise again. But I want you to go out there this afternoon and knock the stuffing out of us ... because that's what we are going to do to you.' I would do that because I am a realist. And as such I am concerned solely with West Bromwich Albion. I sympathize with the sympathizers, but the game goes on. Of course I was stunned by the tragic crash. But my immediate reaction was: what can we do for those killed? Nothing. What can we do for the dependants? As much as we possibly can. That over, then on with the game. Football is like that—a field of human sacrifice. Every season it 'kills' players, not by death or injury but purely

because they're not good enough. At the end of every season some bright-eyed lad is told, 'Sorry, sonny, you'll never be a footballer. Pack your boots and go.' Inhuman? No, fact.

When Manchester United was top of the soccer world they never wanted nor sought help. They alone will decide what is necessary now. Manchester United, I am sure, will again one day be a great team. But it's my job not to let them become great at West Bromwich's expense. My team will play as hard as they have ever played on Saturday. It's their job. It's their duty. Manchester United I know will give us a terrific match next Saturday. The man we will have to watch particularly … is all eleven. Those 15,000 or so Manchester United supporters will din out a vocal encouragement worthy of their own 60,000 home crowd, and I hope those Albion supporters will yell out even louder in sympathy and encouragement to them and us. Finally, again if I were Jimmy Murphy, I would go into the dressing room after Saturday's game to say, 'Thanks for the game, lads … that's the best memorial you could have ever paid to players who died at Munich.

At Buckingham's request, the fee for his article was sent to the Lord Mayor's Disaster Fund.

As a United supporter, young as I was, I knew that what he was saying was right. There were still plenty of tears being shed for the departed—there still are whenever 6 February comes round, or whenever I look at the words of 'The Flowers of Manchester'—but nothing could change what had happened; nothing could bring back the dead; and the best tribute to the players who'd lost their lives was to carry on ... and win.

West Brom was going to be a tough game, though, a real test. They were flying high up near the top of the league and playing attractive attacking football. On the morning of the match all the papers were saying Bobby Charlton would be back in the line-up. Lance Corporal Bobby Charlton, the third survivor hero of Munich, was 'rarin' to go'; the prediction was that he would be taking his place at outside-left in place of two-goal hero Shay Brennan. This was a change of position for Bobby: before the crash he'd taken Billy Whelan's place at inside-right. Since his debut in October 1956 he'd emerged as a brilliant creative player, quick and intelligent, who packed a power-house of a shot. He was seen as the best inside-right prospect England had for a long time. So did he mind playing on the wing? Not at all. He'd play anywhere, he told Jimmy Murphy, and his inclusion would give United's attack that extra touch of experience.

Charlton did indeed play that afternoon, and the game at The Hawthorns ended in a 2–2 draw. Again it was played in a highly charged emotional atmosphere, and it was the diminutive five-foot-four-inch Ernie Taylor who dominated the match and provided the inspiration for the new Babes. The tactics were simple: give it to Ernie. And they paid off. During the course of the ninety minutes he provided a master class in the art of the inside-forward—feinting, wriggling, passing and shooting. He ran unceasingly into space to receive the ball from his young team-mates, constantly twisting and turning to change the pattern of play, one minute setting up an attack, the next falling back to help out in defence. He scored the first goal after the Albion defence got into a tangle from a Bobby Charlton cross, and the second was put in by Alex Dawson after Taylor's shot had crashed off the bar. With four minutes to go United were winning 2–1, but in spite of some heroics from Harry Gregg they couldn't hold out and Albion snatched a late equalizer to earn an Old Trafford replay. It was a moment of terrible disappointment for United and the fifteen thousand supporters who had made the trip to the Midlands.

Against all the odds, though, United had nearly beaten one of the top teams in the league. It was a triumph for team spirit and the motivational powers of Jimmy Murphy. Throughout the game Murphy's Marvels, as they were now being called in the papers, never allowed Albion to play the football they were capable of; United's pressurizing and challenging tackling put them right out of their stride. It was a fact remarked on by the future England manager Bobby Robson, who was in the Albion side that afternoon. 'I applaud United's tremendous spirit,' he said, 'but they must be careful not to carry it to the point where they lose their heads.' Central to the performance, though, was the genius of Ernie Taylor and his brilliant controlling inside-forward play. Taylor had been an inspired signing by Murphy, and it was significant that while he was in the game United always looked like winning it. It was only after the ageing Taylor faded in the last twenty minutes after running himself into the ground that West Brom got on top for the first time. Even then the United defence, with Harry Gregg, Bill Foulkes, Ian Greaves and Ronnie Cope all outstanding, played so well that Albion only just made it.

Ernie Taylor was wonderfully supported by Bobby

Charlton. Taylor now had somebody playing beside him who could match him for vision and flair, and with the two of them at the heart of the attack United produced the most penetrative play for more than three-quarters of the game. Bobby Charlton was back. With Duncan Edwards and seven of his team-mates dead, and five others still in hospital, Charlton had joined Bill Foulkes and Gregg to honour his fallen comrades by continuing to play football in the great tradition of the Busby Babes.

With so many players drafted into the main squad, United's reserves were also receiving a welcome boost. Playing against Burnley that afternoon was one of England's most distinguished amateur footballers. Bob Hardisty, the former Bishop Auckland captain and England amateur international, had come out of retirement to help United's youngsters in their Central League games for the rest of the season. He was joined by two Bishop Auckland colleagues, Derek Lewin and Warren Bradley. 'That is what we want them for,' Jimmy Murphy said, 'to provide the experience that the very young men we must now play in our reserve team require around them.' Bishop Auckland were Britain's most famous and successful amateur football club, and they had come to the aid of United, Britain's outstanding professional side, in what Murphy described as 'perhaps the most historic and certainly the most generous transaction in our country's football life. I have been in soccer a long time now and I have never heard of such a happening, a big professional club approaching a big amateur club for the loan of its stars . . . and getting them. Auckland have been magnificent. Manchester United will be long indebted to them and to the players for the spontaneous manner in which they agreed to come to Old Trafford to help us out.'

After eleven o'clock Mass the next day the talk was all of little Ernie Taylor. In the three games since Munich Taylor had been Dad to the new Babes, and in each of the three games he had emerged head and shoulders above the rest as man of the match. What a buy he was proving to be, and what great judgement on the part of Jimmy Murphy! Murphy had always stayed in the shadows, but now that his time had come what many wise heads like Mr Caesar had been saying for a long time was clearly correct: if he chose to do so, Jimmy Murphy could manage any club in the country. Interviewed in that morning's papers, Taylor was full of praise for Murphy. Ernie had played under Joe Smith, one of the leading managers of the day, at Blackpool, and he had great respect for him, but 'Jimmy Murphy tops even that. He's the finest man I've ever worked under.' Of the team he said, 'The youngsters are getting better and better. I think after a few more matches together we'll have the best defence around. Big fellahs! With big hearts!'

So keen were the team to win the replay on the night of Wednesday, 5 March that they had a special practice match at Old Trafford on the Sunday morning. Sunday was always football's post-match treatment-room day, but not for United this week. Jimmy Murphy said he didn't want to announce his team for the replay until he had conferred with his directors, then added, 'But all the boys who played on Saturday are fit, and what a fantastic display they gave us! I have been in football for over thirty years and the way the lads fought beat anything I have ever seen in that time, even that fantastic game against Bilbao. They were magnificent, every one of them.'

The players themselves were no less fulsome in their praise for Jimmy. 'Mr Murphy deserves a medal,' one of them said. 'We've been unbeaten in our three games since the crash and it's all his doing. He's a marvel.'

Jimmy Murphy had always been the great motivator. Known as 'Tapper' Murphy during his playing days for his tough tackling, he was a forceful, belligerent player, and these were the qualities he tried to instil into the players under his charge. It gave the Busby Babes a bit of steel to go with their silky skills, and it was this as much as anything that was bringing in the results. Wilf McGuinness used to tell a story that illustrates perfectly Murphy's motivational techniques. When Wilf was making his first team debut against Wolves in October 1955, Murphy came up to him, put his arm round his shoulder and said, 'Wilf, son, you're playing against Peter Broadbent today and I want you to mark him tightly. This man wants to pinch money from your dear mother's purse.' What Murphy was referring to was the loss of Wilf's win bonus if Wolves beat them that day, but seventeen-year-old Wilf took what Jimmy had told him literally. Broadbent was a skilful inside-forward and one of the game's gentlemen, so during the kickabout before the game, knowing that it was McGuinness's first game, he walked over to him to shake his hand and wish him the best of luck. 'Fuck off, you thieving bastard' was the reply he got from Wilf. McGuinness had a good game, marking Broadbent tightly throughout, and United won 4–3. As the teams came off the pitch Murphy walked up to Wilf with a smile and said, 'Your dear old mother would be proud of you.' It was this quality more than anything that helped to save United from slipping into oblivion in those desperate days after Munich. Jimmy Murphy worked night and day not just to keep United afloat but to keep them winning by breathing fire, fury and, above all, pride back into this makeshift team.

* * *

The sixth-round replay at Old Trafford was set to be an epic battle. The 2–2 draw at The Hawthorns had shown that West Brom were one of the strongest teams in the First Division, and the replay brought a massive turn-out. Now that the first few games had been played, more fans felt able to go to a match again, and there were a lot of others who had hardly been to a match before who wanted to be there to feel part of the great wave of emotion on which United were being carried along. United said they'd not had time to get tickets printed and sold in the few days between the first game and the replay so it was pay on the gate—and nearly a hundred thousand turned up. The first fans had started to queue at noon, seven and a half hours before kick-off, and as they did it started to rain. Down it poured as the queues lengthened; by four o'clock some of them stretched for more than a hundred yards. By six o'clock roads approaching the ground were at a standstill.

At 6.30 p.m. there was chaos in the city centre as more than six thousand fans packed on to the forecourt of Central Station trying to get trains to the ground, only to be told that no more trains would be running. Among those stranded were West Brom fans who had made the journey from Birmingham; alongside them were many United stalwarts who'd been to every game that season. Beryl and Olga

Townsend had managed to get out of work early and they'd gone straight to the station. It was the way they always travelled to the ground.

> We were at Central Station and by six o'clock we'd been queuing for two hours, but we didn't get any further than that. It was absolutely chocker there. I wouldn't have minded as much if we could have got to the ground because we could have been outside and we would have felt as though we were taking part, but they said there were just so many people there and it was too dangerous to let them take any more trains in. And I said, 'We've been standing here since four o'clock. We couldn't get here any earlier than that.' When it was clear there would be no more trains going to Old Trafford a policeman at the station said to us, 'Why don't you go to Maine Road, because City have got a game on there tonight.' Well, that was all I needed. I wasn't going to watch City and I just went berserk. I hadn't missed a game home or away all season, including the draw at The Hawthorns on the Saturday, and I was devastated that I wasn't going to be there to support them that night.

An announcement was made that those who had bought train tickets would get their money back, but few bothered in the mad rush to find alternative transport. They needn't have made the effort: by this time the gates at the ground had already been locked. In fact it had become a struggle to get anywhere near Old Trafford.

I went with my dad, but we were far too late to get

in. The gates had opened at 5.15 p.m., but by 6.30 the ground-full bells had rung and they were all closed. Another who didn't manage to get in was Norman Williams, who'd been at the ground since about four o'clock. 'I was queuing to get in the seats,' he said, 'because I couldn't stand on the terraces with a broken leg. As I got near the gate it must have been about six or seven o'clock and they closed the terracing down behind the goal so everybody who had been queuing to get in there all rushed to get in the seats, and of course I couldn't cope with that with my broken leg so I didn't get in.'

Sixty-four thousand managed to get into the ground, and when the gates were locked an hour before kick-off it was estimated that at least thirty thousand remained outside. But the sense of oneness with the team was so great that everybody stayed there for the whole match. I stood with my dad in the packed crowd on the forecourt behind the scoreboard end. Around 7 p.m., some of those locked out, desperate to get into the ground, tried to batter down the gates. One group succeeded in getting the gates to one of the turnstiles open, but the turnstile itself and two hefty policemen kept them out until club officials got round to board it up. Mounted policemen ploughed into other groups who were trying to bash some gates down. Other fans tried to climb over the walls, and one youth managed to get up on the roof of a building inside the wall. But from there he had nowhere to go: three policemen were waiting for him on our side of the wall and there were clearly others on the inside stopping him from getting down. Another lad climbed up one of the floodlight pylons to about sixty feet. A policeman climbed after him and ordered him down. The lad was egged on a bit by the crowd to climb further up, but he seemed to get cold feet and came down. When he got to the bottom half a dozen policemen were waiting for him, and he was arrested.

Although we didn't get in we managed to get a match programme, which I've still got. On the front of it were the words that had been on the front of the previous one—'United Will Go On'—but this time they were printed over a picture of the third and decisive goal going in against Sheffield Wednesday in the fifth round, which according to the caption inside the programme 'was greeted by a cheer which reverberated throughout Lancashire'. Again, there were no cartoons. In their place this time was a tribute to Duncan Edwards. 'Still the pages of tragedy turn for us,' it said, 'and the death of Duncan Edwards on 21st February made the sadness we have shared the more pointed. Despite a fifteen-day struggle to save his life by a group of dedicated surgeons and nurses, Duncan Edwards joined his seven team-mates at whose funerals we paid homage so recently. We who thrilled to his awe-inspiring demonstrations of seeming invincibility, coupled with a joy of living that affected his comrades whenever and wherever the going was tough, will always remember Duncan.'

Right from the whistle it was a night of suspense, drama, tension and emotion, and the climax didn't come until the dying seconds of the game. Along with thousands of others we tried to follow the game by listening to the 'oohs' and 'aahs' of the crowd as we stood outside. United started shakily, but before half-time they had got themselves into the game and West Brom started to look a bit uncertain. Again, little Ernie Taylor, the midfield general, was man of the match, closely followed by Bobby Charlton. Charlton was everywhere, tackling like a terrier. And it was he and Taylor who combined to set up United's dramatic last-minute winner. Taylor chipped a brilliant pass out to Charlton on the right wing, and he took it in his stride and hared off on a touchline run. After beating two challenges he cut in along the goal-line, looked up and played a perfect low ball across the goalmouth. There, unmarked, was Colin Webster to tap in what he said later was one of the easiest goals of his life. The stadium erupted, and the roar was picked up and magnified by the crowd outside. I'll never forget it. There had been some remarkable ovations since the United team had first taken the field after Munich, but nothing like the cheers on this night when that all-important goal was scored. John Camkin, a *News Chronicle* reporter who was inside the ground, said, 'I can find no words to describe the explosion inside Old Trafford. It can only be said that neither Hampden Park nor Wembley nor any other ground in Britain has ever heard this concentration of noise.'

The cheers went on long after the final whistle. We were there, part of the thirty thousand or so who'd waited outside all through the match, and we danced on the forecourt of the ground behind the big scoreboard. This was the real moment of release. What had seemed unthinkable a few short weeks earlier was happening. United were back. Against all the odds, the rebuilt team had reached the semi-final of the FA Cup. When the gates opened at the end of the match we were swallowed up by the triumphant homeward-bound crowd sweeping across the United Road bridge and past the little houses near the ground as we made our way to Trafford Bar to get a 94 bus.

Whole families stood on their doorsteps asking, 'What was the score? What were they like?' When they got the news, everyone was finally convinced that United were well and truly back in business.

After the match, West Brom captain Ray Barlow put paid to the idea spreading through the game that teams playing United at Old Trafford were at a disadvantage because they couldn't play full-out for fear of injuring players and upsetting a wildly partisan crowd.

> If teams have got this idea then they can forget it entirely. United are playing it hard and with terrific enthusiasm at the moment. You've got to play hard against them to stand any chance at all. To lay off against a side with the sort of spirit they have got would be suicide. And if United play that way themselves, then they obviously expect other teams to play just as strongly against them. I had read and heard a lot about the Old Trafford crowd and had seen it stated that they were hysterical. But it wasn't like that. They were noisy certainly, and early on they roared even when the home full-backs were in possession going forward. But they weren't so very different from any other madly keen Cup crowd. They were there to encourage the young United players like any crowd, but they made rather more noise over it. It was a very hard game. There were times when fouls were given against us when we put their players down heavily, as they did to us. But the crowd didn't hold it against us. They shouted for a few seconds and then were roaring their own men on. There is absolutely no reason at all why

teams shouldn't play at Old Trafford exactly as they would do elsewhere.

Bill Foulkes reckoned it had been the toughest game of them all. He said he thought West Bromwich were the finest footballing side in the league. 'They play an attacking game from start to finish,' he said, 'and although I think our new reorganized United team is capable of giving any club a good game, I was really worried about Albion.' He went on to talk about the tremendous spirit at Old Trafford—'but,' he added, 'it is not just that which keeps us going. We have a terrific respect for each other's ability as players, and I think these last two games against West Bromwich prove our recovery is no fluke. Last night's game was the hardest and fastest I have ever played in—and that goes for all the European Cup games including the one against Bilbao, which was fought at a terrific pace.'

In his weekly column in the *Manchester Evening News*, Preston North End and England footballing great Tom Finney summed up what he thought was behind the 'Miracle of Manchester'. He said that though the lost players would not be forgotten, one outstanding fact had risen out of the wreckage and shattered dreams: you cannot destroy a football club. In the month since the crash United had proved that real greatness meant much more than a galaxy of great players; it meant possessing a thing called spirit. And behind it all was this incredible man called Jimmy Murphy, for whom the past month must have been the most remorseless ever spent by any man behind the scenes in modern sport. 'Yet,' Finney went on, 'it is still a quality greater than even Jim Murphy possesses which has prompted this

Miracle of Manchester. It is a feeling which can only be built up over many seasons of failure, setback and success. And it has come to comparatively few clubs. Manchester United have proved they are more than worthy to be numbered among that exclusive band. Their phenomenal fight back from calamity these past four weeks has revealed how worthy they are of becoming an immortal club.'

The good news continued the following morning. Johnny Berry, who had been in a coma for a month, opened his eyes for the first time and spoke to his wife. Jackie Blanchflower, who by now was being allowed to walk about, was by Berry's bedside with his wife. Jackie said Johnny had tried to get up but that he immediately lapsed into unconsciousness again. Dr Karl Kessel, the brain surgeon, said it would be a long time before Berry regained full consciousness, but there was a good chance that he would soon be off the danger list. Matt Busby and *News Chronicle* sports writer Frank Taylor were also reported to be making good progress. Dennis Viollet and Ken Morgans arrived back in Manchester the day after the West Brom game.

That day Manchester's courts were busy dealing with those whose enthusiasm to get into the ground the night before had gone a bit too far. Magistrates were told by a police inspector that if the crowd outside Old Trafford had followed the example of the man who had climbed the wall to get in 'you would have had the ingredients of a disaster. An incident like this could have sparked off something much more serious. The police were fully occupied trying to control the crowd of more than thirty thousand outside the ground. When officers were diverted by the climbing incident it meant that other sections of the crowd were not being supervised.'

All this I read about, as usual, in the *Evening News*, which also carried the headline 'Extend Old Trafford!' This would be the finest United memorial, the paper said.

> Today the Lord Mayor of Manchester's Memorial Fund stands at £22,000. Tonight, the *Manchester Evening News* puts this proposal. Although many ideas have been put up to the Fund Committee, no decision has been reached on how best to use the money. Last night's historic match proved that Manchester United are reborn as a team. They are in the semi-finals of the FA and European Cups. Up to 40,000 hardworking, deserving men, women, boys and girls were turned away from the replay last night because the gates were locked. Not for the first time the gates had to be closed. Evening football is here to stay and the Old Trafford ground is simply not big enough. We say: Let the club have the Memorial Fund money. Let the club extend the ground in honour of the 'Babes'. Either extend the terraces or build a big new double-decker stand. Let the people of Greater Manchester see Manchester United in comfort when they desire and cut out the disappointments of last night. What better way to remember them?

That Thursday, 6 March, it was the bookies who were saying that United really were back. They were quoting the club as 7–4 favourites to win the Cup. A lot of Manchester bookmakers were going even further. The win over West Brom frightened them so much that they immediately closed their books for bets on United. One of the city's leading bookmakers said, 'We stand to lose a fortune if United win. We just had to close our books on them. Do you know, some people were still backing heavily on United immediately after the crash? That's support for you. Until last night I was still willing to take bets on them, but then I saw them beat the Albion and, oh brother, so far as I'm concerned, if you want to bet on United to win do me a favour and take your money somewhere else.'

* * *

It was now four weeks after the crash and we'd had time to take in the full effect of the tragedy, but I still felt a great sense of loss and still felt cheated that the great Busby Babes had been taken away from us before the team had reached its prime. Although the new Babes were doing unbelievably well, whatever the reports said they were not as good as the team that had been wiped out. We'd never forget the players who had lost their lives and those whose injuries were so severe that it looked unlikely they would ever play again. And it still felt strange to see all those new faces in the team. I'd found it hard to believe that it wasn't the old team running out for each of the games I'd been to after the crash. What was clear, though, was one outstanding fact that had risen out of the wreckage and the shattered dreams—you cannot wipe out a football club. United were proving, as Tom Finney said, that real greatness meant much more than a squad of great players; it meant possessing spirit, and United had that in abundance.

Carried along on this great wave of emotion

United were winning their Cup games, but it was a different story in the league. On Saturday 8 March I was with my dad packed into a sixty-odd-thousand crowd to see United get beaten 4–0 by West Brom. They'd beaten this side three days earlier in the Cup but they couldn't sustain that form in the league. Before kick-off we cheered as Professor Maurer and members of his staff from the Rechts der Isar Hospital in Munich came out on to the field. To these Germans the British public owed a debt of praise and gratitude, and they paid it back that afternoon. The guests looked understandably surprised by the roar they received and the warmth of the welcome. The club chairman, Harold Hardman, introduced them and spoke about the wonderful treatment they'd given to the injured. There were more cheers when Professor Maurer's wife was presented with a red and white bouquet by captain Billy Foulkes, and when a similar bouquet was given to the youngest nurse in the party by Harry Gregg. Then there was an eerie silence as we waited to hear a tape-recorded message from Matt Busby to be relayed over the loudspeakers. He said that he and the United players at the hospital were now considered out of danger thanks to the wonderful care of Professor Maurer and his staff. He thanked them for this and said he had been delighted to hear about the team's recent successes. Some women near us in the paddock were in tears as Matt's voice echoed across a packed Old Trafford.

Professor Maurer and his team, along with the Oberburgermeister of Munich, had arrived in Manchester the day before. At the airport the Lord Mayor of Manchester, Alderman Leslie Lever, told the party that Manchester was proud of the hospital's work and they came to the city as honoured guests.

After the welcoming speeches they were whisked off to Stretford Town Hall for a civic reception. A party of United supporters about three hundred strong, many of them of school age, had been waiting there up to two hours in the chilly night air to express their gratitude to them with a mini version of the Old Trafford roar. The doctors and nurses in their blue caps looked faintly surprised by everything that was happening to them. Speaking from the balcony of the Town Hall, the Mayor of Stretford, Councillor Reid, said that the hospital's work would never be forgotten. Professor Maurer insisted that they had only been doing their duty, and then, looking down at the sea of appreciative faces, he said that the injured players had come as patients and they had left as friends. Later that night the party attended the Manchester Press Ball at the Locarno in Sale.

On the Saturday morning before going to the match the German delegation went shopping in a city centre that still bore the unmistakable scars of wartime bombing raids. But now they were here as friends; the old enemy had become the angels of Munich, and the whole of Manchester, it seemed, wanted to thank them. So inundated were they with well-wishers that they eventually had to give up after trying several shops. Everywhere they went Manchester men and women walked up, shook their hands and said, 'Nice to see you here. And thanks for everything you have done.' In one of Manchester's biggest stores shoppers crowded round them as they bought records, including the 'Manchester United Calypso'. Staff formed a guard of honour for them as they walked around, and shoppers applauded them.

The people of Manchester were genuinely touched by the care that had been given to the crash victims.

It was a massive boost for the post-war reconciliation process, and subsequently close links were established between the cities of Manchester and Munich. One of the images I always remember from those terrible times was one of the German doctors who had been looking after Duncan Edwards appearing on the news just before he died looking absolutely exhausted. He'd clearly been keeping a constant vigil in a desperate attempt to save him, and he'd probably had no sleep. I know for a fact that after seeing that doctor many people suddenly realized there were a lot of good Germans in Germany.

The only member of the German party who didn't go on the shopping trip that Saturday morning was Professor Maurer's deputy, brain surgeon Professor Karl Kessel. The trip to England meant a lot to him because he had worked at Manchester Royal Infirmary from 1940 to 1950 and, in his words, 'learned a great deal there'. Kessel said he had great respect for British brain surgery, and that morning, while the rest of the party went shopping, he went instead to the Royal Infirmary where the world famous neurosurgeon Sir Geoffrey Jefferson was ill in the private patients' home. 'When I heard he was ill I decided to see him as soon as possible,' said Professor Kessel. 'You could call me a pupil of Sir Geoffrey.'

The match itself on the Saturday afternoon couldn't possibly live up to all this emotion, and the 4–0 loss was United's first setback since the crash. It was the first sign of an end to the emotional tension which by now had probably continued for too long for the good of the team. After the doctors and nurses had received their tumultuous reception from the packed crowd, United had decided to play against a swirling wind on a bitterly cold afternoon. But they were just not in the game that afternoon. West Brom dictated the early proceedings to such an extent that United didn't manage to mount a serious attack for the first quarter of an hour, and by that time they were a goal down.

The only bright spot for us from a footballing point of view was the performance of Bobby Charlton. Ernie Taylor, whom the new Reds had come to rely on so much, was either off the field or ineffective for most of the game after pulling a thigh muscle early on, but Charlton stepped in and gave a superb performance. With Taylor injured he was the only effective forward United had. In the programme he was on the teamsheet as outside-left, but he was everywhere, and by the time the match ended he had played in just about every position except goalkeeper. 'This young man,' said W.R. Taylor in his match report in the *Manchester Guardian*, 'who has not yet completed his National Service, is a born footballer and surely must be considered for the World Cup. Not only does he control the ball magnificently, but he can shoot and dribble with the best, is extremely versatile, and one has never seen him do anything shabby.'

After the match the Munich delegation was given a civic reception and dinner at Manchester Town Hall at which the Lord Mayor handed over a formal resolution expressing the city council's thanks to the people of Munich and the staff of the hospital. He said that no words could have brought together the people of Munich and Manchester in quite the same way as their humanity and untiring devotion. Professor Maurer repeated that his party felt they really did not deserve all the hospitality they had received in Manchester because they had only been doing their duty. He added that he had received five letters offering a kidney to save the life of Duncan Edwards, from two women and three men—a Frenchman, a Belgian, a South African and two Germans. He said it was impossible to perform such an operation, but the offers reflected the range and depth of international sympathy and the will to help which overwhelmed the troubles between nations. Burgermeister Adolf Hieber, who was representing the Munich municipality, took up the friendship-between-nations theme when he suggested that there should be some form of permanent link between Munich and Manchester, and that one way to achieve it was through regular exchange visits by students of the two cities.

The German newspaper *Die Welt* paid tribute to the people of Manchester who had welcomed the surgeons and nurses from the hospital at the West Brom match. The staff at the hospital, the paper wrote, had done no more than their duty so they were all the more gratified by the reception they were given in Manchester. It showed how quick an English public was to appreciate what was natural to the medical profession. The incident could well help to improve Anglo-German relations, still clouded by unsettled issues. An additional tribute was paid to the British press which had not ceased to compliment the Munich doctors on their skill and devotion to duty.

The following week the Lord Mayor and Lady Mayoress of Manchester, Alderman and Mrs Lever, went to Germany to thank the people of Munich and the staff of the Rechts der Isar Hospital for what they had done 'for the survivors of the tragic Manchester

United air crash'. More than a thousand people cheered and waved as they arrived at Munich station. Among the reception party was Professor Maurer, who called for three cheers. The Manchester party's itinerary included a tour of the city, two visits to the hospital and discussions on an exchange of doctors, nurses and municipal officials between Manchester and Munich. A thirty-man brass band played outside the hospital as Alderman Lever and his wife arrived. Inside they visited the five survivors of the crash who were still there: Matt Busby, Johnny Berry, Jackie Blanchflower, Frank Taylor and Captain Kenneth Rayment, the co-pilot. Afterwards the Lord Mayor said, 'Matt was most cheerful, and Blanchflower and Taylor were quite cheerful as well. The others—well, they are as well as could be expected. I told Matt everyone in England is praying for his speedy recovery and return.'

Johnny Berry and the co-pilot, Captain Kenneth Rayment were still on the critical list, but Matt Busby, Jackie Blanchflower and the journalist Frank Taylor were continuing to show signs of improvement. For Busby, though, as his physical injuries healed, mental ones came to the fore. 'To be honest,' he said later, 'I suppose I wasn't sane. I wanted to die. I felt that, in a way, I might have been responsible. That I shouldn't have allowed us to go the third time. What was so special about me that I'd survived? I was absolutely determined that I'd have nothing more to do with football.'

CHAPTER 11

TEDDY BOYS

Against all the odds, Jimmy Murphy's patched-up team had reached the semi-final of the FA Cup, and it wasn't a bad draw. They were to meet Second Division Fulham, avoiding the only other First Division club left in the competition, Bolton Wanderers, who would be contesting the other semi-final with their Lancashire neighbours, Second Division Blackburn Rovers. Things were looking good. Spring was on its way, it was a time of rebirth and renewal. But the Manchester weather was still capable of reminding us that the dark days hadn't yet come to an end. Instead of the big freeze making way for the bright days of spring, it only brought in the oppressive grim greyness of a Manchester fog. In the days before the Clean Air Act when there were still so many house and factory chimneys filling the air with smoke, pea-soupers would envelop the whole city for days on end, and it wasn't a very healthy place to be. When I'd woken up on the Friday I hadn't even been able to see the shed at the end of our garden, let alone the row of houses on the road behind us. But there was one good thing about it: it would probably mean we'd miss that morning's lessons as the bus would take so long to crawl from our house to school.

After breakfast I set off up our road through a strange, silent world. The fog was so thick that I could only see a couple of yards in front of me, and as I approached the bus stop figures loomed up in front of me out of the grey blanket of damp smoke and muck that enveloped everything, scarves across their mouths to stop them breathing in the noxious air. But even with a thick scarf covering your face you could taste it. The bus emerged out of the gloom, just a soft blur of headlights at first; then, as it got to within a few yards of the stop, the interior yellow lights came into view. It crawled up to the stop at no more than walking pace, and as it drew level you could just about make out the shadowy figure of the driver hunched over the wheel in his cab, peering ahead. The conductor was walking along on the grass verge at the front of the bus, helping the driver to stay on the road.

It was going to be a long journey. When the fog was really bad it could take three hours to cover the four or five miles from Newall Green to Alexandra Park, where I got off. That morning was no exception. The fog showed no sign of lifting. In fact, as we got closer to town it seemed to get thicker. To relieve the boredom some of us got off and walked with the conductor, talking to him and the driver as he struggled on. By the time we got to Alexandra Park we were good mates with them. It was half past eleven. I'd missed nearly all of that morning's lessons, and if it stayed as bad that afternoon they'd let us home early.

Throughout that winter the football fixtures had been severely disrupted by snow and frozen pitches, but fog like this could play even more havoc with them, so it was just as well that we only had it that one day because the big problem for United was that by this time they were facing a massive fixture pile-up. With just over six weeks to go to the end of the season they still had twelve league games to fit in, not to mention the Cup semi-final and the two legs of the European Cup semi-final. To meet these commitments they would have to play three matches a week. If they progressed in either of the Cup competitions there would be an even bigger muddle, so the club sought permission to play the two legs of their European Cup semi-final after the English season had ended. Even if this permission were granted, it would still mean that United would be in action at least once every four days until the beginning of May, with three games to play in four days over the Easter holiday. Chairman Harold Hardman said, 'It's necessary to face up to the fact that with so many fixtures still to fulfil some of our boys will be walking on their knees by the time our programme has been completed.'

Emotion, high adrenalin and a passionate crowd continued to drive them on in the Cup, but in the league it was different. After the 4–0 defeat by West Brom there was a tough away game the following Saturday at Burnley. We didn't generally go to away games, but Burnley wasn't far away so my dad booked two tickets on the North-Western coach that went from the newsagent's at Greenbrow Road shops.

The departure time for the 'chara' was twelve o'clock, but before leaving I had to do my usual Saturday-morning round, collecting the football pools bags for church. My last stop, as usual, was the McDaids just round the corner on Frensham Walk, and there I collected a big bag of broken biscuits which they gave me every Saturday morning. Mrs McDaid worked at the biscuit factory on the small industrial estate near us and once a week she was rewarded with a free five-pound bag of broken biscuits. They couldn't eat all of them so they donated some each week to me to share with my sister. After I'd done the pools bag round I had to walk down to Todd's the bakers at the next lot of shops further down Greenbrow Road. There I got two fresh crusty loaves and four meat and potato pies. I always took a pyrex dish with me for the pies so that they could be smothered in the rich, thick, dark brown gravy they also served. As usual I was on the look-out for dogs as I walked down Amberley Drive. There were one or two fierce-looking ones down there and I didn't want to meet up with any of them. 'Don't run,' I'd been told, 'if one of them approaches you. It's the worst thing you can do.' But that day there was no sign of any of them and I got back safely with the bread and the pies.

Once we'd eaten the pies we walked up to the newsagent's to get the red and cream North-Western coach to take us to Burnley. On the way it took us on a tour of the Industrial Revolution and the once-great Lancashire cotton industry, which was now in decline. We went past the great warehouses in the centre of Manchester, many of them now half empty, then we headed out through Rochdale, Littleborough and Todmorden where a forest of mill chimneys still belched smoke into the valleys of the eastern Pennines. My dad told me that he used to get the train and go out walking on the hills around there when he was a lad.

But most people on the coach didn't seem very interested in the scenery. All the conversation on the way to the match centred on whether the Reds would be able to recapture their Cup form. Had the bubble burst, or was the 4–0 licking West Brom had handed out just a reaction after the tense, hard-fought Cup battles against them? Today was going to be a real test. Burnley had one of the best home records in the First Division and they'd got their brilliant Irish inside-forward Jimmy McIlroy back after injury. McIlroy was in the same mould as Ernie Taylor, the old-fashioned schemer, but United's task was going to be harder today because of Ernie's thigh muscle injury which was going to keep him out of the team that afternoon.

Turf Moor was right near the centre of Burnley, and because it was so close to Manchester, United had brought a big following with them. When we got into the ground there was a solid block of red and white scarves behind one of the goals so we made our way to that end. I got down to the fence at the front. It was the first away game I'd ever been to—all very exciting, and so different to going to a match at Old Trafford. For a start, their ground was quite a bit smaller and you could see over the open terracing at the other end. It seemed to be surrounded by mill chimneys, but beyond them were the green hills of the Pennines—a very different outlook to the industrial landscape around Old Trafford. But not very many of those chimneys were smoking. Many Lancashire cotton workers were working short hours and it had just been announced that about twenty thousand would have an extended Easter holiday—an unwanted break that had been forced on the mill owners by dangerously thin order books. The textile workers unions, it was reported, were resigned to widespread stoppages. And it wasn't just the view that was different. There was a noticeably different atmosphere at an away game, more noise and more passion from the travelling Reds all standing together behind the goals.

The sun was shining brightly on the open terrace—a perfect day for watching a football match—and a great roar greeted the Reds as they came out in their change strip of all white. We had something to get excited about straight away when right from the kick-off United swept down the field on the left and a centre from Bobby Charlton found Bobby Harrop perfectly placed in front of goal. It looked like a cert, and we got ready to cheer an early goal, but Harrop shot wide. Burnley were quick to reply, and they soon began to dominate proceedings. It took a couple of cat-like saves from Harry Gregg to keep United in it, and when he dived bravely at the feet of a Burnley forward he got a boot in his face for his troubles.

That was the signal for things to get a bit heated. Soon after Gregg had been treated for the kick in the face he was involved in a scuffle with Burnley's centre-forward Alan Shackleton on the edge of the box. The referee gave Burnley a free kick and lectured Gregg. A couple of minutes later United's left-back Ian Greaves got involved in another altercation. This time it was with Burnley's right-winger, and the Burnley man went in the book. A minute later the referee had his notebook out again; this time it was Stan Crowther's name that went into it after a heavy tackle by the United left-half. The resulting free kick hit the post and was scrambled away … and then the game hit boiling point. Mark Pearson went in to tackle Burnley wing-half Shannon and clipped him on the leg. The next moment, Shannon was up with his fists raised, jostling Pearson. Unbelievably, it was Pearson who was sent off while Shannon stayed on. Reduced to ten men after just half an hour, United battled on. They managed to hold out for the rest of the first half, but the second half was best forgotten as they conceded three goals.

On the coach on the way back from the match the talk was all about Mark Pearson's sending-off. Nobody could understand why Shannon hadn't been sent off as well. To be fair, though, Pearson wasn't entirely innocent, as many people on the coach pointed out, and trouble had been brewing for him for a few weeks. 'Pancho', as he was known because of his long sideburns, was a terrific ball winner with quite an aggressive temperament. In these games just after the crash he was very fired up, and his conduct on the pitch had been picked up on by a number of reporters. At school there was always a copy of the *Manchester Guardian* in the library, and as early as the 4–0 defeat by West Brom, on the day the Munich delegation came to Old Trafford, their reporter had said, 'Yet again Pearson showed he has not yet learned to control his temper. Professional footballers are often accused of rough play (not always justly) but one of the friendliest aspects of recent weeks has been the attitude of far more experienced opponents to some of the new United players. It says much for the self-control, thoughtfulness and tolerance of a number of old sweats that retribution has not already overtaken Pearson. It certainly will soon if he does not mend his ways for, young as he is, he cannot plead inexperience now and referees cannot be so understanding indefinitely.' It was a point that had also been picked up by West Brom's Bobby Robson after the 2–2 draw in the Cup at The Hawthorns. So what happened at Turf Moor was perhaps an incident that had been waiting to happen.

The match turned into a bit of a battle and on the terraces some of the Burnley fans came out with some

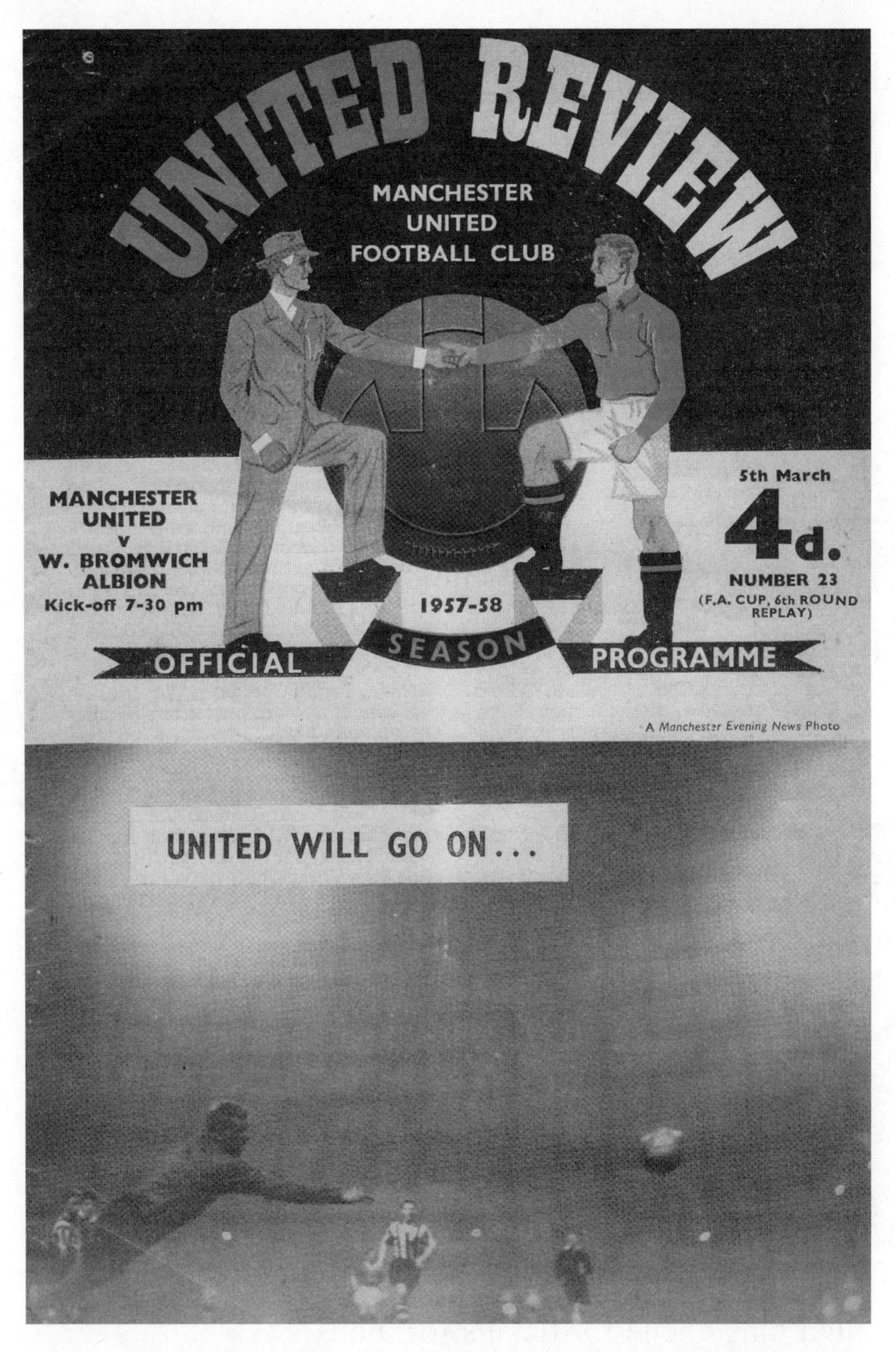

Programme from the West Brom FA Cup Sixth-Round replay, 5 March 1958. The picture is of Alex Dawson scoring United's third goal in the fifth-round tie against Sheffield Wednesday – the first game after the crash.

Right Duncan Edwards on the front cover of *Charles Buchan's Football Monthly*, March 1958. The magazine went on sale just hours before Duncan died from injuries sustained in the crash.

Left (Left to right) Harry Gregg, Jimmy Murphy and Bill Foulkes look from the window of the train as they depart from Munich to travel by land back to Manchester.

Above Jimmy Murphy takes telephone calls from concerned fans in the aftermath of the disaster.

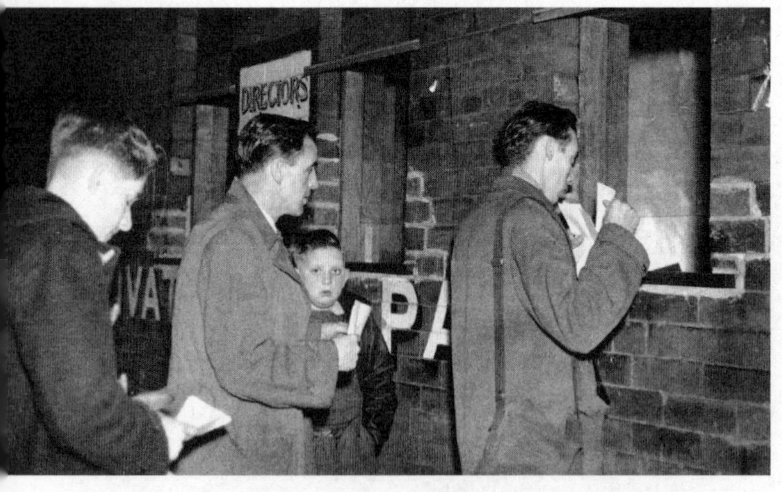

Above Old Trafford, 6 February 1958. United fans queue for tickets for the forthcoming matches against Wolves in the First Division and Sheffield Wednesday in the FA Cup, just before news of the disaster came through.

Above The wives of some of the injured players make their way to the plane that will take them on the first leg of their flight to Munich the morning after the crash.

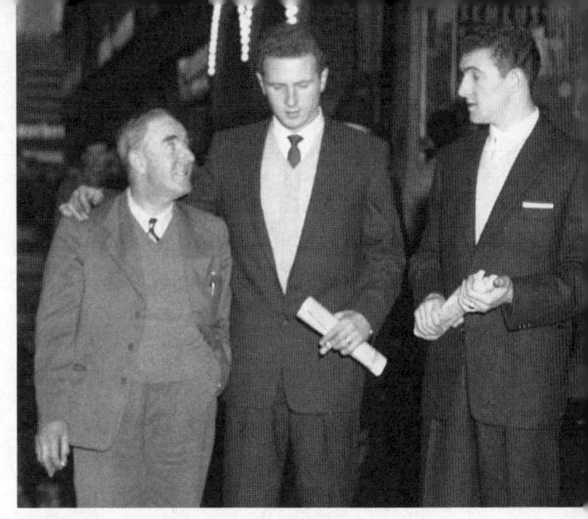

Above (Left to right) John Blanchflower, father of Jackie, with Harry Gregg and Bill Foulkes outside their hotel in Munich, 8 February 1958.

Triumph and tragedy: PictureNews salutes them

BIG VICTORY MEMORY

Two stalwarts of the club

CHAMPIONS, AND A GAY PARTY!

Gregg had premonition of disaster

Their fight back to fame

Bombshell

Triumph

Inside pages of the *Manchester Evening News*, Friday 7 February, 1958.

Above Bobby Charlton and Ray Wood in the Rechts der Isar Hospital in Munich, 11 February 1958.

ver play again—Tragic families fly out

who escaped.

0-50 : EDWARDS : BERRY COMA

"BUSB ACUTE BERRY

Give United the

Right Author's copy of the front page of the *Manchester Evening News*, 7 February 1958, with notes written by his dad on the condition of Duncan Edwards and Johnny Berry as news came through on the radio.

Below Dennis Viollett *(right)* with his wife Barbara, and Albert Scanlon with his wife Josie at the Rechts der Isar Hospital in Munich the day after the crash, 7 February 1958.

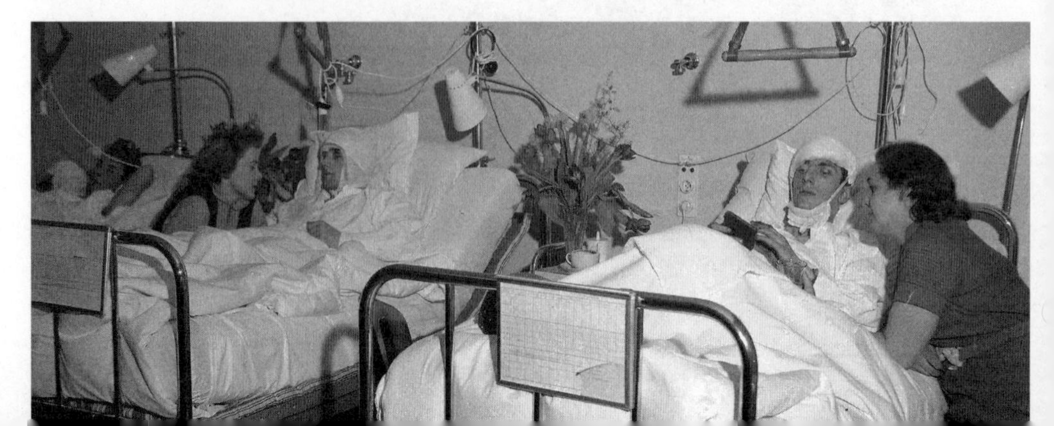

Above West German police form a guard of honour at Munich Airport as the BEA aircraft carrying the coffins of the victims of the crash prepares for take-off, 10 February 1958.

Below Roger Byrne's funeral, Flixton parish Church, 12 February, 1958.

Left Fifth-Round FA Cup tie against Sheffield Wednesday, 19 February 1958. The first goal in the first match after the crash, scored direct from a corner kick by outside-left, Shay Brennan.

Below Manchester United, March 1958: *(back row, left to right)* Bobby Harrop, Ian Greaves, Freddie Goodwin, Harry Gregg, Stan Crowther, Ronnie Cope, Shay Brennan, Bill Inglis (assistant trainer); *(front row, left to right)* Jack Crompton (trainer), Alex Dawson, Mark Pearson, Bill Foulkes (captain), Ernie Taylor, Colin Webster.

Below Training at the Norbreck Hydro, Blackpool, before the Sixth-Round FA Cup tie against West Brom.

Above United fans arrive at Euston station in London for the semi-final replay against Fulham at Highbury, 26 March 1958. United's mascot, Jack Irons, is in the centre with umbrella and bowler hat.

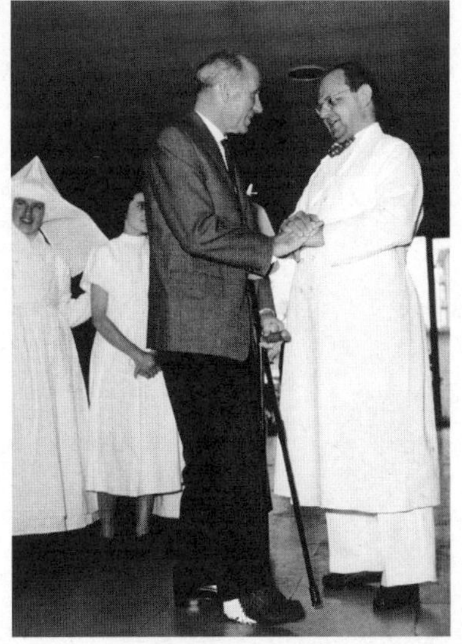

Below Bobby Charlton gets back to playing football with some of the local lads at the back of his home on Beatrice Street, Ashington, Northumberland, 19 February 1958.

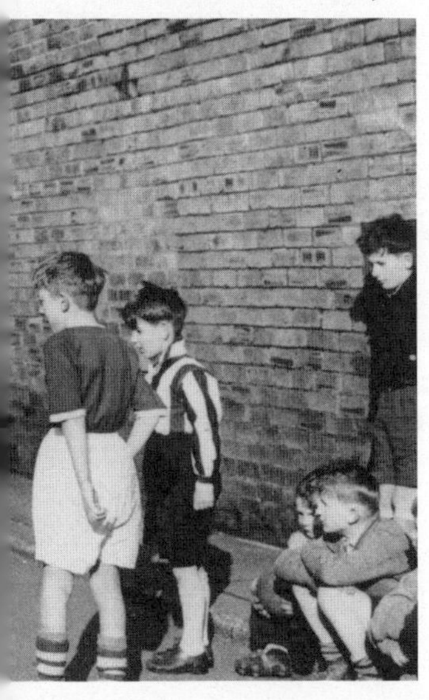

Above Matt Busby says goodbye and thank you to Professor George Maurer as he leaves the Rechts der Isar Hospital in Munich 17 April 1958.

Right Arriving home, 18 April 1958.

United leave Manchester to play a pre-season friendly against Bayern Munich – their first match abroad after the crash – 7 August 1959.

nasty remarks about United. A couple of the lads on our coach had heard a Burnley supporter say it was a pity Bobby Charlton had ever come back from the crash. The atmosphere certainly wasn't very pleasant. Beryl Townsend was at the match, and she told me, 'We heard some Burnley fans near us saying, "It's a pity they didn't all die." I just couldn't believe it. That was the only club where anything like that happened. At every other club the supporters were great. When we went to collect for the Disaster Fund, other supporters were always generous and most other clubs leaned over backwards to help United after the crash. I remember going to West Brom for that Cup tie and every time our coach stopped, their fans were waving and cheering and wishing us good luck. Everywhere we went except this game at Burnley.' It was only a minority of the Burnley fans, but with comments like that going around the ground it's a wonder there wasn't a fight in the crowd as well as on the pitch. There certainly seemed to be a whole lot of ill feeling in Burnley as far as United was concerned—a lot of it, it would seem, whipped up by their chairman Bob Lord. It had to have been his controversial comments immediately after the crash about clubs not giving players to United out of sympathy for them that had laid the foundations for all the unpleasantness. And, unknown to us on the coach as we made our way back to Wythenshawe, there was a whole lot more controversy being stirred up by Mr Lord at the end of the match. The 'Burnley butcher', as he was known throughout the game raised the tempo of his anti-United stand when he said, 'Manchester United played like Teddy Boys. If they are allowed to carry on like they did this afternoon, it means the whole structure of league football will be at stake. They will do the game a great deal of harm, and will lose the sympathy which the public have for them at the moment. Everybody was grieved by the terrible tragedy at Munich, but now I'm afraid that the public spotlight focused on the new United has meant that some of the players are losing their heads.'

Jimmy Murphy was justifiably angry. In the fifties the words 'Teddy Boy' conjured up images of youthful violence and anti-social behaviour. It was a time when the children of the war years were coming of age, and some of them had declared their own war on the values of their parents' and grandparents' generations. In the vanguard of the rebellion was a colourful and often violent minority of youths called Teddy Boys. They'd first made their appearance in the early 1950s, and prided themselves on their distinctive fashion: long 'drape' jackets with velvet collars and cuffs, 'drainpipe' trousers and thick crêpe-soled shoes. They were fans of the rock 'n' roll music that had come into Britain from America with Bill Haley and the Comets, and they developed a reputation for looking for fights in dance halls and cinemas, particularly those playing rock 'n' roll music or showing new 'youth-oriented' films such as *Rock Around the Clock.* By the mid-fifties newspapers were filled with reports of riots at cinemas. Teddy Boys were jiving in the aisles and ripping up seats; hundreds were arrested, charged and fined for insulting behaviour. At the time of the Burnley match the Manchester papers were reporting on two teenage Teddy Boys who had hurled a third through the plate-glass window of a grocer's shop just a hundred yards from a police station in Woodhouse Park, Wythenshawe.

Calling his young United players Teddy Boys,

then, was understandably like a red rag to a bull for Jimmy Murphy and he reacted strongly as he came to the defence of his players. 'Mr Lord's remarks were totally unjustified, and I think this is a shocking thing,' he said. 'It is disgraceful coming from the chairman of a football club. In defence of my team I must say we object most strongly to the remarks about Teddy Boys.'

Bob Lord's jibes were all over the papers on the Sunday morning. 'Manchester people are still swayed by what happened at Munich,' he was reported as saying. 'It isn't good for the game. There is too much sentiment about Manchester United … in Manchester. All the talk since Munich seems to have gone to the heads of some of the United players. All they have had to withstand in recent weeks seems to have been a bit too much for some of these young men.' As we stood talking about it after eleven o'clock Mass, it all seemed particularly nasty and tasteless. Yes, there was a lot of sentiment around, and there was still a lot of grieving. Emotional energy was probably the only thing keeping some of these young lads going. None of us knew what it must have been like in the dressing room at that time, but it can't have been easy. Going out and fighting the good fight for your fallen comrades had to have been part of it. But what Bob Lord seemed to have forgotten, Mr Caesar pointed out, was that it was his players who started the rough stuff with repeated fouls on Harry Gregg. What we all found particularly repugnant about the comments was that they had come so soon after the crash that some of the team were still lying seriously injured in hospital.

Everybody was shocked. There was no hate in football in the 1950s. The yobbish tribalism that afflicts football today only started to creep in during the sixties. These tasteless outbursts of Mr Lord's at such a sensitive time soured relations between United and their Lancashire neighbours for many seasons to come. He'd had so much to say about United that a minority of his club's supporters were now parroting his tasteless comments on the terraces. The vast majority of Burnley fans, though, were as disgusted as everybody else about it. Typical of the views of many of them was this letter to the *Manchester Evening News* in which one woman from Bacup said, 'I am a mere female supporter and I have been following Burnley FC for the past ten years. But I'll never go again as long as I live, because I heard a large portly gentleman sitting in the stands say it was a pity all the Manchester United players had not been destroyed in the Munich disaster.'

That day, while comments like that were being made at Turf Moor, the crash claimed its twenty-third and final victim, Captain Kenneth Rayment, the co-pilot of the aircraft, who had been unconscious since the accident.

* * *

While all this was going on Jimmy Murphy had to get his team prepared for an FA Cup semi-final on the Saturday. He took the players to Blackpool, as he had done before the previous two Cup ties, for another spell of seaside preparation. With them was young Ken Morgans, the eighteen-year-old Welsh winger, who had played his first game of football since the crash for the reserves against Newcastle while the first team were at Burnley. He scored a goal and seemed to be in good form, so there were predictions that he would come into the team at outside-right.

Man of the match for United at Burnley was Bobby Charlton. Just five weeks after he had escaped the wreckage at Munich, the twenty-year-old survivor was playing for the friends he had lost. It was as though he had a sense of duty; of doing it for the boys and for the Boss who was still lying in hospital. So good was Charlton's form that he also jumped to the front of the queue of England's inside-forwards, and he was selected to play for the Football League against the Scottish League at Newcastle. He had only played thirty First Division matches, but here he was challenging Bobby Robson, the West Brom and England inside-forward, for a place in England's World Cup squad.

United's semi-final was being played at Villa Park; Bolton were playing Blackburn at Maine Road. On the day it was reported that plainclothes police were travelling on the trains to Birmingham and on those coming into Manchester for the Maine Road semi-final. They were warned to watch out for hooliganism following recent train-wrecking by soccer fans. Soccer hooliganism was something new. Just a few weeks earlier gangs of Liverpool fans had brought mob violence to Blackburn and had been warned by magistrates that they would not get away with it in the future. As he sent a twenty-five-year-old Liverpool fan to jail for six months for assaulting a policeman, the chairman of Blackburn magistrates said, 'We take a very serious view on the conduct of you people when you come to our town for these football matches. Over a long period you have got away with it very quietly. Two or three times you have come over in gangs and created havoc by assaulting and obstructing policemen.' The jailed fan said, 'I'd had so much to drink, all I can remember is being hit on the head with a truncheon.'

In Birmingham, the ticket touts were having a field day. Many fans jumped at the chance to buy a 2s 6d (12½p) ticket for £2 10s (£2.50). Police, it was reported, repeatedly moved the ticket touts on, but United fans followed the spivs wherever they were moved on to. I couldn't believe it. £2 10s was a lot of money—nearly half my dad's wages—but fans were desperate to get to the match. It promised to be a great personal battle between two master inside-forwards—Ernie Taylor of United and Johnny Haynes of Fulham. Each of them was the brains behind their respective forward lines, and the sixty-five thousand capacity crowd were eager to watch the struggle. For long periods, though, the game didn't live up to expectations. It ended as a 2–2 draw, but much of the play was undistinguished. All the goals came in the first half. Charlton opened the scoring for United, then got a second just before half-time after Fulham had taken a 2–1 lead. No goalkeeper could have touched either of them, all the reports said. In the second half the game became a personal duel between Charlton and Fulham's young goalkeeper Tony Macedo. Five times Macedo thwarted Charlton—the only United forward to threaten any danger. In the meantime Harry Gregg had to make three great saves to keep Fulham out. When we talked about it outside church the next morning it was Gregg's performance more than anything that gave us confidence that United would win the replay and get through to the final against Bolton, who had beaten Blackburn 2–1.

Just after we got back from church a smart-looking coach stopped on the other side of the road right opposite our house. We were all curious and crowded round our front window to see what was going on. As we watched, the coach began to empty. Important-looking men in heavy overcoats got off and stood in groups looking at Johannesburg Gardens, the old people's bungalows opposite us. Then one of them detached himself from the group and began to walk over to our house. My dad opened the front door and went out to meet this official-looking character. They had a brief chat, and when my dad came back in he was quite excited. The party on the coach, he said, was made up of some Manchester city councillors and a delegation of Communist Party officials from the city of Leningrad in Russia. The man who'd spoken to my dad had asked him if it would be all right to bring the Leningrad delegation into our house to meet a typical Manchester family and see the sort of house they lived in.

Within a minute our little living room was packed with big, burly-looking Russians. They spoke to my mam and dad through an interpreter, asking them about the house and about living in Manchester. Then one of them got a couple of gold metal badges out and gave one each to me and our Joan. It was, we were told, the official badge of the city of Leningrad, and they were being given to us as a token of their friendship.

After a conducted tour of our little house the Russian party thanked my mam and dad and emptied the place as quickly as they had filled it. We watched them as they walked up Johannesburg Gardens and went into the community centre—to meet some typical Mancunian old people, I suppose. The whole thing was amazing. It was the height of the Cold War and we had just had a house full of Russians—the people who were going to nuke us out of existence, if a lot of the newspaper reports were to be believed. Britain was at the time gripped by a very real fear of nuclear conflict. The ideological differences between the USSR and the West were a source of tension, and the US and Britain on one side and Russia on the other were building more and more nuclear weapons as a result. All attempts to control, let alone reverse, the process broke down repeatedly. The headlines all through February and March 1958 were about attempts to set up East–West summit talks to discuss nuclear disarmament. They were trying to get talks set up for the summer but it didn't look promising as neither side could agree terms for the talks. There was a real fear of Russia at the time, yet here we were on a Sunday morning with the dreaded enemy in our house, and they were all very friendly. There certainly didn't seem to be anything very frightening about them and I couldn't see any of them dropping H-bombs on us. They all looked too nice for that. What with Germans and Yugoslav Communists being welcomed in the streets of Manchester and on the pitch at Old Trafford, and the big, bad Russians in our front room, these were confusing times. When it came to it, when you met them and talked to them most people seemed to be all right. So why did we have to go to war with each other and try to wipe each other out?

But these were big questions to be thinking about on a Sunday morning, especially when there were reports to read about yesterday's semi-final and a replay to look forward to. It was going to be played at Highbury the following Wednesday. United had not been at their best at Villa Park and Jimmy Murphy had only a few days to try to get his players back to the form that had seen them through the previous rounds of the Cup. One of the main weaknesses had been down the wings. Crash survivor Ken Morgans hadn't been fit enough to play and wasn't expected to get back to full match fitness in time for the replay. On the Monday, more of the crash survivors had made their return to Old Trafford. Albert Scanlon had the plaster removed from his leg when he came to the ground, and Jackie Blanchflower, though he was limping and had one arm in a sling, said he felt quite well. But it was being reported that his doctors in Munich were doubtful about the prospects of him ever being able to play again.

It was now more than six weeks since the crash and by this time concerts and fund-raising events were being held throughout Manchester to raise money for the Lord Mayor's Disaster Fund. These efforts gave many fans the chance to do something in aid of the bereaved families. Among them were Beryl Townsend and her sister Olga.

> We set about trying to organize funds, and everywhere we went people were still just so stunned all they could think of was, what can we do for them? They had these special evenings and we all went to loads of them in pubs and clubs here, there and everywhere. But there was something that didn't feel right about them. Somehow it felt as if it was wrong that somebody was entertaining you at these concerts, singing and playing music. It felt a bit awkward that you were going out enjoying yourself. But it was all to raise funds, and everybody gave something. I remember particularly that the City fans were great. They all came along and contributed. One night we

met Eddie Colman's mum and dad at one of them. It was the night that Mike Todd, the Hollywood film producer, was killed in a plane crash, which seemed strange because we were there because of the Babes who'd just been killed in a plane crash. That was the night when somebody sang 'You flew away, and my heart went with you'. We were all weeping buckets by then.

For the fans in that last week of March there was the problem of trying to get to a semi-final replay in London on a Wednesday afternoon. For the majority there was no chance. The journey to the capital took a long time, and it was expensive. To get to the match would mean having to take two days off work and not many people could afford to lose two days' wages. For me there wasn't a chance. We couldn't afford to go, and even if we could have spared the cash there was no way my mam and dad would have let me have two days off school for a football match, however important it might be. Supporters were angry with the FA about the choice of venue, which was virtually a home match for Fulham. Nobody was doing United or their fans any favours now. When they protested they gained an unlikely ally in Bob Lord, of all people, who made a public stance in support of United. He was still public enemy number one as far as United fans were concerned, but he said,

> My sympathy is with United on this issue. That is sincere. It looks very odd to me that this replay should be at Highbury. There may be extenuating circumstances, but it seems a bit cock-eyed. It certainly isn't fair. It's on the cards

> in my opinion that all semi-finals will be played in London one day. Look what they're doing with internationals. England now play Wales at Wembley. They take Ireland there too instead of to the provinces. It's a fact that if Ireland went to Liverpool or Everton there'd be full houses, which they don't get at Wembley. Soccer started in the North and, in my view, that's where it should finish.

There was one thing you could say about Bob Lord: he was never afraid of coming out and speaking his mind.

But the decision had been made. The replay was going to be at Highbury whether United fans could be there or not. And then television came to the rescue. Apart from the FA Cup Final itself this was long before the days of live matches on the television, but this one was different, and the BBC agreed with the FA to cover it. It was a decision that led to an enormous row. Cardiff City had a league match to play that same afternoon and their manager, Trevor Morris, protested strongly to the Football League:

> The [Football] League is supposed to protect the interests of their member clubs, yet they allowed this match to be put on on an afternoon when we have a league game against Bristol Rovers. It is going to cost us at least a 50 per cent cut in our gate and I take an extremely poor view of the matter. And the Rovers are with me. I appreciate that quite a lot of people in Manchester and in other parts of the country will like to watch the Cup replay and some may regard me as a spoilsport. Quite obviously many people would

like to see a football match on the television every Saturday afternoon. If the Football League allowed that they would very soon be in trouble.

In spite of the difficulties, several thousand diehards took the time off work to go to the match. Two special trains with a capacity of one thousand were put on, leaving London Road Station for Euston at 6.40 a.m. and 7.32 a.m., though many were angry with British Railways who had bumped up the usual London excursion fare from 30s (£1.50) to 38s 3d (£1.91). And getting to London would give no guarantee of getting into the match, because once they got to Highbury United supporters would find themselves at the back of long queues because it was only tickets for seats that could be booked in advance. Those who planned to drive down would have to set off even earlier than the trains: before the days of motorways, driving to London was a major expedition. The AA's recommended route for motorists from Manchester to Highbury involved going on the A34 to Stone in Staffordshire, then taking the A51 to Lichfield before switching to the A5 through Towcester, Dunstable and St Albans, and on through Mill Hill and Highgate. Anybody making the trip could expect the journey to take five or six hours.

On the morning of the match queues began to form outside Highbury at dawn; a crowd of nearly seventy thousand was expected. It was set to be a finely balanced tussle, one that seemingly everybody wanted to see, but when it came to it the actual attendance was only thirty-eight thousand. Outside the ground ticket touts fared badly, and tickets were sold at face value or less. Many reasons were given for the unexpectedly low turn-out. Television was blamed by many, but was it really the widespread-queuing-from-dawn stories that had kept so many people away?

The problem for those who remained in Manchester was that even though it was on television, it was an afternoon match, so how were you going to get to see it? Some were lucky. The boys of Stretford Grammar School, for instance, were given half a day off. As morning lessons finished they hurried out, cheering the headmaster, who said that he had been saving up a half-day holiday which had been granted at the school's speech day, and when he received a request from the boys for time off so that they could watch the semi-final on television, this had seemed a good time to take it. Bobby Charlton would have approved of the headmaster's decision: he had attended the school for a short time when he first moved down from Ashington to join United. But there was no such let-off for me. English and French I think it was that afternoon. It was purgatory. The game kicked off, and there we were doing French verbs. What made it worse was that we had finally got a television, so I could have been sitting at home watching the Reds in our own front room.

As soon as the bell went for the end of that afternoon's lessons it was a race to get down the stairs and out of school as quickly as possible. I'd never run faster than I did that afternoon across Alexandra Park, past the lake and out on to Princess Road. A quick sprint to the 101 bus stop at Great Western Street and, what good luck, the bus came before I'd had time to get my breath back. The good thing about the 101 was that it was a limited stop—only two stops along the whole of Princess Road before it got on to the estate—and that afternoon it was particularly quick. In twenty minutes I was home, just in time for the half-time summary for latecomers like me. And the news was good: the Reds were winning 3–2. The first half had been an open, end-to-end affair, and it seemed we'd been helped by a few howlers by Fulham keeper Tony Macedo, who had played a real blinder on Saturday. United had kicked off, but the first threat had come from Second Division Fulham. A long ball down the middle brought Gregg off his line quickly, and his clearance put United on the attack through Bobby Charlton. This led to a spell of pressure from United, Macedo having to make saves from Freddie Goodwin and Charlton. United, the half-time reporter said, played clever football that had the Fulham defence distinctly rocking, and their reward came after fourteen minutes when they took the lead through Alex Dawson, who flung himself headlong and low to head past Macedo from a Shay Brennan corner. Fulham equalized, only for United to go back in front with another goal from Dawson, but within three minutes Fulham had brought the scores level again. Then, just on the stroke of half-time, Wythenshawe's Shay Brennan had snatched a third for United.

I settled down for the second half. This was great—watching United play a semi-final in London on television in our own front room. It was such a novelty to be able to watch a live football match in your own home. The black and white pictures were a bit snowy and indistinct but it didn't matter, especially when Dawson completed his hat-trick to give United a 4–2 lead early in the second half. But Fulham weren't finished. They came back at United and made it 4–3 with just over a quarter of an hour to go, but so what? This was like the days before the crash when United seemed invincible. It didn't matter how many the opposition scored, we'd always get more, and so it was in this semi-final: Bobby Charlton made it 5–3 in injury time.

Just the sort of game the Babes would have played. The spirit lived on in the reborn team. This was vintage stuff, and Matt Busby would have loved it. In the papers the next day, along with the match report came the news that he was off the danger list. People were beginning to smile again, and with the arrival of spring, the gloom that had hung over Manchester since those dark, cold days of February was beginning to lift. Although they'd slipped down the league, United were in the FA Cup Final and in the semi-final of the European Cup. It was unbelievable. If anybody had said they'd achieve that in the days immediately after the crash no one would have believed them. And the great thing was, they deserved to be there. They'd got to Wembley on merit, playing fine, skilful attacking football, and they seemed to be going from strength to strength. That semi-final replay was their best game since Munich; they stroked the ball from man to man with the style and confidence of the United of old. For the first time the new team spiced their fighting spirit with a dash of the Busby style.

After the semi-final replay United's fixtures really started to pile up. There was a visit to Sheffield Wednesday on Saturday, 29 March, and the rearranged match they had been scheduled to play against Aston Villa on the day of the replay had had to be rearranged again, for the following Monday, 31 March. The Friday of that week was Good Friday, when they were due to play Sunderland at home; on the Saturday they faced Preston at Old Trafford, with a trip to Sunderland to follow on Easter Monday. It meant a hectic spell of five matches in ten days. For Bobby Charlton it was even more. He was still in the Army and had matches to play for them, so his replay appearance at Highbury was the first of three games in four days for him. After that he had to return to his unit near Shrewsbury to play in the final of the Mid-West District Cup at Oswestry, and then he was on duty again for United. It all amounted to seven matches in thirteen days.

There was going to be plenty of football to look forward to over the next few weeks, and at school all the United fans were confident that they were ready to hit a winning run in the league. If they could do it in the Cup, why not in the league? That Friday we were due to break up for our Easter holidays—two weeks off, and in that time United had six First Division matches to play, two at home and four away. By the time we got back after the Easter holidays the Reds, I was sure, would have climbed back up the league again, back to the only place that seemed right for them.

On the last morning at school before the holiday there was the usual end-of-term ordeal of getting your exam results. Everybody in the school packed into the hall, the eleven-year-old Upper Thirds sitting in the first rows right up there in front of the stage, the eighteen-year-old prefects from the Upper Sixth at the back. At exactly half past nine, the rector, Monsignor Duggan—or Tommy as all the lads used to call him, behind his back—came sweeping into the hall in his purple-trimmed cassock and cummerbund, leading a procession of all the masters up the aisle in the middle of the hall and on to the stage. In they came, mortar boards on their heads, gowns with brightly coloured silk trimmings flowing behind them, up the steps at the side of the stage to take their places in a semi-circle facing the assembled school. The organ swelled to the opening notes of the school hymn, and everybody joined in.

In cloistered schools your boys you taught
How England first became
A Catholic land whose people sought
For more than earthly fame.
Teach us today our faith to prize,
Christ's voice alone to heed;
Towards hill eternal raise our eyes,
Let us imitate you, St Bede.

I wanted the hymn to go on for ever because I wasn't looking forward to the next bit—the announcement of the exam results. And our class was going to be first. At the end of the hymn Father Burke, the assistant rector, stood up. 'Upper Third A,' he said, and our class stood up with the eyes of the rest of the school and all the masters on the stage on us. Our form teacher, Father O'Connor—or Kev as he was known—came to the front of the stage with his big black register and started to read the results from it. First, with 87.6 per cent, was Michael Maher. Everybody clapped, and Maher had to walk out of his seat, up the middle aisle towards the stage, across the front of it, then all the way round to the back of the hall and back up the middle aisle to get back to his seat. All eyes were on him as he walked round. It was all right for him: he was one of the boarders at the school, which was the junior seminary for the Salford diocese, and he came from Blackburn so he hadn't been as occupied with Munich and United's matches just after the crash, when we had been doing our exams. While he was still on his way round, Kev O'Connor announced who was second. John Hendy, another of the boarders, from Burnley, began his long walk round.

By the time Kev got to twentieth place I was still standing there, our class group getting noticeably thinner with only ten of us left standing. This was torture. It was inhuman, treating people like this, but this was the ritual we had to face three times every year. It's the way it was in a Catholic grammar school. They could be cruel places. The pressure was enormous: all eyes in the hall on the remaining students, everybody wondering who was going to be last man standing, bottom of the class. Oh, the humiliation of it; please don't let it be me.

Then, relief: 'Twenty-first, with 53.7 per cent, David Hall.' There was no applause. Only those who came first and second in the class got clapped; for the rest it was just the long, lonely walk round. By the time I got back to my place there were only six left standing. The rest of the class looked pityingly at them as they shifted uncomfortably on their feet. Soon it was down to three; then just one. One eleven-year-old boy, singled out for all the school to look at, bottom of the class. It was Danny Connor, little ginger-haired Danny Connor from Stockport, the best footballer in the Upper Third by a mile. Nobody deserved this, let alone Danny.

For the next hour and a half this cruel ritual went on for every form in the school except the sixth form. The lower down the class you were, the longer you were left standing, with everybody's eyes on you, and the longer the walk round the hall seemed. After the results there was about an hour left before school finished for the holidays, at twelve o'clock. This last hour was the most relaxed of the term. We went back to our form rooms for a chat with our form teachers. Kev O'Connor was OK, one of the pleasanter teachers at the school, not one of the hard men who tried to terrorize you. We talked about United and about the way they had risen from the ashes to reach the FA Cup Final. It was a very Catholic theme, particularly appropriate for the Easter feast that was coming up. But more than anything it was hard to believe. Father O'Connor said that if anyone had written a story about a football team coming back from a disaster like Munich in the way United had done nobody would have believed it would be possible. No schoolboy comic story of sporting victory against all the odds would ever be able to approach this one.

* * *

United may have been back, but Matt Busby wasn't. It was reported that the Munich surgeons were doubtful whether he would be able to see the Cup Final. We scanned the Manchester papers anxiously every day for news, and it still wasn't good. Jimmy Murphy was doing a fantastic job, but United wouldn't be the same again without Matt Busby. Our worst fears were confirmed when the *Evening News* carried an interview with Mr Tom Appleby, manager of Manchester Opera House, who was one of Matt's closest friends. He had just returned from a visit to Munich during which he'd had long bedside talks with Matt and spoken to his doctors at length. Busby, it was reported, was nearing the final stages of the grimmest fight for life Germany's leading surgeons had ever seen. His hair had turned white and his brow, now deeply lined, bore unmistakable evidence of the extreme pain he had suffered, and was still suffering. A long convalescence lay ahead.

Appleby said that as he lay in his jacked-up bed in the Rechts der Isar Hospital, Matt's thoughts were not on football, but for the relatives of those who had died in the disaster. Appleby was also concerned at reports suggesting that Matt was experiencing an easy recovery and that he would soon be out and about again, just like his old self.

> It's all wrong. People should realize what a tough time he's had, and is still having. The bulletins tell of progress, but necessarily they are just cold facts. They hide the mental torment and physical pain he is undergoing. He is still very sick. Both his legs are broken and in plaster. The left leg is broken in many places. Certain surgical work has had to be done without anaesthetics both on the lung and, when it was necessary, to reset a leg after removing the plaster casing. The German professor who has superintended everything in such a marvellous manner said that the pain that Matt has suffered must have been very severe, and he'd never experienced a man suffer so grimly and unflinchingly.
>
> At first Mr Busby showed no interest in anything. Once he whispered to me, 'At times I feel broken in spirit as well as in body.' That is why only the closest friends and relatives have been allowed to see him for such a long time. It's been necessary to give him time to fight his own personal battle. Now he's mostly interested

> just in the welfare of those left behind to sorrow. All the time he's worrying about the relatives and wondering what he might do for them. His whole thought is that when he gets well enough he must go round to see all those who were bereaved and make sure they are all right. He's really a very wonderful man, and that's one reason why it is so vitally necessary everyone should know of his great fight.

It was clear from reports like this that along with his physical injuries, Busby was struggling with mental difficulties too. In spite of United's resurrection and their heroic achievement in reaching the Cup Final, Manchester was still a sombre place—no place for a man in such a depressed state. So United sent Matt and his wife Jean to Interlaken, in Switzerland, for an extended period of convalescence. It was only in their last days there a few weeks later that Jean said to him one evening, 'You know, Matt, the lads would have wanted you to carry on.' With that, the melancholic spell was broken. Busby knew that he had to go back, though he said later, 'It was dreadful, facing up to going back.'

United were going on; life was going on. Other things had taken over in the news—Winston Churchill had pneumonia; the Labour Party denounced the South African Government for setting up a white dictatorship in the country; the United States had a third satellite in orbit—but I was still anxiously scanning the *Manchester Evening News* every night for any bit of information I could get. Slowly, things were getting back to normal.

Then death came to our own family. On that Friday, the day school broke up for the Easter holidays, just after we'd finished our tea, Mr O'Malley from next door but one came to say there was a phone call for my mam. He was the only person near us who had a phone, and he'd said we could give people his number if anybody needed to contact us in an emergency, so we knew something must be wrong. When my mam came back she was in tears. 'Mam's dead,' she said to my dad. 'I'll have to get down there.' Then she turned to me and Joan and said, 'Your gran died this afternoon. I'm going to have to go to her house to sort things out. You stay here with your dad.'

That night I lay in bed and thought about Gran Kearney as I looked at the United picture on my bedroom wall. Seven out of the eleven players on that team photo were dead, as well as one who was a reserve, and now my gran had gone to join them. I was missing them, but I was going to miss my gran even more. No more singing 'Danny Boy'; no more sixpences; no more Kendal mints. I thought about what she'd told me on the Saturday just after the crash, about how she'd be joining them soon, and I wondered if she'd seen them play yet, up there in heaven. That night, in my dreams, she did—and Billy Whelan was captain, just like she said.

On the Saturday morning my mam was still at my gran's, making arrangements for the funeral. She didn't want us to go down to her house on Grey Mare Lane because she didn't want us to see her lying there dead. We were too young, and it would have been too upsetting for us to see the dead body of somebody so close to us. I'd lived with death and reports of death for nearly two months. So much had been said and written over that time about United's tragedy being like a death in the family, but now for me this really was family. It hurt, and there were tears, because I was close to my gran and would miss her. But, young as I was, I was aware that her death wasn't tragic in quite the same way that the deaths at Munich had been. It hadn't come out of the blue as it had for those young men who had the world at their feet. My gran was old; she'd had a full life and she and her family were prepared for death. It wasn't nice when it happened, but there was none of that sense of waste that came the day the team died at Munich.

There was no match to go to that afternoon as United were playing away, at Sheffield Wednesday. Even if they had been at home we wouldn't have gone to the match. It wouldn't have seemed right. It felt a bit like the Saturday just after the crash all over again, when so many people were saying it wasn't right to play football that afternoon. But just as football went on that day, life had to go on for us. We tried to keep to some sort of normal routine. I collected the church football pools bags and walked down to Todd's the bakers to get the bread and the meat and potato pies for our dinner. Life had to go on, just as United had to go on after the crash. In a strange way, all that seemed to have prepared me a little bit for this, especially the thought that my gran had put into my head that death wasn't the end; that she may even have been up there watching the old United. After all, it was Saturday.

It might have seemed disrespectful to go to a match that afternoon, but playing was different. St Peter's altar boys had a football team. We didn't play every week and we weren't in a league or anything like that, we just used to play friendlies against the altar boys from other churches in Wythenshawe, so most of our matches seemed to be against St Anthony's from Woodhouse Park or St John's from Benchill. I say 'we', but to be honest I didn't get that many games, or at least my name wasn't often one of the eleven on the teamsheet that was pinned up in the sacristy; it was usually on there as reserve. They knew I was keen and dependable. I'd always turn up in the hope of getting a game if one of the first-choice players forgot about the match or didn't turn up because he had to go to Northenden with his mam to get a new pair of shoes. This meant that I did finish up getting quite a lot of games.

I remember my dad being at one of them, and he very quickly identified the basic problem I had with my game. When we were walking home, he said to me, 'Why are you always running away from the ball? Why is it that you're always miles away from the play?'

'Oh, but I'm not,' I replied. 'I'm always running

into space. I'm always running into dangerous positions where I can set something up—a bit like Ernie Taylor, you know.'

'But it's no use being in space if you never get the ball,' my dad said.

I thought about that for a bit. There must be something in it. But I said, 'That's probably because the rest of them just haven't got the vision that I've got.' I knew that wasn't true, though. We had some good players in that team. Most of them were a bit older than me and nearly all of them played for their school teams. They certainly knew how to pass the ball, but when I was playing I think they probably looked up, saw who it was and thought, 'Oh no, better not give it to 'Orlicks, never know what he's going to do with it.'

Anyway, this particular Saturday afternoon I did get a game. I think it was Pete McLoughlin who hadn't turned up, so I played at inside-right, and I think it must have been one of the high spots of my career because not only did we win, but I got two of our goals. Admittedly they were both tap-ins. I was standing on the goal-line when the ball landed at my feet in the mud and all I had to do for both of them was stick my foot out. It was easier to put them in the net than it would have been to clear them, but two goals were two goals, and as any good striker would claim, it was all about anticipation and good positioning—being in the right place at the right time. That afternoon I was Bobby Charlton, although on reflection I don't remember him getting many goals like that; his were more likely to be thirty-yard thunderbolts. Maybe they were more like Dennis Viollet's poacher's goals.

At the end of the match there was always the same

routine. We played on the school pitch on the field at the back of St Peter's Primary School. Leo Fewtrell's dad, Bert, was the school caretaker, and he always came over to open up the store room at the back of the school hall. There, among the bottles of pop and the bags of sherbet dip and penny chews and Black Jacks from the school tuck shop, we'd get changed. Bert was always in a hurry to get locked up so he'd always come out with the same line: 'Come on, lads, hurry up. United are on the telly.' We knew they weren't—football was very rarely on the television then—but we always wanted to believe it, so we always fell for it. It certainly made me get a move on.

I ran home down Whitburn Road to get back in time for *Sports Report*. All the way back I was thinking about United's match at Hillsborough that afternoon, and there were big question marks over it. United might have reached the Cup Final, but it was the end of March now and they hadn't won a league game since the crash. Surely all this was going to change today? United were going to win this one. It was only three days after the great win over Fulham in the semi-final and the new Reds were riding on a high. They'd swept Wednesday aside in the Cup, and now the Sheffield side were struggling near the bottom of the league. It was a game everybody thought United would win; it was going to be the turning point for them in the league.

I was anxious to get back for the result, but there was a distraction. A stream ran across the fields by the side of Whitburn Road through a little valley, a sort of canyon with steep muddy banks and trees on either side of it. John Shufflebottom, his brother Tom and a few of their mates had slung a rope over one of the branches that went across the valley and they'd made a swing. They called me over and asked me if I wanted to have a go. Normally I'd have said yes; it was a great feeling swinging out into the void high above the stream, doing a big loop and then landing back on the bank—all very exciting, and not to be missed. But on this occasion I hurried on home, and it was a good job I did because as I walked into our house the instantly recognizable *Sports Report* signature tune that is still with us today was playing.

I settled down on the floor in front of the radiogram, but the news that was coming in from Hillsborough wasn't good. We might have won our altar boys' game that afternoon, but the same couldn't be said for United. It was a miserable 1–0 defeat. Yet again they hadn't been able to raise their game and produce anything like their Cup form. It was the same in the rearranged game against Aston Villa at Villa Park on the Monday afternoon. Like Wednesday, Villa were down in the relegation zone and United should have been able to beat them, even without Ernie Taylor who was still injured, but it wasn't to be. It did look as though they were going to pick up a point when with a minute to go they were drawing 2–2, but Villa grabbed a late winner.

Information on mid-week matches like this was scarce at the time, and I didn't find out the score until I looked at the *Manchester Guardian* the next day. The report said that 'Manchester's play was immaculate but it lacked the extra determination, the extra foot of speed and the quicker, surer tackling that determines a game of lasting value from a mere collection of impressions that will disappear with time. But one performance,' the paper's special correspondent continued, 'that will be remembered by the 18,000 spectators was the display of Charlton, the United inside-left. Charlton carried the burden of the attack and his execution of a body swerve, change of pace and direction and tenacity when given half a chance, has not been bettered at Villa Park this season.' In his report in the *Evening News* that night David Meek thought that United had deserved a point. 'Again we saw a balanced attack playing neat football all the way to the penalty box, but then lacking the know-how to burst through and score. Occasionally they clicked, and when it did it brought a goal.' Mark Pearson, it was good to hear, had restrained himself admirably under some provocation and played well. United still hadn't won a league match, but Meek, just like every Red I knew, was confident that the Easter weekend would break the sequence.

Before Easter, though, we'd got the sad business of going to my gran's funeral. After a Requiem Mass at St Brigid's she was buried with her husband—the grandfather I'd never met—at Moston Cemetery. I'd never been to a funeral at Moston, but its reputation went before it. My mam always said it was the bleakest place in Manchester, and it certainly was that day. It was the first day of April, but the arctic conditions we'd experienced for so much of that winter had returned. Although the cemetery was only a few miles from town it really was a desolate spot, very open and exposed, and a biting wind howled across it, chilling me and everybody there to the bone. Figures all in black, or the darkest overcoats they had, huddled together as much as they could to keep out the cold and the sleet that started to whip into our faces.

Standing by a graveside as the priest read the interment prayers wasn't a new experience for me. I'd never been to a family funeral or a funeral at

Moston before, but as an altar boy I'd been to plenty at Southern Cemetery, which was the one near us. In fact I used to look forward to funerals, or at least to any on a Saturday morning or during the school holidays. If we were able to, the altar boys would always go with the priest to the cemetery, and after the burial somebody from the family would always give us five bob (25p) to share between us. At a time when it only cost 9d (less than 4p) to get in the boys' entrance at Old Trafford, that was a lot of money. I was used to seeing coffins being lowered into the earth, the priest sprinkling holy water on to them and the tears of the families as they tossed handfuls of earth into the void. But this time it was my family; the tears were those of my mam and my aunties and my cousins, and the coffin that was being lowered into the big hole was my gran. All those deaths in such a short time. Now my gran had gone to join Roger Byrne and Tommy Taylor and all the rest of them, but it was still hard to come to terms with the fact that I'd never see any of them again.

After the funeral everybody went back to my gran's house on Grey Mare Lane where there were pork pies, sausage rolls and luncheon-meat sandwiches set out in the back room. My mam put the kettle on the gas stove in the scullery at the back, but most of the men got themselves a bottle of Wilson's bitter from the crate under the table. The women stood in little groups, and the talk was all of births, marriages, deaths and illnesses. 'Do you remember Rose Healy?' Yes. 'Well, you know her mother died last week? Lovely woman she was. Always used to do the flowers at St Anne's.' And, 'Did you know May Lee was in hospital? She's in Ancoats. Rushed in to have her appendix out.' Then it all got a bit more light-hearted and there was a bit of chat about fashion, about the two inches that had changed that world—two inches slashed from the hem of a girl's skirt at the Paris dress shows; two inches more leg; two inches that had captured the headlines during the last week. 'Nice legs,' one of my aunties said. 'They're going to be putting the bosomy brigade in the shade.'

Among the men, though, the talk focused on football. Some distant relations I'd not met before were over from Ireland for the funeral. They talked about Billy Whelan and what a sad loss he was to the Irish team. He'd been a real favourite in Ireland and they couldn't understand how he'd lost his place in the United team just before the crash. They soon got on to asking about the new team that seemed to be doing so well. They'd not seen the new Red Devils in action, not even on television, and they wanted to know how these young Babes, fresh up from the reserves and the youth team, compared to the great pre-crash team and were they, as one of the papers in Ireland had said, still one of the top four sides in England? How was it that a team with only five players in it that had any experience of playing in the First Division could have got the results they had in the Cup?

My dad and my Uncle Tommy both said that this side didn't compare in any way with the team that had been wiped out at Munich, or with the 1948 team they had watched week in and week out, except in terms of the results they'd got in the Cup. This was a completely new team, they said, with a very different style, and it all revolved around the genius of Ernie Taylor. But what you had to remember was that a lot of the pre-Munich reserves who'd been brought in were so good that they would have walked into most other First Division teams. Still, apart from Ernie and the survivors of the crash who were back playing, this team was nowhere near as good as the Babes individually; they weren't in the same league; they were being carried along by the emotion of the crowd and had a fanatical will to win. 'Ah,' our Irish relatives said, 'so that explains all that trouble at Burnley. We've already seen some reports that this team Jimmy Murphy has got together are a bit of a dirty lot.' No, they weren't dirty, my dad said. They were tough and they were fit, but above all they were playing their hearts out for Jimmy and for Matt and for all those great players whose boots they had stepped into. This may have led to some over-enthusiasm on the part of some of the younger members of the side, but that couldn't be labelled dirty play. As for being one of the top four teams in the country, my dad wasn't sure. They were doing well in the Cup, but going nowhere in the league. We'd have to wait until next season to see if they were still up there with the best.

By the time of my gran's funeral nearly a week had passed since the semi-final replay and controversy was still raging over the decision to televise the game. Football was very wary of television. If people could watch a top game from the comfort of their own armchair, why would they fork out good money to stand on the terraces to watch? Joe Richards, the president of the Football League, blasted television when he said, 'It is a menace to soccer. I hope we never see again what happened last Wednesday when Fulham played Manchester United in the Cup semi-final replay and Bristol Rovers visited Cardiff City in the league. Attendances at both games were definitely affected because the Highbury match was televised. We all like to see soccer on television, and while in some ways it does the game good, clubs can only live by what they receive at the turnstiles. The four home authorities are determined to do something to control television for the benefit of the game in general.' I couldn't see what all the problem was about. Showing the game on television had seemed the fairest thing to do after the FA had given United fans such a rough deal by choosing a London ground for it. For 99 per cent of United fans, watching it on the screen was the only possible way of seeing it.

Just before the Easter programme there was a big boost for United's Cup Final hopes when Dennis Viollet started training again. Dennis was a great goal-scorer, one of the most prolific in United's history, and goals were what was lacking, especially in the league. A fit Dennis Viollet back from Munich to play alongside Ernie Taylor and Bobby Charlton would make a massive difference. The doctors had given him the all-clear to go ahead and train as hard as he liked, and it was expected that he would be fit for Wembley on 3 May. The big talk when we went down to the fields to play football that week was about where he was going to play. There wasn't an easy answer to that. If he could recover his pre-Munich form Jimmy Murphy would have to find a place for him, but Charlton was now playing brilliantly in Viollet's inside-left position and Taylor had to be the first choice for inside-right. Charlton, a few people suggested, could play on the left wing to make way for Viollet, or even at centre-forward. What was absolutely certain, we all felt, was that there had to be a place for all three of them in the attack.

All of a sudden the big problem Murphy was faced with was not finding a team but deciding who to leave out. Tom Heron, a recent signing from the Irish club Portadown, had just had a good game for the reserves; Kenny Morgans was back in training and recovering his old form; Wilf McGuinness was also back in training, much quicker than expected after his cartilage operation; and two more of the Munich survivors, left-winger Albert Scanlon and goalkeeper Ray Wood, were lapping the pitch and kicking a ball around. This strengthening of the squad would help to see the club through the crowded fixture programme that lay ahead. Viollet's return in particular would save the day if, as was beginning to look increasingly likely, Bobby Charlton was capped for England. England had two World Cup warm-up games scheduled for the dates which United were still hoping AC Milan would agree to for the two legs of the European Cup semi-final.

By Good Friday, winter was back with a vengeance. Roads in the North-West were almost deserted and holiday resorts, which had prepared for a bumper Easter, reported the worst bank holiday business for years. In Manchester it was the coldest Easter for nearly twenty years, and along the east of Britain snowstorms raged from Dundee to Dover. In London a popular peace movement was born when thousands of people gathered in Trafalgar Square to protest against Britain's first H-bomb tests, carried out at Christmas Island in the Pacific Ocean. The Campaign for Nuclear Disarmament had been launched with a massive public meeting in London in February; they'd organized a four-day Easter march to a then unknown place in Berkshire—Aldermaston—where, they had discovered, a secret atomic weapons plant was being built. The march started with the Good Friday rally in Trafalgar Square, and around ten thousand protesters turned out. People from all walks of life waved banners, pushed children in prams and sang peace songs from sheets handed out by the organizers. Hiroshima was the reason so many were there: in a world with the weapons of mass destruction that had brought the Second World War to an end there must never be another war. The speeches in Trafalgar Square emphasized this theme and advocated unilateral nuclear disarmament—the proposal that Britain should take the initiative and get rid of its own nuclear weapons because the alternative, multilateral disarmament—by negotiation between countries—was clearly not working.

As the marchers set out on their pilgrimage a full league football programme was being played throughout Britain. United were at home to Sunderland, and they managed to salvage their first point in the league since the draw with Nottingham Forest on 22 February, but it wasn't a very distinguished performance. Like Wednesday and Villa, Sunderland were struggling at the bottom of the table, but it looked as though they were going to win the game until Dawson side-stepped two opponents and scored with a fine drive to give United a last-minute equalizer. By this time, though, hundreds of disillusioned Reds were halfway down Chester Road, having seen enough. The second half was particularly bad, United going behind and showing no real sense of urgency to get back into the game. Maybe they had got the Cup Final on their minds, or was it just that they were young and they were having to play far too many games? United had now slipped to eighth in the league and they were playing like the relegation candidates they'd only managed to take one point off in the last three games.

On Easter Saturday they were up against it, with Preston at home. Eighteen-year-old Ken Morgans was back for his first match after the crash, but after the dismal run of results it didn't look as though United would have much chance. Preston were second, and playing well. But when the results came through on *Sports Report*, there was a surprise: United had managed to hold them to a goalless draw.

I didn't get to either of those games. On Good Friday I couldn't, because as an altar boy I had to be at church for the long-drawn-out service which started at three o'clock. It was the longest of the year, and church was always packed for it. It was also one of the most dramatic—all about death. This year it was all very much in keeping with the still sombre mood of the time. Easter Saturday, however, was different. We could have gone to the Preston match, and I thought we would, but my dad said he didn't want to go and my mam said I was too young to go on my own. With my dad, it increasingly seemed as though he just couldn't bear to go and see his beloved United playing such pedestrian football. Preston were a good team, but if it hadn't been for the crash United would almost certainly have been above them, well on their way to a third league title in a row. Now it looked as though it might be years before they were at the top again.

I knew how my dad felt, and how a lot of other supporters, especially of his age, felt. There was an empty feeling about football; a tremendous sense of loss. I felt it as well. I couldn't get over this sense of having been cheated. We shouldn't have been losing all these matches; we would have been top of the league again by now. Instead we were sliding further and further down, and it was difficult to accept. I'd probably been spoiled. The first football team I'd been taken to see have been acknowledged far and wide as one of the greatest teams ever. The first matches I saw are still spoken of as some of the best ever. Who, for instance, from that vast crowd that packed Maine Road on 6 February 1957 for the Bilbao game could ever forget the drama and excitement of that night? It was matches like this that I kept thinking about that Easter. United might have reached the Cup Final, but were we ever going to be thrilled like that again? There was something in what people were saying about the new Reds being rougher and cruder than the old team. Beryl Townsend can recall her shock at the signing of Stan Crowther just before the Sheffield Wednesday Cup tie. 'We had a problem with that first game when Stan Crowther came,' she said, 'because he was such a dirty player and we weren't used to dirty players at Old Trafford.'

But all this didn't really matter to me. It was still United, and I still wanted to go to every game, so I wasn't happy that we were missing two home games on consecutive days. I knew Good Friday was out because going to church had to come first, but I really thought we would have been going to the Preston game on the Saturday. Instead we had to go to the CWS stores on Downing Street near London Road Station to get new shoes for me and our Joan with my mam's divi cheques (the dividend the Co-op used to pay its customers). Going down to town on the bus that afternoon it was cold, wet and smoggy—not the sort of thick smog we'd had recently, just a sort of browny-grey mist that made buildings more than fifty yards away indistinct shadows. We used to have so much rain and smog in those days but somehow the cold, wet, greyness that hung over Manchester for much of the time in the weeks after Munich seemed appropriate to the mood of the city. I can still picture what it was like sitting upstairs on that double-decker bus in the warmth looking through a blue haze of cigarette smoke down at the shop lights shining on the cold, wet pavements and the cobblestone streets. There always seemed to be lots of condensation running down shop windows, and down the windows of other buses as they passed by in the gloom. Lowryesque figures battled against the elements, an amazing number of them carrying umbrellas. Most of the men wore flat caps, trilbys or bowler hats. Some of the smarter women wore hats, but most had their heads covered in a scarf or a hair net which concealed curlers or clips. Older women had woollen shawls over their heads and wrapped around their shoulders to protect themselves from the rain.

The only day that was different was Sunday and the next day, when we went to see my Gran Hall in Beswick and nearly everybody was in their best clothes for Easter Sunday. A lot of the kids round there, though, seemed to be doing their best to ruin them as they played out in the surrounding streets and on the crofts. When we got to my gran's my Uncle Jack was there. He was my dad's elder brother, and like my dad he'd always been a United supporter, although since the war he'd not been to anything like as many matches as my dad. We sat round the big scrubbed table in the scullery in front of the black leaded open-range fire and they conducted their analysis of the problems with the team. The coal glowed in the grate, and my gran cut a slice of white bread for me and gave me the toasting fork so that I could make myself some toast while my dad and my Uncle Jack talked. It was the way we always did toast. You'd stick the fork into the top edge of a thick slice of bread and hold it in front of the embers of a coal fire. We didn't have butter; we used margarine, and, if you were lucky, some jam. At my Gran Hall's we always put Tate and Lyle's golden syrup on our toast.

As my gran got the syrup out for me, my Uncle Jack was making the point that I'd read in the papers and heard so many times before. The biggest problem for United, he said, was the fact that they'd taken so many reserves to Belgrade. Why, when they could only play eleven men, had they taken seventeen? It was now two months after the crash and six of the first choice eleven at the time of the Belgrade match and four of its leading reserves could not be considered in any reckoning of the club's current playing strength. No team could withstand losses like that.

Then he and my dad went through the present team, player by player. In goal we couldn't do any better: Harry Gregg was the best keeper around, and Ray Wood was a very able deputy. At full-back things weren't too bad either. Before the crash Bill Foulkes, and occasionally Ian Greaves, was the steady, pedestrian part of the partnership with the much more constructive Roger Byrne, who was often able to start an attack going. Now, with Foulkes and Greaves in partnership at the back, a lot of the creativity that had come from Byrne's play was missing; but they were still a good pair of full-backs, as good as any in the First Division. Of the reserves who'd been brought in, centre-half Ronnie Cope had been the biggest success, especially when you considered that he had been third choice after Mark Jones and Jackie Blanchflower. At right-half, Freddie Goodwin couldn't really be regarded as a stopgap player and he'd been showing the sort of class that at one time had kept Eddie Colman out of the team. But how do you replace Duncan Edwards? Stan Crowther had been a good signing who had brought much-needed experience to the young team. Defensively he'd been very good, but he didn't have Edwards's ability to complement his defensive duties with forward surges. Overall, though, they agreed that the defence wasn't too bad. It was the attack that was the problem.

Ernie Taylor had been an inspired buy. My dad said Ernie would have been able to hold his own in the 1948 team, or in the Babes team that had been wiped out. And Bobby Charlton was showing that he had the makings of a world-class forward. The trouble was he was still young, and he was having to play too many matches. Why did he have to play games for the Army when he had so many to play for United? But Charlton and Taylor were the only two class forwards we'd got. Colin Webster was at best a hard-working trier, and Alex Dawson was too young; he'd been brought in much too early. He'd got the makings of a good centre-forward, but he could have done with another few seasons in the reserves. He just wasn't ready for the first team, and his career had probably taken a step back as a result of being played. The same was definitely true of Mark Pearson. Many Reds who'd been to all the reserve and youth team games before Munich also believed that promising young careers were harmed by the fact that they had to be thrust into the first team before they were ready. 'Alex Dawson and Mark Pearson's future was ruined by Munich,' Norman Williams said. 'They were both brought on too early and both of them suffered because of it. Alex Dawson looked a great centre-forward. I'd seen him in the youth team; scored five goals in one match. Brilliant! And we always called him the Black Prince, because he was such a magnificent figure, a great player, or at least he would have been. And Mark Pearson too looked like a top footballer in the making, yet both never lived up to their early promise. Both were pitched in too early.'

* * *

Three days after playing Sunderland at Old Trafford United had to travel up to Roker Park to play them again. Three games in four days. Stan Crowther was rested, and in at left-half came twenty-year-old Wilf McGuinness, who had made a rapid recovery from his cartilage operation. If they'd been at home I'm sure we would have gone to the match, but instead that Easter Monday we had a change of sport: my dad took me to the Harris Stadium in Fallowfield for the Daily Express International Cycling and Athletics meeting.

It was freezing, and a bitterly cold wind blew across the track, but the cycle racing was great. I'd never been to a cycle track before and I was hooked on it straight away. It was all very exciting and dramatic. We stood up against the track wall on the banking as it swept down to the finishing straight where the riders jockeyed for position to swoop down for their sprint finish. On the athletics track there were some big names, including Derek Ibbotson, but he could only finish a disappointing seventh in the Fallowfield Mile. I couldn't understand that. Ibbotson was a four-minute miler up there in the Roger Bannister and Chris Chataway class and I'd never heard of most of the other runners. There were no four-minute miles that afternoon, but it was good sport, made even better when we received the news that United had managed to record their first league win since Munich with a 2–1 victory over Sunderland. Colin Webster, who had been coming in for a lot of criticism, had scored both goals.

When we got home for our tea there was more good news, and it wasn't just that we were having tinned salmon followed by jelly and evaporated milk for our tea (because it was a holiday). When we sat down my mam said she'd got something to tell me and our Joan. We were going to have a baby. It was due in the summer. Obviously my mam and dad had known for quite a few months, but for me and Joan the news came right out of the blue. I was eleven and Joan was ten; Mam and Dad were both over forty. People didn't have babies when they were as old as that, and we didn't know many kids of our age who had baby brothers or sisters. It was a massive surprise for us but we were very pleased. It would be nice to have a new baby in the house. I thought it would be particularly good for Joan. One of her favourite summer pastimes was taking someone's baby for a walk (with permission, of course). Mind you, she always seemed more interested in the prams than the babies themselves, and she'd only pick babies who had nice prams. My mam would have to get a good pram if she wanted Joan to take our baby for a walk.

Inevitably, me and our Joan started to ask questions. Where did babies come from? Our knowledge of the facts of life was just about non-existent. It wasn't something they told you about in a Catholic primary school, or in a grammar school where would-be priests were educated, and it certainly wasn't anything that had ever been brought up in our house—far too embarrassing, and not the sort of thing you talked about in front of the children, or in front of anybody I suspect. But now my mam couldn't avoid the issue, and eventually we got an answer of sorts from her, through a process of elimination. It wasn't going to come out of her mouth and it wasn't going to come out of her bottom, so there was only one place left, and even I knew enough about the difference between boys and girls to know where that was. But how the baby had got there in the first place was a bit of a dark secret that remained untouched, and we didn't push the matter. The fact that my dad might have had something to do with it didn't really come into it. Being good Catholics, I think we just thought it was something to do with the Immaculate Conception. If that's the way Jesus came into the world, that's probably the way it was for all babies.

That week, the excitement of having a baby on the way began to make up for the sadness I was still feeling over the death of my Gran Kearney. It seemed odd that a new life was following on so quickly from one that had only just left us. It was all a bit like United really: death, and then almost immediately a new team being born. Easter, and all the Easter services I'd been to, was clearly affecting the way I was thinking: death on Good Friday followed so quickly by resurrection and new life. Something had definitely happened to me over the last few weeks. I'd become aware of things I'd never really thought anything about. These were big thoughts, though, too much for an eleven-year-old to be dwelling on for too long. After all, the dark nights of winter were coming to an end and summer was on its way.

CHAPTER 13

ONE GAME TOO MANY

With the nights growing lighter there was more time to play out after school—that is, if there wasn't too much homework to do. Football on the road in front of our house: two lots of jumpers down at either end for the goals, and the edgings made a good touchline that you could bounce the ball off—a bit like modern five-a-side where you use the walls of the gym, only on our pitch the edgings were about three inches high so you had to keep the ball down or it would be out for a throw-in. Because our road was a dead end there was no problem having our pitch on it, and the concrete made a good playing surface, except when you took a flyer and grazed your knees or your elbows. And it wasn't just football we played out there. Summer was coming, so thoughts were turning to cricket. The grass verge over on the other side of the road made a perfect cricket pitch, and there were always a couple of old milk crates hanging around somewhere to use for wickets.

I also remember making 'stilts' from golden syrup cans and string, and going up to the shops for my mam on metal roller skates with metal wheels that you wore over your shoes. Then there would always be lots of time playing 'allies' (marbles) and riding home-made 'bogeys', made from an old plank and some wheels, down the little hill round the corner on Frensham Drive. We'd also go fishing for tadpoles and sticklebacks in the pond near the top of the road. We'd sometimes play with the girls—games like whip and top, jacks, two-balls, hide and seek and rally-vo, and sometimes we'd join in their skipping games. They would have a skipping rope made from an old washing line right across the street as there was so little traffic. The trouble was, it went right across our football pitch, so you had to join them because they wouldn't move out of the way. The girls had lots of skipping rhymes, and rhymes for two-balls, which involved throwing two balls up at the wall and catching them while chanting what seemed like a nonsense verse.

One of the best games the lads played was the Mystery Riders. I don't know who the Mystery Riders were; maybe they were on at the ABC Minors kids matinée at the Forum cinema in Northenden. I wouldn't know, because we were never allowed to go to that; but that didn't stop me joining in with the rest of the lads, charging down the road and across the grass in front of the flats, our dark blue gabardine macs draped over our shoulders with just the top button fastened to make it into a cape. If we weren't the Mystery Riders we were all Flash Gordon, or we'd be galloping on our imaginary white horses, slapping our backsides with one hand to create the rhythm and sound of horses' hooves. As we galloped across the field behind the old people's bungalows where Farmer Shenton kept his cows we'd be Hopalong Cassidy or the Lone Ranger and Tonto riding the Texas plains, firing our imaginary gun (two pointed fingers and a cocked thumb) at any strangers or Injuns who got in our way.

Soon after Easter the weather started to get warmer, so much so that one day while we were still on holiday all the kids from our road went for a picnic down the lanes. Everybody had a bottle of water, which we called 'Corporation Pop', and some butties. Most of the kids had jam butties, but I had Marmite on mine. On another day we made tents on Shenton's field. We borrowed my mam's clothes horse, or maiden as we used to call it, and an old blanket to put over it, and set up camp on the field. We sat in the tent drinking our Corporation Pop and all was quite peaceful—until Jeannie Jampot from Amberley flats appeared on the scene. This meant trouble. My mam had told us not to play with her. I wasn't sure why, but she didn't like her and didn't want us associating with her. Jeannie insisted on coming into the tent and straight away suggested that we should play doctors and nurses. I was a bit uneasy: doctors and nurses involved touching each other and examining each other, and, if it was done properly, taking some of your clothes off and showing the doctor or the nurse bits you weren't supposed to show. Jeannie was insistent: that's what she wanted to play, and she wanted to do it properly. She said she would be the patient, and she needed her knickers down so that she could be examined. I was petrified. Our Joan was there so it was bound to get back to my mam, and we'd be in dead trouble. Jeannie wasn't bothered though. 'Come on! You're the doctor,' she said. 'You're not scared, are you?' Of course I wasn't scared, or at least I didn't want her to think I was scared but now I knew why my mam didn't want us to play with her. Fortunately Jeannie soon lost interest. I don't think she thought I was very good at the game and she went off to find someone else to play with.

* * *

With so many interesting diversions, it's not surprising that I don't remember a great deal about the matches in the last few weeks of the 1957/58 season. There just seemed to be so many of them, and the one common factor was that United were still not winning any of them. The win against Sunderland on Easter Monday turned out to be a bit of a flash in the pan, and we went straight back to some pretty dismal results.

One bright spot was the form of Bobby Charlton. Since his return he had impressed, so much so that Preston's legendary England winger Tom Finney said he was one of the best youngsters he had ever seen. Charlton was beginning to look like the complete footballer, and soon after Easter the news came through that he had won his first England cap. He was named in the side to play Scotland at Hampden Park on 19 April, at inside-right. Only a couple of months earlier he'd been lying in a hospital in Munich; no player could have had a quicker rise to the top. Bobby had just been coming to the forefront at the time of the crash, but it was since his return from Munich that he had hit the brilliant form that had attracted the England selectors and kept United's name alive in the England set-up. For the rest of the team the selectors had chosen largely as expected, Fulham full-back Jim Langley, Wolves left-half Bill Slater and West Brom centre-forward Derek Kevan filling the places left vacant by Roger Byrne, Duncan Edwards and Tommy Taylor.

What an achievement it was for Bobby Charlton. Paying tribute to him in his *Evening News* column, his captain Bill Foulkes said, 'Charlton is my idea of the perfect sportsman—and the near perfect footballer. When he came back from Germany and took his place in the crippled United side he hit form that startled—and delighted—all connected with the club. It was as though the added responsibility of being one of the old hands had brought out of him a new-found brilliance,' Foulkes said. 'He has always been a very promising boy, but I am sure all fans would agree that he has never played better than in recent weeks. He is one of soccer's gentlemen. By that I don't mean a "softy" for he is a hard and courageous tackler, but he is scrupulously fair and I have never known him to lose his temper even when severely provoked.' Never was there a truer description of Bobby Charlton, and those words about him when he was still only twenty were to apply throughout his long and distinguished career.

Later in the week came the news that everybody in Manchester had been waiting for: Matt Busby was going to leave hospital the following week. He'd be back in time for the last few matches of the season, and for the FA Cup Final. A BEA spokesman said, 'He has not yet recovered his full strength but he is well enough to travel. And I think he is keen to be getting back to his Babes.' The plan was for him to travel by train from Munich and come back to Manchester via the Hook of Holland and Harwich. After Busby's departure, the only survivors left in the hospital would be Johnny Berry and the *News Chronicle* sports writer Frank Taylor, and both were improving daily, the spokesman added.

On the same day it was announced that Professor Georg Maurer had been made an honorary CBE by the Queen in recognition of his services to the victims of the Munich air disaster. The news went down particularly well in Manchester, where he had achieved some sort of heroic status. The commendation, which was released by the British Embassy in Bonn, stated that the award was in recognition of Professor Maurer's efficiency and devotion. 'The people injured in the crash were nearly all taken to his hospital, where they received care and treatment of the highest order. All those who have been able to see the work of Professor Maurer and his staff are agreed that no praise could be too high for the skill and selflessness with which they have looked after their patients. The honour which Her Majesty has conferred is intended to symbolize the appreciation and gratitude, not only of the injured, but of the many thousands of British people who have anxiously followed the progress of their recovery.' The commendation also pointed out that the disaster had had one fruitful result, that of promoting Anglo-German friendship.

I talked to my dad about it before going to bed that night. Just over a decade earlier he'd fought in a war against Germany. Professor Maurer and many of his team of doctors were on the other side. We were killing them and they were killing us, yet here they were, not very long after, saving so many British lives. But then we learned it wasn't the first time that British lives had been saved by this devoted surgeon. On the beaches of Dunkirk, eighteen years earlier, he had been decorated with the Iron Cross for his heroism under fire, saving the lives of British as well as German soldiers. This benign-looking roly-poly doctor must be the only person in history to have been decorated with Germany's highest military honour and a CBE from the Queen. In Manchester he was, and has always been, a hero.

For United in these opening weeks of April, as the most traumatic season in the club's history drew to a close, it was a question of how best to honour fixture commitments. To get all their games played before the end of the season would mean playing another six matches within the space of fifteen days. Then there was the FA Cup Final and the European Cup. Both legs of the semi-final against AC Milan were due to be played by 30 April, but once allowance had been made for the time it would take to travel overland for the away leg, that was going to be impossible. If they were to continue in the European Cup, which is what they wanted to do, the only way they would be able to do it would be to play both legs of the semi-final after the FA Cup Final on 3 May. Milan had suggested dates in April, but United told them that the crush of domestic league fixtures was so heavy there was no way they would be able to accommodate them.

While the negotiations dragged on, the Boss set out on his return journey to Old Trafford. On Thursday, 17 April, exactly ten weeks on from the disaster that had nearly cost him his life along with so many members of his team, Matt Busby left hospital. The headline in that night's *Evening News* read 'Busby Promises: I Will Be Back As Boss Next Year—And I Won't Miss Final'. Before leaving the hospital he shook hands warmly with Professor Georg Maurer. 'Thank you. Thank you ever so much for everything. Thank you for making me well again,' Matt said. 'Don't forget you must come to London to see the Cup Final.' Then he was driven to a hotel for a press conference at which he said he would be taking over his job again the following season.

On Friday, 18 April I got home from school and read the *Evening News* report on Matt Busby's arrival. Joy had returned to Kings Road, Chorlton-cum-Hardy that day, the report said. In the morning caller after caller had knocked at the door of the Busby household with bouquets of flowers. There were football people like Joe Mercer, the Sheffield United manager; crash survivors like Ray Wood, the United goalkeeper, who came with his wife Betty; and many members of the public, like the four workmen who left a bunch of flowers propped up against the green garage doors, and the supporter from Sale who left two bunches of grapes. Inside the house a triumphal avenue of flowers awaited Matt in the hall.

At just after three o'clock a black Humber carrying Matt and his wife arrived outside his house. Matt Busby was home. The long, anxious wait in hospital was over. Children and neighbours gathered around the car as Matt tried to swing himself out of it on his crutches. Standing at his front gate, he thanked the cheering crowd and told them he was glad to be home. As he hobbled slowly up his drive, his daughter Sheena opened the front door and his pet poodle raced out, barking loudly, and jumped up at him. Sheena ran forward and kissed her father. Then Matt, smiling broadly, with one arm around his daughter and the other around his wife, asked reporters and photographers, 'Are you all right, lads? How have you been while I've been away?' He stood at the door posing for the photographers, and he was still smiling, but he looked tired. When asked about the future he said, 'The first thing is to get back to full health. That at the moment is the most important thing.' Then Matt, who had now been joined by his son Sandy and son-in-law Don Gibson, hobbled into the home he had left seventy-five days earlier, followed by Sheena, who was unable to hold back the tears.

The next day United were playing Birmingham City at Old Trafford, but there was no question of the Boss being fit enough to attend a match yet. It was the first home game since Easter. In the meantime there had been two away games: a 1–0 defeat against Spurs and a 3–3 draw with Portsmouth. In spite of their poor form in the league, a win against Birmingham would edge United closer to the last-ditch fight that was going on for the top four talent money places which were paid to the top four teams in the First Division. United went into the game in a confident mood. In the Portsmouth game on the Wednesday night they'd found their goal-scoring touch, but a defence weakened by injuries and international call-ups had let in as many as were scored. Now for the Birmingham game they were back to full strength in defence and Jimmy Murphy continued his experimental wing plan which had worked for him when he first tried it at Portsmouth by playing right winger Ken Morgans on the left. The only notable absentee from the team was Bobby Charlton, who was making his England debut against Scotland that afternoon.

A huge amount of sympathy was still being shown by the supporters of other clubs, and the Birmingham fans were no exception: before kick-off the Lord Mayor of Manchester, Alderman Leslie Lever, received a cheque for £141 from the chairman of Birmingham City Supporters Club. But on the pitch, once the game kicked off, the Birmingham players were single-minded. Within two minutes they had taken the lead, and they went on to win 2–0.

The following Monday night, 21 April, United's fixture scramble continued with the rearranged game against Wolves. This was the one I and so many others had been looking forward to on the Saturday after the crash. At that time it was the game that was going to put United back to within striking distance of the top; by the time it was played Wolves were already the new champions. And how it showed: they put on a magnificent display and ran out 4–0 winners. The gulf between the teams seemed enormous that night. If anybody needed reminding how big a blow the crash had been to United, they didn't need to look beyond this match.

Matt Busby was still not fit enough to attend this match but, disappointing as it must have been for him to see Wolves in the place that had been occupied by United for the previous two seasons, it was at his request that the players formed a lane near the tunnel and clapped Wolves on to the pitch. One of those players was Dennis Viollet. He'd played for the reserves two days earlier and scored a goal, but tonight was going to be his opportunity to prove that he was fit enough for the Cup Final, which was only twelve days and two more matches away. Dennis was the fifth Munich survivor to make his way back into the first team after Bill Foulkes, Harry Gregg, Bobby Charlton and Ken Morgans. In his pre-Munich form he could be a match-winner at Wembley, but it was still only ten weeks since the disaster and he would need to play in United's last three league matches to prove that he was fully match fit for the big occasion. Ernie Taylor, Stan Crowther and Bobby Charlton were all rested, so Dennis came into the team in his old inside-left position, which Charlton had been occupying with such distinction. Where he would play if he was fit for the final, and where Bobby would play, was anybody's guess. It was a constant topic of discussion at school over the next week.

The Boss's return to Old Trafford came two days after the postponed Wolves game. He was using two elbow sticks to get around, but in spite of this he looked quite fit, and as he went round he had a few words of encouragement for each of the players. By this time Johnny Berry, the last of the survivors, was back home, and on the day that the Boss made his surprise visit, Bill Foulkes and Dennis Viollet called at Johnny's house to see him. It was the first time Johnny had seen either of them since the crash. Bill and Dennis took him out by car to the golf club to meet up with the rest of the boys. Now everybody was back, but still a great sadness hung over the club. So many old friends had been lost.

For the new Babes, though, there was an FA Cup Final to play. Three days after a 1–1 draw with Newcastle came the last league game of the season, at Stamford Bridge. Jimmy Murphy treated the match against Chelsea as a dress rehearsal for the Cup Final. He picked what everybody thought might be his Wembley line-up, and in it was a place for Dennis Viollet in a new-look attack that had Charlton at centre-forward, Taylor and Viollet as inside-forwards, Dawson on the right wing and Webster on the left. Over the previous few weeks Murphy had been experimenting by switching Ken Morgans from the right wing, where he had played before Munich, to fill what had become the problem berth of outside-left. But, apart from a fine game against Portsmouth when he made all three of United's goals, he hadn't yet hit his pre-Munich form. So on to the left wing came Colin Webster, who'd started on the right wing for the new-born Reds in the Sheffield Wednesday match. In the short time since Munich he was the sixth man to play on the left wing: Brennan, Pearson,

Charlton, Heron and Morgans had all been tried in an attempt to fill the place so superbly shared by David Pegg and Albert Scanlon before the crash. With Alex Dawson playing well on the right wing, Ken lost out on the position he'd been in for the final game in Belgrade.

Chelsea ran out 2–1 winners, but Murphy's experimental forward line was deemed to be a success. Colin Webster was easily the most impressive left-winger of the six that had been tried there in recent weeks, Alex Dawson confirmed that he was the best on current form for the right-wing berth, and although the Taylor–Charlton–Viollet middle three showed a bit of reluctance to shoot, they played well together and moved intelligently.

Nevertheless, in the week leading up to the final there was a heated debate in Manchester's pubs and works canteens about who should be in the team. It looked as though the young players like Shay Brennan and Mark Pearson who had performed such heroics in the rounds just after Munich were going to lose out, and not everybody agreed with this. Dennis Viollet, the player who had been such an integral part of the pre-Munich Babes, became a target for people who thought he didn't deserve a Wembley place. A steady stream of letters had been arriving at Old Trafford ever since it had been suggested that he might play in the final, saying that it would be unfair if he were selected.

I learned about this from my usual source, the back page of the *Manchester Evening News*, on the Monday of Cup Final week. Dennis had written a piece himself:

> I don't know for sure that I will be in the Wembley side, but I make no secret of the fact

> that has been my aim and my deeply cherished hope. Some supporters apparently don't share my feelings and have written to say it would be unfair on the lads who battled through after Munich against seemingly hopeless odds. One letter finished up: 'So don't play, Dennis. You are only going to play a stinker and let the side down and you'll never forgive yourself for that.' I don't mind telling you that that letter came as a bit of a shock for I must admit that as I trained and kept my fingers crossed for a place at Wembley I never even thought that I should do anything else but try to get in the team. When I came back from Munich, although it took a few weeks before I stopped hating football, I determined to try my hardest to get fit in time to be available for selection for May 3. No one has more admiration for the lads who battled through the fifth round against Sheffield Wednesday, fought magnificently against West Bromwich in the sixth round and then shattered the football world by finally beating Fulham to get to Wembley. It has been a wonderful effort, and I certainly sympathize with anyone who played in those matches and then misses the big day itself. But that doesn't mean I would voluntarily turn down one of their places—as these letter writers seem to think I should.

I couldn't believe it, and neither could my dad when I showed him the paper when he got in from work. He'd always liked Dennis. He was a skilful player and a good goal-scorer, an integral part of the team before the crash. On top of that, what some of these people seemed to have forgotten was that he played in the early rounds at Workington and Ipswich before the crash, so it wasn't as though he was just walking into the final without being involved in the hard work of getting there. He'd also missed out the season before with a groin injury when he'd played in every round of the Cup. But emotions were still running high and many supporters had formed an allegiance to players like Brennan and Pearson, who had been so much a part of those highly charged occasions that had got United to the final.

Jimmy Murphy had some tough decisions to make. After three days' careful thought about the forward line he had put out against Chelsea, he named his Cup Final team. It was, as everybody suspected it would be, the team that had played at Stamford Bridge. The unluckiest man was Ken Morgans, who had been in wonderful form before the crash, but who had been only a shadow of his former self since his return from Munich. The tragedy of Morgans was that he was never to recapture the form and confidence that had got him into the team before the crash. He'd survived the accident and had been passed fit to play within two months, but he was never the same again. Kenny, then, was another of the victims of Munich.

The team went to their usual pre-Cup match hotel at Blackpool, and there was great excitement when the players learned that Matt Busby would be joining them there. But would the Boss go to Wembley and lead the team out? Jimmy Murphy hoped he would. 'To complete a grand day out,' he said, 'it would be just right to have my very good friend and boss Matt Busby with me at Wembley.' That week we were still learning about the effects of the crash, on Busby and on others. One big surprise was Harry Gregg, who had appeared to have come out of it unscathed: he'd been suffering in silence from the after-effects. Although he had played in nearly every game since Munich he revealed that he had been suffering from splitting headaches and dizziness. Few people knew because he had kept it a closely guarded secret. When he walked on to the field for a game the pain was so bad that it made him dizzy, but he didn't tell anyone or report unfit because he found that as soon as the match started his head cleared. Thankfully he hadn't had a single attack for a week now.

The build-up to the Cup Final was different from any before or since. There was more talk of emotion than of football. It reached such a height that it prompted an appeal for 'football, not emotional sentiment' by spokesmen for the two main political parties on Bolton Town Council. Alderman James Vickers, a former mayor and leader of the Labour group, hoped that both Bolton Wanderers and Manchester United would play good football and that victory would go to the better team. 'There has naturally been a tremendous amount of national publicity about the disaster which overcame Manchester United,' he said. 'While I am sure everyone in our town is very sorry indeed for what happened, we believe that the nation is getting a little bit tired of the emotional outbursts which are taking place from time to time. We would remind people that at Winter Hill, near Bolton, there was a similar disaster which left thirty-eight to forty orphan children in the Isle of Man, and little national publicity was focused on this tragic event. In other words, let us not have emotional sentiment at Wembley, but football.' Alderman Vickers added that he had been moved to speak out after hearing reference to the coming Cup Final as an emotional event on a television programme, during an interview with the Footballer of the Year Danny Blanchflower. Alderman Taylor, the Conservative leader, supported Alderman Vickers: 'As things stand there is a real danger that Bolton Wanderers will be playing the rest of the country.' For the Bolton players, too, it was going to be a difficult day. The England centre-forward Nat Lofthouse was their captain, and many of those who had perished he numbered among his friends. 'Some of the fellows who died at Munich,' he recalled later, 'were among my pals. Barely a fortnight before the disaster I was having a drink with them at Old Trafford after they had thrashed us 7–2.'

But the emotion surrounding United couldn't be contained, particularly now that Matt Busby was back. Two days before the final he limped out of the team's hotel to watch training on a nearby golf links. He said he was a much happier man now that he was close to the team again. The next day, wearing sunglasses and smiling broadly, he hobbled on a crutch on to the coach taking United from the Blackpool hotel to London. Holidaymakers and sightseers crowded into the hotel car park to give the team a send-off. Several got on to the coach to shake Matt's hand. As he travelled with the team to their Cup Final hotel at Weybridge, he was at pains to point out that although he was with the squad, Jimmy Murphy remained in complete charge. He was planning to appear with his players in front of the Wembley crowd, but whether he would walk the two hundred yards with them from the tunnel or meet them in front of the royal box was something he wasn't going to decide until the morning of the match.

On Cup Final eve I looked enviously at the guide to things to do in London and the adverts aimed at supporters who'd got tickets for the final which was printed in that night's *Evening News*. The New Bagatelle Restaurant in Mayfair was advertising a Cup Final Night Grand Gala Dinner Dance and Glamorous Cabaret with the Midnight Lovelies—not that I'd ever have been allowed to go to see that, of course. The Blue Angel on Berkeley Street in Mayfair extended a welcome to the teams and supporters from Manchester and Bolton and promised that a pleasant evening was a certainty at their establishment, while the Lido Restaurant welcomed supporters of Bolton and Manchester United to London with a dinner dance and spectacular floor show from 9 until 3 a.m. for 27s 6d (£1.37). Dancing partners would be available, it added. How nice of them, I thought, and how thoughtful of them to go to the trouble of providing dancing partners for all those men who'd be down on their own. I was even more envious when I read about the two nurses from the Manchester blood transfusion centre who would be cheering United on at Wembley: newly appointed director Louis Edwards had presented the centre with two 25s (£1.25) Cup Final tickets and they had won them in a ballot. Mr Edwards said he'd presented the tickets because it was nurses who had looked after the injured players at Munich so well.

On the day of the Cup Final it seemed that unless you came from Bolton, everybody wanted United to win. Even City fans. In his book *Manchester United Ruined My Life*, the screen writer Colin Shindler, a lifetime Blue, said it was the only match he ever wanted United to win. The incredible fightback after

Munich had captured the imagination of the world. Getting to Wembley had seemed like a miracle, but there had also been some kind of inevitability about it. There seemed to be a bond between the team and the fans; they just had to do it; there was no other way. United had to get back there and show the world what had been printed on the front of the programmes just after the crash: 'United Will Go On'. And the closer they'd got to Wembley, the stronger the feeling had grown that they were doing it for the lads who died at Munich.

In an emotional few minutes before Jimmy Murphy led the team out on to the Wembley turf, Matt Busby went into the dressing room to give a few words of encouragement to the players who were going out to represent Manchester United in the biggest game of the season. The previous year his Babes had been in there; now, as he looked around the room, those lads weren't there. Instead there was this new team made up of young lads from the reserves, a couple of new signings and the few who had survived the disaster. When Murphy led the new young side out, all eyes were on Busby as he made his way slowly to the bench, on crutches. Nat Lofthouse recalled it as an incredibly charged atmosphere as the teams walked out from the tunnel. We sat at home watching it all on our own television for the first time.

Bolton Wanderers were a good team, and they were a hard team, with the toughest defence I've ever seen: Hartle and Banks at full-back, and a half-back line of Hennin, Edwards and Higgins. They weren't going to let sentiment get in the way. When the game kicked off, centre-forward Nat Lofthouse, England's Lion of Vienna, wasn't going to let emotions get the better of him either. He was a professional playing for Bolton Wanderers; in spite of what the rest of the country seemed to want, all that mattered to him was for Bolton to win the Cup. Within five minutes he'd put them in front with a low drive that gave Harry Gregg no chance. Then he made himself the villain of the piece by barging Gregg and the ball into the back of the net as Harry jumped to catch it. No goal, we thought. It couldn't be a goal; it was a foul on the goalkeeper. But, incredibly, the referee was pointing to the centre circle. Even Lofthouse couldn't believe his luck; he admitted later that he thought he had fouled Gregg. No modern referee would have given a goal, but here we were again with a foul on the goalkeeper costing us dearly.

When that second goal was allowed the bubble burst and the events of the past few months seemed to catch up with the team. The players had run on adrenalin for a month or so after the crash, but then the inevitable reaction had set in, and they had won just one of their last fourteen league games to finish ninth in the table. Wembley was one game too many; too much of an emotional strain. Less than three weeks before the disaster they had thrashed Bolton 7–2; now they lost tamely, 2–0. It was all too much for the survivors. 'I'd rather have been anywhere but there,' Bill Foulkes said later, 'but somehow we got through it.'

Appropriately, United's shirts that day were emblazoned with a phoenix rising from the flames. With eight dead and two severely injured they had lost ten of their best players, but they'd kept going. Reaching the Cup Final had been a tremendous achievement, but losing that day was for me and for many others effectively the end of the season. The players had run out of emotional steam. But the hard-earned draw against Red Star in Belgrade just three months earlier meant that United still had European commitments. It all seemed so long ago now; part of a different world; but just five days after losing to Bolton at Wembley they had to face up to AC Milan at Old Trafford in the first leg of the European Cup semi-final.

Mentally and physically they were shattered. Since their semi-final replay win over Fulham at the end of March they'd played twelve games in just over a month. Many of the team were raw, inexperienced young players; now they had to face one of Europe's top teams. To make matters more difficult it seemed that any sentimental good will there had been for United in high places had finally run out: Bobby Charlton was selected to play in a friendly against Portugal on the night of the first leg. Since his return Charlton had been a beacon of hope, and United really needed him for the game against Milan. Instead they had to call up young Mark Pearson again. The crowd was low—less than forty-five thousand. It was almost as though the supporters, who had given so much, were as exhausted as the players.

Strangely, I don't remember much about the game—not many of the people I spoke to do—but United won that first leg with a penalty from Ernie Taylor and a goal from Dennis Viollet. Astonishingly, they were only one match away from meeting Real Madrid in the final, but it was a slim lead to take to the San Siro for the second leg six days later. The occasion was all too much for what was still a makeshift team, and United crashed out 4–0 in front of a noisy, passionate Italian crowd of about eighty thousand. It would be five years before United qualified again for a European tournament.

So the 1957/58 season ended with defeat at Wembley and in Europe, but as the players who had ensured that United would go on recuperated during the summer months there was one more twist to come in the European tale when the club received an invitation to play in the European Cup the following season in addition to Wolves, the new English champions. Initially the FA gave their blessing, but the Football League, apparently resentful of the way United had flouted their authority to enter the European Cup in the first place, said they couldn't give their consent. United wanted to play in the competition so they went to the Board of Appeal of the Football League, who came down in their favour. But still the League wouldn't have it. They didn't want United in the competition so they referred the matter to the joint FA and League Consultative Committee, who decided that United were ineligible because the European Cup was for champion clubs only.

No more sympathy, no more concessions.

CHAPTER 14

FOR EVER AND EVER

My dad never went to watch United again. I never really asked him why, but I think like many others of his generation he felt that nothing would ever live up not just to the standards of the Busby Babes but to the potential they had to be the greatest club side ever. By the start of the 1958/59 season I was twelve and deemed old enough to go to matches on my own, or at least with my friends, which I have continued to do to this day.

Always there, though, the one constant through the ups and downs of following a football team, has been the memory of those events and their consequences; because something happened in those weeks after Munich that turned United from the football team I supported from the great northern industrial city I came from into an object of affection for people all over Britain and the world. Out of the death and destruction of Munich and the determination that despite the disaster United would go on, a legend was born. It was a story of sporting heroics that was reported around the world, and it inspired millions. One of them was Alex Wexler from the USA, who was quoted on a United website recently:

> I was 13 years old on that dark day in February 1958. As a US citizen, I had no inkling of what football was. Upon reading the local newspaper, I came across a small article which sketchily described the crash. My heart went out to the

players, passengers and families of those who perished and those who survived. Because of the Busby Babes, whom I never saw play, I learned about this wonderful game. Following the sport as best I could over here with minimal coverage, I became a Manchester United fan, and finally got to come over and see some matches a few years ago. Now it's an annual pilgrimage, and in a few hours I'll be boarding British Airways Flight 1502 to Manchester and will see the Manchester Derby and FA Cup match next week.

The Munich air disaster has become part of the soul of Manchester United. It's embedded in there with Matt Busby's dream as he stood in the bombed-out ruins of Old Trafford in 1945 and in his realization of that dream in the Busby Babes. At its heart is a passion and an iron resolve; a passion not just to win, but to win in style, to play the beautiful game, to attack and entertain; and an iron resolve to fight back whatever the odds. Both were evident in that first season after Munich when to the astonishment of much of the football world the team I was now going to see regularly with my mates rather than my dad finished as runners-up behind Wolves. They were there nearly a decade later in the Bernabéu when an ageing and injured Bill Foulkes came galloping out of defence to score the dramatic late winner against the great Real Madrid to put United in the European Cup Final; and there in the final itself at Wembley when Bobby Charlton leapt higher than I'd ever seen him leap to head the opening goal, and in the dazzling wing play of young John Aston, who tore the Benfica defence to shreds and did much to seal the victory that finally made United champions of Europe. They were there in those last three unforgettable minutes in the Nou Camp in 1999 when, after being outplayed by Bayern Munich for so much of the match, United scored the two goals that secured the Treble.

Every time I go to Old Trafford I glance at the Munich clock, and think of the team I first went to watch there, the team that embodied Matt Busby's dream of what football was all about. As I walk round the ground to my seat at the top of the Stretford End I always think of what it used to be like, with the factories and the chimneys and the railway sidings at the back of the Popular Side, and the smell—of industry and of the soap works—that always hung over the place. All very different from the monolithic structure that stands there now, the shiny glass-and-steel shrine to the commercialization of football and the global brand that Manchester United has become.

Everything has changed. The Emirates is a far cry from the Highbury where the Babes played their last great game in England before the fateful trip to Belgrade; the City of Manchester Stadium is as far removed as it is possible to imagine from the Maine Road I used to go to for those first nights of European football and the great Manchester derbies. But nowhere has changed more than Old Trafford—the now rather tackily rechristened Theatre of Dreams. Roy Keane's prawn sandwich brigade going in through the big flash doors to their cheerless, atmosphere-less suites and boxes; day-trippers clutching their megastore bags; first-timers buying the fanzines, thinking it's the programme. Looking at them, I always feel a strange mixture of resentment and superiority. United are my team, and they were my dad's team before me; they are the team of thousands of Mancunians like me who've supported them through thick and thin. We were there at Maine Road for the Bilbao game, at Wembley for the European Cup Final in 1968, and in the Nou Camp in 1999; but we were also at Bootham Crescent in 1975 when we were playing York City in the old Second Division, and at Old Trafford the season before when Denis Law hung his head as his backheel gave City the 1–0 win that helped to put us down, and on New Year's Day 1992 when a reserve centre-forward scored a hat-trick to give QPR a 4–1 win over us. So who are all these interlopers I see around me now, and what do they know about my team? I wonder if some of them have even heard of Munich and of the great Busby Babes.

But then, why shouldn't they be there? Manchester United are the greatest football team in the world, they play exciting and entertaining football, so it's no wonder that people want to come from all over the place to see them play. And I look at the excited faces of the kids hurrying along with their dads for their big day out to see United for the first time and I think of the first time I came 'walking down the Warwick Road to see Matt Busby's aces', and the resentment gives way to a strange kind of pride. All these people coming from far and wide to see my team, the team that embodies the heart and soul of the great city I come from, and they're coming because they're the best and they know they are going to be entertained by them. Whether they come from Swindon or Singapore, Cornwall or Copenhagen, they've come to see United; they want to be associated with them; they want to wear the shirt; they want to say they support Manchester United. And what's wrong with that? Just because I'm from Manchester and I've been a Red for over fifty years doesn't give me any ownership or any more right to be there than them.

It's still strange though. It's still hard to come to terms with your team being a global brand, particularly one that is owned by Americans who don't seem to know very much about football or care very much about the great traditions of the club. What's happened to the soul of Manchester United? And then you're up in your seat at the top of the Stretford End and the boys are out on the pitch and the game is on.

We love United, we do,
We love United, we do,
We love United, we do,
Oh United we love you.

A stepover from Ronaldo and a run reminiscent of George Best; a volley from Rooney, as hot to handle as a Bobby Charlton thunderbolt; a sweet flowing passing move starting from Gary Neville at the back, one touch, two touches, moving up the field, ending with a delicate little flick into the net from Tevez that either Viollet or Law would have been proud of. The soul of Manchester United is once again laid bare on the pitch; they still play in the only way a United team can, with passion and flair. Winning the Premiership in style again in 2007 was a victory for football, for style and skill and entertainment over the dour pragmatism of Mourinho's Chelsea—the legacy of Matt Busby and the Babes who perished in the snow and slush that terrible afternoon in Munich.

In those first days after the crash the future for Manchester United looked grim. The team had been destroyed; nothing could ever be the same again. There were rumours that the team would fold, that they would withdraw from that season's competitions. The chairman came out straight away and said United would go on, but amid the despair of those cold, dark February days it didn't seem possible. But cometh the hour, cometh the man. Jimmy Murphy made sure that United would go on. He played a massive part in the history of Manchester United, and I, along with many Reds who were there at the time, don't think he has been given as much credit as he deserved. How many of those millions around the world who we are told support Manchester United have even heard of Jimmy Murphy? In the weeks and months after the crash it was he who worked the miracle United needed. Working night and day in the most difficult circumstances imaginable for any football manager, he breathed fire, fury and pride back into a makeshift team and kept the heart of the club beating. In getting them to Wembley against all the odds, he put pride back into the team and convinced players and supporters alike that Manchester United would be great again. That United did achieve greatness again when Matt Busby came back, and more recently under Alex Ferguson, is in no small measure due to the miracle this warm-hearted Welshman achieved when he kept the heart of Manchester United beating.

And the soul? Some say it's gone, sold to the commercialism and the marketing and the money men, and the attempts to turn our beloved football team into nothing more than a brand that sells shirts, insurance, credit cards and television channels. But none of that has touched the soul of Manchester United. Football and the lives of modern footballers have changed beyond all recognition, but the soul is still there out on the pitch; the vision of Matt Busby and the style of his Babes. It's there in Gary Neville, Paul Scholes and Ryan Giggs, the lads brought in straight from the classroom and schooled in the ways of Manchester United in just the same way that Duncan Edwards, Eddie Colman and David Pegg were before them. It's there in the way they play and in a manager who understands the soul of Manchester United; a manager who is as committed to a football philosophy of winning and entertaining as his great predecessor was. Above all, it's there in the fans. Yes there are some interlopers, and yes the atmosphere isn't what it used to be, but don't believe the media myth that none of the fans are from Manchester. Where I sit, or more accurately where I stand for most of the match, on the Stretford End, just about everybody around me is a Manc, and if they are not they are from somewhere close by. Some of them may have moved to the coast in North Wales or Blackpool, some to the posher bits of Cheshire or to the countryside in Derbyshire or Cumbria, where I live now; others have had to go to London because that's where their work has taken them. But they're Mancs. Even if they weren't born there, their mams and dads who started taking them to see the Reds were, so they're Mancs at least as much as the Irish World Cup team are Irish, even though most of them weren't born in the Emerald Isle. So the soul of Manchester United is still there, all around me on the Stretford End, and it's there in front of me on the pitch and it's there in the bond between a player like Gary Neville and the fans.

Owners of football clubs come and go, so do managers and players, some more frequently than others. The one constant of any football club is its fans, and that's where the soul of Manchester United is—the repository of Matt Busby's vision, Munich and the legacy of the Babes. We've never owned the team; we never will; but it's our team. I don't even know who owned Manchester United when I started watching them in 1956, and I didn't care. I was only interested in what was happening on the pitch and the fact that I supported the greatest football team in Britain who were on their way to becoming the best in the world. The club is owned by a bunch of Americans now but, other than the huge hikes in ticket prices and a certain contempt for the loyalty of the supporters, I can't say anything is very different from the pre-Glazer days. I had no more ownership of the club in the days when the Edwards dynasty made so much money out of it, or even in the days of the PLC than I do now.

The great debate since the Glazer takeover about ownership and the marginalization of the fans is all about the soul of Manchester United, or the loss of it, as some see it. I'm a founder member of FC United of Manchester, the breakaway team set up by United fans at the time of the Glazer takeover, because I agree with all they stand for about giving football back to the fans. I go to some of their matches. They're great, they're affordable, and they've brought a lot of the fun back to going to a football match. They're doing well, too: they've won their league and gained promotion each season so far, and I'm really pleased for them. The fans who have moved over to them have a real sense of ownership because they are the owners. Look around at any FC match and Little United, as the fans call them, have taken a sizeable chunk of the diehard support from

Big United. But they are not United. When you've followed the Busby Babes and you were a Red in Manchester at the time of Munich, there's only one United.

There's a lot about Manchester United now that I'm not happy with, but there's a lot about modern football I don't like, and the two go together. It is way beyond the scope of this book to explore that, but for those who want to know more I recommend David Conn's excellent book *The Beautiful Game*. For my part, I've just paid my annual subscription to MUST, the Independent Manchester United Supporters' Trust, not out of any strong belief that it will make the slightest bit of difference to the ownership of Manchester United or the way it is run, but because, like just about every Red, I don't believe that huge debts are good for the club. I share their belief that football fans, not just of Manchester United but of all our football teams, should have some say, however small, in how their club is run. MUST offers an alternative ownership vision for United which does not mean ever-higher prices and contempt for supporters' loyalty. It's an idealistic vision, one that I would like to be part of, and it's one that is beginning to be shared by some European governments, and by UEFA, who are now recognizing the need for good corporate governance of clubs which gives their fans some say. But how compatible is this with running a successful football club, capable not just of competing and winning at the highest level but also of upholding the great tradition of Manchester United of entertaining and winning in style? Has the soul of the team we support been sold to Mammon, or is it only through the marketing and the money men that the soul can be kept alive?

For more than twenty years Sir Alex Ferguson has ensured that the soul of Manchester United is still there, out there on the pitch where it matters. He's brought back all the skill, passion, excitement, entertainment and above all success that were the very soul of Manchester United. It's the legacy of Matt Busby and his vision; of his famous Babes and their stirring achievements, and of Bobby Charlton, Bill Foulkes, Harry Gregg and the rest of the lads who came back from Munich determined to remember their dead friends by making United great again. But the football world in which Sir Alex has operated so successfully for so many years is very different to that of his illustrious predecessor. In a world in which a central defender like John Terry—very good, but not one of the all-time greats—can sign a contract that puts him on £130,000 a week, what price Duncan Edwards? The Busby Babes were on £20 a week, but what would the modern-day wage bill have been for that first team squad that flew out to Belgrade in February 1958? In a world of inflated transfer fees and players' wages, to maintain a team that is true to the traditions of Manchester United—not just winning, but winning in style—you have to have players who have the skill, the flair and the style of the Rooneys and Ronaldos, and that means being able to pay for them.

So perhaps in the real world of modern football Manchester United—my team from the great Northern industrial city where I was born and bred—have to be a global brand. Maybe we have to learn to co-exist with the prawn sandwich brigade and the day-trippers who take away so much of the atmosphere from the ground. Maybe we have to accept the megastores and the insurance and the credit cards and the tours of Asia and America and all the rest of the commercial, money-making trappings. Maybe we have to accept it all, because without the money that is generated, how is it going to be possible to attract the players who will be capable of carrying on the great footballing traditions of the club. We have to accept that the world has changed.

Thankfully, some things remain the same and maybe we have to accept that it's only because of the money and the marketing and all the rest of the hype that things can remain the same. Walking out of the ground after the 7–1 demolition of AS Roma in the second leg of the 2006/07 Champions League quarter-final tie, I said to my daughter, Kathy, 'That's what watching the Busby Babes was like.' Attack! Attack! Attack! It was one of the most stunning European performances of all time, a tour de force of attacking brilliance. I had to cast my mind back to the days before Munich for anything that compared. Just like the games back then, on that April night at Old Trafford Roma could, and perhaps should, have scored three or four themselves. And that's the way it was: the Babes played football with the conviction that games are won by going forward, not by sitting back and defending; however many the opposition scored, United were always going to score more. That's my abiding memory of watching the Busby Babes. And on nights like that, when the modern Manchester United of Sir Alex Ferguson demolished Roma, the spirit of the Babes was still out there on the pitch. Their soul goes marching on.

Those European nights that were such a novelty for players and fans alike in that far-off season when Matt Busby's Red Devils faced Anderlecht, Borussia Dortmund, Bilbao and the great Real Madrid have now become regular events. But there is still something special about going to see your team play in great cities like Rome, Milan, Barcelona and Prague. I was in Lisbon for the match against Benfica in September 2006. It was a warm evening, and as I walked round town after the game looking for somewhere to eat, I saw groups of United fans drinking at tables outside bars on the pedestrianized streets. It was the perfect European night. Benfica in the Stadium of Light. Not a great game, but we'd won 1–0 thanks to a late goal from Louis Saha. No trouble; well-behaved fans enjoying the match and the city afterwards, treated with respect by the Portuguese authorities, not caged in the stadium like animals as we are after so many away European ties. It was the way all European away games should be, and it was fifty years almost to the day since United's first ever European Cup matches against Anderlecht. Perhaps these were the sorts of nights Matt Busby had in mind when he defied the English football authorities to take United into Europe all that time ago. Foreign travel; top competition against Europe's elite teams; extending horizons for players and fans alike. That afternoon before going to the match I'd visited the Monument to the Discoveries, the massive angular structure on the Belem waterfront commemorating the great Portuguese explorers who opened up the New World in the fifteenth and sixteenth centuries. Somehow it seemed appropriate to be there watching United on the fiftieth anniversary of the year in which they first set out to conquer Europe, paving the way not just for themselves but for Liverpool, Celtic, Aston Villa and Nottingham Forest to go on and win the European Cup.

As I walked round after the match I passed a group of Reds sitting outside one of the bars. They were just like any of the other groups sitting drinking that night except for the United shirt that one of them was wearing. It had the number 9 on it and the name Charlton. I went over to him. 'It's great to see somebody wearing that shirt!' I said. 'The finest player we've ever had, and the one man above all others who is United through and through. It saddens me that he is never given the honour he deserves by most of the fans today.' The man agreed.

Bobby Charlton is the United legend who embodies all that is great about the team. I have supported the club for as long as he has been associated with it. Today, the views expressed by many fans about Charlton and the lack of respect they show him is something I find deeply disappointing. On the odd occasions when he ventures on to the pitch he graced for so many years, to present an award or hand over a cheque to a charity, the reception he receives is often lukewarm at best. To younger fans in particular Bobby Charlton is the sober figure in the suit who acts as an ambassador for his club, his adopted city or his country; the businessman who is part of the higher echelons of corporate United. He has become synonymous with the things they love to hate about the club—big business, global branding and, above all, the Glazer takeover. It's almost as if it is no longer politically correct to acknowledge the fact that he is one of our footballing legends.

But for those of us who saw him play in those first matches after Munich and at his peak in the sixties, he was the footballing ideal: quick, intelligent and elegant, with a power in his shooting the like of which I've never seen before or since. With that thunderous shot and his sprinter's pace out of midfield, he scored some of the most spectacular goals English football has ever seen. He scored more times for England and United than any other player and made more appearances for United than any other player, records which are still standing in 2007. Bobby Charlton is arguably not just the greatest United footballer of all time, but also the greatest English footballer. He has a well-deserved reputation not just as a scorer of great goals but also as a great goal-scorer—something that is rarely seen in any one player. For me, there has never been a more exciting sight at Old Trafford than Charlton in full flight, running with the ball at his feet down the middle of the pitch and letting fly from twenty or thirty yards out. George Best, who knew a thing or two himself about taking on players, said, 'I've never seen anyone go past players as easily as he did.' So great was his reputation as a footballer, and such was the esteem in which he was held, that in the late 1960s it was said that all over the world there were children who could speak only two words of English: one was 'Bobby', the other was 'Charlton'. I know it was true because I came across many of them myself as a student when I spent my summers hitch-hiking all over Europe. Bobby Charlton—two words that cut across all language barriers wherever you went.

And though he won everything the game had to offer—Championships, Cup winner's medals, a record number of international caps and goals—it wasn't just his tremendous achievements on the field that sparked instant recognition. Nor was it solely his exquisite skills. No, Charlton stood for something that the world admired. He was the perfect sportsman, soccer's great gentleman, the ultimate in old-fashioned sporting heroes. Playing for United and for England, his name became synonymous not just with some of the greatest moments in the English game but also with the highest traditions of sportsmanship and integrity. He was never in trouble, he never argued with referees, and he always showed honesty and respect to opponents. It made him the perfect role model, the essence of the Corinthian ideal. His status as the greatest ambassador in the history of British sport rested unequivocally on his unrivalled sense of fair play.

It goes deeper than that too. He is the figurehead, the living link with the past who represents all the traditions of Manchester United. He is the embodiment of its soul—Matt Busby's vision; Munich; the commitment to make United great again and to honour the memory of the team that died. The disaster at Munich and the death of his team-mates affected Bobby deeply. After the accident he became a more serious and subdued person, haunted by the tragedy and suffering from the consuming guilt of being a survivor when so many of his friends had perished. The carefree lad who had flown out to Belgrade became the solemn, dutiful figure, devoting most of his life to United, determined both on and off the field to do all he could to ensure that his team-mates were remembered in the most appropriate way possible with flair and success on the field of play.

Charlton's finest hour at club level came that May night in 1968, ten years after the disaster, when he captained United to European Cup triumph, scoring twice in the 4–1 victory over Benfica at Wembley. For Charlton and his mentor Matt Busby, that victory capped the post-Munich rebuilding. They had arrived at the destination they had set out for with the Babes who had died at Munich and Charlton famously missed the post-match celebrations, preferring instead to conduct a solitary remembrance of absent friends—the lads who couldn't be there that night. Busby never got over Munich. 'He felt responsible,' Charlton said. 'Those were his kids that died that day.' But it was Charlton, through his achievements, who did so much to ease 'the old man's' pain, and Busby recognized it. 'There has never been a more popular footballer,' said Sir Matt. 'He was as near perfection as man and player as it is possible to be.'

After all he had put into the club, he was rightly made a United director in 1984 and became a respected ambassador for his club, like his old international adversary Franz Beckenbauer at Bayern Munich. But integrity, sportsmanship, staying out of trouble on the pitch and then becoming a diplomatic figurehead does not make you a modern hero. It's the anti-establishment figures who are revered; it's the great players who were rebels and fighters who are worshipped on the Stretford End today. Best, Cantona, Keane—all still have their songs sung at every match. But not the player who is arguably the greatest of them all. It seems sad that while you still hear 'We all live in a Georgie Best world' and 'Ooh Aah Cantona', you never hear the song about Charlton that used to ring around the terraces in the sixties:

Aye, Aye, Aye, Aye,
Charlton is better than Pelé.
For Pele is a no-good bum,
And so is Eusebio.

When Bobby Charlton returned from Munich and started playing again, he was for me and for many a beacon of hope. Because of him, we knew there was a future; that United really would go on. Charlton, Busby's vision and Munich are inextricably woven into the very fibre of Manchester United. The fact that Charlton is not always given the respect and the recognition he deserves by some of the present generation of United fans may sadden me, but the obscene chant about Munich that can be heard coming from a small minority of so-called supporters of some of United's rivals just makes me angry. To me, these people are not real football fans. The vast majority of their own supporters are embarrassed by the insensitivity and callousness of their actions.

Whenever City or Liverpool or Leeds visit Old Trafford and the song about Munich is heard emanating from that mindless minority of idiots, I can't help thinking about Bobby Charlton sitting in the stand close by, and wondering if Bill Foulkes or Harry Gregg or Albert Scanlon is there, having to listen as the memory of their long-dead team-mates is violated. If I feel angry as those unthinking morons sing 'Who's that lying on the runway, who's that dying in the snow?' how do Charlton and the other survivors feel? It was their mates who died; they were on the plane with them. And how do the families feel when they hear their loved ones being sung about in this way? The boys who died were sons and brothers, husbands and boyfriends. Perhaps the cretins who regularly embarrass their clubs and the majority of their fans should be reminded of this, and of the fact that respect for the dead is fundamental to any civilized society.

Beryl and Olga Townsend found it particularly

upsetting when they went to a Manchester derby at Old Trafford with the family of Billy Whelan. They'd kept in touch with Billy's sister Rita and the rest of the family ever since the days just after the crash and had arranged for them to come over from Dublin to meet Sir Alex Ferguson.

> The City fans were singing it that day. The seats I'd got were near the corner where the City fans were, and when they started singing it with Billy's family there, having to listen to it, I was very upset. Singing about death like that is disgusting. It's something that would never have happened years ago; fans would have never dreamt of doing anything like this. Billy's sister, Rita, was particularly upset that day. Nobody should have to hear things like this sung about the deaths of their own families. Afterwards I wrote to [David] Bernstein, who was the chairman at Maine Road, and to the *Manchester Evening News*. Paul Hince, the City reporter, phoned me at home because he was very upset about it. He said, 'Please accept that's not how the majority of City fans are. We're ashamed of them.'

The same is true of the vast majority of Leeds and Liverpool fans. It seems unlikely that we will be seeing very much of Leeds and their fans at Old Trafford in the foreseeable future, but Liverpool will be there, and inevitably, with tension continuing to rise between some sections of the fans of both clubs, so will the songs. Those who sing them bring shame to their team and its supporters—and that applies just as much to the minority of so-called United fans with their 'Murderers!' chants and the Hillsborough graffiti that often greets Liverpool fans on their way to Old Trafford. None of this has anything to do with supporting a football team, and the perpetrators of these acts are an embarrassment to the vast majority of real supporters. When you talk to long-standing Liverpool and United fans, it's clear that most don't want to put up with the hooliganism and nastiness that accompanies the natural rivalry between the two teams. There is a feeling that Liverpool and Manchester are both working-class cities in the North-West that have produced two of the greatest football clubs in the world and that that is something to be proud of. After Munich, Liverpool were one of the first clubs to come to United and offer whatever help they could. The tasteless Munich chants are a slur on the memory of those times and on the sympathy that was extended to United by Liverpool.

The same is true of Manchester City, whose players went to the funerals of their friends from United and whose supporters grieved for them at a time when the whole of the city of Manchester came together. Recently, the official Manchester City supporters' club and other groups associated with the club wrote an open letter to their fans urging them to support their own team rather than goad United supporters with the appalling Munich chant. The letter, entitled 'We Are City, Let's Be Proud To Be Blue', called those who use the chants 'an embarrassment'. Supporters' club chairman Alan Garry—who was, like me, a schoolboy at the time of the crash—said, 'I think it's up to somebody like myself to educate people about what a tragedy and what a terrible day it was. We [the official supporters' club] are taking a lead in trying to stop these people doing it. A lot of us cringe when we hear it and we are trying to do anything we can to stop it. It has gone on for a long, long time and it's about time in our view that it stops. We can only try. It is nasty and it is repugnant. We only hope they'll listen and learn, and stop doing it.'

Those are the words of a true football supporter reflecting the views of the vast majority of City fans. They are passionate about their own team, they want them to beat United more than anybody in the world, which is just as it should be, but they are not filled with the sort of hatred that leads to such lack of respect for the memories of the dead. Fans today would do well to remember that at the time of the Munich disaster the whole of Manchester, red, blue and uncommitted, was united in its grief. It was a tragedy deeply felt, not just by everybody in Manchester but throughout the football world.

VICTIMS AND SURVIVORS

Twenty-three people on board the BEA charter aircraft lost their lives. There were twenty-one survivors.

THE VICTIMS

Players

Geoff Bent, full-back
Roger Byrne, Captain, left-back
Eddie Colman, right-half
Duncan Edwards, left-half
Mark Jones, centre-half
David Pegg, outside-left
Tommy Taylor, centre-forward
Liam (Billy) Whelan, inside-right

MUFC Staff

Walter Crickmer, secretary
Tom Curry, trainer
Bert Whalley, chief coach

Journalists

Alf Clarke, *Manchester Evening Chronicle*
H. D. (Donny) Davies, *Manchester Guardian*
George Follows, *Daily Herald*
Tom Jackson, *Manchester Evening News*
Archie Ledbrooke, *Daily Mirror*
Henry Rose, *Daily Express*
Eric Thompson, *Daily Mail*
Frank Swift, *News of the World*

Crew
Captain Kenneth Rayment, co-pilot
Tom Cable, cabin steward

Other Passengers
Bela Miklos, travel agent
Willie Satinoff, supporter

THE SURVIVORS

Players
Johnny Berry, outside-right*
Jackie Blanchflower, centre-half*
Bobby Charlton, inside-right
Bill Foulkes, right-back
Harry Gregg, goalkeeper
Ken Morgans, outside-right
Albert Scanlon, outside-left
Dennis Viollet, inside-left
Ray Wood, goalkeeper

MUFC Staff
Matt Busby, manager

Journalist
Frank Taylor, *News Chronicle*

Photographers
Ted Ellyard, *Daily Mail*
Peter Howard, *Daily Mail*

Other Passengers
Mrs Vera Lukic
Mrs Lukic's baby daughter, Venona

Mrs Eleanor Miklos
Nebosja Tomasevich, Yugoslav diplomat

Crew
Rosemary Cheverton, stewardess
Margaret Bellis, stewardess
George William Rodgers, radio officer
Captain James Thain, pilot

PICTURE ACKNOWLEDGEMENTS

Frontispiece

Memorial clock at Old Trafford: Claire Macintosh/ EMPICS Sport/PA Photos.

Illustrations, Section One

Crowds in Warwick Road, September 1959, photo by L. Kaye: Manchester Archives and Local Studies; bottom photos: both courtesy the author.

Bradford colliery, Manchester, 1953; Manchester United Football Club, September 1959, photo by L. Kaye; rainy night, Piccadilly, Manchester, 1959; Market Street, Manchester on a Saturday afternoon, July 1958, photo A. P. Morris: all Manchester Archives and Local Studies.

Manchester United v Atlético Bilbao, Maine Road, 6 February 1957: Topham Picturepoint/PA Photos; Roger Byrne leads his team on to the pitch, 1 February 1958: Lee/Central Press/ Hulton Archives/Getty Images; Matt Busby briefs the team before their match against Red Star: Keystone/Getty Images; Bobby Charlton scores a goal, Belgrade: Topfoto.co.uk; team members board plane: PA Photos; newpapers courtesy the author.

Wreckage of aircraft: PA/PA Archives/PA Photos; newspapers: Manchester Evening News.

Tribute from *Football Monthly*: Football Monthly Archives.

Illustrations, Section Two

Programme, 5 March 1958: courtesy the author.

Football Monthly cover, March 1958: Football Monthly Archives; Jimmy Murphy: PA Photos; team members returning to England, 10 February 1958: PA Photos; John Blanchflower with two survivors, 8 February 1958: AP/PA Photos; wives of players board a plane for Munich, 7 February 1958: PA Photos; fans queue for tickets, 6 February 1958: PA Photos; page of the *Manchester Evening News*, 6 February 1958: *Manchester Evening News*.

Bobby Charlton and Raymond Wood in hospital, 11 February 1958: Getty Images; guard of honour, Munich airport, 11 February 1958: © popperfoto.com; Roger Byrne's funeral, 12 February 1958: *Manchester Evening News*; Dennis Viollet, Albert Scanlon and their wives in hospital in Munich, 7 February 1958: AP/PA Photos; newspaper cutting: courtesy the author.

Brennan scores goal for Manchester United, 20 February 1958: Getty Images; Manchester United supporters, 20 March 1958: Getty Images; Matt Busby leaves hospital, 17 April 1958: © popperfoto.com; Matt Busby at home, Manchester: © Hulton-Deutsch Collection/Corbis; Bobby Charlton with young fans, 19 February 1958: Getty Images; Manchester United team practising, 26 February 1958: PA Photos; Manchester United squad of 1958, March 1958: Getty Images.

Manchester United team leave for Munich, 17 August 1959: © popperfoto.com.

Newspaper extracts, courtesy of:

Daily Mirror and *Daily Herald*: *Daily Mirror*/ Mirrorpix.

Charles Buchan's Football Monthly: above quotes from *Charles Buchan's Football Monthly* with kind permission from Football Monthly Archives.

Manchester Guardian: copyright, Guardian News & Media Ltd, 1958.

Daily Mail & News Chronicle and *Daily Dispatch*: Associated Newspapers.

Doncaster Chronicle: Yorkshire Post Newspapers.

Case Files

Microbiol[illegible]

Second Edition

EUGENE [illegible]
The John S. Dun[illegible] Chief and Program Director
The Methodist Hospit[illegible]
Obstetrics and Gyne[illegible]
Houston, Texas
Clerkship Dir[illegible]ical Associate Prof[illegible]ssor
Department [illegible]tetrics/Gynecology
University of Texas Medical School at Houston
Houston, Texas

CYNTHIA DEBORD, PHD
Former Instructor and Course Director of Medical Microbiology
Department of Microbiology and Molecular Genetics
University of Texas Medical School at Houston
Houston, Texas

AUDREY WANGER, PHD
Associate Professor
Department of Pathology
University of Texas Medical School at Houston
Houston, Texas

GILBERT CASTRO, PHD
Professor (Retired)
Department of Integrative Biology and Pharmacology
University of Texas Medical School at Houston
Vice President for Inter-Institutional Relations (Retired)
University of Texas Health Science Center at Houston
Houston, Texas

JAMES D. KETTERING, PHD
Emeritus Professor
Department of Biochemistry and Microbiology
Loma Linda University School of Medicine
Loma Linda, California

DONALD BRISCOE, MD
Program Director
Family Medicine Residency
The Methodist Hospital-Houston
Medical Director Houston Community Health Centers, Inc.
Denver Harbor Clinic
Houston, Te[illegible]

New York Chicago San Francisco
Lisbon London Madrid Mexico City
Milan New Delhi San Juan Seoul
Singapore Sydney Toronto

1 2 3 4 5 6 7 8 9 0 DOC/DOC 0 9 8

ISBN 978-0-07-149258-4
MHID 0-07-149258-5

Notice

Medicine is an ever-changing science. As new research and clinical experience broaden our knowledge, changes in treatment and drug therapy are required. The authors and the publisher of this work have checked with sources believed to be reliable in their efforts to provide information that is complete and generally in accord with the standard accepted at the time of publication. However, in view of the possibility of human error or changes in medical sciences, neither the editors nor the publisher nor any other party who has been involved in the preparation or publication of this work warrants that the information contained herein is in every respect accurate or complete, and they disclaim all responsibility for any errors or omissions or for the results obtained from use of the information contained in this work. Readers are encouraged to confirm the information contained herein with other sources. For example and in particular, readers are advised to check the product information sheet included in the package of each drug they plan to administer to be certain that the information contained in this work is accurate and that changes have not been made in the recommended dose or in the contraindications for administration. This recommendation is of particular importance in connection with new or infrequently used drugs.

This book was set in Times Roman by International Typesetting and Composition.
The editor was Catherine A. Johnson.
The production supervisor was Catherine Saggese.
Project management was provided by Gita Raman, International Typesetting and Composition.
The cover designer was Aimee Nordin.
RR Donnelley was printer and binder.

This book is printed on acid-free paper.

Library of Congress Cataloging-in-Publication Data

Case files. Microbiology / Eugene C. Toy ... [et al.].—2nd ed.
p. ; cm.
Includes bibliographical references and index.
ISBN-13: 978-0-07-149258-4 (pbk. : alk. paper)
ISBN-10: 0-07-149258-5 (pbk. : alk. paper)
1. Medical microbiology—Case studies. I. Toy, Eugene C. II. Title: Microbiology.
[DNLM: 1. Microbiology—Case Reports. 2. Microbiology—Problems and Exercises.
3. Anti-Infective Agents—Case Reports. 4. Anti-Infective
Agents—Problems and Exercises. 5. Clinical Medicine—Case Reports.
6. Clinical Medicine—Problems and Exercises. QW 18.2 C337 2008]
QR46.C356 2008
616.9'041—dc22 2007038259

DEDICATION

To Phil Robinson, a modern day miracle worker; he came to St. Joseph in 2006 amidst turmoil and uncertainty, and with leadership, vision, and commitment, directed us to a bright and exciting future.

—ECT

To my parents, Darrell and Ruth, for their ongoing support; to my loving husband, Wes, and children Emily, Elliot, and Evan.

—CD

To my wife, Georgia, and daughters, Theresa and Mitzi, who have always been the ultimate motivation for me to do my work, and enjoy it.

—GC

To my patient wife, Betty, and children, Brian, Pamela, and David.

—JK

To Cal, Casey, Peter, Ben, Kristen, Leonard, Eric, and all of their parents.

—DB

Phil Robinson

Chief Operating Officer, Hospital Partners of America

Case Files: Microbiology is dedicated to Phil Robinson, FACHE, MHA, who serves as Chief Operating Officer of Hospital Partners of America and CEO of St. Joseph Medical Center, Houston. With a career in healthcare that has spanned 30 years, Phil Robinson's wide experience has stretched across the country and in for-profit hospitals and not-for-profit facilities. A graduate of Texas A & M University, Phil received his Masters in Health Administration from Washington University in St. Louis. He remains active with mentoring and teaching at both universities.

Mr. Robinson has been listed in Modern Healthcare as an "Up and Comer," is a graduate of Leadership Houston, and recently received the Distinguished Alumnus Award from the Washington University Health Administration Program. He also provides leadership and insight to boards of several national and local healthcare and civic organizations. He has held executive positions with The Methodist Hospital System in Houston, the Alton Ochsner Medical Foundation and Ochsner Foundation Hospital in Louisiana, JFK Medical Center in Florida, and with HCA.

In April 2006, Phil accepted the role of interim CEO of St. Joseph Medical Center in Houston, Texas, while serving as the Vice President of Operations for the Texas Region. Most recently, Phil was promoted to COO for Hospital Partners of America and oversees the operational activities of the seven HPA medical centers in the United States. For our hospital, St. Joseph, he literally resurrected the institution from being money losing to a now dynamic, money making, strong hospital. We at St. Joseph, from doctors to nurses, from pharmacists to technicians, and from patients to their families, are grateful to Phil Robinson. He is our modern day hero.

CONTENTS

SECTION IV

CONTRIBUTORS

Ashley Gullet
Medical Student, Class of 2008
University of Texas Medical School at Houston
Houston, Texas
Cytomegalovirus
Hepatitis

David Parker
Medical Student, Class of 2008
University of Texas Medical School at Houston
Houston, Texas
Clamydia trachomatis
Herpes simplex virus
Human papillomavirus
Treponema pallidum

❖ ACKNOWLEDGMENTS

The inspiration for this basic science series occurred at an educational retreat led by Dr. Maximilian Buja, who at the time was the Dean of the University of Texas Medical School at Houston. It has been such a joy to work together with Drs. DeBord, Wanger, and Castro, who are accomplished scientists and teachers, as well as the other excellent authors and contributors. It has been rewarding to collaborate with Dr. Donald Briscoe, a brilliant faculty member. Dr. James Kettering is an inspiring author, phenomenal scientist, and virologist, and has achieved what all of us strive for a retirement in beautiful Northern California. I would like to thank McGraw-Hill for believing in the concept of teaching by clinical cases. I owe a great debt to Catherine Johnson, who has been a fantastically encouraging and enthusiastic editor. At the University of Texas Medical School at Houston, I would like to recognize Dr. Samuel Kaplan, Professor and Chair of the Department of Microbiology and Molecular Genetics, for his support. At Methodist Hospital, I appreciate Drs. Mark Boom, Karin Pollock-Larsen, H. Dirk Sostman, and Judy Paukert and Mr. John Lyle and Mr. Reggie Abraham. At St. Joseph Medical Center, I would like to recognize our outstanding administrators: Phil Robinson, Pat Mathews, Laura Fortin, Dori Upton, Cecile Reynolds, and Drs. John Bertini and Thomas V. Taylor. I appreciate Marla Buffington's advice and assistance. Without the help from my colleagues, this book could not have been written. Most important, I am humbled by the love, affection, and encouragement from my lovely wife Terri and our four children, Andy, Michael, Allison, and Christina.

Eugene C. Toy

❖ INTRODUCTION

Often, the medical student will cringe at the "drudgery" of the basic science courses and see little connection between a field such as microbiology and clinical problems. Clinicians, however, often wish they knew more about the basic sciences, because it is through the science that we can begin to understand the complexities of the human body and thus have rational methods of diagnosis and treatment.

Mastering the knowledge in a discipline such as microbiology is a formidable task. It is even more difficult to retain this information and to recall it when the clinical setting is encountered. To accomplish this synthesis, microbiology is optimally taught in the context of medical situations, and this is reinforced later during the clinical rotations. The gulf between the basic sciences and the patient arena is wide. Perhaps one way to bridge this gulf is with carefully constructed clinical cases that ask basic science-oriented questions. In an attempt to achieve this goal, we have designed a collection of patient cases to teach microbiological related points. More important, the explanations for these cases emphasize the underlying mechanisms and relate the clinical setting to the basic science data. We explore the principles rather than emphasize rote memorization.

This book is organized for versatility: to allow the student "in a rush" to go quickly through the scenarios and check the corresponding answers and to provide more detailed information for the student who wants thought-provoking explanations. The answers are arranged from simple to complex: a summary of the pertinent points, the bare answers, a clinical correlation, an approach to the microbiology topic, a comprehension test at the end for reinforcement or emphasis, and a list of references for further reading. The clinical cases are arranged by system to better reflect the organization within the basic science. Finally, to encourage thinking about mechanisms and relationships, we intentionally used open-ended questions with the clinical cases. Nevertheless, several multiple-choice questions are included at the end of each scenario to reinforce concepts or introduce related topics.

HOW TO GET THE MOST OUT OF THIS BOOK

Each case is designed to introduce a clinically related issue and includes open-ended questions usually asking a basic science question, but at times, to break up the monotony, there will be a clinical question. The answers are organized into four different parts:

PART I

1. **Summary**
2. A **straightforward answer** is given for each open-ended question
3. **Clinical Correlation**—A discussion of the relevant points relating the basic science to the clinical manifestations, and perhaps introducing the student to issues such as diagnosis and treatment.

PART II

An **approach to the basic science concept** consisting of three parts

1. **Objectives**—A listing of the two to four main principles that are critical for understanding the underlying microbiology to answer the question and relate to the clinical situation
2. **Definitions of basic terminology**
3. **Discussion of topic**

PART III

Comprehension Questions—Each case includes several multiple-choice questions that reinforce the material or introduces new and related concepts. Questions about the material not found in the text are explained in the answers.

PART IV

Microbiology Pearls—A listing of several important points, many clinically relevant reiterated as a summation of the text and to allow for easy review, such as before an examination.

SECTION I

Applying the Basic Sciences to Clinical Medicine

PART 1. APPROACH TO LEARNING MICROBIOLOGY

The student of microbiology should be aware of the scientific characteristics of each microbe, with a particular interest in the relevance to clinical manifestations. The following is a systematic three-pronged approach:

1. **How does one know that a person is infected?**
2. **Where and how is a person infected?**
3. **What can be done if a person is infected?**

1. **How does one know that a person is infected?** The clinician may have a suspicion of a certain etiologic agent based on clinical clues, but this educated guess must be corroborated by laboratory confirmation. This necessitates an understanding of the basis for presumptive and definitive diagnosis. Possible laboratory tests include culture, polymerase chain reaction (PCR) of DNA or RNA, antigen tests, or antibody tests.
2. **Where and how is a person infected?** This question translates to understanding about the mechanisms of disease transmission. For example, if a patient is found to be infected with the hepatitis B virus, the student should be aware that the most common methods of disease acquisition are intravenous drug use, sexual transmission, and vertical transmission. Blood transfusion at one time was a common modality, but now with screening of banked blood, the incidence is very low.
3. **What can be done if a person is infected?** This translates to knowing the best treatment and method of prevention of infection. In other words, once a patient is known to be infected with a certain microbe, what is the best treatment? The student is best served by learning more than one antimicrobial therapy and some of the advantages and disadvantages of each therapeutic choice. For example, a urinary tract infection caused by *Escherichia coli* may be treated empirically with a variety of antibiotics; however, a quinolone antibiotic such as ciprofloxacin is contraindicated in pediatric patients, and gentamicin is relatively contraindicated in those with renal insufficiency.

Likewise, the student should have a systematic approach to classifying microorganisms: viruses, bacteria, protozoa, and fungi.

Virus: A noncellular organism having genetic nucleic acid that requires a host to replicate. They are usually 15 to 450 nanometers (nm) in diameter. Viruses do not have a cell membrane or cell wall, but they have a rigid protein coat called the "capsid." The inner cavity contains DNA or RNA. Viruses come in various shapes including spherical, tetrahedral, polygonal, rod shaped, and polyhedral. One end is usually broader (head), and one end narrower (tail). The tail often has antigenic proteins for attachment to the host. Because viruses do not reproduce without a host, they are considered obligate parasites and not living. See Figure I-1 for a schematic of viruses.

		Genome size (kb)	Envelope	Capsid symmetry
Positive-strand RNA Viruses	Picornaviridae	7.2–8.4	No	Icosahedral
	Caliciviridae	8	No	Icosahedral
	Togaviridae	12	Yes	Icosahedral
	Flaviviridae	10	Yes	Icosahedral
	Coronaviridae	16–21	Yes	Helical
Retroviruses	Retroviridae	3–9	Yes	Icosahedral
Negative-strand RNA Viruses	Rhabdoviridae	13–16	Yes	Helical
	Filoviridae	13	Yes	Helical
	Paramyxoviridae	16–20	Yes	Helical
Segmented Negative-strand RNA Viruses	Orthomyxoviridae	14	Yes	Helical
	Bunyaviridae	13–21	Yes	Helical
	Arenaviridae	10–14	Yes	Helical
Segmented Double-strand RNA Viruses	Reoviridae	16–27	No	Icosahedral
DNA Viruses	Parvoviridae	5	No	Icosahedral
	Papovaviridae	5–9	No	Icosahedral
	Adenoviridae	36–38	No	Icosahedral
	Herpesviridae	100–250	Yes	Icosahedral
	Poxviridae	240	Yes	Complex

Figure I-1. Schematic diagram of selected virus families that are pathogenic to humans, approximately to size.

Bacteria: These single-celled organisms belong in the kingdom Prokaryotae, and they usually have a cell wall as an outer covering consisting of a complex of sugar and amino acids, and often a cell membrane surrounding the cytoplasm. Being prokaryotes, bacteria do not have a membrane around their nuclei. Some bacteria have flagella, which are cytoplasmic fibrous structures for locomotion. Bacteria may be classified according to shape (cocci, bacilli, or vibrio [comma-shaped], or spirilla [corkscrew]). Bacteria may also be classified by Gram stain characteristics, metabolism requirements (anaerobic versus aerobic), and presence or absence of cell wall (*Mycoplasma* do not have a cell wall). See Figure I-2 for cell wall characteristics of gram-negative versus gram-positive bacteria.

Parasites: Usually consisting of the protozoa and helminths. Helminths are parasitic worms usually subdivided into flatworms or platyhelminths and roundworms or nemathelminths.

Protozoa: Parasites in humans belonging to the kingdom Protozoa are classified into three phyla: Sarcomastigophora (flagellates and amebas), Ciliophora (ciliates), and Apicomplexa (sporozoans).

Fungi: Eukaryotic organisms growing in two basic forms: yeasts and molds. The mold form usually consists of multicellular filamentous colonies. Branching cylinder-like tubules form, called hyphae. The yeast form are single cells, usually spherical or ellipsoid in shape. Most yeast reproduce by budding. When the yeast cells bud but fail to break off, they can form elongated yeast cells, called pseudohyphae. Fungi can be classified according to their ability to produce superficial versus deep invasive infection, or by their appearance or sexual reproduction characteristics.

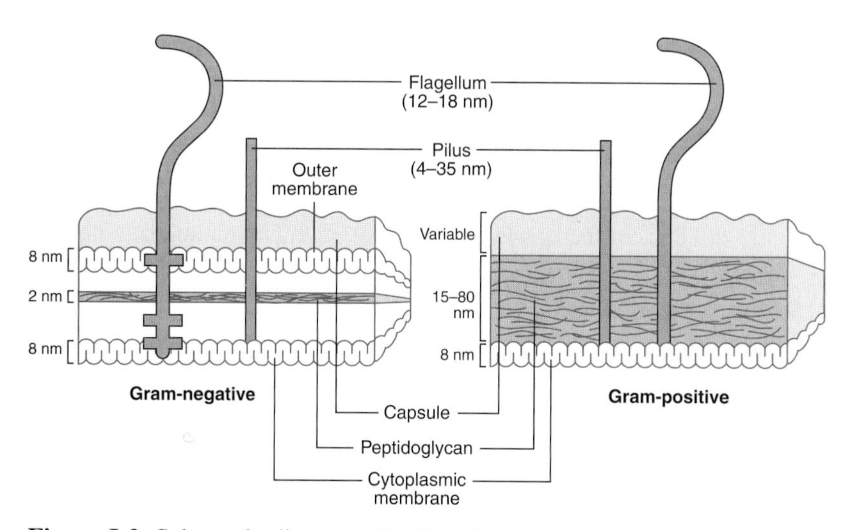

Figure I-2. Schematic diagram of cell walls of gram-negative versus gram-positive bacteria.

PART 2. APPROACH TO DISEASE

Physicians usually approach clinical situations by taking a history (asking questions), performing a physical examination, obtaining selective laboratory and imaging tests, and then formulating a diagnosis. The conglomeration of the history, physician examination, and laboratory tests is called the **clinical database.** After reaching a diagnosis, a treatment plan is usually initiated, and the patient is followed for a clinical response. Rational understanding of disease and plans for treatment are best acquired by learning about the normal human processes on a basic science level, and likewise, being aware of how disease alters the normal physiological processes is understood on a basic science level.

Clinicians should be aware of the laboratory methods of diagnosis, including the advantages and disadvantages, cost, time requirements, and potential morbidity to the patient. Various laboratory techniques include detecting DNA or RNA sequences, identifying certain protein components of the microorganism (antigen), or unique enzyme or toxin; microscopic examination such as Gram stain (most bacteria), acid-fast stain *(Mycobacterium)*, and immunofluorescence techniques (used to detect difficult-to-culture organisms such as *Legionella*). Cultures are the traditional method of diagnosis, and they must be taken in such a way as to minimize contamination and placed on the appropriate media (or mammalian cell for viruses), with temperature and atmospheric conditions for optimal amplification. Thereafter, the correct identification process should be used to assess characteristics such as colony morphology (both grossly and under the microscope), hemolytic pattern on agar, fermentation profile, Gram stain appearance, and the like.

Once the organism is identified, then susceptibility testing is generally performed to assess the likelihood that certain antimicrobial agents will be effective against the particular strain of pathogen. For example, isolates of *Staphylococcus aureus* should be tested against β-lactam antibiotics such as methicillin to aid the clinician in treating with methicillin versus vancomycin. Susceptibility is generally performed in a qualitative manner (susceptible, intermediate, resistant), or quantitative with minimum inhibitory concentrations (MIC) or minimum bactericidal concentrations (MBC) as determined by successive dilutions of the isolate bathed in antimicrobial mixtures.

PART 3. APPROACH TO READING

There are seven key questions that help to stimulate the application of basic science information to the clinical setting.

1. **Given a particular microorganism, what is the most likely clinical manifestation?**
2. **Given a particular microorganism, what is the mechanism whereby clinical or subclinical findings arise?**
3. **Given clinical symptoms of infection, what is the most likely causative microorganism?**

4. **Given clinical findings, what are the most likely associated features of the microorganism (such as cell wall characteristics or viral genome)?**
5. **Given the clinical findings, what is the most likely vector of transmission?**
6. **Given the clinical findings, what is the most likely laboratory culture findings?**
7. **Given a particular microorganism, what is the most likely mechanism of resistance acquisition?**

1. **Given a particular microorganism, what is the most likely clinical manifestation?**

   This is the fundamental knowledge that the student must learn in the broad scope of microbiology, that is, the most likely presentation of clinical disease. Each organism has certain typical patterns of clinical manifestations, based on its characteristics. The interaction between microbe and host, including replication cycle, enzymes released, and host immune response all play roles in the overt symptoms and signs. The student should have an understanding of the common presentations of disease. Likewise, the student should be aware of the mechanisms of the clinical manifestations.
2. **Given a particular microorganism, what is the mechanism whereby clinical or subclinical findings arise?**

   The student of microbiology is often tempted to memorize the extensive list of microorganisms and clinical disease. Unfortunately, this haphazard approach leads to quick forgetfulness and lack of understanding of the basic science underlying this discipline. Instead, the student should approach the field of microbiology by linking the microorganism, and its particular characteristics, to the mechanisms of disease, such as the interaction with host physiological state, cellular abnormalities that develop, and even cell death. It is the ability of the student to understand the mechanisms that allows for rational approaches to diagnosis and treatment.
3. **Given clinical symptoms of infection, what is the most likely causative microorganism?**

   The student of microbiology first learns antegrade from microbe toward disease, but patients present instead with disease symptoms and signs. Thus, the student must be able to work backward from clinical presentation to a differential diagnosis (a list of the most likely etiologies) to the probable causative organism. Again, rather than memorization, the student should incorporate mechanisms in the learning process. Thus, the student would best be served to give a reason why the suspected microorganism causes a certain clinical presentation.

   Microorganism → Host defenses/response to invading organism → Clinical signs

   Clinical signs → Most likely microbe(s)

4. **Given clinical findings, what are the most likely associated features of the microorganism (such as cell wall characteristics or viral genome)?**

   This is similar to question 3, but it goes back to the underlying basic science peculiarities of the microbe. First, the student must use the clinical information to discern the likely microorganism, and then the student must be able to relate the characteristics of the microbe. Because a common and effective method of classifying viruses includes the viral genome, this is an important differentiating point. Likewise, bacteria are often subdivided by their cell wall characteristics, which lead to their Gram stain findings. For example, the clinical information may be: "A 66-year-old male complains of blisters erupting on the right chest wall region associated with pain and tingling." The student should be able to remember that a vesicular rash that is unilaterally associated with pain and tingling is characteristic for herpes zoster. The etiologic agent is varicella-zoster, which causes chickenpox. The virus can lay dormant in the dorsal root ganglia and, then during times of stress or immunocompromised states, travel down the nerve and cause local eruption on the dermatome distribution. The pain and tingling are caused by the stimulation of the nerve. The student may recall that varicella is a herpesvirus, and thus is a double-stranded DNA virus.

5. **Given the clinical findings, what is the most likely vector of transmission?**

   Again, the student must first discern the most likely etiologic agent based on the clinical findings. Then, an understanding of how the microbe causes disease, such as vector of transmission, is important. A related topic is preventive or treatment related, such as how to sterilize equipment exposed to the patient, or the best antibiotic therapy for the described patient.

6. **Given the clinical findings, what are the most likely laboratory findings?**

   Based on the clinical presentation, the student should discern the most likely microbe and then its laboratory characteristics. These laboratory findings should be correlated to its mechanisms of disease. For example, the clinical findings are: "A 10-year-old boy presents with sore throat and fever. On examination, there is exudate in the oropharynx. A Gram stain reveals gram-positive cocci in chains." The student should be aware that a culture would reveal β-hemolytic pattern on blood agar media. Furthermore, the mechanism should be learned, that is, that the group A *Streptococcus* gives off *hemolysin,* which leads to *hemolysis* of the red blood cells.

7. **Given a particular microorganism, what is the most likely mechanism of resistance acquisition?**

   Patterns of antimicrobial resistance are enormous concerns for all involved in medical sciences. Bacteria and viruses are increasingly acquiring mechanisms of resistance, which spurs scientists to design new antibiotics or chemicals that disable the microbial method of resistance. For example, if the mechanism of resistance is a β-lactamase enzyme, then the addition of a β-lactamase inhibitor such as sulbactam may lead to increased efficacy of a β-lactam such as ampicillin.

MICROBIAL PEARLS

- There are seven key questions to stimulate the application of basic science information to the clinical arena.
- The student of microbiology should approach the discipline in a systematic manner, by organizing first by bacteria, viruses, fungi, and protozoa, and then subdividing by major characteristics.
- Learning microbiology can be summarized as a threefold approach: (1) Basis for presumptive and definitive diagnosis (i.e., understanding how one knows that a person is infected), (2) disease transmission (i.e., where and how a person is infected), (3) treatment and prevention of infection (i.e., what can be done if a person is infected).
- The skilled clinician must be able to translate back and forth between the basic sciences and the clinical sciences.

REFERENCES

Brooks GF, Butel JS, Morse SA. The science of microbiology. In: Medical Microbiology. New York: McGraw-Hill, 2004:1–7.

Madoff LC, Kasper DL. Introduction to infectious disease. In: Kasper DL, Fauci AS, Longo DL, eds. Harrison's Principles of Internal Medicine, 16th ed. New York: McGraw-Hill, 2005:695–99.

SECTION II

Antimicrobial Therapy

Antimicrobial agents consist of **antibacterial, antiviral, antifungal, and antiparasitic medications.** These drugs take advantage of the different structures or metabolism of the microbes versus human cells. The student should group classes of drugs together rather than memorize each individual agent. A systematic approach includes learning the agent, the mechanism of action, and the spectrum of activity.

PART 1. ANTIBACTERIAL AGENTS

Antibacterial agents, which target specific components of microorganisms that are unique or more essential to their function than they are to humans, are classified according to their mechanisms of action. The component targets include **enzymes necessary for bacterial cell wall synthesis, the bacterial ribosome, and enzymes necessary for nucleotide synthesis and DNA replication.**

Resistance of pathogens to antibacterial and other chemotherapeutic agents may be the result of a natural resistance or may be acquired. In either case, it occurs through **mutation, adaptation, or gene transfer.** The mechanisms of resistance for any antibacterial agent vary, but are consequences of either changes in uptake of drug into, or its removal from, the bacterial cell, or to changes in the bacterial cell target site of the drug from a gene mutation. **Multiple drug resistance** is also a major impediment to antibacterial therapy and may be **chromosomal or plasmid mediated** where genetic elements from resistant bacteria that code for enzymes that inactivate antibacterial agents are transferred to nonresistant bacteria. The emergence of drug resistance is to a large degree the result of the widespread and often unnecessary or inappropriate use of antibiotics in humans.

The **penicillins** include natural penicillins, penicillins that are resistant to staphylococcal β-lactamase, and extended-spectrum penicillins (see Table II-1). The **cephalosporins** are classified as first to fourth generation according to their antibacterial spectrum (see Table II-2). **Aztreonam,** which is relatively β-lactamase resistant, is the only available **monobactam.** It is nonallergenic and is active only against aerobic gram-negative bacilli (e.g., *Pseudomonas, Serratia*). See Table II-3 for a listing of selected antibacterial agents. The **carbapenems** (imipenem, meropenem, and ertapenem), which are resistant to most β-lactamases, have a wide spectrum of activity against gram-positive and gram-negative rods and anaerobes. To **prevent its metabolism to a nephrotoxic metabolite, imipenem** is administered with an **inhibitor of renal tubule dehydropeptidase, cilastatin. Vancomycin,** which is unaffected by β-lactamases, **inhibits bacterial cell wall synthesis** by covalent binding to the terminal two D-alanine residues of nascent peptidoglycan pentapeptide to prevent their elongation and cross-linking, thus increasing the susceptibility of the cell to lysis. It is **active against gram-positive bacteria.**

Table II-1
PARTIAL LISTING OF PENCILLINS

Natural penicillins: Penicillins G (prototype); Penicillin V
β-lactamase resistant: Nafcillin; Oxacillin; Cloxacillin; Dicloxacillin
Extended-spectrum **Aminopenicillin:** Ampicillin; Amoxicillin **Ureidopenicillins:** Mezlocillin; Piperacillin **Carboxypenicillin:** Ticarcillin

Table II-2
SELECTED LISTING OF CEPHALOSPORINS

REPRESENTATIVE CEPHALOSPORINS (ROUTE)	NOTES
1st generation –Cefazolin (iv) –Cephalexin (po) –Cefadroxil (po)	Active against gram-positive cocci, including staphylococci, pneumococci, and streptococci. They are particularly good for soft tissue and skin infections.
2nd generation –Cefuroxime (po) –Cefoxitin (iv) –Cefotetan (iv)	Marked differences in spectrum of activity; generally, active against certain aerobic gram-negative bacteria and somewhat less active against many gram-positive organisms sensitive to 1st generation cephalosporins. Cefuroxime more active against *Haemophilus influenza,* and cefoxitin more active against *Bacteroides fragilis.*
3rd generation –Cefotaxime (iv) –Ceftazidime (iv) –Ceftriaxone (iv)	Expanded aerobic gram-negative spectrum and cross and blood-brain barrier. Useful to treat bacterial strains resistant to other drugs.
4th generation –Cefepime (iv)	Generally similar activity to 3rd generation cephalosporins but more resistant to β-lactamases.

iv = intravenous; po = oral.

Table II-3

PARTIAL LISTING OF ANTIBACTERIAL AGENTS

ANTIBACTERIAL AGENTS	MECHANISM OF ACTION
β-LACTAM ANTIBIOTICS Penicillins Cephalosporins Monobactams – aztreonam (p) Carbapenems – imipenem (p) – meropenem (p) – ertapenem (p)	Inhibit synthesis of the bacterial cell wall.
Vancomycin (o,p)	Inhibits synthesis of bacterial cell wall.
Chloramphenicol *Tetracyclines* – tetracycline (o,p) – oxytetracycline (o,p) – doxycycline (o,p) – methacycline (o) – minocycline (o,p) *Macrolides* – erythromycin (o,p) – clarithromycin (o) – azithromycin (o) *Ketolides* – telithromycin (o) *Oxazolidones* – linezolid (o,p) *Aminoglycosides* *Spectinomycin* (p) *Lincomycins* – clindamycin (o,p)	Bind to bacterial ribosomes to inhibit protein synthesis.
SULFONAMIDES – sulfadiazine (o) – sulfamethizole (o) – sulfamethoxazole (o) – sulfanilamide (t) – sulfisoxazole (t,o) Trimethoprim	*Sulfonamides:* Structural analogs of p-aminobenzoic acid that inhibit bacterial dihydropteroate synthase to block folic acid synthesis and cell growth. *Trimethoprim:* Selectively inhibits dihydrofolic acid eductase to block folic acid synthesis and cell growth. Acts synergistically with sulfmethoxazole.
Fluoroquinolones (selected) – ciprofloxacin (t,o,p) – levofloxacin (t,o,p) – ofloxacin (t,o,p) – gatifloxacin (o,p) – moxifloxacin (o,p)	Inhibit activity of bacterial topoisomerase (DNA gyrase) that is necessary for replication.

t = topical, o = oral, p = parenteral

PART 2. ANTIVIRAL AGENTS

The **three major classes of antiviral agents** are **DNA polymerase inhibitors, reverse transcriptase inhibitors, and protease inhibitors.** It should be noted that HIV treatment usually includes the use of at least two reverse transcriptase inhibitors and one protease inhibitor. DNA polymerase inhibitors are subdivided into nucleoside and nonnucleoside. Drugs may target viral nucleic acid replication such as DNA polymerase either via nucleoside (purine or pyrimidine analogs) such as acyclovir or ribavirin, or by attacking a unique viral process needed in nucleic acid synthesis such as viral pyrophosphate (nonnucleoside type). Antiviral drugs used to treat herpes simplex virus (HSV), varicella-zoster virus (VZV), and Cytomegalovirus (CMV), can be classified as either nucleosides or nonnucleosides, or according to their site of action in the viral replicative cycle, or according to their clinical use.

Common Antiviral Agents

Influenza. **Amantadine and rimantadine** are primarily used against infections caused by the **influenza A virus.** Their mechanism of action is interfering with **viral uncoating.** Both agents are fairly well absorbed orally and cause some minor central nervous system (CNS) effects (rimantadine less so) and minor gastrointestinal (GI) effects (see Table II-4 for partial listing).

Table II-4

PARTIAL LISTING OF ANTIVIRAL MEDICATIONS

Hepatitis B and C	Lamivudine, adefovir, interferon alfa, and ribavirin.
Influenza	Amantadine and rimantadine (nonnucleosides that inhibit uncoating), zanamivir and oseltamivir (nonnucleosides that inhibit release and budding).
HIV-1	Nucleoside reverse transcriptase inhibitors (NRTIs; abacavir, didanosine, lamivudine, stavudine, zalcitabine, zidovudine) Nucleotide inhibitors (tenofovir) Nonnucleotide reverse transcriptase inhibitors (NNRTIs; delavirdine, efavirenz, nevirapine) Protease inhibitors (amprenavir, indinavir, nelfinavir, ritonavir saquinavir) Fusion inhibitors (enfuvirtide)

Herpes Virus

Acyclovir is used against **herpes simplex virus 1 and 2.** Acyclovir, a **nucleoside DNA polymerase inhibitor,** is a **deoxyguanosine triphosphate (dGTP) analog,** which is incorporated into the viral DNA and causes DNA chain termination. Its specificity is a result of the presence of **herpes specific thymidine kinase** in infected cells, which phosphorylates acyclovir 100 times more efficiently than by uninfected cells. Acyclovir can be used topically, orally for recurrent genital herpes, and intravenously for immunocompromised patients or herpes encephalitis. Its adverse effects include headache, nausea, and rarely nephrotoxicity with intravenous use. **Valacyclovir** is an analog of acyclovir and is converted to acyclovir in the body. Its advantage is **better bioavailability.** See Table II-5 for listing of agents against herpes viruses.

Table II-5
AGENTS USED TO TREAT HERPES VIRUSES
(ROUTE OF ADMINISTRATION)

AGENTS	VIRAL INFECTIONS
Acyclovir (t,o,p)	HSV, VZV
Cidofovir (p)	VZV, CMV
Famciclovir (o)	HSV, VZV
Ganciclovir (o,p)	CMV
Penciclovir (t)	HSV, VZV
Idoxuridine (o)	HSV
Valacyclovir (o)	HSV, VZV
Trifluridine (t)	HSV
Foscarnet (p)	HSV, CMV
Fomivirsen (p)	CMV

HSV = herpes simplex virus; CMV = cytomegalovirus; VZV = varicella-zoster virus; t = topical, o = oral, p = parenteral

Penciclovir is converted to the triphosphate form and inhibits viral DNA polymerase. **Famciclovir** is converted to the active agent penciclovir in the body. Penciclovir is used topically to treat herpes labialis "cold sores;" famciclovir is used for genital herpes or herpes zoster. Headache and GI effects are common. **Ganciclovir** is structurally similar to acyclovir and must be converted to the triphosphate form to be active; it competes with dGTP for incorporation into viral DNA, thereby inhibiting DNA polymerase. Its primary role is against **Cytomegalovirus** and is **far more effective than acyclovir against CMV.** Ganciclovir can induce serious **myelosuppression.**

Foscarnet is a synthetic nonnucleoside analog of pyrophosphate and inhibits DNA polymerase or HIV reverse transcriptase by directly binding to the pyrophosphate binding site. Its use is usually for **acyclovir resistant herpes or CMV retinitis.** Significant **nephrotoxicity** may occur with its use.

Sorivudine is a **pyrimidine nucleoside analog** and, on being converted to the triphosphate form, is active against herpes DNA synthesis. It is effective against **varicella-zoster** and is usually well tolerated. **Idoxuridine** is an **iodinated thymidine analog,** which **inhibits herpes DNA synthesis** in its triphosphate form. It is used primarily topically for **herpes keratitis.** Adverse effects include pain and inflammation. **Vidarabine** is an **adenosine analog,** which also needs to be in its triphosphate form and blocks **herpes specific DNA polymerase.** It has been used for **herpes encephalitis or zoster in immunocompromised individuals,** but because of its **nephrotoxicity,** it has largely been supplanted by acyclovir. **Trifluridine** is a **fluorinated pyrimidine nucleoside analog.** Its monophosphate form inhibits thymidylate synthetase and triphosphate form inhibits DNA polymerase. It is active against herpes 1 and 2 and CMV, and it is used primarily against keratoconjunctivitis and recurrent keratitis.

Anti-HIV Agents

Retrovir (azidothymidine [AZT] or zidovudine [ZDV]) inhibits viral reverse transcriptase when its triphosphate form is incorporated into the nucleic acid and **blocks further DNA chain elongation,** leading to **termination of the DNA.** Also, the monophosphate form of Retrovir may block deoxythymidine kinase and inhibit the production of normal dTTp. Its principal role is treating HIV infection, and adverse effects include headache, **bone marrow suppression,** fever, and abdominal pain.

Didanosine is also a **nucleoside reverse transcriptase inhibitor,** primarily used as an **adjunct to Retrovir,** or for those patients with HIV infection intolerant or unresponsive to zidovudine. **Peripheral neuropathy** and **pancreatic damage** are its side effects. **Stavudine** is a thymidine nucleoside analog that inhibits HIV-1 replication and that is used in HIV patients unresponsive to other therapies.

Protease Inhibitors

Invirase or saquinavir blocks **HIV protease activity,** rendering the virus unable to generate essential proteins and enzymes including reverse transcriptase. It is used in combination with a conventional reverse transcriptase inhibitor.

PART 3. ANTIFUNGAL AGENTS

In addition to the pyrimidine analog, **flucytosine,** and the penicillium-derived antifungal agent, **griseofulvin,** the three major classes of antifungal agents are the **polyene macrolides, azoles, and allylamines** (Table II-6).

Of all the available antifungal agents, **amphotericin B** has the **broadest spectrum of activity,** including **activity against yeast, mycoses, and molds.** It is the **drug of choice for disseminated or invasive fungal infections** in **immunocompromised** patients. The **major adverse effect** resulting from

Table II-6
SELECTED ANTIFUNGAL DRUGS

POLYENE MACROLIDES
Nystatin (o)
Natamycin (t)
Amphotericin B (t, o for GI tract, p)
AZOLES
Miconazole (t)
Ketoconazole (t,o)
Clotrimazole (t)
Itraconazole (o,p)
Fluconazole (o,p)
Voriconazole (o,p)
ALLYLAMINES
Naftifine (t)
Terbinafine (o,t)
OTHER ANTIFUNGAL AGENTS
Flucytosine (o)
Griseofulvin (o)

t = topical; o = oral; p = parenteral

amphotericin B administration is the almost invariable **renal toxicity** that results from decreased renal blood flow and from tubular and basement membrane destruction that may be irreversible and may require dialysis. Other adverse effects of amphotericin B relate to its intravenous infusion and include fever, chills, vomiting, hypotension, and headache that can be ameliorated somewhat by careful monitoring and slow infusion.

The **azole antifungal agents** have a **broad spectrum of activity,** including activity against **candidiasis, mycoses, and dermatophytes,** among many others. As topical agents they are relatively safe. Administered orally, their **most common adverse effect is GI dysfunction.** Hepatic dysfunction may rarely occur. Oral azoles are **contraindicated for use with midazolam and triazolam** because of potentiation of their **hypnotic and sedative effects,** and with β-hydroxy-β-methylglutaryl-coenzyme A **(HMG CoA) reductase inhibitors** because of an **increased risk of rhabdomyolysis. Itraconazole** has been associated with **heart failure when used to treat onychomycosis** and, therefore, **should not be used in patients with ventricular abnormalities.** Monitoring patients who receive itraconazole for potential **hepatic toxicity** is also highly recommended. **Voriconazole** frequently causes an **acute blurring of vision** with changes in color perception that resolves quickly.

The **allylamine antifungal agents, naftifine and terbinafine,** are used **topically** to treat dermatophytes. Contact with mucous membranes may lead to local irritation and erythema and should be avoided. **Terbinafine** administered orally is effective against the **onychomycosis. Monitoring for potential hepatic toxicity is highly recommended.**

Flucytosine is active against only a **relatively restricted range of fungal infections.** Because of rapid development of resistance, it is used concomitantly for its synergistic effects with other antifungal agents. The most commonly reported adverse effect is **bone marrow suppression,** probably because of the **toxicity of the metabolite fluorouracil,** that should be continuously monitored. Other reported less common adverse effects include reversible hepatotoxicity, enterocolitis, and hair loss.

Griseofulvin, the use of which is declining relative to terbinafine and itraconazole, is an effective antifungal agent that is used only **systemically** to treat a very **limited range of dermatophyte infections.** The most common adverse effects include **hypersensitivity** (fever, skin rash, serum-sickness-like syndrome) and **headache.** It is **teratogenic.**

Mechanism of Action

Nystatin and amphotericin B bind to ergosterol, a major component of fungal cell membranes. This disrupts the stability of the cell by forming pores in the cell membrane that result in leakage of intracellular constituents. Bacteria are not susceptible to these agents because they lack ergosterol.

Azoles (imidazoles less so) have a greater affinity for fungal than human **cytochrome P_{450} enzymes** and, therefore, more effectively reduce the synthesis of fungal cell ergosterol than human cell cholesterol.

The allylamine antifungal agents, naftifine and terbinafine, decrease ergosterol synthesis and increase fungal membrane disruption by inhibiting the enzyme squalene epoxidase.

Flucytosine must first be transported into fungal cells via a cytosine permease and converted to 5-fluorouracil and then sequentially converted to 5-fluorodeoxyuridylic acid, which disrupts DNA synthesis by inhibiting thymidylate synthetase. Human cells are unable to synthesize the active flucytosine metabolites.

The mechanism of antifungal action of griseofulvin is not definitely known. It acts only on growing skin cells and has been reported to inhibit cell wall synthesis, interfere with nucleic acid synthesis, and disrupt microtubule function, among other activities.

Administration

Amphotericin B is insoluble in water and, therefore, is generally administered as a colloidal suspension with sodium deoxycholate. Because of its poor absorption from the GI tract, amphotericin B must be given intravenously to treat systemic disease, although it is effective orally for fungal infections within the GI lumen. Likewise, nystatin is poorly absorbed but may also be used for fungal infection of the GI tract. It is too toxic for systemic use and, therefore, is mostly used topically to treat fungal infections of the skin and mucous membranes (e.g., oropharyngeal thrush, vaginal candidiasis). Costly lipid formulations of amphotericin B are available for intravenous use which reduce its nonspecific binding to cholesterol of human cell membranes and, therefore, its potential to cause renal damage. Griseofulvin is administered in a microparticulate form to improve absorption.

PART 4. ANTIPARASITIC AGENTS

Parasitic infections affect half the world's population and are particularly prevalent in developing countries. Immunocompromised individuals such as those with HIV infection are also prone to parasitic disease. These medications can be categorized as active against malaria, toxoplasmosis, cyclospora, cryptosporidia, pneumocystis, amebiasis, leishmaniasis, helminths, trematodes, and cestodes (see Table II-7).

Table II-7
DRUGS FOR PARASITES

	PROPHYLAXIS	TREATMENT	
Malaria (erythrocytic)	• Chloroquine • Mefloquine • Doxycycline	• Chloroquine • Quinine • Quinidine	2nd drug for falciparum: • Fansidar • Doxycycline • Clindamycin
Malaria (hepatic)	• Primaquine • Etaquine	• Primaquine	
Toxoplasmosis	• Trimethoprim/ Sulfamethoxazole	• Pyrimethamine/Sulfadiazine • Pyrimethamine/Clindamycin	
Cyclospora	• Trimethoprim/ Sulfamethoxazole	• Trimethoprim/Sulfamethoxazole • Pyrimethamine/Sulfadiazine	
Cryptosporidiosis		• Antiretrovirals • Paramomycin/Azithromycin	
Pneumocystis	• Trimethoprim/ Sulfamethoxazole • Dapsone • Pentamidine (inhaled) • Atovaquone	• Trimethoprim/Sulfamethoxazole • Trimethoprim/Dapsone • Clindamycin/Primaquine • Atozaquine • Pentamidine (IV)	
Amebiasis		• Metronidazole • Iodoquinol	
Giardiasis		• Metronidazole • Paromomycin	
Leishmaniasis		• Pentamidine • Amphotericin B • Azole antifungal drugs	
Antihelminthics (intestinal worms)		• Mebendazole • Albendazole • Thiabendazole • Pyrantel pamoate	
Antitrematodes & Anticestodes (Flukes, Schistosomiases)		• Praziquantel • Albendazole	

Source: Harrison's Internal Medicine, 2004;1202–8.

ANTIMICROBIAL PEARLS

- β-lactam antibiotics inactivate bacterial transpeptidases and prevent the cross-linking of peptidoglycan polymers essential for cell wall integrity.
- Both penicillin and amoxicillin are susceptible to β-lactamases.
- To prevent its metabolism to a nephrotoxic metabolite, imipenem is administered with an inhibitor of renal tubule dehydropeptidase, cilastatin.
- Vancomycin, which is unaffected by β-lactamases, is active against gram-positive bacteria.
- Chloramphenicol can cause GI disturbances, reversible suppression of bone marrow, and rarely plastic anemia.
- Aminoglycosides may cause ototoxicity or nephrotoxicity and should be used with caution in those patients who have renal insufficiency or who are elderly.
- The primary strategy of antiviral agents is to attack a unique but vital viral enzyme or process.
- The three major types of antiviral agents include DNA polymerase inhibitors, reverse transcriptase inhibitors, and protease inhibitors.
- HIV therapy usually uses at least two reverse transcriptase inhibitors and one protease inhibitor.
- Didanosine is also a nucleoside reverse transcriptase inhibitor for HIV infections and is associated with peripheral neuropathy and pancreatic damage.
- Foscarnet is a synthetic nonnucleoside analog of pyrophosphate and is associated with reversible nephrotoxicity; hypo- or hypercalcemia and phosphatemia that may lead to neural and cardiac dysfunction. Also, hallucinations, genital ulceration, and anemia may occur.
- Itraconazole has been associated with heart failure when used to treat onychomycosis and, therefore, should not be used in patients with ventricular abnormalities.
- A common side effect of griseofulvin is hypersensitivity.
- Because of renal toxicity, amphotericin B is often used to initiate a clinical response before substituting a continuing maintenance dose of an azole.

REFERENCES

Gale EF, Cundliffe E, Reynolds PE, et al. The Molecular Basis of Antibiotic Action, 2nd ed. London: Wiley, 1981.

Groll A, Piscitelli SC, Walsh TJ. Clinical pharmacology of systemic antifungal agents: a comprehensive review of agents in clinical use, current investigational compounds, and putative targets for antifungal drug development. Adv Pharmacol 1998;44:343.

Levy SB. The challenge of antimicrobial resistance. Sci Am 1998;278:46.

Sarosi GA, Davies SF. Therapy for fungal infections. Mayo Clin Proc 1994;69:1111.

Stevens DA, Bennett JE. Antifungal agents. In: Mandell GL, Bennett JE, Dolin R, eds. Principles and Practices of Infectious Diseases, 5th ed. Philadelphia, PA: Churchill Livingstone, 2000:448.

Wright AJ. The penicillins. Mayo Clin Proc 1999;74:290.

SECTION III

Clinical Cases

❖ CASE 1

A 53-year-old male farmer presents for evaluation of a growth on his arm. About a week ago, he noticed some mildly itchy red bumps on his arm. They started to blister a day or two later and then ruptured. During this time he had a low-grade fever, but otherwise felt well. Further questioning reveals that he has had no ill contacts and never had anything like this before. He has cows, horses, goats, sheep, and chickens on his farm. On examination of his right upper arm, you find a 4.5-cm circular black eschar surrounded by several vesicles (blisters) and edema. He has tender axillary lymph node enlargement (adenopathy). A Gram stain of fluid drained from a vesicle and a biopsy from the eschar both show chains of gram-positive bacilli on microscopy.

◆ **What organism is the likely cause of this disease?**

◆ **What are the primary virulence factors of this organism?**

ANSWERS TO CASE 1: *Bacillus anthracis*

Summary: A 53-year-old male farmer has a 4.5 cm circular skin lesion of black eschar surrounded by vesicles and edema. The Gram stain on microscopy shows gram-positive bacilli in chains.

- **Organism most likely causing disease:** *Bacillus anthracis*
- **Primarily virulence factors:** Capsular polypeptide and anthrax toxin

CLINICAL CORRELATION

Bacillus anthracis is the etiologic agent of cutaneous, gastrointestinal, and inhalational anthrax. Approximately 95 percent of anthrax disease is cutaneous. *Bacillus anthracis* is distributed worldwide, and all animals are susceptible, but it is more prevalent in herbivores. Infected animals often develop a fatal infection and contaminate the soil and water with *B. anthracis* that can sporulate and continue to survive in the environment for many years. Oxygen is required for sporulation, and the spores will grow on culture plates, in soil, or in the tissue of dead animals. Human infections are caused by either penetration of these spores through the skin barrier (cutaneous), ingestion of the spores (rare), or inhalation of the spores (so-called wool-sorters' disease), which usually occurs while processing animal products. Person-to-person transmission of anthrax has not been described. Cutaneous anthrax, the most common clinical manifestation, occurs within 2–3 days of exposure to an infected animal or animal product. A papule develops at the site of inoculation, which progresses to form a vesicle. A characteristic **black eschar** is formed after rupture of the vesicle and development of necrosis in the area. In rare cases the disease progresses and becomes systemic with local edema and bacteremia, which can be fatal if untreated.

The only other *Bacillus* species frequently associated with human disease is ***B. cereus,*** which is a cause of gastroenteritis following ingestion of a contaminated food product, most commonly **fried rice.** The spores of *B. cereus* can also survive in the soil and be responsible for traumatic wound infections, particularly to the eye, when soil contamination is involved.

APPROACH TO SUSPECTED ANTHRAX INFECTION

Objectives

1. Know the structure and characteristics of B. anthracis.
2. Know the clinical diseases caused by and virulence of *B. anthracis.*
3. Know the structure and characteristics of *B. cereus.*
4. Know the clinical diseases caused by and virulence of *B. cereus.*

Definitions

Eschar: Skin lesion associated with cutaneous anthrax and resembling a black, necrotic sore.

Wool-sorters' disease: Disease associated with inhalation of anthrax spores from infected animal products, most often associated with sheep wool.

Differential diagnosis: Listing of the possible diseases or conditions that may be responsible for the patient's clinical presentation.

DISCUSSION

Characteristics of *Bacillus* Species

Bacillus species are **large, motile, facultative anaerobic, gram-positive rods with a central spore.** The spore is quite resistant to extreme conditions and can survive in nature for prolonged periods of time. *Bacillus anthracis* is nonmotile and on Gram stain is often seen in chains. **The virulent forms of *B. anthracis* are more likely to be surrounded by a capsule.** The organism can be cultured as large colonies on blood agar plates within 24 hours, often resembling a "Medusa head" (irregular appearance to the colony with swirling projections). The **principal virulence factors** of *B. anthracis* are the **capsular polypeptide and anthrax toxin.** The capsule consists of **poly-D-glutamic acid,** which is thought to **allow the organism to resist phagocytosis. Anthrax toxin** consists of three proteins: **protective antigen, edema factor, and lethal factor.** Protective antigen is named for its ability to confer immunity in experimental situations. Edema factor and lethal factor bind to protective antigen to form edema toxin and lethal toxin. The bound proteins are transported across cell membranes and are released in the cytoplasm where they exert their effects. Once the spores enter the body they are taken up by macrophages. Because of both lethal and edema factors, the spores survive killing, and subsequently germinate.

Diagnosis

The differential diagnosis of a patient (farmer) with fever, adenopathy, and black eschar include other cutaneous lesions such as **furuncles** (staphylococci), **ecthyma gangrenosum** (*Pseudomonas aeruginosa)*, and **spider bites.** However, none of these etiologies are known to cause **eschar formation with surrounding edema.** The specific diagnosis of anthrax is made by growth of the organism from blood (inhalation anthrax), or wound (cutaneous anthrax).

Bacillus anthracis grows easily on most bacteriological culture media within 18–24 hours at 35°C (95°F). The organism is a **nonmotile, spore-forming gram-positive bacillus** that is **nonhemolytic** when grown on blood containing agar medium and produces **lecithinase** on egg yolk agar. Lecithinase is an enzyme produced by both *B. anthracis* and *B. cereus* that **degrades the lecithin in the egg yolk agar leaving a white precipitate.**

Careful review of a Gram stain from a primary specimen of a patient with suspected anthrax is necessary, because the organisms have the propensity to easily decolorize and appear gram-negative. However, the presence of **spores** is a key to the identification of the organism as a gram-positive bacillus. Based on these few tests (large gram-positive bacilli, nonhemolytic, lecithinase positive) a presumptive identification of *B. anthracis* can be made. As a result of the recent events in the world leading to concerns over bioterrorism, definitive diagnosis of anthrax must be performed in a public health laboratory. **Confirmatory testing involves the use of fluorescently labeled monoclonal antibodies as well as DNA amplification assays.** The use of **India ink** can also help to determine the presence of a capsule, a relatively unique aspect. The **capsule of *B. anthracis* is not stained by the India ink,** which can be easily visualized against the dark background.

Treatment and Prevention

Ciprofloxacin is the drug of choice for anthrax, following the identification of weaponized strains that were resistant to penicillin as a result of the production of a β-lactamase. **Prevention** of anthrax involves **vaccination** of animals as well as humans at high risk of exposure (military personnel). Prophylaxis is not recommended for asymptomatic persons. When deemed necessary, prophylaxis with ciprofloxacin must be maintained for up to 30 days because of the potential delay in germination of inhaled spores.

COMPREHENSION QUESTIONS

[1.1] A wound specimen obtained from a person working with wool from a Caribbean island demonstrated a large gram-positive rod from a nonhemolytic colony with swirling projections on blood agar. The most likely method to demonstrate **spores** would be which of the following?

A. Acid-fast stain
B. Gram stain
C. India ink stain
D. Malachite green stain

[1.2] Which of the following is the current preferred antimicrobial treatment of cutaneous anthrax?

A. Aminoglycosides
B. Ciprofloxacin
C. Penicillin
D. Tetracyclines

[1.3] *Bacillus anthracis* is unique to other bacteria. It is the only bacteria to possess which of the following?

A. An endotoxin
B. An exotoxin
C. A polypeptide capsule
D. A polysaccharide capsule
E. Lipopolysaccharide in its outer cell wall
F. Teichoic acid in its outer cell wall

Answers

[1.1] **D.** Spores can be observed as intracellular refractile bodies in unstained cell suspensions. Also, they are commonly observed by staining with malachite green or carbolfuchsin. The spore wall is relatively impermeable, but heating of the preparation allows dyes to penetrate. Alcohol treatment then serves to prevent spore decolorization. Finally, the spores are counterstained.

[1.2] **B.** Penicillin G was considered to be the first choice treatment for patients with cutaneous anthrax and when used should be continued for 7–10 days. However, because some naturally occurring isolates have been reported to be penicillin resistant (but still ciprofloxacin sensitive) and some patients are allergic to penicillin, ciprofloxacin is now considered to be the drug of choice for cutaneous anthrax. Ciprofloxacin belongs to the family of quinolones. As a fluorinated quinolone, it has greater antibacterial activity, lower toxicity, and is able to achieve clinically useful levels in blood and tissues compared to nonfluorinated quinolones. They act against many gram-positive and gram-negative bacteria by inhibiting bacterial DNA synthesis via the blockage of DNA gyrase. Despite the use of antibiotics in the treatment of anthrax, clinically manifested inhalational anthrax is usually fatal. If anthrax is suspected, public health authorities should be notified immediately. Aminoglycosides and tetracyclines have different mechanisms of action and have preferred uses in other disease states and infections. Aminoglycosides inhibit bacterial protein synthesis by attaching to and inhibiting the function of the 30S subunit of the bacterial ribosome. Their clinical usefulness has declined with the advent of cephalosporins and quinolones. Tetracyclines also inhibit bacterial protein synthesis; however they do so by inhibiting the binding of aminoacyl-tRNA to the 30S subunit of bacterial ribosomes.

[1.3] **C.** Virulent forms of *B. anthracis,* the causative agent of anthrax, are more likely to be surrounded by a capsule. This capsule is a polypeptide, composed of a polymer of glutamic acid, and is a unique feature of *B. anthracis.* Lipopolysaccharides (LPS/endotoxin) are unique to gram-negative bacteria (*B. anthracis* is a gram-positive rod). In addition, whereas *B. anthracis* is associated with both teichoic acid (cell wall) and a potent exotoxin, these are not unique features of this bacterium. Other gram-positives (i.e., staphylococci) release exotoxins and have teichoic acid in their cell walls.

MICROBIOLOGY PEARLS

- The most common form of anthrax is cutaneous anthrax in which penetration of the skin by *B. anthracis* spores causes eschar formation with regional lymphadenopathy.
- The organism is a **nonmotile, spore-forming gram-positive bacilli** that is **nonhemolytic** and produces **lecithinase.**
- Inhalation anthrax is a matter of public health concern.
- The drug of choice for treating anthrax is ciprofloxacin.
- The two main methods of anthrax virulence are its capsule and toxin.
- An eschar surrounded by edema is suspicious for anthrax.

REFERENCES

Logan NA, Turnbull PCB. Bacillus and other aerobic endospore-forming bacteria. In: Murray PR, Baron EJ, Jorgensen JH, et al., eds. Manual of Clinical Microbiology, 8th ed. Washington, DC: ASM Press 2003.

Murray PR, Rosenthal KS, Pfaller MA. Bacillus. In: Murray PR, Rosenthal KS, Pfaller MA. Medical Microbiology, 5th ed. St. Louis, MO: Mosby, 2005:265–71.

Ryan KJ. Sherris Medical Microbiology: An Introduction to Infectious Diseases, 3rd ed. New York: McGraw-Hill, 2003.

Swartz MN. Recognition and management of anthrax—an update. N Engl J Med 2001;345:1621–6.

❖ CASE 2

A 60-year-old man presents to the emergency room with severe abdominal pain. He has had mild, left lower abdominal cramping pain for about 3 days, which has worsened in the past 8 hours. He has also had nausea, fever, and chills. On examination, he is in obvious pain, has a fever of 38.6°C (101.5°F) and has an elevated heart rate (tachycardia). His abdominal examination is notable for absent bowel sounds, diffuse tenderness, and rigidity when palpated. An x-ray reveals the presence of free air in the abdominal cavity. He is taken for emergency surgery and found to have severe diverticulitis with a perforated colon. Cloudy peritoneal fluid is collected. An anaerobic culture grows *Bacteroides fragilis.*

◆ **What characteristics are noted on Gram staining of *B. fragilis*?**

◆ **What are its primary mechanisms for resisting phagocytosis?**

ANSWERS TO CASE 2: *Bacteroides fragilis*

Summary: A 60-year-old man has a ruptured diverticulitis leading to peritonitis. The cultures of the purulent drainage reveal *B. fragilis.*

 **Characteristics on gram staining:** *Bacteroides fragilis* appears encapsulated, with irregular staining, pleomorphism, and vacuolization.

 **Primary mechanisms of resisting phagocytosis:** The capsular polysaccharide and succinic acid production.

CLINICAL CORRELATION

Bacteroides fragilis is one of the most clinically significant **anaerobic** organisms. It is part of the **normal flora of the gastrointestinal (GI) tract** and causes clinical infections when it escapes from this environment following surgery, traumatic bowel perforation, or other diseases, such as **diverticulitis.** Although many anaerobes are part of the normal gastrointestinal flora, ***B. fragilis*** **is the most common cause of intraabdominal infections.** *Bacteroides fragilis* is also associated with respiratory tract infections (sinusitis, otitis), genital tract infections, brain, skin, and soft tissue infections.

Diverticulitis is an inflammation of a small food and particle collecting sac in the large intestine; it may lead to colonic rupture and therefore allow the organisms normally present in the GI tract to penetrate the peritoneal cavity and possibly the bloodstream. These infections usually involve a mixture of both aerobes and anaerobes.

APPROACH TO *Bacteroides fragilis*

Objectives

1. Know the microbiologic characteristics of *B. fragilis* and other *Bacteroides* species.
2. Know the virulence factors associated with *B. fragilis.*

Definitions

Anaerobes: Organisms that do not require oxygen for growth and may die in its presence.

Bacteroides bile esculin (BBE) agar: Media selective for *B. fragilis* on which the colonies appear black.

Diverticulitis: Inflammation of a diverticulum, which is a small bulging sac in the colon wall which can trap food particles and become inflamed and painful.

DISCUSSION

Characteristics of *Bacteroides* Species

Bacteroides species include the *B. fragilis* group as well as many other species. Two new genera were recently created, *Prevotella* and *Porphyromas,* to remove the pigmented, bile-sensitive anaerobes previously in the genus *Bacteroides.* All are **small, anaerobic, gram-negative bacilli** and many strains are encapsulated. **Vacuolization, irregular staining, and pleomorphism** are common.

Bacteroides fragilis has a distinct **capsule** composed of two **polysaccharides,** which appears to **inhibit phagocytosis and allow adherence to peritoneal surfaces.** Other virulence factors for this bacterium include the presence of **pili,** which promote adherence to epithelial cells and the production of **succinic acid, which inhibits phagocytosis.** *Bacteroides fragilis* produces an endotoxin that has little biologic activity. It also produces **superoxide dismutase,** an enzyme, **which allows the organism to survive in the presence of small amounts of oxygen.**

Diagnosis

Anaerobes are not usually the primary cause of an infection, but are involved in a mixed aerobic, anaerobic infection. Often diagnosis of **anaerobic infections** is based on clinical features including a **foul smelling wound** with the **presence of gas** in the involved tissue usually located in close proximity to a mucosal surface. Infections that involve spillage of GI material into the peritoneum are likely to involve aerobes and anaerobes. The **most commonly associated anaerobe is *B. fragilis.*** Patients with severe diverticulitis, appendicitis, or colonic injury often develop *B. fragilis* peritonitis.

To increase the chances of recovery of anaerobes from a specimen, the sample must be appropriately collected to allow survival of anaerobes. Anaerobes are organisms that do not require oxygen for growth. Sensitivity of the anaerobic organism can vary from those that **cannot tolerate any oxygen (strict anaerobes)** to those that can grow in the presence of **small amounts of oxygen (oxygen tolerant).** Anaerobes are therefore grown under atmospheric conditions that limit the presence of oxygen and include predominantly nitrogen, as well as hydrogen and carbon dioxide. Tissues or fluids collected and transported under anaerobic conditions are the most optimal; however, if necessary an anaerobic transport swab can also be used.

Bacteroides species produce **small colonies on anaerobic blood agar** medium within 24 hours. Selective media such as kanamycin/gentamicin laked blood agar will support growth of gram-negative anaerobes only. Presumptive identification of *B. fragilis* can be made by growth of **black pigmented colonies on Bacteroides bile esculin agar,** and resistance to kanamycin, colistin, and vancomycin special potency antimicrobial disks. Definitive identification of anaerobes or *B. fragilis* is made with commercial identification systems that are based on the presence of preformed enzymes or in reference laboratories using gas liquid chromatography to determine the specific gases produced by the organism.

Treatment and Prevention

Surgical debridement is usually necessary at least in part for the treatment of anaerobic infections. **β-Lactamase activity is common in *Bacteroides* species,** especially *B. fragilis,* which results in **resistance to penicillin and cephalosporin antibiotics.** Drugs of choice for *Bacteroides* species include β-lactam–β-lactamase inhibitor combinations, such as piperacillin/tazobactam, metronidazole, and imipenem.

COMPREHENSION QUESTIONS

[2.1] During an emergency surgery, a 60-year-old male is found to have severe peritonitis and a perforated colon. Foul-smelling cloudy peritoneal fluid is collected. Subsequent analysis reveals the growth of black pigmented colonies on *Bacteroides* bile esculin agar. No growth is detected in the presence of kanamycin, colistin, or vancomycin. Which of the following microorganisms is most likely involved in this case?

A. *Actinomyces israelii*
B. *Bacteroides fragilis*
C. *Clostridium difficile*
D. *Enterococcus faecalis*
E. *Porphyromonas gingivalis*
F. *Prevotella melaninogenica*

[2.2] Which of the following is the treatment of choice to control this infection in this patient (described in Question [2.1])?

A. Cephalothin
B. Erythromycin
C. Metronidazole
D. Penicillin

[2.3] Among the many virulence factors produced, *B. fragilis* produces an enzyme that allows the organism to survive in the presence of small amounts of oxygen. Which of the enzymes listed below catalyzes the following reaction?

$$2O_2^- + 2H^+ \rightarrow H_2O_2 + O_2$$

A. β-Lactamase
B. Myeloperoxidase
C. Nicotinamide adenine dinucleotide phosphate (NADPH) oxidase
D. NO synthase
E. Oxidase
F. Superoxide dismutase

[2.4] A foul-smelling specimen was obtained from a 26-year-old woman with a pelvic abscess. Culture grew both aerobic and anaerobic gram-negative bacteria. The most likely organisms are which of the following?

A. *Actinomyces israelii* and *Escherichia coli*
B. *Bacteroides fragilis* and *Listeria monocytogenes*
C. *Bacteroides fragilis* and *Neisseria gonorrhoeae*
D. *Clostridium perfringens* and *Bacteroides fragilis*
E. *Escherichia coli* and *Peptostreptococcus*

Answers

[2.1] **B.** *Bacteroides* species are normal inhabitants of the bowel and other sites. Normal stools contain large numbers of *B. fragilis* (10^{11} organisms per gram). As a result, they are very important anaerobes that can cause human infection. Members of the *B. fragilis* group are most commonly isolated from infections associated with contamination by the contents of the colon, where they may cause suppuration, for example, peritonitis after bowel injury. Classification is based on colonial and biochemical features and on characteristic short-chain fatty acid patterns in gas chromatography. These short-chain fatty acids also contribute to the foul-smelling odor emanating from the wound in the above case.

[2.2] **C.** Metronidazole, mainly used as an antiprotozoal agent, is also highly effective against anaerobic bacterial infections, such as those infections caused by *Bacteroides* species. It is the drug of first choice for GI strains of *Bacteroides.* Two other effective antibiotics are imipenem and piperacillin/tazobactam. *Bacteroides* species, such as *B. fragilis,* commonly possess β-lactamase activity resulting in resistance to penicillin and cephalosporin (e.g., cephalothin) antibiotics. Erythromycin is not indicated in the treatment of *Bacteroides* species.

[2.3] **F.** A key feature of obligate anaerobes such as *Clostridium, Bacteroides,* and *Actinomyces* is that they lack catalase and/or super-oxide dismutase (SOD) and are therefore susceptible to oxidative damage. *Bacteroides fragilis,* however, is able to survive (not grow) in environments with low oxygen content because of its ability to produce small amounts of both SOD and catalase. Anaerobes that possess SOD and/or catalase are able to negate the toxic effects of oxygen radicals and hydrogen peroxide and thus tolerate oxygen. Other common enzymes listed above catalyze the following reactions:

Catalase/superoxide dismutase catalyzes: $2H_2O_2 \rightarrow 2H_2O + O_2$
Myeloperoxidase catalyzes: $Cl^- + H_2O_2 \rightarrow ClO^- + H_2O$
NADPH oxidase catalyzes: $NADPH + 2O_2 \rightarrow 2O_2^- + H^+ NADP^+$
NO synthase catalyzes: $^1/_2O_2$ + arginine $\rightarrow$ NO + citrulline
Oxidase catalyzes: $2H^+ + 2e^- + {}^1/_2O_2 \rightarrow H_2O$

[2.4] **C.** In infections, such as intra-abdominal abscesses, *Bacteroides* species are often associated with other organisms. The only other organism in the list above that is solely aerobic and gram-negative is *N. gonorrhoeae. Clostridium* and *Listeria* are both gram-positive. *E. coli* is gram-negative and a facultative anaerobe.

MICROBIOLOGY PEARLS

- The treatment of choice of *B. fragilis* is surgical debridement in addition to metronidazole, imipenem, or piperacillin/tazobactam.
- Most anaerobes are part of mixed infections at mucosal surfaces.
- *Bacteroides fragilis* is the most common anaerobe in the human GI tract.
- *Bacteroides fragilis* usually express superoxide dismutase, an enzyme, which allows the organism to survive in the presence of small amounts of oxygen.

REFERENCES

Brook I, Frazier EH. Aerobic and anaerobic microbiology in intraabdominal infections associated with diverticulitis. J Med Microbiol 2000;49:827–30.

Engelkirk PG, Duben-Engelkirk JD, Dowell VR. Principles and Practice of Clinical Anaerobic Bacteriology. Belmont, CA: Star Publishing, 1992.

Murray PR, Rosenthal KS, Pfaller MA. Anaerobic gram negative bacilli. In: Murray PR, Rosenthal KS, Pfaller MA. Medical Microbiology, 5th ed. St. Louis, MO: Mosby, 2005:421–26.

CASE 3

A 28-year-old woman presents to the office for the evaluation of a rash. She had just returned from a weeklong camping trip in the New England area, when she noted the presence of a circular, red rash on her lower abdomen. Also, she has had a low-grade fever, and some achiness and fatigue. Examination of her abdomen reveals a 10-cm flat, red, circular patch with some central clearing. No other skin rashes are noted, and the remainder of the examination is normal. The blood cultures are negative. You make the presumptive diagnosis of erythema migrans and send blood for confirmatory serologic studies.

- **What organism is the etiologic agent of erythema migrans?**
- **What are the primary reservoir and vector of transmission of this agent?**

ANSWERS TO CASE 3: *Borrelia burgdorferi*

Summary: A 28-year-old woman who has been recently camping in the New England area complains of fever and a skin rash consistent with erythema migrans. Confirmatory serologies are sent.

- **Etiologic agent of erythema migrans:** *Borrelia burgdorferi*
- **Primary reservoir of infection:** Small rodents, primarily the white-footed mouse
- **Primary vector of transmission:** *Ixodes tick*

CLINICAL CORRELATION

Borrelia burgdorferi is the causative agent of Lyme disease and is transmitted to humans by *Ixodes* ticks. This disease was first recognized in Old Lyme, Connecticut, with the identification of cluster cases of arthritis in children. The infection is characterized by a **"bull's eye" skin lesion,** which develops from the site of the tick bite, 1–4 weeks postinfection. Additional initial symptoms include fever, fatigue, headache, joint pain, or mild stiffness of the neck. **Lyme disease is the most common vector-born disease in the United States,** and if left undiagnosed and untreated, the infection usually progresses to involve the nervous or vascular systems and cause fluctuating or chronic arthritis.

APPROACH TO *Borrelia* SPECIES

Objectives

1. Know the characteristics and virulence factors of *B. burgdorferi.*
2. Know the reservoir, vector, and host involved in the transmission of *B. burgdorferi.*

Definitions

Erythema migrans: Skin lesion composed of redness (erythema) with central clearing (target lesion).

Spirochetes: Thin spiral bacteria of which three genera cause significant disease in humans: *Leptospira, Borrelia,* and *Treponema,* which lead to leptospirosis, Lyme disease, and syphilis, respectively (see Table 3-1 for an abbreviated listing).

Table 3-1
ABBREVIATED LISTING OF SPIROCHETES

SPIROCHETE	DISEASE	TREATMENT	COMMENT
Treponema	Venereal syphilis, Yaws, pinta, endemic syphilis	Penicillin	Veneral syphilis usually is sexually or vertically (to fetus/neonate) transmitted, whereas yaws, pinta, endemic syphillis is by skin or shared utensils, usually affecting children
Leptospires	Weil syndrome (severe hepatic renal failure) Anicteric leptospirosis (without jaundice)	Doxycycline or ampicillin	Coiled, highly motile with hooked ends and flagella allowing burrowing into tissue
Borrelia	Relapsing fever Lyme disease	Erythromycin, tetracycline	Usually human or rodent reservoir transmitted by tick bite

DISCUSSION

Characteristics of *Borrelia* Species

Borrelia burgdorferi belongs to the **spirochete** family of **prokaryotes.** It stains **gram-negative,** although spirochetes are considered neither gram-positive nor gram-negative. Spirochetes consist of a **flexible, multilayer outer cell membrane** and a **more rigid, peptidoglycan-containing cytoplasmic membrane.** Between these two layers are **endoflagella** that insert at the ends of the spirochete. **Rotation of these flagella** creates the **characteristic cork-screw shape** of these organisms. This provides for motility of the organism and hides the normally antigenic flagella from host defenses. These organisms are **microaerophilic** and have a doubling time of 8–24 hours. The disease is endemic in several regions of the United States including **Northeastern, Midwest, and Pacific coast** states. However, most reported cases occur in **New York, Connecticut, Pennsylvania, and New Jersey.**

The spirochetes that cause Lyme disease have been divided into genospecies. Three genospecies, *B. burgdorferi* sensu stricto, *B. garinii,* and *B. afzelii,* are known to cause Lyme disease and are known collectively as **B. burgdorferi** sensu lato. The outer membrane of *B. burgdorferi* contains unique outer surface proteins (Osps), which are thought to play a role in their virulence. **Small rodents,** particularly the white-footed mouse, are the

primary reservoirs of *B. burgdorferi,* and the vector of transmission is the *Ixodes* tick. The larva of the tick is born uninfected. The **ticks become infected with the spirochete on feeding on an infected animal.** This usually occurs during the nymph stage of the tick's life cycle. The spirochetes **multiply in the gastrointestinal (GI) tract** of the **tick,** and then are transmitted to the animal host by regurgitation or salivation during a subsequent feeding. *Borrelia burgdorferi* are next **transmitted to humans via tick bite** followed by dissemination through the bloodstream to the joints, heart, and central nervous system (CNS). The nymphal stage of the tick is more infective than the adult and larval stages. Most exposures to *Borrelia* occur between the months of May and July, when the nymphs are most active.

Clinically there are three stages of *B. burgdorferi* infection: **stage 1,** which occurs in the first 4 weeks postinfection, involves the initial characteristic skin lesion referred to as **"erythema migrans"; stage 2** follows for months postinfection with **neurologic and cardiac** involvement; and **stage 3** results in **chronic arthritis** of the joints.

Diagnosis

The diagnosis of Lyme disease is made primarily by **clinical presentation** and patient history of exposure. Confirmation of a clinical **diagnosis is made serologically** via the detection of **antibody** by enzyme-linked immunoabsorbance or indirect immunofluorescence. However, serologic tests are most reliable 2–4 weeks postinfection, because of cross-reactivity with normal flora, and Western blot analysis should be used to confirm a positive serologic test. Alternately, **new PCR-based tests** are available to detect *B. burgdorferi* DNA. *Borrelia burgdorferi* is difficult to grow in culture, requiring complex culture media and a microaerophilic environment. It is also difficult to visualize under light microscopy, but can be seen under darkfield microscopy or when stained with Giemsa or silver stains.

Treatment and Prevention

Initial stages of infection with *B. burgdorferi* can be effectively treated with **doxycycline** or **amoxicillin,** while **later stages of disease** are better treated with **penicillin G or ceftriaxone. Prevention** of infection involves limiting exposure to ticks by **wearing protective clothing in endemic areas,** including long sleeves and long pants tucked into socks. Careful search for and removal of ticks is also an important preventative measure. Use of **repellants** is also helpful and administration of insecticides may reduce the number of active nymphal ticks for a given season. A **vaccine** containing recombinant OspA protein was developed for persons with the highest risk of exposure. The vaccine is approved for adults and shows approximately 75 percent efficacy.

COMPREHENSION QUESTIONS

[3.1] A 9-year-old boy presents with a migratory rash with central clearing on the back of his neck. The child had recently been on vacation with his family in Oregon and had gone hiking. The child's pediatrician observes the rash and suspects an infection with *B. burgdorferi.* Which of the following is thought to be a virulence factor of this organism?

A. Intracellular growth in leukocytes
B. Endotoxin release
C. Localization in reticuloendothelial cells
D. Antiphagocytic capsular antigen
E. Expression of outer surface proteins

[3.2] If the child's infection is left untreated, which of the following symptoms would most likely appear?

A. Urethritis
B. Centripetal spread of rash
C. Biphasic illness with fever and chills
D. Stiffness in the knees
E. Swelling of lymph nodes

[3.3] A small tick, of the genus *Ixodes,* most commonly transmits *B. burgdorferi.* Which of the following diseases is also transmitted by a tick?

A. Q fever
B. Leptospirosis
C. Ehrlichiosis
D. Yellow fever
E. Eastern equine encephalitis

Answers

[3.1] **E.** Differential expression of outer surface proteins is thought to be involved with virulence; answers A, B, C, and D are incorrect: (A) intracellular growth in leukocytes is a virulence factor of *Ehrlichia;* (B) endotoxins are characteristic of gram-negative organisms, not *Borrelia;* (C) localization in reticuloendothelial cells occurs in infections with *Francisella tularensis;* (D) an antiphagocytic capsular antigen is not a virulence factor of *Borrelia.*

[3.2] **D.** Later stages of infection with *B. burgdorferi* include arthritis, meningitis, nerve palsies, and cardiovascular abnormalities; answers A, B, C, E, are incorrect: (A) arthritis, not urethritis, is a later manifestation of infection with *B. burgdorferi;* (B) the skin rash or erythema migrans expands centrifugally, not centripetally; (C) biphasic illness with fever and chills occurs more commonly with *Leptospira* infections; (E) swelling of lymph nodes is more commonly associated with *Yersinia* infections.

[3.3] **C.** Similar to Lyme disease, ehrlichiosis is also transmitted via a tick vector; answers A, B, D, and E are incorrect: (A) Q fever is most commonly transmitted via inhalation of dried feces or urine contaminated with rickettsiae; (B) Leptospirosis is typically transmitted via ingestion of contaminated food or water; (D and E) both yellow fever and eastern equine encephalitis are transmitted by mosquitoes.

MICROBIOLOGY PEARLS

❖ *Borrelia burgdorferi* is a microaerophilic spirochete.

❖ Primary reservoirs of *B. burgdorferi* are small rodents (e.g., white-footed mouse), and the vector of transmission is the *Ixodes* tick.

❖ States with highest incidence include: New York, Connecticut, Pennsylvania, and New Jersey.

❖ Primary treatment is doxycycline or amoxicillin.

❖ Prevention consists of wearing protective clothing, use of insect repellants or insecticides, and a recombinant OspA protein vaccine.

REFERENCES

Brooks GF, Butel JS, Morse SA. Jawetz, Melnick, & Adelberg's Medical Microbiology, 23rd ed. New York: McGraw-Hill, 2004:336–338.

Murray PR, Rosenthal KS, Pfaller MA. Medical Microbiology, 5th ed. St. Louis, MO: Mosby, 2005.

Ryan JR, Ray CG. Sherris Medical Microbiology, 4th ed. New York: McGraw-Hill, 2004:431–434.

Wilske B, Schriefer ME. Borrelia. In: Murray PR, Baron EJ, Jorgensen JH, et al., eds. Manual of Clinical Microbiology, 8th ed. ASM Press, 2003.

CASE 4

A 19-year-old male college student presents to the student health department with abdominal pain, diarrhea, and fever. He says that his symptoms started a day ago. He has had 10 stools in the past day and has noted blood mixed in with the stool on several occasions. He usually eats at home but reports having eaten chicken in the college cafeteria 3 days ago. He has no history of gastrointestinal (GI) disease. On examination, he has a temperature of 37.8°C (100°F) and appears to be in pain. His abdomen has hyperactive bowel sounds and is diffusely tender but without rigidity, rebound tenderness, or guarding. A general surgeon is consulted and is considering the diagnosis of acute appendicitis versus bacterial gastroenteritis possibly related to the chicken eaten. A stool sample tests positive for blood and fecal leukocytes. Stool cultures are sent and are subsequently positive for a pathologic organism.

- **What is the most likely pathologic organism?**

- **In what atmospheric environment does this organism grow?**

ANSWERS TO CASE 4: *Campylobacter jejuni*

Summary: A 19-year-old man presents with a bacterial gastroenteritis that mimics appendicitis.

- **Most likely etiology of this infection:** *Campylobacter jejuni*
- **Preferred atmospheric environment:** Microaerophilic (presence of increased levels of carbon dioxide)

CLINICAL CORRELATION

More than 50 serotypes of *C. jejuni* have been identified based on heat labile (capsular and flagellar) antigens. *Campylobacter jejuni* is endemic worldwide, and **most cases of infection are associated with eating poorly cooked chicken, although milk, water and other meats** have also been implicated. Human-to-human transmission is rare. ***Campylobacter jejuni* is one of the most frequent causes of bacterial diarrhea occurring most often in the summer or early fall.** The incubation period is 1–3 days followed initially by symptoms of fever, malaise, and abdominal pain. *Campylobacter jejuni* can cause bloody diarrhea, mucosal inflammation, and bacteremia, suggesting that it is invasive to the lining of the intestine. Most cases of *Campylobacter* gastroenteritis is self-limited, with symptoms resolving within 7 days; however, relapses can occur in 5–10 percent of cases which are untreated.

Complications of *Campylobacter* gastroenteritis include pancreatitis, peritonitis, or more uncommonly arthritis, osteomyelitis, and sepsis. A serious postinfection sequelae of *Campylobacter* gastroenteritis is **Guillain-Barré syndrome**, an acute demyelinating disease. Antigenic similarities between the lipopolysaccharides on the surface of some serotypes of *C. jejuni* and myelin proteins are thought to be responsible for causing Guillain-Barré disease.

Other *Campylobacter* species such as *C. coli* also cause gastroenteritis, which is clinically indistinguishable from *C. jejuni* infection. *Campylobacter fetus* is primarily a cause of bacteremia, septic arthritis, peritonitis, abscesses, meningitis, and endocarditis in immunocompromised patients.

APPROACH TO SUSPECTED *Campylobacter* INFECTION

Objectives

1. Know the characteristics, virulence factors, and preferred growth environments of *C. jejuni.*
2. Know the sources of infection with and mechanism of transmission of *C. jejuni.*

Definitions

Guillain-Barré syndrome: A demyelinating disease resulting from similarities between the host and the surface of the *Campylobacter* organism.
Fecal leukocytes: White blood cells present in the stool, which correlate loosely with the presence of an invasive pathogen.

DISCUSSION

Characteristics of *Campylobacter*

Campylobacter species are **small motile, nonspore-forming, comma-shaped, gram-negative bacilli.** Its motility is the result of a single **flagellum** located at one or both poles of the organism. Campylobacter does not grow in aerobic or anaerobic environments. It is **microaerophilic,** requiring 5–10 percent oxygen and high concentrations of carbon dioxide for growth. *Campylobacter jejuni* grows better at 42°C (107.6°F) than 37°C (98.6°F). *Campylobacter jejuni* multiplies more slowly than other enteric bacteria, making isolation difficult from stool samples unless selective media are used. When **selective media** are used, the colonies that grow tend to be **gray, mucoid, and wet appearing.** Its outer membrane contains lipopolysaccharides with endotoxic activity. Extracellular toxins with cytopathic activity have also been found; however, little is known regarding the pathogenesis of this organism and the role of these putative virulence factors in disease. The organisms are sensitive to decreased pH, so it is hypothesized that factors that neutralize gastric acid enhance the organisms chances for survival.

Diagnosis

The differential diagnosis of acute gastroenteritis would include *Salmonella, Shigella, Yersinia,* as well as *Campylobacter.* Because of the feature of abdominal pain and cramps, sometimes in the absence of diarrhea, *Campylobacter* gastroenteritis can be misdiagnosed as appendicitis or irritable bowel syndrome. The presence of bloody diarrhea may also suggest enterohemorrhagic *Escherichia coli.*

Definitive diagnosis would be made by **culture of the stool and growth of *Campylobacter*.** *Campylobacter* are more fastidious than most other causes of bacterial gastroenteritis and specimens should be transported to the laboratory in media such as **Cary-Blair.** Selective media such as campy blood agar or Skirrow medium, which includes antibiotics to inhibit the normal stool flora, allows for growth of *Campylobacter* within 48–72 hours. Presumptive identification can be made by growth of **oxidase positive colonies on selective media at 42°C** (107.6°F) **after 48–72 hours** with characteristic **comma-shaped, small, gram-negative bacilli seen on Gram stain.** Confirmation of identification of either *C. jejuni* or *C. coli* can be made by resistance to cephalothin and susceptibility to nalidixic acid antimicrobial disks. As a result of the fastidious nature of these pathogens, a commercial assay for detection of *Campylobacter* antigen in the stool is frequently used for diagnosis.

TREATMENT AND PREVENTION

Most often *C. jejuni* infection is self-limited and does not require specific antimicrobial therapy. Supportive care, that is, hydration, is often the only treatment needed. If specific therapy is needed for severe disease, or infection in immunocompromised patients, **erythromycin** is the drug of choice, because of the recent increase in resistance to fluoroquinolones.

Prevention involves care in food preparation. Foods, especially chicken, should be completely cooked, and exposure to raw or undercooked chicken or unpasteurized milk should be limited, especially in pregnant women or immunocompromised persons.

COMPREHENSION QUESTIONS

[4.1] Which of the following are the special laboratory conditions needed to recover *C. jejuni?*

A. 37°C (98.6°F) aerobic on blood agar plates
B. 37°C (98.6°F) anaerobic on blood agar plates
C. 42°C (107.6°F) microaerophilic on Skirrow medium
D. 42°C (107.6°F) aerobic on Skirrow medium

[4.2] A 21-year-old woman presents to the emergency room with shortness of breath 2 weeks after recovering from a "stomach flu." Physical exam reveals ascending muscle weakness that began in her toes. Cardiac irregularities are also notable. A review of the patient's chart revealed that a bacterial stool culture 2 weeks earlier, during the patient's "flu" episode, found comma-shaped organisms growing at 42°C (107.6°F). Which of the following pairs represents the causative agent of this patient's flu and the postflu condition, respectively?

A. *Campylobacter jejuni,* Guillain-Barré syndrome
B. *Clostridium botulinum,* botulism
C. JC virus, progressive multifocal leukoencephalopathy (PML)
D. Poliovirus, poliomyelitis

[4.3] In a nonimmunocompromised patient with *C. jejuni* as the causative agent of their food poisoning, which of the following is the treatment most often required?

A. Metronidazole
B. Vancomycin
C. Cephalosporin
D. TMP-SMZ
E. Supportive care and hydration

[4.4] A 20-year-old college student develops diarrhea that lasts for approximately 1 week. Stool cultures reveal a motile, microaerophilic gram-negative rod that is isolated by incubation at 41°C (105.8°F) on medium containing antibiotics. This organism is most likely to be which of the following?

A. *Escherichia coli*
B. *Vibrio parahaemolyticus*
C. *Yersinia enterocolitica*
D. *Campylobacter jejuni*
E. *Proteus vulgaris*

Answers

[4.1] **C.** The isolation and identification of *C. jejuni* can be achieved using special culture characteristics. Three requirements must be met. First, a selective medium is needed. There are several widely used selective media: Skirrow's medium uses vancomycin, polymyxin B, and trimethoprim; other selective media contain cefoperazone, other antimicrobials, and inhibitory compounds. The selective media are suitable for isolation of *C. jejuni* at 42ºC (107.6°F); when incubated at 36–37ºC (96.8–98.6°F), other *Campylobacters* and bacteria may be isolated. Finally, incubation must be in an atmosphere with reduced oxygen and added carbon dioxide. The colonies appear to be colorless or gray and may be watery and spreading or round and convex.

[4.2] **A.** Guillain-Barré syndrome (acute idiopathic polyneuritis) is associated with infections such as herpesvirus and *C. jejuni* (comma-shaped bacteria that grows at 42°C [107.6°F]). It is believed that some *C. jejuni* serotypes have surface lipopolysaccharides that are antigenically similar to myelin protein leading to the inflammation and demyelination of peripheral nerves and ventral root motor fibers. Suspected Guillain-Barré in a patient is always a medical emergency because respiratory distress or failure can ensue, and the patient should always be admitted to the hospital for careful treatment and observation. The other answers contain correct matching of the causative agent with the resulting condition, but do not reflect the clinical scenario described.

[4.3] **E.** Most infections with *C. jejuni* are self-limiting and thus do not require specific antimicrobial therapy, except in cases of severe disease and infection in immunocompromised individuals. Therefore, most often the only required therapy is hydration and supportive care. When specific antimicrobial therapy is indicated, the drug of first choice is erythromycin, with alternate drugs being tetracycline, ciprofloxacin, and ofloxacin.

[4.4] **D.** Based on the culture characteristics indicated above, the only possible answer is *C. jejuni*. Please also refer to the discussion for Question [4.1].

MICROBIOLOGY PEARLS

- *Campylobacter* species are small motile, non-spore-forming, comma-shaped, gram-negative bacilli, best grown in a microaerophilic environment at 42°C (107.6°F).
- Guillain-Barré is a rare neurological complication of *C. jejuni* gastroenteritis.
- *Campylobacter jejuni* gastroenteritis is usually self-limited; however, if necessary, erythromycin is the drug of choice.
- *Campylobacter* infection most often occurs several days after consumption of undercooked chicken.
- Symptom of fever and abdominal pain may initially mimic appendicitis.

REFERENCES

Allos BM. *Campylobacter jejuni* infections: update on emerging issues and trends. Clin Infect Dis 2001;32:1201–6.

Murray PR, Rosenthal KS, Pfaller MA. *Campylobacter* and *Helicobacter*. In: Murray PR, Rosenthal KS, Pfaller MA. Medical Microbiology, 5th ed. St. Louis, MO: Mosby, 2005:347–55.

Winn W, Allen S, Janda W, Koneman E, et al. Curved gram negative bacilli and oxidase-positive fermenters; Campylobacteraceae and Vibrionaceae in Koneman's Color Atlas and Textbook of Diagnostic Microbiology, 6th ed., Baltimore, MD: Lippincott, Williams and Wilkins, 2006:392–428.

❖ CASE 5

A 19-year-old woman presents for the evaluation of pelvic pain. The pain has progressively worsened over the past week. She has also been having some burning with urination and a vaginal discharge. She is sexually active, has had four lifetime partners, takes oral contraceptive pills, and occasionally uses condoms. On examination, she appears in no acute distress and does not have a fever. Her abdomen is soft with moderate lower abdominal tenderness. On pelvic examination, she is noted to have a yellow cervical discharge and significant cervical motion tenderness. No uterine or adnexal masses are palpated, but mild tenderness is also noted. A Gram stain of the cervical discharge reveals only multiple polymorphonuclear leukocytes. A direct DNA probe test subsequently comes back positive for *Chlamydia trachomatis.*

◆ **How does *C. trachomatis* enter a target cell?**

◆ **What are the two stages of the *C. trachomatis* life cycle?**

ANSWERS TO CASE 5: *Chlamydia trachomatis*

Summary: A 19-year-old woman with probable pelvic inflammatory disease has a positive DNA probe assay for *C. trachomatis*.

- **How *C. trachomatis* enters a target cell:** The elementary body of *C. trachomatis* binds to receptors on the host and induces endocytosis.
- **Two stages of the *C. trachomatis* life cycle:** The elementary body and the reticulate body.

CLINICAL CORRELATION

Chlamydia trachomatis is the causative agent of the most common sexually transmitted disease in the United States, and it is also the greatest cause of preventable blindness around the world. Chlamydial disease affects women five times more often than men, and approximately two-thirds of those affected lack symptoms and thus, do not know that they are infected. **Many of those infected with gonorrheal disease are also infected with *Chlamydia*,** as both organisms infect the columnar epithelial cells of the mucous membranes. Chlamydial disease usually affects those of lower socioeconomic standing and is prevalent in underdeveloped countries. Children are also a main reservoir, transmitting the disease by hand-to-hand transfer of infected eye fluids or by sharing contaminated towels or clothing.

APPROACH TO SUSPECTED CHLAMYDIAL INFECTION

Objectives

1. Know the characteristics of the *Chlamydia* species.
2. Know the virulence factors and diseases associated with *Chlamydia* bacteria.

Definitions

Elementary body: Nondividing 300-nm infectious particle. This particle has an outer membrane with disulfide linkages which allows it to survive extracellularly.

Chandelier sign: Cervical motion tenderness during the bimanual exam, characteristic of pelvic inflammatory disease (PID).

Exudate: Material, such as fluids, cells or debris, which has extravasated from vessels and has been deposited on tissue surfaces or in tissue.

Papule: Small palpable elevated lesion that is less than 1 cm.

DISCUSSION

Characteristics of *Chlamydia trachomatis*

Chlamydia trachomatis is a **gram-negative obligate intracellular parasite** with a unique life cycle. It is coccoid in morphology and is very small, usually about 350 nm in diameter. Although *C. trachomatis* is classified as gram-negative bacteria, it **lacks a peptidoglycan layer and muramic acid,** which are present in other gram-negative organisms. There are many disulfide linkages present in the outer membrane which stabilize the organism. Its **extracellular form is called the elementary body,** which has a small, spore-like structure. It attaches to columnar, cuboidal, or transitional epithelial cells in structures lined by mucous membranes. The elementary body binds to receptors on susceptible cells and induces endocytosis into the host. These membrane-protected structures are known as inclusions. The elementary body undergoes reorganization into a larger, more metabolically active form known as the **reticulate body.** Reticulate bodies grow and multiply by binary fission to create larger intracellular inclusions. Reticulate bodies transform back into elementary bodies, which are released from the epithelial cell by exocytosis and which can then infect other cells. The life cycle of *C. trachomatis* lasts approximately 48–72 hours. Table 5-1 lists in sequential order are the stages of the life cycle.

Chlamydia trachomatis appears to be an **obligate human pathogen** with approximately 15 serotypes. It is the most common bacterial cause of sexually transmitted diseases in humans and also causes **conjunctivitis and ocular trachoma.** Infection of the conjunctiva by *C. trachomatis* results in scarring and inflammation. This fibrosis pulls the eyelid inward causing the eyelashes to rub against the cornea. Because the eyelid is rolled inward, the individual is unable to completely close the eye resulting in the inability to maintain moisture on the surface of the eye. It is the combination of the lack of surface

Table 5-1

LIFE CYCLE OF *Chlamydia trachomatis*

1. Elementary body attaches to host cell.
2. Host cell phagocytizes the elementary body residing in a vacuole, inhibiting phagosome-lysome fusion.
3. The elementary body reorganizes to form a reticulate body.
4. The reticulate body divides by binary fusion.
5. Some reticulate bodies convert back into elementary bodies; elementary bodies are released into host cell.

moisture and constant abrasion by the eyelashes that causes corneal scarring and blindness. Ocular trachoma is one of the leading causes of blindness worldwide.

Chlamydia trachomatis also causes other diseases including **pneumonia, urethritis, epididymitis, lymphogranuloma venereum, cervicitis, and pelvic inflammatory disease. Lymphogranuloma venereum** presents with a **painless papule on the genitalia that heals spontaneously.** The infection is then localized to **regional lymph nodes** where it resides for approximately 2 months. As time progresses, the lymph nodes begin to swell, causing pain, and may rupture and expel an exudate. Men with **epididymitis** present with fever, unilateral scrotal swelling, and pain. Women with **cervicitis** present with a swollen, inflamed cervix. There may also be a yellow purulent discharge present. PID occurs when the infection spreads to the uterus, fallopian tubes, and ovaries. PID presents with lower abdominal pain, dyspareunia, vaginal discharge, uterine bleeding, nausea, vomiting, and fever. **Cervical motion tenderness** during the bimanual exam is known as the "chandelier sign." Recurrent PID may scar the fallopian tubes, resulting in infertility or ectopic pregnancy. Children may acquire chlamydial disease during birth via passage through an infected birth canal. **Inflammation of the infant's conjunctiva** may occur with a yellow discharge and swelling of the eyelids within 2 weeks after birth. The presence of **basophilic intracytoplasmic inclusion bodies** from the conjunctiva is a helpful diagnostic clue. Neonatal **pneumonia** may also occur from passage through an infected birth canal. An infected child may present 4–11 weeks after birth with respiratory distress, cough, and tachypnea. The direct destruction of host cells due to chlamydial infection and then host's inflammatory response produces the clinical symptoms associated with the various forms of chlamydial disease.

Other *Chlamydial* species are known to cause disease in humans. **Atypical pneumonia** is caused by *Chlamydophila pneumonia,* and presents with fever, headache, and a dry hacking cough. Additionally, **psittacosis** is another atypical pneumonia caused by *Chlamydophila psittaci*. This organism is acquired by inhalation of feces from **infected birds,** which serve as the reservoir.

Diagnosis

Infection with *C. trachomatis* can be rapidly diagnosed by detection of the bacterial nucleic acid in patient samples from the oropharynx, conjunctiva, urethra, or cervix. Other specimens such as the conjunctiva can be cultured using McCoy cells in a tissue culture assay. Diagnostic tests for nucleic acid detection include PCR amplification or direct DNA hybridization assays, measuring for specific 16S ribosomal RNA sequences can be performed on all of above specimens including urine.

Treatment and Prevention

Currently, the best method of preventing chlamydial infection is education and proper sanitation. Ocular infection of *C. trachomatis* can sometimes but not always be prevented by administration of topical tetracycline drops. It is the lack of this antibiotic in underdeveloped countries that makes *C. trachomatis* prevalent in these areas. *Chlamydia trachomatis, C. psittaci,* and *C. pneumonia* are all treated with tetracycline or erythromycin. **Azithromycin** is effective for cervicitis and urethritis. Pelvic inflammatory disease is treated with ceftriaxone and 2 weeks of doxycycline.

COMPREHENSION QUESTIONS

[5.1] A 32-year-old immigrant woman from Tanzania delivers a healthy baby boy. Because this woman had no regular doctor, no preliminary tests were performed prior to delivery. Thirteen days after delivery, the child develops swelling of both eyes with the presence of a yellow discharge. The presence of intracytoplasmic inclusion bodies is detected. Which antibiotic would be most appropriate in this situation?

A. Tetracycline
B. Ceftriaxone
C. Penicillin G
D. Doxycycline
E. Erythromycin

[5.2] Which diagnostic test is best to identify an infection with *C. trachomatis?*

A. Aerobic and anaerobic blood cultures
B. Stool culture
C. DNA probe
D. Urine culture
E. Culture and darkfield microscopy

[5.3] A 29-year-old bird collector presents to the local clinic with what he describes as flu-like symptoms. He doesn't look ill, and has a slight fever, headache, and a dry hacking cough. He denies the production of sputum or hemoptysis. There are no crackles heard on auscultation, and a radiograph shows small streaks of infiltrate. It is determined that he has pneumonia. What is the most likely organism causing his disease?

A. *Streptococcus pneumoniae*
B. *Chlamydophila psittaci*
C. *Haemophilus influenzae*
D. *Staphylococcus aureus*
E. *Chlamydophila pneumoniae*

Answers

[5.1] **E.** The symptoms described are classic for inclusion conjunctivitis caused by *C. trachomatis.* The infection was most likely passed from the mother to child during vaginal delivery. The infection usually presents 2 weeks after delivery and is characterized by swollen eyes and a yellow discharge. The drug of choice for this infection is erythromycin eyedrops. Most children are given erythromycin eye drops prophylactically postbirth. Tetracyclines are not given to young children due to staining of teeth.

[5.2] **C.** The most specific test used to detect a chlamydial infection is a DNA probe. ***C. trachomatis*** is a gram-negative obligate intracellular parasite, and any blood or urine culture would not be helpful for diagnosis. *Chlamydia trachomatis* is not present in stool. Darkfield microscopy is used to view spirochetes, which *C. trachomatis* is not.

[5.3] **B.** Although all of the organisms listed above cause pneumonia, only two of them are atypical. Atypical pneumonia is characterized by a dry hacking cough, fever, and headache. These include *C. psittaci* and *C. pneumoniae.* The mention of birds should point you in the direction of *C. psittaci,* because they are the reservoir for the organism that is inhaled through dry feces. Typical pneumonias are characterized by hemoptysis of pus-laden sputum, and patients appear very sick.

MICROBIOLOGY PEARLS

- Chlamydial disease is the most common STD in the United States.
- Cervical motion tenderness and adnexal tenderness are common findings of pelvic inflammatory disease.
- The elementary body is the infectious stage in *C. trachomatis.*
- *Chlamydia trachomatis* is the most common preventable cause of worldwide blindness (Proper sanitation is important for prevention and the use of tetracycline or erythromycin is important for early treatment.).

REFERENCES

Murray PR, Rosenthal KS, Pfaller MA. Medical Microbiology, 5th ed. St. Louis, MO: Mosby, 2005:412–420.

Schneider AS, Szanto PA. Pathology Board Review Series, 2nd ed. Philadelphia, PA: Lippincott Williams & Wilkins, 2001:272, 280.

Boman J, Gaydos C, Quinn T. Minireview: molecular diagnosis of *Chlamydia pneumoniae* infection. J Clin Microbiol 1999;37:3791–9.

❖ CASE 6

A 52-year-old man presents for the evaluation of diarrhea and abdominal pain, which have been worsening over the past week. He is now having 8–10 watery stools a day and mild cramping pain. He denies vomiting, fever, ill contacts, or having had blood in his stool. He has no history of gastrointestinal diseases. He states that approximately 10 days ago he completed a course of amoxicillin/clavulanate for pneumonia. On examination he is mildly ill appearing, but his vital signs are normal. His abdomen is soft, has hyperactive bowel sounds, and is diffusely, mildly tender. A stool sample is negative for blood but positive for leukocytes. A stool culture is negative, but a specific toxin assay is positive.

◆ **What is the most likely etiologic agent of this disease?**

◆ **Which condition predisposes this organism to cause disease in humans?**

ANSWERS TO CASE 6: CLOSTRIDIA

Summary: A 52-year-old man who recently took oral antibiotics, now has diarrhea. Fecal leukocytes are present in the stool, and a toxin test is positive.

- **Most likely etiologic agent:** *Clostridium difficile*
- **Condition predisposing disease in humans:** Recent antibiotic exposure

CLINICAL CORRELATION

There are approximately 90 bacterial species of *Clostridium,* about 20 of which are known to cause disease in humans. They are found widely in soil, decaying vegetation, and the intestinal tracts of humans and other vertebrates. Infection occurs in patients with predisposing factors including trauma, surgery, immunosuppression, and prior treatment with antibiotics. *Clostridium perfringens* is the most common *Clostridium* species isolated from human infections and is a cause of wound infections including gas gangrene. *Clostridium tetani* is associated with the toxin mediated disease, tetanus, which occurs in unvaccinated persons who come in contact with the organism. The spores of the organism survive for long periods of time in the soil and are introduced into the person following deep puncture wounds. Tetanus is characterized by tonic spasms usually involving the muscles of the neck, jaw (lockjaw), and trunk. *Clostridium botulinum* is the causative agent of botulism. Botulism occurs when spores are consumed usually from improperly canned vegetables. Symptoms of nausea, blurred vision, and weakness of the upper extremities spreading downward occur within 12–36 hours after ingestion of the toxin. Infant botulism is associated with consumption of honey.

Clostridium difficile can be isolated in the stool of fewer than 5 percent of healthy adults; however, up to 70 percent of healthy infants have the organism in their stool. Most cases of *C. difficile* colitis occur during or after a course of antibiotics. Antibiotics alter the intestinal flora allowing for an overgrowth of *C. difficile,* which either already exists in the intestinal tract or is introduced from an environmental source. Disease can range from asymptomatic carriage of the organism to mild diarrhea to pseudomembranous colitis, which can be further complicated by toxic megacolon and bowel perforation.

APPROACH TO SUSPECTED *Clostridium difficile* INFECTION

Objectives

1. Know the characteristics of the *Clostridium* species.
2. Know the virulence factors and diseases associated with *Clostridium* bacteria.

Definitions

Antibiotic-associated diarrhea: Gastroenteritis caused by *C. difficile*
Pseudomembranous colitis: Presence of nodules or plaques on erythematous (red) colonic mucosa seen by sigmoidoscopy, associated with *C. difficile* colitis

DISCUSSION

Characteristics of *Clostridium difficile*

Clostridium difficile is an **anaerobic, spore-forming, toxigenic gram-positive rod.** Some strains have a thin capsule and some have fimbriae, although the significance of these is uncertain. *Clostridium difficile,* so named because of the initial difficulty in isolating and culturing the organism, requires a selective medium for growth which also inhibits normal stool flora.

The **virulence factors** of *C. difficile* include **toxin production** as well as production of other enzymes, such as **hyaluronidase. Toxin A is an enterotoxin,** and **Toxin B,** the more biologically active toxin in humans, is a **cytotoxin.** The specific role each component plays in disease in humans is unknown. The enterotoxin is chemotactic and initiates the release of cytokines, hypersecretion of fluids in the intestinal tract, and hemorrhagic necrosis. Depolarization of actin microfilaments occurs, which leads to destruction of the cellular cytoskeleton disruption of tight junctions between epithelial cells. A new strain of *C. difficile* has been recently identified, which is more virulent and more likely to cause megacolon. This strain has been found to produce larger quantities of Toxins A and B in addition to a new toxin, binary toxin. Formation of spores allows the organism to survive under stressful situations in the environment for extended periods of time. Spore formation also allows the organisms to survive in the hospital environment and can be transferred from patient to patient on fomites.

Diagnosis

Antibiotic-associated diarrhea is the most common cause of diarrhea that develops in patients who have been hospitalized for 3 or more days. Clinical diagnosis can be made by visualization of the **pseudomembrane** (fibrin, bacteria, cell debris, white blood cells).

The **gold standard for laboratory diagnosis** of antibiotic-associated diarrhea caused by *C. difficile* is **detection of toxin production in the stool** using a tissue culture assay, where a specific antibody neutralizes the toxin and therefore, the production of cytopathic effect. However, this assay requires tissue culture facilities as well as approximately 3 days for completion. Culture of *C. difficile* can be performed on selective media, cycloserine, cefoxitin, and fructose agar in an egg yolk agar base (CCFA medium), in an anaerobic environment. After 24–48 hours, incubation colonies will fluoresce chartreuse on

CCFA and have a barnyard odor. Specific identification can be made using commercially available rapid methods that detect fatty acids produced by the organism or by gas-liquid chromatography. Growth of the organism would have to be followed up by detection of toxin for a specific diagnosis of disease.

Commercially available membrane or microwell based **enzyme immunoassays** are available for rapid detection of Toxin A or Toxin A and B in a stool specimen. For optimal recovery testing of three stools on 3 days is recommended.

Treatment and Prevention

The first-line treatment for *C. difficile* disease is oral metronidazole, with oral vancomycin reserved for those who fail first-line treatment. Unfortunately, relapse can occur in 20–30 percent of adequately treated patients because of the resistance of the spores to treatment. A second round of treatment is usually successful. Failure is not usually attributed to resistance of the organism to vancomycin or metronidazole. Prevention of *C. difficile* in hospitalized patients involves good infection control procedures that include isolation of the infected patient.

COMPREHENSION QUESTIONS

[6.1] Which organism listed below may cause a life-threatening gastroenteritis as a result of use of a broad spectrum antimicrobial agent?

A. *Bacillus anthracis*
B. *Bacillus cereus*
C. *Clostridium botulinum*
D. *Clostridium difficile*
E. *Clostridium tetani*

[6.2] *Clostridium difficile*, as the causative agent in antibiotic-associated diarrhea, can best be detected using which of the following gold standard laboratory tests?

A. Gas-liquid chromatography
B. Pseudomembranous visualization
C. Rapid fatty acid detection assays
D. Tissue culture toxin detection assay

[6.3] A hospitalized patient developed severe diarrhea and pseudomembranous colitis within 5 days after antibiotic therapy was initiated. The severe diarrhea and pseudomembranous colitis occurred as a result of which of the following?

A. Collagenase
B. Fibrinolysin
C. Hyaluronidase
D. Lecithinase
E. Mucinase
F. Toxin A and B

Answers

[6.1] **D.** The use of broad spectrum antibiotics such as ampicillin and clindamycin has been associated with pseudomembranous colitis. Antibiotic administration results in the proliferation of drug-resistant *C. difficile* that produces Toxin A (a potent enterotoxin with cytotoxic activity) and Toxin B (a potent cytotoxin). This disease is best treated by discontinuing the use of the offending antibiotic and administering oral doses of metronidazole or vancomycin. Administration of antibiotics may also lead to a milder form of diarrhea, called antibiotic-associated diarrhea. This form is associated with *C. difficile* about 25 percent of the time.

[6.2] **D.** All of the above tests may be used as detection assays for *C. difficile*. However, only the tissue culture toxin detection assay is the gold standard laboratory test. This test involves a specific toxin neutralizing antibody that detects toxin (Toxin A and B) production in the stool using a tissue culture detection assay. Not all *C. difficile* strains produce toxins, and the tox genes are not carried on either plasmids or phages.

[6.3] **F.** *Clostridium difficile* produces two toxins, Toxins A and B. Both toxins are present in stool samples. Toxin A is enterotoxic causing the severe diarrhea, whereas Toxin B is cytotoxic leading to the destruction of enterocytes resulting in pseudomembranous colitis. For additional information please refer to the discussions for Questions 6.1 and 6.2.

MICROBIOLOGY PEARLS

- ❖ The most common cause of diarrhea in a patient who has been hospitalized for 3 or more days is *C. difficile.*
- ❖ The initial treatment for pseudomembranous colitis is metronidazole. Oral vancomycin is used for those who fail to respond to metronidazole.
- ❖ Detection of toxins in the stool is the method of choice for diagnosis of *C. difficile* colitis.

REFERENCES

Allen SD, Emery CL, Lyerly DM. In: Murray PR, Baron EJ, Jorgensen JH, et al., eds. Manual of Clinical Microbiology, 8th ed. Washington, DC: ASM Press, 2003:835–56.

Murray PR, Rosenthal KS, Pfaller MA. Clostridium. In: Murray PR, Rosenthal KS, Pfaller MA. Medical Microbiology, 5th ed. St. Louis, MO: Mosby, 2005:401–20.

❖ CASE 7

A 6-year-old girl is brought into the office for evaluation of a sore throat and fever, which she has had for approximately 4 days. Her parents have immigrated to the United States from Russia about 6 months ago. She has not had much medical care in her life, and her immunization status is unknown. On examination the child is anxious, tachypneic, and ill appearing. Her temperature is 38.6°C (101.5°F), and her voice is hoarse. Examination of her pharynx reveals tonsillar and pharyngeal edema with the presence of a gray membrane coating of the tonsil, which extends over the uvula and soft palate. She has prominent cervical adenopathy. Her lungs are clear. You immediately transfer her to the local children's hospital with the presumptive diagnosis of pharyngeal diphtheria and order confirmatory tests.

◆ **What Gram stain characteristics does *Corynebacterium diphtheriae* have on microscopy?**

What factor is required for the expression of diphtheria toxin?

ANSWERS TO CASE 7: *Corynebacterium diphtheriae*

Summary: A 6-year-old girl who recently arrived from Russia is diagnosed with pharyngeal diphtheria.

- **Characteristics of *C. diphtheriae* on Gram stain:** The club-shaped appearance of the gram-positive bacillus, often characterized as "Chinese letters" because of adherence of cells following division.

- **Factor required for the expression of diphtheria toxin:** Lysogenic bacteriophage.

CLINICAL CORRELATION

Corynebacteria are ubiquitous in nature and are part of the normal flora of the human respiratory tract and skin. Although most species of *Corynebacterium* can be opportunistic pathogens, only a few species are commonly associated with human disease. One of those species is *Corynebacterium jeikeium,* which is most commonly associated with **bacteremia** and line-related infection in immunocompromised patients. This organism is one of the few species of *Corynebacterium* that tends to be multidrug resistant. *Corynebacterium diphtheriae,* the cause of diphtheria, is one of the most pathogenic of the species. Humans are the only known reservoir and transmission is thought to occur by contact with aerosolized droplets, respiratory secretions, or infected skin lesions. Respiratory diphtheria occurs 2–6 days after inhalation of infected droplets. Patients develop nonspecific signs and symptoms of an upper respiratory infection as the organisms multiply locally with in epithelial cells in the respiratory tract. Toxin is then produced eliciting systemic symptoms including fever. An exudate, containing organisms, fibrin, and white and red blood cells, is formed, which is called a **pseudomembrane.** This grayish membrane covers the tonsils, uvula, and palate and can extend as far as the nasopharynx or larynx. Complications of membrane formation can be respiratory compromise by aspiration of the pseudomembrane, which is a common cause of death in this disease. Symptoms include fever and cervical lymphadenopathy (bull neck).

Cutaneous diphtheria, although rare in the United States, occurs from invasion of the organism from the patient's skin into the subcutaneous tissue. A papule develops at the site of contact that later becomes covered by a grayish membrane. As in respiratory diphtheria, toxin production by the organism elicits a systemic response with fever. Diphtheria toxin can also have effects on the heart (myocarditis) and nervous system (dysphagia, paralysis).

APPROACH TO SUSPECTED DIPHTHERIA INFECTION

Objectives

1. Know the characteristics and virulence factors of *C. diphtheriae.*
2. Know the factors involved with the expression of and the mechanism of action of the *C. diphtheriae* exotoxin.

Definitions

Lysogenic bacteriophage: Virus that infects bacteria.
Elek Test: An immunodiffusion test to detect the production of diphtheria toxin in a strain of *C. diphtheria.*
Pseudomembrane: Membrane formed in diphtheria, which consists of dead cells, leukocytes, and fibrin.

DISCUSSION

Characteristics of *Corynebacterium diphtheriae*

Corynebacterium diphtheriae is a **nonencapsulated gram-positive bacillus.** It is **nonmotile, non-spore-forming, and club shaped.** The cells often remain attached after division and form sharp angles, giving a **characteristic "Chinese letter" appearance** on microscopy.

Corynebacterium diphtheriae is divided into **three subtypes—gravis, intermedius, and mitis—**based on colony morphology and biochemical testing.

In the presence of a lysogenic β-phage, *C. diphtheriae* can produce a highly potent **exotoxin.** The toxin, which is the **major virulence factor** of this organism, consists of two components. The **B segment binds to specific receptors on susceptible cells.** Following proteolytic cleavage, the **A segment** is released into the host cell, where it can **inhibit protein synthesis.** The exotoxin targets a factor present in mammalian cells but not in bacterial cells, thus causing host tissue damage without affecting bacterial replication. Toxin-related tissue necrosis causes the characteristic pseudomembrane seen in clinical diphtheria.

Diagnosis

The **differential diagnosis** in the presence of sore throat, fever, and cervical lymphadenopathy would include streptococcal pharyngitis and infectious mononucleosis.

Clinical diagnosis of diphtheria can be made by visualization of the characteristic **pseudomembrane** formation. The **membrane should not be removed** because of the tight adherence to the epithelial surface and the chance for subsequent bleeding. Cultures should be collected from the throat or nasopharynx. A Gram stain would reveal the characteristic **gram-positive club-shaped bacilli.**

Corynebacterium with the exception of a few lipophilic species will grow well on most nonselective media within 24 hours. Colonies are usually **nonpigmented and small, without hemolysis on blood agar.** However, *C. diphtheriae* is more fastidious and specimens should be plated on a selective medium such as Tellurite in addition to the nonselective media. Colonies of *C. diphtheriae* will appear black on Tellurite media. Colonies growing on Loeffler media can be stained with methylene blue to observe the characteristic metachromatic granules. Definitive identification is made by biochemical tests usually performed at a reference or state public health laboratory, where the isolate will be further tested for toxin production. The Elek test is an immunodiffusion assay for detection of production of *C. diphtheria* toxin by the isolate.

Treatment and Prevention

Therapy for diphtheria is a combination of **antimicrobial therapy** (erythromycin) and **antitoxin.** The **antitoxin must be administered rapidly,** before the toxin binds to epithelial cells. Diphtheria can be prevented by **vaccination** with diphtheria toxoid (DPT). Infected patients should be isolated from other susceptible persons to prevent secondary spread of the disease. Prophylaxis with erythromycin can also be given to close contacts who are at risk.

COMPREHENSION QUESTIONS

[7.1] The mechanism of action of the exotoxin produced by *C. diphtheriae* can be characterized by which of the following?

A. Acting as a superantigen that binds to MHC class II protein and the T-cell receptor.
B. Blocking the release of acetylcholine causing anticholinergic symptoms.
C. Blocking the release of glycine (inhibitory neurotransmitter).
D. Inhibits protein synthesis via EF-2 adenosine diphosphate (ADP) ribosylation.
E. Stimulation of adenylate cyclase by ADP ribosylation of G-protein.

[7.2] Which of the following most accurately describes the therapy available for the prevention and treatment of *C. diphtheriae?*

A. Antimicrobial therapy for prophylaxis only
B. Antimicrobial therapy and prophylaxis, antitoxin, and toxoid (DPT)
C. Antitoxin only
D. Diphtheria toxoid (DPT) booster vaccination only

Answers

[7.1] **D.** *Corynebacterium diphtheriae* produces a potent exotoxin encoded by a lysogenic β-prophage. Following proteolytic cleavage, the A segment is released into the host cell where it inhibits *only* mammalian protein synthesis (ribosomal function) via ADP ribosylation of EF-2. Inhibition of protein synthesis disrupts normal cellular physiologic functions that are believed to be responsible for the necrotizing and neurotoxic effects of diphtheria toxin. An exotoxin with a similar mode of action is produced by some *Pseudomonas aeruginosa* strains. *Staphylococcus aureus* is responsible for producing the toxic shock syndrome toxin that acts as a superantigen leading to T-cell activation. *Clostridium tetani* blocks the release of glycine, leading to "lock-jaw." *Clostridium botulinum* blocks the release of acetylcholine, causing central nervous system (CNS) paralysis and anticholinergic symptoms. Finally, the heat-labile toxin produced by *Escherichia coli* causes watery diarrhea by stimulating adenylate cyclase.

[7.2] **B.** Protection against *C. diphtheriae* can be established through both active and passive immunity. Active immunity consists of a toxoid administered in the form of the DPT vaccine. Passive immunity is established by administering diphtheria antitoxin (immunoglobulins). Antimicrobial therapy (erythromycin) can be used to effectively treat patients with clinical diphtheria.

MICROBIOLOGY PEARLS

- The club-shaped appearance of the gram-positive bacillus *C. diphtheriae* is often characterized as "Chinese letters" as a result of adherence of cells following division.
- The typical clinical feature of diphtheria is pseudomembrane formation.
- Diphtheria is preventable by administration of DPT vaccine, which provides immunity for diphtheria, pertussis, and tetanus.

REFERENCES

Holmes, RK. Biology and molecular epidemiology of diphtheria toxin and the tox gene. J Infect Dis 2000;181(suppl 1):S156–67.

Murray PR, Rosenthal KS, Pfaller MA. Corynebacterium and other gram-positive bacilli. In: Murray PR, Rosenthal KS, Pfaller MA. Medical Microbiology, 5th ed. St. Louis, MO: Mosby, 2005:279–85.

CASE 8

A 72-year-old female nursing home resident is transferred to the hospital because of fever and altered mental status. She has advanced Alzheimer disease, is bed bound, and has an indwelling Foley catheter as a consequence of urinary incontinence. Her baseline mental status is awake and talkative, but oriented only to person. In the hospital now, she has a temperature of 38.3°C (101°F) and tachycardia (a rapid heart rate). She mumbles incoherently and is otherwise nonverbal. Her skin is cool, dry, and without ulceration. Her mucous membranes are dry. Her abdomen is soft, has normoactive bowel sounds, and is apparently tender in the suprapubic region. Her urinary catheter is draining cloudy urine. A urinalysis reveals too numerous to count white blood cells and bacteria. Gram stain of the urinary sediment reveals gram-positive cocci. Blood and urine cultures also grow gram-positive cocci.

 **What is the most likely cause of this infection?**

How does this organism acquire antibiotic resistance?

ANSWERS TO CASE 8: *Enterococcus faecalis*

Summary: A 72-year-old woman with an indwelling urinary catheter has a urinary tract infection and bacteremia. Gram-positive cocci are isolated from the urine and blood cultures.

 **Most likely etiology of infection:** *Enterococcus faecalis*

◆ **Mechanism of development of antibiotic resistance:** DNA mutation, or plasmid or transposon transfer

CLINICAL CORRELATION

Enterococci are normal flora of the gastrointestinal (GI) tract and are therefore more likely to cause infections in patients with a history of preceding abdominal or genital tract procedures. Although a common cause of community acquired urinary tract infections (UTIs), enterococci are most often associated with nosocomial UTI, particularly in patients with urinary catheters. Bacteremia and rarely endocarditis can result as complications of enterococcal urinary tract or wound infections, with the GI tract the most likely source. Patients at higher risk for enterococcal endocarditis are elderly patients and those with underlying heart disease, particularly the presence of artificial heart valves. **Enterococci** usually are a cause of **subacute left-sided or mitral valve endocarditis.**

APPROACH TO SUSPECTED ENTEROCOCCAL UTI

Objectives

1. Know the characteristics of *E. faecalis.*
2. Know the nature of the intrinsic and acquired antibiotic resistances of *E. faecalis.*

Definitions

Tachycardia: Increased heart rate above 100 beats per minute.

Transposons: Small pieces of DNA that can replicate and insert randomly in the chromosome.

Leukocyte esterase: An enzyme present in leukocytes, therefore used as an indirect marker of their presence.

DISCUSSION

Characteristics of *Enterococcus* Species

Enterococcus faecalis is an **aerobic gram-positive coccus** commonly found as **normal fecal flora** of healthy humans and other animals. It is capable of growing in extreme conditions, including a wide range of temperatures, high pH, the presence of high concentrations of bile salts, and saline concentrations of up to 6.5 percent. Enterococci have also been isolated from soil, food, and water. Enterococci are difficult to distinguish morphologically from streptococci, and for years were considered a member of the *Streptococcus* family. They **possess the group D streptococcal carbohydrate antigen on their cell surface.** Like streptococci, enterococci are often seen **singly, in pairs, or short chains on microscopy.** Little is known about the virulence factors associated with *E. faecalis.* Some strains of *Enterococcus* produce factors, not totally elucidated, which allow their adherence to both heart valves and urinary epithelial cells. One of its other major virulence factors is an **intrinsic resistance to multiple antibiotics,** including ampicillin, penicillin, and aminoglycosides, which are effective against other gram-positive bacteria. There is also evidence for acquired antibiotic resistance, either by **mutation** of **native DNA** or **acquisition of new DNA** from **plasmid or transposon transfer.** It is capable of acquiring resistance both from other enterococci and from other bacterial species and has recently been shown to transfer the gene for vancomycin resistance to *Staphylococcus aureus.*

Diagnosis

Clinical diagnosis of UTI is made by typical clinical symptoms of urgency and/or dysuria followed by a urinalysis and bacterial culture. The presence of white blood cells (positive leukocyte esterase) and bacteria in the urine are indicative of cystitis. The specific etiologic agent can only be determined by culturing the urine in a quantitative manner. The presence of greater than 10^5 colony-forming units (CFUs) per milliliter of clean catch urine or 10^4 CFU/mL of catheterized urine is considered significant for a UTI. Colonies of *Enterococcus* appear **nonhemolytic** or, in rare cases, α-hemolytic on blood agar and can be specifically identified using a **rapid PYR** (L-pyrrolidonyl-β-naphthylamide) test. **Conventional, overnight identification includes growth in 6.5 percent sodium chloride and esculin hydrolysis in the presence of bile.** Further identification of enterococci to the species level is not commonly done in routine clinical laboratories. Although most commercially available identification methods can speciate enterococci difficulties in accurate speciation occurs without the use of DNA sequence analysis. Most clinically significant enterococci are either *E. faecalis* or *E. faecium. Enterococcus faecium* tends to be more resistant to antibiotics particularly ampicillin and vancomycin.

Treatment and Prevention

Although enterococci are intrinsically resistant to low concentrations of β-lactam antibiotics, such as **ampicillin,** these agents are still the first choice for uncomplicated enterococcal urinary tract infections in cases in which the affecting strain is not highly resistant. For complicated UTI or endocarditis, bactericidal therapy is necessary and includes **ampicillin or vancomycin plus an aminoglycoside,** assuming that the infecting strain is susceptible to ampicillin or vancomycin and high levels of aminoglycosides. An alternative would be vancomycin if it is susceptible; or if resistant, alternative agents such as linezolid or quinupristin/dalfopristin might be appropriate.

Although there is no specific prevention for enterococci because they are able to survive for extended periods of time on inanimate objects, nosocomial outbreaks have been associated with antibiotic-resistant strains of enterococci and proper disinfection and infection control measures are necessary to prevent further spread.

COMPREHENSION QUESTIONS

[8.1] Testing of blood culture isolates from a hospitalized patient revealed gram-positive cocci, β-lactamase positive, vancomycin-resistant, PYR-positive, and the presence of Lancefield group D antigen. Which of the following is the most likely isolate identification?

A. *Enterococcus faecalis*
B. *Streptococcus agalactiae*
C. *Streptococcus bovis*
D. *Streptococcus pneumoniae*

[8.2] Which of the following is the most serious condition that can result as complications of enterococcal urinary tract or wound infections?

A. Cellulitis
B. Gastroenteritis
C. Scarlet fever
D. Subacute endocarditis
E. Toxic shock syndrome

[8.3] After an abdominal surgery for removal of ovarian cysts, this 56-year-old woman has had low-grade fever for the past 2 weeks. She has a history of rheumatic fever as a child. Three of the blood cultures grew gram-positive cocci. Which of the following is the most likely etiologic agent?

A. Group A streptococci
B. Group B streptococci
C. Group C streptococci
D. Group D streptococci
E. Viridans streptococci

Answers

[8.1] **A.** All bacteria listed are gram-positive cocci. *Streptococcus pneumoniae* does not have a Lancefield grouping, whereas *S. agalactiae* has a group B classification. *Streptococcus bovis* is PYR-negative. Thus, only *E. faecalis* fulfills all laboratory test results in the above question.

[8.2] **D.** In patients, the most common sites of enterococci infection are the urinary tract, wounds, biliary tract, and blood. In neonates, enterococci can cause bacteremia and meningitis. In adults, enterococci may cause endocarditis. Thus, bacteremia and/or endocarditis are rare and very serious complications that can result from enterococcal UTI. Cellulitis and toxic shock syndrome are typically associated with both staphylococci and streptococci, whereas scarlet fever is associated only with streptococci. Finally, gastroenteritis can be associated with a number of organisms such as *Clostridium difficile.*

[8.3] **D.** *Streptococcus bovis* is among the nonenterococcal group D streptococci. They are part of the enteric flora and have the ability to cause endocarditis.

MICROBIOLOGY PEARLS

❖ Enterococci, gram-positive cocci, are normal flora of the human and animal GI tract.

❖ Enterococci are a common cause of wound infections following procedures involving the GI or genitourinary (GU) tracts.

❖ Bacteremia and/or endocarditis are rare complications of enterococcal UTIs.

❖ Enterococcal UTIs are often nosocomial infections, especially in elderly patients with urinary catheters.

❖ Ampicillin and vancomycin are the principal antibiotics used to treat enterococcal infections.

REFERENCES

Moellering, RC. Enterococcus species, streptococcus bovis, and leuconostoc species. In: Mandell GL, Bennett JE, Dolin R, eds. Principles and Practice of Infectious Diseases, 5th ed. Philadelphia, PA: Churchill Livingstone, 2000:2147–56.

Murray PR, Rosenthal KS, Pfaller MA. Enterococcus and other gram-positive cocci. In: Murray PR, Rosenthal KS, Pfaller MA. Medical Microbiology, 5th ed. St. Louis, MO: Mosby, 2005:259–63.

CASE 9

A 21-year-old woman presents with a 3-day duration of discomfort with urination and increased urinary frequency. She has noted that her urine has a strong odor as well. She denies fever, abdominal pain, back pain, vaginal discharge, or skin rash. She is sexually active and takes oral contraceptive pills. On examination, she is comfortable appearing and afebrile. She has no costovertebral angle tenderness. Abdominal exam is notable only for suprapubic tenderness. Microscopic examination of the sediment of a centrifuged urine sample reveals 10–15 white blood cells per high power field and numerous bacteria.

- **What type of organism would a Gram stain of the urine most likely show?**
- **What is the most common etiologic agent of this infection?**
- **What is the most likely reservoir of this infection?**
- **What is the most likely mechanism by which this organism infects the urinary tract?**

ANSWERS TO CASE 9: *Escherichia coli*

Summary: A 21-year-old woman has urinary frequency and dysuria. The urinalysis shows numerous white blood cells.

- **Organism most likely to be seen on Gram stain:** Gram-negative rod
- **Most common etiologic agent:** *Escherichia coli*
- **Most likely reservoir for the organism:** Patient's own gastrointestinal (GI) tract
- **Most likely mechanism of introduction of organism into the urinary tract:** Urethral contamination by colonic bacteria followed by ascension of the infection into the bladder

CLINICAL CORRELATION

Escherichia coli is the most commonly found aerobic, gram-negative bacilli in the GI tract of humans. *Escherichia coli* is responsible for **over 80 percent of all urinary tract infections (UTIs),** along with other clinical diseases including gastroenteritis, sepsis, and neonatal meningitis. The *E. coli* that causes diarrhea is usually acquired from the environment, whereas most other infections caused by *E. coli* are acquired endogenously. Much of the diarrhea resulting from *E. coli* is acquired in developing countries particularly in travelers to these countries. The serotypes that are associated with travelers' diarrhea can be grouped based on their method of pathogenesis: enterotoxigenic, enterohemorrhagic, enteroaggregative, and enteroinvasive strains. These strains produce toxins, which account for their invasiveness as well as decreased absorption in the GI tract. Most of these cause a self-limited diarrhea with the exception of **enterohemorrhagic *E. coli,* frequently associated with *E. coli* serotype O157:H7, causing a bloody diarrhea**, which is usually acquired from eating **poorly cook meat from an infected cow**. Complications of infection with this organism include hemolytic uremic syndrome (HUS), which is a triad of hemolytic anemia, thrombocytopenia, and renal failure. HUS is a significant cause of acute renal failure in children.

UTIs caused by *E. coli* are associated with organisms from the GI tract or vagina ascending up to the bladder. These organisms can colonize the vagina and be introduced into the bladder during instrumentation or sexual intercourse. Those serotypes that produce adhesions, which mediate adherence of the organisms to epithelial cells in the urinary tract are more likely to cause infections. The majority of cases of uncomplicated and complicated pyelonephritis are caused by *E. coli,* a complication of a UTI, where the organisms continue to ascend from the bladder to the kidney.

APPROACH TO SUSPECTED *Escherichia coli* UTI

Objectives

1. Know the structure, characteristics, and virulence factors of *E. coli.*
2. Know the pathogenic groups and toxins involved in diarrhea caused by *E. coli.*

Definitions

Pyelonephritis: Infection of the kidney.
Cystitis: Infection of the bladder.
Hemolytic uremic syndrome (HUS): A syndrome characterized by hemolytic anemia, thrombocytopenia (low platelets), and acute renal failure.

DISCUSSION

Characteristics of *Escherichia coli*

Escherichia coli is a member of the family **Enterobacteriaceae (see Table 9-1 for an abbreviated list).** All members of this family have in common the fact that they **ferment glucose, are oxidase negative, and reduce nitrates to nitrites.** Many members of the family Enterobacteriaceae, like *E. coli,* are normal flora of the human GI tract.

Escherichia coli produces numerous **adhesins,** which allow the organism to attach to cells in the urinary and gastrointestinal tracts. This prevents the bacteria from being flushed from these organs by the normal passage of urine or intestinal motility. *Escherichia coli* also can produce several **exotoxins,** involved in the pathogenesis of diarrhea, including shiga toxins, heat-stable toxins, heat-labile toxins, and hemolysins. **Hemolysin HlyA** is particularly

Table 9-1
ABBREVIATED LISTING OF ENTEROBACTERIACIAE

Shigella
Salmonella
Escherichia
Enterobacter
Klebsiela
Serratia
Proteus

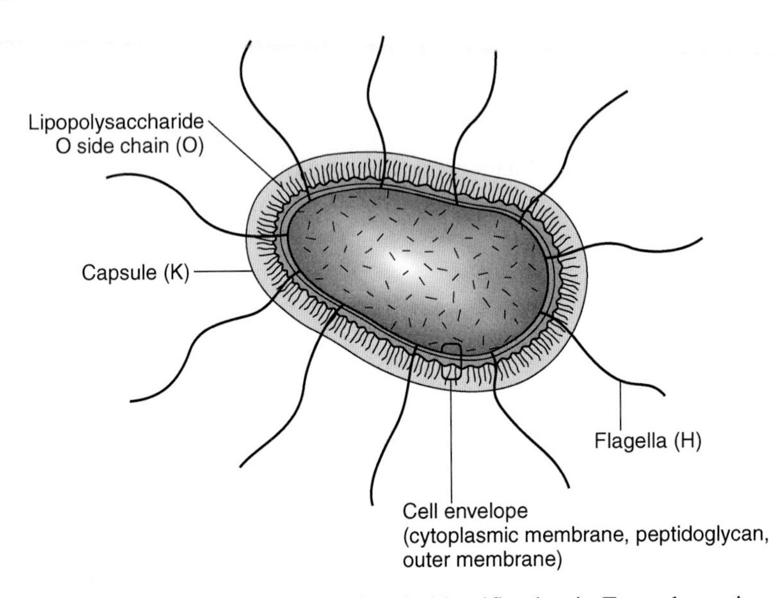

Figure 9-1. Structures used for antigenic identification in Enterobacteriaceae.

important in producing an **inflammatory response in the urinary tract,** whereas most of the other exotoxins are more pathogenic in the GI tract.

Escherichia coli are divided into **serogroups** based on the **O antigen** found on the **lipopolysaccharide (LPS)** of the cell membrane and the **H antigen found on the flagella (Figure 9-1).**

Diagnosis

The diagnosis of a UTI is made by urinalysis and urine culture. Complications such as pyelonephritis would be indicated by fever and flank pain. On urinalysis, the presence of white blood cells or leukocyte esterase and bacteria are suggestive of a true infection. Definitive diagnosis of the etiology is made by culture of the urine. *Escherichia coli* is easily grown on most culture media. A quantitative urine culture from a symptomatic patient should demonstrate greater than **10^5 colony-forming units (CFUs) bacteria/mL urine** to be considered significant. *Escherichia coli* would appear as **pink colonies on MacConkey agar** indicating **fermentation of lactose.** A rapid spot **indole** test would give a preliminary identification of *E. coli,* which would be confirmed by biochemical analysis.

Treatment and Prevention

Treatment of UTIs is based on the affecting organism and its susceptibility to antibiotics. Common antimicrobials chosen include trimethoprim sulfamethoxazole, or a fluoroquinolone. Most *E. coli* are resistant to ampicillin and penicillin. Recurrent UTIs are quite common, particularly in young women. Prevention can include consumption of large amounts of liquid and attention to totally emptying the bladder during urination. Fluid and electrolyte replacement should be administered to patients with *E. coli* diarrhea; however, antimicrobial treatment should not be administered. *Escherichia coli* diarrhea is best prevented by improved hygiene.

COMPREHENSION QUESTIONS

[9.1] *Escherichia coli* can be classified by their characteristic virulence properties and different mechanisms that cause disease. To which group does the verotoxin producing *E. coli* 0157:H7 serotype belong?

A. Enteroaggregative *E. coli* (EAEC)
B. Enterohemorrhagic *E. coli* (EHEC)
C. Enteroinvasive *E. coli* (EIEC)
D. Enteropathogenic *E. coli* (EPEC)
E. Enterotoxigenic *E. coli* (ETEC)

[9.2] Several children are hospitalized with bloody diarrhea and severe hematological abnormalities. A 4-year-old girl dies of kidney failure shortly after admittance. An epidemiological investigation establishes that all of the patients developed symptoms following consumption of hamburgers from the same fast-food restaurant chain. Which of the following organisms is most likely to be responsible for the outbreak?

A. *Campylobacter jejuni*
B. non-O1 serogroup of *Vibrio cholerae*
C. O157:H7 serotype of *Escherichia coli*
D. *Shigella dysenteriae*
E. *Salmonella typhimurium*

[9.3] A Gram stain of an isolate from voided urine in a patient with a UTI reveals the presence of pink rods. Further biochemical analysis reveals that these bacteria ferment glucose, reduce nitrates to nitrites and are unable to synthesize the following reaction:

$$2H^+ + 2e^- + {}^1/_2O_2 \rightarrow H_2O$$

Which of the following characterize the above test results?

A. *Escherichia coli*
B. *Neisseria gonorrhoeae*
C. *Proteus vulgaris*
D. *Pseudomonas aeruginosa*
E. *Staphylococcus aureus*
F. *Streptococcus pyogenes*

[9.4] A 7-year-old child with bloody diarrhea is admitted after laboratory results indicating anemia and abnormal kidney function. After testing, it is determined that the etiologic agent is an *E. coli* that is most likely to produce which of the following?

A. Endotoxin
B. Exotoxin
C. LT toxin
D. ST toxin
E. Verotoxin

[9.5] Several days after an appendectomy a patient develops a high fever, dangerously low blood pressure, and disseminated intravascular coagulation (DIC). Based on these and other findings, a diagnosis of septicemia as a result of an enteric gram-negative rod is made. Which of the following cytokines is most likely to be responsible for the fever, low blood pressure, and DIC?

A. IFN-γ
B. IL-2
C. IL-10
D. TGF-β
E. TNF-α

Answers

[9.1] **B.** All of the above classes of *E. coli* cause diarrhea. However, only EHEC produce a verotoxin that has many properties that are similar to Shiga toxin. EHEC has been associated with hemorrhagic colitis, a severe form of diarrhea, and with HUS. HUS is a disease resulting in acute renal failure, microangiopathic hemolytic anemia, and thrombocytopenia.

[9.2] **C.** *Escherichia coli* 0157:H7 strains are classically associated with outbreaks of diarrhea after ingestion of undercooked hamburger at fast-food restaurants. Many cases of hemorrhagic colitis and its associated complications can be prevented by thoroughly cooking ground beef. The other organisms listed can cause GI disturbances; however, *E. coli* is the classic disturbing pathogen in this case. *Shigella dysenteriae* produces a heat-labile enterotoxin that affects the gut and central nervous system and is a human disease that is transmitted via a fecal-oral route. *Salmonella* and *Campylobacter* are associated with poultry and eggs primarily, whereas *Vibrio* is associated mainly with seafood.

[9.3] **A.** The biochemical reaction described above is catalyzed by the enzyme oxidase. Thus, *E. coli* is the only bacteria listed that is a gram-negative rod (pink), ferments glucose, converts nitrates to nitrites, and is oxidase negative.

[9.4] **E.** The verotoxin produced by *E. coli* is similar to Shiga toxin, causing bloody diarrhea. Please refer to the discussion for Question 9.1.

[9.5] **E.** The acute phase response involves the increase in the levels of various plasma proteins (C-reactive protein and mannose-binding proteins) and is part of innate immunity. These proteins are synthesized and secreted by the liver in response to certain cytokines such as IL-1, IL-6, and TNF-α (produced after exposure to microorganisms) as nonspecific responses to microorganisms and other forms of tissue injury. Specifically, endotoxin (LPS) from gram-negative bacteria has the ability to activate macrophages that, in turn, synthesize TNF-α. TNF-α then functions to cause fever and hemorrhagic tissue necrosis (inflammatory reaction/immune response).

MICROBIOLOGY PEARLS

- *Escherichia coli* is the most common cause of UTIs in otherwise healthy patients.
- *Escherichia coli* can easily be identified following growth of a flat lactose fermenter on MacConkey agar that is indole positive.
- Many serotypes of *E. coli* are associated with traveler's diarrhea.

REFERENCES

Murray PR, Rosenthal KS, Pfaller MA. Enterobacteriaceae. In: Murray PR, Rosenthal KS, Pfaller MA. Medical Microbiology, 5th ed. St. Louis, MO: Mosby, 2005:323–38.

❖ CASE 10

A 48-year-old man presents for the evaluation of a 2-month history of upper abdominal pain associated with nausea. It is made worse when he drinks coffee, soda, or alcohol. He has taken multiple over-the-counter antacid medications that provide temporary relief. He admits to a 20-pack-year smoking history and drinking one or two alcoholic beverages a week but denies significant use of nonsteroidal anti-inflammatory drugs (NSAIDs). His general physical examination and vital signs are normal. His abdominal examination is notable for epigastric tenderness without the presence of masses, rebound tenderness, or guarding. A rectal examination reveals his stool to be heme positive. A complete blood count (CBC) shows a mild hypochromic, microcytic anemia. He is referred to a gastroenterologist for an upper GI endoscopy, which shows diffuse gastritis and a gastric ulcer.

- **What organism is most likely to be visualized on histologic evaluation of a gastric biopsy specimen?**

- **Besides microscopic evaluation, what other clinical test may provide a rapid detection of this organism?**

- **What two factors facilitate this organism's ability to colonize the stomach?**

ANSWERS TO CASE 10: *Helicobacter pylori*

Summary: A 48-year-old man has diffuse gastritis and a gastric ulcer on endoscopic examination.

- **Organism on histologic evaluation of a gastric biopsy:** The organism likely to be visualized on biopsy specimen is *Helicobacter pylori.*
- **Other clinical test for rapid detection of this organism:** The urease test.
- **Factors facilitating this organism's ability to colonize the stomach:** Blockage of acid production by a bacterial acid-inhibitory protein and neutralization of acid by ammonia produced by urease activity.

CLINICAL CORRELATION

Helicobacter pylori has been implicated in the development of multiple GI diseases, including gastritis, ulcers, and gastric cancers. Humans are the primary reservoir of the infection and human-to-human transfer, via fecal-oral contact, is likely to be an important mode of transfer. *Helicobacter pylori* is a curved gram-negative bacillus with motility facilitated by corkscrew motion and polar flagella. Culture of this organism requires a complex medium and microaerophilic environment. *Helicobacter pylori* that colonize the stomach produce urease, an enzyme that has many effects. Urease activity produces ammonia, which neutralizes gastric acid. This, along with a specific acid-inhibitory protein that directly blocks gastric acid production, facilitates the colonization of the acidic stomach environment. Urease by-products also cause local tissue damage and stimulate an inflammatory response. Urease activity is enhanced by the presence of a heat shock protein, HspB, which exists on the surface of *H. pylori.* The identification of urease activity in a gastric biopsy sample is highly specific for the presence of an active *H. pylori* infection, making it the basis for a widely used clinical test for the rapid detection of *H. pylori* infections.

APPROACH TO SUSPECTED *Helicobacter pylori* INFECTION

Objectives

1. Be able to describe the characteristics of *Helicobacter* bacteria.
2. Understand the role of *H. pylori* in causing gastric ulcers.

Definitions

Urease: *Helicobacter pylori* uses this enzyme to convert urea into ammonia and carbon dioxide. This chemical reaction is the basis of the rapid urea breath test for diagnosis of *H. pylori.* The increased ammonia produced by this reaction neutralizes gastric acid, which allows the organism to survive the normally harsh gastric environment and damages the gastric mucosa.

Type B gastritis: Type B gastritis is gastritis of the antrum caused by *H. pylori* infection (compare with Type A of the fundus, caused by autoimmune disorders).

Corkscrew motility: *Helicobacter pylori* is highly motile because of 5–6 polar flagella.

Microaerophilic organisms: Organisms that require reduced oxygen concentration (5%) to grow optimally (include: *H. pylori* and *Campylobacter jejuni*).

Upper endoscopy: Visual examination of the mucosa of the esophagus, stomach, and duodenum using a flexible fiberoptic system introduced through the mouth.

DISCUSSION

Characteristics of *Helicobacter pylori* Impacting Transmission

Helicobacter pylori is a **curved gram-negative bacilli** that requires **microaerophilic** environments to grow. Discovered in 1983, the organism was originally classified under the *Campylobacter* genus, but eventually was reclassified under a new and separate genus, *Helicobacter,* as understanding of the organism has evolved. **Urease production** is the most important enzyme that distinguishes *H. pylori* from *Campylobacter* species and other various *Helicobacter* species, and **allows the organism to survive the harsh gastric environment.** *Helicobacter pylori* also has **oxidase, catalase, mucinase, phospholipase enzymes, and vacuolating cytotoxin,** which aid in the virulence and pathogenesis of the organism. Infections of *H. pylori* are ubiquitous, worldwide, and extremely common in developing nations and among lower socioeconomic groups. Humans are the primary reservoir, and no animal reservoir has been identified at the present time. The primary mode of transmission is person to person (usually by the fecal-oral route), and the infection commonly is clustered in families or among close contacts. Some speculation has been made that contaminated water or food sources may be a reservoir, but at the present time there are no data to support this.

Diagnosis

Helicobacter pylori has been clearly associated with **Type B gastritis, gastric ulcers, gastric adenocarcinoma of the body and antrum, and gastric mucosa-associated lymphoid tissue (MALT) B-cell lymphomas.** Diagnosis of *H. pylori* should be considered in patients with symptoms of these diseases. The most rapid test to detect *H. pylori* is the **urease test or urea breath test** that detects by-products of the **urease reaction cleaving urea into ammonia and carbon dioxide; however, the invasiveness of biopsy or the expense of breath detection instruments limits the use of these assays. Microscopy** is both extremely sensitive and specific for diagnosis of *H. pylori* in gastric biopsy specimens when stained with **Warthin-Starry silver stain, hematoxylin-eosin, or Gram stain.** Antigen detection in stool samples via a commercial polyclonal enzyme immunoassay is highly sensitive and specific, while also inexpensive and easy to perform. **Serology** is another preferred diagnostic test, whereby *H. pylori* stimulates a humoral immune response (IgM early in infection; IgG and IgA later in infection and persisting), but it cannot distinguish between past and present infections. Culture is a more challenging and time-consuming way to diagnose *H. pylori,* because it must be grown in a microaerophilic atmosphere on an enriched medium containing charcoal, blood, and hemin.

Treatment and Prevention

Because *H. pylori* is primarily **transmitted person to person via fecal-oral route,** the best prevention is improving hygiene by **frequent hand washing,** especially before meals. In symptomatic patients who are positive for infection with *H. pylori,* combination therapy is needed. This therapy includes (1) acid suppression, usually with a proton pump inhibitor, (2) one or more antibiotics, and (3) occasional additive therapy with bismuth.

COMPREHENSION QUESTIONS

[10.1] A 45-year-old man presents to the hospital vomiting blood. He is diagnosed with a perforated peptic ulcer. The causative agent discovered by gastric biopsy is a spiral gram-negative bacillus. What other long-term complications could this organism cause if not treated?

A. Skin ulcers
B. Esophageal varices
C. Gastric MALT lymphomas
D. Colon cancer

[10.2] Which of the following is an important distinguishing characteristic of *H. pylori* as compared to *Campylobacter* species?

A. Oxidase production
B. Catalase production
C. Urease production
D. Curved shape
E. Polar flagellum

[10.3] A 58-year-old man presents to the clinic with decreased appetite, nausea, vomiting, and upper abdominal pain. If the causative agent is a curved gram-negative rod with urease production, what treatment should be given to this patient?

A. Proton pump inhibitor and antibiotic
B. Proton pump inhibitor, antibiotic, and bismuth
C. Over-the-counter antacids and antibiotics
D. Nonsteroidal anti-inflammatory drugs (NSAIDs)

Answers

[10.1] **C.** *Helicobacter pylori* is the causative agent that can cause Type B gastritis, peptic ulcers, gastric adenocarcinoma, and gastric MALT B cell lymphomas.

[10.2] **C.** Both *Campylobacter* species and *H. pylori* have a curved shape, are oxidase and catalase positive, with polar flagellum. Urease production is the distinguishing factor of *H. pylori,* and it is the basis of the rapid urease breath test that diagnoses *H. pylori* infection.

[10.3] **B.** The combination therapy of proton pump inhibitor, antibiotic, and bismuth is required to eradicate an infection with *H. pylori.*

MICROBIOLOGY PEARLS

- *Helicobacter pylori* are *characterized* as being curved gram-negative bacilli and microaerophilic, and by having multiple polar flagella and urease activity.
- Clinical manifestations include Type B gastritis, gastric ulcers, gastric adenocarcinoma, gastric MALT lymphomas conjunctivitis, or gastroenteritis.
- It is transmitted via the fecal-oral route.
- Antimicrobial treatment includes acid suppression, antibiotics, and adjunctive treatments (i.e., bismuth).

REFERENCES

Johnson AG, Hawley LB, Lukasewycz OA, Jiegler RJ. Microbiology and Immunobiology, 4th ed. Baltimore, MD: Lippincott Williams & Wilkins, 2002.

Levinson W, Jawetz E. Medical Microbiology and Immunology, 7th ed. New York: McGraw-Hill, 2002.

Murray PR, Rosenthal KS, Pfaller MA. Medical Microbiology, 5th ed. St. Louis, MO: Mosby, 2005:291–295.

Passaro D, Chosy EJ, Parssonet J. *Helicobacter pylori*: Consensus and controversy. Clin Infect Dis 2002;35:298–304.

Weingart V, Rüssmann H, Koletzko S, et al. Sensitivity of a novel stool antigen test for detection of *Helicobacter pylori* in adult outpatients before and after eradiacation therapy. J Clin Microbiol 2004. 42:1319–21.

Youngerman-Cole S. Digestive disorders health centre: *Helicobacter pylori* tests. http://www.webmd.com/digestive-disorders/Helicobacter-pylori-Tests. Last updated January 12, 2006.

❖ CASE 11

A 19-month-old child is brought to the emergency room following a seizure. His mother says that he had a cold for 2 or 3 days with a cough, congestion, and low-grade fever, but today he became much worse. He has been fussy and inconsolable, he would not eat and has slept most of the morning. He then had two grand-mal seizures. He has no history of seizures in the past. His mother reports that he has not received all of his immunizations. She is not sure which ones he's had, but he's only had two or three shots in his life. On examination his temperature is 38.1°C (100.5°F), his pulse is 110 beats per minute, and he appears very ill. He does not respond to your voice but does withdraw his extremities from painful stimuli. He grimaces when you try to bend his neck. His skin is without rash and his HEENT (head, eyes, ear, nose, throat), cardiovascular, lung, and abdominal examinations are normal. His white blood cell count is elevated, and a CT scan of his head is normal. You perform a lumbar puncture, which reveals numerous small gram-negative coccobacilli.

◆ **What organism is the most likely etiology of this illness?**

◆ **What component of this organism is the target of vaccine-induced immunity?**

ANSWERS TO CASE 11: *Haemophilus influenzae*

Summary: A 19-month-old boy who has not received many immunizations presents with meningitis. The lumbar puncture shows multiple gram-negative coccobacilli.

- **Organism most likely causing this infection:** *Haemophilus influenzae* type B.
- **Component of this organism that is the target of vaccine-induced immunity:** Purified polyribitol phosphate, a component of the *H. influenzae* type B polysaccharide capsule.

CLINICAL CORRELATION

Haemophilus species, particularly *H. parainfluenzae* and *H. influenzae* non-type B are normal flora in the human upper respiratory tract. These strains can, however, be associated with respiratory infections such as otitis media and bronchitis. *Haemophilus influenzae* type B was the most common cause of pediatric meningitis (ages 2 months to 2 years of age) until the introduction of routine childhood immunization against this bacterium.

Transmission of *H. influenzae* occurs by close contact with respiratory tract secretions from a patient colonized or infected with the organism. Prior viral infection promotes colonization of the respiratory tract with *H. influenzae.* Invasive infections such as meningitis occur when the colonizing organisms invade the bloodstream and subsequently the meninges. Usually as a result of *H. influenzae* type B, the capsule aids in adherence of the organism and evasion of phagocytosis. Neurological sequelae can occur in up to 20 percent of cases of meningitis. *Haemophilus influenzae* type B can also be a cause of epiglottitis in young children, which can result in respiratory obstruction requiring intubation.

Haemophilus aphrophilus and *H. paraphrophilus* are causes of culture negative endocarditis named thus because of the fastidious nature and difficulty in recovering these organisms from the blood of infected patients. *Haemophilus ducreyi* is a cause of an uncommon sexually transmitted disease *chancroid.* Chancroid is characterized by genital skin lesions and lymphadenopathy, leading to abscess formation if remains untreated.

APPROACH TO SUSPECTED *Haemophilus influenza* MENINGITIS

Objectives

1. Know the structure and physiology of *Haemophilus.*
2. Know the significance of the capsule of *Haemophilus* in the virulence, infection, and development of protective immunity.

Definitions

Epiglottitis: Inflammation of the epiglottis usually caused by *H. influenzae,* which presents as sore throat, fever, and difficulty breathing.

Meningitis: Inflammation of the meninges leads to headache, stiff neck, and fever with increase in cells in the cerebrospinal fluid.

Grand-mal seizure: Seizure that results in loss of consciousness and generalized muscle contractions.

DISCUSSION

Characteristics of *Haemophilus* Species

Haemophilus are **small, pleomorphic, gram-negative bacilli or coccobacilli.** Humans are the only known reservoir. They are **facultative anaerobes** and grow on media that contain growth-stimulating factors known as X factor (hematin) and V factor (NAD). **Heated sheep blood agar, chocolate agar,** contains both of these factors and is used to grow *Haemophilus.* Many strains of *Haemophilus* have a **polysaccharide capsule,** and specific capsular antigens are used to identify strains of *H. influenzae.* Six types, *A* through *F,* have been identified. The **polysaccharide capsule of *H. influenzae* type B** represents its major virulence **antiphagocytic** factor. The **capsule** contains **ribose, ribitol, and phosphate, known collectively as polyribitol phosphate (PRP).** Phagocytosis and complement-mediated activity are stimulated in the presence of antibodies directed at the *H. influenzae* type B capsule. This represents the **basis for the *H. influenzae* type B vaccine,** which contains **purified PRP antigens** conjugated to specific protein carriers.

Diagnosis

Acute meningitis typically involves the rapid onset (over several days) of **headache, fever, and stiff neck,** although in young children only fever and irritability may be evident. Rash may also be present in some forms of meningitis. Without treatment, progression of the disease includes loss of consciousness and/or seizures and coma. Specific diagnosis is based on culture of the etiologic organism from the cerebrospinal fluid (CSF). Prior to culture a rapid presumptive diagnosis of bacterial meningitis is based on increased number of polymorphonuclear leukocytes (PMNs) in the CSF as well as an elevated protein and a decreased glucose. **Gram stain** of the CSF may reveal the presence of bacteria if the number of organisms is high enough. In the case of *H. influenzae* meningitis, the presence of tiny gram-negative coccobacilli is seen in a Gram-stained smear of the CSF.

Haemophilus influenzae **require both X and V factors for growth;** therefore no growth would be seen on blood agar unless growth of *Staphylococcus aureus* on the agar allowed for lysis of the blood and release of the required factors into the media. Good growth would be evident on chocolate agar as grayish colonies after 24 hours incubation at 35°C (95°F) and 5 percent carbon dioxide. Identification of *Haemophilus* to the species level can be made by requirement for X or V for growth. More specifically, a commercially available identification system could be used that is based on the presence of preformed enzymes and can be made within 4 hours. *Haemophilus* species other than *H. influenzae* grow much more slowly, particularly *H. ducreyi,* which may require 5–7 days of incubation after culture of an infected lymph node or genital abscess.

Treatment and Prevention

Up to 50 percent of strains of *H. influenzae* produce a β-lactamase, rendering them resistant to ampicillin. Treatment for *H. influenzae* meningitis involves the use of a **third-generation cephalosporin (cefotaxime, ceftriaxone).** Respiratory infections caused by *H. influenzae* may be treated with antibiotics such as **amoxicillin-clavulanate or a macrolide** (such as azithromycin). Routine pediatric immunization with the vaccine against *H. influenzae* type B has reduced the incidence of invasive disease by approximately 90 percent and has also reduced respiratory colonization. *Haemophilus ducreyi* is usually treated with **erythromycin** or a newer macrolide antibiotic. An alternative for therapy of chancroid includes a **fluoroquinolone.**

COMPREHENSION QUESTIONS

[11.1] A 2-year-old child has high fever, is irritable, and has a stiff neck. Gram-stain smear of spinal fluid reveals gram-negative, small pleomorphic coccobacillary organisms. Which of the following is the most appropriate procedure to follow to reach an etiologic diagnosis?

A. Culture the spinal fluid in chocolate blood agar and identify the organism by growth factors.
B. Culture the spinal fluid in mannitol salt agar.
C. Perform a catalase test of the isolated organism.
D. Perform a coagulase test with the isolate.
E. Perform a latex agglutination test to detect the specific antibody in the spinal fluid.

[11.2] *Haemophilus influenzae* synthesizes immunoglobulin A (IgA) protease, which enables the bacterium to penetrate and invade the host's respiratory epithelium. This is an example of a bacterium's ability to evade which of the host's immune system responses?

A. Cellular or cell-mediated immunity (CMI) against *H. influenzae*
B. Nonspecific humoral immunity
C. Nonspecific innate immunity
D. Phagocytic function and intracellular killing of bacteria
E. Specific humoral immunity against *H. influenzae*

[11.3] An 18-month-old baby girl is suspected to have *H. influenzae* meningitis. She has not been immunized with the HIB vaccine. A rapid latex agglutination test is performed with the spinal fluid to make a definitive diagnosis. What chemical component in the spinal fluid are we detecting with this assay?

A. IgG antibody
B. IgM antibody
C. Lipopolysaccharide (LPS)
D. Polypeptide
E. Polysaccharide capsule

[11.4] The *H. influenzae* vaccine contains which of the following?

A. Lipopolysaccharide (LPS)
B. Live attenuated *H. influenzae*
C. Polypeptide antigens containing D-glutamate
D. Polyribitol phosphate antigens
E. Teichoic acid
F. Toxoids

[11.5] Cerebrospinal fluid from a spinal tap of a patient complaining of a severe headache, fever, and nuchal rigidity revealed the presence of gram-negative coccobacilli. Further testing revealed growth of the organism on growth factor X and V supplemented chocolate agar, and no hemolysis when grown on blood agar. Which of the following organisms represents the above description?

A. *Bordetella pertussis*
B. *Haemophilus ducreyi*
C. *Haemophilus haemolyticus*
D. *Haemophilus influenzae*
E. *Haemophilus parainfluenzae*

Answers

[11.1] **A.** The organism in the above description is *H. influenzae.* This organism is differentiated from other related gram-negative bacilli by its requirements of a chocolate media supplemented with growth factors, such as X and V factors, and by its lack of hemolysis on blood agar.

[11.2] **E.** Immunoglobulin A (IgA) is associated with immunological protection of the host at the epithelial boundary. An IgA protease has the ability to breakdown IgA and thereby act as a virulence mechanism enabling the bacterium to invade the host through an unprotected epithelial boundary. Because IgA is an antibody associated with the humoral (specific) arm of the immune system, IgA protease allows the bacterium the ability to evade the specific humoral immunity of the host.

[11.3] **E.** The latex agglutination test involves the use of latex beads coated with specific antibody that become agglutinated in the presence of homologous bacteria or antigen. This test is used to determine the presence of the capsular polysaccharide antigen of *H. influenzae* in serum or spinal fluid.

[11.4] **D.** Encapsulated *H. influenzae* contains capsular polysaccharides of one of six types (A–F). *Haemophilus influenzae* type B is an important human pathogen with its polyribose phosphate capsule being its major virulence factor. As a result, active immunity is built using polyribitol phosphate antigens (capsular polysaccharide) of *H. influenzae.*

[11.5] **D.** *Haemophilus haemolyticus* and *H. influenzae* are the only organisms listed above that require both growth factors X and V for growth; however, they can be distinguished from each other in that *H. influenzae* is hemolysis negative on blood agar, whereas *H. haemolyticus* is hemolysis positive.

MICROBIOLOGY PEARLS

- ❖ *Haemophilus* species other than *H. influenzae* type B are still a significant cause of systemic infections.
- ❖ The widespread use of *H. influenzae* vaccines in developed countries has decreased the incidence of *H. influenzae* meningitis.
- ❖ *Haemophilus influenzae* meningitis is treated with cefotaxime or ceftriaxone.
- ❖ *Haemophilus* species are a significant cause of otitis (middle ear infections), sinusitis, and epiglottitis in young children.

REFERENCES

Murray PR, Rosenthal KS, Pfaller MA. Pasteurellaceae. In: Murray PR, Rosenthal KS, Pfaller MA. Medical Microbiology, 5th ed. St. Louis, MO: Mosby, 2005:367–76.

Slack MPE. Gram-Negative Coccobacilli in Infectious Diseases. Philadelphia, PA: Mosby, 1999;8(20):1–18.

❖ CASE 12

A 45-year-old homeless alcoholic man presents to the emergency room with fever and cough of 4-day duration. The cough is productive of thick, bloody phlegm. He complains of pain in the right side of his chest with coughing or taking a deep breath. He denies any other medical history and says he can't remember the last time he saw a doctor. He doesn't smoke cigarettes, drinks a pint of whiskey whenever he can get it, and denies drug use. On examination, he is dirty, disheveled, and appears malnourished. His temperature is 38.9°C (102°F), pulse 105 beats per minute, and respiratory rate is 30 breaths per minute. The lung examination is notable for decreased breath sounds and crackles in the right lower, posterior field. His white blood cell count is elevated. A chest x-ray reveals a dense right lower lobe infiltrate with evidence of a pulmonary abscess. Sputum samples are collected for Gram stain and culture, and a blood culture is sent. A bacterial etiology is suspected.

What is the most likely organism to be isolated in the sputum and blood cultures?

◆ **By what mechanism does this organism commonly develop antibiotic resistance?**

ANSWERS TO CASE 12: *Klebsiella pneumoniae*

Summary: A 45-year-old alcoholic man has developed a bacterial cavitary pneumonia with evidence of a pulmonary abscess.

- **Most likely organism to be isolated:** *Klebsiella pneumoniae*
- **Mechanism whereby *Klebsiella* commonly develops antibiotic resistance:** Plasmid acquisition

CLINICAL CORRELATION

Klebsiella causes lower respiratory infections, wound soft tissue infections and is a common cause of hospital-acquired urinary tract infections (UTIs). *Klebsiella pneumoniae* is also associated with lobar pneumonia in a person with an underlying debilitating condition such as alcoholism or diabetes. Pneumonia caused by this organism tends to be necrotic, inflammatory, and hemorrhagic and has a high propensity for cavitation or abscess formation. Patients often produce thick, bloody sputum. Because of the destructive nature of the infection and the underlying debility of the patient, pneumonia caused by *K. pneumoniae* carries a high mortality.

Community-acquired pneumonia is usually the result of spread of organisms that normally reside in the upper respiratory tract into the lower respiratory tract. Organisms that have virulence factors that allow them to survive the host response in the lung can establish an infection. Patients with disruption of their immune defenses are at greater risk of infection. *Klebsiella pneumoniae* pneumonia is therefore considered an opportunistic infection because it is not a common cause of pneumonia in normally healthy patients. Symptoms of bacterial pneumonia are usually nonspecific and include malaise, anorexia, headache, myalgia, arthralgia, and fever. *Klebsiella pneumoniae* produces a severe acute, necrotic, and hemorrhagic pneumonia, which is evidenced by cavitary lung lesions on chest x-ray, pleural effusions, and possible abscess formation or empyema. Because of the hemorrhagic nature of the pneumonia, patients tend to have blood-tinged sputum.

Two uncommon species of *Klebsiella* are also causes of respiratory disease. *Klebsiella rhinoscleroma* is associated with chronic granulomatous disease of the upper respiratory mucosa (predominantly outside the United States), and *K. ozaenae* is associated with chronic atrophic rhinitis.

APPROACH TO SUSPECTED *Klebsiella pneumoniae* PNEUMONIA

Objectives

1. Know the structure, physiology, and virulence factors of *K. pneumoniae.*
2. Know the nature of the native and acquired antibiotic resistance of *K. pneumoniae.*

Definitions

Chronic obstructive pulmonary disease (COPD): A progressive lung disease that commonly results from heavy smoking and is evident by difficulty breathing, wheezing, and a chronic cough.

Empyema: Accumulation of pus in the pleural space around the lung.

DISCUSSION

Characteristics of *Klebsiella* Species

The genus *Klebsiella,* which belongs to the family **Enterobacteriaceae** includes five species, with the most clinically significant being *K. pneumoniae. Klebsiella pneumoniae* is a **large, nonmotile, gram-negative rod** with a **prominent polysaccharide capsule.** The **capsule is antiphagocytic** and retards leukocyte migration into an infected area.

Another virulence factor of *K. pneumoniae* is its propensity to develop **resistance** to multiple antibiotics. All strains of *K. pneumoniae* are innately **resistant to ampicillin,** because of the production of **β-lactamase.** Acquisition of resistance to other antibiotics usually occurs by **transfer of plasmids** from other organisms. Recently strains of nosocomially acquired *K. pneumoniae* have been isolated that produce an extended spectrum β-lactamase and therefore are resistant to all β-lactam antibiotics.

Diagnosis

Diagnosis of community-acquired pneumonia is made clinically based on symptoms of cough, especially with blood, and chest x-ray indicating infiltrates, cavitary lesions, or pleural effusions. Specific diagnosis of pneumonia is made by culture of expectorated sputum. Sputum samples must be of good quality (many white blood cells and rare squamous epithelial cells) represent the flora of the lower respiratory tract and not mouth flora. In a small percentage of cases of community-acquired pneumonia blood cultures will also be positive for the affecting organism.

Klebsiella pneumoniae will **grow rapidly producing large mucoid colonies** on routine laboratory media. Colonies are often extremely mucoid and will tend to **drip into the lid of the plate** while incubating in an inverted position. **Pink colonies** will be evident on MacConkey agar indicating their fermentation of lactose. Confirmatory identification is made for other members of the family Enterobacteriaceae by commercially available identification systems using a combination of **sugar fermentation and enzyme production.** Both *K. oxytoca* and especially *K. rhinoscleromatis* are slower growing than *K. pneumoniae* and the other Enterobacteriaceae. All *Klebsiella* species are very closely related with nearly identical biochemical reactions, except for the fact that *K. pneumoniae* is indole negative, and *K. oxytoca* is indole positive. Commercial identification systems have a difficult time differentiating these species.

Treatment and Prevention

Treatment of *K. pneumoniae* pneumonia would be based on the susceptibility of the isolate. Treatment can be complicated by the presence of multidrug-resistant strains. Most strains are susceptible to **extended spectrum cephalosporins** such as cefepime as well as **fluoroquinolones** such as moxifloxacin. In cases of strains that produce an extended spectrum β-lactamase, the treatment of choice would be imipenem or meropenem.

Prevention of community-acquired pneumonia would involve avoidance of high-risk activities such as smoking or drinking in excess. Prevention of spread in the hospital would involve appropriate infection control procedures to isolate patients with multidrug-resistant organisms. *Klebsiella oxytoca* has similar susceptibility patterns as *K. pneumoniae* and can also produce extended spectrum β-lactamases.

COMPREHENSION QUESTIONS

[12.1] The most common mechanism by which *K. pneumoniae* attains its antibiotic resistance is by plasmid acquisition. Which of the following best describes the direct transfer of a plasmid between two bacteria?

A. Competence
B. Conjugation
C. Recombination
D. Transduction
E. Transformation

[12.2] A specimen of thick, bloody sputum from a hospitalized 80-year-old patient with diabetes mellitus and difficulty in breathing is sent for laboratory analyses. The tests yield heavy growth of a lactose-positive, nonmotile, gram-negative rod with a large capsule. Which of the following bacteria is most likely to be the cause of the pulmonary problems?

A. *Enterobacter aerogenes*
B. *Escherichia coli*
C. *Klebsiella pneumoniae*
D. *Pseudomonas aeruginosa*
E. *Yersinia pseudotuberculosis*

[12.3] A 65-year-old diabetic man presents to the emergency room with a severe productive cough producing thick bloody sputum resembling a "currant-jelly" like appearance. Culture using MacConkey agar reveals pink colonies, with large mucoid colonies on routine laboratory media. Which of the following organisms is most likely responsible for this patient's pneumonia?

A. *Enterobacter cloacae*
B. *Escherichia coli*
C. *Klebsiella pneumoniae*
D. *Pseudomonas aeruginosa*
E. *Serratia marcescens*

[12.4] The O antigens that are used to help characterize members of the Enterobacteriaceae family are found on which of the following?

A. Capsules
B. Endotoxins
C. Exotoxins
D. Fimbriae
E. Flagella

Answers

[12.1] **B.** The three important processes by which DNA is transferred between bacteria are via transformation, transduction, and conjugation. Transformation is defined as the uptake of soluble DNA by a recipient cell. Transduction refers to the transfer of DNA by a virus from one cell to another. Conjugation refers to the direct transfer of soluble DNA (plasmids) between cells. Examples of such plasmids are the sex factors and the resistance (R) factors.

[12.2] **C.** Whereas all of the above listed organisms are gram-negative rods, only *K. pneumoniae* fulfill all of the laboratory criteria listed in the question, such as the presence of a very large capsule, which gives a striking mucoid appearance to its colonies.

[12.3] **C.** Patients with *K. pneumoniae* infections usually have predisposing conditions such as alcoholism, advanced age, chronic respiratory disease, and diabetes. The "currant-jelly" sputum distinguishes *K. pneumoniae* from the other organisms. Infections can lead to necrosis and abscess formation. Please refer to the discussion for Question 12.2.

[12.4] **B.** There are three surface antigens associated with several members of the Enterobacteriaceae. The cell wall antigen (somatic or O antigen) is the outer polysaccharide portion of the lipopolysaccharide (LPS/endotoxin). The H antigen is on the flagellar proteins (*Escherichia* and *Salmonella*). The capsular or K polysaccharide antigen is particularly prominent in heavily encapsulated organisms such as *Klebsiella.*

MICROBIOLOGY PEARLS

- *Klebsiella pneumoniae* are a common cause of hospital-acquired UTIs.
- Patients with diabetes or COPD or who drink alcohol excessively are predisposed to pneumonia with *K. pneumoniae.*
- *Klebsiella pneumoniae* produces a large mucoid colonies on agar plates as a result of the presence of a polysaccharide capsule that also acts to allow the organism to avoid phagocytosis.

REFERENCES

Baldwin DR, MacFarlane JT. Community Acquired Pneumonia in Infectious Diseases. Philadelphia, PA: Mosby, 1999;2(27):1–10.

Eisenstein BI, Zaleznik DF. Enterobacteriaceae. In: Mandell GL, Bennett JE, Dolin R, eds. Principles and Practice of Infectious Diseases, 5th ed. Philadelphia, PA: Churchill Livingstone, 2000:2294–310.

Murray PR, Rosenthal KS, Pfaller MA. Enterobacteriaceae. In: Murray PR, Rosenthal KS, Pfaller MA. Medical Microbiology, 5th ed. St. Louis, MO: Mosby, 2002:223–38.

❖ CASE 13

An 18-day-old female infant is brought to the pediatric emergency room by her panicked mother. The child has developed a fever and has been crying nonstop for the past 4 hours. She has fed only once today and vomited all of the ingested formula. The baby was born by vaginal delivery after an uncomplicated, full-term pregnancy to a healthy 22-year-old gravida$_1$ para$_1$ (one pregnancy, one delivery) woman. The mother has no history of any infectious diseases and tested negative for group B *Streptococcus* prior to delivery. The immediate postpartum course was routine. The baby had a routine check-up in the pediatrician's office 3 days ago, and no problems were identified. On examination, the child has a temperature of 38.3°C (100.9°F), pulse of 140 beats per minute, and respiratory rate of 32 breaths per minute. She is not crying at the moment. She has poor muscle tone, will not regard your face or respond to loud stimuli. Her anterior fontanelle is bulging. Her mucous membranes are moist, and her skin is without rash. Her heart is tachycardic but regular, and her lungs are clear. Her white blood count is elevated, a urinalysis is normal, and a chest x-ray is clear. A Gram stain of her cerebrospinal fluid (CSF) from a lumbar puncture shows gram-positive coccobacilli.

◆ **What organism is responsible for this infection?**

 **How does this organism avoid antibody-mediated host defenses?**

ANSWERS TO CASE 13: *Listeria monocytogenes*

Summary: An 18-day-old infant presents with meningitis and Gram stain of the CSF reveals gram-positive coccobacilli.

 **Organism responsible for this infection:** *Listeria monocytogenes*

◆ **Mechanism of avoidance of antibody-mediated defenses:** Intracellular replication and spread from cell to cell by phagocytosis

CLINICAL CORRELATION

Listeria is found in the environment but is not normal fecal flora in humans. Infection with *Listeria* is more common in the summer months. Disease is often the result of ingestion of the organism from infected foods such as milk, soft cheese, undercooked meat, or unwashed vegetables. *Listeria monocytogenes* causes asymptomatic or mild gastrointestinal infections in persons with intact immune systems and severe disease, most commonly meningitis, in those with impaired cellular immunity, such as pregnant women, neonates, AIDS patients, and posttransplant patients on immunosuppressive medications. Two types of neonatal disease have been described. Early-onset disease, which occurs with in the first 2 days of life, is the result of transplacental infection. Initial signs and symptoms include difficulty breathing and pneumonia. This infection is also called granulomatosis infantiseptica, because severe disease can be associated with a granulomatous rash with abscesses. Late-onset disease, which usually occurs 2–3 weeks after birth, is thought to result from exposure to *Listeria* either during or shortly after delivery. This infection most commonly presents as meningitis. Clinically these syndromes can be difficult to distinguish from that seen with group B streptococci.

APPROACH TO SUSPECTED *Listeria monocytogenes*

Objectives

1. Know the structure and physiology of *L. monocytogenes.*
2. Know the life cycle, virulence factors, and diseases associated with *L. monocytogenes.*

Definitions

Cold enrichment: Used to enhance growth of *Listeria,* particularly from food.

Granulomatosis infantiseptica: Severe form of *Listeria* infection of neonates in which granulomatous skin lesions are evident.

Anterior fontanelle: An opening of the neonatal skull between the sutures.
Gravida: Number of total pregnancies.
Para: Number of deliveries (usually after 20-week gestation); a pregnancy that ends prior to 20-week gestation is an abortus.

DISCUSSION

Characteristics of *Listeria*

Listeria monocytogenes is a **small, facultative anaerobic, gram-positive bacillus.** It may appear as **coccobacilli in pairs or chains,** so it can be mistaken for *Streptococcus pneumoniae* or *Enterococcus* on Gram stain. *Listeria monocytogenes* is an **intracellular** pathogen, which allows it to avoid antibody-mediated defenses of the host. It initially **enters host cells via the action of a protein, internalin,** which induces phagocytosis of the bacteria. *Listeria* produces a **toxin,** which then lyses the phagosome, releasing the bacteria into the host cell's cytoplasm. It replicates in the host cytoplasm and moves to the host membrane. By pushing against the membrane, a protrusion, known as a **filopod,** is produced, which can be phagocytized by adjacent cells.

This cycle is then repeated in the new host cell, allowing *Listeria* to spread without being exposed to antibodies or other humoral immunity factors. For this reason, host cellular immunity factors protect against infection and those with impaired cellular immunity are vulnerable.

Diagnosis

Clinical diagnosis is difficult based on the nonspecific signs and symptoms. Clinically *L. meningitis* in neonates resembles group B streptococci, both are a significant cause of bacteria meningitis in that age group. Definitive diagnosis of *Listeria* is made by **culture of the CSF and/or blood.** Gram stain of the CSF would demonstrate **small gram-positive bacilli,** appearing similar to corynebacteria or *S. pneumoniae.*

Listeria will grow on routine agar media within 24–48 hours. On blood agar media *Listeria* demonstrate **β-hemolysis,** which differentiates it from *Corynebacterium,* but adds to the difficulty in distinguishing them from streptococci. Specific identification is made in part by observation of characteristic tumbling motility on a wet preparation after room temperature incubation. A reaction of **catalase positive** helps to distinguish *Listeria* from streptococci.

Culture of *Listeria* from food may require cold enrichment, which would enhance the growth of *Listeria.* Food samples would be sent to a public health laboratory where some of the food would be enriched in a selective broth media at room temperature or lower.

Treatment and Prevention

Treatment of *Listeria* septicemia or meningitis is with **ampicillin** plus or minus gentamicin. Of significance is the inherent resistance of *Listeria* to cephalosporins, which are commonly chosen as empiric therapy for meningitis in adults and would be appropriate for treatment of streptococcal meningitis in children. Prevention involves the avoidance of the consumption of **under-cooked foods,** especially in high-risk patients.

COMPREHENSION QUESTIONS

[13.1] A 22-year-old medical student suffers diarrhea for more than a week since his return from a short vacation in Mexico. While in Mexico, he consumed a large quantity of raw cheeses almost every day. Which of the following is the most likely organism causing his diarrhea?

A. *Bacillus cereus*
B. *Escherichia coli*
C. *Listeria monocytogenes*
D. *Salmonella enteritidis*
E. *Shigella dysenteriae*

[13.2] A premature neonate suffers pneumonia and sepsis. Sputum culture on blood agar plate yields pinpointed β-hemolytic colonies. Which of the following is a simple test to determine whether the organism is *S. agalactiae* or *L. monocytogenes* (these two organisms are important neonatal pathogens)?

A. Bacitracin test
B. Catalase test
C. Coagulase test
D. Polymerase chain reaction
E. Sugar fermentation test

[13.3] The most frequent source of infection with *L. monocytogenes* is through which of the following?

A. Human feces
B. Livestock
C. Raw milk
D. Soil
E. Ticks

Answers

[13.1] **C.** Outbreaks of gastroenteritis, as a consequence of *L. monocytogenes,* are related to the ingestion of unpasteurized milk products, for example, cheese. *Bacillus cereus,* causing food poisoning, is associated with spore survival and germination when rice is held at warm temperatures. *Escherichia coli* is usually associated with the enterohemorrhagic *E. coli* (EHEC) form (verotoxin) that causes a bloody diarrhea and is associated with improperly cooked hamburger. *Salmonella* causes a diarrhea associated with contaminated chicken consumption. Finally, *Shigella* is usually associated with enterocolitis outbreaks among children in mental institutions and day care centers.

[13.2] **B.** *Streptococcus agalactiae* (group B streptococci) is the leading cause of neonatal sepsis and meningitis. All streptococci (including *S. agalactiae*) are catalase-negative, whereas staphylococci are catalase-positive. *Listeria monocytogenes* is also catalase-positive.

[13.3] **C.** Unpasteurized milk is a common vector for transmission of **Listeria.** See answer to Question 13.1.

MICROBIOLOGY PEARLS

❖ *Listeria meningitis* clinically resembles group B streptococcal meningitis and needs to be distinguished because of the resistance of *Listeria* to cephalosporins.

❖ *Listeria* grown on blood agar media will be β-hemolytic and resemble streptococci; however, by Gram stain *Listeria* are small bacilli and not chains of cocci.

❖ *Listeria* infection is commonly associated with consumption of undercooked food or unpasteurized milk or cheese products.

REFERENCES

Bortolussi R, Schlech WF. Listeriosis. In: Infectious Diseases of the Fetus and Newborn infant, 4th ed. Philadelphia, PA: W.B. Saunders, 1995:1055–73.

Murray PR, Rosenthal KS, Pfaller MA. Listeria and erysipelothrix. In: Murray PR, Rosenthal KS, Pfaller MA. Medical Microbiology, 5th ed. St. Louis, MO: Mosby, 2005:273–78.

❖ CASE 14

A 50-year-old man, a recent immigrant from Vietnam, is brought to the emergency room with a cough productive of bloody sputum. He first noticed a cough approximately 2 months ago, but there was not much sputum. In the past several days his sputum production has increased and become mixed with blood. He reports having lost approximately 15 lb in this time frame as well. He also notes that he's had drenching night sweats 2 or 3 nights a week for the past month. He has a 50-pack-year smoking history but no other medical history. He came to the United States from Vietnam 7 months ago. On examination, he is a thin, frail-appearing male. His vital signs are normal. His head and neck exam is normal. He has no palpable adenopathy in his neck or axilla. His lung exam is notable only for decreased breath sounds diffusely. A chest x-ray shows a cavitary infiltrate of the left upper lobe.

◆ **What type of organism is likely to be seen on Gram stain of a sputum sample?**

What technique of staining is most commonly used to identify this organism?

◆ **What is the histologic characteristic of Langhans cells?**

ANSWERS TO CASE 14: *Mycobacterium*

Summary: A 50-year-old Vietnamese man presents with chronic bloody sputum, weight loss, and a cavitary lesion on chest radiograph, all consistent with tuberculosis.

- **Likely Gram stain findings of sputum sample:** *Mycobacterium tuberculosis* appear as colorless ("ghost") cells
- **Most commonly used staining technique for *M. tuberculosis*:** Acid-fast staining
- **Histologic characteristics of Langhans cells:** Multinucleated giant cells of fused macrophages

CLINICAL CORRELATION

It is estimated that *M. tuberculosis* infects approximately one-third of the world's population. *Mycobacterium tuberculosis* is spread from **person to person via aerosolized respiratory droplets** that travel to the terminal airways. The bacteria are phagocytized by alveolar macrophages but inhibit destruction by the phago-some and proceed to replicate. Circulating macrophages are attracted to the site of infection and create **multinucleated giant cells, composed of fused macrophages called Langhans cells.** Extrapulmonary sites are infected through the spread of infected macrophages via lymphatic or hematogenous dissemination. Because of the **intracellular** nature of *M. tuberculosis* infections, **antibody mediated defenses are relatively ineffective.** Persons with conditions of reduced cellular immunity, such as AIDS, alcoholism, or drug abuse, or persons living in crowded, close quarters, such as prisoners, are at increased risk for infection. Organisms can remain **dormant in granulomas** for many years and reactivate following immunosuppression at a later date. At that time the organisms can infect extra-pulmonary sites.

Mycobacterium avium-intracellulare is found in the environment and is an opportunistic pathogen that causes disease in **AIDS patients.** Disease can range from pneumonia to gastroenteritis to disseminated disease.

Mycobacterium kansasii can clinically mimic pulmonary tuberculosis, but it is most often seen in middle-aged men with prior lung damage such as **silicosis or asbestosis.** ***Mycobacterium leprae*** is acquired by contact with the **nine-banded armadillo.** Most infections are seen in the southern United States including Texas and Louisiana. Thought to be lepers (skin lesions and deformation of the features of the face), these patients were contained in sanitariums and left to die. Infection can be either of the lepromatous or tuberculous type. Most infections caused by rapidly growing *Mycobacteria* are chronic wound infections, because this organism is found in the soil.

APPROACH TO SUSPECTED MYCOBACTERIAL INFECTION

Objectives

1. Know the structure and physiology of *Mycobacterium.*
2. Know the reservoirs, transmission, and diseases caused by *Mycobacterium.*
3. Know the mechanisms of host defenses and treatments for mycobacterial diseases.

Definitions

Langhans cells: Multinucleated giant cells composed of fused macrophages.
Granuloma: Chronic inflammatory response to either *Mycobacterium* or fungi, composed of macrophages and multinucleated giant cells.
PPD: Purified protein derivative, prepared from *M. tuberculosis* antigens inoculated intradermally and a positive reaction is indicative of exposure to *M. tuberculosis.*

DISCUSSION

Characteristics of Mycobacteria Species

Mycobacterium are **small rod-shaped bacilli that stain as ghost cells with Gram stain,** but because of the presence of **mycolic acids in their cell wall** stain with an **"acid-fast stain"** such as Kinyon or Ziehl-Neelsen. This complex, lipid-rich cell wall also makes the organisms resistant to many commonly used laboratory stains and is responsible for the resistance of this organism to many common detergents and antibiotics.

In general, *Mycobacterium* species are **slow-growing organisms,** with a generation time of 15–20 hours, compared to about 1 hour for most bacteria. *Mycobacterium* can be divided into groups as characterized by **Runyon,** based on their growth characteristics, particularly **pigment production.** The **photochromogens,** which are pigmented only in the presence of light, include *M. kansasii,* as well as other saprophytic *Mycobacterium.* The **scotochromogens,** which are **pigmented even without the presence of light,** include *M. szulgai,* as well as the nonpathogenic *M. gordonae,* which has an orange pigment. The **nonchromogens** are **not pigmented in the light or dark** including *M. avium-intracellulare,* as well as *M. haemophilum.* The fourth runyon group is composed of the **rapidly growing *Mycobacteria*** such as *M. fortuitum, M. chelonae,* and *M. abscessus.* The *M. tuberculosis* complex includes *M. tuberculosis, M. africanum, M. ulcerans,* and *M. bovis,* as well as other rarely identified *Mycobacterium.* These colonies appear buff or tan color and are dry when growing on Lowenstein-Jensen agar. *Mycobacterium leprae* is not considered in that classification because it cannot be cultured in the laboratory.

One of the virulence factors of *M. tuberculosis* is **cord factor.** This can be visualized microscopically as organisms grown in broth culture will demonstrate a **ropelike pattern** indicating cording. The rapid growing *Mycobacterium* include *M. fortuitum* complex, *M. chelonae* complex, and *M. abscessus,* as well as other uncommonly isolated nonpathogenic *Mycobacterium.* These organisms by definition will grow within seven days of subculture onto routine microbiological media such as a blood agar plate.

Diagnosis

Diagnosis of tuberculosis is initially made based on a history (exposure to patient with tuberculosis, immigration, a stay in a jail or homeless shelter) and physical exam in patients with a productive cough, night sweats, and fever. A **positive PPD test** would indicate exposure to *M. tuberculosis* and warrant further testing with chest x-ray. Patients with the characteristic upper lobe cavitary lesion would have sputum collected and cultured for *Mycobacterium.* **The classic chest radiograph findings include lower lobe consolidation in active infection, and apical lobe scarring with reactivation.**

A **fluorescent, direct smear, of the respiratory specimen** after decontamination to remove bacterial flora is reported within 24 hours of receipt of the respiratory specimen in the laboratory. Several first early morning deep cough specimens should be collected. Growth of *M. tuberculosis* on Lowenstein-Jensen (LJ) agar can take 3–8 weeks because of the slow dividing time of the organism; however, with the use of broth medium growth time has been decreased to as short as 1 week. Newly designed automated broth systems read bottles for growth based on carbon dioxide production of the organisms on a daily basis for up to 8 weeks. Bottles which are determined to be positive are stained by Kinyoun stain to visualize the presence of *Mycobacterium.* Positive bottles can be tested directly for *M. tuberculosis, M. kansasii, M. avium-intracellulare,* or *M. gordonae* using **DNA probes.** Other *Mycobacterium* species are identified either by routine biochemical tests, which require several weeks, or by high-pressure liquid chromatography, which can speciate *Mycobacterium* based on mycolic acids extracted from their cell surface. Optimal growth temperature for *Mycobacterium* species is 35°C (95°F); however, the *Mycobacterium* that infect the skin such as *M. haemophilum* grow best at lower temperatures, and organisms such as *M. szulgai* prefer 42°C (107.6°F). Growth on solid media is also enhanced in the presence of 5–10 percent carbon dioxide.

Treatment and Prevention

Prophylaxis for tuberculosis consists of oral **isoniazid** for 6–9 months and is given to all patients with a recent conversion of their PPD to positive and a negative chest x-ray. Treatment for tuberculosis based on **culture** of

M. tuberculosis from any patient specimen is initially (first 2 months) with a **multiagent regimen** based on likely resistance patterns; one such combination is isoniazid, rifampin, ethambutol, and pyrazinamide. Once the results indicate susceptibility to all of the four firstline drugs, treatment can continue with two drugs (usually isoniazid and rifampin) for the remaining 4–6 months. Because of the interaction of rifampin with other drugs, particularly HIV drugs and antifungals, this therapy may need to be individualized.

Prevention of tuberculosis besides prophylactic isoniazid includes isolation of patients in the hospital to prevent spread. Patients with a positive acid-fast smear must remain in isolation until a diagnosis of tuberculosis is ruled out, until they leave the hospital, or following several weeks of appropriate anti-tuberculous therapy with obvious clinical improvement. All known close contacts (family members) of the index case should have a PPD test to determine if they should be given therapy and/or worked up for disease.

Vaccination with BCG, (an attenuated strain of *M. bovis*) is not routinely performed in the United States because of the comparatively low incidence of tuberculosis. Protection from tuberculosis is not 100 percent with the vaccine and can confuse the results of the PPD for screening of recent converters.

Treatment of the other atypical mycobacteria varies based on the species. *Mycobacterium avium-intracellulare* is usually treated with clarithromycin or azithromycin and ethambutol plus or minus amikacin. Current treatment for leprosy is dapsone and rifampin for at least 6 months.

COMPREHENSION QUESTIONS

[14.1] An emaciated prisoner in a New York prison began coughing up sputum streaked with blood. Examination of the sputum revealed the presence of acid-fast bacilli. Which of the following would confirm a diagnosis of tuberculosis?

A. Inclusion bodies of the nuclei of macrophages
B. Presence of gram-positive pleomorphic organisms
C. Rough, nonpigmented colonies
D. Rapid growth on Lowenstein-Jensen medium

[14.2] A 45-year-old traveler discovers that he has converted from negative to positive on the tuberculin (PPD) skin test. This indicates which of the following?

A. He has active tuberculosis.
B. He has delayed-type hypersensitivity against *M. tuberculosis.*
C. He is most likely to be infected with an "atypical" *Mycobacterium.*
D. He needs to be immediately isolated to prevent spread of *M. tuberculosis.*
E. He will eventually develop tuberculosis.

[14.3] A 60-year-old man with a chronic cough, bloody sputum, and marked weight loss is diagnosed as having tuberculosis. A "serpentine-like" colonial morphology is noted on Lowenstein-Jensen agar. This latter finding is caused by which of the following factors?

A. A large "slimy" capsule
B. An endotoxin
C. Coagulase
D. Cord factor
E. Wax D

[14.4] A 25-year-old man known to have AIDS experiences a gradual onset of malaise and anorexia, proceeding within a few weeks to photophobia, impaired consciousness, and oculofacial palsy. An acid-fast bacterium with trehalose-6, 6'-dimycolate is isolated. The identity of this organism is which of the following?

A. *Mycobacterium fortuitum-chelonei*
B. *Mycobacterium kansasii*
C. *Mycobacterium marinum*
D. *Mycobacterium scrofulaceum*
E. *Mycobacterium tuberculosis*

Answers

[14.1] **C.** To mount a protective immune response against a specific microorganism requires that the appropriate population of cells play a role in the response. A lipoprotein of *M. tuberculosis* stimulates a specific "toll-like receptor" on the macrophage. Activated macrophages then synthesize IL-12, which causes differentiation of naïve helper T cells into the Th-1 type of helper T cells that participates in the cell-mediated (delayed hypersensitivity) response. In addition, delayed hypersensitivity (not humoral) reactions are produced against antigens of intracellular pathogens such as *M. tuberculosis.* Thus, humoral immunity is not protective against *M. tuberculosis,* and the patient will suffer severe tuberculosis if cell-mediated immunity is not functional. Therefore, an agglutination test for antibodies is useless as *M. tuberculosis* is an intracellular pathogen and will not elicit a humoral (antibody-formation) immune response that will protect the patient against *M. tuberculosis.* The growth is usually slow, and the colonies are rough and nonpigmented.

[14.2] **B.** The purified protein derivative (PPD) skin test, or tuberculin skin test, contains several proteins from *M. tuberculosis,* which when combined with waxes elicits a delayed hypersensitivity. It does not assess for the status of infection, but only speaks about prior exposure. The clinical presentation and/or chest radiograph would be the next steps in evaluation.

[14.3] **D.** Virulent strains of *M. tuberculosis* grow in a characteristic "serpentine" cord-like pattern, whereas avirulent strains do not. Virulence of the organism is correlated with cord factor (trehalose dimycolate).

[14.4] **E.** *Mycobacterium tuberculosis* commonly has the trehalose dimycolate factor (see answer to Question 14.3).

MICROBIOLOGY PEARLS

- ❖ *Mycobacterium tuberculosis* is a slow growing organism that causes pulmonary infection after close contact with an infected individual.
- ❖ A positive skin test (PPD) indicates exposure to the organism and not necessarily disease.
- ❖ *Mycobacterium* species stain positive with an acid-fast stain because of components in their cell wall.
- ❖ Initial therapy for tuberculosis requires multiple agents to avoid the development of resistance, and culture susceptibilities will dictate which agents should be continued.

REFERENCES

Haas DW. Mycobacterium tuberculosis. In: Mandell GL, Bennett JE, Dolin R, eds. Principles and Practice of Infectious Diseases, 5th ed. Philadelphia, PA: Churchill Livingstone, 2000:2576–607.

Murray PR, Rosenthal KS, Pfaller MA. Mycobacterium. In: Rosenthal KS, Kobayashi GS, Pfaller MA. Medical Microbiology, 5th ed. St. Louis, MO: Mosby, 2005:297–310.

❖ CASE 15

A 15-year-old teenager is brought to the office for evaluation of a cough and fever. His illness began several days ago with low-grade fever, headache, myalgias, and fatigue, and has slowly worsened. He now has a persistent cough. He has tried multiple over-the-counter cold and cough medications without relief. He has no significant medical or family history. No family members have been ill recently, but one of his good friends missed several days of school approximately 2 weeks ago with "walking pneumonia." On examination he is coughing frequently but is not particularly ill-appearing. His temperature is 38.1°C (100.5°F), pulse is 90 beats per minute, and respiratory rate is 22 breaths per minute. His pharynx is injected (red and inflamed); otherwise, a head and neck exam is normal. His lung exam is notable only for some scattered rhonchi. The remainder of his examination is normal. A chest x-ray shows some patchy infiltration. A sputum Gram stain shows white blood cells but no organisms.

- **What is the most likely etiology of this infection?**

- **What is the explanation for no organisms being seen on Gram stain?**

- **What rapid, although nonspecific, blood test can provide presumptive evidence of infection by this organism?**

ANSWERS TO CASE 15: *Mycoplasma*

Summary: A 15-year-old adolescent presents with a persistent cough, patchy infiltrate on chest x-ray, and exposure to a friend with "walking pneumonia."

- **Most likely infectious agent:** *Mycoplasma pneumoniae*
- **Reasons no organisms are seen on Gram stain:** *Mycoplasma pneumoniae* does not stain because it does not have a cell wall.

- **Rapid blood test for presumptive evidence of *M. pneumoniae:*** Cold agglutinins

CLINICAL CORRELATION

Mycoplasma pneumoniae is transmitted from person to person by aerosolized respiratory droplets and is most common in children and adolescents. Disease caused by *M. pneumonia* usually has an insidious onset and can progress to tracheobronchitis or **pneumonia,** which is often **patchy or diffuse, as opposed to lobar.** Because of the inability to diagnose this on microscopy, and the difficulty and length of time required for culture, serologic testing is often used to identify this organism.

APPROACH TO SUSPECTED *Mycoplasma pneumoniae* PATIENT

Objectives

1. Know the structure and physiology of *M. pneumoniae* and other *Mycoplasma* organisms.
2. Know the clinical diseases associated with and tests for identification of *M. pneumoniae.*

Definitions

Tracheobronchitis: Inflammation of the trachea in addition to the bronchi; causing swelling & narrowing of the airways.

Rhonchi: A coarse rattling sound heard on auscultation of the lungs of a patient with partially obstructed airways.

Pruritus: Itching; can have many causes: food allergy, drug reation, kidney/liver disease, aging or dry skin, cancers, infectious agents or other unknown causes.

DISCUSSION

Characteristics of *Mycoplasma pneumoniae* That Impact Transmission

Mycoplasma pneumoniae is a **short, strictly aerobic rod.** It has a trilamellar, sterol-containing cell membrane but **no cell wall,** therefore it is **not identifiable with Gram or other stains.** The lack of a cell wall also confers resistance against **β-lactams** and other antibiotics that act on the cell walls of bacteria. It is the **smallest free-living bacterium,** even during infection, it remains extracellular. It divides by binary fission and has a doubling time of approximately 6 hours, much slower than most bacteria. This contributes to the difficulty in isolating this organism by culture, as up to 6 weeks of incubation is required. *Mycoplasma* has the **adherence protein Pl** at one end, which is responsible for its attachment to a protein on target cells and may confer its preference for respiratory epithelium. When attached to ciliated respiratory epithelial cells, first the cilia and then the cell is destroyed. This interferes with normal mucociliary clearance and allows the lower airways to be irritated and contaminated with infectious agents.

Mycoplasma pneumoniae is **transmitted from person to person by aerosolized respiratory droplets and secretions,** and close association with an index case is usually required. No seasonal peak is observed. There is usually a **1–3 week incubation period** before the onset of clinical disease. Although it can infect those of all ages, disease more commonly occurs in children and young adults. *Mycoplasma pneumoniae* is responsible for 15–20 percent of community-acquired pneumonias. Clinical presentation consists of a low-grade fever, headache, malaise, and later a nonproductive cough, with a slow resolution.

Diagnosis

Diagnosis is primarily made from clinical presentation. Because of the inability to diagnose the infection with microscopy and the difficulty and length of time required for culture, serologic testing is often used to confirm a clinical diagnosis. Antibody-directed enzyme immunoassays and immunofluorescence tests or complement fixation tests are used in diagnosis. Another useful test is to analyze the titer of **cold agglutinins.** *Mycoplasma pneumoniae* infection often results in the stimulation of **an IgM antibody against the I-antigen on erythrocytes.** This antigen-antibody complex binds at 4°C (39.2°F) causing the clumping of erythrocytes. Although this response can be triggered by other organisms, titers of these antibodies of 1:128 or greater, or a fourfold increase with the presence of an appropriated clinical presentation are considered presumptive evidence of *M. pneumoniae* disease.

Another *Mycoplasma, M. hominis,* causes **pelvic inflammatory disease (PID), nongonococcal urethritis (NGU), pyelonephritis, and postpartum**

fever. Another cause of NGU and an organism that is detected with cold agglutinins is *Ureaplasma urealyticum,* a facultative anaerobic rod. Although this organism can also be a commensal, it can also lead to the sexually transmitted disease NGU and infertility. It is diagnosed via serology, by both cold agglutinins and specific serology with complement fixation and ELISA (enzyme-linked immunosorbent assay) for IgM. Like *Mycoplasma,* culture is not reliable and takes many weeks. PCR probes are also used for diagnosis. The clinical picture of NGU consists of urethral discharge, pruritus, and dysuria. Typically, systemic symptoms are absent. The onset of symptoms in NGU can often be subacute. There are 3 million new cases of NGU (including *M. hominis, U. urealyticum, Chlamydia trachomatis,* and *Trichomonas vaginalis*) a year, and 10–40 percent of women suffer PID as a result, compared to only 1–2 percent of males, with morbidity from NGU because of stricture or stenosis. NGU occurs equally in men and women, though can be asymptomatic in 50 percent of women.

Treatment and Prevention

Mycoplasma pneumoniae-related pneumonia, as well as other *Mycoplasma* infections resulting in NGU, can be effectively treated with **tetracycline** and **macrolides.** Tetracyclines can be used to treat most *mycoplasmas,* as well as *Chlamydia;* whereas macrolides can be used to treat *Ureaplasma* infections, which are resistant to tetracycline. *Mycoplasma pneumoniae* infections are difficult to prevent because patients are infectious for extended periods of time, even during treatment. Several attempts have been made to produce inactivated and attenuated live vaccines without success.

COMPREHENSION QUESTIONS

[15.1] A 33-year-old woman is diagnosed with "walking pneumonia" caused by *Mycoplasma.* Which of the following best describes the characteristics of the etiologic organism?

A. Absence of a cell wall
B. Belonging to the class of Eukaryotes
C. Often evoke an IgM autoantibody response leading to human erythrocyte agglutination
D. Typically colonize the gastrointestinal tract

[15.2] Which of the following antibiotics is the best treatment for the above patient?

A. Ampicillin
B. Ceftriaxone
C. Erythromycin
D. Gentamicin
E. Vancomycin

[15.3] *Mycoplasma* organisms may also cause disease in nonpulmonary sites. Which of the following is the most commonly affected nonpulmonary site?

A. Meningitis
B. Prosthetic heart valve
C. Septic arthritis
D. Urethritis

[15.4] A 20-year-old man presents to the clinic with a history of fever and nonproductive cough. The patient's chest x-ray shows consolidation of the right lower lobe. An infection with *M. pneumoniae* is considered as the cause of the patient's pneumonia. Which of the following methods would confirm this diagnosis?

A. Culture of sputum specimen on solid medium
B. Detection of organism by microscopy
C. Complement fixation test of acute and convalescent sera
D. PCR amplification of patient's sputum specimen
E. Enzyme immunoassay to detect cell wall antigens

Answers

[15.1] **A.** *Mycoplasma* are the smallest living organisms, and they do not have cell walls but rather have cell membranes. Thus, they are typically resistant to antibiotics that interfere with cell wall synthesis. Also, because of their absence of a cell wall, they are not usually detected on Gram stain. They have a propensity for attaching to respiratory, urethral, or genital tract epithelium.

[15.2] **C.** Erythromycin, clarithromycin, or azithromycin (macrolides) are effective against mycoplasma species.

[15.3] **D.** *Mycoplasma* and *Ureaplasma* species are commonly isolated from the lower genital tract. They are likely the most common cause of nonchlamydial nongonococcal urethritis.

[15.4] **C.** Diagnosis is primarily made from serologic testing (enzyme immunoassays, immunofluorescence, cold agglutinins) Answers A, B, D, and E are all incorrect: (A) culturing *M. pneumoniae* is difficult and slow and is not used for diagnosis; (B) *Mycoplasmas* lack a cell wall making microscopy inappropriate; (D) PCR amplification of a sputum specimen is not an appropriate method of diagnosis; (E) *M. pneumoniae* lacks a cell wall and thus, cell wall antigens.

MICROBIOLOGY PEARLS

- *Mycoplasmas* are small free-living microorganisms that lack a cell wall.
- *Mycoplasma pneumoniae* is a common cause of atypical pneumonia in children and adolescents.
- Symptoms include nonproductive cough, fever, headache, and "walking pneumonia."
- Effective treatment is with erythromycin or tetracycline.

REFERENCES

Baseman JB, Tully JG. Mycoplasmas: sophisticated, reemerging, and burdened by their notoriety. Emerg Infect Dis 1997;3:21. www.cdc.gov/ncidod/EID/vol3no1/baseman.htm.

Murray PR, Rosenthal KS, Pfaller MA. Medical Microbiology, 5th ed. St. Louis, MO: Mosby, 2005:395–9.

Loens K, Ursi D, Goossens H, et al. Molecular diagnosis of *Mycoplasma pneumoniae* respiratory tract infections. J Clin Microbiol 41:4915–23. 2003.

Ryan JR, Ray CG. Sherris Medical Microbiology, 4th ed. New York: McGraw-Hill, 2004:409–11.

❖ CASE 16

A 19-year-old woman presents to the physician's office for the evaluation of a swollen knee. She states that for the past 1–2 week she has had some achiness in several of her joints and a low-grade fever, but it seemed to localize to her left knee approximately 3 days ago. It has been red, hot, and swollen. She has had no injury to the area and has never had anything like this before. Her past medical history is significant for having been treated for *Chlamydia* at the age of 17. She takes oral contraceptive pills regularly. She is sexually active, has been with her most recent boyfriend for about a month, and has had 5 partners in her lifetime. On examination, her vital signs are normal, but you notice that she walks with a limp. Her general examination is normal, and her skin is without rash. Her left knee is erythematous and warm to the touch. There is a visible effusion. Movement is limited because of pain and stiffness from the swelling. She refuses a pelvic examination because she doesn't see what that has to do with her sore knee. However, she does allow you to perform a joint aspiration.

◆ **What are the most likely Gram stain findings of the aspirated joint fluid?**

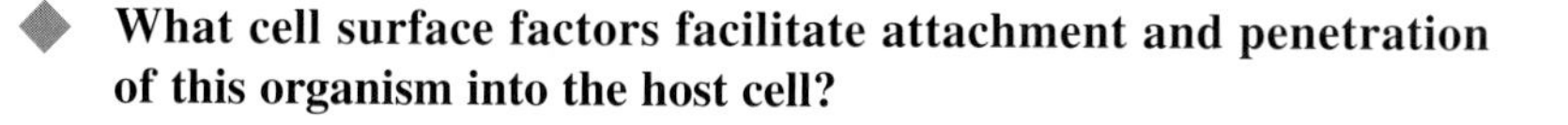

◆ **What cell surface factors facilitate attachment and penetration of this organism into the host cell?**

ANSWERS TO CASE 16: *Neisseria*

Summary: A 19-year-old woman presents with septic arthritis. She has had an infection previously with *Chlamydia*.

- **Likely findings on Gram stain of the joint fluid aspirate:** Multiple polymorphonuclear leukocytes with intracellular gram-negative diplococci.
- **Cell surface factors facilitating attachment and penetration into the host cell:** Pili, which attach to epithelial cells, and Opa protein, which promotes firm attachment and cell penetration.

CLINICAL CORRELATION

Humans are the only known reservoir of *Neisseria* species. *Neisseria gonorrhoeae* is transferred from person to person by sexual contact. Approximately half of infected women have an asymptomatic carrier state. This is much less common in men. *Neisseria gonorrhoeae* causes urethritis in men and cervicitis in women. Complications of genital infections include pelvic inflammatory disease. The organism can also infect the rectum and oropharynx. Newborns passing through an infected birth canal may develop conjunctivitis by direct contact, a disease called ophthalmia neonatorum. Disseminated disease, including bacteremia with resultant joint and/or skin infections is more common in patients with complement deficiencies. Septic arthritis as a complication of disseminated disease may present in two forms, either as a systemic disease with fever, chills, and polyarticular syndrome, or as a monoarticular suppurative infection of a single joint without skin lesions or systemic symptoms. Most cases of disseminated gonococcal disease occur in persons with an asymptomatic genital infection.

Neisseria meningitidis is carried as normal upper respiratory flora in approximately 10 percent of the population. The polysaccharide capsule allows the organism to avoid phagocytosis and under unknown circumstances enter the blood and in some cases the central nervous system. The subsequent inflammatory response induced by the organism causes shock and disseminated intravascular coagulation. This is evidenced by skin lesions, which can mimic those seen in disseminated gonococcal infection. Bacteremia with or without meningitis usually occurs in teenage children. If untreated, the disease has a high mortality rate.

APPROACH TO SUSPECTED GONORRHOEAE PATIENT

Objectives

1. Know the structure and characteristics of *Neisseria* species.
2. Know the factors associated with the development on *Neisseria* infections and diseases.

Definitions

Disseminated intravascular coagulation (DIC): A complication of septic shock usually caused by endotoxin produced by the affecting organism.
Ophthalmia neonatorum: Conjunctivitis in the first month of life usually as a result of *N. gonorrhoeae* or *Chlamydia trachomatis.*

DISCUSSION

Characteristics of *Neisseria* Species

Neisseria species are **aerobic, nonmotile, nonspore-forming, gram-negative cocci.** They usually are arranged in **pairs** (diplococci) with adjacent sides flattened, resembling **kidney beans.** *Neisseria* are **fastidious organisms** that require a complex medium and an atmosphere supplemented with **carbon dioxide** for optimal growth. *Neisseria gonorrhoeae* has specific cell surface components related to its adherence, cellular penetration, toxicity, and evasion of host defenses. Cellular adherence is conferred by the presence of **pili,** which attach to host epithelial cells and also provide resistance to killing by host neutrophils. The **outer membrane also contains the Opa proteins** (opacity proteins), which promote tight attachment and migration of the bacteria into the host. Then **Por proteins** (porin), which form channels (pores) in the outer membrane, **prevent phagolysosome fusion,** allowing intracellular survival. **Rmp proteins** (reduction-modifiable proteins) stimulate antibodies, which inhibit host bactericidal antibodies, protecting the other surface antigens from host attack.

Plasmid acquisition and transfer appear to play significant roles in the development of **antibiotic resistance** by *N. gonorrhoeae.* Multiple plasmids, which confer **β-lactamase,** have been identified. A conjugative plasmid that causes high-level tetracycline resistance has also been identified. These plasmids are becoming more common, resulting in more antibiotic-resistant gonococcal disease. LOS (lipooligosaccharide), also present in the cell wall, produces the inflammatory response responsible for most of the symptoms associated with gonococcal disease by its release of tumor necrosis factor-α.

Neisseria meningitidis appear the same as *N. gonorrhoeae* on Gram stain. They also produce a polysaccharide capsule that prevents phagocytosis. *Neisseria meningitidis* is divided into 13 serogroups, the most common of which are A,C,Y, W135, and B.

Diagnosis

Septic arthritis must be differentiated from other noninfectious forms of arthritis such as rheumatoid arthritis and gout. **Definitive diagnosis** is made by **analysis of cells and Gram stain from an aspirate of the joint.** Gram stain would reveal **intracellular gram-negative diplococci.** A presumptive diagnosis of gonorrhea can be made from a smear from a male urethra; otherwise, culture is required for diagnosis.

Neisseria species are **fastidious organisms** in that they require carbon dixide **atmosphere,** and *N. gonorrhoeae* also require **chocolate agar.** *Neisseria gonorrhoeae* also may require at least 48 hours for production of small grey colonies. **Selective media** such as **Thayer Martin** or **Martin Lewis** is usually needed to isolate *N. gonorrhoeae* from nonsterile sites such as the cervix or urethra. *Neisseria gonorrhoeae* are quite sensitive to drying, so plates must be placed in a warm environment quickly to maintain viability. If a delay in transit to the laboratory is expected to be longer than several hours, a transport media such as Jembec is required. Rapid identification can be made from gram-negative diplococci, growing on selective media that are **oxidase positive.** Isolates are specifically identified by acid production from select sugars. *Neisseria gonorrhoeae* ferments glucose only, and *N. meningitidis* ferments both glucose and maltose. Because of the fastidious nature of *N. gonorrhoeae,* genital infections are identified using DNA probes, which detect both *N. gonorrhoeae* and *C. trachomatis,* which commonly occur together and don't require live organisms for detection.

Treatment and Prevention

Penicillin is the treatment of choice for meningococcemia. Approximately 30 percent of ***N. gonorrhoeae*** **produce β-lactamase and are therefore resistant to penicillin.** Treatment with **ceftriaxone** or a quinolones is usually recommended, although increase in **resistance to quinolones** has been demonstrated in some geographic locations. **Prevention of meningococcal disease is by vaccination.** A recent CDC recommendation advises vaccinating all adolescents for meningococcus at the age of 11–12 years. Other susceptible persons, such as military personnel, college students who will be living in dormitories and asplenic patients, should be vaccinated as well. Prophylaxis of close contacts is also recommended to prevent spread of the disease. Prevention of *N. gonorrhoeae* includes practicing safe sex and use of a condom, as well as screening sexually active persons. Screening of pregnant women for congenitally transmitted infections with appropriate treatment would prevent infection of the neonate with *N. gonorrhoeae,* as well as other congenitally transmitted infections.

COMPREHENSION QUESTIONS

[16.1] The source of *N. meningitidis* is the nasopharynx of human carriers who exhibit no symptoms. The ability of this bacterium to colonize the respiratory mucosa is associated with its ability to synthesize which of the following?

A. Coagulase
B. Collagenase
C. Hyaluronidase
D. Lipases
E. Pili

[16.2] Several *Neisseria* species are a part of the normal flora (commensals) of the human upper respiratory tract. Which of the following statements accurately describes the significance of these bacteria?

A. As a part of the normal flora, *Neisseriae* provide a natural immunity in local host defense.
B. As a part of the respiratory flora, they are the most common cause of acute bronchitis and pneumonia.
C. Commensal bacteria stimulate a cell-mediated immunity (CMI).
D. Commensal *Neisseriae* in the upper respiratory tract impede phagocytosis by means of lipoteichoic acid.
E. Normal flora such as nonpathogenic *Neisseriae* provide effective nonspecific B-cell–mediated humoral immunity.

[16.3] A 22-year-old man presents to the STD clinic with a 5-day history of burning on urination and a 3-day history of a nonpurulent urethral discharge. He is sexually active with many female partners and does not use condoms. There is no history of prior sexually transmitted diseases. Laboratory findings from endourethral exudate are most likely to show which of the following?

A. A negative gonorrhea culture
B. Abundant intracellular diplococci in neutrophils
C. Immunofluorescence using monoclonal antibodies to serotypes A–C
D. Intracellular elementary bodies

[16.4] The two pathogenic *Neisseria* species, *N. meningitidis* and *N. gonorrhoeae,* differ from the nonpathogenic *Neisseria* species in what way?

A. The former are less resistant to certain antibiotics than the nonpathogenic species.
B. The pathogenic species are oxidase positive.
C. The pathogenic species grow well in enriched chocolate agar.
D. The pathogenic species do not grow well at room temperature.

Answers

[16.1] **E.** Both *N. gonorrhoeae* and *N. meningitidis* adhere to the mucous membrane tissues by means of pili (short protein appendages from the membrane through the cell wall). Coagulase and lipase are products of streptococci, whereas collagenase and hyaluronidase are enzyme products of streptococci.

[16.2] **A.** The normal or usual flora seldom cause disease in humans, except the several species that may be opportunistic in the right circumstances. One mechanism that has been suggested as to how the normal flora help to protect humans from pathogenic strains of bacteria is to stimulate the immune system to produce antibodies (or CMI) that would recognize related pathogens and inhibit their growth. An unexplained component of this mechanism is how the normal flora continue to exist as part of the body flora in spite of these immune mechanisms.

[16.3] **B.** This presentation is classic for gonorrhea infection and symptoms. Abundant gram-negative diplococci will be found both intracellularly and outside of the phagocytic cells. Interestingly, gonococci may even divide within the phagocytic cell. This evidence (Gram stain of the exudate) is presumptive evidence of gonococcal infection, and treatment should be made immediately. Such a specimen should be positive for culture with the correct medium (e.g., Thayer-Martin) and incubation conditions (37°C [98.6°F], increased carbon dioxide atmosphere). Serotypes A–C refers to *N. meningitidis,* and elementary bodies would indicate *Chlamydia* microorganisms.

[16.4] **D.** *Neisseria gonorrhoeae* and *N. meningitidis* are true human pathogens, surviving best in the human host. They are more fastidious in their nutritional requirement, requiring an enriched selective medium for growth. All *Neisseria* are oxidase positive. Normal flora (nonpathogenic) *Neisseria* will grow at room temperature on simple medium. Because of β-lactamase production, sensitivities should be done to ensure proper antimicrobial selection for treatment.

MICROBIOLOGY PEARLS

- ❖ *Neisseria meningitidis* is a highly contagious organism, which can cause meningitis in otherwise healthy young people.
- ❖ *Neisseria meningitidis* can be successfully prevented with the use of the vaccine for high-risk individuals.
- ❖ *Neisseria gonorrhoeae* is a treatable sexually transmitted disease and should be ruled out in high-risk patients to prevent further complications including disseminated disease.

REFERENCES

Apicella, MA. Neisseria meningitidis. In: Mandell GL, Bennett JE, Dolin R, eds. Principles and Practice of Infectious Diseases, 5th ed. Philadelphia, PA: Churchill Livingstone, 2000:2228–41.

Murray PR, Rosenthal KS, Pfaller MA. Neisseria. In: Murray PR, Rosenthal KS, Pfaller MA. Medical Microbiology, 5th ed. St. Louis, MO: Mosby, 2005:311–21.

Sparling, PF, Handsfield, HH. Neisseria gonorrhoeae. In: Mandell GL, Bennett JE, Dolin R, eds. Principles and Practice of Infectious Diseases, 5th ed. Philadelphia, PA: Churchill Livingstone, 2000:2242–58.

❖ CASE 17

A 35-year-old woman presents to the emergency department with right flank pain. She reports that she had a few days of urinary urgency, frequency, and burning which she tried to treat herself by drinking cranberry juice. Earlier today she started having a severe, colicky pain on her whole right side. She has had a fever, and when she urinated this morning she noticed that it appeared to have blood. She's had a few urinary tract infections (UTIs) in the past but nothing like this. She is on no medications regularly and has no other significant medical history. On examination, she has a temperature of 37.5°C (99.5°F), her other vital signs are normal, and she appears to be in pain. Notable on examination is some tenderness on the right flank but no masses, rebound tenderness, or guarding on palpation of her abdomen. She has costovertebral angle tenderness on the right side but not the left. Her peripheral white blood cell count is elevated. A urinalysis shows the presence of leukocyte esterase, blood, and a high pH. An abdominal CT scan reveals an obstructing stone in the right ureter causing hydronephrosis of the right kidney.

◆ **What organism is likely to be responsible for this infection?**

◆ **What is the cause of the high pH of this patient's urine?**

ANSWERS TO CASE 17: *Proteus mirabilis*

Summary: A 35-year-old woman presents with a UTI and nephrolithiasis (kidney stones). The urine has a high pH.

- **Organism most likely to be responsible for this infection:** *Proteus mirabilis.*
- **Mechanism of high pH in urine:** *Proteus* produces urease, which splits urea into carbon dioxide and ammonia, raising the urinary pH.

CLINICAL CORRELATION

Proteus species are normal flora of the gastrointestinal tract and predominantly associated with hospital-acquired UTIs as well as bacteremia, osteomyelitis, empyema, and neonatal encephalitis. *Proteus* causes UTIs after urethral contamination with fecal bacteria followed by ascension into the bladder. Most infections occur in patients with structural abnormalities or long-term catheters of the urinary tract. *Proteus* infections can result in significant renal damage by several mechanisms. *Proteus* produces large amounts of urease, which breaks down urea into carbon dioxide and ammonia and results in elevated urinary pH levels. **High urinary pH** can contribute to direct renal toxicity and also can result in increased urinary stone formation. Urinary stones can result in further renal damage by obstructing urine flow and serving as a focus of ongoing infection. Crystalline material tends to build up inside of a long-term catheter leading to biofilm formation. This can essentially block flow through the catheter. *Proteus* is also among the most common causes of bacteremia in the family Enterobacteriaceae often associated with underlying disease such as diabetes, malignancy, or heart or lung disease. Bacteremia is usually secondary to a primary UTI. Pediatric meningitis with *Proteus* species, especially in the first week of life, has a high mortality rate and a predilection for abscess formation when the organism gains access to the brain. It is hypothesized that the organisms gain entry into the blood through the umbilicus and from the blood they disseminated into the brain.

APPROACH TO *Proteus mirabilis* INFECTION

Objectives

1. Know the structure and characteristics of *P. mirabilis.*
2. Know the mechanisms by which *P. mirabilis* produces renal damage.

Definitions

Nephrolithiasis: The presence of calculi (solid, crystalline) that develop in the kidney and pass through the genitourinary tract.

Hydronephrosis: Enlargement of the kidney because of an abnormality such as the presence of stones.

DISCUSSION

Characteristics of *Proteus* Species

The genus *Proteus* includes five species, the most common of which are *P. mirabilis* and *P. vulgaris. Proteus* species are commonly found in the environment and as normal flora in the intestinal tract of humans and other animals. *Proteus mirabilis,* like other members of the Enterobacteriaceae family, is a **nonspore-forming, facultative anaerobic, gram-negative bacillus.** *Proteus* has **fimbriae,** which facilitate attachment to uroepithelium, and **flagellae,** which provide the **motility** required for ascending infection. *Proteus* also has the ability to transform from a **single cell form to a multicell elongated (swarmer)** form. The swarmer cells are more likely to be associated with cellular adherence in the kidney as demonstrated in an animal model of infection. **Hemolysin,** which induces cell damage by forming pores, may also play a role in establishment of pyelonephritis.

Diagnosis

Diagnosis of a UTI is initially by the urinalysis followed by a culture. The presence of **leukocyte esterase,** which is an indicator of the presence of white blood cells, in this patient indicated a presumptive UTI. The **increased urinary pH** as well as the evidence of a stone by CT indicated an obstructive process. Gram stain of the urine may be helpful if a significantly large number of organisms are present in the urine (greater than 10^5 colonies per milliliter). Culture of urine would likely be diagnostic after 24 hours. Members of the family Enterobacteriaceae, the most common cause of UTIs in an otherwise healthy young person, should grow rapidly on blood as well as MacConkey agars. The presence of greater than or equal to 10^5 CFU/mL in the urine of a single organism would indicate a significant pathogen. *Proteus* is easily identified on a MacConkey agar plate as a **clear colony (nonlactose fermenter).** The **obvious swarm** seen on blood agar would indicate a *Proteus* species. Definitive confirmation of *P. mirabilis* would be made by biochemical tests included in most commercially available identification systems. A quick test to differentiate *P. mirabilis* and *P. vulgaris* would be indole positivity in the latter.

Treatment and Prevention

Proteus species are usually among the most susceptible genera of all of the Enterobacteriaceae, **most susceptible to penicillin,** although it is not uncommon for them to be resistant to tetracyclines. *Proteus vulgaris,* however, tends to be resistant to more antimicrobials than *P. mirabilis.* As is the case with most bacteria, new resistance mechanisms are being seen in otherwise susceptible organisms.

COMPREHENSION QUESTIONS

[17.1] A 78-year-old patient with an episode of acute urinary retention was catheterized. Three days later, he developed fever and suprapubic pain. Culture of the urine revealed a thin film of bacterial growth over the entire blood agar plate, and the urease test was positive. Which of the following is the most likely organism to cause this infection?

A. *Escherichia coli*
B. *Helicobacter pylori*
C. *Morganella morganii*
D. *Proteus mirabilis*
E. *Enterococcus faecalis*

[17.2] A urinary tract infection as a result of *P. mirabilis* facilitates the formation of kidney stones because the organism does which of the following?

A. Destroys blood vessels in the kidney
B. Exhibits "swarming" motility
C. Ferments many sugars
D. Produces a potent urease
E. Secretes many exotoxins

[17.3] A 55-year-old woman is noted to have pyelonephritis with shaking chills and fever. Blood cultures are obtained, and the Gram stain is read preliminarily as consistent with *Proteus* species. Which of the following bacteria also may be the etiology?

A. *Escherichia coli*
B. Group B *Streptococcus*
C. *Staphylococcus aureus*
D. *Streptococcus pyogenes*

Answers

[17.1] **D.** *Proteus* species produce infections in humans only when the bacteria leave the intestinal tract. They are found in UTIs and produce bacteremia, pneumonia, and focal lesions in debilitated patients or those receiving intravenous infusions. *Proteus mirabilis* is a common cause of UTI. *Proteus* species produce urease, making urine alkaline and promoting stone formation. The rapid motility of these organisms is evidenced by "swarming," a thin film of organisms over the entire agar plate.

[17.2] **D.** *Proteus* species produce a urease, which hydrolyzes urea leading to ammonia, which alkalinizes the urine (leading to a higher pH).

[17.3] **A.** Both proteus and *E. coli* are gram-negative rod bacilli. *Escherichia coli* is the most common isolate in UTIs.

MICROBIOLOGY PEARLS

❖ The ability of *Proteus* species to swarm is an important virulence mechanism in causing UTIs.

❖ The swarming nature of *Proteus* also is an early diagnostic indicator as to the organism's identity.

❖ *Proteus* species have the ability to produce obstructive stones because of the presence of the urease enzyme.

❖ *Proteus mirabilis* is the most common cause of *Proteus* infections.

REFERENCES

Mobley HLT, Belas R. Swarming and pathogenicity of proteus mirabilis in the urinary tract. Trends Microbiol 1995;3:280–84.

Murray PR, Rosenthal KS, Pfaller MA. Enterobacteriaceae. In: Murray PR, Rosenthal KS, Pfaller MA. Medical Microbiology, 5th ed. St. Louis, MO: Mosby, 2005:323–38.

O'Hara CM, Brenner FW, Miller JM. Classification, identification, and clinical significance of proteus, providencia and morganella. Clin. Microbiol. Rev 2000;13:534–46.

❖ CASE 18

A 73-year-old man with a history of hypertension and type II diabetes mellitus presents to the physician's office with excruciating left ear pain for the past 3 days. He also has noticed today that his speech seems a bit slurred, and his wife says that the left side of his face looks "droopy." He has had so much pain and swelling that he hasn't been able to put his hearing aid in for several days. He has had "swimmer's ear" in the past, which responded to treatment with ear drops, but has not had any ear problems in several years. He cleans his ears daily with cotton swabs prior to putting in his hearing aid. He denies having a fever, but says that his blood sugars have been higher than usual for the past 2 days. On examination, his vital signs are normal, and he is in obvious pain. He has a prominent left-sided facial droop. His left ear is diffusely swollen, and he is tender on the pinna, the entire periauricular area, and mastoid. There is purulent drainage from the ear canal. You are unable to insert a speculum into the canal because of the swelling and pain. He has evidence of facial nerve palsy on the left side. Blood tests show an elevated white blood cell count and a markedly elevated erythrocyte sedimentation rate (ESR). Your diagnosis is malignant external otitis infection.

◆ **What organism is the most likely cause of this infection?**

◆ **Which two toxins contribute to most of the systemic toxicity of this organism?**

ANSWERS TO CASE 18: *Pseudomonas aeruginosa*

Summary: A 73-year-old man is diagnosed with malignant otitis externa.

Organism most likely to cause this infection: *Pseudomonas aeruginosa*

Which two toxins contribute to most of the systemic signs of infection: Lipopolysaccharide endotoxin and exotoxin A

CLINICAL CORRELATION

Pseudomonas causes numerous types of infections, with the common factor being that they are usually in a debilitated host. *Pseudomonas aeruginosa* is an opportunistic pathogen that is most commonly associated with nosocomial pneumonia. Pulmonary infections primarily occur in patients with underlying disease such as cystic fibrosis or chronic lung or heart disease, who have immune suppression, or who are on ventilators. Skin infections occur in patients whose skin has been disrupted either by burn or trauma. Skin lesions can also be a secondary effect of disseminated disease and are known as ecthyma gangrenosum. Other common infections include urinary tract infection in catheterized patients and chronic otitis. Malignant otitis externa, a severe external ear infection, which can potentially invade through the cranial bones and nerves, is seen primarily in the elderly and in diabetics. Other complications are uncommonly a result of *Pseudomonas* bacteremia, such as endocarditis, meningitis, and bone and joint infections.

APPROACH TO SUSPECTED *Pseudomonas* PATIENT

Objectives

1. Know the structural and physiologic characteristics of *P. aeruginosa*.
2. Know the virulence factors associated with *P. aeruginosa*.

Definitions

Periauricular: Around the external ear.

Erythrocyte sedimentation rate (ESR): A measure of the time it takes for red blood cells to settle, which is a nonspecific measure of inflammation.

Ecthyma gangrenosum: Pustular skin lesions that later become necrotic ulcers and can lead to gangrene.

DISCUSSION

Characteristics of *Pseudomonas* Species

Pseudomonas species is a **ubiquitous, aerobic gram-negative bacillus.** At least ten species are included in the genus that can cause disease in humans. Some of the closely related organisms have been transferred to their own genus, such as *Burkholderia cepacia,* formerly *Pseudomonas cepacia.* ***Pseudomonas aeruginosa* is the most common cause of human infections.** It is motile as a result of the presence of **polar flagellae.** It is found commonly in the environment and has a predilection for **moist areas.** Reservoirs in nature include soil, vegetation, and water. **Reservoirs in a hospital include sinks, toilets, mops, respiratory therapy, and dialysis equipment.** It exhibits **intrinsic resistance** to many **antibiotics and disinfectants.** It has minimal growth requirements and can be easily cultured on many media in a wide range of temperatures. It has multiple virulence factors. *Pseudomonas* adheres to host cells by pili and nonpili adhesins. It produces a **polysaccharide capsule** that allows the organism to adhere to epithelial cells, inhibits phagocytosis, and confers protection against antibiotic activity. Patients with **cystic fibrosis** are more likely to be infected with a strain whose colony appears **mucoid** because of the presence of the **capsule.**

Pseudomonas produces **multiple toxins and enzymes,** which contribute to its virulence.

Its **lipopolysaccharide endotoxin and exotoxin A** appear to cause most of the systemic manifestations of *Pseudomonas* disease. **Exotoxin A blocks protein synthesis** in host cells, causing direct **cytotoxicity.** It mediates systemic toxic effects as well. It is similar in function to diphtheria toxin but is structurally and immunologically distinct. **Endotoxin** contributes to the development of many of the symptoms and signs of **sepsis,** including fever, leukocytosis, and hypotension.

Antibiotic resistance is another important aspect of its virulence. It is **intrinsically resistant to numerous antibiotics** and has acquired resistance to others through various means. The **polysaccharide capsule prevents the penetration of many antibiotics** into *Pseudomonas.* Penetration of antibiotic into the *Pseudomonas* cell is usually through pores in the outer membrane. **Mutation of these porin proteins** appears to be a primary mechanism of its antibiotic resistance. **Multidrug efflux pumps and β-lactamase production** also contribute to the antibiotic resistance that so frequently complicates the treatment of *Pseudomonas* infections.

Some *P. aeruginosa* strains produce a diffusable pigment: **pyocyanin,** which gives the colonies **a blue color;** fluorescein, which gives them a **yellow color; or pyorubin,** which gives them a red-brown color. **Pyocyanin** also seems to aid in the virulence of the organism by stimulating an inflammatory response and by producing toxic oxygen radicals.

Diagnosis

Diagnosis of malignant otitis externa is by the common clinical features of otorrhea, painful edematous ear canal with a purulent discharge. Culture of the discharge from the internal ear grows *P. aeruginosa* in most cases. *Pseudomonas aeruginosa* grows readily on routine laboratory media. Preliminary identification can be made by **colony morphology** particularly if **typical green pigment** is produced. *Pseudomonas aeruginosa* appears as a clear to dark colony on MacConkey agar, indicating that it **does not ferment lactose.** Colonies of *P. aeruginosa* are β-hemolytic and dark colored, as a result of pigment production and blood agar media. The organisms are motile, and therefore colonies appear spread. It does not ferment glucose, is oxidase positive, and is therefore not a part of the Enterobacteriaceae family, but is considered a **nonfermenter.** *Pseudomonas aeruginosa* can be distinguished from some of the other closely related species by its ability to grow at a wide range of temperatures, up to as high as 42°C (107.6°F). The colonies also have a distinct odor, sometimes considered a grape-like odor. Confirmatory identification can be made by numerous commercially available identification systems.

Treatment and Prevention

Treatment of malignant otitis externa includes **surgery** to remove necrotic tissue and pus **and appropriate antibiotics. Treatment with two antibiotics** to which the organism is susceptible is optimal. *Pseudomonas aeruginosa* is usually inherently resistant to multiple antibiotics. Most are susceptible to the **antipseudomonal penicillins,** such as piperacillin and ticarcillin and to the newer **fluoroquinolones** as well as the **aminoglycosides.** Imipenem is often reserved for treatment of infections caused by drug-resistant strains.

COMPREHENSION QUESTIONS

[18.1] A severely burned firefighter develops a rapidly disseminating bacterial infection while hospitalized. "Green pus" is noted in the burned tissue and cultures of both the tissue and blood yield small oxidase-positive gram-negative rods. Which of the following statements most accurately conveys information about this organism?

A. Endotoxin is the only virulence factor known to be produced by these bacteria.
B. Humans are the only known reservoir hosts for these bacteria.
C. The bacteria are difficult to culture because they have numerous growth requirements.
D. These are among the most antibiotic resistant of all clinically relevant bacteria.
E. These highly motile bacteria can "swarm" over the surface of culture media.

[18.2] The fluoroquinolone resistance seen with increasing frequency in *P. aeruginosa* infections is best explained by which of the following mechanisms?

A. Changes in the structure or composition of the cell envelope that make it more difficult for the antibiotic to gain entrance
B. Enzymatic cleavage of the antibiotic molecule
C. Inactivation of the antibiotic by enzymatic acetylation
D. Overproduction of the cellular target that the antibiotic attacks
E. Removal of the antibiotic from the cell interior by a membrane pump

[18.3] An aerobic, oxidase positive organism is isolated from the sputum of a 12-year-old cystic fibrosis patient with pneumonia and lung abscesses. On culture the organisms have a "fruity" odor and form greenish colonies. The etiologic agent of the respiratory tract infection is most likely to be which of the following?

A. *Chlamydia pneumoniae*
B. *Klebsiella pneumoniae*
C. *Pseudomonas aeruginosa*
D. *Serratia marcescens*
E. *Streptococcus pneumoniae*

Answers

[18.1] **D.** *Pseudomonas aeruginosa* is an obligate aerobe that grows on many types of culture media, sometimes producing a sweet or grape-like odor. It often produces a nonfluorescent bluish pigment (pyocyanin) which diffuses into agar or pus fluids. Many strains also produce a fluorescent pigment (pyoverdin), which gives a greenish color. One of the most significant problems with *Pseudomonas* infections is the high level of natural resistance to many antimicrobials that this widespread environmental opportunist exhibits.

[18.2] **E.** Clinically significant infections with *P. aeruginosa* should not be treated with single-drug therapy, because the bacteria can develop resistance when single drugs are employed. The newer quinolones, including ciprofloxacin, are active against *Pseudomonas*. Quinolones inhibit bacterial DNA synthesis by blocking DNA gyrase. The fluorinated forms of ciprofloxacin and norfloxacin have low toxicity and greater antibacterial activity than the earlier forms. Plasmids code for enzymes that determine the active transport of various antimicrobials across the cell membrane.

[18.3] **C.** All of the options are potential etiologic agents for pneumonias in humans. The laboratory descriptions of the organism best fits *P. aeruginosa* (also see the answer for Question 18.1).

MICROBIOLOGY PEARLS

- *Pseudomonas aeruginosa* is most commonly treated with a β-lactam such as piperacillin or cefepime plus an aminoglycoside such as tobramycin.
- *Pseudomonas aeruginosa* is an opportunistic pathogen that is most often found in hospital environments as a source of nosocomial infection.
- *Pseudomonas aeruginosa* is a nonfermentative gram-negative bacilli that is oxidase positive.

REFERENCES

Murray PR, Rosenthal KS, Pfaller MA. Pseudomonas and related organisms. In: Murray PR, Rosenthal KS, Pfaller MA. Medical Microbiology, 5th ed. St. Louis, MO: Mosby, 2005:587–615.

Sparling PF, Handsfield HH. Pseudomonas aeruginosa. In: Mandell GL, Bennett JE, Dolin R, eds. Principles and Practice of Infectious Diseases, 5th ed. Philadelphia, PA: Churchill Livingstone, 2000:2310–27.

CASE 19

A 48-year-old man presents to the emergency room with 2 days of crampy abdominal pain, nausea, vomiting, diarrhea, and fever. He has not had any blood in his stool. He denies contact with anyone with similar symptoms recently. He has not eaten any raw or unprocessed foods recently. The only food that he did not prepare himself in the past week was a breakfast of eggs "sunny-side up" and bacon that he had at a diner the day before his symptoms started. On examination, he is tired appearing; his temperature is 37.7°C (99.9°F); and his heart rate is 95 beats per minute while he is lying down, but it increases to 120 beats per minute when he sits up. His blood pressure is 145/85 mm Hg while lying down and 110/60 mm Hg when sitting. The physician interprets this as a positive "tilt test," indicating significant volume depletion. His mucous membranes appear dry. His abdominal exam is notable for diffuse tenderness but no palpable masses, rebound, or guarding. A rectal exam reveals only heme-negative watery stool.

- **What is the most likely etiologic agent of this infection?**

- **What are the most common sources of human infections with this organism?**

ANSWERS TO CASE 19: *Salmonella* AND *Shigella*

Summary: A 48-year-old man with acute gastroenteritis has fever, a positive tilt test, abdominal pain, and diarrhea after eating eggs a day before.

- **Most likely etiology of infection:** *Salmonella*
- **Most common sources of infection:** Undercooked poultry, eggs, dairy products, or foods prepared on contaminated work surfaces

CLINICAL CORRELATION

This individual has the acute onset of diarrhea and vomiting. The first priorities as with any patient are the ABC's: airway, breathing, circulation. Circulatory status is assessed by monitoring the pulse rate and blood pressure, which may be normal at rest, but abnormal on changing of position. This patient had a rise in 10 beats per minute heart rate from the lying to the sitting position, and a fall of 10 mm Hg of blood pressure. This constitutes a **positive tilt test** and may indicate a volume depletion of 10–25 percent. Thus, the first therapeutic goal would be volume repletion, such as with intravenous normal saline.

In humans, most cases of nontyphoidal *Salmonella* result from ingesting contaminated food products. Poultry, eggs, dairy products, or other foods prepared on contaminated work surfaces are the most common sources. Fecal-oral spread is common among children. Live animals, especially exotic pets such as reptiles, have also been identified as sources of infection. Host gastric acid is a primary defense against the organism, and conditions or medications that reduce gastric acidity may predispose to infection. The primary site of invasion of *Salmonella* is the M (microfold) cells in the Peyer's patches of the distal ileum. M cells internalize and transfer foreign antigens from the intestinal lumen to macrophages and leukocyte. The infection can then spread to adjacent cells and lymphoid tissue. Host inflammatory responses usually limit the infection to the gastrointestinal (GI) tract, but bacteremia can occur. Bacteremia is more common in the children, elderly patients, or those with immune deficiencies, such as AIDS. Gastroenteritis is the most common clinical manifestation of *Salmonella* infection. Nausea, vomiting, nonbloody diarrhea, fever, and abdominal cramps starting 8–48 hours after ingestion of contaminated food are typical. The illness is generally self-limited and will last from 2 to 7 days.

Enteric fever, or typhoid fever, is a more severe form of gastroenteritis with systemic symptoms that are caused by either *Salmonella typhi* or *Salmonella paratyphi.* Symptoms include chills, headache, anorexia, weakness, and muscle aches; and later fever, lymphadenopathy, and hepatosplenomegaly; and in a third of patients a maculopapular rash (rose spots). Symptoms persist for a longer period of time than nontyphoidal gastroenteritis as does the carrier state in a small percentage of infected patients.

Gastroenteritis caused by *Salmonella* can mimic the signs and symptoms of other forms of infections such as *Shigella.* Infection with *Shigella* produces predominantly diarrhea, sometimes grossly bloody as a result of invasion of the mucosa. The infection is also usually self-limited; however, dehydration can occur if diarrhea is severe.

APPROACH TO SUSPECTED *Salmonella* AND *Shigella* INFECTION

Objectives

1. Know the structure, characteristics, and clinical diseases associated with *salmonella.*
2. Know the virulence, epidemiology, and pathogenesis of *salmonella* infections.
3. Know the structure, characteristics, and clinical diseases associated with *shigella.*
4. Know the virulence, epidemiology, and pathogenesis of *shigella* infections.

Definitions

Rose spots: Papular rash usually on the lower trunk leaving a darkening of the skin, characteristic of typhoid fever.

Fecal leukocytes: White blood cells found in the stool, nonspecific finding of an invasive process.

Hepatosplenomegaly: Enlargement of both the liver and the spleen which can be a feature of many diseases, including typhoid fever.

DISCUSSION

Characteristics of *Salmonella* and *Shigella*

Salmonella are **motile, facultative anaerobic, nonspore-forming, gram-negative bacilli** that are part of the family Enterobacteriaceae. The genus *Salmonella* consists of more than 2400 serotypes capable of infecting almost all animal species. However, *S. typhi* and *S. paratyphi* only colonize humans. *Salmonella* is **protected from phagocytic destruction** by two mechanisms: an **acid tolerance response gene,** which protects it both from gastric acid and from the acidic pH of the phagosome, and *Salmonella*-**secreted invasion proteins (Sips or Ssps).** These rearrange M-cell actin, resulting in membranes that surround and engulf the *Salmonella* and enable intracellular replication of the pathogen with subsequent host cell death.

Shigella is a **nonmotile gram-negative bacilli** that is also part of the family Enterobacteriaceae. There are 40 serotypes of *Shigella* that are divided into four groups or species, based on biochemical reactivity. *Shigella dysenteriae* is group A, *Shigella flexneri* is group B, *Shigella boydii* is group C, and *Shigella sonnei* is group D. Virulence mechanisms of *Shigella* include their ability to **invade the intestinal mucosa and production of shiga toxin,** which acts to destroy the intestinal mucosa once the organism has invaded the tissue. Some strains of *Escherichia coli* are closely related to *Shigella* species and are also capable of producing shiga toxin.

Diagnosis

The diagnosis of gastroenteritis is based on the patient's age, risk factors, exposures, and symptoms. **Collection of stool and blood cultures,** if fever and other systemic symptoms are present, is necessary for the definitive diagnosis. A direct exam for **fecal leukocytes and occult blood** may initially help narrow down the differential diagnosis. For example, blood in the stools usually indicates invasive bacterial infection. In cases of bacterial gastroenteritis, final diagnosis is made by culture of the stool for enteric pathogens such as *Campylobacter, Shigella,* and *Salmonella.* Although culture of *Campylobacter* requires specialized media and incubation conditions, both *Salmonella* and *Shigella* grow rapidly on routine microbiologic media. Because of the fact that stool contains many organisms that are normal flora, stools are also cultured onto selective media to aid in more rapid diagnosis.

Both *Salmonella* and *Shigella* are nonlactose fermenters that appear as clear colonies on MacConkey agar. The use of a medium that contains an indicator for production of H_2S helps differentiate the two genera. ***Shigella* does not produce H_2S and appears as clear or green colonies on a media such as Hektoen enteric (HE) agar,** whereas *Salmonella* appears black as a result of production of H_2S. This is only presumptive and further biochemical testing needs to be performed because other organisms also produce black colonies on HE agar. The diagnosis of *Shigella* can also be made by **testing for Shiga toxin** directly in the stool. This cannot differentiate *Shigella* from the **enterohemorrhagic *E. coli*** that also produce **shiga toxin** and are associated with **hemolytic uremic syndrome.**

Treatment and Prevention

Nontyphoid *Salmonella* gastroenteritis is usually not treated because it is a self-limited disease, and antibiotics have not been shown to alter the course of the infection. Primary treatment should be supportive including fluid replacement if necessary. **Antibiotic treatment is recommended for treatment of bacteremia, long-term carriers, or typhoid fever.** Amoxicillin, sulfamethoxazole and trimethoprim (SMX-TMP), or, in areas where antibiotic resistant strains are prevalent (India, Asia and Africa), quinolones can be used. The specific choice of antimicrobial agent should be based on susceptibility testing of the patient's isolate.

In the case of infection caused by ***Shigella,*** **antibiotic therapy has been shown to be useful,** especially in the prevention of person-to-person spread of the disease. **Quinolones** can also be used to treat, although *Shigella* therapy should be based on antimicrobial susceptibility testing of the isolate.

Prevention of disease caused by enteric pathogens is based on control of the contaminated source in the environment and good personal hygiene. The thorough cooking of poultry and cooking eggs until the yolk is hard can kill *Salmonella* and prevent infection. A vaccine does exist for prevention of typhoid fever, which is useful for travelers to endemic areas of the world. The efficacy of the vaccine is thought to be between 50 and 80 percent.

COMPREHENSION QUESTIONS

[19.1] In which of the following sites is *S. typhi* most likely to be found during the carrier state?

A. Blood
B. Gallbladder
C. Kidney
D. Liver
E. Spleen

[19.2] A 4-year-old has fever and diarrhea. Blood culture grows a gram-negative rod. This is most likely to be which of the following?

A. Group B *Streptococcus*
B. *Listeria* species
C. *Salmonella* species
D. *Shigella* species

[19.3] Which of the following is a frequent cause of osteomyelitis in patients with sickle cell anemia?

A. Group A *Streptococcus*
B. Group B *Streptococcus*
C. *Salmonella* species
D. *Streptococcus pneumoniae*

[19.4] Which of the following is mismatched?

A. Ecthyma gangrenosum – *Pseudomonas aeruginosa*
B. Halophilic – *Salmonella typhi*
C. K1 antigen – neonatal meningitis caused by *Escherichia coli*
D. Red pigment – *Serratia marcescens*
E. Severe dehydration – *Vibrio cholerae*

Answers

[19.1] **B.** The feces of persons who have unsuspected subclinical disease or are carriers is a more important source of contamination than frank clinical cases that are promptly isolated. The high incidence of *Salmonellae* in commercially prepared chickens has been widely publicized, possibly related to the use of animal feeds containing antimicrobial drugs that favor the proliferation of drug-resistant *Salmonellae* and their potential transmission to humans. Permanent carriers usually harbor the organisms in the gallbladder or biliary tract and, rarely, in the intestine or urinary tract.

[19.2] **C.** Enterocolitis is the most common manifestation of *Salmonella* infection. In the United States, *S. typhimurium* and *S. enteritidis* are prominent, but enterocolitis may be caused by more than 1400 strains of *Salmonella.* Bacteremia is rare (2–4 percent) except in immunodeficient persons. Stool cultures may remain positive for *Salmonella* weeks after clinical recovery. *Streptococci* and *Listeria* stain gram-positive, and *Shigella* organisms rarely, if ever, enter the blood stream from the intestines.

[19.3] **C.** Hematogenous infections account for about 20 percent of cases of osteomyelitis and primarily affect children, in whom the long bones are infected. More than 95 percent of these cases are caused by a single organism, with *Staphylococcus aureus* accounting for 50 percent of the isolates. Group B *streptococci* and *E. coli* are common during the newborn period and group A *streptococci* and *Haemophilus influenzae* in early childhood. *Salmonella* species and *S. aureus* are major causes of long-bone osteomyelitis complicating sickle cell anemia and other hemoglobinopathies. Septic arthritis may be encountered in sickle cell disease with multiple joints infected. Joint infection may result from spread of contiguous osteomyelitis areas. *Salmonella* infection is seen more often in osteomyelitis than in septic arthritis.

[19.4] **B.** Organisms requiring high salt concentrations are called halophilic. Usually, this refers to microorganisms that are capable of living or surviving in an ocean or saltwater area. *Vibrios* are especially well known for this ability. *Salmonella typhi* (typhoid fever) multiply in intestinal lymphoid tissue and are excreted in stools. They are hardy survivors in water sources, but they do not survive in halophilic conditions as well as *Vibrios*.

MICROBIOLOGY PEARLS

- *Shigella* is a common cause of gastroenteritis, which can be bloody as a result of the ability of the organism to invade the mucosa. Because of the low inoculum required for infection, person-to-person transmission may occur in close contacts.
- *Salmonella* nontyphi is associated with a self-limited diarrhea associated with ingestion of contaminated food products such as undercooked eggs.
- *Salmonella* and *Shigella* are nonlactose fermenters that are differentiated in the laboratory by production of H_2S; the appearance of black colonies on Hektoen enteric agar result from *Salmonella* species.

REFERENCES

Dupont HL. Shigella species (bacillary dysentery) In: Mandell GL, Bennett JE, Dolin R, eds. Principles and Practice of Infectious Diseases, 5th ed. Philadelphia, PA: Churchill Livingstone, 2000:2363–69.

Mandell GL, Bennett, JE, Dolin, R eds. Principles and Practice of Infectious Disease. 5th ed. Philadelphia, PA: Churchill Livingstone, 2000:2344–63.

Miller SI, Pegues DA. *Salmonella species,* including *salmonella typhi.* In: Mandell GL, Bennett JE, Dolin R, eds. Principles and Practice of Infectious Diseases, 5th ed. Philadelphia, PA: Churchill Livingstone, 2000.

Murray PR, Rosenthal KS, Pfaller MA. Enterobacteriaceae. In: Murray PR, Rosenthal KS, Pfaller MA. Medical Microbiology, 5th ed. St. Louis, MO: Mosby, 2005:266–80.

❖ CASE 20

A 59-year-old man with emphysema secondary to a 50-pack-year smoking history presents with a fever, chills, chest pain, and cough. He had a "cold" with mild cough and congestion for approximately 3 days but then had the abrupt onset of more severe symptoms. His temperature has been as high as 39.4°C (103°F), and he's had shaking chills. His cough is productive of sputum that looks like "rust." When he coughs or takes a deep breath, he gets a sharp, stabbing pain in his left lower chest. He has been taking numerous over-the-counter cold medications without relief and has had to use his ipratropium inhaler more often than usual. On examination, he is quite ill appearing. His temperature is 38.8°C (101.9°F), pulse is 110 beats per minute, blood pressure 110/60 mm Hg, and respiratory rate is 28 breaths per minute. His pulmonary examination is significant for the presence of crackles and rhonchi in the left lower fields and expiratory wheezing heard in all other fields. His heart is tachycardic but otherwise normal on auscultation. The remainder of his examination is normal. His white blood cell count is markedly elevated. An electrocardiogram is normal. A chest x-ray shows a dense infiltration of the left lower lobe along with a pleural effusion on the left side.

◆ **What would you expect to see on Gram stain of a sputum sample?**

◆ **What is the likely reservoir from which this patient's pneumonia occurred?**

ANSWERS TO CASE 20: *Streptococcus*

Summary: A 59-year-old male complains of fever and cough, with "rust" colored sputum. A chest x-ray shows a dense infiltration of the left lower lobe and a left pleural effusion.

- **Most likely Gram stain findings:** multiple polymorphonuclear leukocytes (PMNs) and encapsulated gram-positive cocci in pairs and short chains.
- **Likely reservoir of this infection:** colonization of the upper airway (naso- or oropharynx) and aspiration into the lower airways.

CLINICAL CORRELATION

Streptococci cause a wide range of diseases from localized skin and soft tissue infections to systemic infections such as necrotizing fasciitis, endocarditis, and arthritis. *Streptococcus pyogenes* is commonly associated with pharyngitis and its sequelae of rheumatic fever and glomerulonephritis, in addition to the skin and soft-tissue infections previously mentioned. *Streptococcus agalactiae* is most well known for its association with neonatal meningitis following vaginal colonization of the pregnant women.

Streptococcus pneumoniae is a cause of otitis media, sinusitis, bronchitis, pneumonia, and meningitis. *Streptococcus pneumoniae* (pneumococcus) is the most frequent cause of bacterial pneumonia, otitis, and meningitis. It commonly colonizes the upper airways in humans, more frequently in children than adults. Pneumococcal diseases occur when organisms spread from the site of colonization to a distant, susceptible site. Pneumonia occurs when pneumococcus is aspirated into the distal airways and multiplies in the alveoli. Pneumococcal pneumonia typically follows a milder upper respiratory infection. Symptoms of pneumococcal pneumonia include cough, fever, chills, and shortness of breath. Patients may also have increased white blood cells and anemia. A common complication of pneumococcal pneumonia is pleural effusion, which occurs in up to 40 percent of patients. Meningitis either follows sinusitis or otitis or occurs as a result of bacteremic spread of the organisms. Patients that are immunocompromised, elderly, or have underlying heart or lung disease, as well as those that are asplenic, are at higher risk than normal for developing serious disease with *S. pneumoniae.*

APPROACH TO SUSPECTED PNEUMOCOCCUS INFECTION

Objectives

1. Know the structure and physiologic features common to the genus *Streptococcus.*
2. Know the virulence factors, epidemiology, and diseases associated with specific *Streptococcus* species.

Definitions

Rhonchi: A vibration of the chest wall that can be felt with the hand and sounds like a dull roaring or murmuring.

Cytokines: Proteins produced by leukocytes that act as mediators of a further inflammatory response.

DISCUSSION

Characteristics of *Streptococcus*

The genus *Streptococcus* contains multiple species that are differentiated either by their **cell wall carbohydrate group antigen,** their **hemolysis on blood agar,** or their **biochemical reactivity.** Not all streptococci, including *S. pneumoniae,* possess a carbohydrate cell wall antigen. Streptococci are **facultative anaerobes** that require carbon dioxide for growth. Streptococci are **gram-positive cocci that form either pairs or chains, whereas *S. pneumoniae* are elongated, lancet shaped, gram-positive cocci,** and are usually in pairs or short chains.

Virulent strains of pneumococcus are **encapsulated by a polysaccharide capsule.** Strains that are unencapsulated are easily cleared by host defenses. Colonization is facilitated by binding of the pneumococcus to epithelial cells by surface protein adhesins, producing **secretory IgA protease,** which prevents host immunoglobulin A from binding to it and producing **pneumolysin,** which **destroys phagocytic and ciliated epithelial cells** by creating pores in their cell membranes. Phagocytosis is limited by the **antiphagocytic nature of the polysaccharide capsule** and by the pneumolysin's inhibition of the oxidative burst required for intracellular killing. Much of the tissue damage caused by pneumococcal infections is mediated by the inflammatory response of host defense systems. The complement system is activated by teichoic acid, peptidoglycan fragments, and pneumolysin. Cytokine production is stimulated, causing more inflammatory cells to migrate to the site of infection. **Hydrogen peroxide** is produced by pneumococcus, which **causes tissue damage** via reactive oxygen intermediates.

Antibiotic resistance in pneumococcus is an increasing problem. **Penicillin resistance** has developed, primarily via mutations in penicillin-binding proteins in the cell wall. This is a consequence of mutations in the cellular DNA and from acquisition of DNA from both other pneumococci and other bacteria with which pneumococcus comes in contact. **Efflux pumps** also confer some degree of resistance to antibiotics.

Diagnosis

Diagnosis of pneumococcal pneumonia is made based on clinical signs and symptoms, chest x-ray demonstrating infiltration of a single lobe, and sputum Gram stain with many PMNs and gram-positive cocci in pairs and chains. Confirmation of the diagnosis can be made by culturing the organisms from the sputum and/or blood. *Streptococcus pneumoniae* grows rapidly on routine laboratory media including blood and chocolate agar. Colonies on blood agar demonstrate **β-hemolysis (green color)** and may be slightly to extremely **mucoid** because of their polysaccharide capsule. Colonies are differentiated from viridans streptococci by **sensitivity to optochin and bile solubility.** Although optochin susceptibility is considered definitive, the addition of bile to a colony will identify the organism as *S. pneumoniae* if the colony lyses and disappears within a few minutes.

More rapid diagnosis of pneumococcal pneumonia can be made using the urinary antigen test.

Treatment and Prevention

Treatment of uncomplicated pneumonia is usually with either a **quinolone** or a **macrolide** such as azithromycin. Complicated or disseminated pneumococcal disease is usually treated with **penicillin or cefotaxime** depending on susceptibility of the isolate to penicillin. Treatment of the other streptococcal species is usually with penicillin, but in serious infections should be based on the individual isolate susceptibility. Adult and pediatric **vaccines directed against pneumococcal capsular antigens** are available, and current guidelines recommend universal vaccination of children, persons over the age of 65, and others at high risk for pneumonia, such as persons with diabetes or chronic lung disease.

COMPREHENSION QUESTIONS

[20.1] A newborn has a temperature of 39.4°C (103°F). Blood culture grows gram-positive cocci in chains. This is most likely to be which of the following?

A. Group A *Streptococus (Streptococcus pyogenes)*
B. Group B *Streptococcus (Streptococcus agalactiae)*
C. *Salmonella* species
D. *Streptococcus pneumoniae*

[20.2] A 3-year-old is diagnosed with bacterial meningitis. Cerebrospinal fluid grows out gram-positive cocci in short chains and diplococci. This is most likely to be which of the following?

A. Group B *Streptococcus*
B. *Salmonella*
C. *Staphylococcus aureus*
D. *Streptococcus pneumoniae*

[20.3] Which of the following is the primary virulence factor of *S. pneumoniae?*

A. Bile solubility
B. Optochin production
C. Pili
D. Polypeptide capsule
E. Polysaccharide capsule

[20.4] Which of the following is true regarding meningitis with *S. pneumoniae?*

A. Cephalosporins are always effective.
B. One desires a concentration of antibiotics in the cerebral spinal fluid 10 times the minimal inhibition concentration.
C. Penicillin is always effective.
D. Resistance is not increasing in *S. pneumoniae.*

Answers

[20.1] **B.** Most human infections caused by streptococci involve the group A organisms *(S. pyogenes).* The group B streptococci are members of the female genital tract and are important causes of neonatal sepsis and meningitis. They are usually β-hemolytic (similar to group A), hydrolyze hippurate and give a positive response in the so-called CAMP test (Christie, Atkins, Munch-Peterson). Detection of the infection and prompt antimicrobial treatment is necessary because the infections may become life-threatening. *Streptococcus pneumoniae* organisms are important in meningitis cases in young children, but are more frequently seen as diplococci forms rather than long chains.

[20.2] **D.** *Streptococcus pneumoniae* is responsible for 10–20 percent of meningitis cases in children ages 1 month to 15 years. *Neisseria meningitidis* range from 25 to 40 percent, whereas *Haemophilus influenzae* may be involved in 40–60 percent. Group A and B streptococci appear to be involved only 2–4 percent of the time. Under the conditions described above, *S. pneumoniae* would be the most likely etiologic agent.

[20.3] **E.** Bile solubility and optochin sensitivity are presumptive identification tests that identify *S. pneumoniae* from other α-hemolytic streptococci. The polysaccharide capsule occurs in dozens of antigenic types, but types 1–8 are responsible for approximately 75 percent of the cases of pneumococcal pneumonia. Vaccines are available that give approximately 90 percent protection and usually contain 23 types of carbohydrates for the United States–licensed preparation.

[20.4] **B.** Because pneumococci are sensitive to many antimicrobial drugs, early treatment usually results in rapid recovery. Antibody response (host's active immunity) seems to play a diminished role today. Penicillin G is the drug of choice, but 5–10 percent of the isolates in the United States are penicillin resistant (MIC ≥2 μg/mL), and 20 percent are moderately resistant (0.1–1 μg/mL). Resistance to cephalosporins, tetracycline, and erythromycin has been demonstrated, although pneumococci remain susceptible to vancomycin. In reference to penicillin therapy, one rule of thumb is to aim for a concentration of 10 times the MIC in the CSF.

MICROBIOLOGY PEARLS

- *Streptococcus pneumoniae* is a common cause of otitis media and meningitis.
- Because of the increasing incidence of penicillin resistance of *S. pneumoniae* empiric therapy of disseminated disease is with ceftriaxone.
- *Streptococcus pneumoniae* is an α-hemolytic streptococci susceptible to optochin.

REFERENCES

Murray PR, Rosenthal KS, Pfaller MA. Streptococcus. In: Murray PR, Rosenthal KS, Pfaller MA. Medical Microbiology, 5th ed. St. Louis, MO: Mosby, 2005:237–58.

Musher, DM. *Streptococcus pneumoniae.* In: Mandell GL, Bennett JE, Dolin R, eds. Principles and Practice of Infectious Diseases, 6th ed. Philadelphia, PA: Churchill Livingstone, 2005:2392–2411.

❖ CASE 21

While on call on a Saturday night in July, you receive a call from the mother of a 15-year-old man who developed the acute onset of nausea, vomiting, and diarrhea shortly after returning from an outdoor party that was held at the home of a friend. At the party, a picnic lunch of hamburgers, hot dogs, potato salad, baked beans, and lemonade was served. The food was served on an outdoor picnic table, and the guests were free to eat at any time during the party. None of the food tasted spoiled or tainted. His symptoms started abruptly about an hour after he returned home, which was approximately 4 hours after he had eaten. He currently is unable to keep down anything. He does not have a fever and has not passed any blood in his stool or vomitus. Prior to calling you, your patient's mother spoke with the hostess of the party, who said that she had heard from three other guests who became ill with similar symptoms.

◆ **What organism is the most likely cause of this patient's illness?**

◆ **Your patient's mother requests that you call in a prescription for an antibiotic to treat the infection. What is your response?**

ANSWERS TO CASE 21: STAPHYLOCOCCI

Summary: A 15-year-old male with gastroenteritis after eating food at an outdoor picnic. Several other participants also developed similar symptoms.

- **Most likely organism causing this infection:** *Staphylococcus aureus.*
- **Response to request to treat with antibiotic:** No, the gastroenteritis is caused by a preformed toxin, not by the ingested staphylococci, therefore antibiotic therapy would be of no help.

CLINICAL CORRELATION

Staphylococcus aureus is a common colonizer of the human nasopharynx and skin. Infection occurs when the normal skin barrier is disrupted by either surgery or trauma.

Staphylococcus aureus causes numerous infections, ranging from simple localized skin and soft tissue infections to disseminated disease, such as bacteremia, endocarditis, osteomyelitis, and septic arthritis. Many of the infections caused by *S. aureus* are toxin mediated, such as toxic shock syndrome, scalded skin syndrome, and gastroenteritis.

Previously thought to be a nosocomial infection seen in hospitalized patients, community acquired MRSA has become a significant public health concern. The majority of these strains produce a toxin called Panton-ValentineLeukocidin (PVL) that is associated with more severe disease, including skin and soft tissue infections and necrotizing pneumonia.

Staphylococcal food poisoning, the second most reported cause of food poisoning in the United States, is a result of the presence of enterotoxin. Food is contaminated by a human carrier, with processed meats, custard-filled baked goods, potato salad, or ice-cream being common vectors. The toxin rapidly produces nausea, vomiting, and diarrhea, usually within 2–6 hours of ingestion. Further toxin is not produced by the ingested *S. aureus,* and the disease also rapidly resolves, usually within 12–24 hours.

Staphylococcal species also frequently colonize human skin but can cause disease in certain situations. Although there are more than 20 other species, the majority of the species isolated are *Staphylococcus epidermidis.* The most common predisposing factor for disease with staphylococci not (*S. aureus*) is the presence of artificial devices in the patient such as catheters and replacement joints. *Staphylococcus epidermidis* produces a slime that allows it to adhere to plastics and form a biofilm that makes it very difficult for antibiotics to penetrate.

APPROACH TO SUSPECTED STAPHYLOCOCCAL INFECTION

Objectives

1. Know the structure, physiology, and virulence factors associated with *S. aureus* and the coagulase-negative staphylococci.
2. Know the diseases caused by staphylococci and the mechanisms by which staphylococci develop antibiotic resistance.

Definitions

Biofilm: Bacteria grow on an artificial surface and form a conglomerate with secreted polysaccharides and glycopeptides.

Superantigens: Antigens, most often bacterial toxins, that recruit a large number of T lymphocytes to an area.

Enterotoxins: Substances produced by bacteria that are toxic to the GI tract that cause diarrhea and/or vomiting.

DISCUSSION

Characteristics of *Staphylococcus*

Staphylococci belong to the family **Micrococcaceae,** which includes the genus *Micrococcus* in addition to *Staphylococcus.* Staphylococci grow rapidly on multiple culture media, in a wide range of environments, including up to 10 percent sodium chloride, and in a broad range of temperatures. *Staphylococcus aureus* is a **nonmotile, nonspore forming, facultative anaerobic gram-positive coccus** that commonly colonizes healthy humans and is a frequent cause of disease. It is frequently identified as growing in **clusters or clumps.** This is a result of the effect of **bound coagulase** ("clumping factor"), which **binds fibrinogen,** converts it to insoluble fibrin, and results in aggregation. ***Staphylococcus aureus* is the only *Staphylococcus* found in humans which produces coagulase;** other staphylococcal species are commonly identified as coagulase-negative staphylocci.

Staphylococcus aureus produces **at least five cytolytic toxins, two exfoliative toxins, eight enterotoxins,** and **toxic shock syndrome toxin.** Some of these toxins act as superantigens, which recruit host defense cells that liberate cytokines and, therefore, produce systemic effects. Heating will kill the *S. aureus* organisms, but not inactivate the **enterotoxins, because they are stable to heating at 100°C (112°F) for 30 minutes** and are resistant to breakdown by gastric acids.

Of growing public health concern is the rapid spread of antibiotic resistance within *S. aureus* isolates. Almost all *S. aureus* produces penicillinase, a β-lactamase specific for penicillin. Many isolates have also acquired a gene that codes for an **altered penicillin binding protein, PBP2,** providing antibiotic resistance to semisynthetic penicillins and cephalosporins as well, including methicillin and nafcillin. Some of these genes will also be associated with resistance to non–β-lactamase antibiotics, such as quinolones and macrolides. Some *S. aureus* isolates have been identified recently with reduced sensitivity to vancomycin. The mechanism of this resistance is unknown. Genes that confer resistance can be transferred between organisms by plasmid transfer, transduction and cell-to-cell contact.

Diagnosis

The initial diagnosis of staphylococcal infection may be difficult because many of the skin and soft tissue infections mimic those of streptococci. Definitive diagnosis is made by Gram stain and culture of the infected site as well as blood. Staphylococci are large **gram-positive cocci grouped in clusters (Figure 21-1).** Staphylococci grow rapidly on routine laboratory media.

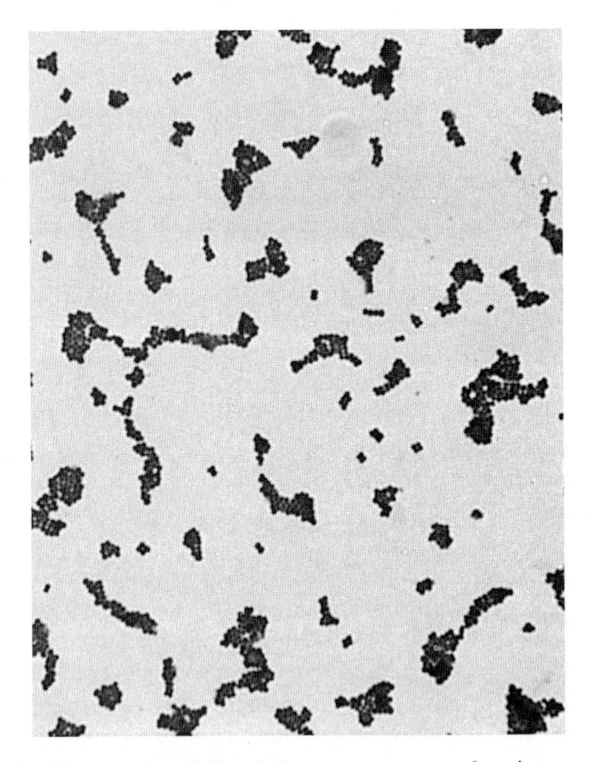

Figure 21-1. Gram stain of *Staphylococcus aureus* showing gram-positive cocci in clusters. (*Reproduced, with permission, from Brooks G, Butel J, Morse S. Jawetz, Melnick, and Aldelburg's Medical Microbiology, 23rd ed. New York: McGraw-Hill, 2004:224.*)

Their colony morphology is different from streptococci in that the colonies are larger, white or yellow instead of grey. They also can be differentiated from streptococci by a **positive catalase test** (reactivity with hydrogen peroxide). *Staphylococcus aureus* is **β-hemolytic on blood agar medium** and is differentiated from the other *Staphylococcus* species by production of coagulase or positive latex agglutination for ***Staphylococcus* protein A.** Further confirmation of the identification of *S. aureus* is not necessary; however, many commercially available identification systems can identify the organism based on biochemical reactivity. A selective media such as mannitol salts agar, which also differentiates *S. aureus* from other staphylococcal species is available, but not often used in clinical laboratories.

Staphylococcal gastroenteritis is usually self-limited with symptoms disappearing within 12 hours, and therefore diagnosis is made clinically based on incubation period and history of others eating similar foods with same symptoms. ***Staphylococcus saprophyticus*** is the only other staphylococcal species that is identified as a consequence of its association with **urinary tract infections in young women.** *Staphylococcus saprophyticus* is differentiated from the other coagulase negative staphylococci by its susceptibility to novobiocin, which is tested by disk diffusion. *Staphylococcus lugdunensis* has recently gained attention as a significant cause of bacteremia and endocarditis. These organisms look morphologically like *Staphylococcus epidermidis*, but clinically resemble *Staphylococcus auereus*. Their distinguishing feature is that they are PYR positive.

Treatment and Prevention

Treatment of local wound infections without systemic symptoms does not usually require treatment with antibiotics; however, in the cases of more complicated infections or presence of fever, antimicrobial therapy is usually warranted. Although **nafcillin** is the drug of choice for staphylococcal infections, because of the high percentage of strains that are resistant to methicillin and nafcillin, initial treatment is usually with **vancomycin** until the susceptibility results are available. Oral antibiotics, such as dicloxacillin, rifampin and sulfamethoxazole and trimethoprim (SMX-TMP) or clindamycin can also be used dependent on the susceptibility of the isolate. **Treatment of *Staphylococcus* non-*aureus*** is with **vancomycin,** because the majority of isolates are resistant to nafcillin.

Control of *S. aureus* involves **strict adherence to hand washing** policies, particularly in the hospital setting. The organism can easily be spread from person to person. Colonization with *S. aureus* is usually transient; however, an attempt can be made in some situations to decolonize the nares by using intranasal mupirocin and/or the skin by using oral anti-staphylococcal antibiotics in combination with topical agents.

COMPREHENSION QUESTIONS

[21.1] A 12-year-old girl was playing soccer when she began to limp. She has pain in her right leg and right upper thigh. Her temperature is 38.9°C (102°F). X-ray of the femur reveals that the periosteum is eroded, suggestive of osteomyelitis. Blood culture yields gram-positive bacteria. The most likely etiologic agent is which of the following?

A. *Listeria monocytogenes*
B. *Salmonella enteritidis*
C. *Staphylococcus aureus*
D. *Staphylococcus saprophyticus*
E. *Streptococcus pneumoniae*

[21.2] An outbreak of staphylococcal infection involving umbilical cords of seven newborn babies was reported in the nursery. Bacteriologic survey reveals that two nurses have a large number of *S. aureus* in the nasopharynx. What test should be performed to determine whether these nurses may have been responsible for the outbreak?

A. Bacteriophage typing
B. Coagulase testing
C. Nasopharyngeal culture on mannitol salt agar
D. Protein A typing
E. Serologic typing

[21.3] Virulence factors of *S. aureus* include all of the following except one. Which one is this exception?

A. β-lactamases
B. Coagulase
C. Enterotoxins
D. M Protein
E. Protein A

[21.4] Short incubation food poisoning, caused by ingestion of preformed enterotoxin, is caused by which bacteria listed below?

A. *Staphylococcus aureus*
B. *Staphylococcus epidermidis*
C. *Enterococcus faecalis*
D. *Streptococcus pneumoniae*
E. *Streptococcus pyogenes*

Answers

[21.1] **C.** Staphylococci, especially *S. epidermidis,* are normal flora of the human skin and respiratory and gastrointestinal tracts. Nasal carriage of *S. aureus,* the pathogen, occurs in 20–50 percent of humans. Abscesses are the typical lesion of *S. aureus.* From any one focus, organisms may enter the bloodstream and lymphatics to spread to other parts of the body. In osteomyelitis, the primary focus is generally in a terminal blood vessel of the metaphysis of a long bone, which may lead to necrosis of bone and chronic suppuration. *Staphylococcus saprophyticus* is usually a nonpathogenic normal flora organism. *Listeria* is usually transmitted in unpasteurized dairy products, whereas *Salmonella enteritidis* is primarily intestinal. *Streptococcus pneumoniae* is primarily a respiratory pathogen, although it is an important central nervous system pathogen in children.

[21.2] **A.** Bacterial viruses (bacteriophages or phages) can attach to separate receptors on the cell walls of various strains of *S. aureus.* Different specific receptors have been identified and used as the basis of epidemiologic typing of pathogenic *S. aureus* strains. Typical cultures from the outbreak and strains obtained from personnel can be subjected to a standardized procedure using a series of bacteriophages that attack *S. aureus* strains. This procedure can readily identify the source of the outbreak organism if it came from a medical care worker.

[21.3] **D.** M proteins are virulence factors of group A streptococci *(S. pyogenes).* All of the other listed virulence factors may be found routinely in *S. aureus* bacteria.

[21.4] **A.** Of the options given the best answer is *S. aureus,* as a result of enterotoxin production in food. None of the other strains listed produce enterotoxins that result in short-term gastroenteritis.

MICROBIOLOGY PEARLS

❖ *Staphylococcus aureus* is a common cause of community-acquired and nosocomial wound infections.

❖ Treatment of *S. aureus* is with nafcillin if the isolate is susceptible, or alternatively with vancomycin.

❖ *Staphylococcus aureus* is differentiated from the other staphylococcal species by production of coagulase.

REFERENCES

Murray PR, Rosenthal KS, Pfaller MA. Staphylococcus and related organisms In: Murray PR, Rosenthal KS, Pfaller MA. Medical Microbiology, 5th ed. St. Louis, MO: Mosby, 2005:202–16.

Moreillon P, Que Y, Glauser MP. *Staphylococcus aureus* (including staphylococcal toxic shock). In: Mandell GL, Bennett JE, Dolin R, eds. Principles and Practice of Infectious Diseases, 6th ed. Philadelphia, PA: Churchill Livingstone, 2005:321–51.

❖ CASE 22

A 20-year-old man presents for evaluation of a rash that he thinks is an allergic reaction. For the past 4 or 5 days he has had the "flu," with fever, chills headache, and body aches. He has been taking an over-the-counter flu medication without any symptomatic relief. Yesterday he developed a diffuse rash made up of red, slightly raised bumps. It covers his whole body, and he says that it must be an allergic reaction to the flu medication. He has no history of allergies and takes no other medications, and his only medical problem in the past was being treated for gonorrhea approximately 2 years ago. On further questioning, he denies dysuria or penile discharge. He denies any genital lesions now, but says that he had a "sore" on his penis a few months ago that never really hurt and went away on its own after a few weeks so he didn't think much about it. On exam, his vital signs are all normal. He has palpable cervical, axillary, and inguinal adenopathy. His skin has an erythematous, maculopapular eruption covering his whole body including his palms and soles of his feet. No vesicles are noted. His genital examination is normal.

- **What organism is the likely etiology of this disease?**
- **What disease and stage does this patient have?**
- **What microscopic examination could confirm this diagnosis?**
- **Which serologic tests could assist in his diagnosis?**

ANSWERS TO CASE 22: *Treponema pallidum*

Summary: A 20-year-old man has adenopathy and a macular papular rash affecting his soles and palms. He had a painless penile "sore" that spontaneously resolved.

- **Most likely causative organism:** *Treponema pallidum.*
- **Disease and stage:** The patient has syphilis, more specifically secondary syphilis.
- **Microscopic examination to confirm the diagnosis:** Examination by darkfield microscopy of exudates from skin lesions could confirm the diagnosis of *T. pallidum* infection and secondary syphilis.
- **Serologic tests to assist in the diagnosis:** The following serologic examinations are useful in diagnosis: Venereal Disease Research Laboratory (VDRL) and rapid plasmin reagin (RPR) tests are used for initial screening, while the fluorescent treponemal antibody-absorption test (FTA-ABS), and the microhemagglutination test for *T. pallidum* (MHA-TP), are the more specific diagnostic tests.

CLINICAL CORRELATION

Treponema pallidum is a gram-negative, microaerophilic spirochete that causes venereal syphilis, the third most common bacterial sexually transmitted disease in the United States. It is transmitted by contact with fluid from an ulcer containing the infectious agent either through sexual contact by penetrating intact mucous membranes or through nonsexual contact with the agent with skin that is broken or abraded. Studies estimate that transmission occurs in over half of sexual encounters where a lesion is present. *Treponema pallidum* infection results in multiple disease phases with distinctive clinical manifestations. Primary syphilis usually involves the formation of a painless ulcer at the site of entry of the organism, called a chancre. Chancres are highly contagious by contact and can spontaneously heal after a few weeks to a few months. Secondary syphilis develops 2–12 weeks after the primary stage and is characterized by a flu-like illness, followed by a rash that typically starts on the trunk but can spread to any skin or mucous membrane surface. Without treatment, the symptoms generally resolve in 3–12 weeks. This is followed by a relatively asymptomatic period known as latency, which can last for years. Some infected persons have no further symptoms; however, some progress to tertiary syphilis, a diffuse disease with many effects on the dermatologic, musculoskeletal, cardiovascular, and central nervous systems. Currently the population most at risk is heterosexual African Americans living in urban areas.

APPROACH TO SUSPECTED *Treponema pallidum* INFECTION

Objectives

1. Know the natural history of syphilis infection.
2. Know the methods of diagnosis and treatment of syphilis.

Definitions

Macule: Flat lesion that is not palpable, of a different color from surrounding skin and smaller than 1 cm.

Microaerophilic: Organisms that can tolerate small amounts of oxygen because they contain superoxide dismutase. They use fermentation in the absence of oxygen.

Tabes dorsalis: A condition characterized by diminished vibratory, proprioceptive, pain, and temperature senses, as well as the loss of reflexes.

Argyll Robertson pupil: Constricts during accommodation but does not react to light.

DISCUSSION

Characteristics of *Treponema pallidum* That Impact Transmission

Treponema pallidum is a **thin spirochete and an obligate human pathogen.** It consists of three subspecies, each of which causes disease in humans. *Treponema pallidum* is labile, unable to survive exposure to drying, and is very difficult to grow in culture. *Treponema pallidum* does not have a capsule and usually contains six axial filaments, located between the outer membrane and the peptidoglycan layer. It produces no toxins that have been currently identified. *Treponema pallidum* is too thin to be seen with standard microscopy with Gram stain but can be seen with **darkfield microscopy** or by staining with antitreponemal antibodies labeled with **fluorescent dyes.** *Treponema pallidum* is transmitted by direct contact with an infectious lesion, transfusion of infected blood, or congenital transfer. It attaches by one or both ends to host cells, although it rarely penetrates the cell. The resultant disease of syphilis occurring primarily because of the host immune response to the treponemal infection, with both humoral and cell-mediated immune systems playing a role.

Syphilis disease presents in **three different stages** with characteristics specific to each stage. **Primary syphilis** presents with a **hard, painless, broad-based chancre.** The chancre has a punched-out base and rolled-up edges, sometimes expelling a serous exudate. This primary lesion presents 3–6 weeks after the initial contact with the infectious agent. It typically resolves in 4–6 weeks and does not leave scar tissue. **Secondary syphilis** presents with a symmetrical widely distributed macular rash. The rash can infect the mucous membranes including the cervix, throat, and mouth. It may also appear on the **palms and soles** of the patient, an important clinical finding because there are few diseases that present with a rash on palms and soles. Patchy hair loss is also seen, typically causing the eyebrows to fall out. There is usually a low-grade fever, weight loss, and general malaise. **Condyloma latum** is a **painless, wart-like lesion** on the scrotum or vulva that may also be present during this stage (Figure 22-1). **Secondary syphilis** occurs several weeks after the lesion of primary syphilis has healed. It is during the secondary stage where syphilis is considered to be most infectious.

After secondary syphilis, there is a **latent period** where the disease is not infectious, although the patient is still seropositive. This stage can range from 2 years to several decades. **Tertiary syphilis** can present with personality

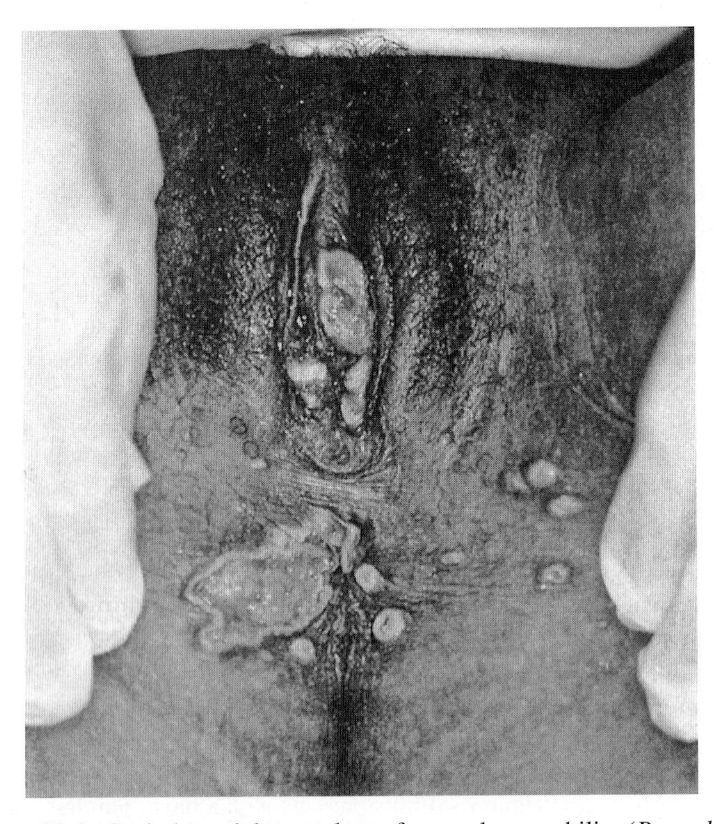

Figure 22-1. Genital condylomata lata of secondary syphilis. (*Reproduced, with permission, from Cunningham FG et al. William's Obstetrics, 21st ed. New York: McGraw-Hill, 2001:1487.*)

changes, blindness, paresis, gummas, **Argyll Robertson pupils** and **tabes dorsalis. Gummas** are granulomatous lesions of the skin and bone which are necrotic and fibrotic. Tabes dorsalis is characterized by diminished vibratory, proprioceptive, pain, and temperature sense, as well as the loss of deep tendon reflexes. It is the damage to the dorsal roots and ganglia which cause the loss of reflexes, pain, and temperature sense, while the loss of proprioception and vibratory sense are because of the posterior column involvement. The Argyll Robertson pupil constricts during accommodation but does not react to light.

Diagnosis

The **diagnosis of syphilis** can be made by **identification of spirochetes by darkfield microscopy** of a chancre or skin lesion sample of the primary and secondary stages, respectively; however, most syphilis is diagnosed by serologic studies.

There are several serologic laboratory tests that may be used to detect syphilis. The **VDRL** and **RPR** are **nonspecific tests** of host production of anticardiolipin antibody. These will be positive in approximately 80 percent of cases of primary and all secondary stages of syphilis. False-positive VDRLs may be encountered in patients with lupus, infectious mononucleosis, hepatitis A, the antiphospholipid antibody syndrome, leprosy, malaria, and occasionally pregnancy. False-negative RPR and VDRLs may be obtained early in the disease. The more specific treponemal tests, the FTA-ABS and the TP-PA, are used for confirmation of infection. They detect the presence of antibodies specific to *T. pallidum.*

Treatment and Prevention

The drug of choice for the treatment of syphilis is **benzathine penicillin.** One injection is given when the infection is less than 1 year duration, whereas injections each week for 3 weeks is administered for infection longer than 1 year. Patients who are allergic to penicillin are treated with erythromycin and doxycycline. However, doxycycline is contraindicated in patients who are pregnant, because it can cross the placenta and is toxic to the fetus. Universal precautions used in the clinical setting are adequate to prevent the transmission of syphilis. Outside of the clinical setting, safe sex should be practiced to prevent the transmission through sexual contact. Currently, there is no vaccine available for the prevention of *T. pallidum* infection.

COMPREHENSION QUESTIONS

[22.1] A 21-year-old Asian woman visits her obstetrician and is later diagnosed with secondary syphilis. On further questioning, it is determined she is allergic to penicillin. Because *T. pallidum* is known to cross the placenta, treatment is started immediately. Which antibiotic would be most appropriate in this situation?

A. Tetracycline
B. Ceftriaxone
C. Penicillin G
D. Doxycycline
E. Erythromycin

[22.2] A 27-year-old white man presents to his family doctor complaining of being tired all the time and having a slight fever for the past 2 weeks. He recently returned from a trip to Las Vegas, where he indulged in some of the infamous nightlife. His physical exam is unremarkable except for a macular rash over his trunk and on the palms of his hands. There are no lesions or ulcers on the penis. What organism is causing this man's illness?

A. *Chlamydia trachomatis*
B. *Neisseria gonorrhea*
C. *Treponema pallidum*
D. *Borrelia burgdorferi*
E. *Rickettsia rickettsii*

[22.3] A sample is taken from a vulvar ulcer in a 25-year-old sexually active African American female. The organism is a weakly staining gram-negative, microaerophilic organism. When attempting to view a smear under a microscope, no organisms are seen. Which method of visualization is most appropriate in this setting?

A. Ziehl-Neelsen stain
B. India ink preparation
C. Congo red stain
D. Darkfield microscopy
E. Giemsa stain

[22.4] A third-year medical student is on his first rotation in internal medicine. His attending physician points out that there are several tests that are used to diagnose syphilis. Which test is most specific for the detection of syphilis?

A. Rapid plasmin reagin (RPR)
B. Fluorescent treponemal antibody-absorption (FTA-ABS)
C. Venereal Disease Research Laboratory (VDRL)
D. Ziehl-Neelsen stain
E. Aerobic and anaerobic blood cultures

[22.5] A 28-year-old sexually active woman presents for her annual well-woman exam. She at times has a low-grade fever and lately has noticed a rash on her face, mainly on the cheeks. She is saddened to learn she has a positive VDRL test for syphilis. However, she is asymptomatic for syphilis and is in a monogamous relationship with her husband who has not had any other sexual contacts. Which of the following is the most likely reason for the positive syphilis test?

A. She has secondary syphilis.
B. She has HIV, altering her immune reaction.
C. She had exposure to syphilis earlier this week.
D. She has systemic lupus erythematosus (SLE).
E. She has *Chlamydia*.

Answers

[22.1] **E.** Erythromycin and doxycycline are used when allergy to penicillin is present. Doxycycline is contraindicated in pregnant women because it crosses the placenta and is toxic to the fetus. Ceftriaxone and tetracycline are not used for the treatment of syphilis. Penicillin is contraindicated because of the patient's allergies.

[22.2] **C.** *Treponema pallidum* is usually transmitted through unprotected sexual activity with an infected individual. This man presents with the symptoms of secondary syphilis, which includes malaise, mild fever, and rash on the palms or soles of the feet. The primary lesion (chancre) may go unnoticed because it is painless and subsides in a few weeks. *Neisseria gonorrhea* is associated with a serous exudate. *Chlamydia* is associated with painful urination. *Rickettsia rickettsii* and *Borrelia burgdorferi* are associated with arthropod vectors.

[22.3] **D.** The organism present is *T. pallidum,* a spirochete. No organisms are seen under light microscopy because spirochetes are too small to be visualized by this technique. Use of darkfield microscope allows for visualization of the corkscrew morphology. The Ziehl-Neelsen stain is used to detect acid-fast bacteria such as mycobacteria. India ink preparations are used to visualize a capsule that is present in *Cryptococcus neoformans* but that spirochetes do not have. Giemsa stain is used to detect *Borrelia, Plasmodium, Trypanosomes,* and *Chlamydia* species.

[22.4] **B.** There are two classes of test used to detect the presence of an infection. The nontreponemal tests detect the presence of antibodies against lipids present on the organism. The nontreponemal tests include RPR and VDRL. Specific tests that detect antibodies against the organism itself, include TP-PA and FTA-ABS. Aerobic and anaerobic cultures are not specific tests used to identify syphilis. The Ziehl-Neelsen stain is used to identify acid fast bacteria.

[22.5] **D.** In the presence of a woman with no known contacts with syphilis and a low-grade fever and rash, it is most likely that she had a false-positive reaction to the VDRL test because of lupus (SLE). This is often a common finding in lupus patients, and may be the first sign that they have lupus. In contrast, the VDRL test would be positive in secondary syphilis, often in high titer (greater than 1:32). Her being positive for HIV, while she may also have a false-positive reaction to the VDRL test if HIV positive, is not the most likely answer choice for this patient. The presence of the malar rash makes SLE more likely. Recent exposure to syphilis would lead to a false-negative test result; antibodies form between 4 and 8 weeks from exposure. *Chlamydia trachomatis* infection would not lead to a positive test result for syphilis.

MICROBIOLOGY PEARLS

- ❖ Some of the nontreponemal nonspecific tests are the VDRL and RPR.
- ❖ The specific treponemal tests include the FTA-ABS and TP-PA.
- ❖ Primary syphilis generally consists of a painless chancre.
- ❖ Secondary syphilis consists of a generalized macular popular rash especially affecting the palms or soles, or condyloma latum.
- ❖ Tertiary syphilis is typified by gummas, neurosyphilis, tabes dorsalis, Argyll Robertson pupil.
- ❖ The best treatment for syphilis is penicillin.

REFERENCES

Murray PR, Rosenthal KS, Pfaller MA. Medical Microbiology, 5th ed. St. Louis, MO: Mosby, 2005:339–45.

Ryan JR, Ray CG. Sherris Medical Microbiology, 4th ed. New York: McGraw-Hill, 2004:422–30.

Schneider AS, Szanto PA. Pathology: Board Review Sseries, 2nd ed. Philadelphia, PA: Lippincott Williams & Wilkins, 2001:272, 278, 281.

❖ CASE 23

A 35-year-old woman presents to the emergency room with a 2-day history of severe diarrhea and vomiting. Her symptoms started shortly after returning from a mission trip that she took with her church to a rural area in central Africa. She recalls eating shrimp that seemed undercooked. Her symptoms started abruptly, with watery diarrhea followed by vomiting. She has not had a fever and denies abdominal pain. On examination, her temperature is 37.2°C (98.9°F), pulse is 115 beats per minute, and blood pressure is 80/50 mm Hg. Her mucous membranes are dry, and her eyes appear sunken. Her skin is dry and tents when lightly pinched. Her abdomen has hyperactive bowel sounds but is soft and nontender. Her stool is watery and tests negative for blood. A complete blood count shows an elevated white blood cell count and an elevated hematocrit. A metabolic panel shows hypokalemia, low serum bicarbonate, and prerenal azotemia. You assess this patient to be in hypovolemic shock and metabolic acidosis, and institute appropriate therapy.

◆ **What organism is most likely to be identified on stool culture?**

◆ **What is the cause of this patient's diarrhea?**

ANSWERS TO CASE 23: *Vibrio cholerae*

Summary: A 35-year-old woman recently traveled to Africa and developed diarrhea causing hypovolemic shock and metabolic acidosis. She remembers eating undercooked shrimp.

- **Most likely etiologic agent:** *Vibrio cholerae*
- **Cause of the diarrhea:** Hypersecretion of water and electrolytes into the intestinal lumen caused by cholera toxin

CLINICAL CORRELATION

The first priorities as with any patient are the ABCs: airway, breathing, circulation. This patient is in hypovolemic shock, meaning insufficient circulation to maintain tissue perfusion needs. The most important step in intervention is volume repletion, usually with intravenous isotonic saline solution. A likely therapy would be 3 L of normal saline intravenously.

Vibrio species are found in saltwater and infections usually occur in the spring and summer. Transmission is by either consumption of contaminated shellfish or traumatic injury associated with infected water. The disease cholera is caused by toxigenic strains of *V. cholerae* (01 and 0139 serotypes). *Vibrio cholerae* is spread by ingestion of contaminated water or food. The organism is sensitive to gastric acid; therefore, the dose required to cause an infection is high. Conditions that reduce gastric acid, such as antacid medications or achlorhydria, increase the risk of infection.

The hallmark of cholera is severe watery diarrhea with mild to severe dehydration because of production of toxin by the organism. In cases of severe dehydration, patients have a nonpalpable pulse and very low blood pressure. **Fever is usually not present.** Patients may become obtunded with sunken eyes and dry mucous membranes.

Vibrio parahaemolyticus is associated with gastroenteritis that is self-limited even though patients present with explosive watery diarrhea, with abdominal pain and fever. The disease rarely progressed to the severity of dehydration of *V. cholerae. Vibrio vulnificus* is more often associated with wound infections, that is, cellulitis, rather than gastroenteritis. In alcoholic patients or those with other underlying liver disease, the organism can become disseminated and be associated with a high mortality rate.

APPROACH TO SUSPECTED *Vibrio* INFECTION

Objectives

1. Know the structure, physiology, and virulence factors of *V. cholerae*.
2. Know the reservoirs and mechanisms of spread of *V. cholerae* and the mechanism of action of the cholera toxin in causing disease.

Definitions

Azotemia: Buildup in the blood of nitrogenous end-products of protein metabolism.

Obtunded: Loss or dulling of sensations.

DISCUSSION

Characteristics of *Vibrio*

Vibrio species are **motile, curved, gram-negative bacilli with a single polar flagellum.** They are **facultative anaerobic organisms.** Their natural environment is **saltwater,** where they can multiply freely, and it has been found in **shellfish and plankton.** The major human pathogens are *V. parahaemolyticus, V. vulnificus,* and *Vibrio cholerae.*

Over 200 serotypes of *V. cholerae* have been identified, based on their **O antigen** serogroup. Serotype O1 has been responsible for the major cholera pandemics of the past 200 years, but serotype O139 has been identified as contributing to disease since 1992.

The major virulence of this organism is its **enterotoxin.** The toxin consists of five B subunits, which bind to mucosal cell receptors and allow for release of the single A subunit into the cell. **The A subunit activates adenyl cyclase,** resulting in the **hypersecretion of water, sodium, potassium, chloride, and bicarbonate** into the intestinal lumen.

Bacteria that survive transit through the stomach can colonize the upper small intestine. Colonization pili facilitate attachment to the intestinal mucosa. The volume of the secreted fluid and electrolytes can overwhelm the gastrointestinal tract's ability to reabsorb them, resulting in large volumes of watery diarrhea. **The loss of an isotonic, bicarbonate-containing fluid results in dehydration, hypovolemia, metabolic acidosis, hemoconcentration, and hypokalemia.**

Diagnosis

The presumptive diagnosis of *Vibrio* disease can be made after history of association with saltwater, either involving trauma or consumption of **raw shellfish.** The watery diarrhea associated with *V. parahaemolyticus* cannot be easily distinguished clinically from other forms of bacterial gastroenteritis. **Cellulitis** caused by *V. vulnificus* should be diagnosed rapidly to avoid mortality. History of recent exposure to seawater is helpful in making a presumptive diagnosis.

The diagnosis of cholera should be suspected in those with severe diarrheal illness who live in or have traveled to an endemic area. Diagnosis of *Vibrio* infection can be confirmed by culturing stool or wound samples. **Gram stain** of wound or blood cultures may demonstrate a **characteristic curved appearance to the gram-negative bacilli.**

Most of the *Vibrio* species require salt for growth and therefore specialized media, such as thiosulfate citrate bile salts sucrose (TCBS) agar. Most of the *Vibrio* species will grow on blood agar and may appear β-hemolytic, but poor growth is seen on MacConkey agar. *Vibrio cholerae* appear as yellow colonies, and ***V. parahaemolyticus*** **and *V. vulnificus* appear as green colonies** on TCBS agar.

Treatment and Prevention

The **treatment** of cholera involves **volume replacement** with **isotonic, bicarbonate-containing fluids,** either using oral rehydration solutions in mild to moderate dehydration or IV fluids, such as Ringer lactate, in the profoundly dehydrated or those unable to tolerate oral intake. **Oral antibiotics** can be given to kill the bacteria and decrease the duration of the illness, but do not take away the need for appropriate rehydration therapy. Most commonly administered antimicrobial is **doxycycline.**

Treatment with antimicrobials is not usually needed for gastroenteritis caused by *V. parahaemolyticus.* **Wound infections or bacteremia caused by *V. vulnificus* require rapid administration of antimicrobials such as tetracycline or a quinolones.** Prevention of cholera includes improvement of hygienic practices including treatment of the potable water supply with either heat or chlorine and ensuring thorough cooking of seafood. Research is ongoing to perfect a vaccine to prevent cholera.

COMPREHENSION QUESTIONS

[23.1] An individual experiences diarrhea after eating raw shellfish in San Francisco. What is the most probable cause of the problem?

A. *Campylobacter jejuni*
B. *Salmonella choleraesuis*
C. *Shigella dysenteriae*
D. *Vibrio parahaemolyticus*
E. *Yersinia enterocolitica*

[23.2] Which of the following statements is true of cholera enterotoxin?

A. Appears to produce its effect by stimulating adenyl-cyclase activity in mucosal cells
B. Causes destruction of the intestinal mucosa allowing for invasive infection
C. Causes a net efflux of ions and water from tissue into the lumen of the large intestine
D. Is a protein with a molecular weight of approximately 284,000 daltons

[23.3] Fever, leukopenia, disseminated intravascular coagulation, and hypotension caused by members of the Enterobacteriaceae family are most strongly associated with which of the following structures?

A. H antigens
B. K antigens
C. Lipid A
D. Polysaccharides
E. R antigens

[23.4] A 50-year-old man recently visited India and developed diarrhea before returning to the United States. *Vibrio cholerae* O1 (El Tor, Ogawa) was isolated from his stool. Which of the following is the biotype of the *V. cholerae* strain?

A. Classical
B. El Tor
C. 10
D. Ogawa

Answers

[23.1] **D.** *Vibrio parahaemolyticus* is a halophilic bacterium that causes acute gastroenteritis following ingestion of contaminated seafood such as raw fish or shellfish. After 12–24 hours, the patient develops nausea and vomiting, abdominal cramps, fever, and watery to bloody diarrhea. It is usually self-limited in 1–4 days, requiring only restoration of water and electrolytes. All other answer options could produce episodes of gastroenteritis, but the halophilic nature of *V. parahaemolyticus* and seafood is recognized as a classic combination.

[23.2] **A.** The clinical correlation section of this case study summarizes the action of the *V. cholerae* enterotoxin quite well. It can be the cause of 20–30 L/day diarrheal output, resulting in dehydration, shock, acidosis, and death. It is antigenically related to the LT of *Escherichia coli,* has a molecular weight of approximately 84,000 daltons, does not damage the mucosa, and affects the small intestine.

[23.3] **C.** The lipopolysaccharide (LPS) of gram-negative cell walls consists of a complex lipid, lipid A, to which is attached a polysaccharide made up of a core and a terminal series of repeat units. LPS is attached to the outer membrane by hydrophobic bonds and is required for the function of many outer membrane proteins. LPS is also called endotoxin. All the toxicity resides in the lipid A component. Endotoxin (lipid A) can activate complement, resulting in inflammation and the clinical features referred to in the question.

[23.4] **B.** The O antigen of *Vibrio* species has been given numbers to indicate biotype, a form of subdivision for strains of cholera organism. *Vibrio cholerae* serogroups O1 and O139 have long been recognized as strains responsible for epidemic and pandemic cholera. There have been six pandemics from 1817 to 1923, most likely caused by the O1 subtype. A new pandemic caused by the El Tor biotype started in Asia in 1961 and spread to Central and South America by 1991. The disease and biotype is rare in North America, but it does have an endemic focus on the Gulf of Mexico coastal areas (Louisiana and Texas).

MICROBIOLOGY PEARLS

- The A subunit of the *Vibrio* enterotoxin activates adenyl cyclase, resulting in the hypersecretion of water, sodium, potassium, chloride, and bicarbonate into the intestinal lumen.
- The predominant clinical presentation of *Vibrio* gastroenteritis is watery diarrhea.
- The *Vibrio* organism appears as gram-negative, curved, motile bacilli. *Vibrio* gastroenteritis or cholera is associated with consumption of contaminated seafood or water.
- *Vibrio vulnificus* is associated with cellulitis caused by trauma incurred in a seawater environment and carries a high mortality rate if not treated rapidly.
- *Vibrio* species require salt for growth and can be differentiated from other organisms by growth on TCBS agar.

REFERENCES

Murray PR, Rosenthal KS, Pfaller MA. Vibrio, Aeromonas, and Plesiomonas. In: Murray PR, Rosenthal KS, Pfaller MA. Medical Microbiology, 5th ed. St. Louis, MO: Mosby, 2005:339–45.

Neill MA, Carpenter CCJ. Other pathogenic vibrios. In: Mandell GL, Bennett JE, Dolin R, eds. Principles and Practice of Infectious Diseases, 6th ed. Philadelphia, PA: Churchill Livingstone, 2005:2544–48.

Seas C, Gotuzzo E. Vibrio cholerae. In: Mandell GL, Bennett JE, Dolin R, eds. Principles and Practice of Infectious Diseases, 6th ed. Philadelphia, PA: Churchill Livingstone, 2005:2553–44.

❖ CASE 24

A 5-year-old girl is brought to the physician's office because of "pink eye." She was sent home from kindergarten yesterday by the school nurse because her left eye was red. When she awakened this morning, the right eye was red as well. She has had watery drainage but no purulent discharge. She's had a mild head cold with a runny nose and a mild sore throat but no fever. When her mother called the school this morning, she was told that five of her daughter's classmates were out with pink eye today. On examination, the child has injected conjunctiva bilaterally with clear drainage. No crusting of the lashes is noted, and the corneas are clear. She has mildly tender preauricular adenopathy. The remainder of her examination is unremarkable.

◆ **What organism is the most likely cause of this infection?**

◆ **How does this organism gain entry into host cells?**

ANSWERS TO CASE 24: ADENOVIRUS

Summary: A 5-year-old girl with conjunctivitis of both eyes, with nonpurulent drainage associated with an upper respiratory infection.

- **Most likely organism causing the infection:** Adenovirus.
- **Method that the organism gains entry into host cells:** Adenoviruses gain entry into host cells by binding to the coxsackie adenovirus receptor (CAR) followed by receptor-mediated endocytosis.

CLINICAL CORRELATION

Conjunctivitis is a normal feature of many childhood infections. However, the most common cause of conjunctivitis is related to infection with adenoviruses. In addition to being the most common cause of viral conjunctivitis, adenoviruses also commonly cause upper respiratory infections and gastrointestinal infections. Most adenoviral diseases are mild and self-limiting in immune-competent persons. Children are infected more frequently than adults.

APPROACH TO SUSPECTED ADENOVIRAL INFECTION

Objectives

1. Be able to describe the characteristics of adenovirus.
2. Understand how adenovirus causes infection.
3. Know the strategies of prevention.

Definitions

Conjunctivitis: Inflammation of the eye tissue.
Lymphadenopathy: Enlargement of a lymph node occurring singly or in multiple nodes.
Preauricular adenopathy: Enlargement of a lymph node occurring singly or in multiple nodes anterior to the ear.

DISCUSSION

Characteristics of Adenoviruses That Impact Transmission

Adenoviruses are **nonenveloped viruses that contain linear, double-stranded DNA** with a terminal protein attached to both 5′ ends of the genome. The **viral capsid** is composed of an **icosadeltahedral** structure that contains a penton base and fiber at each vertex. The fibers contain viral attachment proteins that determine the target cell specificity among viral serotypes. The fiber also serves as a **hemagglutinin.** Over 100 different serotypes have been recognized, more than 49 of which are known to infect humans.

To gain entry into the host cell, the **viral fiber proteins bind to the coxsackie adenovirus receptor on host cell surfaces** and become **internalized by receptor-mediated endocytosis.** The virus then lyses the endosome, and the viral DNA is delivered to the host nucleus still within the viral capsid. Viral DNA replication occurs in the nucleus, via a virally encoded DNA polymerase, and the viral capsid proteins are made in the cytoplasm and then transported to the nucleus for viral assembly. Adenoviral genes are transcribed from both strands of the DNA genome in either direction at different times during viral replication. A single viral replication cycle takes approximately 32–36 hours and produces around 10,000 new virions. Figure 24-1 shows the replication cycle. However, errors in assembly and replication are common, resulting in a much lower number of infectious viral particles.

Adenoviruses infect **epithelial cells of the respiratory tract, conjunctiva, and enteric organs.** Infections are **spread from person to person by aerosolized respiratory droplets, close contact, or a fecal-oral route. Fomite** transmission is also common because adenoviruses are nonenveloped, making them more resistant to detergents and desiccation. They can cause **lytic infections** in epithelial cells and tend to cause latent infections in lymphoid tissue. **Persistence in lymphoid tissues** involves integration of viral DNA into the host genome. Reactivation of virus can occur with stress. Viremia may occur and cause spread to distant organs such as the kidney, bladder, liver, and lymphoid tissue. **Viremia is especially common in immunosuppressed patients.**

Diagnosis

Adenoviruses primarily infect **children under 3 years** and appear clinically with a variety of symptoms including **fever, cough, nonstreptococcal exudative pharyngitis, cervical adenitis, conjunctivitis, or gastroenteritis.** Symptoms can last from 3 to 5 days. More severe respiratory diseases include laryngitis, bronchiolitis, and pneumonia. Reactivated viral disease occurs primarily in immune compromised individuals. Adenoviral follicular **conjunctivitis, or "pink eye,"** outbreaks in children often involve swimming pools as a common source of infection. Gastroenteritis is also a major clinical manifestation of adenoviral infection. Adenoviral types 40, 41, and 42 have been shown to be associated with **gastrointestinal disease** in infants and hospitalized patients.

In addition to clinical presentation of infection, laboratory diagnostic tests, including **cell culture, ELISA** (enzyme-linked immunosorbent assay), **PCR, and DNA-probe analysis** are available and can be used to detect the viral type in clinical samples and tissue culture. However, their primary use is for epidemiological studies, and they are not used widely in clinical practice for diagnostic purposes. Typically, diagnosis is made by clinical presentation and patient history.

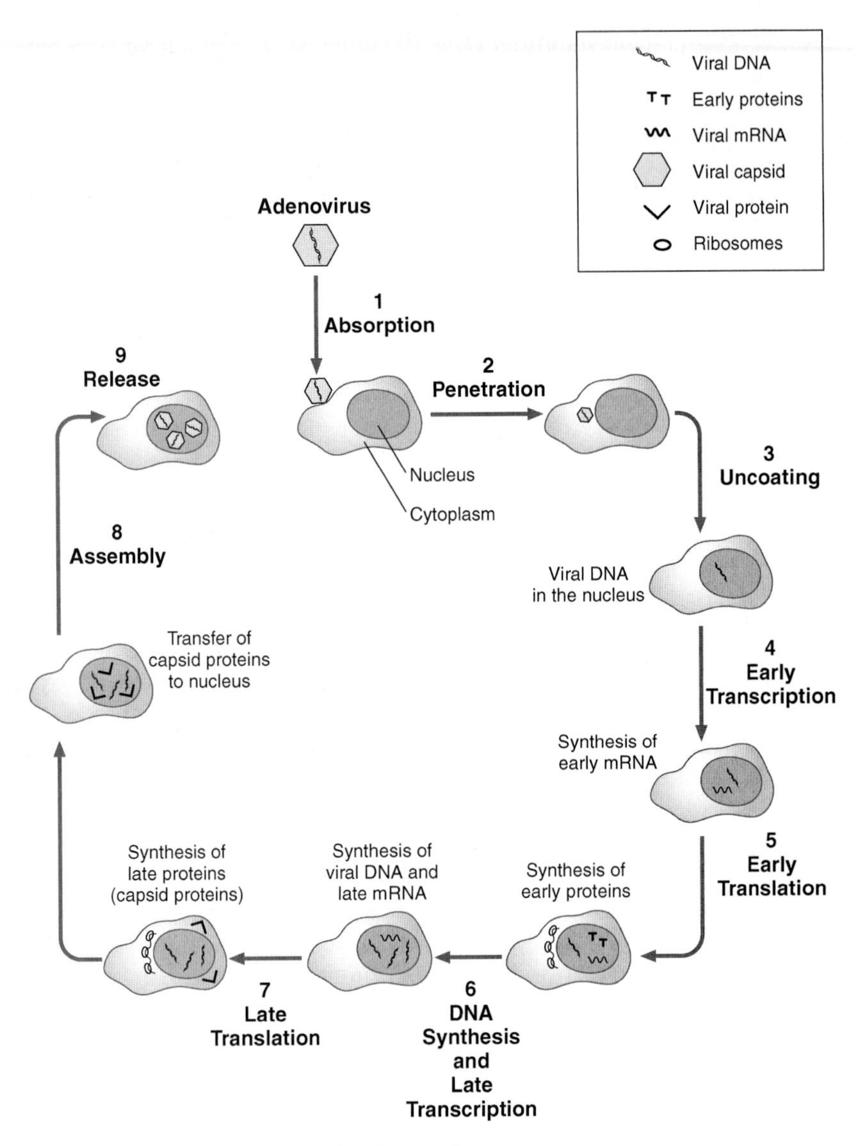

Figure 24-1. Adenovirus replication cycle.

Treatment and Prevention

Currently, there is no treatment for adenoviral infection. Live oral vaccines have been developed for adenovirus types 4 and 7, which cause acute respiratory tract infections, and have been used primarily in military settings. However, because some adenoviruses are oncogenic, such vaccines have not been made available to the general population. Thus, prevention is the most important aspect involving careful hygiene, handwashing, and isolation of infected individuals.

COMPREHENSION QUESTIONS

[24.1] An 11-year-old boy attending summer Boy Scout camp develops symptoms of sore throat, headache, fatigue, and conjunctivitis. He is seen by the camp medical staff and on examination is found to have a slight fever of 39.8°C (103.6°F), but no rash. Within the next 1–2 days, several of the other campers develop similar symptoms, which last for 5–7 days. The larger number of campers with similar symptoms indicates that a common source of infection is causing the outbreak. Which of the following activities is the most likely source of the campers' infection?

A. Hiking in wooded areas with tall grass
B. Sharing water canteens with other campers
C. Sleeping outdoors without protective netting
D. Swimming in the camp pond
E. Walking barefoot in the bath house

[24.2] The causative agent in the question above was determined to be an adenoviral infection. Which of the following best describes this viral agent?

A. Nonenveloped, double-stranded DNA virus with fibers at its vertices
B. Nonenveloped, double-stranded, circular DNA virus
C. Enveloped, single-stranded, negative-sense RNA virus
D. Enveloped, double-stranded, linear DNA virus with glycoprotein spikes
E. Enveloped, double-stranded, circular DNA virus

[24.3] A 2-year-old child attending day care develops diarrhea and gastroenteritis as a result of an adenoviral infection. Which of the following adenoviral serotypes would most likely be responsible for this girl's illness?

A. Type 4
B. Type 7
C. Type 19
D. Type 37
E. Type 41

Answers

[24.1] **D.** The campers' symptoms are consistent with adenoviral conjunctivitis, which is commonly spread through contaminated swimming pools or ponds; answers A, B, C, and E are incorrect.

[24.2] **A.** Adenoviruses are nonenveloped, double-stranded linear DNA viruses with fiber structures projecting from their vertices or penton bases; answers B, C, D, and E are incorrect: (B) describes polyoma viruses such as human papillomavirus; (C) describes viruses such as rhabdoviruses, orthomyxoviruses, paramyxoviruses, and the like; (D) describes herpesviruses; (E) describes hepatitis B virus.

[24.3] **E.** Adenoviral types 40, 41, and 42 have been shown to be associated with gastrointestinal disease in infants; answers A, B, C, and D are incorrect: Adenoviral types 4 and 7, commonly cause upper respiratory infections in military recruits; adenoviral types 19 and 37 have been implicated in causing epidemic keratoconjunctivitis.

MICROBIOLOGY PEARLS

- ❖ Adenoviruses commonly cause conjunctivitis, in combination with pharyngitis, and upper respiratory infections.
- ❖ Children under 3 years and immunocompromised adults are at particular risk.
- ❖ Clinical manifestations are fever, cough, nonstreptococcal exudative pharyngitis, cervical adenitis, conjunctivitis, or gastroenteritis.
- ❖ No treatment or vaccination is available for the general public.

REFERENCES

Brooks GF, Butel JS, Morse SA. Jawetz, Melnick, & Adelberg's Medical Microbiology, 23rd ed. New York: McGraw-Hill, 2004:420–8.

Ryan JR, Ray CG. Sherris Medical Microbiology, 4th ed. New York: McGraw-Hill, 2004:507–10.

Shenk TE. Adenoviridae: the viruses and their replication. Fields Virology, 4th ed. Philadelphia, PA:Lippincott Williams & Wilkins, 2001:2111–35.

❖ CASE 25

You are called to examine a 1-day-old male because the nurse is concerned that he is jaundiced. He was born by spontaneous vaginal delivery to a 19-year-old gravida$_1$ para$_1$ after a full-term, uncomplicated pregnancy. The mother had no illnesses during her pregnancy; she did not use tobacco, alcohol, or drugs; and the only medication that she took was prenatal vitamins. She denied any significant medical history, and there is no family history of genetic syndromes or illnesses among children. The infant is mildly jaundiced but has a notable abnormally small head circumference (microcephaly). His cardiovascular examination is normal. His liver and spleen are enlarged on palpation of the abdomen. Neurologic exam is notable for the lack of a startle response to a loud noise. CT scan of his head reveals intracerebral calcifications. The pediatrician explains to the child's mother that the virus involved is the most commonly transmitted transplacental viral infection in the United States.

◆ **What is the most likely cause of this infant's condition?**

◆ **How did he likely acquire this?**

◆ **What is the test of choice to confirm the diagnosis?**

ANSWERS TO CASE 25: CYTOMEGALOVIRUS

Summary: A 1-day-old male with microcephaly, jaundice, hepatosplenomegaly, and deafness caused by a viral infection.

- **Most likely cause of this infant's condition:** The infant is most likely suffering from a congenital infection with cytomegalovirus (CMV).
- **Likely acquisition of this infection:** Transplacental spread of the virus during a primary CMV infection of the pregnant mother.
- **Test of choice to confirm the diagnosis:** The definitive diagnostic test to confirm CMV infection in this patient is to demonstrate the presence of CMV in the infant's urine.

CLINICAL CORRELATION

Human cytomegalovirus (CMV) is the largest member of the human Herpesviridae family. It is lymphotrophic and commonly produces asymptomatic infections in immune competent hosts. However, it can cause serious primary and recurrent infections in immunosuppressed individuals and neonates. CMV is the most common transplacentally transmitted infection in the United States.

APPROACH TO SUSPECTED CMV INFECTION

Objectives

1. Be aware of the genomic characteristics of CMV.
2. Be able to describe how CMV causes infection, including transplacental infection.

Definitions

Lymphotrophic: Having a specific affinity for lymph cells or their precursors.
Microcephaly: Abnormally smaller sized head, which may be associated with mental retardation.
Hepatosplenomegaly: Enlargement of the liver and spleen.
Subclinical infection: Without the presence of noticeable clinical disease.

DISCUSSION

Characteristics of CMV That Impact Transmission

CMV belongs to the **Betaherpesvirinae** subunit of the Herpesviridae family and is the **largest known virus to infect humans.** The genome of **linear, double-stranded DNA is housed in an icosadeltahedral capsid.** Between the envelope and the capsid is a layer called the **tegument,** a phosphoprotein-containing matrix that plays a role in initiating replication. CMV, like other herpesviruses, has a lipid envelope that contains glycoproteins that facilitate attachment and entry into host cells. The virus often establishes **latent infection in lymphocytes, leukocytes, and organs like the kidney, heart, and lung.** Cell-mediated immunity is required for the control of CMV infections. Suppression of the immune system by medications or infection, such as **AIDS,** can result in **reactivation of the virus and severe, symptomatic disease.**

CMV has a ubiquitous distribution and approximately **10–15 percent of children are infected before the age of 5.** Most CMV infections in immune competent hosts are asymptomatic, although occasionally a **mononucleosis-like syndrome** can occur. Yet, even in subclinical infections, CMV can be isolated from saliva, cervical secretions, semen, urine, and white blood cells for months to years following infection. Although CMV is found in many host secretions, its major routes of **transmission** are via contact with **blood, oral secretions, sexual contact, organ transplant, or congenital infection.** CMV is the **most common viral cause of congenital disease** and infection, and its spread is thought to occur via **transplacental** transfer. The risk to the fetus is particularly high when the **mother** has a **primary infection during her pregnancy.**

Diagnosis

Although most CMV infections during childhood and in adults are asymptomatic, infants and immunocompromised patients can develop severe clinical symptoms from either primary infection or reactivation. Of the 1 percent of infants infected in utero or during delivery, 90 percent will develop asymptomatic infections, while the other 10 percent will develop symptomatic infections with congenital defects or disorders. **Nearly all of the infants with symptomatic infections are born of mothers with primary infections during their pregnancies.** Congenital CMV can cause a devastating syndrome that includes **microcephaly, intracerebral calcifications, hepatosplenomegaly, thrombocytopenia, chorioretinitis, deafness, mental retardation, jaundice, and rash.** Many of the infants with severe CMV congenital syndrome die within a short time, and those who survive have been shown to have persistent neurologic deficits. Reactivation of a latent infection during pregnancy confers a much lower risk, as the fetus is protected by the maternal immune response.

In addition to assessing the clinical symptoms, more definitive approaches to diagnosing CMV infection include direct detection of **CMV antigen or DNA in tissues or fluids via immunoassays or quantitative PCR.** Diagnosis of CMV infection can be confirmed by identification of the virus in the **infant's urine** during the first week of life. Histologically, CMV infection can also be detected by its ability to produce characteristic **enlarged cytomegaly of infected cells with pronuclear inclusions, or "owl's eyes."**

Treatment and Prevention

CMV infections are primarily treated with **ganciclovir, immune globulin plus ganciclovir, or foscarnet.** Treatment with ganciclovir has been used to prevent CMV disease in AIDS patients and transplant recipients. Use of this agent also reduces the severity of CMV syndromes such as retinitis and gastrointestinal disease. Treatment with both immune globulin and ganciclovir has been used to reduce the high mortality of CMV pneumonia in bone marrow transplant patients.

Unfortunately, congenital and perinatal transmission of CMV cannot be prevented once acquired by the pregnant woman. Thus, hygiene and handwashing may play a role in prevention. Isolation of infants with CMV infections can prevent spread to other infants. Prevention of transplantation-acquired CMV infection can be obtained by transplanting organs and blood products from seronegative donors into seronegative recipients. In situations where it is not possible to use organ or blood products from seronegative donors, prophylactic treatment of all transplant patients or preemptive therapy of those patients with evidence of active CMV infection should be used. Such therapies include the use of hyperimmune CMV globulin, anti-CMV agents or a combination of both. Additionally, safe sex practices also reduce transmission of new CMV infections. CMV vaccines are currently under development; however, none are currently available.

COMPREHENSION QUESTIONS

[25.1] An 18-year-old female presents to her physician with a 1-week history of fever, sore throat, fatigue, and myalgia. Physical examination reveals enlarged tonsils and exudative pharyngitis. Based on her clinical presentation, her physician diagnoses her with infectious mononucleosis. Because there are multiple causes of infectious mononucleosis-like illnesses, which of the following diagnostic assays would rule out CMV as the causative agent of this patient's infection?

A. A negative Gram stain of a throat swab
B. A lack of atypical lymphocytes in the patient's blood
C. A positive histological finding of cytomegaly
D. A positive Monospot test

[25.2] A previously healthy 8-year-old boy develops a classic childhood illness as a result of a primary viral infection. Which of the following agents would most likely produce symptomatic disease in a boy of this age?

A. Cytomegalovirus
B. Epstein-Barr virus (EBV)
C. Herpes simplex virus 2 (HSV-2)
D. Poliovirus
E. Varicella-zoster virus (VZV)

[25.3] A 32-year-old HIV infected male is noted to have acute CMV infection causing acute gastrointestinal symptoms. The treating physician has ordered that antiviral therapy be administered. Which of the following is most likely to be targeted by the antiviral agent?

A. Protease cleavage
B. Nuclear transport of virus
C. Synthesis of viral DNA
D. Transcription of viral proteins
E. Viral-cell fusion

Answers

[25.1] **D.** Both CMV and EBV infections can cause infectious mononucleosis disease; however, only EBV produces heterophile antibodies that would result in a positive Monospot test; answers A, B, and C, incorrect: A negative Gram stain of the patient's throat culture would rule out group A *Streptococcus;* atypical lymphocytes are commonly present in EBV infection but not CMV-related infections; and cytomegaly is typically present in CMV infections.

[25.2] **E.** VZV is a classic childhood disease that produces symptomatic primary infections; answers A, B, C, and D are incorrect: Most primary CMV, EBV, and poliovirus infections are asymptomatic, whereas HSV-2 infections would rarely occur in a child of this age.

[25.3] **C.** Ganciclovir has been used primarily to treat severe CMV infections, and its method of action involves inhibition of DNA synthesis; answers A, B, D, and E are incorrect methods of antiviral therapy for CMV infection.

MICROBIOLOGY PEARLS

- ❖ CMV is the most common viral cause of congenital infection in the United States with the mechanism being primarily transplacental infection.
- ❖ CMV establishes latent infection in lymphocytes and leukocytes.
- ❖ CMV can be excreted in saliva, semen, urine, blood, and cervical secretions for months to years following infection.
- ❖ Clinical manifestations include a mononucleosis-like disease in immune competent individuals; microcephaly, hepatosplenomegaly, deafness, neurological deficits, and jaundice in congenital infections.
- ❖ CMV cytopathology involves cytomegaly or enlargement of infected cells with pronuclear inclusions, or "owl's eyes."

REFERENCES

Murray PR, Rosenthal KS, Pfaller MA. Medical Microbiology, 5th ed. St. Louis, MO: Mosby, 2005:558–62.

Ryan JR, Ray CG. Sherris Medical Microbiology, 4th ed. New York: McGraw-Hill, 2004:566–9.

Sia IG, Patel R. New strategies for the prevention and therapy of *Cytomegalovirus* infection and disease in solid-organ transplant recipients. Clin Microbiol Rev 2000;13:83–121.

❖ CASE 26

A 17-year-old female is brought to the physician's office for evaluation of a sore throat and fever. Her symptoms started approximately 1 week ago and have been worsening. She has been extremely fatigued and has spent most of the last 3 days in bed. She denies any ill contacts. She has no significant medical history, takes no medications, and has no allergies. On examination, she is tired and ill appearing. Her temperature is 38.5°C (101.3°F). Examination of her pharynx shows her tonsils to be markedly enlarged, almost touching in the midline. They are erythematous and covered with white exudates. She has prominent cervical adenopathy, which is mildly tender. A cardiovascular examination is normal, and her abdomen is soft, nontender, and without palpable organomegaly. A rapid streptococcal antigen test in the office is negative. You send a throat culture and decide to start amoxicillin for strep pharyngitis, assuming that the office test was a false-negative. Two days later, you get a call from her mother stating that she has had an allergic reaction to the amoxicillin, and she now has a red rash from head to toe.

- **What is the most likely diagnosis of this patient?**

- **What is the most likely cause of her infection?**

- **In what human cells can this virus replicate? In what cells can it cause latent infection?**

ANSWERS TO CASE 26: EPSTEIN-BARR VIRUS

Summary: A 17-year-old female with fever, exudative pharyngitis, and adenopathy develops a prominent macular-papular rash after ampicillin is instituted.

- **Most likely diagnosis:** Infectious mononucleosis.
- **Most likely etiology:** Epstein-Barr virus (EBV).
- **In the human cells this virus can replicate, and in the cells it can cause latent infection:** EBV preferentially replicates in epithelial cells and B cells, and is known to cause latent infections in B cells.

CLINICAL CORRELATION

Epstein-Barr virus (EBV) is a member of the human herpesvirus family, and more specifically a member of the Gammaherpesvirinae subfamily. Humans are the only known natural host for these viruses. EBV infections are most commonly known for causing infectious mononucleosis in adolescents and young adults, and it is often referred to as the "kissing disease." Viral transmission occurs via repeated close intimate contact or through the sharing of items contaminated with saliva, because virus is intermittently shed in the saliva of most seropositive individuals. Secondary attack rates with family and household contacts tend to be low because 90–95 percent of adults have previously been exposed to EBV. Most primary infections are asymptomatic, whereas symptomatic infections are marked with fever, fatigue, pharyngitis, tender lymphadenitis, and possible hepatosplenopathy. Infections with these symptoms can be mistakenly diagnosed as streptococcal pharyngitis, and the resulting inappropriate treatment with amoxicillin can produce an allergic rash.

APPROACH TO SUSPECTED EBV INFECTION

Objectives

1. Be aware of the genomic and other characteristics of EBV.
2. Be able to describe the clinical disease caused by EBV, mode of transmission, and strategies for treatment.

Definitions

Lymphocytosis: A larger than normal number of T lymphocytes.

Atypical lymphocytes: Enlarged T lymphocytes, also referred to as "Downey cells," with eccentric nuclei and a vacuolated cytoplasm.

Heterophile antibodies: Nonspecific antibodies, including an IgM antibody, that recognizes the Paul-Bunnell antigen on sheep, horse, and bovine erythrocytes.

DISCUSSION

Characteristics of EBV That Impact Transmission

Similar to other members of the **Herpesviridae (Table 26-1), EBV is an enveloped virus** with a **double-stranded linear DNA genome** that is approximately 172 kb in size and encodes more than 70 viral proteins. The DNA core is surrounded by an **icosadeltahedral nucleocapsid, with a protein tegument** located between the capsid and viral envelope, containing viral enzymes and proteins necessary for replication. The outer membrane of EBV contains virally encoded **glycoprotein spikes,** important for host cell attachment to **human B cells and epithelial cells** of the oro- and nasopharynx via the receptor for the C3d component of the complement system. As an **enveloped virus,** EBV is easily disrupted by acids, detergents, and desiccation and, thus, is effectively transmitted via intimate contact and saliva.

There **are two infectious subtypes of EBV, EBV-1, and EBV-2,** which are closely related except for **differences in their nuclear antigens.** The various EBV antigens are expressed in different phases of productive viral replication or in latent infection and can be used in diagnoses. **Early EBV antigens,** such as **early antigens (EAs)** and **nuclear antigens (NAs),** are nonstructural proteins

Table 26-1
PROPERTIES OF HERPES VIRUSES

VIRUS	TARGET CELL	SITE OF LATENCY	TRANSMISSION
Herpes simplex virus type 1	Epithelial cells of the mucosa	Neurons	Close contact
Herpes simplex virus type 2	Epithelial cells of the mucosa	Neurons	Close contact (sexually transmitted)
Varicella-zoster virus	Epithelial cells of the mucosa	Neurons	Respiratory and close contact
Epstein-Barr virus	B cells and epithelial cells	B cell	Person to person via saliva
Kaposi sarcoma-related virus	Lymphocytes	Unknown	Close contact (sexually transmitted)
Cytomegalovirus	Monocytes, lymphocytes, epithelial cells	Monocytes lymphocytes	Close contact, blood, and tissue transplantation, and congential

expressed at the onset of lytic viral infection and are followed by the expression of late viral antigens, including the structural components of the viral capsid (VCA) and membrane (MA). Latent phase antigens are expressed in latently infected B cells and include Epstein-Barr nuclear antigens (EBNAs), latent proteins (LPs), and latent membrane proteins (LMPs).

EBV was first discovered in association with African **Burkitt lymphoma,** a common malignancy of young children in sub-Saharan Africa. The **highest occurrence of Burkitt lymphoma** appears to occur in regions with **high incidence of malaria,** indicating malaria as a possible disease cofactor. Other EBV-related diseases include **nasopharyngeal carcinoma** and, in immunocompromised patient populations, B-cell **lymphomas, interstitial lymphocytic pneumonia,** and **hairy leukoplakia** of the **tongue.**

EBV can cause lytic infections of epithelial cells and latent infection or immortalization of B cells. The lytic infection of epithelial and B cells promotes virus shedding into the saliva of the host, allowing for viral transmission to other hosts and spread within the host. In B cells, EBV promotes cell growth and prevents apoptosis. The proliferating B cells produce an IgM antibody to the Paul-Bunnell antigen, called a **heterophile antibody,** which serves as a diagnostic indicator of infectious mononucleosis. In this stage of infection, antibody is produced against several EBV antigens, and a T-cell response is mounted. This response contributes to the symptoms and signs of mononucleosis, such as lymphadenopathy, splenomegaly, and atypical lymphocytosis. Latent infection of B cells may occur after the resolution of the acute infection, with periodic reactivation and shedding of the virus in the saliva for months, years, or even lifetime. Persons with inadequate T cell immunity may not be able to suppress EBV infection and may progress to lymphoproliferative disease, B-cell lymphomas, or Hodgkin disease. Nasopharyngeal carcinoma, seen primarily in Asian and Aleutian populations, is thought to be associated with EBV infection in conjunction with some other genetic or environmental component.

Diagnosis

EBV-related **infectious mononucleosis** is clinically recognized by **high fever, malaise, lymphadenopathy, pharyngitis, and occasional hepatosplenomegaly.** Young children, who have a less active immune response, tend to have milder or subclinical infections. Symptoms from infection can last for days to weeks and then tend to resolve slowly on their own. Some of the rarer, but serious, complications of EBV infection include laryngeal obstruction, meningitis, encephalitis, hemolytic anemia, thrombocytopenia, and splenic rupture. A macular papular rash often erupts when amoxicillin is taken by an EBV infected patients.

Definitive diagnosis of EBV infections involves the finding of lymphocytosis with the presence of **atypical lymphocytes, heterophile-positive antibodies,** and **antibody to EBV antigens.** Atypical lymphocytes appear with the onset of infection, whereas a positive heterophile antibody response can be detected approximately 1 week after the onset of symptoms and remain present for several months. The Monospot test and ELISA (enzyme-linked immunosorbent assay) are widely used for detection of heterophile antibody.

Treatment and Prevention

Currently, there is **no effective treatment** for EBV infection, nor is a viral vaccine available. However, because EBV infections in children tend to be less severe, and the immunity developed is lifelong, it is speculated by some clinicians that early exposure to EBV may be a means of preventing more severe infections and symptomatic disease.

COMPREHENSION QUESTIONS

[26.1] Which of the following statement regarding the serologic diagnosis of infectious mononucleosis is correct?

A. A heterophile antibody is formed that reacts with the membrane protein of EBV.
B. A heterophile antibody is formed that agglutinates sheep or horse red blood cells.
C. A heterophile antigen occurs that cross-reacts with atypical lymphocytes.
D. A heterophile antigen occurs following infection with both EBV and CMV.

[26.2] A transplant patient taking high levels of immunosuppressive drugs becomes infected with EBV and develops a lymphoma. The dosage of immunosuppressive drugs given to the patient is subsequently decreased, and the tumor regresses. Which of the following properties of EBV infection is related to the patient's tumor development?

A. Immortalization of B cells
B. Increased white blood cell count
C. Presence of atypical lymphocytes
D. Production of heterophile antibodies

[26.3] A 21-year-old man visits the student health center suffering from a sore throat, swollen glands, fatigue, and a temperature of 39.4°C (103°F). Examination of the patient's peripheral blood smear shows 10 percent atypical lymphocytes, an elevated white blood cell count, and a positive heterophile antibody test. The patient asks for antimicrobial therapy. Which of the following statements would best dictate the clinician's response?

A. α-Interferon is helpful in EBV infections but has multiple side effects.
B. Ribavirin is effective in patients over 60 years.
C. Attenuated-viral vaccine has been developed but not effective in this case because the infection has already occurred.
D. There is no effective treatment.

Answers

[26.1] **B.** A nonspecific heterophile agglutination test (Monospot test) is commercially available and can be used to diagnose EBV infectious mononucleosis within a week to months of infection. Infectious mononucleosis-like infection caused by CMV is heterophile negative.

[26.2] **A.** Aggressive monoclonal B-cell lymphomas can develop in patients with reduced T-cell function. The immortalization of B cells in the absence of functional T cell immunity can give rise to lymphoproliferative disease such as Hodgkin lymphoma, Burkitt lymphoma, and nasopharyngeal carcinoma.

[26.3] **D.** Currently, there are no effective treatments or vaccines available for EBV infection. Ribavirin is useful in treating respiratory syncytial virus-related and hepatitis C virus-related infections, while α-interferon has been used in treating the following viral infections: condyloma acuminatum, chronic hepatitis B and C, and Kaposi sarcoma.

MICROBIOLOGY PEARLS

❖ EBV-related infectious mononucleosis is heterophile antibody-positive.

❖ Clinical manifestations are fever, malaise, lymphadenopathy, pharyngitis, with presence of lymphocytosis and atypical lymphocytes.

❖ No current treatment or vaccines are available.

REFERENCES

Cohen JL. Epstein-Barr virus infection. N Engl J Med 2000;343:481–92.

Murray PR, Rosenthal KS, Pfaller MA. Medical Microbiology, 5th ed. St. Louis, MO: Mosby, 2005:553–8.

Ryan JR, Ray CG. Sherris Medical Microbiology, 4th ed. New York: McGraw-Hill, 2004:567–73.

CASE 27

A 62-year-old male presents to your office for follow-up of some abnormal blood test results. You had seen him 2 weeks ago as a new patient for a routine physical examination. You ordered blood tests and found that his liver enzymes were elevated by approximately three times the upper limits of normal. The patient says that to his knowledge he's never had abnormal liver tests before, although he has not been to a doctor in several years. He denies alcohol or drug use and is not taking any medications. He gives no history of jaundice. His past medical history is significant only for hospitalization at the age of 45 for a bleeding stomach ulcer. He required surgery and had transfusion of 4 units of blood. He recovered from this episode without further complication and has had no recurrences. Your complete physical examination 2 weeks ago was normal, and a focused physical examination today shows no signs of jaundice, no hepatosplenomegaly, and no physical exam findings suggestive of portal hypertension. You diagnose an infectious etiology for the laboratory findings (elevated liver enzymes).

- **What is the most likely infectious cause of his abnormal liver function tests?**

- **How did he most likely acquire this infection?**

ANSWERS TO CASE 27: HEPATITIS VIRUSES

Summary: A 62-year-old man with abnormal liver function tests who had a blood transfusion previously, likely caused by an infectious etiology.

- **Most likely infectious etiology:** Hepatitis C virus
- **Most likely route of transmission:** Blood transfusion

CLINICAL CORRELATION

Hepatitis C virus (HVC) is transmitted parenterally by **blood transfusions or intravenous drug use** and rarely by sexual contact. It is uncommonly diagnosed as a cause of acute hepatitis, often producing subclinical infection, but it is frequently diagnosed later as a cause of chronic hepatitis. The natural history of infection is not completely understood, but 50–85 percent of patients with hepatitis C will develop chronic infection.

On initial infection, approximately 15 percent of persons will develop an acute hepatitis syndrome and recover completely. However, most infected individuals will appear asymptomatic yet progress to chronic infection. This chronic infection may progress to cirrhosis, liver failure, or hepatocellular carcinoma. HCV is transmitted from person to person, primarily via contact with infected blood or sexual contact. Routine screening of the donated blood supply for HCV was started in 1992. Prior to this, HCV was the primary cause of posttransfusion hepatitis. The high percentage of infections that are asymptomatic contributes to the spread of the virus in the population. Diagnosis is made by the presence of circulating antibody to HCV. HCV-polymerase chain reaction is also used to quantitate the amount of circulating virus present in an infected person. This serves as a measure of disease activity and as a monitor of response to therapy. Recombinant interferon, which induces host antiviral and antiproliferative activity, is the most widely used therapy for HCV.

APPROACH TO VIRAL HEPATITIS

Objectives

1. Know the structure and characteristics of the viruses that cause hepatitis.
2. Know the specific diseases associated with and routes of transmission of the hepatitis viruses.
3. Understand the mechanisms of development of acute and chronic hepatitis infections.

Definitions

Hepatitis: Inflammation of the liver; viral causative agents include hepatitis viruses A, B, C, D, E, and G. The clinical presentation can include fever, nausea or vomiting, jaundice, dark urine, pale feces, and elevated liver enzymes (AST and ALT).

Dane particle: A 42-nm particle that is the hepatitis B virion.

Fulminant hepatitis: Severe acute hepatitis that causes rapid destruction of the liver.

DISCUSSION

Characteristics of Hepatitis Viruses

Because of its rich vascular supply, the liver may be involved in any systemic blood-borne infection, but the most common and clinically significant infections are those with one of five hepatotropic viruses: Hepatitis A, B, C, D, or E. They can produce virtually indistinguishable clinical syndromes. Affected individuals often complain of a prodrome of nonspecific constitutional symptoms including fever, nausea, fatigue, arthralgias, myalgias, headache, and sometimes pharyngitis and coryza. This is followed by the onset of visible jaundice as a result of hyperbilirubinemia, with tenderness and enlargement of the liver, and dark urine caused by bilirubinuria. The clinical course, outcomes, and possible complications then vary depending on the type of virus causing the hepatitis. A comparison of features of these five viruses is shown in Table 27–1.

Hepatitis A

Hepatitis A and **E** are both very contagious and transmitted by **fecal-oral route,** usually by contaminated food or water where sanitation is poor and in day care by children. **Hepatitis A virus (HAV) is found worldwide,** and is the **most common cause of acute viral hepatitis in the United States. Hepatitis E** is much less common, and it is found in Asia, Africa, and Central America. Both hepatitis A and E infections usually lead to self-limited illnesses and generally resolve within weeks. Almost all patients with hepatitis A recover completely and have no long-term complications.

HAV is a member of the **Picornaviridae family.** It is a nonenveloped, linear, positive-sense, single-stranded RNA virus with only one serotype. Its average incubation period is approximately 30 days, and it results in 25,000 symptomatic cases in the United States annually. However**, nearly 90 percent of HAV infections in children and 30–50 percent in adults are asymptomatic.** Clinical symptoms vary according to the age of the patient; infections in children are mostly asymptomatic or present with nonspecific symptoms, whereas adults generally have a more severe clinical course. Only 1–4 percent of patients develop fulminant liver failure, and there is 1 percent mortality

Table 27-1
COMPARISON OF HEPATITIS VIRUS

	VIRUS TYPE	TRANSMISSION	INCUBATION	MARKERS SEROLOGIC	CARRIER STATE	CHRONIC HEPATITIS	PREVENTION
Hepatitis A	RNA	Enteral (fecal-oral)	15–45 days	Anti-HAV IgM	No	No	Vaccine, avoid contaminated food and water
Hepatitis B	DNA	Sexual, parenteral	30–180 days (mean 60–90 days)	+HBsAg, anti-HBcIgM (acute)	Yes	Yes	Vaccine, avoid blood and fluids
Hepatitis C	RNA	Parenteral	15–160 days (means 50 days)	Anti-HCV HCV RNA or ELISA	Yes	Yes	No vaccine, avoidance
Hepatitis D	Defective RNA	Parenteral	Same as HBV	Anti-HDV IgM	Yes	Yes	Vaccine for HBV, avoidance
Hepatitis E	RNA	Enteral (fecal-oral)	14–60 days (mean 40 days)	Anti-HEV	No	No	Avoid contaminated food and water

from HAV infection. It is not **known to cause chronic infection.** The virus is **contagious before symptoms appear.** Serologically, HAV infection can be diagnosed as ALT level rise initially with the appearance of symptoms. Then, **anti-HAV IgM antibodies** are produced and can be detected by enzyme-linked immunoassay. Then 1–3 weeks later, anti-HAV IgG antibodies are made, providing lifelong immunity to the host.

Proper hand washing, avoidance of contaminated food and water, and the administration of a **vaccine** for travelers are all methods for prevention of HAV infection. The CDC now recommends universal vaccination against HAV for all children 1 year and older. Alternatively, exposed persons can be treated **with HAV immunoglobulin intramuscularly** within 14 days of exposure. Additional treatment for infected patients is supportive.

Hepatitis B

Hepatitis B virus (HBV) is a member of the Hepadnavirus family and has a **DNA genome,** making it unique among the hepatitis viruses. It is an enveloped virus with a circular and partially double-stranded DNA genome. The HBV virion, known as the **Dane particle,** consists of the genome, a viral DNA polymerase, and P protein, which is attached to the genome. The DNA polymerase also contains reverse transcriptase and ribonuclease H activity, allowing HBV to use an RNA intermediate during replication.

HBV has a specific affinity for liver cells, with attachment to these cells being mediated by viral glycoproteins. Once attached, HBV is taken up by the hepatocytes and the genome is converted into fully double-stranded DNA which is then delivered to the nucleus. The host cell's transcription and translation machinery are then used to make new HBV virions. These virions are then released from the hepatocyte via exocytosis.

Several viral proteins can be detected during HBV infection and are useful in diagnosis and monitoring of disease. The virion is surrounded by a core protein antigen (HBcAg), and the presence of HBcAg in a patient's serum indicates that the patient has been exposed to HBV. Other HBV antigens include surface antigen (HBsAg) and the "e" antigen (HBeAg). **HBsAg can be detected when live virions** are present in an infection, and HBeAg is a glycoprotein cleavage product of the core which is shed into the serum. The **presence of HBeAg and HBsAg correlate with active HBV infection** and thus, **active disease.** Antibodies to these viral antigens can help to determine whether infection is recent or not. IgM anti-HBc indicates a new infection, whereas IgG anti-HBc indicates past infection. Figure 27-1 shows a hepatitis B serology diagram.

HBV is the **second most common type of viral hepatitis** in the United States, and it is usually **sexually transmitted.** It may also be acquired **parenterally,** such as from intravenous drug use, or during birth, from chronically infected mothers. The outcome then depends on the age at which the infection was acquired. Up to **90 percent of infected newborns develop chronic hepatitis B infection,** which places the affected infant at significant risk of **hepatocellular**

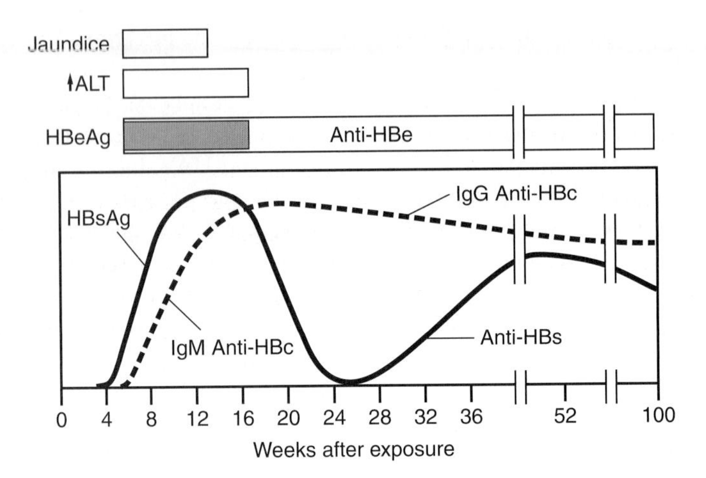

Figure 27-1. Clinical and laboratory features of acute viral hepatitis B infection.

carcinoma later in adulthood. For those individuals infected later in life, approximately 95 percent of patients will recover completely without sequelae. Between **5 and 10 percent of patients will develop chronic hepatitis,** which may progress to cirrhosis. Also, a **chronic carrier state** may be seen in which the virus continues to replicate but does not cause hepatic damage in the host.

A **vaccine** consisting of recombinant HBsAg is available and is a scheduled immunization given to all infants and adolescents, as well as to persons with increased risk of exposure (i.e., health-care workers and IV drug users). The incidence of HBV infection has decreased with the onset of the HBV vaccine and the screening of pregnant women prior to delivery. Yet, HBV remains in high rates in Southeast Asia and the Mediterranean areas. Nonimmunized persons exposed to HBV can be treated with immunoglobulin within 1 week of exposure. HBV infection can be treated with reverse transcriptase inhibitors or α-interferon.

Hepatitis C

Hepatitis C virus (HCV) is a member of the **Flaviviridae family.** It is a lipoprotein-enveloped virus with a positive-sense RNA genome. There are hundreds of HCV genotypes as a result of a hypervariable region in the envelope region. The virus is more or less virulent depending on the hypervariable region, thus making it very difficult to produce an effective vaccine against HCV. The virus enters cells through endocytosis after binding to the CD81 surface receptor. The acidity of the endosome causes fusion of the viral envelope with the endosomal membrane and results in release of the viral RNA into the host cytoplasm. The viral RNA acts as messenger RNA, directing the production of the viral polyprotein. The polyprotein anchors to the host cell endoplasmic reticulum and the virus remains cell-associated. The HCV proteins inhibit apoptosis and the action of interferon-α. By remaining associated with the cell and inhibiting apoptosis, HCV can cause chronic infection and persistent liver disease. The incubation period for infection can vary from 2 to 26 weeks, with an average of 6–7 weeks.

Most initial HCV infections are asymptomatic or result in mild nonspecific symptoms such as malaise or abdominal pain. On initial infection, approximately 15 percent of persons will develop an acute hepatitis syndrome and recover completely. **More than 70 percent of infected patients will be asymptomatic, yet many will progress to chronic hepatitis.** Yet, another 15 percent of infected patients rapidly develop cirrhosis. Chronic infection can also progress to more serious disease including: cirrhosis, liver failure, or hepatocellular carcinoma. The high percentage of infections that are asymptomatic also contributes to the spread of the virus in the population.

HCV infection is diagnosed by demonstrating the presence of circulating **IgG antibodies** to HCV antigens through enzyme immunoassay. Unfortunately, these antibodies may not be detected until up to 4 months postinfection, making it difficult to diagnose an acute HCV infection. Additionally, such tests cannot distinguish between acute, chronic, or resolved HCV infections. Alternatively, **reverse transcriptase polymerase chain reaction** (RT-PCR) testing can be used to diagnose infection and to quantitate the amount of circulating HCV RNA in an infected person. This assay serves as both a measure of HCV disease activity and as a monitor of response to therapy.

Numerous antiviral agents are used as therapy for HCV infection, including **recombinant interferon-α,** which helps to induce host antiviral and antiproliferative activity. End-stage chronic HCV hepatitis may require liver transplantation; however, the risk of graft reinfection is 50 percent for HCV. Currently, there is no effective vaccine to prevent HCV infection. However, the establishment of routine screening of donated blood and organs has reduced the spread of HCV via these modes of transfer.

Hepatitis D

Hepatitis D virus (HDV) is a **defective RNA virus** that **requires the presence of the hepatitis B virus** to replicate. Specifically, it lacks genes for envelope proteins, and thus to replicate it requires infection with HBV. It then consists of an envelope (provided by HBV) with HBsAg, delta antigen, and **single-stranded, circular** RNA. If infection with HDV occurs during a superinfection of preexisting HBV, there is a higher risk of chronic liver infection and chronic HDV infection. This type of superinfection is also more likely to lead to fulminant hepatitis and has a 5–15 percent mortality rate. However, when HDV coinfects a person simultaneously with HBV, it typically presents as severe acute disease with a low risk of developing chronic liver infection or mortality. HDV is spread similarly to HBV, via percutaneously, mucosally, or through sexual contact.

Laboratory diagnosis of HDV is made by detection of the RNA genome (via RT-PCR) or the delta antigen (via enzyme-linked immunosorbent assay, ELISA) from blood samples. Additionally, anti-HDV antibodies can also be detected by ELISA; however, antibodies are present only transiently. To prevent coinfection with HBV, prophylaxis to HBV can be administered. To prevent a

HDV superinfection, it is important to educate HBV-positive patients about reducing risk factors for infection. The only treatment available for HDV infection is α-interferon, which lessens clinical symptoms.

Hepatitis E

Hepatitis E virus (HEV), also called **"enteric non-A, non-B hepatitis,"** is a member of the **Caliciviridae family.** It is nonenveloped, and its genome consists of linear, positive-sense, single-stranded RNA. HEV is similar in many ways to HAV. Both are transmitted by the fecal-oral route, most frequently through contaminated water sources. It is not endemic to the United States and is therefore seen most often in travelers. The average incubation period is 40 days. HEV infection is most often diagnosed by exclusion, because laboratory testing is not available.

Like HAV, it has a l**ow mortality rate (1–2 percent),** except for infection in **pregnancy where a 15–25 percent mortality rate** is noted, and there is **no chronic stage.** Like all of the hepatitis viruses, the clinical severity of infection increases with the age of the patient. The immunological response is also similar to that of HAV. To protect from HEV infection while traveling to endemic areas, travelers are advised not to drink the water (or ice) and not to eat unpeeled fruits or vegetables. There is no vaccine available, and immunoglobulin does not prevent infection with HEV.

Hepatitis G

The hepatitis G virus (HGV), has been more recently identified. As a member of the **Flavivirus family** it resembles HCV in its viral structure (positive-sense RNA genome), transmission (blood-borne) and in its high production of chronic hepatitis disease. Lab diagnosis involves identifying the HGV genome via RNA detection methods (i.e., RT-PCR).

Hepatitis Serologies

Clinical presentation does not reliably establish the viral etiology, so serologic studies are used to establish a diagnosis. **Antihepatitis A IgM** establishes an **acute hepatitis A infection.** If Antihepatitis C antibody is present, an acute hepatitis C is diagnosed, but it may be negative for several months. The hepatitis C PCR assay, which becomes positive earlier in the disease course, often aids in the diagnosis. Acute hepatitis B infection is diagnosed by the presence of **hepatitis B surface antigen (HBsAg)** in the clinical context of elevated serum transaminase levels and jaundice. HBsAg later disappears when the antibody (anti-HBs) is produced.

There is often an interval of a few weeks between the disappearance of HBsAg and the appearance of anti-HBsAb, which is referred to as the **"window period."** During this interval, the presence of antihepatitis B core antigen IgM (anti-HBc IgM), will prove indicate an acute hepatitis B infection. Hepatitis B precore antigen (HBeAg) represents a high level of viral replication. It is almost always present during acute infection, but its persistence after 6 weeks of illness is a sign of chronic infection and high infectivity. Persistence of HBsAg or HBeAg are markers for chronic hepatitis or a chronic carrier state; elevated or normal serum transaminase levels distinguish between these two entities, respectively.

COMPREHENSION QUESTIONS

[27.1] A 33-year-old nurse suffered a needle stick injury. The patient used illicit intravenous drugs. One month later, the nurse develops jaundice. Which of the following findings would implicate hepatitis B as the etiology?

A. Positive antihepatitis B surface antibody
B. Positive antihepatitis B-core antibody
C. Positive hepatitis B surface antigen
D. Positive antihepatitis A antibody

[27.2] A 25-year-old male tests positive for a hepatitis C infection. Which of the following is the most likely method of transmission?

A. Fecal-oral
B. Fomite
C. Intravenous drug (needles)
D. Sexual transmission

[27.3] A 12-year-old teenager is brought into the emergency room with skin "turning yellow" and abdominal discomfort. The liver function tests reveal serum transaminase levels in the 2000 IU/L range. Which of the following is the most accurate statement about probable complications?

A. Significant likelihood of hepatocellular carcinoma
B. Almost no chance of long-term sequelae
C. About a 10 percent chance of a chronic carrier state
D. Long-term complications usually respond to α-interferon therapy

[27.4] A 28-year-old woman presents with symptoms of jaundice, right upper quadrant pain, and vomiting. She also has elevated ALT. It is determined that she acquired hepatitis A from a church picnic where several other adults also became infected. What should be done to protect the family members?

A. One dose of HAV immunoglobulin should be administered intramuscularly.
B. No treatment is necessary.
C. A series of three vaccinations should be administered at 0, 1, and 6 months.
D. α-Interferon should be administered.
E. Household contacts should be quarantined and observed.

Answers

[27.1] **C.** The presence of hepatitis B surface antigen means actively replicating virus, and in the context of the recent needle stick injury, this likely represents a hepatitis B infection. The presence of HBeAg is a marker of active disease and infectivity. For example, pregnant mothers infected with HBV who have the absence of serum HBeAg, there is a greater than 10 percent transmission rate to the fetus, whereas in pregnant mothers with HBeAg in their serum, there is a greater than 90 percent transmission rate to the fetus.

[27.2] **C.** Intravenous drug use is the primary method of transmission of hepatitis C virus.

[27.3] **B.** This is most likely hepatitis A infection, which carries a very low chance of long-term sequelae.

[27.4] **A.** HAV immunoglobulin should be given to household contacts in one IM dose. This must be done within 14 days of exposure to the index patient as prophylaxis against hepatitis A. Answer (C), the series of three vaccinations at time 0, 1, and 6 months, refers to the immunization schedule for hepatitis B, not hepatitis A. This would not be protective for those exposed to HAV. (D) α-Interferon is used to treat symptomatic patients with HBV and HCV, not prophylaxis of family members of patients with HAV. (E) Quarantining the household contacts of the patient is not the appropriate treatment.

MICROBIOLOGY PEARLS

- ❖ HCV is an enveloped virus with a positive-sense RNA genome.
- ❖ HCV transmission occurs primarily via infected blood/parenteral transmission.
- ❖ Although most acute infections are asymptomatic, HCV produces high rates of chronic infection and mortality.
- ❖ Treatment of HCV infection includes recombinant interferon-α.
- ❖ No vaccine is available for HCV.

REFERENCES

Brooks GF, Butel JS, Morse SA. Jawetz, Melnick, & Adelberg's Medical Microbiology, 23rd ed. New York: McGraw-Hill, 2004:466–86.

Howley PM, Knipe DM. Fields Virology, 4th ed. Philadelphia, PA:Lippincott Williams & Wilkins, 2001.

Murray PR, Rosenthal KS, Pfaller MA. Medical Microbiology, 5th ed. St. Louis, MO: Mosby, 2005:675–90.

Ryan JR, Ray CG. Sherris Medical Microbiology, 4th ed. New York: McGraw-Hill, 2004:541–53.

National Institute of Allergy and Infectious Disease. Hepatitis. www.niaid.nih.gov/publications/hepatitis.htm

CASE 28

The mother of a 3-year-old girl brings the child in for the evaluation of a "wart" on her thumb. It has been present for 3 or 4 days and seems to cause some pain. The week prior, the child had a "head cold" and "cold sores" around her mouth, all of which have resolved. She has never had warts, and the mother says that the child is otherwise healthy. On examination, you see a well appearing child who is sitting in her mother's lap and sucking her thumb. Her head and neck exam is normal. On her left thumb, just proximal to the base of the thumbnail, is the lesion about which the mother is concerned. It is a cluster of small vesicles with a faint area of surrounding erythema. The remainder of the child's examination is normal.

- **What virus is the most likely cause of this skin lesion?**
- **How was it transmitted to this patient's thumb?**

ANSWERS TO CASE 28: HERPES SIMPLEX VIRUSES

Summary: A 3-year-old girl had "cold sores" previously and now a cluster of small vesicles with a faint area of surrounding erythema on the thumb, consistent with herpetic whitlow.

◆ **Most likely viral cause of this skin lesion:** The most likely cause of the girl's skin lesion is herpes simplex type 1 (HSV-1).

◆ **How was it transmitted to this patient's thumb:** The patient most likely acquired the infection at this secondary site via self-inoculation of the skin by sucking her thumb.

CLINICAL CORRELATION

There are two serotypes of herpes simplex viruses, types 1 and 2 (HSV-1 and HSV-2), which both cause vesicular lesions via infection of mucosal membranes and or compromised epithelial cells. Both HSV-1 and HSV-2 are known to replicate in the basal epithelium of these vesicular lesions and then establish latent and recurring infections within the innervating neurons of these cells. HSV primarily cause clinical symptoms at the site of inoculation of the virus. Although there is some overlap, HSV-1 tends to cause disease above the waist, and HSV-2, which is more commonly transmitted via sexual contact, causes disease below the waist.

APPROACH TO SUSPECTED HSV INFECTION

Objectives

1. Know the structure and characteristics of HSV.
2. Know the clinical disease caused by HSV, mode of transmission, and strategies for treatment.

Definitions

Vesicular lesions: Small, blister-like lesions filled with clear fluid.

Syncytia: Fusion of neighboring cells infected with virus, resulting in multinucleated giant cells.

Gingivostomatitis: Localized inflammation and or ulcerative lesions in the mucous membranes of the oral cavity.

Prodrome: Early symptoms of HSV infection, including itching and tingling of skin 12–24 hours prior to lesion formation.

DISCUSSION

Characteristics of HSV That Impact Transmission

The **herpes simplex viruses (HSV)** are members of the **Alphavirinae subfamily of human herpesviruses.** As with other herpesviruses, they **are large, enveloped viruses** containing linear, **double-stranded DNA** genomes surrounded by an **icosadeltahedral nucleocapsid,** with a protein tegument (space containing viral enzymes and transcription factors) located between the capsid and viral envelope. The structures of the **HSV-1 and HSV-2 genomes** are similar and share approximately **50 percent homology.** They can infect many cell types in humans and in other animals. They tend to cause lytic infections in fibroblast and epithelial cells and latent infections in neurons. HSV enters host cells via fusion at the cell membrane and releases gene transcription proteins, protein kinases, and proteins that are cytotoxic to the host cell. Once inside the host, the viral genome is delivered to the nucleus of the cell. HSV uses the host transcription/translation machinery; yet it is a viral-encoded DNA polymerase that replicates the DNA genome. Newly formed enveloped virions are released from the cell by either exocytosis or cell lysis.

The **virus enters through mucosal membranes or breaks in the skin.** It replicates in cells at the infection site and then establishes latent infection of the neuron that innervates the primarily infection site via retrograde transport. HSV avoids antibody-mediated defenses by cell-to-cell spread by the formation of **syncytia. Cell-mediated immunity is necessary for control of HSV infections,** and persons with impaired cellular immunity can get more severe and diffuse disease. The **latent infection of neurons** also helps the virus to avoid host defenses and provides the potential for recurrent disease. **Recurrences** can be triggered by many events, including stress and other illnesses. Recurrent HSV disease is usually less severe than primary disease because of the memory response of the host immune system. HSV-1 tends to be transmitted via contact with saliva or direct contact with skin or mucous membrane lesions. It causes gingivostomatitis, cold sores, and pharyngitis. **Herpetic whitlow,** an infection of the finger with **HSV-1,** results from direct contact with herpes lesions and is most commonly seen in **children who suck their fingers or in health-care workers** who care for infected patients.

Diagnosis

Clinical signs of HSV-1 and HSV-2 infections include (1) oropharyngeal disease, with symptoms of fever, sore throat, gingivostomatitis, and submandibular lymphadenopathy; (2) keratoconjunctivitis, with recurrent lesions of the eye and eyelid; (3) cutaneous infections, with vesicular lesions of the mouth, fingers, and genital tract (Figure 28-1); and (4) encephalitis. Neonatal infections occur most commonly during vaginal delivery in pregnant mothers experiencing primary or recurrent genital lesions. HSV neonatal infections are

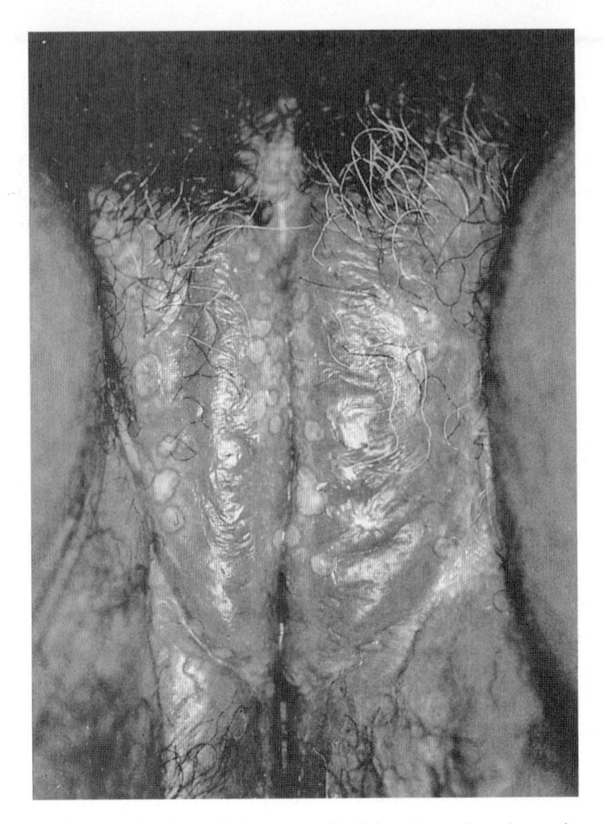

Figure 28-1. First episode primary genital herpes simplex virus infection. *(Reproduced, with permission, from Cunningham FG, et al. William's Obstetrics, 21st ed. New York: McGraw-Hill, 2001:1495.)*

nearly always symptomatic and have high mortality rates if not promptly diagnosed and treated. Signs of infection include localized vesicular lesions of the skin, eye or mouth, encephalitis, and/or disseminated disease.

Cytopathologically, HSV can be diagnosed by visualizing **multinucleated giant cells** on direct examination of cells from the base of a vesicular lesion, referred to as a **Tzanck smear.** However, this assay **lacks both sensitivity and specificity,** because it does not distinguish among HSV-1, HSV-2, and varicella-zoster virus (VZV) infections. **Isolation of virus from herpetic lesions,** cerebral spinal fluid, or stool specimens remains the definitive diagnostic approach, where the appearance of characteristic HSV cytopathic effects on cells can be observed. Other rapid diagnostic tests include: detecting viral antigen (via immunofluorescence) or DNA (via PCR) in tissue samples or vesicle fluid. HSV-1 and HSV-2 **serotyping** can be performed by several biochemical, nucleic acid, or immunologic methods, with DNA probe analysis being the most widely used in current clinical practice.

Treatment and Prevention

Several antiviral drugs have been developed to treat HSV infections, including **acyclovir, valacyclovir, and famciclovir.** All of these drugs function as inhibitors of viral DNA synthesis and are capable of shortening the duration of clinical symptoms and suppressing viral reactivation.

Prevention of HSV infection relies on the avoidance of direct contact with the virus or viral lesions. Asymptomatic shedding of virus can occur in infected persons in saliva, urethral, and cervical sources, and because only about one-fourth of individuals infected with HSV know that they are infected, safe sex practices are highly recommended to avoid spread. The vast majority of HSV infections in newborns can be prevented by cesarean delivery of neonates in women experiencing primary HSV-2 infection or recurrent genital lesions. This practice has significantly decreased the rate of neonatal infection and mortality. Additionally, experimental recombinant HSV-2 vaccines are currently being developed and tested. One prospective trial has shown efficacy in preventing genital herpes infections in HSV-1 and HSV-2 seronegative women.

COMPREHENSION QUESTIONS

[28.1] Which of the following cell types are specific to a latent genital infection with HSV-2?

A. Trigeminal ganglia
B. Sacral ganglia
C. Vagal nerve ganglia
D. Neural sensory ganglia

[28.2] Which of the following viruses, in addition to HSV-1 and HSV-2, produces the cytopathologic findings of multinucleated giant cells?

A. Adenovirus
B. Cytomegalovirus
C. Epstein-Barr virus
D. Human papillomavirus
E. Varicella-zoster virus

[28.3] Which of the following statements most accurately describes HSV infections?

A. HSV establishes lytic infection in neural ganglion cells.
B. Latent HSV infections can be prevented in persons with functional cell-mediated immunity.
C. Primary and recurrent HSV infections are treated with drugs that inhibit the viral DNA polymerase.
D. HSV infection is transmitted via direct contact with symptomatic shedding of viral particles in active lesions.
E. Severe neonatal herpes infections are commonly associated with in utero transmission.

Answers

[28.1] **B.** Latent infection by HSV-2 has been shown to occur primarily in the sacral ganglia, whereas HSV-1 latency has been demonstrated in trigeminal, superior cervical, and vagal nerve ganglia. Varicella-zoster virus remains latent in neural sensory ganglia.

[28.2] **E.** A Tzanck smear assay can be used to identify the characteristic cytopathologic effects of multinucleated giant cells in herpetic skin lesions; however, this assay cannot distinguish among HSV-1, HSV-2, and VZV infections.

[28.3] **C.** Most antiviral therapies for HSV are nucleoside analogues or other inhibitors of the viral DNA polymerase; answers A, B, D, and E are incorrect: HSV establishes lytic infections in fibroblast and epithelial cells and latent infections in neurons; infection with HSV results in lifelong latent infection even in persons with functional cell-mediated immunity; HSV is transmitted most commonly from direct contact with active lesions (however, virus may be shed asymptomatically in saliva and urethral and cervical fluids); although in utero transmission of HSV is possible, it is very uncommon, and most neonatal HSV infections occur via vaginal delivery in mothers with primary genital infections.

MICROBIOLOGY PEARLS

- ❖ Clinical manifestations include painful vesicular lesions of the mouth, fingers, and genital tract.
- ❖ Characteristic viral cytopathology includes syncytia, cells with "ballooning" cytoplasm, and Cowdry A type inclusion bodies.
- ❖ Diagnosis of infection is made by viral isolation; HSV-1 and HSV-2 serotyping is performed by nucleic acid restriction mapping or DNA probe analysis.
- ❖ Effective treatment of primary and recurrent infections is with viral DNA polymerase inhibitors: acyclovir, valacyclovir, and famciclovir.

REFERENCES

Murray PR, Rosenthal KS, Pfaller MA. Medical Microbiology, 5th ed. St. Louis, MO: Mosby, 2005:543–50.

Ryan JR, Ray CG. Sherris Medical Microbiology, 4th ed. New York: McGraw-Hill, 2004:555–62.

Whitley, RJ, Kimberlin, DW, Roizman, B. Herpes simplex viruses. J Clin Infect Dis 1998;26:541–55.

❖ CASE 29

A 28-year-old man presents to the physician's office for evaluation of a rash on his chest. He started with one oval-shaped purplish area that he thought was a bruise but has subsequently developed multiple new lesions. The growths don't hurt, itch, or bleed, but he continues to get new ones, and the existing ones are getting larger. He has never had anything like this before, has no history of allergies and denies exposure to any new medications, foods, lotions, or soaps. His past medical and family histories are unremarkable. His review of systems is significant for a 15-lb weight loss in the past 2 months, approximately 6 weeks of diarrhea, and a 3-week history of a sore throat. On examination, he is a thin but generally well appearing male. His vital signs are normal. Examination of his pharynx shows thick white plaques on the posterior pharynx and soft palate. On the skin of his chest are multiple oval-shaped purple or brown macules. They are firm on palpation and vary in size from 0.5 to 4 cm in length. Several of them appear to be growing together into larger, confluent plaques. You perform a punch biopsy of one of the lesions. In 5 days you get the pathology report with the diagnosis of Kaposi sarcoma.

- ◆ **With what virus is this patient likely infected?**
- ◆ **What specific cell types are most commonly infected with this virus? What cell surface receptor is the binding site of this virus?**
- ◆ **What serologic testing is most frequently performed to make this diagnosis?**

ANSWERS TO CASE 29: HUMAN IMMUNODEFICIENCY VIRUS

Summary: A 29-year-old man has weight loss, white plaques on the pharynx, and purple lesions on the abdomen, which on biopsy reveals Kaposi sarcoma.

- **Virus with which this patient is most likely infected:** Human immunodeficiency virus (HIV)
- **Specific cells infected by and binding site of HIV:** CD4 surface receptor protein on macrophages and T lymphocytes
- **Serologic testing to confirm diagnosis:** HIV enzyme-linked immunosorbent assay (ELISA) and Western-blot analysis, or PCR

CLINICAL CORRELATION

The HIV is a human retrovirus in the Lentivirinae subfamily. It is a spherical, enveloped RNA virus with a cone-shaped capsid that contains two copies of a positive-strand RNA genome. HIV infects cells of macrophage lineage and helper T cells by binding to the CD4 surface receptor protein on these target cells, resulting in fusion of the viral envelope with the cellular plasma membrane to gain entry. On entry into the host cell cytoplasm, an RNA-dependent DNA polymerase enzyme (reverse transcriptase), which is present in the viral capsid, uses the viral RNA to synthesize viral DNA. The viral DNA is transported to the host nucleus, where it is spliced into the host genome. The integrated viral DNA acts as a host cellular gene and is transcribed by host RNA polymerase II to produce new copies of viral RNA and proteins, which assemble into new HIV virions. HIV initially infects cells of macrophage lineage, but quickly reaches the lymph nodes where CD4 T cells are infected. The immunosuppression caused by HIV is primarily caused by a reduction in the helper and delayed type hypersensitivity responses mediated by CD4 T cells. Infected macrophages probably serve as reservoirs and means of distribution of HIV. HIV avoids the host immune system in several ways. Infection of macrophages and helper T cells inactivates central components of the host immune system. Also, HIV has an intrinsic genetic instability as a result of errors caused by reverse transcriptase which may contribute to an antigenic drift in the virus, resulting in reduced host immune system recognition. Symptomatic disease caused by HIV is proportionate to the loss of CD4 T cells and the resulting immune dysfunction. Acquired Immune Deficiency Syndrome (AIDS) is defined by the presence of HIV, a reduction of CD4 T cells, and the acquisition of characteristic opportunistic infections. Serologic diagnosis of HIV infection is primarily made by ELISA testing and, when this is positive, confirmation by Western blot analysis. Current HIV treatment involves using medications, individually or in combinations, which interfere with the actions of reverse transcriptase and block the proteases that activate the virion.

APPROACH TO HUMAN IMMUNODEFICIENCY VIRUS

Objectives

1. Know the structure and characteristics of the human immunodeficiency virus.
2. Know the mechanism by which HIV is transmitted, infects target cells, replicates, and causes immune deficiency.
3. Know the diagnosis, treatment, and opportunistic infections associated with AIDS.

Definitions

Retrovirus: An RNA virus. Retroviruses have an enzyme called reverse transcriptase that gives them the unique property of transcribing RNA into DNA. The retroviral DNA can then integrate into the chromosomal DNA of the host cell to be expressed there.

HAART: Highly active antiretroviral therapy. It is the treatment for human immunodeficiency virus (HIV) infection that uses a combination of several antiretroviral drugs. The drugs inhibit the ability of the virus to multiply in the body, and they slow down the development of AIDS.

AIDS: Acquired immunodeficiency syndrome. A cell-mediated immunity caused by infection by the HIV leading to depletion of CD4 helper T lymphocyte cells.

DISCUSSION

Characteristics of Human Immunodeficiency Virus

HIV appears to have been derived from primate (chimpanzee, especially) lentiviruses and are the etiologic cause of AIDS. AIDS was described in 1981, and the virus was isolated in 1983. AIDS is one of the most significant public health problems worldwide at the current time.

HIV is a **retrovirus** (reverse transcriptase or RNA-dependent DNA polymerase) in the **lentivirus subgroup.** It is a medium-sized virus (approximately 100 nm) with two copies of a positive-sense (same as messenger RNA [mRNA]) single-stranded RNA genome. This genome is the most complex of all retroviruses. The **lipid envelope contains glycoproteins** that undergo **antigenic variation,** making vaccine development difficult, if not impossible, at the present time. **Protease enzymes are coded for by the viral genome,** and these are required for the production of infectious viruses. The reverse transcriptase makes a double-stranded DNA copy (provirus) of the viral genomic RNA, which is incorporated into a host chromosome. The proviral DNA later serves as a template for viral mRNA's and new virion genomes. Virions bud from the plasma membrane of the host cell. Heterogeneous populations of viral genomes are found in an infected individual, especially the *env* gene, which codes for envelope glycoproteins. **The gp120 viral receptor** contains binding domains responsible for **viral attachment to the CD4 molecule** (host receptor) and coreceptors and determines cell tropisms (lymphocytes versus macrophages). These glycoproteins cause antibodies to be formed by the host and are only weakly neutralizing to the virus. The **gp41 product** contains a transmembrane domain that **anchors the glycoprotein in the viral envelope** and a **fusion domain** that facilitates viral entry into the target (host) cells. The virus is inactivated by treatment at room temperature for 10 minutes by any of the following: 10 percent bleach, 50 percent ethanol, 35 percent isopropanol, 0.5 percent paraformaldehyde, or 0.3 percent hydrogen peroxide. HIV in blood in a needle or syringe, however, requires exposure to undiluted bleach for 30–60 seconds for inactivation. Heating at 56°C (132.8°F) for 10 minutes (same as for complement inactivation) will inactivate HIV in 10 percent serum, but HIV in dried protein-containing mixtures is protected. Lyophilized blood products need to be heated to 68°C (154.4°F) for 72 hours to ensure inactivation of contaminating viruses.

Diagnosis

HIV infection can be diagnosed by virus isolation, detection of **antiviral antibodies,** or measurement of **viral nucleic acid or antigens.** HIV may be cultured from lymphocytes in peripheral blood primarily. Virus numbers vary greatly in an individual. The magnitude of plasma viremia is an excellent correlate of the clinical stage of HIV infection compared to the presence of antibodies. The most sensitive viral isolation technique requires cocultivation of the test sample with uninfected mitogen-stimulated peripheral blood mononuclear cells. Virus growth is usually detected in 7–14 days by measuring viral reverse transcriptase activity or virus-specific antigens. Virus isolation of HIV is usually considered a research technique, and most medical center viral diagnostic laboratories will not offer this service.

Antibody detection is the most common way to diagnose HIV infection. Seroconversion in HIV infection is generally found to occur in approximately 4 weeks. **Most individuals are seropositive within 6–12 weeks after infection,** and essentially all will be antibody positive in 6 months. Commercially available **enzyme-linked immunoassays** (EIA, ELISA) are routinely used as **screening tests.** If done properly, the reported sensitivity and specificity are at least 98 percent. Two separate EIA tests need to be positive for antibodies in the usual screening situation, and a confirmation test (Western blot usually) will be done to rule out EIA false-positives. **Western blot tests** (also commercially available) will usually detect antibodies to **viral core protein p24 or envelope glycoproteins gp41, gp120, or gp 160. An oral swab test is commonly used.**

Amplification assays (RT-PCR, DNA PCR. or bDNA tests) are used to detect viral RNA in clinical specimens. These tests may be quantitative when reference standards are used in each test. These molecular-based tests are very sensitive and form the basis for plasma viral load measurements. **HIV RNA levels** are important predictive markers of disease progression and monitors of the effectiveness of antiviral therapies.

Treatment and Prevention

Treatment of HIV infection uses classes of drugs that inhibit the virally-coded **reverse transcriptase** and inhibitors of the **viral protease enzymes.** Unfortunately, current treatments are biostatic, not virucidal. Therapy with combinations of antiretroviral drugs is called **highly active antiretroviral therapy** (HAART). It appears to lower viral replication below the limits of laboratory detection but is not curative. The virus persists in reservoirs of long-lived, latently infected cells. When HAART is discontinued, viral production rebounds. Monotherapy usually results in the rapid emergence of drug-resistant mutants of HIV. HAART therapy has turned HIV infection into a chronic, treatable disease. Unfortunately, large numbers of HIV-infected persons worldwide do not have access to the drugs.

A safe and effective vaccine would be the best hope for controlling HIV infection. Currently, many candidate vaccines are under development and in clinical trials. We have seen that viral vaccines are best when used in a preventative manner. Uninfected individuals are given the vaccine and develop antibodies that prevent infection or disease if the wild-type virus is encountered. HIV vaccine development is difficult because HIV mutates so rapidly. There appears to be so much variation in immune responses in HIV infections that no vaccine has been able to be protective to all individuals in a population. Nothing being currently developed appears to be close to approval in this area, although many organizations are working to produce an effective vaccine. A big hurdle for this, in part, is the lack of an appropriate and cost-effective laboratory animal model for HIV. The SIV-macaque model of simian AIDS is only partially useful for the development of a human HIV vaccine.

COMPREHENSION QUESTIONS

[29.1] During a medical check-up for a new insurance policy, a 60-year-old grandmother is found to be positive in the ELISA screening test for antibodies against HIV-1. She has no known risk factors for exposure to the virus. Which of the following is the most appropriate next step?

A. Immediately begin therapy with azidothymidine.
B. Perform the screening test a second time.
C. Request that a blood culture be done by the laboratory.
D. Tell the patient that she is likely to develop AIDS.
E. Test the patient for *Pneumocystis carinii* infection.

[29.2] In a person with HIV-1 infection, which of the following is the most predictive of the patient's prognosis?

A. CD4+ cell count
B. CD4:CD8 cell ratio
C. Degree of lymphadenopathy
D. Level of HIV-1 RNA in plasma
E. Rate of decline in anti-HIV antibody

[29.3] Highly active antiretroviral therapy against HIV infection includes one or more nucleoside analogue reverse transcriptase inhibitors in combination with representatives of which class of antiretroviral agents?

A. Inhibitors of viral binding
B. Inhibitors of viral protein processing
C. Inhibitors of viral release
D. Inhibitors of viral uncoating
E. Nonnucleoside antiretroviral agents

[29.4] Which of the following is the pathogen responsible for blindness in advanced HIV infections?

A. *Cytomegalovirus*
B. Epstein-Barr virus
C. Fungus
D. Toxoplasma

Answers

[29.1] **B.** Because HIV cannot be safely isolated and grown in the standard medical center diagnostic laboratory, diagnosis of HIV infections relies on detection of antibodies against the virus. The standard screening test is done by ELISA (enzyme-linked immunosorbent assay). ELISA test formats are quite reliable and accurate and can be used for antibody or antigen detection. By definition, however, screening tests are not 100 percent accurate for sensitivity and specificity. HIV infection, especially, is a tragic infection that requires utmost accuracy in laboratory diagnosis results to aid the physician in counseling the involved patient and family. Under the conditions described in Question 29.1, no known risk factors for HIV contact are claimed or identified. For this situation and any other requiring diagnostic laboratory testing for HIV infection, extra effort is taken to ensure accuracy and correct results. Because it is widely accepted that HIV ELISA screening is not 100 percent sensitive and specific (approximately 98 percent accurate, however), a second blood sample is collected for retesting by ELISA. If both ELISA results are positive, a second confirming test is done. This is usually a Western blot technique. If the Western blot test is positive, then HIV infection is confirmed and related to the patient.

[29.2] **D.** Amplification assays (RT-PCR, DNA PCR, and b DNA tests) are routinely used to detect viral RNA in clinical specimens. The tests can be quantitative when reference standards are used, and appropriate positive and negative controls must be included in each test. Because these molecular based tests are very sensitive, they form the basis for plasma viral load determinations. It is generally agreed that the amount of HIV in the blood (viral load) is of significant prognostic value. There are continual rounds of viral replication and cell killing in each patient, and the steady-state level of virus in the blood varies with individuals. A single measurement of plasma viral load approximately 6 months after infection can predict the risk of development of AIDS in men several years later. In women, viral load appears to be less predictive. The plasma viral load appears to be the best predictor of long-term clinical outcome, whereas CD4 lymphocyte counts are the best predictor of short-term risk of developing an opportunistic disease. Plasma viral load measurements are a critical element in assessing the effectiveness of antiretroviral drug therapy.

[29.3] **B.** A growing number of drugs have been approved for treatment of HIV infections. It must be remembered that all HIV drug treatments are only virostatic and not virucidal at this point in time. Classes of drugs include nucleoside and nonnucleoside inhibitors of the viral reverse transcriptase and inhibitors of the viral protease enzyme. The protease inhibitors are significant because protease activity is absolutely essential for production of infectious virus, and the viral enzyme is distinct from human cell proteases. These inhibitors (approved in 2003) block virus entry into host cells.

[29.4] **A.** The predominant causes of morbidity and mortality among patients with late-stage HIV infection are opportunistic infections. These are defined as severe infections induced by agents that rarely cause disease in immune-competent individuals. Opportunistic infections usually do not occur until CD4 T cell counts drop from normal (1000 cells per microliter) to less than 200 cells per microliter. The common opportunistic infections in untreated AIDS patients are caused by protozoa, fungi, bacteria, and other viruses. Coinfection with DNA viruses are reported to lead to enhanced expression of HIV in cells in vitro. Herpesvirus infections are common in AIDS patients, and cytomegalovirus (CMV) has been shown to produce a protein that acts as a chemokine receptor and is able to help HIV infect cells. CMV retinitis is the most common severe ocular complications of AIDS.

MICROBIOLOGY PEARLS

- HIV is a retrovirus and requires reverse transcriptase to make a double-stranded DNA copy of the viral genomic RNA.
- Antibody detection is the most common method of diagnosing an infection.
- The treatment of HIV largely depends on targeting viral reverse transcriptase and protease enzymes.

REFERENCES

Brooks GF, Butel JS, Morse SA, Jawetz, Melnick, & Adelberg's Medical Microbiology, 23rd ed. New York: McGraw-Hill, 2004:605–22.

Knipe DM, Howley PM. Fields Virology, 4th ed. Philadelphia, PA:Lippincott Williams and Wilkins, 2001:1971–2094.

Murray PR, Rosenthal KS, Pfaller MA. Medical Microbiology, 5th ed. St. Louis, MO: Mosby, 2005:657–74.

Ryan JR, Ray CG. Sherris Medical Microbiology, 4th ed. New York: McGraw-Hill, 2004:601–16.

❖ CASE 30

A 42-year-old woman presents to the physician's office for a routine gynecologic exam. She is feeling well and has no specific complaints at this visit. While reviewing your records, you see that she has not come in for a Papanicolaou (Pap) smear in approximately 5 years. She admits that she has not come in because she has been feeling fine and didn't think it was really necessary. She has a history of three pregnancies resulting in three full-term vaginal deliveries of healthy children. She was treated at the age of 22 for *Chlamydia*. She has never had an abnormal Pap smear. Her social history is notable for a one-pack per day smoking history for the past 25 years. She is divorced from her first husband and is sexually active with a live-in boyfriend for the past 3 years. She has had 7 sexual partners in her lifetime. Her examination today is normal. You perform a Pap smear as part of the examination. The report arrives 10 days later with the diagnosis "high-grade squamous intraepithelial lesion."

- **What is the most likely infectious etiology of this lesion?**

- **What specific virus types confer a high-risk of cervical neoplasia?**

- **Where on a cellular level does this organism tend to replicate in benign diseases? In malignancies?**

ANSWERS TO CASE 30: HUMAN PAPILLOMAVIRUS

Summary: A 42-year-old woman has high-grade squamous intraepithelial neoplasia on a Pap smear.

- **Most likely infectious etiology of this lesion:** Human papillomavirus (HPV)-related infection.
- **Specific virus types confer a high risk of cervical neoplasia:** HPV types 16 and 18 are most commonly associated with anogenital neoplasias.
- **Location of replication in benign diseases and malignancies:** The site of replication in benign HPV infections occurs in the host neoplasm where the viral DNA remains extrachromosomal. However, in HPV-related malignancies the viral DNA is integrated into the host genome.

CLINICAL CORRELATION

Human papillomavirus (HPV) preferentially infects the squamous epithelium of skin and mucous membranes causing epithelial proliferation and the development of cutaneous warts and genital, oral, and conjunctival papillomas. Although most HPV infections are benign, and most warts or lesions regress spontaneously with time, some HPV viral types have been shown to be linked to cervical and anogenital carcinomas (Table 30-1). Major risk factors for infection and progression to carcinomas include: multiple sexual partners, smoking, and immunosuppression.

Table 30-1

CLINICAL SYNDROMES AND THEIR ASSOCIATED HPV TYPES

CLINICAL SYNDROME	ASSOCIATED HPV TYPES
Cutaneous warts:	
Plantar wart	1
Common wart	2, 4
Flat wart	3, 10
Benign head & neck tumors:	
Laryngeal papilloma	6, 11
Oral papilloma	6, 11
Conjuncrival papilloma	11
Anogenital warts:	
Condyloma acuminatum	6, 11
Cervical intraepithelial neoplasia	16, 18

APPROACH TO SUSPECTED HPV INFECTION

Objectives

1. Know the characteristics of the HPV.
2. Know the mechanism of infection and strategies for prevention and treatment.

Definitions

Koilocytes: Enlarged keratinocytes with shrunken nuclei.
Poikilocytosis: Presence of perinuclear cytoplasmic vacuolization and nuclear enlargement of epithelial cells.
Papillomas: An epithelial neoplasm producing finger-like projections from the epithelial surface.
Condylomas: Epithelial neoplasm and hyperplasia of the skin, resulting in the formation of a large cauliflower-like mass.

DISCUSSION

Characteristics of HPV That Impact Transmission

HPV is a member of the **Papillomaviridae family.** Over 100 distinct types of HPV have been identified based on DNA sequence studies. It has **circular, double-stranded DNA genome** contained within a small, nonenveloped capsid. HPV has a predilection for infecting the squamous epithelium of skin and mucous membranes. HPV is transmitted from **person to person by direct contact, sexual intercourse,** or via **delivery through an infected birth canal.** As a nonenveloped virus, HPV is more environmentally resistant to acids, detergents, and desiccation, which allows for transmission via contaminated fomites.

HPV gains entry through breaks in the skin and **replicates in the basal cell layer** of the epithelium. HPV DNA is replicated, and the viral particles are assembled in the nucleus of epithelial cells with late viral gene expression occurring in the upper layers of differentiated keratinocytes. In **benign lesions,** such as **common skin warts,** the viral DNA **remains extrachromosomal in the nucleus of the infected epithelial cell.** However, more commonly in **carcinomas or high-grade intraepithelial lesions** viral DNA becomes **integrated into the host genome.** The viral genome encodes transforming genes, which have been shown to cause the inactivation of proteins that inhibit cellular growth, making infected cells more susceptible to mutation or other factors that may lead to the development of dysplasia and cancer.

HPV DNA, primarily **types 16 and 18,** has been shown to be present in more than 95 percent of cervical carcinoma specimens. Because of their high occurrence in cervical cancers, these HPV types are considered to be high-risk, whereas **HPV types 6 and 11 are considered low-risk** and many other HPV types are considered benign. Yet, because many HPV-related infections (even those with types 16 and 18) are benign with lesions that can regress spontaneously, the utility of characterizing specific HPV types in clinical specimens remains to be determined.

Diagnosis

HPV infection presents clinically with the growth of a variety of cutaneous warts and papillomas. Warts result from HPV replication stimulating **excessive growth** of the **epidermal layers above the basal layer** (Figure 30-1). The presence of koilocytotic squamous epithelial cells can be detected in a Pap smear. While the use of DNA probes and PCR can be used in diagnosis and in viral serotyping.

Different types of warts (flat, plantar, or common), genital condylomas, and laryngeal papillomas can develop depending on the infecting viral type and the site of infection. Laryngeal papillomas can occur in infants born to mothers with active HPV genital lesions. While rare, these papillomas often require repeated surgical removal. Anogenital warts occur on the squamous epithelium of the external genitalia and anorectum and are most commonly caused by HPV types 6 or 11, however, these lesions rarely undergo malignant transformation. HPV types 16 and 18 are responsible for most cases of cervical intraepithelial neoplasia and cancer. Cervical cancer usually develops after a progression of cellular changes from cellular atypia to low-grade intraepithelial lesion, high-grade intraepithelial lesion and subsequently to carcinoma. Although the mechanisms of host defenses against HPV are not well understood,

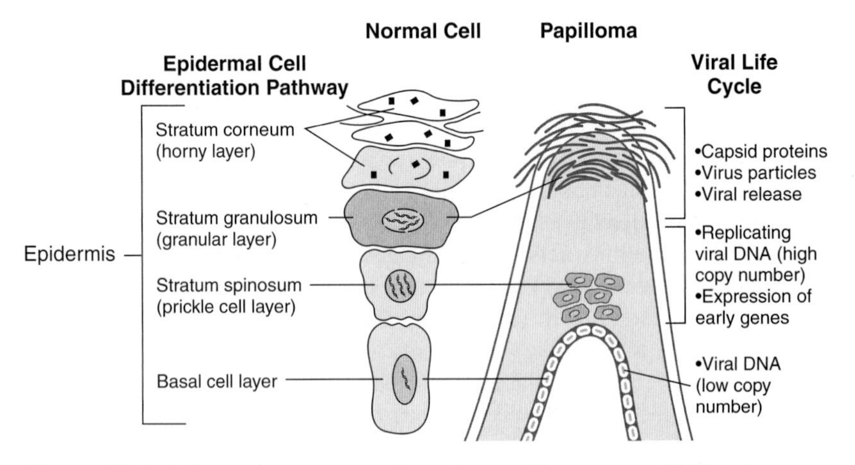

Figure 30-1. Schematic representation of a papilloma wart. HPV is incorporated in the basal layer and affects the maturing cells (left) and results in the skin wart or papilloma (right).

the immune system, especially cellular immunity, are important in the control of HPV infections. HPV diseases occur more frequently and tend to be more severe in immunocompromised hosts.

Treatment and Prevention

Although many HPV infections are benign with the resulting warts or lesions regressing spontaneously with time, because of the strong association of HPV with cervical carcinomas and transmission via vaginal delivery, physical treatment and removal of lesions is often performed. **Physical treatment** of warts and other lesions involves local cellular destruction by means of cryotherapy, acid application or electrocautery. Alternatively, **immune stimulant therapy** is used to promote immunologic clearance of the abnormal cells using either the injection of interferon or topical applications of imiquimod. Cervical cancer usually develops after a progression of cellular changes from cellular atypia to low-grade intraepithelial lesion, high-grade intraepithelial lesion, and subsequently to carcinoma. The introduction of routine screening of women for cervical cancer with Pap smears has resulted in finding more abnormalities in earlier, more treatable stages, and a marked reduction in the death rate from cervical cancer. Most deaths from cervical cancer now occur in women who have not had adequate Pap smear screening. A new qaudrivalent HPV vaccine, Gardasil, was FDA approved in 2006. The vaccine is composed of major capsid proteins assembled into virus-like particles and provides protection against infection with HPV types 6, 11, 16, and 18, which together cause 70 percent of cervical cancers (HPV 16 & 18) and 90 percent of genital warts (HPV 6 & 11). Additionally, infection with HPV can be prevented by avoiding direct contact with infected skin lesions, and by safe sex practices.

COMPREHENSION QUESTIONS

[30.1] Which of the following types of cancers is HPV most commonly associated with?

A. Anogenital
B. Breast
C. Lung
D. Oral
E. Prostate

[30.2] HPV-related cervical intraepithelial neoplasia can be diagnosed by the presence of which of the following histologic features?

A. Central, basophilic intranuclear cellular inclusions
B. Cowdry type A intranuclear cellular inclusions
C. Enlarged multinucleated cells
D. Cytoplasmic vacuolization and nuclear enlargement of cells
E. Numerous atypical lymphocytes

[30.3] Which of the following viral families is known to be causally associated with tumor formation in healthy appearing human adults?

A. Flaviviruses
B. Papovaviruses
C. Paramyxoviruses
D. Polyoma viruses

Answers

[30.1] **A.** Of the types of cancers listed, HPV is most commonly associated with anogenital carcinomas, which includes cervical carcinomas.

[30.2] **D.** HPV produces characteristic cytoplasmic vacuolization and nuclear enlargement of squamous epithelial cells, referred to as koilocytosis; answers A, B, C, and E are incorrect: Both Cowdry type A intranuclear inclusions and enlarged multinucleated cells can be seen with herpes simplex virus (HSV) and varicella-zoster virus (VZV) infections; central, basophilic intranuclear inclusion bodies are seen in CMV infections, whereas the presence of atypical lymphocytes is seen specifically in Epstein-Barr virus (EBV) infections.

[30.3] **B.** HPV is a member of the Papillomaviridae family and is causally associated with cervical cancer in otherwise healthy individuals; answers A, C, D, and E are incorrect: Hepatitis C virus is a member of the flaviviruses family and causes chronic hepatitis and in severe cases is a factor in liver cancer development; paramyxoviruses include agents such as respiratory syncytial virus and measles virus and are not associated with carcinomas; human polyoma viruses include BK and JC viruses, which have been associated with immunocompromised patients, and their role in formation of human tumors is still under investigation.

MICROBIOLOGY PEARLS

❖ HPV has a tropism for squamous epithelium of skin and mucous membranes.

❖ HPV types 16 and 18 are most commonly associated with cervical carcinomas.

❖ Treatment of HPV-related lesions include immunologic agents, cryotherapy, acid application, and electrocautery.

REFERENCES

Bosch FX, Lorincz A, Meijer CJ, et al. The causal relationship between human papillomavirus and cervical cancer. J Clin Pathol 2002;55:244.

Murray PR, Rosenthal KS, Pfaller MA. Medical Microbiology, 5th ed. St. Louis, MO: Mosby, 2005:523–4.

Ryan JR, Ray CG. Sherris Medical Microbiology, 4th ed. New York: McGraw-Hill, 2004:617–20.

National Institute of Allergy and Infectious Disease. Human papillomavirus. www.niaid.nih.gov/factsheets/stdhpv.htm

National Cancer Institute. About HPV vaccines. www.cancer.gov/cancertopics/hpv-vaccines

❖ CASE 31

A 4-year-old girl is brought in by her mother for the evaluation of multiple skin growths on her neck and upper chest. They have been present for a month or two. They are not pruritic or painful. The mother thinks that they are "pimples" because she squeezed a couple of them and some white material was expressed. She has been treating the lesions with an over-the-counter acne preparation, but it hasn't helped. The child has no significant medical history, takes no medications, and has no allergies. On examination you see multiple discrete, isolated 1–2-mm papules on her upper chest and lower neck. They are flesh colored, have a central umbilication, and feel firm on palpation. The remainder of her examination is normal. You suspect Molluscum contagiosum.

- **How did the girl most likely acquire this infection?**

- **What would you see microscopically on a stained slide of material expressed from the core of one of these lesions that would confirm your diagnosis?**

ANSWERS TO CASE 31: MOLLUSCUM CONTAGIOSUM

Summary: A 4-year-old girl with multiple discrete 1–2-mm papules on her upper chest and lower neck that are flesh colored, have a central umbilication, consistent with Molluscum contagiosum.

- **Most likely mechanism of acquisition of infection:** Direct contact with the virus or via contact with contaminated fomites.
- **Microscopic findings of expressed material confirming diagnosis:** Microscopic observation of the core material would show eosinophilic cytoplasmic inclusions, also known as molluscum bodies.

CLINICAL CORRELATION

Molluscum contagiosum is a poxvirus that causes benign cutaneous disease worldwide. It is transmitted via direct contact with infected cells or with objects contaminated with virus particles. It causes small wart-like growth on infected skin, and occurs more frequently in children than adults.

APPROACH TO SUSPECTED MOLLUSCUM CONTAGIOSUM INFECTION

Objectives

1. Be aware of the characteristics of the poxvirus.
2. Be able to describe the mechanism of infection and strategies for prevention and treatment.

Definitions

Molluscum bodies: Eosinophilic cytoplasmic inclusions seen in epidermal cells infected with Molluscum contagiosum.
Umbilicated lesions: Lesions with cup-shaped crater and a white core.
Papules: Lesions that are raised and well circumscribed.

DISCUSSION

Characteristics of Molluscum Contagiosum That Impact Transmission

Poxviruses are among the **largest, most complex viruses known.** They have a linear, **double-stranded DNA genome** that is fused at both ends. The virion binds to a cell surface receptor and enters the target cell by fusion of the outer envelope with the cell membrane. Replication of poxviruses occurs entirely in the host cytoplasm, making them unique among DNA viruses and requiring them to provide all enzymes necessary for viral replication. For example, poxviruses encode proteins for mRNA synthesis, DNA synthesis, nucleotide scavenging, and immune escape mechanisms. Viral DNA replication and virion assembly occurs in **cytoplasmic inclusions** called **Guarnieri inclusions.** The newly assembled virions are released on cell lysis.

Because the worldwide eradication of smallpox has been documented, **Molluscum contagiosum is the only poxvirus specific for humans.** Viral inoculation occurs through small skin abrasions, either from direct contact with infectious particles or via contaminated fomites. The **incubation period** for Molluscum contagiosum infection is approximately **2 weeks to 6 months.** Some documented forms of viral spread include direct contact with lesions during **wrestling matches, in swimming pools,** sharing of **towels,** and **sexual contact.** Molluscum contagiosum infection is more common in children than in adults, and in adults it is most often transmitted by sexual contact. Immunocompromised persons who are infected with Molluscum contagiosum may develop hundreds of lesions. Patients who are at greatest risk for this presentation are those with late-stage AIDS, with a CD4 count <200 cells/μL.

Diagnosis

Molluscum contagiosum clinically causes discrete, **flesh-colored papules with a central umbilication.** These nodular lesions most commonly form in groups of 5–25 occurring on the trunk, genitalia, and extremities. They are also known to cause **"kissing lesions"** via direct contact of a lesion with an uninfected area of skin on the same host; such as a lesion on the lateral chest may cause a "kissing lesion" on the inner arm. The semisolid core of these lesions can be expressed and examined **microscopically** for the presence of **large, eosinophilic inclusions, known as molluscum bodies.**

Treatment and Prevention

The lesions of Molluscum contagiosum generally develop within 2–3 months of contact and usually resolve within 1–2 years. Cell-mediated and humoral immunity both appear to be important for disease resolution. When indicated, the lesions can be removed by **curettage, electrocautery, or liquid nitrogen** applications.

COMPREHENSION QUESTIONS

[31.1] The incidence of Molluscum contagiosum as a sexually transmitted disease is increasing in young adults and results in the formation of small wart-like lesions in the genital region. Which of the following viruses might also be suspected in such a case of sexually acquired lesions?

A. Cytomegalovirus
B. Varicella-zoster virus
C. Human papillomavirus
D. Human immunodeficiency virus

[31.2] Which of the following statements best describes the viral characteristics of Molluscum contagiosum?

A. A large and complex virus containing single-stranded linear RNA
B. A double-stranded DNA virus encoding a DNA-dependent RNA polymerase
C. A double-stranded linear DNA virus that integrates into the chromosome
D. A single-stranded DNA virus that replicates in the host cytoplasm
E. A double-stranded circular DNA virus

[31.3] A sexually active 17-year-old man presents to the local free clinic to check some small papules that appeared on his penis. The papules are small and white and contain a central depression in their center. There is no penile discharge, nor is there pain on urination. To what group is the organism most likely associated with?

A. Poxviridae
B. Papovaviridae
C. Adenoviridae
D. Parvoviridae
E. Arenaviridae

Answers

[31.1] **C.** Human papillomavirus; answers A, B, and D are incorrect; cytomegalovirus is known as a sexually transmitted disease but does not characteristically form lesions in or around the genitalia; varicella-zoster virus does form vesicular lesions but appears clinically as a vesicular rash of the head, trunk, or extremities in a dermatomal pattern, not as a genital infection; human immunodeficiency virus is also known to be transmitted via sexual contact, yet it manifests clinically primarily through suppression of the host immune response, not through the formation of genital lesions.

[31.2] **B.** Molluscum contagiosum is a poxvirus and therefore is a double-stranded DNA virus encoding a DNA-dependent RNA polymerase; answers A, C, D, and E are incorrect: (A) describes the characteristics of rabies virus; (C) more appropriately describes herpes simplex viruses; (D) poxviruses do replicate in the host cytoplasm, and Molluscum contagiosum is a double-stranded DNA virus; (E) more appropriately describes human papillomaviruses.

[31.3] **A.** The disease in question is Molluscum contagiosum, which belongs to the Poxviridae and is characterized by small white papules with a central umbilication usually found in the genital region; answers B, C, D, and E are incorrect: (B) Papovaviridae include human papillomavirus and BK, JC polyomavirus, and although HPV causes genital warts, they do not have the central umbilication present in Molluscum contagiosum; (C) Adenoviridae include a variety of viral serotypes which cause respiratory, ocular, and gastrointestinal diseases; (D) Parvoviridae include erythema infectiosum characterized by the slapped cheek appearance; (E) Arenaviridae include lymphocytic choriomeningitis and Lassa virus, which are not described in the question stem.

MICROBIOLOGY PEARLS

- Molluscum contagiosum is a poxvirus transmitted via direct contact with infected cells, sharing of towels, or via sexual contact.
- Clinical manifestations are small flesh colored umbilicated lesions occurring on the trunk, extremities, or genitalia.
- Lesions will resolve spontaneously over time, or can be removed via scraping or treatment with liquid nitrogen.

REFERENCES

Brooks GF, Butel JS, Morse SA. Jawetz, Melnick, & Adelberg's Medical Microbiology, 23rd ed. New York: McGraw-Hill, 2004:463–4.

Murray PR, Rosenthal KS, Pfaller MA. Medical Microbiology, 5th ed. St. Louis, MO: Mosby, 2005:523–4.

Ryan JR, Ray CG. Sherris Medical Microbiology, 4th ed. New York: McGraw-Hill, 2004:528–9.

CASE 32

A 6-year-old boy is brought to your office for evaluation of fever, ear pain, and swollen cheeks. His mother reports that he's had 3 or 4 days of low-grade fever and seemed tired. Yesterday he developed the sudden onset of ear pain and swelling of the cheeks along with a higher fever. He is an only child, and neither of the parents has been ill recently. He has had no significant medical illnesses in his life, but his parents decided not to give him the measles, mumps, rubella (MMR) vaccine because they read that it could cause autism. On examination, his temperature is 38.6°C (101.5°F), and his pulse is 105 beats per minute. He has swollen parotid glands bilaterally to the point that his earlobes are pushed up, and the angle of his mandible is indistinct. His tympanic membranes appear normal. Opening his mouth causes pain, but the posterior pharynx appears normal. You do note some erythema and swelling of Stensen duct. He has bilateral cervical adenopathy.

What is the cause of this child's illness?

◆ **What factor has reduced the incidence of this disease by over 99 percent in the United States?**

ANSWERS TO CASE 32: MUMPS

Summary: A 6-year-old boy has tender inflammation of the parotid glands (parotitis) and fever.

 **Most likely cause of this child's disease:** Mumps virus

◆ **Factor decreasing disease incidence by over 99 percent in the United States:** Routine vaccination with live, attenuated mumps virus

CLINICAL CORRELATION

The mumps virus is primarily a childhood disease that causes acute, painful swelling of the parotids and other glands. It is a highly communicable disease that has one known serotype and infects only humans. Mumps is endemic around the world, with approximately 90 percent of children being infected by the age of 15. It is now an uncommon illness in countries such as the United States, where a live attenuated vaccine is widely used. The MMR vaccine, a combination vaccine of measles, mumps, and rubella, has resulted in a greater than 99 percent reduction in the incidence of mumps. Almost all cases of mumps now seen are in the unvaccinated or in persons with depressed cellular immunity.

APPROACH TO SUSPECTED MUMPS VIRUS INFECTION

Objectives

1. Be able to describe the characteristics of the mumps virus.
2. Be able to describe the strategies for prevention and treatment of the infection.

Definitions

Parotitis: Inflammation of the parotids; large salivary glands located on each side of the face below and in front of the ear.

Hemagglutinin-neuraminidase protein: A viral capsid glycoprotein involved with viral attachment, fusion, and enzymatic hydrolysis of various proteins; also produces nonspecific agglutination of red blood cells used for diagnostic assay.

Orchitis: Inflammation of the testes.

Oophoritis: Inflammation of one or both ovaries.

DISCUSSION

Characteristics of the Mumps Virus That Impact Transmission

The mumps virus is a member of the family **Paramyxoviridae.** As a paramyxovirus, it is an **enveloped, virus with a single-stranded, negative-sense RNA genome.** The viral envelope contains two glycoproteins: a **hemagglutinin-neuraminidase protein** involved in attachment and a **membrane fusion protein.** The mumps virus is transmitted to epithelial cells of the mouth or nose via direct contact with contaminated respiratory droplets or saliva or via fomites. The virus then fuses with the host cell membrane via the specific viral attachment and surface fusion proteins, which results in binding to sialic acid on the target cell membrane. Transcription, replication, protein synthesis, and assembly occur in the cytoplasm of the host cell. Newly formed virions acquire their outer envelope by budding through the host cell membrane and are released to infect other host cells. After initial infection and replication in the nasal or upper respiratory tract, viral infection spreads to the salivary glands. Virus infects the **parotids or other salivary glands** either by ascending infection into the gland through Stensen duct or by viremia. Viral particles are also transmitted to distant organs, such as the kidneys, testes, ovaries, and central nervous system (CNS) through viremic spread.

The symptoms of mumps are often the result of the inflammatory response of the host immune system. Many mumps infections are subclinical, and this, along with the fact that infected persons are contagious even 1–2 weeks prior to developing symptoms, promotes person-to-person spread of the disease. The cell-mediated immune system is responsible for defense against this infection and acquired immunity is lifelong. Passive immunity is transferred from mothers to newborns, and thus, mumps is rarely seen in infants less than 6 months old.

Diagnosis

Cases of mumps are now relatively uncommon, but can be diagnosed primarily by clinical presentation along with a patient history that lacks mumps virus immunization. Clinical symptoms include acute onset of **fever and malaise, followed with painful bilateral or unilateral swelling of the parotid or other salivary glands.** Ten to twenty percent of cases may progress to more severe infections with CNS involvement, resulting in aseptic meningitis or meningoencephalitis. In adolescent children and adults, additional complications may occur including: orchitis, oophoritis, and pancreatitis. These more severe symptoms are rarer and occur primarily in immunocompromised hosts.

Laboratory diagnosis is not typically required; however, rapid confirmation of mumps infection can be obtained through direct **viral antigen detection** via immunofluorescence analysis. Appropriate clinical samples for analysis include saliva, CSF, and urine. Alternately, serology can be used to detect a fourfold rise in mumps-specific IgM or IgG antibody in clinical samples. Also, clinical specimens can be cultured in cells for observation of cytopathic effects such as cell rounding and syncytia formation.

Treatment and Prevention

Though mumps is usually self-limiting, it is treated with supportive care: fluids, rest, anti-inflammatories. Patients with mumps or suspected mumps should be isolated for up to a week after symptoms begin or until infection is ruled out. There is no specific antiviral therapy for mumps. However, immunization with the live attenuated mumps virus vaccine provides effective protection against infection.

COMPREHENSION QUESTIONS

[32.1] A 6-year-old child presents to their pediatrician with symptoms of fever, fatigue, and swollen glands. Which of the following patient information would confirm a diagnosis of infection with the mumps virus?

A. A history of exposure to mumps
B. Clinical evidence of orchitis
C. Detection of mumps-specific IgM antibody
D. Resolution of fever followed by signs of encephalitis

[32.2] Which of the following statement regarding infection with the mumps virus is correct?

A. After initial replication, viremic spread can occur to various organs.
B. Diagnosis is made solely on symptoms, as virus cannot be cultured.
C. Passive immunization is the only means of preventing infection.
D. Reinfection is possible, because of the presence of two viral serotypes.
E. Virus is transmitted via the fecal-oral route.

[32.3] Which of the following organs would most commonly exhibit signs of mumps infection?

A. CNS
B. Ovaries
C. Pancreas
D. Parotids
E. Testes

Answers

[32.1] **C.** The detection of mumps-specific IgM antibody indicates active mumps virus infection; answers A, B, D, and E are incorrect; (A) exposure to mumps does not necessarily cause infection, particularly if the child has been immunized; (B) symptoms of orchitis because of mumps infection occurs only in adolescent males; (D) encephalitis is a more rare complication of mumps infection and is not specific to the mumps virus.

[32.2] **A.** After initial replication in the upper respiratory tract and salivary glands, viral particles are also transmitted to distant organs such as the kidneys, testes, ovaries, and CNS through viremic spread; answers B, C, D and E are incorrect.

[32.3] **D.** Swollen parotid glands are a common symptom during infection with the mumps virus; answers A, B, C, and E are possible complications of infection with the mumps virus, but are less commonly occurring.

MICROBIOLOGY PEARLS

- Nearly all cases of mumps are seen in unvaccinated children or persons with depressed cellular immunity.
- Clinical manifestations: acute fever and painful swelling of the parotids and other glands.
- Immunization with a live attenuated mumps virus vaccine has resulted in nearly 100 percent reduction in the incidence of infection.

REFERENCES

Brooks GF, Butel JS, Morse SA. Jawetz, Melnick, & Adelberg's Medical Microbiology, 23rd ed. New York: McGraw-Hill, 2004:560–2.

Ryan JR, Ray CG. Sherris Medical Microbiology, 4th ed. New York: McGraw-Hill, 2004:513.

Centers For Disease Control and Prevention. Vaccines and preventable diseases: mumps vaccines. http://www.cdc.gov/vaccines/vpd-vac/mumps/default.htm.

CASE 33

An 8-year-old boy is brought in to the physician's office with a 3-day history of fever and a rash. He has also had a mild sore throat and felt somewhat fatigued. His mother is concerned that he could have "scarlet fever." The rash started on his face and then spread to his arms and legs. He has only been given acetaminophen for the fever. He takes no other medications, has no known allergies, has no significant medical history, and has had no contact with anyone known to be ill. On examination, his temperature is 37.7°C (99.8°F), and his other vital signs are normal. His cheeks are notably red, almost as if they had been slapped. His pharynx is normal appearing, and the remainder of his head and neck exam is normal. On his extremities there is a fine, erythematous, maculopapular rash but no vesicles or petechiae. A rapid group A streptococcal antigen test done in the office is negative.

 **What virus is the likely cause of this illness?**

◆ **In which human cells does this virus cause lytic infections?**

ANSWERS TO CASE 33: PARVOVIRUSES

Summary: An 8-year-old boy with fever and "slapped cheek" appearance has erythema infectiosum or fifth disease.

- **Most likely viral cause of this illness:** Infection with parvovirus B19
- **Human cells in which the virus causes lytic infections:** Mitotically active erythroid precursor cells

CLINICAL CORRELATION

Parvovirus B19 is the only parvovirus known to cause disease in humans. Infection occurs typically in school-age children resulting in a mild febrile upper respiratory illness followed by an exanthematous rash on the face or "slapped cheek" appearance which later spreads to the extremities. It is classically described as fifth disease because it was the fifth childhood exanthem to be described after varicella, rubella, roseola, and measles. Adults are less commonly infected, and primarily present with polyarthritis of the hands, knees, and ankles, occurring with or without rash. Chronic infection occurs in immunodeficient patients with more serious consequences, such as severe anemia and aplastic crisis. Additionally, infection occurring in pregnant seronegative mothers can lead to serious infection and fetal death.

APPROACH TO SUSPECTED PARVOVIRAL INFECTION

Objectives

1. Be able to describe the characteristics of the virus.
2. Be able to describe the strategies for prevention and treatment of the infection.

Definitions

Exanthem: An eruptive disease or eruptive fever appearing on the skin.
Enanthem: An eruptive disease appearing on mucous membranes.
Petechiae: Tiny reddish or purplish spots containing blood and appearing on the skin or mucous membranes.
Hydrops fetalis: Serious edema of the fetus which can result in congestive heart failure.
Erythroid progenitor cells: Precursors to erythrocytes.

DISCUSSION

Characteristics of Parvovirus That Impact Transmission

Parvoviruses are small, **nonenveloped viruses with a linear, single-stranded DNA** genome. They are the **smallest of the DNA animal viruses,** and their virions contain either a positive- or negative-sense copy of the viral genome. Parvovirus B19 belongs to the **Parvoviridae family** and is the only parvovirus known to cause human disease. It is spread from **person to person by respiratory and oral secretions,** replicating first in the nasopharynx, then spreading by viremia to the bone marrow. It binds to the **erythrocyte blood group P antigen on erythroid precursor cells** and is internalized through coated pits. After internalization, the viral DNA is uncoated and transported to the nucleus, where a complementary DNA strand is created by the host DNA polymerase. Inverted repeat sequences on the 5′ and 3′ ends of the viral DNA genome fold back and hybridize to provide a primer for the initiation of DNA replication. The resultant double-stranded viral DNA is then further replicated and transcribed via host cell machinery, and newly formed virions are assembled in the nucleus. Additionally, other factors only available in the S phase of mitosis are required for parvoviral replication. The newly assembled infectious particles are then released by lysis of the host nuclear and cytoplasmic membranes, resulting in cell death. The major site for parvoviral replication is in adult bone marrow and fetal liver cells. Because replication in these cells results in cell lysis and death, there is a **disruption of red cell production and resultant anemia** that occurs with viral infection.

Clinical symptoms caused by parvovirus B19 are related to the immune system response to the infection. The most common clinical illness associated with parvovirus B19 is **erythema infectiosum, or fifth disease.** It is commonly seen in children and usually causes a biphasic infection with mild upper respiratory symptoms, low-grade or no fever, and a rash. The initial stage lasts for approximately 1 week and involves the infection and killing of erythroid cells followed by viremic spread. This stage is the infectious stage and produces flu-like symptoms with mild fever and upper-respiratory symptoms. The second stage of infection is immune-mediated, with the formation of host antibody-virus immune complexes, a reduction in viremia, and the emergence of a spreading lacy skin rash and/or anthralgias. The rash usually starts on the face and is classically described as causing a **"slapped cheek"** appearance. A maculopapular rash will then frequently develop on the extremities. Adults may get a rash, but more often develop arthralgias or frank arthritis. The production of rash, arthralgias, and arthritis are all results of circulating antibody-virus immune complexes. These symptoms are usually self-limited. Yet, persistent infections can occur in immune-compromised hosts who fail to produce virus-neutralizing antibodies, because host antibody-mediated immunity is necessary for defense against the infection and prevention of reinfections.

More rare but potentially life-threatening complications of parvovirus B19 infection can occur. **Aplastic crisis** can occur in hosts with a chronic hemolytic anemia, such as **sickle cell disease** or other acquired hemolytic anemias. In this setting, the combination of viral replication in red cell precursors along with the reduced circulatory life span of existing red cells may result in a profound anemia. Additionally, parvoviral B19 infection in immunodeficient patients can result in persistent infections with chronic bone marrow suppression and anemia. There is also an increased risk of fetal loss because of anemia caused by **transplacental infection of the fetus** when a seronegative mother becomes infected during pregnancy. Fetal parvoviral infection can result in hydrops fetalis, severe anemia, and often, fetal death before the third trimester. The fetus of a seropositive mother is protected from infection by maternal circulating antibodies.

Diagnosis

Diagnosis is primarily made from clinical presentation. While definitive diagnosis of parvovirus B19 infection relies on the detection of **viral DNA** via **PCR or DNA hybridization** assays using patient serum, blood or tissue samples. Additionally, **serologic detection of viral IgM or IgG antibodies** via ELISA (enzyme-linked immunosorbent assay) can be used for diagnoses.

Treatment and Prevention

At present, there is **no specific treatment** for parvovirus B19 infections. Infection control measures are used in hospitals to avoid parvoviral spread, such as rigorous hand washing and isolation of infected patients. Although vaccines are available for dogs and cats, there is currently no parvoviral B19 vaccine available for humans.

COMPREHENSION QUESTIONS

[33.1] Which of the following statements is most accurate regarding infection with parvovirus B19?

A. Parvovirus B19 replicates in the host cell nucleus utilizing a virally encoded DNA polymerase to create a double-stranded DNA intermediate.

B. Parvovirus B19 causes severe anemia because it preferentially infects erythrocyte precursors.

C. Parvovirus B19 can be diagnosed by detection of viral RNA using PCR or hybridization assays.

D. Parvovirus B19 can cause hydrops fetalis via transplacental infection of a fetus in a seropositive mother.

E. Parvovirus B19 is transmitted primarily by fecal-oral transmission and is highly prevalent in infants and young children.

[33.2] A normally healthy 7-year-old girl is sent home from school with a suspected case of fifth disease as a result of her presenting with the initial symptoms of the infection. After being at home for a few days, her symptoms change indicating her transition into the second phase of the illness. Which of the following symptoms is the girl most likely experiencing during the second phase of parvoviral infection?

A. Aplastic crisis
B. Diarrhea
C. High fever
D. Skin rash
E. Swollen glands

[33.3] Which of the following conditions would put an individual at increased risk for serious chronic illness following an infection with parvovirus B19?

A. Immunization with a live measles vaccine
B. Having sickle cell disease
C. Caring for a pet with canine parvoviral infection
D. Coinfection with influenza A virus
E. Not being immunized for poliovirus

Answers

[33.1] **B.** Parvovirus B19 binds preferentially to the erythrocyte blood group P antigen on erythroid precursor cells; answers A, B, C, and E are incorrect: (A) after entry the single-stranded viral DNA genome is transported to the cell nucleus where the host DNA polymerase synthesizes the complimentary DNA strand; (C) Parvovirus B19 infection can be diagnosed by direct detection of viral DNA not RNA; (D) the fetus of a seropositive mother is protected from infection by maternal circulating antibodies; (E) Parvovirus B19 is transmitted primarily by respiratory secretions and is prevalent in school-age children.

[33.2] **D.** The second stage of parvoviral B19 infection is immune-mediated, and results in formation of a lacy skin rash occurring first on the face and then moves to the extremities; answers A, B, C, and E are incorrect: (A) aplastic crisis occurs in hosts with sickle cell disease or other acquired hemolytic anemias, not in normally healthy individuals; (B) parvoviral infection does not cause gastrointestinal symptoms; (C) mild fever, not high fever, is a symptom that occurs in the initial stage of fifth disease; (E) parvoviral infection does not result in swollen glands.

[33.3] **B.** More serious complications of parvoviral B19 infection, such as aplastic crisis, can occur in hosts with sickle cell disease or other chronic hemolytic anemias; answers A, C, D, and E are incorrect as they are not associated with serious complications of parvovirus B19 infection.

MICROBIOLOGY PEARLS

- Parvovirus B19 is the smallest human DNA virus and replicates in mitotically active erythroid progenitor cells.
- Clinical manifestations in children: mild fever followed by rash with "slapped cheek" appearance; fetal infections: hydrops fetalis and death.
- Clinical manifestations in adults: polyarthritis of hands, knees, and ankles with or without rash; chronic infection may result in chronic anemia or aplastic crisis.
- No specific treatment or vaccination.

REFERENCES

Brooks GF, Butel JS, Morse SA. Jawetz, Melnick, & Adelberg's Medical Microbiology, 23rd ed. New York: McGraw-Hill, 2004:414–9.

Heegaard ED, Hornsleth A. Parvovirus: the expanding spectrum of disease. Acta Paediatr 1995;84:109–17.

Ryan JR, Ray CG. Sherris Medical Microbiology, 4th ed. New York: McGraw-Hill, 2004:522–3.

CASE 34

A 62-year-old man presents to the emergency room after suddenly losing the use of his right leg. He reports that he had a few days of headache, fever, and sore throat, which was treated with oral antibiotics and resolved approximately 4 days ago. He was feeling fine until this morning, when he could not lift his right leg to get out of bed. All of his other limbs are functioning normally, and he has normal sensation in them. He has a medical history significant for lung cancer for which he is receiving chemotherapy, with his most recent cycle having been completed a few days prior to the onset of his febrile illness. He denies having any recent falls, injuries, current headache, or neurologic symptoms other than in the right leg. He has not traveled outside of the United States. His only current medication is amoxicillin/clavulanic acid, which was prescribed for his recent febrile illness. He lives with his son, daughter-in-law, and two young grandchildren. The children are healthy, and each had their routine well-child checkups and vaccinations about a month ago, including an oral vaccine. On examination, he is anxious appearing but has normal vital signs and has unremarkable head and neck, cardiovascular, pulmonary, and abdominal examinations. He has flaccid paralysis with normal sensation of the right leg, with normal movement and strength in all other extremities and a normal cranial nerve examination. A head CT scan and lumbar magnetic resonance imaging (MRI) are also normal.

- **What is the most likely infectious cause of this man's flaccid paralysis?**

- **Assuming that he was infected at home, what is the most likely source of his infection?**

ANSWERS TO CASE 34: POLIOVIRUS

Summary: A 62-year-old man with flaccid paralysis of the right leg. He lives with his grandchildren, who were recently given an oral vaccine.

- **Most likely infectious cause of this man's flaccid paralysis:** Poliomyelitis, caused by poliovirus.

- **Most likely source of his infection:** Fecal-oral transmission of viral particles shed from one of his grandchildren recently vaccinated with live attenuated poliovirus vaccine.

CLINICAL CORRELATION

Poliovirus is an exclusive human pathogen, which causes an acute infectious disease that can result in flaccid paralysis from the destruction of motor neurons in the spinal cord. Although most childhood infections tend to be subclinical, the risk of more serious paralytic disease increases with age. Infections are spread through fecal-oral transfer and poor sanitation and crowded conditions help to promote viral spread. Both attenuated live (orally administered) and inactivated poliomyelitis (injected) viral vaccines have been available for over 40 years, and most industrialized countries have been free from wild poliovirus infections since the late 1990s or early 2000s. Use of the killed-virus vaccine for childhood immunizations is currently recommended in the United States because of safety issues with the live-attenuated vaccine, including possible transfer of live virus to close contacts. Efforts are being continued to globally eradicate poliovirus from residual areas such as Africa and India.

APPROACH TO SUSPECTED POLIOVIRUS INFECTION

Objectives

1. Be able to describe the characteristics of the virus.
2. Be able to describe the strategies for prevention and treatment of the infection.

Definitions

Poliomyelitis: Inflammation and destruction of the gray matter of the spinal cord, which can result in paralysis.

Attenuated live poliovirus vaccine or oral polio vaccine (OPV): A viral vaccine consisting of a less virulent form of poliovirus, obtained through multiple passages of three types of poliovirus through tissue culture cells.

Inactivated poliomyelitis vaccine (IPV): A viral vaccine consisting of a large dose of viral antigen that will elicit a protective antibody response without risk of spreading the infection.

DISCUSSION

Characteristics of Poliovirus That Impact Transmission

Poliovirus is a member of the **enterovirus genus of the Picornaviridae family.** It is a **small, nonenveloped virus with a single-stranded, positive-sense RNA genome** that resembles cellular mRNA. It is contained within an icosahedral capsid composed of four polypeptides (VP1-VP4) that are necessary for maintaining virion structure, attachment to specific host cell receptors, and entry into cells. The viral genome contains a small protein at the 5′ end, termed VPg, and is polyadenylated at the 3′ end. The genome is transcribed into a single polyprotein that is proteolytically cleaved to produce all of the virally encoded proteins. One of these proteins is a viral protease, which specifically degrades the 5′ cap proteins from cellular mRNAs and thus preferentially inhibits translation of host mRNA. The 5′ viral VPg protein promotes cap-independent association of the poliovirus genome with host cell ribosomes and allows translation of viral proteins to occur. Polioviruses are **cytolytic** and cause direct damage to infected cells.

As with other *enteroviruses,* poliovirus is transmitted primarily by the **fecal-oral route.** Viral particles enter through the mouth and primary replication is thought to occur in the oropharynx, tonsils, and lymph nodes or in the intestinal epithelium and adjacent lymphoid tissue. The virus is resistant to a wide range of pH levels, allowing it to survive the acidity of the stomach. Depending on the host immune response and the ability of the virus to spread, infection with poliovirus can result in one of four different types of infection: asymptomatic illness, abortive poliomyelitis, nonparalytic poliomyelitis, or paralytic poliomyelitis. After initial viral replication, an immune competent host will make specific antibodies to the virus, and if the infection is limited to this stage the infection remains asymptomatic. Host antibodies provide the major immune response to poliovirus infections. However, if infection is not contained by the host antibody response, there may be a "minor" viremic spread to cells containing a specific receptor recognized by the capsid VP proteins. The specificity of poliovirus infection via these receptors restricts the tropism for poliovirus to cells such as the **anterior horn cells of the spinal cord, dorsal root ganglia, motor neurons, skeletal muscle cells, and lymphoid cells.**

After binding to the receptor, the RNA genome is inserted into the host cytoplasm through a channel created in the cell membrane. Viral transcription and replication occur in the cytoplasm, and new virions are released by cell lysis. Replication in these cells can then lead to a "major" viremia that, when controlled by host antibody response, produces the "minor" illness of abortive poliomyelitis. Abortive poliomyelitis causes nonspecific symptoms that include fever, sore throat, and headache. In a small percentage of infected people, the virus may continue to spread to involve the central nervous system (CNS) or the meninges. This can occur either as a result of viremic dissemination or ascending infection through peripheral nerves into the CNS. This can then result in nonparalytic poliomyelitis, aseptic meningitis, or, when anterior horn cells of the spinal cord or motor cortex are involved, paralytic poliomyelitis. Paralytic poliomyelitis is the least common complication of poliovirus infection and appears less than a week following initial symptoms of abortive poliomyelitis. Paralytic disease is caused by cytolytic damage caused by the virus, not by the immune response.

Diagnosis

In addition to the presentation of the above clinical findings, a suspected poliovirus infection can be diagnosed by the **recovery and culture of the virus from clinical samples.** The best clinical specimens include throat swabs if collected shortly after the onset of infection or rectal swabs and stool specimens collected up to 30 days post onset. Cells inoculated with poliovirus will show cytopathic effects of viral infection in less than a week of culture. Even when there is CNS and meningeal involvement, poliovirus is rarely recovered from CNS fluid. RT-PCR can also be used to detect RNA sequences in tissues and body fluids, increasing the sensitivity and speed of diagnosis.

Treatment and Prevention

Universal vaccination has eliminated wild-type polio from the western hemisphere and has greatly reduced the incidence of the disease worldwide. Two vaccine types exist—a **live, attenuated virus vaccine given orally** and an **inactivated vaccine given by injection.** The live, attenuated virus vaccine has the advantages of creating a secretory antibody in the gastrointestinal (GI) tract and is easily administered. However, viral shedding in the stool of the vaccinated person does occur and has been a source of polio infections during the era of widespread vaccination. In very rare cases, the polio vaccine caused disease either in the vaccinated individual or a close, usually immunocompromised, contact. Because of this, the current recommendation in the United States is to give only the inactivated vaccine, which induces humoral antibodies, but does not carry the risk of vaccine-induced disease. A primary series of four inoculations is recommended within a 1–2 year period, with periodic boosters administered as necessary later in life. However, the inactivated vaccine does not induce local intestinal immunity, allowing poliovirus to still replicate in the GI tract.

COMPREHENSION QUESTIONS

[34.1] Which of the following statements best describes an advantage of the oral polio vaccine when compared to the inactivated poliomyelitis vaccine?

A. It can be administered to immunocompromised patients.
B. It is not associated with vaccine-related cases of poliomyelitis.
C. It induces local intestinal immunity.
D. It is easily administered as a series of multiple injections.
E. It can be given to young children with other scheduled immunizations.

[34.2] The primary pathologic effect of polioviral infection is a result of which of the following?

A. Destruction of infected cells
B. Paralysis of muscle cells
C. Immune complex formation
D. Aseptic meningitis
E. Persistent viremia

[34.3] The majority of nonimmunized patients infected with poliovirus would be expected to experience which of the following symptoms?

A. Flu-like illness
B. Aseptic meningitis
C. Muscle spasms and pain
D. Flaccid paralysis of one or more extremities
E. Asymptomatic infection

Answers

[34.1] **C.** The oral polio vaccine or "live" vaccine produces not only IgM and IgG antibodies in the blood but also secretory IgA antibodies in the intestine, resulting in intestinal immunity; the inactivated poliomyelitis vaccine produces humoral immunity, but not localized intestinal immunity. Answers A, B, D, and E are incorrect: (A) only the inactivated poliomyelitis vaccine is administered to immunocompromised patients; (B) the oral polio vaccine has been associated with transfer of live poliovirus to close contacts of immunized patients, and therefore, use of the inactivated poliomyelitis vaccine is currently recommended in the United States for childhood immunizations; (D) it is easily administered in multiple oral doses, not injections; (E) both the oral polio vaccine and the inactivated poliomyelitis vaccine can be given to young children with other scheduled immunizations.

[34.2] **A.** Polioviruses are cytolytic and cause direct damage to infected cells; answers B, C, D, and E are incorrect: (B) paralysis results in less than 2 percent of patients infected with poliovirus and is a direct result of the destruction of infected neurons in the spinal cord and brain; (C) paralytic disease is caused by cytolytic damage because of the virus, not by the immune response; (D) aseptic meningitis is a result of poliovirus infection which occurs in less than 1–2 percent of patients infected, and is a result of the destruction of infected cells; (E) if not contained by the host antibody response, polioviral infection may result in "minor" and "major" viremic spread within the patient, however, the primary pathologic effect of poliovirus is still the cell lysis of infected cells.

[34.3] **E.** Greater than 90 percent of infections with poliovirus result in asymptomatic infections; answers A, B, C, and D are incorrect; all are potential outcomes of polioviral infections that remain uncontrolled by a host immune response, but are much less common outcomes of poliovirus infection.

MICROBIOLOGY PEARLS

- Poliovirus is a small, nonenveloped virus with a single-stranded, positive-sense RNA genome.
- More than 90 percent of poliovirus infections are asymptomatic.
- Clinical manifestations: "minor" illness of abortive poliomyelitis includes fever, sore throat, and headache; "major" illness of nonparalytic poliomyelitis or paralytic poliomyelitis also includes back pain, muscle spasm, aseptic meningitis, and spinal paralysis of one or more limbs.
- Vaccines available: attenuated live poliovirus vaccine or oral polio vaccine (OPV) and inactivated poliomyelitis vaccine (IPV).

REFERENCES

Brooks GF, Butel JS, Morse SA. Jawetz, Melnick, & Adelberg's Medical Microbiology, 23rd ed. New York: McGraw-Hill, 2004:491–2.

Ryan JR, Ray CG. Sherris Medical Microbiology, 4th ed. New York: McGraw-Hill, 2004:532–7.

Plotkin SA, Vidor E. Poliovirus vaccine–Inactive. In Plotkin SA, Orenstein WA. Vaccines, 4th ed. Philadelphia, PA: WB Saunders, 2004.

Sutter RW, et al. Poliovirus–Live. In Plotkin SA, Orenstein WA. Vaccines, 4th ed. Philadelphia, PA:WB Saunders, 2004.

CASE 35

A 3-year-old male infant is brought to the emergency room in the middle of January with fever, vomiting, and diarrhea for the past day. He has not been able to keep anything down by mouth and has had profuse, very watery stools. He attends day care, and several of his classmates have been out sick recently as well. No adult members of the household have been ill. He has no significant past medical history. On examination, his temperature is 37.9°C (100.2°F), and he has tachycardia. His mucous membranes are dry, and eyes appear somewhat sunken. His abdomen has active bowel sounds and is nontender. His stool is watery and pale. The stool tests negative for blood and fecal leukocytes.

- **What is the most likely cause of this child's illness?**

- **How is this virus activated to form an infectious particle?**

ANSWERS TO CASE 35: ROTAVIRUS

Summary: A 3-year-old boy who attends day care develops gastroenteritis in the winter.

- **Most likely cause of this child's illness:** Rotavirus.
- **How is this virus activated to form an infectious particle:** Activation of rotavirus occurs when the outer capsid layer is lysed by gastrointestinal (GI) proteases to create an infectious subviral particle (ISVP).

CLINICAL CORRELATION

Rotaviruses are ubiquitous worldwide and are estimated to cause more than 50 percent of gastroenteritis cases occurring in children less 2–3 years of age, resulting in approximately 4 billion annual cases. Infections typically occur in the cooler months and result in abrupt onset of vomiting followed with frequent watery diarrhea. Illness is typically self-limiting; however, severe infection can result in immunocompromised or malnourished children and may be fatal. Outbreaks are common in day care, preschool, and hospital settings. Adults may also become infected but usually have few if any symptoms.

APPROACH TO SUSPECTED ROTAVIRUS INFECTION

Objectives

1. Be able to describe the characteristics of the virus.
2. Be able to describe the strategies for prevention and treatment of the infection.

Definitions

Tachycardia: An increased heart rate.

Reassortment: The formation of new virions with hybrid genomes assembled in cells with mixed viral infections, which occurs among viruses containing segmented genomes (i.e., influenza viruses and reoviruses), resulting in high genetic variation.

Intussusception: Blockage of the intestines as a result of the bowel telescoping into itself.

DISCUSSION

Characteristics of Rotavirus That Impact Transmission

Rotavirus is one of the **four genera of the family Reoviridae** and is a common cause of childhood gastroenteritis around the world. The virus consists of a **double-layered protein capsid** that contains a genome made of **11 segments of double-stranded, negative-sense RNA.** The double capsid **looks like a wheel with short spokes** connecting the outer capsid to the inner capsid and core, thus the name **Rotavirus.** As a nonenveloped virus, it retains its infectivity in a wide range of pH and temperatures and is resistant to many common detergents as well. **Rotavirus** is spread through fecal-oral contact, and because of its stability, fomite transmission can also occur. The virus would be inactivated by the pH of a normal, empty stomach but can survive in a buffered stomach or in the gastric environment following a meal. The outer capsid of the virus is partially digested by GI proteolytic enzymes, creating an infectious subviral particle (ISVP). A surface protein of the virus, VP4, is also cleaved by GI proteases, allowing it to bind to the surface of intestinal epithelial cells and allow the ISVP to enter by direct penetration. The RNA genome remains in the viral core and is transcribed into mRNA by a viral polymerase. The mRNA is then transported out of the core to the cell cytoplasm, where it is translated and assembled into new virions. The initial assembly of rotaviral virions is similar to enveloped virions. As the newly formed rotaviral virions bud through the endoplasmic reticulum (ER), they acquire the membrane as an "envelope." However, this "envelope" is soon lost as the virions continue through the ER, and the infectious rotaviral particles are then released from the host cell by cell lysis.

Rotaviruses have been classified into at least **three different major subgroups** and nine different serotypes based on antigenic epitopes of the inner capsid protein VP6. There are primarily four serotypes that are important in causing human disease. Because of the segmented nature of the genome, rotaviruses are capable of producing virions with high genetic variation as a result of the reassortment of genome sequences in mixed infections. This high genetic variability results in increased numbers of serotypes for this viral group and allows for reinfection of persons previously exposed to one rotaviral serotype. Reinfections are common, yet successive infections appear to cause less severe symptoms.

The mechanism by which rotaviral infection causes diarrhea is not entirely understood. Rotaviral particles infect the cells of the small intestinal villi and multiply in the cytoplasm of enterocytes. Damaged cells are sloughed off, releasing large numbers of viral particles into the stool. Virus can be excreted for days to weeks after infection. The infection prevents absorption of water, sodium, and glucose, resulting in a loss of water and electrolytes. A virally encoded nonstructural protein also acts as an enterotoxin, similar to those of *Escherichia coli* and *Vibrio cholerae.* Typical symptoms of rotaviral infection include fever, vomiting, abdominal pain, and watery diarrhea without blood or mucus. The net result is a profuse watery diarrhea that can cause dehydration without appropriate fluid and electrolyte replacement. Symptoms may last for approximately 1 week, with viral excretion lasting weeks longer. Severe and prolonged illness can occur in immunodeficient and malnourished children and without supportive therapy infection can be fatal. Infection with rotavirus stimulates a humoral response; however, protection against reinfection is temporary and incomplete. The presence of high levels of rotavirus IgA in the lumen of the intestine confers relative protection.

Diagnosis

Because the symptoms of rotaviral infection resemble those of other viral diarrhea producing agents, the definitive diagnoses of rotaviral infection requires the **detection of viral antigens in stool samples.** Enzyme immunoassay and latex agglutination are two easy, rapid assays used to confirm rotaviral infection. Additionally, PCR can be used for genotyping viral nucleic acid in stool specimens. Viral culture is both difficult and unreliable and therefore is not used for diagnoses.

Treatment and Prevention

Treatment of rotaviral infection is **supportive,** including the replacement of fluids and electrolytes to restore physiologic balance and prevent dehydration. Both oral and intravenous rehydration therapy are effective, and which one is used depends on the severity of dehydration. Because rotaviruses can retain infectivity over a wide range of pH and temperatures and are resistant to many common detergents, strict hand washing and use of gloves is necessary to limit nosocomial spread.

An **attenuated recombinant Rotavirus vaccine** was developed and used in children for several years. However, its **approval was withdrawn,** and its use stopped because of concerns with the development of **intussusception** among vaccine users. A new rotavirus vaccine was approved by the FDA and released in 2006; to date, it has not been shown to be associated with intussusception. Another difficulty with the production of such a vaccine is that a single vaccine may not protect against all Rotavirus serotypes.

COMPREHENSION QUESTIONS

[35.1] You isolate a virus from the stool of a 1-year-old infant with signs of fever, vomiting, and diarrhea. Laboratory results show that the viral genome is composed of multiple segments of double-stranded RNA, which leads you to suspect that rotavirus is the causative agent of infection. Which of the following statements is true regarding rotavirus replication?

A. The viral genome integrates into the host chromosome.
B. The virus uses the host RNA polymerase for replication of its genome.
C. The segmented genome contributes to the antigenic variation of the virus.
D. The viral agent has a single antigenic type.
E. The newly assembled viral particles are released via budding through the host cell membrane.

[35.2] Similar to rotavirus, which of the following viral agents is also a nonenveloped RNA virus known to cause gastroenteritis diarrhea in young children?

A. Calicivirus
B. Paramyxovirus
C. Parainfluenza virus
D. Coxsackie virus
E. None of the above

Answers

[35.1] **C.** The segmented genome of rotaviruses, allows for the assembly of new virions with mixed genomes in cells multiply infected as a result of reassortment; answers A, B, D, and E are incorrect: (A) the rotaviral genome consists of double-stranded RNA and replicates in the cytoplasm and thus does not integrate into the host chromosome; (B) as an RNA virus that replicates in the cytoplasm, the rotoviral genome is replicated by a viral RNA polymerase; (D) the high genetic variability of rotaviruses because of reassortment results in multiple viral serotypes, at least nine different serotypes have currently been classified in human illness; (E) newly assembled nonenveloped rotaviral particles are released by cell lysis.

[35.2] **A.** Like rotaviruses, caliciviruses are nonenveloped RNA viruses that cause watery diarrhea, especially in children; answers B, C, D, and E are incorrect: (B) Paramyxoviruses are enveloped RNA viruses that cause childhood respiratory and exanthemous infections; (C) Parainfluenza viruses are enveloped RNA viruses which cause respiratory infections such as croup, bronchiolitis, and pneumonia in children; (D) Coxsackie viruses are nonenveloped RNA viruses that cause nonspecific respiratory tract infections, febrile rashes, and meningitis.

MICROBIOLOGY PEARLS

- ❖ Rotaviruses are ubiquitous, causing greater than 50 percent of gastroenteritis cases in children under 2–3 years.
- ❖ Rotaviruses are composed of a double-layered protein capsid and a segmented double-stranded RNA genome, allowing the new virions to have high genetic variation as a result of reassortment.
- ❖ Clinical manifestations: abrupt onset of fever, vomiting, abdominal pain, and watery diarrhea without blood or mucus.
- ❖ Only supportive treatment of infection including fluid and electrolyte replacement.

REFERENCES

Brooks GF, Butel JS, Morse SA. Jawetz, Melnick, & Adelberg's Medical Microbiology, 23rd ed. New York: McGraw-Hill, 2004:505–8.

Centers for Disease Control and Prevention. Intussusception among recipients of rotavirus vaccine—United States, 1998–1999. Morb Mortal Wkly Rep 1999; 48:577–81.

Ryan JR, Ray CG. Sherris Medical Microbiology, 4th ed. New York: McGraw-Hill, 2004:577–81.

❖ CASE 36

A 10-month-old female is brought to the pediatric emergency room in late December with a cough and fever. She started getting sick with a mild cough and runny nose approximately 3 days ago, but has progressively worsened. She is now coughing frequently and has vomited after coughing. She has no history of asthma or other respiratory illness. She was born after an uncomplicated, full-term pregnancy and has no significant medical history. She attends day care 3 days a week. On examination, her temperature is 38.3°C (100.9°F), pulse is 110 beats per minute, respiratory rate is 30 breaths per minute, and her oxygen saturation is low at 91 percent by pulse oximetry. Her head and neck examination shows her to have a right otitis media but is otherwise normal. Her cardiac exam is notable only for tachycardia. Her pulmonary examination shows her to be in moderate respiratory distress. She has prominent nasal flaring and subcostal retractions on inspiration. She has loud expiratory wheezes in all lung fields. The remainder of her examination is normal. A chest x-ray shows hyperaeration but no infiltrates.

◆ **What is the likely infectious cause of her respiratory illness?**

◆ **Following resolution of this illness, her mother asks whether she is protected from getting this disease again. How do you respond?**

ANSWERS TO CASE 36: RESPIRATORY SYNCYTIAL VIRUS

Summary: A 10-month-old female presents with bronchiolitis. A chest x-ray shows hyperaeration but no infiltrates.

- **Likely infectious cause of her respiratory illness:** Respiratory syncytial virus (RSV).
- **Is she protected from getting this disease again:** The immunity developed with an RSV infection is incomplete, and reinfections are common. However, the severity of disease with repeat infections appears to be reduced, especially in older children and adults.

CLINICAL CORRELATION

RSV is a ubiquitous and highly contagious viral infection and is the single most common cause of fatal respiratory tract infections in infants under 12 months of age. It accounts for approximately 25 percent of pediatric hospitalizations of this age group, resulting in severe respiratory illnesses such as bronchiolitis, pneumonia, and respiratory failure. It is also highly prevalent in childcare settings, with 70–95 percent of children attending day care being infected by 3–4 years of age. Less severe illness occurs in older children and adults and may present as a common cold.

APPROACH TO SUSPECTED RSV INFECTION

Objectives

1. Be able to describe the characteristics of the virus.
2. Be able to describe the strategies for prevention and treatment of the infection.

Definitions

Bronchiolitis: Inflammation of the bronchioles or thin-walled branches of the lungs.

Right otitis media: Inflammation of the right middle ear marked with pain, fever, dizziness, and abnormal hearing.

DISCUSSION

Characteristics of RSV That Impact Transmission

RSV belongs to the Pneumovirus genus of the family Paramyxoviridae. It is a common cause of upper and lower respiratory tract infections in all age groups, but tends to cause more severe, lower respiratory disease in **infants and young children.** RSV is an **enveloped virus with a single-stranded, negativesense RNA genome.** It is transmitted by the inhalation of aerosolized respiratory droplets. It can survive on nonporous surfaces, such as countertops, for 3–30 hours but is inactivated by many detergents and does not tolerate changes in temperature or pH well. RSV infections primarily remain localized in the respiratory tract. The virus infects target respiratory epithelial cells by fusion of its envelope with the host cytoplasmic membrane via the action of two viral envelope glycoproteins. However, unlike the related influenza and parainfluenza viruses, RSV envelope glycoproteins do not possess hemagglutinin or neuraminidase activities. RNA transcription, protein synthesis, replication, and assembly all occur in the cytoplasm and newly formed virions are released by budding from the host cell. RSV is also capable of promoting cell-cell fusion, resulting in multinucleated giant cells known as syncytia, an ability for which it derives its name.

RSV is initially transmitted to the nasopharynx through contact with **infected secretions and fomites,** resulting in localized infections of respiratory epithelium. Although viremia is rare, progressive infections can extend to the middle and lower airways. Disease caused by RSV is primarily the result of the host immune system mediating damage to infected respiratory epithelial cells. In adults and older children, mild upper respiratory tract symptoms such as a runny nose or mild cough usually develop with clinical symptoms lasting for 1–2 weeks. In **infants or younger children,** more serious illness such as **bronchiolitis** can occur. This occurs when there is inflammation and plugging of the bronchi and bronchioles with mucous and necrotic tissue from immune-mediated cellular damage. The smaller airways of infants and young children are especially susceptible and may result in cough, tachypnea, respiratory distress, wheezing, and hypoxia.

Mortality is high in infants with underlying disease or reduced immune function, and causes of death often include respiratory failure, cor pulmonale (right-sided heart failure), or bacterial superinfection. The immune response to RSV is not entirely understood, but both humoral and cell-mediated systems appear to play a role. The immunity developed with an infection does not appear to be complete. Repeat infections with RSV are common, but symptoms tend to be less severe with subsequent infections. Although outbreaks of RSV infection can occur in **elderly patients** resulting in severe illness, particularly in those residing in long-term care facilities.

Diagnosis

In addition to the presenting clinical symptoms, RSV can be diagnosed more definitively through **viral genome or antigen detection.** Direct identification of RSV antigens is performed via immunofluorescence analysis on exfoliated epithelial cells or with ELISA (enzyme-linked immunosorbent assay) testing on nasal secretions. Large amounts of viral particles are present in **nasal washings,** particularly from infected children, making it a good clinical specimen for viral genome detection via RT-PCR. When attempting to isolate the virus in culture, clinical samples should be inoculated immediately into cell cultures, because of the labile nature of RSV. The presence of RSV can be recognized by the formation of giant cells or syncytia formation in inoculated cultures in 1–2 weeks.

Treatment and Prevention

Treatment of RSV infections relies mainly on **supportive care including oxygenation, ventilatory support, IV fluids, and nebulized cold steam.** These modalities are used in an effort to remove or reduce mucus secretions in the airways and allow for adequate oxygen exchange. The antiviral agent ribavirin has been approved for use via aerosolization in high-risk infants exposed to RSV and in severe lower respiratory tract illnesses caused by RSV infection. Close observation of severe cases is critical. Currently there is no vaccine approved for RSV. However, passive immunization with anti-RSV immunoglobulin is available for premature infants, using monoglonal antibodies, Synagis. Premature infants especially with bronchopulmonary dysplasia and congenital heart disease should be vaccinated.

Additionally, preventative measures are particularly important in hospital and specifically neonatal intensive care units, because **RSV is highly contagious.** Prevention of nosocomial spread requires strict enforcement of the following precautions: hand washing; isolation of RSV infected infants; and changing of gloves, gowns, and masks between patients.

COMPREHENSION QUESTIONS

[36.1] Which of the following paramyxoviruses lacks an envelope viral attachment protein with hemagglutinin activity?

A. Parainfluenza virus
B. Mumps virus
C. Measles virus
D. Respiratory syncytial virus

[36.2] An 8-month-old infant is brought to the emergency room with a suspected RSV infection. Which of the following clinical illnesses would you be most concerned about this child having as a result of infection with this virus?

A. Bronchiolitis
B. Encephalitis
C. Meningitis
D. Pancreatitis
E. Pharyngitis

[36.3] Which of the following statements most accurately describes the chemical and physiologic properties of RSV?

A. RSV is a nonenveloped virus with a single-stranded, negative-sense RNA genome.
B. Newly formed RSV particles are released via host cell lysis.
C. RSV infects erythroid precursor cells via fusion of its viral envelope glycoproteins with the host cytoplasmic membrane.
D. Transcription of the RSV genome occurs in the nucleus of the host cell, while protein synthesis, replication, and assembly occur in the cytoplasm.
E. RSV is sensitive to detergents and is inactivated by changes in temperature and pH.

Answers

[36.1] **D.** Respiratory syncytial virus, differs from other paramyxoviruses in that it does not have a hemagglutinin protein in its viral envelope; answers A, B, and C all have viral envelope proteins with hemagglutinin activity.

[36.2] **A.** Bronchiolitis is a common clinical manifestation of RSV infection in infants, which results from inflammation and plugging of the bronchi and bronchioles with mucous and necrotic tissue; answers B, C, D, and E are incorrect as they are not symptoms specific to infection with RSV.

[36.3] **E.** RSV is an enveloped virus and is inactivated by many detergents as well as changes in temperature and pH.; answers A, B, C, and D are incorrect: (A) RSV is an enveloped virus with a single-stranded, negative-sense RNA genome; (B) RSV virions are released by budding from the host cell membrane, not by cell lysis; (C) RSV infects respiratory epithelial cells, not erythroid precursor cells, via fusion with the host membrane; (D) RSV is an RNA virus, and transcription, protein synthesis, replication, and assembly of new virions occurs in the cytoplasm of the host cell.

MICROBIOLOGY PEARLS

- ❖ RSV is highly contagious and is the primary cause of respiratory tract infections in infants under 1 year of age.
- ❖ Clinical manifestations: respiratory symptoms including rhinitis, pneumonia, and blockage of airways leading to respiratory distress.
- ❖ Vaccination for RSV is available for children at high-risk for the disease.
- ❖ Treatment with ribavirin in severe cases or in high-risk infants exposed to the virus.

REFERENCES

Brooks GF, Butel JS, Morse SA. Jawetz, Melnick, & Adelberg's Medical Microbiology, 23rd ed. New York: McGraw-Hill, 2004:558–60.

Ryan JR, Ray CG. Sherris Medical Microbiology, 4th ed. New York: McGraw-Hill, 2004:503–6.

❖ CASE 37

You are asked to consider being vaccinated with smallpox vaccine to serve as a first-responder in the event of a biological warfare attack. After considering the risks and benefits, you consent. You are given the vaccine by the standard technique—a small, bifurcated needle is used to create multiple punctures in the skin overlying your deltoid. The area is covered, and you are instructed not to touch the actual site. In 2 days, a small papule and erythema appear at the vaccine site. A few days later, multiple vesicles are noted. These progress to form larger pustules. In approximately 2 weeks, the whole vaccine site has formed a scab and this subsequently falls off in another week. When complete recovery has occurred, you have a scar left at the vaccine site.

◆ **What is the actual virus used as the smallpox vaccine?**

◆ **Why must the virus used in the vaccine carry or encode its own enzymes for DNA and mRNA synthesis?**

ANSWERS TO CASE 37: SMALLPOX

Summary: A physician has received the smallpox vaccine.

- **Actual virus used as the smallpox vaccine:** Vaccinia, which is a form of the cowpox virus.
- **Reason variola carries or encodes its own enzymes for DNA and mRNA synthesis:** Variola virus must produce its own enzymes for DNA and mRNA synthesis because viral replication occurs entirely in host cell cytoplasm, and therefore it cannot use the enzymes located in the host nucleus.

CLINICAL CORRELATION

Variola, the virus that causes smallpox, is a member of the poxvirus family. Smallpox is a highly contagious and severe disease that once caused high mortality in human populations. It was discovered in 1796 by Edward Jenner that the closely related but less virulent cowpox virus could confer resistance to smallpox. This discovery, along with the fact that humans were the only reservoir for variola, eventually led to an effective global vaccination program, using the vaccinia virus as the live viral vaccine. Vaccinia shares antigenic determinants with variola but primarily causes clinical disease in nonhuman animals. Rare, but potentially severe, adverse events such as postvaccinial encephalitis, progressive vaccinia necrosum, or fetal vaccinia can occur after vaccination, primarily in persons with suppressed immunity, severe allergies, eczema, or pregnant women. Additionally, smallpox vaccination is also contraindicated for persons in close contact with individuals with the conditions listed.

Because of worldwide vaccination and disease control efforts, the last case of indigenously acquired smallpox was seen in Somalia in 1977. The World Health Organization declared that smallpox was eradicated in 1980. Routine smallpox vaccination was discontinued after 1980, as the risk of vaccination was thought to outweigh the risk of acquiring smallpox. Concerns about the risk of smallpox being used as a bioterror weapon have led to the reinstitution of vaccination programs, primarily among military, public health, and safety workers.

APPROACH TO SUSPECTED SMALLPOX INFECTION

Objectives

1. Be able to describe the characteristics of the virus.
2. Be able to describe the strategies for prevention and treatment of the infection.

Definitions

Bifurcated needle: A specialized needle that forks into two prongs at its distal end; the prongs use capillary action to administer a specific amount of smallpox vaccine via multiple inoculations at the same site.

Maculopapular: The clinical presentation combination of both macules (rash) with papules (lesions).

Guarnieri's inclusion bodies: Electron-dense intracytoplasmic acidophilic inclusions within infected cells which serve as assembly sites for new smallpox virions.

DISCUSSION

Characteristics of Smallpox That Impact Transmission

Variola is a member of the poxvirus family, and a member of the genera Orthopoxvirus. There are several diseases caused by orthopoxviruses: variola, vaccinia, cowpox, and monkeypox. **Variola** is the causative agent of smallpox, a virulent human virus that causes high mortality, while cowpox and monkeypox are zoonotic viruses causing accidental cutaneous infections in humans. **Vaccinia** is a form of the **cowpox** virus and has been used effectively as a live viral vaccine against smallpox disease. **Poxviruses are the largest and most complex viruses known.** Poxviruses are **enveloped and contain a linear, double-stranded DNA genome,** which is fused at both ends. They are the only DNA viruses, which replicate entirely in the host cell cytoplasm. Because of this, poxviruses must carry and/or encode all of the proteins required for both DNA and mRNA synthesis.

Transmission of the smallpox virus occurs via **inhalation of infected respiratory droplets,** exposure to infectious skin lesions, or through contact with contaminated fomites. Once inhaled, initial replication of the virus occurs in the respiratory tract, where the virus binds to a target cell surface receptor and the envelope fuses with the cell membrane. The core of the virus is then released into the cellular cytoplasm where DNA replication and transcription takes place. New virions are assembled in cytoplasmic inclusions, referred to as **Guarnieri inclusion bodies.** Unlike other enveloped viruses, poxviruses assemble their own viral membranes around these viral inclusions instead of acquiring them from host membranes. The new viral particles are then released either by cell lysis or exocytosis. After initial infection of the respiratory tract occurs, the virus spreads through lymphatic channels causing primary viremia and infection of reticuloendothelial cells. Viral replication in these cells causes a secondary viremia and results in clinical manifestations of the skin and internal organs. Variola virus exists as at least two strains—**variola major and variola minor. Variola major** is associated with **high mortality rates** (20–50 percent), whereas **variola minor** is associated with a **mortality rate of less than 1 percent.**

Diagnosis

Diagnosis of smallpox is typically made by clinical presentation. Clinical smallpox has an incubation period of approximately 2 weeks, followed by an **abrupt onset of malaise, fever, chills, and myalgia.** A few days post-onset, a characteristic **maculopapular rash begins** to develop and progresses in a centrifugal pattern over the head and extremities. During approximately a 2-week period, the rash progresses to a **single crop of maculopapular lesions to firm vesicles, then to pustules** that scab and slowly heal. The high mortality associated with this smallpox results from either the overwhelming primary viral infection or from potential secondary bacterial superinfection.

Highly suspected cases of smallpox should be referred immediately to the Centers for Disease Control, where new variola and orthopox PCR tests are available.

Treatment and Prevention

As previously discussed, successful **global vaccination** efforts have eliminated naturally acquired cases of smallpox worldwide, with routine smallpox vaccinations ending in 1980 in the United States. However, new concerns of biological weapons development have led to the testing of old vaccine stocks and the development of new stocks for use primarily among military, public health, and safety workers. Chemotherapeutic agents such as **methisazone or cidofovir** may have some efficacy as prophylaxis against smallpox infection; however, currently there are no treatments available for use in established smallpox disease.

COMPREHENSION QUESTIONS

[37.1] Which of the following statements describes a characteristic that enabled the worldwide eradication of smallpox in 1980?

A. The inactivated smallpox vaccine is easily prepared and safe.
B. Smallpox has no known reservoir outside of humans.
C. Mass vaccination of the world was possible as a result of easy administration of the vaccine in the field.
D. Subclinical smallpox infections were also inhibited through worldwide mass vaccinations.
E. All stocks of smallpox virus were destroyed worldwide in 1979.

[37.2] Due to the potential of a bioterrorist threat, emergency health-care responders in New York City are being considered for smallpox vaccination. Which of the following would be a candidate for vaccination?

A. Household contact is breast-feeding
B. Mild asthma
C. Is pregnant
D. Has eczema
E. Household contact is HIV-positive

[37.3] A college student is reading about the Middle Ages and notices that many people during that era contracted a deadly disease with similar symptoms including acute fever, chills, and myalgia followed by a characteristic rash with small blister-like lesions. Those that did not die from the illness were left with disfiguring scars. The inciting agent has a double-stranded linear DNA genome that replicates in the cytoplasm. Which of the following agents is the most likely culprit?

A. Varicella virus
B. Herpes simplex virus
C. Rubeola virus
D. Papilloma virus
E. Variola virus

Answers

[37.1] **B.** Smallpox has no known reservoir outside of humans, which was one of the factors which enabled its eradication; answers A, C, D, and E are all incorrect: the vaccination for smallpox consists of a live vaccinia virus and does not contain smallpox virus; mass vaccination of the world was not performed or required because there are no known nonhuman reservoirs of smallpox and subclinical infections do not occur. Thus, large numbers of vaccinations occurring in many populations, such as in the United States, along with strict epidemiologic reporting of smallpox cases worldwide allowed for immunization of those exposed and the elimination of smallpox disease. Not all stocks of smallpox virus were destroyed, and there are still two locations where smallpox virus strains are held: one in Atlanta, and one in Moscow.

[37.2] **B.** Smallpox is a live attenuated vaccine and is contraindicated for individuals or those who are household contacts who are immunocompromised or who may be susceptible to the adverse effects of the vaccine. Those with eczema and similar skin conditions, infection with HIV, transplant patients, those on high dose corticosteroids, those patients who are pregnant or who are breast-feeding are a partial listing of patients for whom the vaccine is contraindicated.

[37.3] **E.** Smallpox (variola virus) killed many people during the Middle Ages. The clinical presentation was that of fever, malaise, and myalgia followed by pus-filled or vesicular rash, which often left disfiguring scars.

MICROBIOLOGY PEARLS

- ❖ Variola is a poxvirus and etiologic agent of smallpox.
- ❖ Vaccinia is a form of the cowpox virus and has been used effectively as a live viral vaccine against smallpox disease.
- ❖ Clinical manifestations of smallpox: a severe rash followed by a single crop of maculopapular lesions that transition into vesicles and pustules, and then slowly crust and heal. The lesions are at the same stage.
- ❖ Contraindications for vaccinia vaccination: suppressed immunity, severe allergies, eczema, pregnancy, or close contact with such persons.

REFERENCES

Brooks GF, Butel JS, Morse SA. Jawetz, Melnick, & Adelberg's Medical Microbiology, 23rd ed. New York: McGraw-Hill, 2004:561–6.

Cono J, Casey CG, Bell DM: Smallpox vaccination and adverse reactions. Guidance for clinicians. MMWR Recomm Rep 2003;52(RR-4):1.

Ryan JR, Ray CG. Sherris Medical Microbiology, 4th ed. New York: McGraw-Hill, 2004:525–7.

Centers for Disease Control and Prevention. Acute, generalized vesicular or pustular rash illness testing protocol in the United States. http://www.bt.cdc.gov/agent/smallpox/ diagnosis/rashtestingprotocol.asp

CASE 38

A 65-year-old man comes to your office for the evaluation of lower back pain. For the past 3 days, he has had a sharp, burning pain in his left lower back, which would radiate to his flank and, sometimes, all the way around to his abdomen. The pain comes and goes, feels like an "electric shock," is unrelated to activity, and can be severe. He has had no injury to his back and has no history of back problems in the past. He denies fever, urinary symptoms, or gastrointestinal symptoms. His examination today, including careful back and abdominal examination, is normal. You prescribe a nonsteroidal anti-inflammatory drug for the pain. The next day, he returns to your office stating that he has had an allergic reaction to the medication because he's developed a rash. The rash is in the area where he had the pain for which he was seen the day before. On examination now, he has an eruption consisting of patches of erythema with clusters of vesicles extending in a dermatomal distribution from his left lower back to the midline of his abdomen.

What is the cause of this rash?

What is the mechanism for the dermatomal distribution of the rash?

ANSWERS TO CASE 38: VARICELLA-ZOSTER

Summary: A 65-year-old man has a painful, dermatomal rash.

- **Cause of this rash:** The most likely cause of this man's rash is reactivation of varicella-zoster virus, causing the appearance of shingles.
- **Mechanism for the dermatomal distribution of the rash:** The dermatomal distribution of this rash is caused by reactivation of a latent varicella infection of a dorsal root ganglion with viral spread along the pathway of the nerve distribution.

CLINICAL CORRELATION

Varicella-zoster virus (VZV) is the causative agent of both chickenpox and shingles. Primary infection with chickenpox occurs mostly in children, with 90 percent of the population acquiring antibodies to VZV by age 10. After primary infection, the virus becomes latent in the dorsal root ganglia, where it may be reactivated later in life. Reactivation of VZV infection results in the unilateral eruption of a painful rash known as herpes zoster or shingles.

APPROACH TO SUSPECTED VZV INFECTION

Objectives

1. Be able to describe the characteristics of the virus.
2. Be able to describe the strategies for prevention and treatment of the infection.

Definitions

Dermatome: An area of skin served by one sensory spinal nerve.
Neuropathic pain: Pain disseminating from the peripheral nervous system.

DISCUSSION

Characteristics of VZV That Impact Transmission

VZV is a member of the **Alphaherpesvirinae** subfamily of the **herpesviruses,** which also include HSV-1 and HSV-2. Similar to other herpesviruses, VZV is a **large, enveloped virus with a double-stranded DNA genome.** As an enveloped virus, VZV is sensitive to drying and many detergents, necessitating its spread from **person to person via respiratory droplets or direct contact with skin lesions.** Initial VZV infection and replication occur in the epithelium of the **respiratory tract, followed by viremic spread to the skin** The virus binds to specific receptors, and the viral envelope fuses with the cell membrane. The capsid delivers the genome to the host cell nucleus where transcription and replication occur.

VZV can cause both lytic and latent infections. In lytic infections, new virions are assembled in the host nucleus, acquire an envelope from the nuclear or Golgi membrane, and are released by exocytosis or lysis of the host cell. In latent infections, the viral genome is not replicated, and only certain viral genes are transcribed. Latent infection of dorsal root or cranial nerve ganglia can occur during the initial infection. The virus spreads by viremia or lymphatic dissemination to the reticuloendothelial system. A secondary viremia then occurs, which disseminates VZV to the skin and other organs. VZV can also form syncytia and spread directly from cell to cell.

Diagnosis

Viremic spread to the skin results in classic varicella infection or chickenpox. Typically, **crops of vesicles and pustules form on erythematous bases,** starting on the head and trunk and progressing centripetally to the extremities. The appearance of these lesions is often described as **"dewdrops on a rose petal."** Both humoral and cell-mediated immunity contribute to control of the infection. VZV is a common childhood disease, and infection usually confers lifelong immunity against future disseminated disease. However, reactivation of latent VZV infections of **nerve root ganglia** may result and is classically described as **herpes zoster or shingles**. The causes of the reactivation are not entirely known, but it tends to be more common in older persons as cellular immunity decreases, in immunosuppressed individuals or in otherwise immune-competent individuals during times of emotional stress. The **reactivated virus replicates and is released along the dermatomal distribution of the nerve,** causing the characteristic **unilateral vesicular eruption of shingles.** The rash is frequently preceded by pain along the course of a sensory nerve days to weeks prior to the onset of rash. Neuropathic pain may continue to persist for weeks or months after the rash clears, indicating damage to the nerve root. Secondary bacterial infections may also complicate reactivation. Reactivations of VZV tend to be infrequent and sporadic.

Similar to HSV-1 and HSV-2, VZV can be diagnosed by examining a **Tzanck smear** of cells scraped from vesicular lesions for the presence of **multinucleated giant cells.** However, **direct fluorescent-antibody staining** of vesicular lesion scrapings remains the most rapid, sensitive, and specific assay for diagnosing VZV infections.

Treatment and Prevention

Several **viral DNA polymerase inhibitors** are available for treating VZV infections including: **acyclovir, famciclovir, and valacyclovir.** Treatment with these drugs has shown to be effective in reducing fever and skin lesions if treatment is begun within 3 days of onset of infection, prior to the eruption of lesions. These drugs have also shown some efficacy in reducing viral dissemination in immunocompromised patients. Additionally, analgesics and other pain killers can help with the patient's neuralgia.

Prevention of infection spread involves respiratory and contact isolation of infected patients. **Passive immunization of high-titer varicilla-zoster immunoglobulin (VZIg)** can be administered to immunocompromised patients if given within 3 days of exposure. This treatment is effective only for inhibiting primary infection in high-risk patients. More recently, a **live vaccine** has been used in the United States since 1995 to prevent primary childhood infections. A single dose has been shown to be 80 percent effective in children 1–13 years of age, and two doses have been shown to be 70 percent effective in adults. A new, live-attenuated virus vaccine, Zostavax, is recommended to reduce the incidence of shingles for adults over the age of 60.

COMPREHENSION QUESTIONS

[38.1] A Tzanck smear is obtained from a scraping of a patient's skin lesion, and analysis of the smear shows the presence of multinucleated giant cells. Which of the following viruses are known to cause this type cytopathic effect in infected cells?

A. Cytomegalovirus
B. Epstein-Barr virus
C. Herspes simplex virus- type 2
D. Human papillomavirus
E. Human herpesvirus 8

[38.2] A 3-year-old girl presented to her pediatrician's office with fever, swollen lymph nodes, and a vesicular rash on her chest and upper arms. The vesicles were at various stages of development: some were newly forming, while some were crusted over. Which of the following infectious agents is the most likely cause of this girl's rash?

A. Smallpox
B. Parvovirus B19
C. Epstein-Barr virus
D. Measles virus
E. Varicella-zoster virus

[38.3] Based on information provided in the previous question, which of the following clinical specimens should be collected to confirm diagnosis of VZV infection?

A. Saliva
B. Blood
C. Vesicle fluid
D. Cerebrospinal fluid
E. Urine

Answers

[38.1] **C.** HSV-1, HSV-2, and VZV are all known to produce multinucleated giant cells resulting in a positive Tzanck smear, whereas CMV, EBV, HPV, and human herpesvirus 8 do not.

[38.2] **E.** VZV produces a vesicular rash commonly seen in children, and different "crops" of vesicles generally appear on the head and trunk then moving outward; answers A, B, C, and D are incorrect, smallpox infection produces a vesicular rash with all lesions being at the same stage of development, whereas parvovirus B19, EBV, and the measles virus does produce a rash, but not consisting of vesicular lesions.

[38.3] **C.** VZV-specific antigens or viral DNA can be detected in vesicle fluid leading to a definitive diagnosis of VZV infection; answers A, B, D, and E are incorrect: CMV can be detected in saliva, blood, and urine; VZV is not commonly detected in CSF specimens.

MICROBIOLOGY PEARLS

- ❖ Primary lytic infection: chickenpox or varicella; recurrent latent infection: shingles or zoster.
- ❖ Clinical manifestations: unilateral eruption of a painful rash in a single dermatome.
- ❖ Prevention of varicella is by immunization of children and adults over the age of 60, respiratory and contact isolation of infected persons.
- ❖ Treatment: viral DNA polymerase inhibitors such as acyclovir, famciclovir, and valacyclovir.

REFERENCES

Fields BN, Knipe DM, Howley PM, et al. Herpesviridae. Fields Virology, 3rd ed. Philadelphia, PA: Lippincott-Raven, 1996:2525–41.

Murray PR, Rosenthal KS, Pfaller MA. Medical Microbiology, 5th ed. St. Louis, MO: Mosby, 2005:550–3.

Ryan JR, Ray CG. Sherris Medical Microbiology, 4th ed. New York: McGraw-Hill, 2004:562–6.

❖ CASE 39

A 42-year-old woman with chronic asthma presents for evaluation of a cough. She has had severe asthma for most of her life and currently uses both inhaled and oral corticosteroids, oral leukotriene modifiers, and inhaled albuterol to manage her symptoms. While in the process of tapering down her dose of oral steroids, she developed a cough productive of brown mucous and, occasionally, blood. She has had a low-grade fever as well. Her asthma control has been significantly worsened since she developed the cough. On examination, she has a temperature of 37.7°C (99.9°F) and a respiratory rate of 22 breaths per minute, and her saturation of oxygen is slightly low (96 percent on room air). She is coughing frequently. Her head and neck exam is unremarkable. Her pulmonary examination is notable for diffuse expiratory wheezing. A chest x-ray shows a lobular infiltrate that is reminiscent of a cluster of grapes. A complete blood count (CBC) shows a mildly elevated white blood cell count with a markedly elevated eosinophil count. A microscopic examination of her sputum is also notable for the presence of numerous eosinophils.

◆ **What organism is most likely causing her cough?**

◆ **What is the characteristic morphology of this organism seen on microscopic examination?**

ANSWERS TO CASE 39: *Aspergillus*

Summary: A 42-year-old asthmatic woman has allergic bronchopulmonary aspergillosis.

- **Most likely etiologic agent:** *Aspergillus fumigatus*
- **Characteristic morphology of this organism seen on microscopic examination:** Septate hyphae with 45° angle branching

CLINICAL CORRELATION

Aspergillus is a ubiquitous fungal organism that is capable of causing disease in both healthy and immunocompromised hosts. Infection occurs following either inhalation of the organism into the respiratory tract or introduction through the skin via a wound or surgery. *Aspergillus fumigatus* causes about 90 percent of invasive disease in humans, with *A. flavus* causing approximately 10 percent. Other *Aspergillus* species can cause disease but are less common. *Aspergillus* primarily infects the lungs and may cause a hypersensitivity reaction, chronic necrotizing pneumonia, aspergillomas ("fungal balls"), or systemic infection. *Aspergillus* can also cause keratitis and sinusitis. The hypersensitivity reaction, known as allergic bronchopulmonary aspergillosis (ABPA), is seen primarily in chronic asthmatics and persons with cystic fibrosis (CF). Approximately 25 percent of asthmatics and about half of patients with CF are allergic to *Aspergillus,* although the percentages that develop symptomatic disease are much lower. ABPA causes a cough productive of brown mucous plugs and, often, blood. Examination of the mucous will reveal eosinophils and the characteristic fungus. The symptoms initially tend to be mild but become more severe as the patient ages. Repeated episodes may cause bronchiectasis and chronic fibrotic pulmonary disease.

Systemic disease most often occurs in patients who are severely immunocompromised such as subsequent to bone marrow transplantation.

APPROACH TO THE SUSPECTED *Aspergillus* PATIENT

Objectives

1. Know the morphology, environmental sources, and pathogenic properties of *Aspergillus* species.
2. Know the clinical syndromes and diseases associated with *Aspergillus* infections.

Definitions

Allergic bronchopulmonary aspergillosis (ABPA): A hypersensitivity response to inhaled *Aspergillus* in patients with underlying asthma or lung disease.

Aspergilloma: A fungal ball most commonly in the sinus or within an old tuberculous cavity.

Bronchiectasis: Chronic inflammation of the bronchi with dilatation and loss of elasticity of the walls.

DISCUSSION

Characteristics of *Aspergillus* Species

Aspergillus* species** is found in every country in the world, and its **primary habitat is decomposing vegetation.** It is an **opportunistic pathogen** of animals and humans that causes a spectrum of disease ranging from **allergic bronchopulmonary disease** to **disseminated disease** in severely immunosuppressed patients. There are more than 40 species of *Aspergillus*, not all of which cause disease in humans. Therefore species identification is helpful in determining the clinical significance of an isolate. ***Aspergillus fumigatus is responsible for the majority of serious infections as a result of these organisms; however, *A. terreus* and *A. flavus* can be associated with disease in patients on cancer chemotherapy.

A **virulence factor** common to most *Aspergillus* species is **mycotoxin production.** One of the toxins, **gliotoxin,** can affect phagocytosis by macrophages as well as induce apoptosis.

Several factors contribute to the ability of *A. fumigatus* to cause infection. *Aspergillus fumigatus* grows more readily at normal human body temperature than other *Aspergillus* species. It has a very small spore size, which allows the spores to penetrate deep into the lung. It also is the most rapidly growing of all *Aspergillus* species.

Diagnosis

Diagnosis of allergic aspergillosis is usually made clinically, although these patients may have **positive respiratory cultures** for *Aspergillus*. Patients typically have a long-standing **history of asthma** with a history of **infiltrates on chest x-ray.** Other diagnostic criteria include presence of **specific antibody to *Aspergillus*** as well as elevated levels of IgE in the serum and **peripheral blood eosinophils.** The lack of systemic symptoms helps differentiate ABPA from *Aspergillus* pneumonia or disseminated disease. Diagnosis of disseminated disease is by culture of the organism from a normally sterile site and/or demonstration of hyphae invading blood vessels in a tissue biopsy. Disseminated disease can also be presumptively diagnosed by presence of antibody or galactomannan antigen in the patient's serum.

Fungal hyphae can be seen on **direct smear using KOH or calcofluor white,** which is a more sensitive fluorescent stain. ***Aspergillus hyphae*** can be identified by their **frequent septae, and branching at regular intervals at a 45° angle** (Figure 39-1); however, these characteristics are not specific or diagnostic for *Aspergillus.* Definitive diagnosis would be made by microscopic observation of the fungus after culture of the organism. *Aspergillus* species can be **cultured from sputum or bronchoalveolar lavages** of infected patients. The fungus grows rapidly on most laboratory media including blood agar, although a more selective media such as Sabouraud agar is commonly used to culture fungus. Growth is enhanced by incubation at room temperature versus 35°C (95°F). Visualization of the characteristic structure with a conidiophore, a vesicle to which the phialides are attached would confirm the diagnosis of *Aspergillus.* Although speciation can be preliminarily made by the color of the front and reverse of the colony on Sabouraud dextrose agar and their microscopic features, *A. fumigatus* is differentiated from the others by growth at a temperature at or above 50°C (122°F).

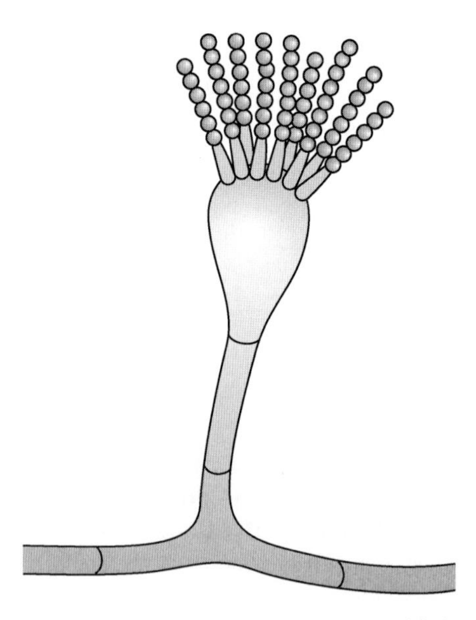

Figure 39-1. *Aspergillus fumigatus.* Frequent septa with branching pattern is characteristic.

Treatment and Prevention

Treatment of ABPA is usually not warranted; however because this is a hypersensitivity reaction, systemic **corticosteroids** are effective treatment, whereas inhaled corticosteroids are not. Therapy for **invasive aspergillosis** is with **amphotericin B, itraconazole, or voriconazole.** Antifungal agents may be used for prophylaxis of patients who are severely immunocompromised to prevent disseminated disease, particularly bone marrow transplant patients. These patients should also be protected from exposure to the organism by use of air filters.

COMPREHENSION QUESTIONS

[39.1] A biopsy of an infected lung from a 76-year-old woman who suffered a third-degree burn 2 months ago revealed uniform hyphae with regularly spaced septation and a parallel arrangement. No yeast cells were observed. Which of the following is the most probable diagnosis?

A. Actinomycosis
B. Aspergillosis
C. Blastomycosis
D. Cryptococcosis
E. Zygomycosis

[39.2] Which of the following is the probable source of infection in aspergillosis in the patient in Question 39.1?

A. Contact with an infected animal
B. Implantation
C. Ingestion
D. Inhalation
E. Water used in preparing lemonade

[39.3] An examination of sputum for a suspected case of fungal infection may reveal hyphae in which of the following?

A. Aspergillosis
B. Cryptococcosis
C. Histoplasmosis
D. Paracoccidioidomycosis
E. Sporotrichosis

Answers

[39.1] **B;** [39.2] **B.** Aspergillosis is a spectrum of diseases that may be caused by a number of *Aspergillus* species. These species are widespread in nature. *Aspergillus* species grow rapidly in vivo and in vitro and bear long conidiophores with terminal vesicles on which phialides produce chains of conidia. In healthy individuals, alveolar macrophages are able to phagocytize and destroy the conidia. Macrophages from immunocompromised patients have a diminished ability to do this. In the lung, conidia swell and germinate to produce hyphae that have a tendency to invade preexisting cavities (abnormal pulmonary space as a result of tuberculosis, sarcoidosis, or emphysema). Sputum and lung tissue specimens produce colonies which are hyaline, septate and uniform in width. Blastomyces and Cryptococcus from yeast cells, while Zygomycoses species have hyphae that are sparsely septate. Actinomyces may be considered a branching bacterium. Aspergillus tends to invade either via inhalation or implantation through skin wounds. In this patient with a 3rd degree [full-thickness skin] burn, implantation through the wound would be the most likely source of infection.

[39.3] **A.** Cryptococcosis, histoplasmosis, paracoccidioidomycosis and sporotrichosis are all caused by dimorphic fungi. At 37°C (98°F), the yeast form predominates. Aspergillosis, on the other hand, is caused by an organism that produces only hyphae (no-yeast component).

MICROBIOLOGY PEARLS

- *Aspergillus* is commonly found in the environment and cause a spectrum of disease ranging from allergic bronchopulmonary disease to disseminated disease.
- Microscopically *aspergillus* has septated, hyphae that branch at 45° angles and a vesicle with condida in either a single row (uniserate) or a double row (biserate).
- Although steroids are used to treat allergic disease, disseminated disease is difficult to treat and has a high mortality rate in severely immunosuppressed patients such as following bone marrow transplant.

REFERENCES

Denning DW. Aspergillus species. In: Mandell GL, Bennett JE, Dolin R, eds. Principles and Practice of Infectious Diseases, 6th ed. Philadelphia, PA: Churchill Livingstone, 2005:2958–73.

Murray PR, Rosenthal KS, Pfaller MA. Opportunistic mycoses In: Murray PR, Rosenthal KS, Pfaller MA. Medical Microbiology, 5th ed. St. Louis, MO: Mosby, 2005:779–800.

❖ CASE 40

A 52-year-old man presents to the physician's office for the evaluation of a cough and fever. He has had these symptoms for approximately a week. He has also noted a sharp chest pain that is worse when he coughs or takes a deep breath. He has had some associated fatigue, headaches, achy joints, and sweatiness at night. He has been using an over-the-counter flu medication, which helps to reduce the cough, but he wanted to be checked because his symptoms are lingering. He has no history of pulmonary diseases and has never smoked cigarettes. He has had no exposure to ill contacts. His only recent travel was a weeklong golf vacation to Phoenix, which he took 3 weeks ago. On examination, he is comfortable appearing and in no respiratory distress. His temperature is 37.7°C (99.9°F), and his vital signs are otherwise normal. His pulmonary examination is notable for some faint expiratory wheezing and crackles in the left upper lung field. The remainder of his physical examination is unremarkable. A chest x-ray shows hilar adenopathy. A CBC shows a normal total white blood cell count but with a high percentage of circulating eosinophils. Microscopic examination of a fresh sputum sample treated with KOH reveals numerous spherules.

◆ **What organism is the likely cause of this patient's symptoms?**

◆ **For this organism, how do spherules form and what is their role in propagating infection?**

ANSWERS TO CASE 40: BLASTOMYCOSIS, COCCIDIODOMYCOSIS, AND HISTOPLASMOSIS

Summary: A 52-year-old man who recently traveled to Phoenix complains of a cough, fatigue, and night sweats. A chest x-ray shows hilar adenopathy. The sputum reveals numerous spherules.

- **Organism most likely to cause his symptoms:** *Coccidioides immitis.*
- **How do spherules form and what is their role in propagating infection:** Inhaled arthroconidia lose their hydrophobic outer wall and remodel into spherical cells, or spherules. Nuclear division and cell multiplication occur and multiple septae develop within the circular cell, dividing it into endospore-containing compartments. The external wall of the spherule thins as growth occurs and then ruptures, releasing multiple spores and propagating the infection.

CLINICAL CORRELATION

Coccidioides immitis is a dimorphic fungus endemic in the western hemisphere. It is typically found in semiarid climates within the north and south 40° latitudes. Common endemic regions in the United States include the San Joaquin Valley, southern Arizona, and southwestern Texas. Transmission occurs by inhalation of the arthroconidia from the soil. The arthroconidia are taken into the bronchioles, where they form a spherule. When symptoms do occur, they usually start 1–3 weeks after exposure and typically include cough, fever, and fatigue. Chest pain, dyspnea, arthralgias, and skin rashes may occur as well. Most infections are self-limited, but it can take several weeks to months for symptomatic resolution. A small percentage of infections result in progressive pulmonary disease or chronic pulmonary complications, and an even smaller percentage may result in dissemination outside of the lung the most common site being the skin. Other areas of dissemination include the bones, joints, and the central nervous system (CNS). Most patients who develop disseminated disease have an underlying risk factor of severe immunosuppression, including those infected with HIV.

APPROACH TO THE SUSPECTED *Coccidoides* PATIENT

Objectives

1. Know the morphology, growth, and reproductive characteristics of *C. immitis.*
2. Know the sources of infection, modes of transmission, and clinical diseases associated with *C. immitis* infection.

Definitions

Dyspnea: Shortness of breath or difficulty breathing.
Dimorphic fungi: Fungi that grow as a mold at room temperature and in the environment and as yeast at 35°C (95°F) or in the body.
Arthroconidia: Barrel-shaped structures that are the mold and infectious form of *C. immitis.*

DISCUSSION

Characteristics of *Coccidioides* Species

Coccidioides is one of several **systemic and dimorphic fungi. *Histoplasma*** *capsulatum,* ***Blastomyces*** *dermatitidis,* and ***Paracoccidioides*** *braziliensis* are the others. ***Cryptococcus neoformans*** is also a **systemic** fungus but is **not dimorphic.** *Sporothrix schenckii* is dimorphic but not usually systemic. These fungi are commonly found in the environment in differing parts of the world and are transmitted by the aerosol route. In the majority of cases, fungi are inhaled into the lungs, and disease is unrecognized because patients remain asymptomatic.

Coccidioides immitis **grows in the soil as mycelia by apical extension.** Maturation results in the development of arthroconidia, which have a hydrophobic outer layer and can remain viable for a long period of time. They form fragile attachments to adjacent cells that are easily broken. Physical trauma, even a mild wind, can break these attachments and result in airborne dissemination of arthroconidia. If inhaled, the arthroconidia can deposit in the lung, where they lose their hydrophobic outer wall. The cell remodels into a spherical form known as a spherule. Within the spherule, cells multiply and septae form that divide the spherule into multiple compartments. These compartments contain endospores that are released as the spherule grows and eventually ruptures. The endospores are capable of generating new spherules or reverting to mycelial growth if removed from the site of an infection.

Spherule growth and rupture result in a host inflammatory response that includes the action of neutrophils and eosinophils. T lymphocytes also play an important role in the control of *C. immitis* infection. Most infections with this organism are asymptomatic or cause mild, nonspecific upper respiratory symptoms that are not diagnosed.

Diagnosis

Initial preliminary diagnosis is made by consistent clinical symptoms in a patient with recent travel to a *Coccidioides* endemic area of the country. **Definitive diagnosis is made by direct observation of spherules** with subsequent culture of the organism in a specimen, usually of respiratory origin. Direct examination can be made using either KOH or calcofluor white stains.

***Coccidioides immitis* is a dimorphic fungus** that forms spherules in the patient (35°C [95°F]) and arthroconidia in the environment (room temperature). The **arthroconidia are the infectious form** and can be transmitted in the laboratory if proper biosafety precautions are not adhered to. *Coccidioides immitis* grows rapidly (within 1 week) on routine laboratory media. Colonies appear as a white fluffy mold, whose appearance is indistinguishable from the other dimorphic fungi, including *Histoplasma capsulatum* and *Blastomyces dermatitidis. Coccidioides immitis* can be specifically identified by immunodiffusion of extracted *C. immitis* antigen and commercially prepared antibody or by DNA probes specific for *C. immitis* RNA.

In cases in which culture is not possible, or negative, serology or skin testing may be helpful for diagnosis. The disadvantage of both is that a positive conversion may last for life and make diagnosis of a current infection difficult.

Treatment and Prevention

Treatment is not usually provided to patients with uncomplicated respiratory disease without risk factors for dissemination. Patients with complicated disease are treated with either an **azole or amphotericin B.**

COMPREHENSION QUESTIONS

[40.1] A 35-year-old man is HIV antibody-positive and has a CD4 count of 50 cells/mm^3 (normal: 500–1000 cells/mm^3). He has had a fever of 38.3°C (101°F) for a few weeks and "feels tired all the time." He has no other symptoms, and findings on physical examination are normal. Complete blood count, urinalysis, and chest x-ray are normal. A bone marrow biopsy reveals granulomas, and a culture grows an organism that is a budding yeast at 37°C (98.6°F), but produces hyphae and tuberculated chlamydospores at 25°C (77°F). Of the following, which is the most likely cause?

A. *Aspergillus fumigatus*
B. *Coccidioides immitis*
C. *Cryptococcus neoformans*
D. *Histoplasma capsulatum*
E. *Mucor* species

[40.2] A 4-year-old girl who lives in Bakersfield, CA, has had a low-grade fever. Skin tests performed for the first time give the following results:

Tuberculin (PPD)	Positive (10 mm induration)
Coccidioidin test	Positive (15 mm induration)
Dick test	Positive (with erythema)
Dick control test (heated toxin)	Negative (no erythema)
Schick test	Negative (no erythema)
Schick control test (heated toxin)	Negative (no erythema)

The test results suggest which of the following?

A. The patient has been exposed to *Coccidioides immitis.*
B. The patient has been immunized against *Coccidioides immitis.*
C. The patient has had scarlet fever.
D. The patient has IgG antibody to *Mycobacterium tuberculosis.*
E. The patient lacks immunity to *Corynebacterium diphtheriae.*

[40.3] A 50-year-old immunocompromised woman is diagnosed as having meningitis. A latex agglutination test on the spinal fluid for capsular polysaccharide antigen is positive. Of the following organisms, which one is the most likely cause?

A. *Aspergillus fumigatus*
B. *Cryptococcus neoformans*
C. *Histoplasma capsulatum*
D. *Nocardia asteroides*
E. *Toxoplasma gondii*

[40.4] Which of the following is the most common portal of entry in *Blastomyces dermatitidis* infection?

A. Genitourinary tract
B. Lymphatic system
C. Mouth
D. Respiratory tract
E. Skin

Answers

[40.1] **D.** An HIV-positive individual may have normal immune capacity as measured by laboratory parameters, but still be more at risk for opportunistic organisms. Respiratory infections may be caused by fungi, bacteria, or viruses. As a result, laboratory results may be crucial in determining the exact organism causing an infection. In this case, the bone marrow biopsy revealed a budding yeast form at 37°C (98.6°F), but hyphae and tuberculated chlamydospores at room temperature (25°C [77°F]). In disseminated histoplasmosis, bone marrow cultures are often positive. Tuberculate macroconidia are characteristic for *H. capsulatum's* mycelial form.

[40.2] **A.** The Dick and Schick tests are related to streptococcal infections, specifically scarlet fever. The young girl has been exposed to a *Mycobacterium,* most likely *M. tuberculosis,* but the positive reaction observed is based on a cellular immune reaction, not one mediated by antibodies. The location is a region where *Coccidioides* is endemic and should be one of the suspected pathogens to be considered. No vaccine is available for *C. immitis.* Therefore, a positive coccidioidin test indicates that the young girl has been exposed to the agent and has developed a cellular immune reaction in response.

[40.3] **B.** *Cryptococcus neoformans* is a yeast characterized by a thick polysaccharide capsule. It occurs worldwide in nature and in very large numbers in pigeon feces. *Cryptococcus* infection is usually associated with immunosuppression. Tests for capsular antigen can be performed on cerebrospinal fluid and serum. The latex agglutination test for cryptococcal antigen is positive in 90 percent of patients with cryptococcal meningitis. With effective treatment (amphotericin B and possibly flucytosine), the antigen titer usually drops except for AIDS patients.

[40.4] **D.** *Blastomyces dermatitidis* grows as a mold culture, producing septate hyphae and conidia. In a host, it converts to a large, singly budding yeast cell. It is endemic in North America. Human infection is initiated in the lungs. Diagnosis may be difficult because no skin or serologic tests exist. Chronic pneumonia is a common presentation. Sputum, pus, exudates, urine, and lung biopsy material can be examined microscopically, looking for thick walled yeast cells with broadly attached buds. It may also be cultured.

MICROBIOLOGY PEARLS

- *Coccidioides immitis* is a dimorphic, systemic fungus, commonly found in the soil of arid areas.
- Most patients exposed to the arthroconidia of *C. immitis* develop an asymptomatic or respiratory infection. Disseminated disease occurs rarely in severely immunosuppressed patients.
- Person-to-person transmission of *C. immitis* is not known to occur.

REFERENCES

Galgiani J. Coccidioides immitis. In: Mandell GL, Bennett JE, Dolin R, eds. Principles and Practice of Infectious Diseases, 6th ed. Philadelphia, PA: Churchill Livingstone, 2005:3040–51.

Murray PR, Rosenthal KS, Pfaller MA. Systemic mycoses In: Murray PR, Rosenthal KS, Pfaller MA. Medical Microbiology, 5th ed. St. Louis, MO: Mosby, 2005:765–78.

CASE 41

A 28-year-old woman presents complaining of 2-days of itchy vaginal discharge. One week ago you saw and treated her for a urinary tract infection (UTI) with sulfamethoxazole and trimethoprim (SMX-TMP). She completed her medication as ordered and developed the vaginal discharge shortly thereafter. She denies abdominal pain, and her dysuria has resolved. She is not currently taking any medications. On examination, she is comfortable appearing and has normal vital signs. Her general physical examination is normal. A pelvic examination reveals a thick, curd-like, white discharge in her vagina that is adherent to the vaginal sidewalls. There is no cervical discharge or cervical motion tenderness, and bimanual examination of the uterus and adnexa is normal.

- **What is the most likely cause of these symptoms?**

- **What are the most likely reservoirs of this organism in this patient?**

ANSWERS TO CASE 41: *Candida*

Summary: A 28-year-old woman who recently took antibiotics now presents with a vaginal discharge consistent with candidiasis.

- **Most likely etiologic organism:** *Candida albicans*
- **Most likely reservoirs of infection:** Gastrointestinal (GI) and vaginal colonization

CLINICAL CORRELATION

Most *Candida* infections come from the host's endogenous flora. Both humoral and cell-mediated immune functions play a role in defense against *Candida* infections. Those with impaired or suppressed immunity are predisposed to more severe or diffuse disease. Neutropenic persons, such as those on chemotherapy or posttransplant patients, are at risk for severe disease, which disseminates in the blood stream. In contrast, AIDS patients often develop oral, pharyngeal, or esophageal candidiasis but rarely disseminated disease. Intact skin also plays a key role in preventing cutaneous infections, because breaks in the skin of even healthy hosts may result in *Candida* skin infections. The use of antibiotics is probably the most significant predisposing factor for the development of *Candida* infections. Antibiotics that suppress the growth of the normal host bacterial flora can allow *Candida* to proliferate. This is a frequent contributing cause of the development of vaginal candidiasis in women and *Candida* diaper dermatitis in infants.

Candida is the cause of a wide range of infections from oral lesions (thrush) to disseminated disease including endocarditis and meningitis. *Candida albicans* is the most common cause of vaginitis. Predisposing factors include diabetes, previous antimicrobial use, pregnancy, and use of oral contraceptives. Although the pathogenesis and the virulence mechanisms of *Candida* infection is unclear, the presence of pseudohyphae seems to indicate active disease versus colonization. Pseudohyphae are able to adhere to epithelial cells, then the blastoconidia.

APPROACH TO THE SUSPECTED *Candida* PATIENT

Objectives

1. Know the morphology, reservoirs, and reproduction of *Candida* species.
2. Know the clinical syndromes, risk factors, and routes of transmission of diseases associated with *Candida* infection.

Definitions

Neutropenia: A decrease in the number of neutrophils circulating in the blood to less than 2.0×10^9/L, with significant neutropenia being less than 0.5×10^9/L.

Thrush: Form of oral candidiasis in which a membrane forms in the oral cavity consisting of *Candida,* desquamated cells and white blood cells and debris. The appearance is of a creamy white, curd-like exudative plaque on the tongue and in the mouth.

DISCUSSION

Characteristics of *Candida*

Candida are **yeasts** that **exist as both sexual and asexual forms, reproduce by budding** and form **blastospores,** which are small, thin-walled ovoid cells. Blastospores, **pseudohyphae** may be seen on examination of clinical specimens. There are over 150 species of *Candida,* 9 of which appear to cause disease in humans. *Candida albicans* is the most common cause of human candidiasis. It can be found in soil and on inanimate objects and foods. It is also found in the normal flora of the human GI tract, vagina, and skin.

Diagnosis

Diagnosis of vaginitis is made by a combination of physical examination and testing the vaginal exudate. Ruling out other causes of vaginitis may be aided by determining the pH of the exudates as well as stain and culture of the material. **Yeast cells are larger than bacteria** and can be visualized easily by direct wet preparation of the exudates with KOH. *Candida* will grow with 24–48 hours on most routine laboratory media; however, Sabouraud dextrose agar can be used to inhibit the normal flora bacteria in cultures for mucosal candidiasis. *Candida* colonies are smooth and creamy, although some species may be dry and can be identified as yeast by a wet preparation. *Candida* species produce round or oval blastoconidia, and some species also produce **pseudohyphae** (chains of elongated blastoconidia), as in Figure 41-1. Preliminary differentiation of *Candida albicans* from the other *Candida* species can be made by observation of the presence of a germ tube. *Candida albicans* will make a germ tube after several hours incubation in the presence of serum. *Candida albicans* can also be differentiated from other yeast based on their microscopic morphology on corn meal agar. *Candida albicans* produce chlamydospores, large rounded structures in the middle of the pseudohyphae. Yeasts that are germ tube-negative can be further identified by assimilation of different substrates. Several commercial kits are available that identify *Candida* to the species level.

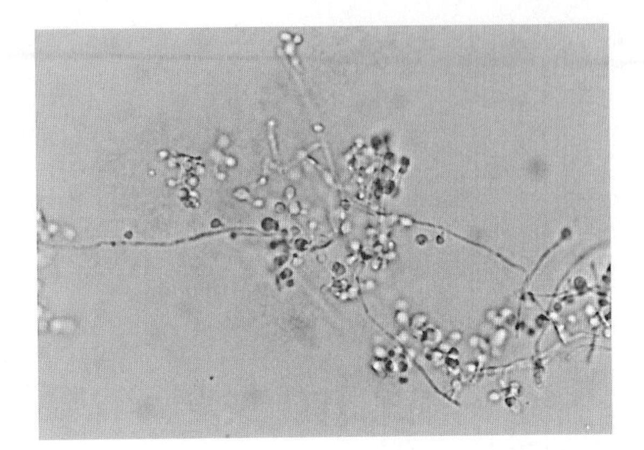

Figure 41-1. *Candida albicans.* Pseudohyphae noted on microscopy. (*Reproduced, with permission, Brooks G, Butel J, Morse S. Jawetz, Melnick, & Adelberg's medical microbiology, 23rd ed. New York: McGraw-Hill, 2004:646.*)

Treatment and Prevention

Therapy for *Candida* vaginitis is usually topical **antifungal agent such as nystatin** or **clotrimazole.** It is not uncommon for patients to remain or be recurrently colonized with vaginal yeast after appropriate therapy. This may or may not lead to a symptomatic recurrence. **Oral or intravenous therapy with either an azole antifungal such as fluconazole, amphotericin B,** or the new agent, **caspofungin,** are used for treatment of disseminated infections with *Candida.* The agent of choice is dependent on the species of *Candida* isolated and the susceptibility of the isolate to the antifungal. Prophylaxis for *Candida* infections is not routinely recommended because of the selection of strains of *Candida* that are resistant to antifungal agents. The only population in which some benefit has been seen with prophylaxis is in bone marrow transplant patients. Partly as a result of the increased use of fluconazole, the incidence of *Candida* species not *albicans,* or the species more likely to be fluconazole resistant have also increased.

COMPREHENSION QUESTIONS

[41.1] *Candida albicans* can be differentiated from other *Candida* species on cornmeal agar by its unique ability to form which of the following?

A. Arthrospores
B. Aseptate hyphae
C. Chlamydospores
D. Germ tubes
E. Tuberculate macroconidia

[41.2] A young man in his mid-twenties presented with mucosal lesions in his mouth. Based on his CD4 cell count and other signs during the past few months, he was diagnosed as having AIDS. Which of the following is the most likely etiology of the oral lesions?

A. *Aspergillus*
B. *Candida*
C. *Cryptococcus*
D. *Mucor*
E. *Rhizopus*

[41.3] Which of the following morphologic structures is not associated with *Candida albicans?*

A. Chlamydospore
B. Hyphae
C. Pseudohyphae
D. Sporangium
E. Yeast

[41.4] Which of the following is the main reason that individuals taking tetracycline often develop candidiasis?

A. *Candida albicans* is capable of degrading the antibiotic.
B. The action of the antibiotic is neutralized by the protein of *C. albicans.*
C. The antibiotic damages the host mucous membrane.
D. The antibiotic is nutritionally favorable for the growth of *C. albicans.*
E. The normal bacterial flora is drastically altered by tetracycline.

Answers

[41.1] **C.** Although multiple *Candida* species may cause disease in humans, *C. albicans* is the most frequent species identified. Chlamydospores (chlamydoconidia) are round, thick-walled spores formed directly from the differentiation of hyphae in which there is a concentration of protoplasm and nutrient material. They may be intercalary (within the hyphae) or terminal (end of hyphae). Germ tubes appear as hyphal-like extensions of yeast cells, usually without a constriction at the point of origin from the cell. Approximately 75 percent of the yeasts recovered from clinical specimens are *C. albicans,* and the germ-tube test can usually provide identification within 3 hours. The morphologic features of yeasts on cornmeal agar containing Tween 80 allow for the differentiation of *C. albicans* from five other *Candida* species.

[41.2] **B.** The risk factors for cutaneous and mucosal candidiasis include AIDS, pregnancy, diabetes, young or old age, birth control pills, and trauma. Oral thrush can occur on the tongue, lips, gums, or palate. It may be patchy to confluent, and it forms whitish lesions composed of epithelial cells, yeasts, and pseudohyphae. Oral thrush commonly occurs in AIDS patients. Although the other genera listed may be opportunistic, only *Candida* routinely presents with mucosal lesions.

[41.3] **D.** A sporangium is a sac enclosing spores, seen in certain fungi, but not *Candida* species. Spores produced within a sporangium, usually located at the tip of a long hyphal stalk are released by rupture of the sporangial wall. All other options (chlamydospore, hyphae, pseudohyphae, and yeasts) are routinely observed in *C. albicans* cultures, depending on conditions of growth.

[41.4] **E.** Patients with compromised host defenses are susceptible to ubiquitous fungi to which healthy people are exposed but usually resistant. *Candida* and related yeasts are part of the normal microbial flora, but are kept at low numbers by faster-growing normal flora bacteria. If broad-spectrum antimicrobials are used, much of the usual flora bacteria may be eliminated. No longer held in check, the opportunist yeast may become more predominant and opportunistic. Discontinuation of use of the broad-spectrum antibiotic is an important first step in patient management, allowing for reestablishment of the normal or usual flora and control of the yeast species.

MICROBIOLOGY PEARLS

- *Candida albicans* is a germ tube—positive yeast that is the most common cause of vaginitis.
- *Candida albicans* can be distinguished from the other *Candida* species by formation of a germ tube after incubation in serum.
- The incidence of *Candida* species other than albicans has increased because of the increased use of azoles and their propensity to develop resistance to those antifungal agents.

REFERENCES

Edwards JE. Candida species. In: Mandell GL, Bennett JE, Dolin R, eds. Principles and Practice of Infectious Diseases, 6th ed. Philadelphia, PA: Churchill Livingstone, 2005:2938–57.

Murray PR, Rosenthal KS, Pfaller MA. Opportunistic mycoses. In: Murray PR, Rosenthal KS, Pfaller MA. Medical Microbiology, 5th ed. St. Louis, MO: Mosby, 2005:779–800.

❖ CASE 42

A 32-year-old man with known AIDS is brought to the emergency room with headache and fever for the past 3 days. According to family members who are with him, he has been confused, forgetful, and irritable for a few weeks prior to the onset of these symptoms. They state that he has advanced AIDS with a low CD4 count and has had bouts of pneumocystis pneumonia, candidal esophagitis, and Kaposi sarcoma. He is on multiple medications, although they don't know whether he is actually taking them. On examination, he is cachetic and frail appearing. He is confused and only oriented to his name. His temperature is 37.8°C (100°F), and his other vital signs are normal. Examination of his cranial nerves is normal. He has minimal nuchal rigidity. Cardiovascular, pulmonary, and abdominal examinations are normal. He is hyperreflexic. A head CT scan is normal. A report of the microscopic examination of his cerebrospinal fluid obtained by lumbar puncture comes back from the laboratory and states that there were numerous white blood cells, predominantly lymphocytes, and no organisms identified on Gram stain but a positive India ink test.

◆ **What organism is the likely cause of this illness?**

◆ **What characteristic of this organism is primarily responsible for its virulence?**

ANSWERS TO CASE 42: *Cryptococcus neoformans*

Summary: A 32-year-old male with advanced AIDS presents with meningitis. The India ink test is positive.

- **Most likely etiology for this man's meningitis:** *Cryptococcus neoformans.*
- **Characteristic of this organism is primarily responsible for its virulence:** *Cryptococcus neoformans* is known characteristically to produce a mucopolysaccharide capsule. This is a key feature of this organism's virulence, because it is antiphagocytic and also interferes with leukocyte migration to sites of infection.

CLINICAL CORRELATION

Cryptococcus neoformans is an encapsulated monomorphic fungi that commonly causes chronic meningitis in immune-suppressed individuals and occasionally in immune-competent persons. The lungs are the primary site of infection, although the organism appears to have specific affinity for the brain and meninges on systemic spread. ***Cryptococcus neoformans*** **is the leading cause of fungal meningitis and is an important cause of mortality in AIDS patients.**

APPROACH TO SUSPECTED *Cryptococcus neoformans* INFECTION

Objectives

1. Be familiar with the characteristics and disease presentation of *C. neoformans* fungi.
2. Know the methods of diagnosis of infection with *C. neoformans*.
3. Be able to describe the treatment and prevention of infection.

Definitions

Meningitis: Inflammation of the meninges.
Nuchal rigidity: Stiffness of the neck associated with meningitis.
Cachetic: Weight loss or wasting because of disease or illness.

DISCUSSION

Characteristics of *Cryptococcus neoformans* That Impact Transmission

Cryptococcus neoformans is an **encapsulated yeast, 4–6 mm in diameter,** which is distributed globally. The most common serotypes are found in high concentrations in **pigeon and other bird droppings,** although they do not appear to cause disease in these hosts. The most common route of transmission to humans is via aerosolization of the organism followed by inhalation into the lungs. Direct animal-to-person transmission has not been shown. Unlike other systemic fungi, *C. neoformans* is **monomorphic,** not dimorphic, and **grows as budding yeast cells** at both 25°C (77°F) in culture and at 37°C (98.6°F) in tissues. When grown in culture, *C. neoformans* produces white- or tan-colored mucoid colonies in 2–3 days on a variety of common fungal media. Microscopically, the organism appears as spherical budding yeast, surrounded by a thick capsule. *Cryptococcus neoformans* differs from the other nonpathogenic cryptococcal strains by its ability to produce phenol oxidase and growth at 37°C (98.6°F).

The **capsule** is an **important virulence factor** of *Cryptococcus,* and it consists of long, unbranched polysaccharide polymers. Capsule production is normally repressed in environmental settings and is stimulated by physiologic conditions in the body. The **capsule is antiphagocytic,** because of its large size and structure and has also been shown to interfere with antigen presentation and the development of T-cell-mediated immune responses at sites of infection. This suppression of an immune response can allow for multiplication of the organism and promotion of its spread outside the respiratory tract. Once outside the lung, the organism appears to have an affinity for the central nervous system (CNS), possibly because of its ability to bind C3 and the low levels of complement found in the CNS.

Diagnosis

Inhalation of these aerosolized yeast cells leads to a primary pulmonary infection. The infection may be asymptomatic or may result in a flu-like respiratory illness or pneumonia. Commonly, cryptococcal pulmonary infection is identified only as an incidental finding on a chest x-ray being performed for other reasons. Often the infection and resulting lesions appear suspicious for a malignancy, only to be diagnosed properly after surgical removal. The most commonly diagnosed cryptococcal disease is meningitis, which results from hematogenous spread of the organism from the lung to the **meninges.** It occurs most commonly in persons with **AIDS** or those who are **immunosuppressed** for other reasons, but it can occasionally occur in persons without underlying conditions. Outside the lungs, *C. neoformans* appears to have a preference for the cerebrospinal fluid (CSF), but disseminated disease can also cause infections of the skin, eye, and bone. Cryptococcal meningitis may be insidious in its onset, slowly causing mental status changes, irritability, or confusion that occurs over weeks to months, or it can occur acutely, with immediate changes in mentation and meningeal symptoms. Clinical disease may present with intermittent headache, irritability, dizziness, and difficulty with complex cerebral functions and may even be mistaken as psychoses. Seizures, cranial nerve signs, and papilledema may appear in late clinical course.

A diagnosis of *C. neoformans* infection is made primarily by clinical presentation and examination of CSF for increased pressure, increased number of white cells, and low glucose levels. Serum and CSF specimens should also be tested for polysaccharide capsular antigen by latex agglutination or enzyme immunoassay. Another classic test for *C. neoformans* is the India ink test, which is an easy and rapid test that is positive in approximately 50 percent of patients with cryptococcal disease. **A drop of India ink** is placed on a glass slide and mixed with a loopful of CSF sediment or a small amount of isolated yeast cells. A cover slip is added and the slide is examined microscopically for encapsulated yeast cells that exclude the ink particles.

Treatment and Prevention

Cryptococcus neoformans infections can be treated with antifungal agents such as **amphotericin B or fluconazole.** Amphotericin B is a broad-spectrum chemo-therapeutic agent and is the most effective drug for severe systemic mycoses. However, it is an extremely nephrotoxic agent to which all patients have adverse reactions such as fever, chills, dyspnea, hypotension, and nausea. Fluconazole is less toxic than amphotericin B and produces fewer side effects; however, resistance to fluconazole has been shown to occur. AIDS patients with cryptococcosis are required to continue lifelong suppressive therapy with fluconazole to prevent relapse of fungal infection.

COMPREHENSION QUESTIONS

[42.1] A 32-year-old man who lives in downtown Philadelphia presents to his physician with a 4-day history of terrible headache, fever, and stiff neck. He has always been in good health and attributes this to his healthy eating habits and his daily running through the city parks near his apartment. The physician suspects the man may have cryptococcal meningitis and collects CSF for examination. Which of the following results would you most likely expect from this patient's CSF studies?

A. Elevated CSF pressure with increased white cell counts
B. Elevated polymorphonuclear cells with high protein levels
C. Elevated lymphocytes with normal glucose levels
D. Normal CSF pressure with a positive Gram stain reaction
E. Normal CSF pressure with negative Gram stain reaction

[42.2] Which of the following laboratory tests would best definitely diagnose cryptococcal infection in the above patient?

A. Quelling reaction capsular swelling
B. Latex agglutination test for polysaccharide capsular antigen
C. Ouchterlony test for fungal infection
D. India ink test for the presence of capsulated yeast
E. Gram stain reaction

[42.3] A 35-year-old man with AIDS presents to the local clinic with complaints of nausea, vomiting, confusion, fever and staggering gait. A lumbar puncture is performed, and an organism with a halo is noted with India ink preparation. What drug would be most beneficial?

A. Ketoconazole and amphotericin B
B. Fluconazole and amphotericin B
C. Nystatin and ketoconazole
D. Nystatin and miconazole
E. Griseofulvin

[42.4] A 34-year-old white homeless man in New York city is brought in by the police to the emergency room because he was found wandering the streets confused with a staggering gait. On physical exam, he is noted to have acne like lesions over a large part of his body accompanied with skin ulcers. He is febrile and has some cranial nerve deficits. A short time later the man becomes short of breath, which was determined to be caused by severe cerebral edema compressing the medulla. Which of the following is the most likely causative agent?

A. *Histoplasma capsulatum*
B. *Coccidioides immitis*
C. *Exophiala werneckii*
D. *Sporothrix schenckii*
E. *Cryptococcus neoformans*

Answers

[42.1] **A.** Meningitis caused by *C. neoformans* infection typically results in increased CSF pressure with an increased number of white cells and low glucose levels; answers B, C, D, and E are incorrect: both (B) and (D) appropriately describe meningitis caused by a bacterial agent such as *Neisseria meningitides;* (C) appropriately describes meningitis caused by a viral agent such as herpes simplex virus; (E) describes normal CSF findings.

[42.2] **B.** answers A, C, D, and E are incorrect: (A) is a test useful for diagnosing *Streptococcus pneumoniae* and uses capsule-specific antibody to cause capsule swelling; (C) is an immunodiffusion test useful in diagnosing *Histoplasma* and *Blastomyces* fungal infections; (D) does provide rapid diagnosis of *Cryptococcus neoformans;* however, this assay is positive in only 50 percent of cryptococcal cases; (E) the Gram stain is more useful in diagnosing bacterial infections, because it would show the presence of yeast cells, but the capsule would not be visible.

[42.3] **B.** The organism present is *C. neoformans,* the usual treatment for cryptococcosis is amphotericin B and fluconazole. The other drugs listed are not indicated for cryptococcosis. Ketoconazole is usually used for chronic mucocutaneous candidiasis. Nystatin is used for candidiasis, and griseofulvin is indicated for dermatophytes of the hair, skin, and nails. Miconazole is used for topical fungal infections, oral thrush, and vaginitis.

[42.4] **E.** The symptoms described including acne-like lesions, skin ulcers, fever, confusion, staggering gait and cranial nerve deficits are a classic example of *Cryptococcus neoformans* infection. In some patients the cerebral edema progresses to a fatal stage compressing the medulla reducing respiratory efforts. The other yeast listed do not cause cerebral edema. *Exophiala werneckii* causes tinea nigra characterized by dark patches on the hands and soles of the feet. *Sporothrix schenckii* is usually associated with a prick from a rose thorn. *Coccidioides immitis* is associated with the desert southwest. *Histoplasma capsulatum* is usually associated with a Mississippi river valley history, as well as lesions that calcify.

MICROBIOLOGY PEARLS

- *Cryptococcus neoformans* is transmitted via aerosolized pigeon or bird droppings.
- Clinical manifestations: headache, altered mental state, nuchal rigidity, often associated with AIDS.
- Identification: clinical symptoms, examination of CSF for increased pressure and number of white cells with low glucose levels, and a positive capsular antigen latex agglutination and India ink tests.
- Current treatment: amphotericin B or fluconazole.

REFERENCES

Brooks GF, Butel JS, Morse SA. Jawetz, Melnick, & Adelberg's Medical Microbiology, 23rd ed. New York: McGraw-Hill, 2004:647–9.

Murray PR, Rosenthal KS, Pfaller MA. Medical Microbiology, 5th ed. St. Louis,MO: Mosby, 2005:779–800.

Ryan JR, Ray CG. Sherris Medical Microbiology, 4th ed. New York: McGraw-Hill, 2004:647–9.

CASE 43

A 29-year-old woman comes into the clinic for evaluation of a cough. Her symptoms started a few weeks ago and have progressively worsened. The cough is not productive. She has had intermittent, low-grade fevers and feels short of breath. She has tried some over-the-counter cough medications, which don't seem to help. She smokes approximately a half-pack of cigarettes a day. She denies any history of pulmonary diseases. On examination, her temperature is 37.5°C (99.5°F), pulse is 100 beats per minute, respiratory rate is 26 breaths per minute, and oxygen saturation is 89 percent on room air. Her blood pressure is normal, but when applying the blood pressure cuff, you notice numerous scars in her antecubital region consistent with "needle tracks." In general, she is a thin woman who appears to be in moderate respiratory distress and is coughing frequently. Her head and neck examination is normal. Her lung examination is notable for decreased breath sounds and rhonchi in all fields. Her cardiovascular and abdominal examinations are normal. A chest x-ray shows a bilateral interstitial infiltrate with a "ground-glass" appearance. She confides that she is HIV positive.

◆ **What organism is the likely cause of her symptoms?**

 **Describe the sexual phase of reproduction of this organism.**

ANSWERS TO CASE 43: *Pneumocystis jiroveci*

Summary: A 29-year-old woman intravenous drug user who is HIV positive has an interstitial pneumonia.

- **Most likely etiologic agent:** *Pneumocystis jiroveci.*
- **Sexual phase reproduction of *P. jiroveci:*** Haploid trophic forms conjugate to form diploid zygotes that become sporocysts; sporocysts undergo meiosis and mitosis to form the spore case that contains eight haploid spores. The spores are released by rupture of the spore case wall.

CLINICAL CORRELATION

Pneumocystis is an opportunistic organism found primarily in the lungs of humans and other animals. The reservoir of the organism in the environment is at this point unknown. Transmission of the organism is from person to person by respiratory droplet inhalation into the lungs. It is unclear whether disease results from the reactivation of a latent infection or acquisition of a new infection. The cellular immune system is primarily responsible for host defenses, with alveolar macrophages and CD4 cells playing a particularly important role. In HIV patients, the risk of developing symptomatic disease from *Pneumocystis* is highly correlated to the number of circulating CD4 cells, with the highest risk in those persons with CD4 counts below 200/mm^3. The use of corticosteroids or other immunosuppressive drugs, treatment for malignancies, or severe malnutrition are risk factors for disease in non–HIV infected people. Classic *Pneumocystis* pulmonary infection is an interstitial pneumonia with plasma cell infiltrates. Typical symptoms are nonproductive cough, fever, dyspnea, and hypoxia. Chest x-rays commonly show a bilateral interstitial infiltrate extending from the hilum with a "ground-glass" appearance. In severely immunosuppressed patients *Pneumocystis* can disseminate most commonly to the thyroid, liver, bone marrow, lymph nodes, or spleen.

APPROACH TO THE SUSPECTED *Pneumocystis* PATIENT

Objectives

1. Know the life cycle, morphology, and reproduction of *Pneumocystis.*
2. Know the epidemiology, modes of transmission, and clinical syndromes associated with *Pneumocystis* infection.

Definitions

Hypoxia: Reduction of oxygen supply to the tissues despite adequate blood perfusion.

Dyspnea: Shortness of breath leading to labored breathing.

DISCUSSION

Characteristics of *Pneumocystis*

Pneumocystis was **originally characterized as a trypanosome;** however, advanced molecular biological techniques have shown it to be closely related to fungi. It is unusual among fungi because it **lacks ergosterol in its cell membranes** and is insensitive to many antifungal drugs. Its life cycle has **both sexual and asexual components.** The trophic form of *Pneumocystis* is small and often seen in clusters. It multiplies asexually by binary fission and sexually by conjugation of haploid trophic forms to diploid cells that become sporocysts. These uninuclear cells undergo miosis then mitosis to form a spore case, which contains eight haploid spores. The spores are released by rupture of the cell wall, although the cyst wall remains and can be identified as empty structures.

Pneumocystis is thought to be ubiquitous in the environment, and most adults have been exposed to the organism during childhood and develop an asymptomatic infection. *Pneumocystis* is found in many mammalian species and is not thought to cross species lines. *Pneumocystis* that infects humans was recently renamed *P. jirovecii.*

Diagnosis

The **diagnosis** is confirmed by the **presence of the organisms in sputum or bronchial samples** obtained by bronchoalveolar lavage or other techniques, such as sputum induced by respiratory therapy. *Pneumocystis* can be identified microscopically by using numerous stains, such as **methenamine silver, Giemsa, chemofluorescent agents such as calcofluor white, or specific** immunofluorescent monoclonal antibodies. The monoclonal antibody fluorescent stain increases the sensitivity and specificity of the test. The diagnostic stage seen is usually the cyst form. The organism cannot be grown in culture.

Treatment and Prevention

Treatment for *Pneumocystis* is usually with **sulfamethoxazole and trimethoprim (SMX-TMP);** however, in allergic patients there are other options such as **dapsone** or **pentamidine. Prophylaxis with SMX-TMP** is recommended for severely immunosuppressed patients including HIV patients with a **CD4 count of less than 200 cells/mm^3.**

COMPREHENSION QUESTIONS

[43.1] *Pneumocystis jiroveci* is now considered a fungus. Which of the following statements accurately describes this organism?

A. In immunocompromised patients the organism invades blood vessels causing thrombosis and infarction.
B. It grows best in a culture medium containing tissue fluid.
C. It is now classified as a fungus because it grows into septate hyphae in Sabouraud agar.
D. It is sensitive to antifungal agents such as amphotericin B.
E. Methenamine silver stain is used to visualize the organism in the clinical specimen.

[43.2] Which of the following statements best describes the laboratory diagnosis of *Pneumocystis jiroveci?*

A. India ink stain of bronchoalveolar lavage material
B. KOH stain of lung biopsy tissue
C. Growth of the organism on Sabouraud agar
D. Methenamine silver stain of induced sputum

[43.3] *Pneumocystis jiroveci* produces disease under what conditions listed below?

A. In individuals with CD4 lymphocyte counts above 400/μL
B. In the presence of immunosuppression
C. Infection in early childhood
D. Prophylaxis with SMX-TMP

Answers

[43.1] **E.** *Pneumocystis jiroveci* is often reported as the organism responsible for the described case. *Pneumocystis carinii* is found in rats, whereas *P. jirovecii* is found in humans. These species are not grown in the laboratory and do not respond to traditional antifungal chemotherapy. Being found primarily in the lungs, respiratory infections occur in immunocompromised individuals, and dissemination is rare. Specimens of bronchoalveolar lavage, lung biopsy, or induced sputum are stained (e.g., Giemsa or methenamine silver) and examined for cysts or trophozoites.

[43.2] **D.** Because *Pneumocystis* species are not able to be grown in the laboratory, staining procedures constitute the primary diagnostics techniques used. See the answer to Question 43.1 for further discussion.

[43.3] **B.** *Pneumocystis jiroveci* and *P. carinii* are present in the lungs of many animals, including humans. This organism rarely causes disease except in immunocompromised hosts. No other natural reservoir has ever been demonstrated, and the mode of infection is unclear. Transmission by aerosols may be possible.

MICROBIOLOGY PEARLS

- *Pneumocystis* that infects humans was recently renamed from *P. carinii to P. jirovecii.*
- *Pneumocystis* has a predilection for the lungs of humans and animals.
- Diagnosis of *Pneumocystis* is made by induced sputum or bronchoscopy with microscopic visualization of the cyst forms with either Papanicolaou, Giemsa, silver stain, or monoclonal antibodies.

REFERENCES

Murray PR, Rosenthal KS, Pfaller MA. Opportunistic mycoses. In: Murray PR, Rosenthal KS, Pfaller MA. Medical Microbiology, 5th ed. St. Louis, MO: Mosby, 2005:664–72.

Thomas CF, Limper AH. Pneumocystis pneumonia. NEJM 2004;350:2487–98.

Walter PD. Pneumocystis carinii. In: Mandell GL, Bennett JE, Dolin R, eds. Principles and Practice of Infectious Diseases, 5th ed. Philadelphia, PA: Churchill Livingstone, 2000:2781–95.

❖ CASE 44

A 44-year-old woman presents to the physician's office for evaluation of skin growths on her right arm. She reports that a few weeks ago she developed some small, red bumps on her right palm, which seemed to come together into a larger nodule. This then ulcerated, but it never was painful. She has been putting topical antibiotic on this area, and it seemed to be improving. However, in the past week she has noticed new growths extending up her forearm that appear just like the original lesion. She denies having skin lesions anywhere else, denies systemic symptoms such as fever, and has no history of anything like this before. She has no significant medical history and takes no medications. She is employed as a florist and floral arranger. On examination, she is comfortable appearing and has normal vital signs. On her right palm you see a circular, 1-cm-diameter, ulcerated area with a surrounding red, raised border. There are two identical appearing, but smaller, lesions on the forearm. Microscopic examination of a biopsy taken from one of the lesions reveals numerous white blood cells and cigar-shaped yeast forms.

◆ **What is the most likely infectious cause of these lesions?**

What is the most likely route by which this infection was transmitted?

ANSWERS TO CASE 44: *Sporothrix schenckii*

Summary: A 44-year-old florist has painless, ulcerated lesions on her right hand and arm.

- **Most likely infectious etiology:** *Sporothrix schenckii.*

- **Most likely route by which this infection was transmitted:** Most likely mechanism of infection is inoculation into the skin via a puncture of the hand with an infected plant (most likely a rose thorn).

CLINICAL CORRELATION

Cutaneous sporotrichosis results from the inoculation of the organism into the skin via a puncture or other minor trauma. Most cases occur in persons with occupational or avocational exposure to infected material, such as in gardening or farming. The most common exposures are to rose thorns and sphagnum moss. The initial lesions are usually in areas that are prone to trauma, such as the extremities. They are often erythematous papules or nodules, which then ulcerate. Secondary lesions develop along the lines of lymphatic drainage. The lesions are usually painless, can wax and wane, and systemic symptoms are rare. Extracutaneous infections with *S. schenckii* have occurred, most commonly involving the joints, particularly hand, elbow, ankle, or knees. Cases of pulmonary sporotrichosis as well as meningitis have been described. Invasive and disseminated disease may occur in the severely immunosuppressed, particularly patients with advanced HIV disease.

APPROACH TO THE SUSPECTED SPOROTRICHOSIS PATIENT

Objectives

1. Know the morphologic characteristics of the yeast and mycelial forms of *S. schenckii.*
2. Know the common sources, routes of transmission, and clinical syndromes associated with *S. schenckii* infections.

Definitions

Dematiaceous fungi: Fungi with dark colored (brown or black) conidia and/or hyphae.

Lymphadenitis: Inflammation of the lymph node(s).

DISCUSSION

Characteristics of *Sporothrix schenckii*

Sporothrix schenckii is a **dimorphic fungus** that is most often isolated from **soil, plants, or plant products.** When cultured at 37°C (98.6°F) or *in vivo,* it exists as **cigar-shaped yeast.** At lower temperatures, it exists as a white, fuzzy mold that on further incubation develops a brown pigment. The hyphal form has numerous conidia, which develop in a rosette pattern at the ends of conidiophores. The fungus is found in the soil and on vegetation in all parts of the world, but most commonly in the tropical regions of North and South America. Transmission from animals to man has also been rarely described.

Diagnosis

Skin lesions associated with sporotrichosis can resemble those of other infectious and noninfectious entities, such as other fungal infections, *Mycobacterium* infections, or collagen vascular diseases. Diagnosis can be made by culture of biopsy material or demonstration of the **characteristic cigar-shaped yeast forms** on microscopic examination of a biopsy specimen. Multiple attempts at biopsy and culture may be required to recover the organism.

Sporothrix schenckii grows well within several days to several weeks on routine fungal media such as Sabouraud dextrose agar. Colonies initially are small and white to cream color that eventually turn brown to black. Laboratory confirmation of *S. schenckii* can be established by demonstration of characteristic mold structures after culture at room temperature. The **rosette formation of the conidia** on the conidiophore is characteristic, but not diagnostic. Conversion from the hyphal form to the yeast form on subculture of a specimen at 37°C (98.6°F) can aid in the specific identification of the fungus.

Treatment and Prevention

Cutaneous sporotrichosis is usually **treated orally with either a saturated solution of potassium iodide** or an **antifungal agent such as itraconazole.** Extracutaneous or disseminated disease is difficult to treat, but usually treated with **itraconazole.** Patients with concomitant HIV and sporotrichosis are usually treated prophylactically for the rest of their life with oral itraconazole.

COMPREHENSION QUESTIONS

[44.1] Which of the following fungi is most likely to cause cutaneous disease?

A. *Aspergillus fumigatus*
B. *Candida albicans*
C. *Cryptococcus neoformans*
D. *Histoplasma capsulatum*
E. *Sporothrix schenckii*

[44.2] A woman who pricked her finger while pruning some rose bushes develops a local pustule that progressed to an ulcer. Several nodules then developed along the local lymphatic drainage. The *most reliable* method to identify the etiologic agent is which of the following?

A. Culture of the organism in the laboratory
B. Gram stain of smear prepared from the lesion
C. India ink preparation
D. Skin test for delayed hypersensitivity
E. Stain the culture with potassium iodide

Answers

[44.1] **E.** *Aspergillus, Cryptococcus,* and *Histoplasma* infections routinely involve the respiratory system and form cellular components recognizable in the diagnostic laboratory. *Candida* species are usually endogenous flora that may be opportunistic under the right circumstances (e.g., immunocompromised patient). Cutaneous and systemic infections are possible under these conditions. *S. schenckii* is typically introduced into the skin by trauma, often related to outdoor activities and/or plants. About three-fourths of the cases are lymphocutaneous, with multiple subcutaneous nodules and abscesses along the lymphatics.

[44.2] **A.** The most reliable method of diagnosing *S. schenckii* is by culture. Specimens are usually biopsy materials or exudate from granulose or ulcerative lesions and are usually streaked on a selective medium such as Sabouraud agar containing antibacterial antibiotics. Initial incubation is usually 25°C–30°C (77°F–86°F), followed by growth at 35°C (95°F) and confirmation by conversion to the yeast form. Staining procedures are usually nonspecific unless fluorescent antibody.

MICROBIOLOGY PEARLS

- *Sporothrix schenckii* is a dimorphic fungus found in the soil of many areas of the world and associated with skin lesions following traumatic implantation most commonly from rose thorns.
- Cutaneous sporotrichosis is commonly treated with oral potassium iodide.
- Extracutaneous sporotrichosis, although rare, occurs in severely immunocompromised patients such as those with HIV.

REFERENCES

Fitzpatrick TB, Johnson RA, Polano MK, et al. Color Atlas and Synopsis of Clinical Dermatology, 2nd ed. New York: McGraw-Hill, 1992.

Gorbach SL, Bartlett JG, Blacklow NR. Infectious Diseases, 2nd ed. Philadelphia,PA: W.B. Saunders, 1998.

Harmon EM, Szwed T. Aspergillosis. eMedicine, 2002. http://www.emedicine.com/med/topic174.html

Mandell GL, Bennett JE, Dolin R, eds. Principles and Practice of Infectious Diseases, 5th ed. Philadelphia, PA: Churchill Livingstone, 2000.

Murray PR, Rosenthal KS, Pfaller MA. Medical Microbiology, 5th ed. St. Louis, MO: Mosby, 2005:738,799.

Rex JH, Okhuysen PC. Sporothrix schenckii. In: Mandell GL, Bennett JE, Dolin R, eds. Principles and Practice of Infectious Diseases, 6th ed. Philadelphia, PA: Churchill Livingstone, 2005:2695–702.

Shafazand S, Doyle R, Ruoss S, et al. Inhalational anthrax: epidemiology, diagnosis and management. Chest 1999;116(5):1369–76.

Todar K. University of Wisconsin-Madison Dept. of Bacteriology, 2002; http:www.bact.wisc.edu/bact330/lymelecture

❖ CASE 45

An 8-year-old boy, a child of immigrants from El Salvador who moved to the southwestern United States 3 months ago, presents to the emergency room with abdominal pain and vomiting. He was ill for a day, but his symptoms have worsened in the past few hours, and his parents panicked when they saw a worm in his vomitus. He has no significant medical history and has taken no medications. On examination, he appears very ill and in obvious pain. His temperature is 37.7°C (99.9°F), his pulse is 110 beats per minute, and his blood pressure is normal. His mucous membranes are dry, but his head and neck exam is otherwise normal. He is tachycardic, and his lungs are clear. His abdomen has high-pitched, tinkling bowel sounds on auscultation and is diffusely tender to palpation. There is, however, no rebound tenderness. An abdominal x-ray shows air-fluid levels consistent with a small bowel obstruction. His parents saved and brought in the worm that he vomited. It is 5 inches long and reddish-yellow in color.

◆ **What organism is most likely responsible for the patient's illness?**

◆ **How did the patient become infected?**

ANSWERS TO CASE 45: ASCARIASIS

Summary: An 8-year-old boy with a small bowel obstruction and who vomited a worm.

 **Most likely organism responsible for the patient's illness:** The nematode, *Ascaris lumbricoides.*

◆ **How did the patient become infected:** By ingesting eggs of the parasite that have matured in an external environment to contain a larval form.

CLINICAL CORRELATION

Infections with *Ascaris* are frequently asymptomatic or may be accompanied by numerous symptoms. The pathology that underlies symptoms is conditioned by the number of worms harbored and the sequential location of larvae in the lungs and adult worms in the intestine.

Larvae released when ingested eggs hatch make a so-called "heart-lung circuit" in which they are carried via the blood to various tissues (Figure 45-1). Migrating larvae elicit eosinophilia and granulomatous lesions. During the larval migration stage, symptoms are associated mainly with larvae present in the liver and lungs. Larvae that reach the lungs may cause pneumonitis. Patients may cough up exudates that are blood-tinged and contain polymorphonuclear leukocytes, mainly eosinophils. Fever may accompany pneumonitis, which usually disappears when the larvae move to the small intestine, as part of their life cycle. *Ascaris* is highly allergenic, stimulating inordinately high IgE levels. Therefore, pneumonitis may be especially severe in individuals who are sensitized by a primary infection and encounter a challenge or secondary infection. Thus, increased severity of pneumonitis is caused by immune-mediated inflammation.

Gastrointestinal (GI) symptoms depend on the number and location of adult worms in the GI tract. Light infection may cause GI upset, colic, and loss of appetite and impair digestion or absorption of nutrients. In heavy infections, the adult worms may ball up in the small intestine, resulting in physical obstruction, a rare but serious occurrence. From their usual location in the small intestine, adult worms infrequently migrate down and out of the anus or up and through the mouth or nose. Adult worms may cause symptoms by migrating to obstruct the bile ducts or penetrate into the gallbladder or liver. Adult worms may be seen in the stool or vomitus.

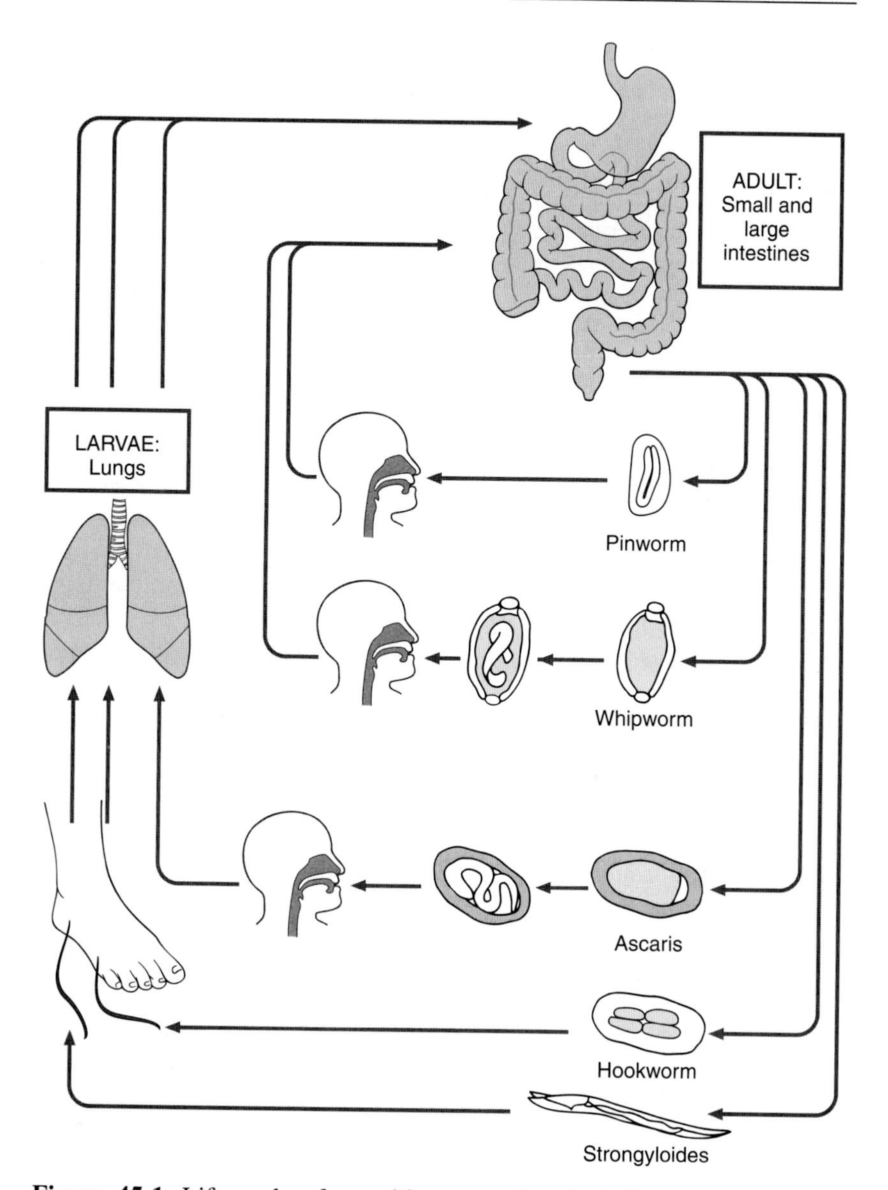

Figure 45-1. Life cycle of parasitic nematodes, including *Ascaris lumbricoides.* (*With permission from Barron S, ed. Medical Microbiology, 4th ed. Galveston, TX: University of Texas Medical Branch, 1996.*)

APPROACH TO SUSPECTED *Ascaris* INFECTION

Objectives

1. Learn the life cycle of *A. lumbricoides* and the epidemiology and clinical course of infection.
2. Be able to describe three basic aspects of infection: transmission, diagnosis, and treatment/prevention.

Definitions

Nematode: A helminth characterized by a cylindrical body and separate sexes, in contrast to cestodes and trematodes (tapeworms and flukes) that are flatworms and generally hermaphroditic.

"Giant intestinal roundworm": Common name for *Ascaris lumbricoides.*

Egg (ova), larva, and adult: Sequential developmental stages in life cycle of helminths.

Larva: Preadult or juvenile stage of helminths; nematodes have four larval stages in their life cycle prior to reaching the adult stage. Each stage is preceded by a molt or shedding of the cuticle or "skin."

DISCUSSION

Characteristics of *Ascaris*

***Ascaris* is one of several nematodes that infect the GI tract and, like all of these, develops through egg, larva, and adult stages.** *Ascaris lumbricoides* is very similar in size and life cycle to *Ascaris suum,* which is the species found in pigs. Parasitologists debate the point that there is only one species of *Ascaris* that infects both pigs and humans. If a human ingests eggs of *A. suum,* the larvae will migrate to the lungs and die, but in the process can cause a serious form of "ascaris pneumonia." Adult worms of *A. suum* do not develop in the human intestine. Other ascarids that infect humans are *Toxocara canis* and *Toxocara cati,* which are parasites of dogs and cats, respectively. Although humans can become infected by ingesting eggs of these species, neither worm develops to maturity. After hatching in the intestine, *Toxocara* larvae migrate chronically in visceral tissue, giving rise to the condition termed "visceral larvae migrans."

Infection Transmission

Typical of nematodes, *A. lumbricoides* has separate sexes and a life cycle that involves **egg, larva, and adult stages.** Growth involves **four larval stages.** Transition from one stage to another and to the adult stage is preceded by a molt. A person **becomes infected by ingesting eggs** that are usually acquired through hand-to-mouth transmission from the soil or via contaminated food or water. Eggs **hatch in the duodenum,** releasing larvae that **penetrate the small intestinal wall to enter the bloodstream.** Larvae are **carried hematogenously** to various organs. On reaching the **lungs, they penetrate into the alveoli.** Larvae reside in the lung for approximately 3 weeks, growing and advancing to a subsequent larval stage. They then **migrate up the bronchi and trachea, where they are then swallowed** and returned to the small intestine. In the **intestine, larvae develop to the adult stage** and reach reproductive maturity in approximately 2 months. Adults can survive for up to 2 years and grow to 15–35 cm in length. A single female worm lays approximately 200,000 eggs daily that are passed in the feces. Eggs can survive for years in the soil, tolerating a wide range of temperatures and other environmental variables. Under optimal conditions, eggs reach an infective, larvated stage in 2–3 weeks. Development is arrested at this stage until the egg is ingested.

Ascariasis is a chronic disease of the small intestine and can be transmitted as long as adult worms are in the intestine and feces containing *Ascaris* eggs are allowed to contaminate the environment. Ascariasis is more prevalent in tropical climates but is found in temperate regions of the world. It is most common where sanitation is poor and where human feces are used as fertilizer in agricultural practices. Infections occur in all ages but are more common in children. In endemic areas, most of the population has some worm burden. With the **exception of pinworm infection, ascariasis is the most common helminthic infection of humans on a global scale.**

Diagnosis

A presumptive diagnosis may be based on clinical symptoms. However, symptoms are not pathognomonic. The **pneumonitis** phase of infection cannot be diagnosed as *Ascaris*-induced because it is a generalized symptom that precedes the intestinal phase of infection by several weeks. Intestinal symptoms are normally absent or mild and, in most cases, go undetected.

A definitive diagnosis is based on **identifying egg or adult stages.** As in this case, the first clue of infection may be adult worms that are vomited or passed in a stool. Intestinal obstruction, especially in children, often prompts medical attention. Because of its uniquely large size, an adult *A. lumbricoides* is unmistakable. The adult females are reddish-yellow in color and can measure up to 7–13 inches long (males are generally shorter) and one-fourth of an inch in diameter. Although a definitive diagnosis can be made by identifying adult worms, ascariasis is more commonly diagnosed by identifying eggs in the stool. Both fertile and infertile eggs are passed in the stool. Because female worms pass thousands of eggs daily, diagnosis can be made by direct examination of a stool sample without the need for specialized laboratory techniques to concentrate eggs. The eggs are ovoid, measure 45 by 75 μm and have a thick transparent inner shell covered by an albuminous coat that is wrinkled and usually stained light brown by bile pigments. Unfertilized eggs are commonly seen in a stool. These are more elongated, measuring 40 by 90 μm. The inside of the unfertilized egg is amorphous instead of containing a well defined single cell of the fertilized egg.

Treatment and Prevention

Adult worms are the target of several drugs available to treat ascariasis. The drug of choice is **mebendazole,** a benzimidazole derivative that has a high therapeutic index. The effectiveness of treatment can be assessed by the disappearance of eggs in stool samples and alleviation of symptoms. In cases of intestinal obstruction, the first action should be directed at ridding the patient of worms through the use of chemotherapeutic agents, such as mebendazole. If the worms can be dislodged the patient may void them in the stool. If the bolus of worms cannot be dislodged, surgery may be an option. If surgery is chosen, it is imperative that the worms be killed or paralyzed with a drug such as piperazine prior to physically removing them from the intestine. The reason for this procedure is that a live, active worm releases an aerosol of eggs through its uterine pore. Eggs are invisible to the naked eye. However, if eggs fall on exposed viscera they elicit granulomatous lesions and adhesions that can lead to severe complications. Preventive measures relate to instructing the patient on how the infection was acquired and on the proper disposal of feces to avoid soil contamination and reinfection.

Synopsis

The synopsis of ascariasis is presented in Table 45-1.

Table 45-1

Synopsis of Ascariasis			
Infective stage of etiologic agent	Location of Pathogenic stage	Laboratory diagnosis based on identification of:	Drugs used in treatment
Egg of: *Ascaris lumbricoides*	Lungs (larvae, transient) Small intestine (adult, chronic)	Egg (stool exam) or Adult (vomitus; passed in stool)	Mebendazole

COMPREHENSION QUESTIONS

[45.1] A definitive diagnosis of ascariasis can be made by observing which of the following?

A. An eosinophilia in a differential white blood cell count
B. Motile larvae in a stool sample
C. Larvae in x-ray of lungs
D. An adult worm passed during a bowel movement

[45.2] Ascariasis is most effectively treated with which of the following drugs?

A. Mebendazole
B. Metronidazole
C. Niclosamide
D. Praziquantel

[45.3] A person presents to his physician complaining of chronic GI symptoms. A diagnosis of *A. lumbricoides* is made. Human nematodes infect individuals via different routes. This patient is most likely infected by which of the following?

A. Larvae penetrating unprotected skin
B. Ingesting larvated eggs
C. Eating uncooked pork
D. Internal autoinfection

Answers

[45.1] **D.** Identification of adult worms passed by an individual can ensure a definitive diagnosis. Although an eosinophilia accompanies ascariasis, this condition can be caused by other infections and by various allergic conditions. Motile larvae in a stool are indicative of infection with *Strongyloides stercoralis.* Nematode larvae cannot be seen in an x-ray.

[45.2] **A.** Mebendazole is a broad spectrum antihelminthic that is the drug of choice for treating *Ascaris* and several other intestinal nematodes. Metronidazole is used primarily to treat infections with protozoa, such as *Giardia lamblia* and *Trichomonas vaginalis.* Niclosamide is the drug of choice in treating most adult cestode or tapeworm infections. Praziquantel is used to treat infections with blood flukes or schistosomes and can also be used to treat adult tapeworms.

[45.3] **B.** *Ascaris* is acquired by ingesting infective eggs, as are the whipworm, *Trichuris trichiura,* and the pinworm, *Enterobius vermicularis.* Filariform larvae penetrating unprotected skin is the route by which a person becomes infected by other intestinal nematodes, hookworms and *Strongyloides;* eating uncooked pork could lead to trichinosis; and internal autoinfection is caused only by *Strongyloides.*

MICROBIOLOGY PEARLS

- ❖ The fertilized eggs are unsegmented when laid by the female worm.
- ❖ Mebendazole, one of several available benzimidazole compounds used to treat nematodes, is the drug of choice in treating *Ascaris* infection.

REFERENCES

Centers for Disease Control. DPDx. Laboratory identification of parasites of public concern. Ascariasis. 2007. http://www.dpd.cdc.gov/dpdx/HTML/Ascariasis.htm.

Centers for Disease Control. DPDx. Laboratory identification of parasites of public concern. Image Library. Ascariasis. 2007. http://www.dpd.cdc.gov/dpdx/HTML/ImageLibrary/Ascariasis_il.htm.

Medical Letter on Drugs and Therapeutics. Drugs for parasitic infections. New Rochelle, NY. 2004. http://www. medletter.com/freedocs/parasitic.pdf. This reference has been updated and "superseded by the special report *Drugs for Parasitic Infections,* which can be purchased (on-line) for $25." This reference has been provided because it is a comprehensive and clinically useful reference that is regularly updated and could be of value to those who are involved in treating parasitic infections.

❖ CASE 46

A 32-year-old man with known HIV is brought to the hospital with diarrhea. He has had between 15 and 25 watery stools a day for the past 2 weeks. He has had a low grade fever and felt very fatigued, but denies vomiting. He has not passed any blood in his stool. He says that he has lost 8 lb in this time frame. He is on a "triple therapy cocktail" of AZT, 3TC, and a protease inhibitor for his HIV. His last CD4 cell count was 150 cells/mm^3. On examination, his temperature is 37.2°C (98.9°F), pulse is 110 beats per minute, blood pressure is 95/75 mm Hg, and respiratory rate is 24 breaths per minute. In general, he appears cachectic. His eyes are dry and sunken. His mucous membranes are moist. His cardiovascular exam is notable for tachycardia, and he has orthoscopic changes on sitting up from lying down. His abdomen has hyperactive bowel sounds, but is soft and only mildly tender. His stool is heme negative. A modified acid-fast stained stool sample reveals multiple red and pink, round oocysts.

- **What is the most likely cause of diarrhea?**
- **How is this infection most commonly acquired?**

ANSWERS TO CASE 46: CRYPTOSPORIDIOSIS

Summary: A 32-year-old man with HIV and diarrhea. A modified acid-fast stained stool sample reveals multiple red and pink, round oocysts.

Most likely etiologic agent: *Cryptosporidium parvum.*

◆ **The most common mode of acquiring this infection:** Ingestion of oocysts in contaminated water or food or fecal-oral transmission from infected animals or person to person.

CLINICAL CORRELATION

Cryptosporidium parvum belongs to a group of protozoans known as coccidians. The infective oocyst is approximately 3–8 μm in diameter. The parasite, on emerging from the oocyst, attaches to the surface of intestinal epithelium where it multiplies both asexually and sexually. The parasite causes changes in the mucosa that include crypt hyperplasia and villous atrophy. Associated with its presence in the intestine, and after an incubation period of approximately 2–12 days, is an acute illness characterized by nausea, abdominal cramps, weight loss, anorexia, malaise, low-grade fever, and diarrhea. The frequency of diarrheal episodes and voluminous fluid loss is often debilitating. During infection there may be periods in which symptoms are absent. Although any individual can acquire the infection, children in day care centers and individuals with AIDS or HIV infection represent populations that are especially vulnerable to cryptosporidiosis. In immunocompetent individuals, the disease will resolve on its own, usually within 7–14 days. In immunocompromised hosts, the disease is generally more severe and chronic, sometimes lasting for life. Five to ten percent of patients with AIDS acquire infection with *Cryptosporidium.* **Persistence of infection in HIV-infected individuals is closely associated with CD4 lymphocyte counts of less than 180 cells/mm^3**. Protracted diarrhea may lead to dehydration, wasting, and death. Severe intestinal distress, usually in immunodeficient individuals, is sometimes associated with pulmonary and tracheal cryptosporidiosis that is associated with coughing and low-grade fever. The strains that infect the intestine and lungs are, to date, indistinguishable.

APPROACH TO SUSPECTED *Cryptosporidium* INFECTION

Objectives

1. Learn the life cycle of *C. parvum* and the epidemiology and clinical course of cryptosporidiosis, and compare this disease with those caused by related organisms, such as *Cyclospora* and *Isospora.*
2. Be able to describe the three basic aspect of infection: transmission, diagnosis, and treatment/prevention.

Definitions

Coccidia: The specific taxonomic group of protozoans to which *C. parvum* belongs.

Oocyst: The stage in the life cycle of *C. parvum* that transmits the disease and is also sought in making a definitive diagnosis. Each oocyst contains four sporozoites.

Sporozoite: The stage released from the oocyst following ingestion and which initiates infection.

Zoonosis: A disease that is transmitted from lower vertebrate hosts to humans.

Acid-fast stain: A type of stain that renders oocysts highly visible in a fecal sample. It is used to support the microscopic diagnosis of the parasite.

DISCUSSION

Characteristics of *Cryptosporidium* That Impact Transmission

***Cryptosporidium* species are ubiquitous, worldwide enteric pathogens of humans** and multiple other animal species. Of the many species of the genus, *C. parvum* is responsible for most clinical disease in humans and other mammals. The life cycle of *C. parvum* occurs within a single host and, like other coccidia, involves sexual and asexual reproduction. Misdiagnosis with cyclosporiasis may be made, in part because clinical symptoms are similar. **Protracted, watery diarrhea is the hallmark of infection.** *Cyclospora cayetanensis,* which infects humans, has a worldwide distribution. Another related organism that causes diarrhea in humans is *Isospora belli.*

The **small intestine is the usual host habitat for *Cryptosporidium,*** where it lives in a unique intraepithelial niche. The life cycle is initiated with the ingestion of oocysts that contain four sporozoites. When oocysts are ingested, they undergo excystation as the outer wall is removed by digestive processes. Sporozoites that are released attach to the host's intestinal epithelial cells and become surrounded by a host-derived membrane, making them intracellular but extracytoplasmic. Sporozoites undergo multiple fission to form meronts that contain multiple merozoites. The merozoites are released to infect other cells. Following another round of asexual division and on release of the second and subsequent generations of merozoites, they penetrate new cells to form gametes. Most gametes undergo enlargement into macrogametes (female). Some become microgametocytes that undergo fission multiple times to form sperm-like microgametes (male). Microgametes leave the microgametocyte and fertilize a macrogamete to form a zygote. The zygote then becomes covered by a wall, forming an oocyst that is highly resistant to chemical and physical changes in the internal and external environment. Sporozoites develop within the oocyst that are sloughed, along with intestinal epithelial cells, and voided in the feces. Because oocysts are passed in the feces in a sporulated stage (i.e., contain sporozoites), they are immediately infective and can retain infectivity for long periods because of their protective wall. In having oocysts that are immediately infective, *Cryptosporidium* is different from *Cyclospora,* which has oocysts that require 1–2 weeks to develop to an infective stage.

Presumably ingestion of one oocyst can initiate an infection that can be contracted by eating contaminated food or drinking contaminated water. Touching the stool of infected individuals or animals or anything contaminated with feces and then touching your mouth can also initiate infection.

Infection can be transmitted by ingestion of oocysts passed in feces of infected humans or animals. Thus, infection can be transmitted from one person to another or from animals to humans, from eating and drinking food or water contaminated with fecal material or from transfer of oocysts from contaminated material to the mouth or from person to person.

Diagnosis

A **definitive diagnosis is based on identifying oocysts in a fecal sample.** A technique, such as sugar flotation, is used to concentrate the oocysts and acid-fast staining is used to identify them. A **fluorescent antibody technique** is also available to stain the isolated oocysts, augmenting visualization. **Oocysts contain four sporozoites.** It is important to make a differential diagnosis with *Cyclospora* oocysts, which are similar in size but are not sporulated when passed. *Cryptosporidium* oocysts contain four sporozoites and are approximately 8 μm in diameter. When sporulated, the oocysts of *Cyclospora* are the same size, but contain two sporocysts, each with two sporozoites. *Isospora* oocysts can also be found in the stool; however, they can be differentiated by their larger size, 15 by 30 μm ovoid. Like *Cyclospora,* oocysts of *Isospora* are excreted in an unsporulated stage, and, after becoming sporulated, contain two sporocysts, each with two sporozoites. **Pulmonary infections of *Cryptosporidium* are diagnosed by biopsy and staining** (Table 46-1).

Table 46-1
DIFFERENTIATION OF HUMAN COCCIDIAN OOCYSTS

SPECIES	NUMBER OF SPOROCYSTS	NUMBER OF SPROROZOITES	OOCYSTS SPORULATED IN STOOL	SIZE OF OOCYST μM
Cryptosporidium parvum	0	4	Yes	4–8
Cyclospora cayetanensis	2	4	No	4–8
Isospora belli	2	4	No	12 × 30

Treatment and Prevention

As noted, infection is self-limiting in immunocompetent hosts and chronic in immunosuppressed individuals. **While nitazoxanide is effective in the treatment of immunocompetent hosts, it has not proven so for immunosupressed patients.** Because of massive fluid loss, due to diarrhea, infected individuals may require rehydration therapy.

Because there **is no effective agent to treat infection specifically in immunosuppressed patients,** the best measure to control infection is avoidance of situations that are conducive to transmission. Thus, knowledge about sources of infection and how infection is transmitted is the key to prevention. Most surface water, such as streams, lakes, and rivers contain some *Cryptosporidium* oocysts. Many public supplies of treated and filtered water derived from these sources are contaminated with low levels of oocysts. **Cryptosporidiosis can be prevented** by thoroughly **washing hands before eating** and after any contact with animals or soil or after changing diapers. In people with weakened immune systems, cryptosporidiosis can be life-threatening. These individuals must take extra precautions to drink only water that has been purified; wash with purified water; cook all food; do not swim in lakes, rivers, streams, or public pools; avoid sexual practices that might involve contact with stool; and avoid touching farm animals.

Synopsis

The synopsis of cryptosporidiosis is presented in Table 46-2.

Table 46-2

Synopsis of Cryptosporidiosis			
Infective stage of etiologic agent	Location of Pathogenic stage	Laboratory diagnosis based on identification of:	Drugs used in treatment
Oocyst of: *Cryptosporidium parvum*	Small and large intestine	Oocyst (stool exam)	Nitazoxanide

COMPREHENSION QUESTIONS

[46.1] A 33-year-old woman has chronic diarrhea. A fecal sample is obtained. Microscopic identification of which of the following stages of the organism would provide the strongest evidence for cryptosporidiosis?

A. Cyst
B. Oocyst
C. Egg
D. Sporocysts
E. Merozoites

[46.2] A 24-year-old male scientist is diagnosed with chronic cryptosporidiosis. He asks about the epidemiology of this disorder. Which of the following accurately describes the disease or the etiologic agent?

A. Is self-limiting in immunocompromised patients
B. Reproduces sexually and asexually in different hosts
C. Can be acquired through sporozoites transmitted by an insect vector
D. Is transmitted through drinking water contaminated with animal feces
E. Is the only human parasite that produces oocysts

[46.3] Chronic, debilitating cryptosporidiosis is most likely to affect which of the following individuals?

A. Dairy farmers
B. Individuals with AIDS
C. Infants placed in day care centers
D. Zoo animal handlers
E. Hikers who drink from streams and lakes

Answers

[46.1] **B.** Oocyst is the correct answer. Egg and cyst stages are not part of the life cycle of *Cryptosporidium.* Eggs are produced by helminths, and cyst stages are produced by other intestinal protozoans, such as *Entamoeba* and *Giardia.* Merozoites occur within infected epithelial cells but are not the target of diagnostic tests or procedures. Sporocysts are not found in the life cycle of *cryptosporidium* as a feature of the oocyst. Sporocysts are a feature of the genus Cyclospora and important in differential diagnosis.

[46.2] **D.** Infection can be acquired from oocysts transferred from farm animals. In immunocompromised individuals, such as those with AIDS or cancer patients being treated with immunosuppressive agents, infection is not self-limiting but rather chronic and sometimes life-threatening. The life cycle of *Cryptosporidium* involves both asexual and sexual reproduction, but both forms occur in a single host. Sporozoites are stages in the life cycle that are released from ingested oocysts. There is no insect that serves as a biological or mechanical vector in the life cycle. Oocysts are also produced by other species of coccidians that infect humans, such as *Isospora, Cyclospora, Toxoplasma,* and *Plasmodium. Toxoplasma* oocysts only occur in feline hosts; *Plasmodium* species cause malaria in which only the mosquito definitive host harbors oocysts; *Isospora* and *Cyclospora* are intestinal coccidian parasites that produce oocysts that are passed in the feces and must be considered in making a differential diagnosis.

[46.3] **B.** All individuals (A–E) are susceptible to infection. However, persons that are at high risk of severe, protracted infection are those with AIDS, or those who have cancer or organ transplants who are treated with drugs that weaken the immune system, or individuals who are genetically immunodeficient.

MICROBIOLOGY PEARLS

- ❖ Often there is misdiagnosis between cryptosporidiosis and cyclosporiasis.
- ❖ Immunologically compromised patients with cryptosporidiosis do not respond to specific therapy with nitazoxanide.

REFERENCES

Centers for Disease Control. DPDx. Laboratory identification of parasites of public concern. Cryptosporidiosis. 2007. http://www.dpd.cdc.gov/dpdx/HTML/Cryptosporidiosis.htm.

Centers for Disease Control. DPDx. Laboratory identification of parasites of public concern. Image Library. Cryptosoridiosis. 2007. http://www.dpd.cdc.gov/dpdx/HTML/ImageLibrary/Cryptosporidiosis_il.htm.

Medical Letter on Drugs and Therapeutics. Drugs for parasitic infections. New Rochelle, NY. 2004. http://www.medletter.com/freedocs/parasitic.pdf. This reference has been updated and "superseded by the special report *Drugs for Parasitic Infections,* which can be purchased (on-line) for $25." This reference has been provided because it is a comprehensive and clinically useful reference that is regularly updated and could be of value to those who are involved in treating parasitic infections.

CASE 47

A 4-year-old girl is brought to the physician's office by her mother because of anal itching. The mother has noticed her daughter scratching and rubbing her anal area frequently for the past few days. Her anal area has been getting red and raw from all the scratching. Mother has used some petrolatum and hydrocortisone cream, but it hasn't helped much. The child has not had any obvious skin rashes and is not scratching any other part of her body. She has not had diarrhea. She takes no medications and has no significant medical history. She attends day care 4 days a week. On examination, she is a well-appearing child. Her vital signs and general examination are normal. Examination of her perianal area reveals some erythema and excoriation from scratching. You perform a microscopic examination of a sample collected by touching the perianal region with a piece of clear cellophane tape.

◆ **What diagnostic finding are you likely to see on this microscopic examination?**

 **What is the organism responsible for this infection?**

ANSWERS TO CASE 47: ENTEROBIASIS OR PINWORM INFECTION

Summary: A 4-year-old girl has perianal pruritus. The diagnosis is made by microscopic examination of a sample collected by touching the perianal region with a piece of clear cellophane tape.

 **Diagnostic finding likely to see on this microscopic examination:** Thin-walled, ovoid eggs that are flattened on one side and contain a nematode larva.

◆ **Organism responsible for this infection:** *Enterobius vermicularis.*

CLINICAL CORRELATION

Enterobius vermicularis, commonly called the pinworm, is the most common cause of helminthic infections in the United States and is endemic around the world. Humans are the only known host for *E. vermicularis,* but other vertebrates can be infected with different species of this nematode. Adult worms, approximately 1 cm in length, white and thread-like in appearance, inhabit the large intestine. Gravid females migrate to the perianal and perineal regions at night to lay eggs that are immediately infective. Infection is more common in children than adults and is often asymptomatic. However, a variety of symptoms are ascribed to pinworms. Atypically, worms are sometimes found in an inflamed appendix and there are rare reports of worms reaching the genital tract and producing vaginitis. By far the most common signs of infection occur in children and include restless sleep and tiredness during the day. However, more common symptoms consist of anal or perianal itching because of the adult worms crawling on the skin. The eggs can also cause local itching, which may be more intense in secondary infections as a result of allergic reactions to their antigenic coating. Frequent scratching results in transfer to the hands and areas under the fingernails. Eggs are frequently transferred to clothing, bedding, toys, and dust, where they can survive for several weeks. Through hand-to-mouth transmission, the eggs are ingested and hatch in the duodenum. Larvae released from eggs reside in the cecum and reach adult stage in about a month. Infections are acute, generally lasting 4–8 weeks. Considering the relatively short duration of a single infection, chronic enterobiasis is caused by reinfection.

APPROACH TO THE SUSPECTED *Enterobius* INFECTION

Objectives

1. Learn the life cycle of *E. vermicularis* and the epidemiology and clinical course of infection.
2. Be able to describe three basic aspects of infection: transmission, diagnosis, and treatment/prevention.

Definitions

Pinworm: Common name for *Enterobius vermicularis.*

Cervical alae: An extension of a lateral cuticular protuberance or lateral line on the body surface of the pinworm that extends to the head region and appears microscopically as a "flared" region or collar. Adult worms are identified, in part, by the presence of cervical alae which are prominent structures when examined microscopically.

Nocturnal migration: Refers to the tendency of pinworms to migrate at night from the colon, out the anus, to the perianal and perineal regions to deposit eggs.

Larvated egg: Refers to eggs that contain a larval stage and are deposited by pinworms on the skin.

DISCUSSION

Characteristics of Enterobiasis That Impact Transmission

A patient acquires infection by **ingesting the pinworm eggs containing infective larvae.** Ingested eggs hatch in the small intestine releasing larvae that migrate to the cecal area and mature into adult male and female worms that are free or insecurely attached to the mucosa. The period between ingestion of eggs to maturation takes approximately 3–4 weeks. Following copulation, the female pinworms produce eggs. Rather than release eggs in the bowel, the **female worms migrate out the anus onto the surrounding skin and release eggs. Worm migration usually occurs at night.** Each female will lay thousands of microscopic, larvated eggs. Pinworm eggs are infective within a few hours after being deposited on the skin. They can survive up to 2 weeks on clothing, bedding, or other objects. Individuals can become infected after accidentally swallowing infective pinworm eggs from contaminated surfaces or fingers. The duration of a single infection is 4–8 weeks.

Diagnosis

Although *Enterobius* is an intestinal parasite, eggs are rarely found during laboratory examinations of stools. If a person is suspected of having pinworms, the so-called **"scotch tape test"** should be used to identify the parasite. Transparent adhesive tape, sometime attached to the end of tongue depressor or "pinworm paddle," is pressed in the anal region. This procedure involves the help of a patient or parents of suspected children. The tape is then transferred to a glass slide, sticky side down. The slide should then be examined microscopically for eggs. Pinworm eggs are approximately 20 × 50 μm characteristically flattened on one side and usually contain an active larva. Because bathing or having a bowel movement may remove eggs, the scotch tape impression should be made on awakening in the morning. In children, samples taken from under the fingernails may also contain eggs because scratching of the anal area is common.

A definitive diagnosis may also be made on **recovery and identification of adult worms** seen directly in bedclothes or around the anal area. The **female** pinworm has a **sharply pointed tail and anterior alae** that form a **collar-like structure** around the mouth. The female worm is about 1 cm long with a diameter approximately 0.5 mm. In female worms that are gravid, the uterus filled with easily identifiable eggs is a common feature.

Treatment and Prevention

Highly effective drugs in the treatment of enterobiasis are **pyrantel pamoate** and **mebendazole,** given as a single dose, with a repeat dose administered 2 weeks later. Mebendazole is a broad spectrum antinematode agent that has a high therapeutic index. Close family contacts of infected individuals should be treated as well. If reinfection occurs, the source of the infection should be identified. Therefore, playmates, schoolmates, close contacts outside the house, and household members should be considered. Each infected person should receive the two-dose treatment and, if necessary, more than two doses. In short, the importance of determining infection in the entire family or contacts should be explained in terms of the life cycle of the worm and personal, and group hygiene should be stressed.

Synopsis

The synopsis of enterobiasis is presented in Table 47-1.

Table 47-1

Synopsis of Enterobiasis			
Infective stage of etiologic agent	Location of pathogenic stage	Laboratory diagnosis based on identification of:	Drugs used in treatment
Egg of : *Enterobius vermicularis*	Large intestine	Egg (anal swab) or Adult	Mebendazole

COMPREHENSION QUESTIONS

[47.1] In which of the following life cycle stages is enterobiasis transmitted?

A. Larva
B. Egg
C. Adult
D. Cyst
E. Oocyst

[47.2] Which of the following is the drug of choice in treating enterobiasis?

A. Mebendazole
B. Metronidazole
C. Piperazine
D. Praziquantel
E. Chloroquine

[47.3] A parent of a child suffering from disturbed sleep and restlessness calls the family physician and states that her child is once again infected with pinworms and asks if she can administer the same medicine that was used to cure an earlier infection. After the physician is convinced that the pinworm infection is the problem, she advises on giving the same treatment and provides direction on how to clean up the environment to prevent further reinfection. The physician should have been convinced by which of the following facts?

A. The parent knew that reinfection was a possibility.
B. The parent had collected worms from bed linen and accurately described them.
C. The parent described symptoms of enterobiasis.
D. The parent had the child's stool examined by her veterinarian who identified telltale eggs.
E. The parent noted that the family's pet cat continued to sleep on the child's bed.

Answers

[47.1] **B.** The egg stage is the stage transmitted from person to person. A larval form (A) is found inside the egg but does not escape to initiate infection until the egg is ingested. Adult forms (C) live in the intestine but are not the stage directly responsible for transmission of the infection. Cyst (D) and oocyst (D) stages are not a part of the life cycle of *E. vermicularis.*

[47.2] **A.** Mebendazole is the most appropriate of several available benzimidazole compounds to treat enterobiasis. This drug of choice is a highly effective, broad-spectrum antihelminthic. Metronidazole (B) is used to treat various protozoan infections, but is not efficacious in treating pinworms. Piperazine (C) is an anthelminthic that was used prior to the discovery of mebendazole to treat enterobiasis and is less effective, and its dose regimens are more complicated. Praziquantel (D) is effective in treating tapeworm and fluke (flatworms) infections but is not useful against pinworms or other nematodes. Chloroquine is a potent antimalarial drug but of no use against helminths.

[47.3] **B.** Finding and identifying adult pinworms is one way to make a definitive diagnosis. Reinfection (A) is a definite possibility but not convincing evidence that the child is actually infected. Symptoms described (C) are associated with enterobiasis but are only presumptive, not definitive, evidence of infection. A stool exam (D) is not an appropriate or effective method to diagnose enterobiasis. Cats (E) are in no way associated with transmission of infection.

MICROBIOLOGY PEARLS

- The egg (larvated) is the infective stage.
- The life cycle is direct, meaning that the adults develop from larvae without leaving the gastrointestinal tract. Adult worms are the primary cause of pathology.
- Pamental pamoate and mebendazole, a broad spectrum antihelminthic, are drugs of choice.

REFERENCES

Centers for Disease Control. DPDx. Laboratory identification of parasites of public concern. Enterobiasis. 2007. http://www.dpd.cdc.gov/dpdx/HTML/Enterobiasis.htm.

Centers for Disease Control. DPDx. Laboratory identification of parasites of public concern. Image Library. Enterobiasis. 2007. http://www.dpd.cdc.gov/dpdx/HTML/ImageLibrary/Enterobiasis_il.htm.

Medical Letter on Drugs and Therapeutics. Drugs for parasitic infections. New Rochelle, NY. 2004. http://www.medletter.com/freedocs/parasitic.pdf. This reference has been updated and "superseded by the special report *Drugs for Parasitic Infections,* which can be purchased (on-line) for $25." This reference has been provided because it is a comprehensive and clinically useful reference that is regularly updated and could be of value to those who are involved in treating parasitic infections.

CASE 48

A 50-year-old woman presents to your office with the complaints of fever, chills, nausea, and vomiting for the past 5 days. She is especially concerned because she just returned from a 3-week long church mission trip to central Africa during which she did not take the recommended malaria prophylaxis. She was careful about using insect repellent and wearing long-sleeved clothing, but she did not take the recommended weekly dose of mefloquine because it made her nauseous. Starting a few days after her return, she has had episodes of shaking chills followed by fever spikes as high as 39.7°C (103.5°F) and then profuse sweating. After these episodes she would feel so exhausted that she would sleep for hours. These severe episodes have been occurring every other day. In between these episodes, she has had low-grade fever, myalgias, nausea,vomiting, and diarrhea. On examination, she appears very fatigued and pale. Her temperature is 37.7°C (99.9°F), pulse 100 beats per minute, blood pressure 110/80 mm Hg, and respiratory rate 18 breaths per minute. Other than signs of dehydration, her examination is unremarkable. A complete blood count shows her to be anemic. She has elevated blood urea nitrogen, creatinine, and lactate dehydrogenase levels. A thin-blood smear is sent to the laboratory, which shows erythrocytes with ring forms at the periphery of the cell and multiple erythrocytes with three or four ring forms present.

- **What is the most likely etiology of her infection?**

- **What findings on the thin blood smear are specific for this organism?**

ANSWERS TO CASE 48: MALARIA

Summary: A 50-year-old woman has fever and body aches. A thin-blood smear shows erythrocytes with ring forms at the periphery of the cell and multiple erythrocytes with three or four ring forms.

- **Most likely etiology of her infection:** *Plasmodium falciparum.*
- **Findings on the thin blood smear are specific for this organism:** Multiple ring forms in a single erythrocyte and ring forms located at the periphery of the erythrocytes.

CLINICAL CORRELATION

Malaria is caused by one of the four species of plasmodia involved in a human-mosquito-human life cycle. Plasmodia are coccidian parasites of erythrocytes. Their life cycle involves asexual reproduction in humans and sexual reproduction in the mosquito. Human infection is initiated by the bite of an infected mosquito, which introduces sporozoites into the bloodstream. The sporozoites travel to the liver where they mature and reproduce asexually by schizogony. *Plasmodium ovale* and *P. vivax* may also establish a dormant—hypnozoite—stage in the liver; *P. falciparum* and *P. malariae* are incapable of this. On completion of the hepatic growth and reproductive stage, merozoites are released from hepatocytes and infect erythrocytes, initiating the erythrocytic cycle. Asexual reproduction continues, resulting in rupture of erythrocytes and release of more infectious merozoites. The classic symptoms of malaria relate to the paroxysm of shaking chills, fever, and sweating and correspond with the cyclical lysis of erythrocytes and release of merozoites. *Plasmodium vivax, P. ovale,* and *P. falciparum* species of malaria tend to produce paroxysms in 48-hour cycles (tertian malaria), whereas *P. malariae* causes paroxysms in 72-hour cycles (quartan malaria).

A series of paroxysms of decreasing intensity constitutes a primary malarial attack. After the primary attack, parasites tend to disappear from the blood. In infections with *P. falciparum* or *P. malariae* this would constitute a cure. In *P. vivax* and *P. ovale* infections, relapses may occur as a result of hypnozoites persisting in the liver.

Complicating pathologic changes such as anemia, hepatomegaly, and splenomegaly may occur. In the case of falciparum malaria, capillaries are blocked by infected erythrocytes that typically tend to become "sticky" and sequestered in capillary beds. Erythrocyte destruction leads to anemia. Capillary blockage leads to ischemia, anoxia, and subsequent organ damage. This is the basis for cerebral symptoms and kidney damage that leads to black water fever, a condition in which hemoglobin and erythrocytes appear in the urine; "blackwater fever" is associated with a poor prognosis. Falciparum malaria is the most virulent and lethal form of malaria, sometimes called malignant tertian malaria.

APPROACH TO THE SUSPECTED MALARIA INFECTION

Objectives

1. Learn the life cycle of *Plasmodium* species and the epidemiology and clinical course of infection.
2. Be able to describe the three basic aspects of infection: transmission, diagnosis, and treatment/prevention.

Definitions

Relapse malaria: Infection derived from hypnozoites (hypnos = sleeping; zoites = animals) or residual liver stages that persist after a primary infection with *P. vivax* and *P. ovale.*

Appliqué form: Parasite on the periphery of erythrocytes, as in *P. falciparum* infection.

Ring stage: Stage in the life cycle of *Plasmodium* in an erythrocyte consisting of a thin ring of protoplasm with a nucleus at one side.

Schizogony: Asexual division or "splitting" carried out by all *Plasmodium* species.

Blackwater fever: A dangerous complication of malaria, especially falciparum, characterized by passage of red to black urine and associated with high mortality.

DISCUSSION

Characteristics of *Plasmodium* That Impact Transmission

Plasmodium is a genus in the phylum Apicomplexa, which contains other human parasites such as *Toxoplasma, Cryptosporidium, Cyclospora,* and *Isospora.* All of these organisms belong to a phylogenetic class in which all species are parasitic.

Malaria infections are endemic in **tropical developing countries.** Although endogenous malaria has occurred in the United States, most cases are imported by travelers. There are numerous species of *Plasmodium,* but only four species cause human malaria—***P. falciparum, P. vivax, P. malariae,* and *P. ovale.*** All species are transmitted by an infected **anopheline mosquito.** *Plasmodium* **sporozoites** are the infective forms injected into the bloodstream when the mosquito takes a blood meal. The sporozoites circulate in the bloodstream and then invade **hepatocytes** to initiate a **preerythrocytic** cycle. In the liver parenchymal cells the parasite multiplies asexually by a process called schizogony or splitting. Asexual reproduction gives rise to multiple individual stages or merozoites. These **merozoites** become blood-borne and invade erythrocytes to initiate the **erythrocytic cycle.** In the case of *P. vivax* and *P. ovale,* the liver phase can be sustained for years by sporozoite-derived dormant stages known as **hypnozoites.** It is the prevalence of the hypnozoites that leads to relapses of malarial symptoms, possibly occurring several years after the first acute disease has been cured.

When merozoites parasitize erythrocytes, their development takes two routes. Some merozoites develop into micro (male) and macro (female) gametocytes. When a female anopheline mosquito bites an infected person and ingests the gametocytes, **fertilization of the macrogametocyte by the microgametocyte takes place in the mosquito** with the subsequent and sequential formation of diploid zygotes, oocysts, and, eventually, sporozoites. **Sporozoites travel to enter the salivary glands of the mosquito** where they are capable of initiating a new infection when the mosquito takes a blood meal. Through the second route in the erythrocytic cycle, the parasite develops successively through ring, trophozoite and schizont stages. As a result of schizogony, the erythrocyte breaks open and releases many new merozoites. These parasites then infect more erythrocytes, repeat the development cycle, ultimately causing the destruction of massive numbers of erythrocytes. The characteristic **chill, fever, and sweating paroxysm** occur when the **parasites are released from the erythrocytes.** Because the release of parasites becomes synchronized and periodic, the paroxysms are also periodic, occurring at 48 or 72 hours depending on the species. The destruction of erythrocytes and release of cell and parasite debris elicit host responses that contribute to pathologic changes.

Diagnosis

Diagnosis is made by finding the **characteristic organisms on thick and thin blood smears.** Differential diagnosis rests on knowing the specific morphologic characteristics of each species, which are revealed in a thin blood smear (Table 48-1). *Plasmodium vivax* and *P. ovale* appear as **ring shapes,** and in other advanced stages of development in enlarged erythrocytes that contain numerous **granules, known as Schüffner dots.** *Plasmodium malariae* has characteristic "band or bar" pattern and do not enlarge the host erythrocytes. *Plasmodium falciparum* can be identified by the presence of multiple ring forms within a single erythrocyte, in contrast to other plasmodia that will have only one ring form per erythrocyte. *Plasmodium falciparum* ring forms also tend to occur at the periphery of the erythrocyte; these "appliqué" forms are distinctive for this species. Mixed infections with more than one species of *Plasmodium* may occur.

Table 48-1
APPEARANCE OF MALARIA PARASITES IN BLOOD SMEARS

CHARACTERISTIC	*Plasmodium* SPECIES
Crescent or sausage shapes present	*P. falciparum*
Trophozoites older than ring stages	*P. vivax, P. malariae, P. ovale*
Schizonts with more than 12 nuclei	*P. vivax*
Enlarged erythrocytes	*P. vivax*
Band forms	*P. malaria*
Ring stages only	*P. falciparum*
Fimbriated oval cell	*P. ovale*

Treatment and Prevention

From the perspective of patient management, drugs to treat malaria fall into three categories: **prophylactic, schizonticidal, and antirelapse.** Prophylactics are designed to prevent infection by attacking the sporozoite stages or preventing the development of clinical symptoms by preventing schizogony in the erythrocytic cycle. **Schizonticidal** compounds may be used in prophylactic measures and to affect a clinical cure in an acute infection. Antirelapse drugs are directed against hypnozoite stages, as in vivax infection. A radical cure in *P. vivax* and *P. ovale* infections requires the use of drugs that eradicate both the erythrocytic and exoerythrocytic schizonts in the liver.

Chloroquine is a schizonticidal compound and drug of choice in treating clinical cases of malaria. Mefloquine, referred to in the case presentation, is used in prophylaxis and also to treat chloroquine resistant strains of *Plasmodium.* Drug resistance of certain strains of *Plasmodium* is a practical problem. In this case, back-up drugs are **quinine** or chemically related **mefloquine,** or a combination of **sulfadoxine** (a sulfonamide) and **pyrimethamine** (pyrimidine derivative). Antirelapse or tissue schizonticidal drugs are aimed at hypnozoites (liver schizonts). The drug of choice in this category is **primaquine.**

Synopsis

The synopsis of malaria is presented in Table 48-2.

Table 48-2

Synopsis of Malaria			
Infective stage of etiologic agent	Location of pathogenic stage	Laboratory diagnosis based on identification of:	Drugs used in treatment
Sporozoite (injected by mosquito) of: *P. vivax* *P. malariae* *P. falciparum* *P. ovale*	Liver (primary schizogony) Erythrocytes (Schizogonic cycle)	Blood smears (Stages in erythrocytes)	*Prophylaxis* Mefloquine *Acute* Chloroquine *Chloroquine Resistant* Quinine or Pyrimethamine +Sulfadoxine *Antirelapse* Primaquine

COMPREHENSION QUESTIONS

[48.1] Microscopic examination of a thin blood smear from a patient suspected of having malaria reveals numerous normal size erythrocytes without stippling but with ring stages, many with multiple ring stages and appliqué forms. Several erythrocytes show developing trophozoites that are spread across the erythrocytes in a band fashion. Which of the following is the most likely cause of infection?

A. *Plasmodium vivax*
B. *Plasmodium malariae*
C. *Plasmodium ovale*
D. *Plasmodium falciparum*
E. A mixed infection with two *Plasmodium* species

[48.2] A patient in California was diagnosed with malaria acquired through a blood transfusion. A discussion of this case by physicians included the following statements. Which statement is correct?

A. The infected blood used in transfusion contained sporozoites.
B. The patient should be treated with chloroquine and primaquine.
C. The patient should be treated to eradicate the stages responsible for symptoms.
D. The blood donor had chloroquine-resistant malaria.
E. The patient would not be infective to mosquitoes.

[48.3] Cerebral malaria most commonly attends infection with which of the following?

A. Any two species of *Plasmodium*
B. *Plasmodium malariae*
C. *Plasmodium falciparum*
D. *Plasmodium ovale*
E. *Plasmodium vivax*

Answers

[48.1] **E.** Multiple ring stages and appliqué forms are indicative of *P. falciparum;* several erythrocytes show developing trophozoites that are spread across the erythrocytes in a band fashion that is indicative of *P. malariae* infection. Normal size erythrocytes without stippling (Schüffner dots) would exclude *P. vivax* and *P. ovale.*

[48.2] **C.** The primary goal should be to treat the patient to eliminate the erythrocytic cycle that is the cause of symptoms. This would constitute a radical cure because the liver phase only occurs if infection is initiated by sporozoites. Thus, treating with primaquine (B) is not necessary because the patient will not harbor hypnozoites. Likewise, (A) is not correct because sporozoites are only acquired from mosquitoes. Transfusion malaria is caused by schizonts and merozoites present in the transferred blood. There is no way to know that the malaria is chloroquine resistant until after treatment with chloroquine (D) and the patient, although not likely to occur, could transmit the infection to mosquitoes (E) because gametocytes would be present in the blood and susceptible *Anopheles* species occur in the United States.

[48.3] **C.** Cerebral malaria involves the clinical manifestations of *Plasmodium falciparum* malaria that induce changes in mental status and coma and is accompanied by fever. Without treatment, cerebral malaria is fatal in 24–72 hours and the mortality ratio is between 25 to 50 percent. The common histopathologic finding is the sequestration of parasitized and nonparasitized red blood cells in cerebral capillaries and venules.

MICROBIOLOGY PEARLS

- In a laboratory diagnosis, in which blood smears are treated with Giemsa or Wright stain plasmodia can be identified when the nucleus and cytoplasm are seen.
- Chemotherapy is directed at erythrocytic stages to provide a clinical cure and hypnozoites in the liver to affect a radical cure. Treatment of specific cases remains an active area of continuous investigation.

REFERENCES

Centers for Disease Control. DPDx. Laboratory identification of parasites of public concern. Malaria. 2007 http:// www.dpd.cdc.gov/dpdx/HTML/Malaria.htm

Centers for Disease Control. DPDx. Laboratory identification of parasites of public concern. Image Library. Malaria. 2007. http://www.dpd.cdc.gov/dpdx/HTML/ImageLibrary/Malaria_il.htm

Medical Letter on Drugs and Therapeutics. Drugs for parasitic infections. New Rochelle, NY. 2004. http://www.medletter.com/freedocs/parasitic.pdf. This reference has been updated and "superseded by the special report *Drugs for Parasitic Infections,* which can be purchased (on-line) for $25." This reference has been provided because it is a comprehensive and clinically useful reference that is regularly updated and could be of value to those who are involved in treating parasitic infections

Centers for Disease Control. Malaria. Part 2: Treatment: General Approaches and Treatment: uncomplicated malaria.2007. http://www.cdc.gov/malaria/diagnosis_treatment/clinicians2.htm

❖ CASE 49

A 40-year-old man presents for a routine examination. He is generally feeling well but complains of some mild dysuria and increasing urinary frequency. He has never had a urinary tract infection (UTI) and thought that the increasing urinary frequency was a normal part of aging. He has not seen any blood in his urine but says that the urine does appear darker than it used to look. He has no other complaints and his review of systems is otherwise entirely negative. He has no significant medical or family history. He smokes a pack of cigarettes a day and denies alcohol use. He is an immigrant from Egypt who has lived in the United States for 3 years. His vital signs and physical examination, including genital and prostate exams, are normal. A urinalysis shows many red blood cells, a few white blood cells, and oval-shaped parasite eggs with terminal spines.

- **What organism is the likely cause of his hematuria?**

- **How does this organism gain entry into humans?**

ANSWERS TO CASE 49: SCHISTOSOMIASIS

Summary: A 40-year-old Egyptian man has hematuria. A urinalysis shows many red blood cells, a few white blood cells, and oval-shaped eggs with terminal spines.

 **Organism likely cause of his hematuria:** *Schistosoma haematobium*

◆ **Method organism gains entry into humans:** Penetration through intact skin by the cercarial stage of the organism

CLINICAL CORRELATION

Schistosomiasis is a human disease syndrome caused by infection with one of several **parasitic trematodes or flukes** of the genus ***Schistosoma.*** These parasites are known commonly as **blood flukes** because the adult worms live in blood vessels of the definitive host. The human disease syndrome is characterized by dermatitis that is caused by entry of the infective stage and by acute and chronic systemic symptoms caused by host responses to eggs deposited by adult worms. *Schistosoma haematobium, S. mansoni,* and *S. japonicum* are the major species that infect over 200 million humans in Asia, Africa, the Middle East, and South America. *Schistosoma japonicum* is considered a zoonotic infection. In addition to these three major species, others, such as *S. mekongi* and *S. intercalatum,* also with potential zoonotic properties, rarely infect humans. Schistosomes with avian or nonhuman mammalian hosts can cause severe dermatitis or swimmer's itch in humans, but not infection with adult worms.

The disease syndrome parallels the development of the parasite in the definitive host. **Swimmer's itch,** an allergic dermatitis, is caused shortly after humans make skin contact with microscopic, infective larval forms called **cercariae** that live in an aquatic environment. Following exposure to human schistosomes, the dermatitis is mild and may go unnoticed. However, when exposed to cercariae of schistosomes that normally infect birds, swimmer's itch can present as an itchy maculopapular rash. Cercariae penetrate the intact skin, enter the circulation and **migrate to the liver** where they mature into adult male and female worms. The adult worms migrate via the bloodstream to their final locations. *Schistosoma mansoni* and *S. japonicum* descend to the mesenteric veins and *S. haematobium* to the **vesical plexus.** Gravid female worms may release 300–3000 eggs per day over a 5–10 year life span. Eggs of *S. haematobium* can work their way through the wall of the urinary bladder into the lumen and are eliminated in urine, while eggs of *S. mansoni* and *S. japonicum* work their way through the walls of the small intestine and colon and are voided in feces. **Acute schistosomiasis or Katayama syndrome** develops one to two months after initial infection and includes **fever, chills, abdominal pain, lymphadenopathy,** and **hepatomegaly and splenomegaly** The pathophysiologic etiology of acute schistosomiasis is not known.

However, the association of its manifestations with heavy infection suggests that it is a form of serum sickness as a result of circulating antigen-antibody complexes. Chronic schistosomiasis results from the inflammatory response to eggs, with granulomas, fibrosis, and scar tissue occurring at the site where eggs are deposited in tissues. Chronic schistosomiasis results from the inflammatory response to the presence of eggs, with granulomas, fibrosis, and scarring around the eggs. Eggs in the bowel wall may result in symptoms of abdominal pain, diarrhea, and blood in the stool. Schistosomiasis of the bladder can cause **hematuria,** dysuria, frequent urination, and a reduction in bladder capacity. With **intestinal schistosomiasis,** the liver is frequently involved as a result of eggs being carried by the portal circulation and becoming trapped in the liver. Pathology involves **inflammation and fibrosis,** leading to **cirrhosis** with resulting **portal hypertension, splenomegaly, ascites, and abdominal and esophageal varices.** Ectopic lesions may rarely be associated with eggs reaching the brain and/or lungs.

APPROACH TO THE SUSPECTED SCHISTOME INFECTION

Objectives

1. Learn the life cycle of blood flukes and the epidemiology and clinical course of infection.
2. Be able to describe three basic aspects of infection: transmission, diagnosis, and treatment/prevention.

Definitions

Cercaria: Infective, aquatic larval form of schistosomes; characterized by a forked tail.

Miracidium: Ciliated larval form of schistosomes (and other flukes) that escapes from the egg and infects a snail intermediate host.

Intermediate host: The host in the life cycle of a helminth that harbors the larval stage(s) of the parasite.

Bilharziasis: A synonym for schistosomiasis.

Swimmer's itch: Dermatitis in humans caused by cercariae penetrating the skin, commonly involving cercariae of schistosomes that parasitize birds or mammals but which cannot complete their life cycle in humans.

Dioecious fluke: A fluke that has separate sexes, as opposed to hermaphroditic flukes.

DISCUSSION

Characteristics of Schistosomes That Impact Transmission

The life cycle of all human schistosomes is similar, except in fine details. **Eggs voided in feces or urine hatch in fresh water,** releasing **ciliated miracidia** that penetrate a **snail intermediate host.** The species of snail varies with the species of schistosome. Miracidia undergo morphologic development through other larval stages, eventually reproducing asexually. The product is hundreds of **cercariae** with forked tails that emerge from the snail and swim freely. On contacting humans that enter their environment, the **cercariae penetrate the intact skin, losing their tails in the process,** and enter the circulation and are **disseminated to all parts of the body.**

The cercariae, now termed **schistosomula,** are carried via the **portal vein** into the **intrahepatic portal system** where they mature in approximately 3–4 weeks. After maturing, the worms migrate against the blood current and move into branches of veins that drain the **urinary bladder** (*S. hematobium*) or the **lower ileum and cecum** (*S. japonicum*) or the **colon** (*S. mansoni*). Female worms lay several hundred eggs per day. The eggs of each species have characteristic morphology. All eggs leaving the host contain a fully developed miracidium.

Diagnosis

Infections can be definitively diagnosed by **finding characteristic eggs in the urine or feces.** Eggs of *S. hematobium* are in the shape of an **elongated oval with a terminal spine;** *S. mansoni* eggs are also oval shaped but with a distinct lateral spine; and *S. japonicum* eggs are round to oval with a short lateral spine or knob that often is unseen. In suspected cases where stools are negative, eggs of *S. mansoni* may be seen in microscopic examination of a rectal biopsy.

Treatment and Prevention

Praziquantel is the drug of choice in the treatment of human schistosomiasis and is effective against all human species. Because the drug has been reported to be effective as a prophylactic, **larval stages and adult forms are presumed to be susceptible.** The treatment of cercarial dermatitis is symptomatic. Prevention is based on avoiding skin exposure to groundwater in endemic areas.

Synopsis

The synopsis of schistosomiasis is presented in Table 49-1.

Table 49-1

Synopsis of Schistosomiasis			
Infective stage of etiologic agent	Location of pathogenic stage	Laboratory diagnosis based on identification of:	Drugs used in treatment
Cercariae: *Schistosoma mansoni*	Adults: Mostly inferior mesenteric veins	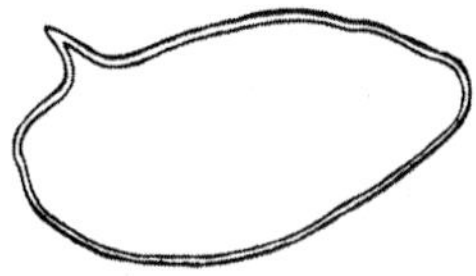 Eggs (stool exam, rectal biopsy)	*Praziquantel*
Schistosoma japonicum	Mostly superior mesenteric veins	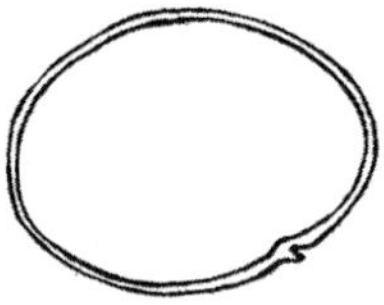 Eggs (stool exam, rectal biopsy)	
Schistosoma hematobium	Vesicular veins	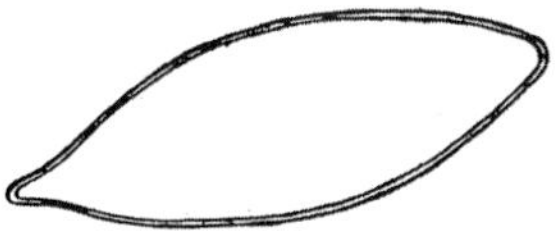 Eggs (urine)	
Swimmer's Itch—Cercarial dermatitis *(Various species of non human schistosomes)*	Skin	Clinical diagnosis	None specific

COMPREHENSION QUESTIONS

[49.1] Which of the following is a host in the life cycle of all trematodes that infect humans?

A. Flea
B. Mosquito
C. Mollusk
D. Flour weevil
E. Sand fly

[49.2] An oil field worker who has lived in Brazil for 10 years has mild gastrointestinal symptoms. Brazil is the only country ever visited by the patient outside of the United States. The patient is diagnosed by his physician of having *S. mansoni* because of which of the following?

A. Round eggs with a prominent terminal spine were observed in a rectal biopsy.
B. Blood was detected in the stool.
C. Nonoperculated eggs with a miracidium inside were observed in stool samples.
D. Eggs were found in a urine sample.
E. Symptoms were relieved by treatment with praziquantel.

[49.3] A 12-year-old boy reports feeling tingling and itching of his legs 30 minutes after swimming in a lake. Over the next day, small papules develop followed by blisters of the legs. Dermatitis due to schistosome infection is diagnosed. What larval stage most likely caused the infection?

A. Filariform larva
B. Cysticercus
C. Cercaria
D. Miracidium
E. Sparganum

Answers

[49.1] **C.** Snails are mollusks. All flukes have snails as intermediate hosts. Fleas, mosquitoes, flour weevils, and sand flies serve as intermediate or definitive hosts to various helminth and protozoan parasites, but not to flukes.

[49.2] **C.** Eggs with a miracidium inside is indicative of a fluke infection; nonoperculated eggs are characteristic of schistosomes and differentiate them from all other human flukes, which have eggs with opercula. Also, *S. mansoni* is the only human schistosome endemic to Brazil and to the western hemisphere. A round egg with a terminal spine (A) is characteristic of *S. hematobium* but would not be expected in a rectal biopsy; furthermore, *S. hematobium* is not endemic to the western hemisphere. Blood in the stool (B) may be a finding in *S. mansoni* infection but would not be a definitive diagnosis. Finding eggs in a urine sample (D) is consistent with *S. hematobium* but not *S. mansoni* infection; again, *S. hematobium* is not endemic to the western hemisphere. Vague gastrointestinal symptoms are not pathognomonic of schistosome infections. Praziquantel (E) is used to effectively treat all intestinal tapeworms of humans, as well as schistosomes. Symptoms could have been caused by adult tapeworms.

[49.3] **C.** Forked-tail cercariae are infective for humans. A filariform larva is the infective stage for hookworm and strongyloides, both nematode parasites. A cysticercus larva (B) is the infective stage of *Taenia* species of tapeworms. A miracidium (D) is the stage of flukes that infects snails, not humans. A sparganum larva (E) is involved in the life cycle of pseudophyllidean tapeworms, such as the broad fish tapeworm.

MICROBIOLOGY PEARLS

- ❖ Swimmer's itch, a symptom of schistosomiasis, is also transmitted by bird schistosomes.
- ❖ Egg stages cause pathology in blood fluke infections and are critical in diagnosis of infection.
- ❖ Praziquantel is effective for all species of human schistosomes.

REFERENCES

Centers for Disease Control. DPDx. Laboratory identification of parasites of public concern. Schistosomiasis. 2007. http://www.dpd.cdc.gov/dpdx/HTML/Schistosomiasis.htm.

Centers for Disease Control. DPDx. Laboratory identification of parasites of public concern. Graphic Library. Schistosomiasis. 2007. http://www.dpd.cdc.gov/dpdx/HTML/ImageLibrary/Schistosomiasis_il.htm.

Medical Letter on Drugs and Therapeutics. Drugs for parasitic infections. New Rochelle, NY. 2004. http://www.medletter.com/freedocs/parasitic.pdf. This reference has been updated and "superseded by the special report *Drugs for Parasitic Infections,* which can be purchased (on-line) for $25." This reference has been provided because it is a comprehensive and clinically useful reference that is regularly updated and could be of value to those who are involved in treating parasitic infections.

CASE 50

A 19-year-old woman presents to the physician's office for the evaluation of an itchy vaginal discharge that she has had for about a week. She has had no fever, abdominal pain, or dysuria. She became involved with a new sexual partner approximately 3 weeks ago. She takes birth control pills but does not regularly use condoms during intercourse. Her partner is asymptomatic. On examination, her vital signs are normal, and a general physical examination is unremarkable. On pelvic examination, her external genitalia are normal. After inserting a speculum you see a bubbly, thin, yellow vaginal discharge. Her cervix is erythematous but without discharge. She has no cervical motion or uterine or adnexal tenderness. A wet mount of the vaginal discharge examined microscopically reveals numerous motile, flagellated, pear-shaped organisms along with numerous white blood cells.

- **What is the most likely infectious cause of her vaginal discharge?**
- **What is the most likely source of her infection?**

ANSWERS TO CASE 50: TRICHOMONIASIS

Summary: A 19-year-old woman with vaginal discharge, which on microscopy reveals numerous motile, flagellated, pear-shaped organisms along with numerous white blood cells.

 **Most likely infectious cause of her vaginal discharge:** *Trichomonas vaginalis*

 **Most likely source of her infection:** Sexual contact with infected but asymptomatic partner

CLINICAL CORRELATION

Trichomonas vaginalis is a **motile, pear-shaped protozoan with four flagella** and an **undulating membrane.** It multiplies by **binary fission** and exists only in its trophozoite form; no cyst form has been identified. It is a common cause of both symptomatic and asymptomatic infections. Many infected women are asymptomatic or have only a small amount of thin vaginal discharge. Others develop symptomatic disease with vaginal **inflammation, itching, and copious vaginal discharge.** The discharge may be white, yellow, or green, and bubbles are often seen. Cervical inflammation with punctate hemorrhages may produce a **"strawberry cervix."** The vast majority of infections in men are asymptomatic, although urethritis, prostatitis, and epididymitis can occur. The parasite is almost always passed by **sexual contact,** although fomite transmission has been documented. The diagnosis is most often made by the microscopic evaluation of a sample of vaginal discharge in a saline wet mount. Flagellated, motile trichomonads will be visible in most symptomatic infections. The diagnosis can also be made by the identification of organisms on Pap smears, by culture of the vaginal discharge, or by the use of specific monoclonal antibody stains or nucleic acid probes. This infection is usually treated with oral **metronidazole,** and both partners should be treated to prevent reinfection. Because of its route of transmission, the identification of infection with *Trichomonas* should prompt the consideration of evaluation for other sexually transmitted diseases.

APPROACH TO THE SUSPECTED *Trichomonas* INFECTION

Objectives

1. Learn the life cycle of *Trichomonas vaginalis* and the epidemiology and clinical course of infection.
2. Be able to answer the three basic aspects of infection: transmission, diagnosis, and treatment/prevention.

Definitions

Trophozoite: Feeding stage of protozoans, in contrast to the vegetative cyst stage that may be present in the life cycles of some protozoa.

Axostyle: A hyaline rod-like structure that runs through the length of *T. vaginalis* and exits at the posterior end.

Fomite: A substance other than food that may harbor and transmit infectious agents.

DISCUSSION

Characteristics of *Trichomonas* That Impact Transmission

The life cycle of trichomonads in general is the simplest of protozoan life cycle because the organism exists only as a trophozoite that divides by binary fission. Transmission is presumed to be by **direct transfer of trophozoites** because a cyst stage does not exist.

Sexual intercourse is considered the usual means of transmitting this infection that is common worldwide. The organism is transmitted cyclically from a woman to a man and back to the same or another woman. Infected men, who play a key role in transmission, are usually asymptomatic. *Trichomonas vaginalis* trophozoites in vaginal discharge are known to live for 30 minutes or more on toilet seats, supporting the possibility that some infections could be acquired through **fomites** such as towels and toilet seats. However, this means of transmission is not well supported by evidence.

Diagnosis

If infection with *T. vaginalis* is suspected, a first step is to diagnose infection by **microscopically examining a wet mount preparation** of vaginal discharge from the patient. The live parasite appears as a **pear-shaped trophozoite with active flagella** that give it motility. Sometime the undulating membrane provides a waving movement. Propagation and concentration of the organism in culture is a possibility if wet mounts are negative. However, examination of wet mounts is usually sufficient to find and identify the organism.

Treatment and Prevention

Metronidazole is effective in treating *T. vaginalis*. Treatment of both sexual partners is recommended to prevent reinfection. Using condoms correctly and consistently will lower the risk of individuals contracting trichomoniasis and other sexually transmitted diseases.

Synopsis

The synopsis of vaginal trichomoniasis is presented in Table 50-1.

Table 50-1

Synopsis of Vaginal Trichomoniasis			
Infective stage of etiologic agent	Location of pathogenic stage	Laboratory diagnosis based on identification of:	Drugs used in treatment
Trophozoite *Trichomonas vaginalis*	Genito-urinary tract	Trophozoite (vaginal discharge)	Metronidazole

COMPREHENSION QUESTIONS

[50.1] Trichomoniasis is transmitted by which stage?

A. Cyst
B. Oocyst
C. Egg
D. Sporozoite
E. Trophozoite

[50.2] What is the drug of choice in treating vaginal trichomoniasis?

A. Metronidazole
B. Mebendazole
C. Mefloquine
D. Niclosamide
E. Niridazole

[50.3] Laboratory diagnosis of vaginal trichomoniasis is most commonly made by which of the following methods?

A. Identifying cyst stages in an iodine stained preparation of vaginal secretion.
B. Finding trophozoites in a saline wet mount of vaginal discharge.
C. Using an acid-fast stain to highlight the parasite.
D. Staining a thin blood smear with common blood stains.
E. Testing for specific antibodies against *T. vaginalis* in the patient's serum.

Answers

[50.1] **E.** *Trichomonas vaginalis* exists only as a trophozoite; no cyst stage has been identified. A cyst (A), oocyst (B) and sporozoite (D) are stages involved in transmitting other protozoan infections, and an egg (C) is the means of transmission in a number of helminth infections.

[50.2] **A.** Metronidazole is the drug of choice. Mebendazole (B) is a broad-spectrum antinematode agent. Mefloquine (C) is used as a prophylactic drug to prevent malaria and also used to treat chloroquine-resistant clinical malaria. Niclosamide is a broad-spectrum agent effective in the treatment of adult tapeworm infections. Niridazole (E) is a drug used to treat schistosomiasis if praziquantel is not available.

[50.3] **B.** Trophozoites are usually visible in saline mounts of vaginal discharge or scrapings. Cysts (A) are not present in the *T. vaginalis* life cycle, and iodine is used primarily to observe cysts of intestinal protozoa. Acid-fast stains (D) are used to search for oocysts of coccidian intestinal parasites, such as *Cryptosporidium* and *Cyclospora.* Thin blood smears are used to diagnose malaria. Serologic diagnoses (E) are helpful in the diagnosis of several "deep tissue" parasites but are not used in diagnosing *T. vaginalis.*

MICROBIOLOGY PEARLS

- *Trichomonas vaginalis* is an important sexually transmitted parasite throughout the world.
- Only trophozoite stages occur and frequently are difficult to find in a saline wet mount.
- Males and females are host, although males are generally asymptomatic.
- Metronidazole is the drug of choice for treating trichomoniasis.

REFERENCES

Centers for Disease Control. DPDx. Laboratory identification of parasites of public concern. Trichomoniasis. 2007. http://www.dpd.cdc.gov/dpdx/HTML/Trichomoniasis.htm.

Centers for Disease Control. DPDx. Laboratory identification of parasites of public concern. Image Library. Trichomoniasis. 2007. http:www.dpd.cdc.gov/dpdx/HTML/ImageLibrary/Trichomoniasis_il.htm.

Medical Letter on Drugs and Therapeutics. Drugs for parasitic infections. New Rochelle, NY. 2004. http://www.medletter.com/freedocs/parasitic.pdf. This reference has been updated and "superseded by the special report *Drugs for Parasitic Infections,* which can be purchased (on-line) for $25." This reference has been provided because it is a comprehensive and clinically useful reference that is regularly updated and could be of value to those who are involved in treating parasitic infections.

SECTION IV

Listing of Cases

LISTING BY CASE NUMBER

LISTING BY DISORDER (ALPHABETICAL)

INDEX

Note: Page numbers followed by *f* or *t* indicate figures or tables, respectively.

B

C

E

F

I

Q

R

S

W

X

Y

Z